M & E PROFESSIONAL DICTIONARIES

A DICTIONARY OF LAW

M & E PROFESSIONAL DICTIONARIES

A DICTIONARY OF LAW

L. B. Curzon
Barrister

SECOND EDITION

*In verbis non verba sed res et
ratio quaerenda est:* Jenk. Cent. 132

Pitman Publishing Ltd
128 Long Acre, London WC2E 9AN

A Longman Group Company

© Pitman Publishing Ltd 1983

First published 1979
Second edition 1983

Reprinted with corrections 1986

British Library Cataloguing in Publication Data

Curzon, L.B.
A dictionary of law.—2nd ed.—(M & E
professional dictionaries)
1. Law—England—Dictionaries
I. Title
344.208'6   KD313

ISBN 0-7121-0439-9

Printed in Great Britain by
Richard Clay (The Chaucer Press) Ltd,
Bungay, Suffolk

Preface to the Second Edition

This dictionary has been compiled primarily for the use of students at home and abroad as a guide to the specialised vocabulary of the principles, practices and procedures of English law. It is hoped that general readers also will find it of interest and use.

The basic vocabularies of those subjects constituting the foundation of legal studies—criminal law, land law, contract, law of torts, equity and the law of evidence, for example—have been combed so as to extract the fundamental language of our law. Other vital areas, such as jurisprudence, legal history and EEC law, have been searched and a selection of their most important words and phrases has been made.

The words and phrases which make up the dictionary are explained in a variety of ways, including straightforward definition, reference to the reports and other legal literature. In many entries references to statutes and cases are given so that students may be led on to explore further the use of words in the context of current law.

English law is a living, and, therefore, a changing, thing. Recording its vocabulary at any moment is analogous to attempting to record the motion of a mountain torrent by the use of a still camera; one can record the object only at one "frozen moment in time". In general, this dictionary has attempted to record legal terminology as it was in September, 1983; some later material was added at proof-reading stages. Parliament has increasingly allowed the use of delayed commencement provisions; so far as possible the text contains the law as it would be if all the affected statutes were fully in force.

I wish to record my thanks to Peter Drew of the editorial staff of Macdonald & Evans for his help in the preparation of the text, to Emlyn Williams, LL.B., for his careful perusal of the manuscript, and to the law teachers and students whose constructive criticisms of the first edition were extremely valuable.

1983   L.B.C.

How to use this Dictionary

1. The entries in this dictionary are arranged invariably in *strict alphabetical order*. This may be illustrated by the following example of a series of entries:

> **privilege**
> **privilege, absolute**
> **privilege, claim of**
> **privileged communication**
> **privileged will**
> **privilege, legal professional**
> **privilege of witness**
> **privilege, parliamentary**
> **privilege, public**
> **privilege, qualified**
> **Privileges, Committee of**
> **privileges, marital**

2. The titles of some Acts which are referred to repeatedly are abbreviated in accordance with the list below. In every case the abbreviation is followed by the appropriate date of the Act, thus: B.A. 1914; Th.A. 1968.

Abbreviations used for the titles of some Acts:

A.E.A.	Administration of Estates Act
A.J.A.	Administration of Justice Act
B.A.	Bankruptcy Act
B.Ex.A.	Bills of Exchange Act
B.N.A.	British Nationality Act
C.C.A.	Consumer Credit Act
Ch.A.	Children Act
C.J.A.	Criminal Justice Act
C.J.J.A.	Civil Jurisdiction and Judgments Act
C.L.A.	Criminal Law Act
Cos.A.	Companies Act
County C.A.	County Courts Act
C. & Y.P.A.	Children and Young Persons Act
D.P.A.	Domestic Proceedings and Magistrates' Courts Act
E.P.A.	Employment Protection Act
E.P.(C.)A.	Employment Protection Consolidation Act

F.L.R.A.	Family Law Reform Act
H.A.	Housing Act
H.S.W.A.	Health and Safety at Work, etc., Act
I.A.	Interpretation Act
J.A.	Judicature Act
L.C.A.	Land Charges Act
L.G.A.	Local Government Act
L.G.P.L.A.	Local Government Planning and Land Act
Lim.A.	Limitation Act
L.P.A.	Law of Property Act
L.R.A.	Land Registration Act
Mat. C.A.	Matrimonial Causes Act
M.C.A.	Magistrates' Courts Act
M.H.A.	Mental Health Act
O.P.A.	Offences against the Person Act
P. & A.A.	Perpetuities and Accumulations Act
P.C.C.A.	Powers of Criminal Courts Act
S.C.A.	Supreme Court Act
S.G.A.	Sale of Goods Act
S.L.A.	Settled Land Act
S.O.A.	Sexual Offences Act
S.S.A.	Social Security Act
T.C.P.A.	Town and Country Planning Act
Th.A.	Theft Act
Tr.A.	Trustee Act
T.U.L.R.A.	Trade Union and Labour Relations Act
W.A.	Wills Act

3. The abbreviation "O" stands for "Order" and refers to grouping in the form of Orders of the Rules of the Supreme Court; "r" refers to "rules"; thus O. 88, r. 7.

4. Cross-reference is achieved by the use of the abbreviation qv, which appears in brackets following words that are further explained elsewhere, and by words in capital letters which stand at the conclusion of the particular entry. Thus, consider the following entry:

life estate. An estate for the life of the tenant (eg, by express limitation, such as a grant "to X for life") or by operation of law (as in curtesy (qv)) or *autre vie* (qv). *See* ESTATE.

After studying the entry above, further reference ought to be made to *curtesy*, *autre vie* and, finally, *estate*.

5. Many entries contain references to cases, statutes, orders, statutory instruments, Law Commission Reports, etc. They have been included for those who wish to make an intensive study of the subject-matter of the entries.

A

A1. A classification in *Lloyd's Register of Shipping* of a ship, the hull and equipment of which are considered first-class. *See* LLOYD'S.

A and B lists. In the event of the winding-up of a company (qv), those on the "A" list, which is a list of present members, are liable in accordance with any guarantee, or in so far as their shares are unpaid. Those on the "B" list, which is a list of persons who have ceased to be members within one year preceding winding-up, are liable (if the contributions of those on the "A" list are insufficient) to the extent unpaid on their shares in respect of debts incurred while they were members. See the Cos.A. 1948, s. 212; *Helbert* v *Banner* (1871) LR 5 HL 28. *See* WINDING-UP.

abandonment. 1. Surrender or relinquishing of a chattel, right or claim, with the intention of not reclaiming it. 2. An action in the High Court is considered abandoned when a notice of discontinuance (qv) is served: see O. 21. 3. In the case of a constructive total loss (qv) in marine insurance, the assured may abandon the subject-matter to the insurer and treat the loss as if it were an actual total loss, after giving notice of abandonment. 4. Abandonment of a child means leaving it to its fate: *Watson* v *Nikolaisen* [1955] 2 QB 286. See the C. & Y.P.A. 1963; Ch.A. 1975, Sch 4. 5. Abandonment of appeal is the withdrawal of appeal by leave of the court or on notice. See O. 59, r. 5; *R* v *Keating* [1982] Crim LR 228.

abatement. 1. Abatement of action is the bringing to an end or the suspending of an action: see O. 15, r. 7; O. 28, r. 11; O. 34, r. 9. 2. Abatement of debts refers to proportionate reduction of payments where a fund cannot meet claims. 3. Abatement of legacies (qv) refers to receipt by legatees of only a fraction, or none, of their legacies when assets are insufficient to pay legacies in full. Pecuniary or general legacies abate proportionately before specific legacies. 4. Abatement of nuisances (qv) refers to their removal. Abatement notices may be served by a local authority in respect of a statutory nuisance. See the Public Health Act 1936, s. 93; Public Health (Recurring Nuisances) Act 1969; *Salford CC* v *McNally* [1975] 2 All ER 860.

abdication. Voluntary renunciation of an office. See, concerning Royal abdication, the Declaration of Abdication Act 1936 (concerning Edward VIII).

abduction. Wrongful leading away of a person. It is an offence under the S.O.A. 1956, s. 20, to abduct an unmarried girl under 16 from her parent or guardian. See *Fam Div Practice Note*, 22.7.80. See *R* v *Tegerdine* (1982) 75 Cr App R 298.

abet. To assist in the commission of an offence when one is present actively or constructively. *See* ACCESSORY; ACCOMPLICE; AID OR ABET.

ab extra. From outside.

abeyance. An estate is in abeyance when there exists no person in whom it can vest.

abeyance of seisin. *See* SEISIN, ABEYANCE OF.

ab initio. From the beginning. 1. A trespasser *ab initio* is one who, being entitled by law to perform an act, abuses his authority, so that his act becomes wrongful from the very beginning. See *The Six Carpenters' Case* (1610) 8 Rep 146a; *Chic Fashions Ltd* v *Jones* [1968] 2 QB 299 (in which continuing existence of doctrine was doubted). 2. A marriage is void *ab initio* if, eg, either party was under 16 at the date of marriage.

ab intestato. From an intestate. "Succession *ab intestato*" refers to succession to property of one who has not disposed of it by will. *See* INTESTACY.

abjuration. Renunciation by oath, eg, as in an oath to leave the realm. See the Promissory Oaths Act 1871.

abode. A place of residence (qv). Usually a question of fact rather than law: *Courtis* v *Blight* (1862) 31 LJCP 48. "A man's residence, where he lives with his family and sleeps at night, is always his place of abode in the full sense of that expression": *R* v *Hammond* (1852) 17 QB 772. See *R* v *Bundy* [1977] 2 All ER 382 and *R* v *Barnet LBC ex p Shah* [1983] 2 WLR 16.

abode in UK, right of. A person has such a right if he is a British citizen or a Commonwealth citizen who immediately before the commencement of the B.N.A. 1981 was a Commonwealth citizen having the right of abode in the UK by virtue of the Immigration Act 1971, s. 2(1)(d) and has not ceased to be a Commonwealth citizen in the meanwhile: Immigration Act 1971, s. 2, as substituted by the B.N.A. 1981, s. 39.

abominable crime. Phrase used in the O.P.A. 1861, s. 61, to refer to sodomy (qv) and bestiality (qv).

abortion. Expulsion of a human foetus before gestation is completed. Procuring an abortion was a felony, but under the Abortion Act 1967, a person is not guilty of an offence relating to abortion when a pregnancy is terminated by a registered medical practitioner, if two registered medical practitioners are of the bona fide opinion that continued pregnancy would involve risk to the woman's life, or injury to the physical or mental health of the woman or existing children of her family, or that there is a substantial risk that if the child were born it would be seriously handicapped by physical or mental abnormalities. See also the O.P.A. 1861, ss. 58, 59; *Royal College of Nursing* v *DHSS* [1981] AC 800. A husband has no enforceable right to prevent wife having a legal abortion: *Paton* v *Trustees of BPAS* [1978] 2 All ER 987.

abrogate. To repeal, annul, cancel, abolish.

abscond. To depart secretly or to hide oneself from the jurisdiction of the court so as to avoid legal process. It may amount to an act of bankruptcy (qv): B.A. 1914, ss. 1, 23.

absconding by person released on bail. Failure, without reasonable cause, by one who has been released on bail in criminal proceedings, to surrender to custody. An offence under the Bail Act 1976, s. 6(1). A warrant (qv) for his arrest may be issued: s. 7(1).

absence. 1. Non-appearance by a party to a writ or subpoena (qv). 2. Continuous absence of a spouse for seven years may be a defence to a charge of bigamy. See *R* v *Curgerwen* (1865) 29 JP 820. 3. Absence "beyond the seas" (qv) refers to absence from the UK and those adjacent islands belonging to the Sovereign.

absolute. Without conditions, complete, as in decree absolute (qv).

absolute assignment. Assignment of the entire interest of a chose in action (qv) so that it is transferred unconditionally to the assignee. It includes an assignment by way of mortgage: *Hughes* v *Pump House Hotel Co* [1902] 2 KB 190. See the L.P.A. 1925, s. 136.

absolute decree. *See* DECREE.

absolute discharge. Where a court by or before which a person is convicted of an offence (not being an offence the sentence for which is fixed by law) is of the opinion, having regard to the circumstances including the nature of the offence and the character of the offender, that it is inexpedient to inflict punishment and that a probation order is not appropriate, the court may make an order discharging him absolutely: P.C.C.A. 1973, s. 7.

absolute duties. Duties to which there are no corresponding rights (eg, according to Austin, a subject's duties to the Crown).

absolute liability. *See* STRICT LIABILITY IN CRIMINAL LAW.

absolute privilege. *See* PRIVILEGE, ABSOLUTE.

absolute title. In the case of a freehold (qv) registered with absolute title, the registered proprietor has a guaranteed title subject only to, eg, entries on the register. In the case of a leasehold (qv) absolute title guarantees that the registered proprietor is the owner of the lease and that it was validly granted. *See* LAND REGISTRATION.

abstract and epitome of title. Narrative summary, which must be supplied by a landowner to a purchaser under contract of sale, of documents and events affecting title. The abstract states the history of title; the epitome is a schedule of documents going back to the root of title (qv). See the L.P.A. 1925, s. 10.

abstracting electricity. *See* ELECTRICITY, DISHONEST ABSTRACTION OF.

abuse. Words of vituperation, insult, invective. It does not generally amount to defamation (qv): *Thorley v Kerry* (1812) 4 Taunt 355. See, however *M'Gregor v Gregory* (1843) 11 M & W 287; *Lane v Holloway* [1968] 1 QB 379.

abuse of distress. Use of an animal or chattel that has been distrained. It renders distrainor liable for conversion (qv). *See* DISTRESS.

abuse of process. Tort based on damage caused by use of a legal process for some purpose other than that for which it was designed. See O. 18, r. 19; *R v Brentford Justices ex p Wong* [1981] QB 445; *Hunter v Chief Constable of W. Midlands* [1982] AC 529.

ACAS. Advisory, Conciliation and Arbitration Service (qv).

acceleration clause. Provision in an agreement for repayment of a loan by instalments whereby if a stated number of instalments is not paid, all outstanding payments become due at once.

acceleration, doctrine of. Where interests in property have been conferred by a testator in succession, eg, "to X for life, remainder to Y" and the gift to X is determined before the time envisaged by the testator, Y's interest is accelerated. If it is discovered that, eg, X cannot take under the will (because he witnessed it), Y's interest becomes immediate. The doctrine does not apply to a contingent gift: *Re Scott* [1975] 2 All ER 1033. See *Re Hodge* [1943] Ch 300; *Re Davies* [1957] 1 WLR 922.

acceptance. 1. Acceptance of an offer to create a contract (ie, an assent to all the terms of the offer) must be unqualified, and may be by words or conduct. It must generally be communicated to the offeror and must conform with the offer. See *Adams v Lindsell* (1818) 1 B & Ald 681; *Hyde v Wrench* (1840) 3 Beav 334; *Carlill v Carbolic Smoke Ball Co* [1893] 1 QB 256. Acceptance "subject to contract" means that the parties intend to be bound only when a formal contract is prepared and signed: *Chillingworth v Esche* [1924] 1 Ch 97. 2. Acceptance of goods under the S.G.A. 1979, s. 35, is deemed to have taken place when a person indicates to the seller that he has accepted them, or when they have been delivered to him and he does an act in relation to them which is inconsistent with the seller's ownership, or when he retains them without informing the seller after a reasonable time that he has rejected them. *See* CONTRACT; OFFER.

acceptance, conditional. 1. Acceptance of offeror's offer by offeree, subject to a stipulation being met. 2. In relation to a bill of exchange (qv), where payment by the acceptor is made subject to a condition. See the B. Ex. A. 1882, s. 19.

acceptance of a bill. Written signature by the drawee of a bill of exchange and the word "accepted" across the bill: B.Ex.A. 1882, ss. 17–19. He thereby undertakes to pay the bill when due. Acceptance *supra protest* (or "acceptance for honour") is acceptance of a bill when it has been dishonoured by one who has no interest in the bill so as to safeguard the drawee's good name: B.Ex.A. 1882, ss. 65–68. Acceptance may be general or qualified (qv). *See* BILL OF EXCHANGE.

acceptance of service. Statement by a solicitor, written on a writ of summons, accepting service and undertaking to appear. Failure to appear may render the solicitor liable in negligence to his client. See O. 10, r. 1.

acceptance, special. *See* SPECIAL ACCEPTANCE.

access. 1. The existence of opportunity of sexual intercourse between husband and wife. Evidence of impossibility of access may be given to rebut the presumption of legitimacy (qv). See the Mat.C.A. 1973, s. 48. 2.

Where one parent has been granted care and control of a child, the other parent or grandparent may be entitled to visit or look after child for periods as part of the right of access. See D.P.A. 1978, s. 14; *S.* v *S.* [1962] 1 WLR 445; *M.* v *M.* [1973] 2 All ER 81. For supervised access, see *Practice Direction* [1980] 1 All ER 1040. 3. The owner of adjoining land has right of access to a highway: *Rowley* v *Tottenham UDC* [1914] AC 95.

accession. Procedure whereby property belonging to X becomes property of Y because it has been affixed to or annexed with that which belongs to Y. *See* FIXTURES.

accessory. One who is concerned in the commission of an offence otherwise than as principal. An accessory *before* the fact was one who "being absent at the time of the felony committed doth yet procure, counsel, command or abet to commit [it]": 1 Hale PC 615. An accessory *after* the fact was one who, knowing that a felony had been committed, subsequently harboured or relieved the felon or in any way secured or attempted to secure his escape. See the Accessories and Abettors Act 1861; *R* v *Fisher* [1969] 1 WLR 8. *See* PRINCIPAL.

accident. "An unlooked for mishap, or an untoward event which is not expected or designed" by the person injured: *Boyle* v *Wright* [1969] VLR 699. "The word 'accident' is not a technical legal term with a clearly defined meaning. Speaking generally, but with reference to legal liabilities, an accident means any unintended and unexpected occurrence which produces hurt or loss": per Lord Linley in *Fenton* v *Thorley* [1903] AC 443. *See* INEVITABLE ACCIDENT.

accommodation bill. A bill of exchange (qv) to which a person who has not received value for it (the "accommodation party") has given his name, thus accepting liability and becoming, in effect, a surety for the person accommodated. See the B.Ex.A. 1882, s. 28.

accommodation, priority need for. *See* HOMELESS PERSON.

accomplice. One person associated with another, whether as principal or accessory (qqv), in the commission of an offence. Evidence of an accomplice may be admissible, but it is the judge's duty to warn the jury that it should be corroborated: *Davies* v *DPP* [1954] AC 378. See *R* v *Beck* [1982] 1 All ER 807.

accord and satisfaction. This occurs where, following the conclusion of a contract, one party obtains his release from his obligation by promising or giving consideration (qv) other than that which the other party has to accept under the contract. The agreement is the accord; the consideration is the satisfaction. See *British Russian Gazette* v *Ass. Newspapers* [1933] 2 KB 616; *D. & C. Builders Ltd* v *Rees* [1966] 2 QB 617.

account. Record of debts and credits, or items to be balanced. See the Cos.A. 1981, Sch. 1.

accounting, false. An offence under the Th.A. 1968, s. 17(1) "where a person dishonestly, with a view to gain for himself or another or with intent to cause loss to another, (*a*) destroys, defaces, conceals or falsifies any account or any record or document made or required for any accounting purpose; or (*b*) in furnishing information for any purpose produces or makes use of any account, or any such record or document as aforesaid, which to his knowledge is or may be misleading, false or deceptive in a material particular." See *R* v *Solomons* [1909] 2 KB 980 for the falsification of taximeter reading; *R* v *Mallett* [1978] 1 WLR 820. See *A.-G.'s Ref. (No. 1 of 1980)* [1981] 1 WLR 34 and *Edwards* v *Toombs* [1983] Crim LR 43.

accounting records. Records kept in accordance with the Cos.A. 1976, s. 12, containing details of company's liabilities and assets and entries from day to day of receipts and expenditure and matters in respect of which the receipts and expenditure take place.

accounting reference periods. Company directors have a duty to prepare, lay and deliver accounts by reference to accounting reference periods (usually 12 and, exceptionally, not more than 18 months), as set out in the Cos.A. 1976, s. 2.

account, order for. Order made by the court so that sums due from one party to another resulting from transactions between parties may be investigated, eg, as between principal and agent. See O. 43, r. 2; *O'Connor v Spaight* (1804) S & L 305; *Neilson v Betts* (1871) 19 WR 1121.

accounts, company. *See* COMPANY ACCOUNTS.

accounts, company, publication of. *See* COMPANY ACCOUNTS, PUBLICATION OF.

account, settled. Statement of accounts between parties, in writing, agreed and accepted by them as correct. A defence to a claim for an account. See *Re Webb* [1894] 1 Ch 83.

account stated. An admission of a sum of money due from one person to another where neither is under a duty to account to the other. Accounts stated with infants (qv) are generally void: Infants Relief Act 1874, s. 1. See *Joseph Evans & Co v Heathcote* [1918] 1 KB 434; *Siqueira v Noronha* [1934] AC 332.

accretion. Growth of land resulting from gradual and imperceptible accumulation by natural causes. See *A.-G. for S. Nigeria v John Holt & Co* [1915] AC 613; *Southern Centre of Theosophy v State of S. Australia* [1982] AC 706. *See* AVULSION.

accumulation. Process whereby interest is invested as it accrues. Under the L.P.A. 1925, s. 164(1) no person may direct accumulation of income for any longer period than the grantor's or settlor's life, or a term of 21 years from the death of the grantor, settlor or testator, or duration of minority of a person living or *en ventre sa mère* (qv) at the death of the grantor, settlor or testator, or duration of minority of person(s) who under limitations of the instrument directing accumulation would, for the time being, if of full age, be entitled to income directed to be accumulated. Under the P. & A.A. 1964, s. 13(1) additional periods are: 21 years from the date disposition was made; duration of minority of

any person in being at that date. The rule does not extend to accumulation of produce of timber or wood, provisions for payment of debts and raising of portions (qv).

accumulation and maintenance settlement. Settlement (qv) in which there is no interest in possession, but one or more beneficiaries will become entitled to an interest in possession on attaining a specified age not exceeding 25 years. See, eg, the Finance Act 1975, Sch 5.

accusatorial procedure. System in most common law countries whereby parties and their representatives have primary responsibility for finding and presenting evidence. The judge does not investigate the facts. *See* INQUISITORIAL PROCEDURE.

accused. One charged with an offence.

accused, non-appearance of. If the prosecutor appears, but the accused does not, the court may proceed in his absence: M.C.A. 1980, s. 11(1). Where a summons has been issued, the court must be satisfied that it was served on the accused a reasonable time before the trial: s. 11(2). A person may not be sentenced to imprisonment in his absence: s. 11(3). *See* POST, PLEA OF GUILTY BY; PROSECUTOR, NON-APPEARANCE OF.

accused, self-incrimination of. *See* SELF-INCRIMINATION.

ac etiam. And also. Phrase used to precede statement of real, as distinct from fictitious, cause of action.

acknowledgment. Avowal or assent to. 1. Acknowledgment of debt. Where right of action has accrued to recover a debt and the person liable acknowledges claim, the right is deemed to have accrued on and not before the date of acknowledgment: Lim.A. 1980, s. 29(5). 2. Acknowledgment of signature to will (qv). Testator's signature must be made or acknowledged in the presence of two witnesses. See the W.A. 1837, s. 9; *Gaze v Gaze* (1843) 3 Curt 451; *Re Colling* [1972] 3 All ER 729.

acquiescence. Consent which is expressed or implied from conduct. "Quiescence under such circumstances as that assent may be reasonably inferred from it": *De Bussche v*

Alt (1880) 8 Ch D. 314. *See* LACHES.

acquittal. Discharge from prosecution following verdict of not guilty or successful plea in bar (qv), etc. There is generally no appeal against acquittal unless under the appropriate statutory authority.

acquittance. "A discharge in writing of a sum of money or other duty which ought to be paid or done": *Termes de la Ley.*

act. 1. Act of Parliament (qv). 2. That which is done by a person, generally consequent on volition. It may include a deliberate omission: see, eg, the Sex Discrimination Act 1975, s. 82.

action. Formal exercise of a right of suing for that which is due. Usually commences by writ (qv) or other mode as prescribed by the Rules of Court. See the S.C.A. 1981, s. 151(1).

action, cause of. "A factual situation the existence of which entitles one person to obtain a remedy against another person": *Letang* v *Cooper* [1965] 1 QB 232.

action, circuity of. *See* CIRCUITY OF ACTION.

action, collusive. *See* COLLUSIVE ACTION.

action, derivative. *See* DERIVATIVE ACTION.

action, discontinuance of. *See* DISCONTINUANCE, NOTICE OF.

action, dismissal of. *See* DISMISSAL OF ACTION.

action on the case. Remedy for wrongs first given by the Statute of Westminster II 1285, whereby in a case in which a writ was found and in a similar case (*in consimili casu*) "falling under like law and requiring like remedy is found none", the clerks of Chancery could agree to make a new writ, or consult Parliament. *Assumpsit* (qv) is an example.

action, removal of. *See* REMOVAL OF ACTION.

actions civil and penal. An action brought to enforce civil rights is a *civil action*. A *penal action* is aimed at the punishment of the party sued, eg, by monetary penalty; the term is also used of an action for the recovery of a penalty given by statute.

actions, consolidation of. *See* CONSOLIDATION OF ACTIONS.

actions, county court. Under the County Court Rules 1981, the "ordinary action" was abolished. The two main classes of action are the "fixed date" action (in which a claim is made for any relief other than payment of money) and the "default" action (ie, any action that is not a "fixed date" one). See O. 3, r. 2.

action, setting down of. *See* SETTING DOWN OF ACTION.

action, settlement of. *See* SETTLEMENT OF ACTION.

actions real and personal. *Real* actions (*res* = thing) were brought at common law for the recovery of his land by a freeholder. See the Real Property Limitation Act 1833 by which they were, in general, abolished. *Personal* actions, eg, actions on contracts, derive from those relating to the enforcement of remedies against persons, in contrast to the recovery of things in real actions. *See* PROPERTY.

actio personalis moritur cum persona. A personal action dies with a party to the cause of the action. The rule was reversed by the Law Reform (Misc. Provs.) Act 1934: "On the death of any person . . . all causes of action . . . vested in him shall survive for the benefit of his estate." Thus, all causes of action in tort, save for defamation (qv) and the claim for damages for bereavement (qv) survive the deceased.

active trust. A trust (qv) which requires the trustee, known as an "active trustee" to perform active duties, eg, to collect rent and profits and transfer proceeds to the beneficiary (qv). *See* BARE TRUST.

act, juristic. Act whereby legal persons create, alter or destroy rights and duties and, as a consequence, affect legal relationships between legal persons. A juristic act may be *unilateral* (eg, disposing of property by will) or *bilateral* (eg, agreement by contract). Elements of a juristic act are: actor (A) must direct his will to an end; A's will must be made manifest; A must have capacity in law to achieve desired result; A's aim must be legal.

act of God. "An extraordinary circumstance which could not be foreseen, and which could not be guarded against": *Pandorf* v *Hamilton* (1886) 17 QBD 675. "Something in opposition to the act of man": *Forward* v *Pittard* (1785) ITR 27. See *Nichols* v *Marsland* (1875) LR 10 Ex 255—extraordinary rainfall; *Nugent* v *Smith* (1876) 1 CPD 423—unusually bad weather at sea. *See* VIS MAJOR.

Act of grace. A free, general pardon granted by an Act of Parliament, usually originated by the Sovereign, eg, at the commencement of a reign.

Act of indemnity. An Act legalising certain activities which were illegal at the time they were carried out, or exempting certain persons from particular penalties following on breaches of the law. See, eg, 4 Hen VIII c. 8; Indemnity Act 1920.

act of law. An event, eg, acquisition of title (qv), resulting other than from an act of the parties. *See* PURCHASER.

Act of Parliament. The will of the legislature, ie, law made by the Queen in Parliament (ie, Queen, Lords and Commons). Concurrence of the Lords may be dispensed with under certain circumstances: see the Parliament Acts 1911 and 1949. An Act comes into force on the day it receives the Royal Assent (qv), unless otherwise stated. Acts may be public or private, local, general or personal. In construing an Act, the intention of the legislature predominates: *A.-G. for Canada* v *Hallett & Carey Ltd* [1952] AC 427. *See* INTERPRETATION OF STATUTES.

Act of Parliament, citation of. *See* STATUTE, CITATION OF.

act of state. An act of the executive, ie, the sovereign power of a country, that "cannot be challenged, controlled or interfered with by municipal courts. Its sanction is not that of Law, but that of Sovereign power and, whatever it may be, municipal courts must accept it as it is, without question": *Salaman* v *Sec of State for India* [1906] 1 KB 639. See *Nabob of the Carnatic* v *E India Co* (1792) 2 Ves Jun 56; *A.-G.* v *Nissan*

[1970] AC 179; *Cubazucar* v *IANSA* [1983] Com LR 58. *See* PREROGATIVE, ROYAL.

acts of bankruptcy. *See* BANKRUPTCY, ACTS OF.

Act, structure of. Constituent elements of a statute, including: long title; preamble; enacting words; short title; principal, subsidiary, administrative and transitional provisions; interpretation and definitions; repealing clause; date of coming into operation; area of operation clause (eg, "This Act shall not extend to Scotland"); schedules.

actual military service. Phrase referring to a privileged will (qv) which allows, eg, a soldier or airman "in actual military service" to make an informal will. It has been given a wide meaning so as to include, eg, an airman undergoing training in Canada (*Re Wingham* [1943] P 187), a minor serving in the BAOR nine years after the end of the war (*Re Colman* [1958] 2 All ER 35). The phrase was reviewed extensively in *Re Wingham*.

actual notice. *See* NOTICE.

actus non facit reum nisi mens sit rea. An act does not itself constitute guilt unless the mind is guilty. The maxim contains a cardinal doctrine of English criminal law. See *Fowler* v *Padget* (1798) 7 TR 509; *Younghusband* v *Luftig* [1949] 2 KB 354.

actus reus. A phrase referring to elements of the definition of an offence (save those which concern the condition of the mind of the accused) eg, his conduct, its results and surrounding circumstances. Thus, the *actus reus* of false imprisonment (qv) is X's unlawful restraint of Y. Should any element of the *actus reus* not be present, the offence has not been committed. The phrase derives from "a mistranslation of the Latin aphorism . . . Properly translated, this means, 'an act does not make a *man* guilty of a crime unless his mind be also guilty'. It is thus not the *actus* which is *reus*, but the man and his mind respectively": *per* Lord Hailsham in *Haughton* v *Smith* [1973] 3 All ER 1109. See *R* v *Miller* (1983) (*The Times*, 18.3.1983). *See* CRIME.

ad colligenda bona. To collect the goods. Grant of administration made to preserve property when no next of kin, creditor or other person applies for administration and the property is in danger of perishing. See *Re Clore* [1982] Ch 456. *See* GRANT.

ad diem. On the appointed day.

address. Desires or opinions of either House of Parliament made known to the Sovereign.

address for service. Address where writs and summons may be delivered. See O. 6, r. 5.

adduce. To present, or bring forward, eg, evidence in support of some proposition or statement already made.

ademption. A specific legacy is said to be adeemed when, as result of implied revocation by testator, it is withheld or extinguished, wholly or in part. There is ademption in the following cases: 1. Testator makes a gift of "my gold watch" and sells it before his death: *Re Dowsett* [1901] 1 Ch 398. 2. Father or person *in loco parentis* (qv) may bequeath a legacy to a child and later make other provisions which, in effect, constitute a portion (qv): *Earl of Durham* v *Wharton* (1836) 10 Bli NS 526. *See* LEGACY.

ad hoc. For this purpose.

ad hoc settlements. *See* SETTLEMENTS, AD HOC.

ad hoc trust for sale. Where trustees for sale of land are either two or more persons approved or appointed by the Court, or their successors in office, or a trust corporation (qv), a sale overreaches certain prior interests: L.P.A. 1925, s. 2(2). The sale is known as an *ad hoc*, or special, trust for sale.

ad idem. Of the same mind; similar in essential matters. A binding contract, for example, requires *consensus ad idem* (agreement as to the same thing) by both parties. See *Raffles* v *Wichelhaus* (1864) 2 H & C 906.

adjacent. "Means close to or nearby or lying by: its significance or application in point of distance depends on the circumstances in which the word is used": *English China Clays* v *Plymouth Corporation* [1974] 2 All ER 239.

adjective law. That portion of the law

dealing with procedure and practice in the courts. *See* SUBSTANTIVE LAW.

adjoining. Touching. Includes "abutting on": Highways Act 1980, s. 329(1). See *Bucks CC* v *Trigg* [1963] 1 WLR 155.

adjourn. To postpone or suspend the hearing of a case until a further date. An adjournment *sine die* (without day) is for an indefinite time. "Adjournment of the House" refers to the suspension of a sitting of the Lords or Commons until the following or a later day.

adjournment of trial. The postponing of a trial of action by a judge who thinks it expedient "in the interest of justice" to adjourn "for such time, and to such place, and upon such terms, if any, as he thinks fit": O. 35, r. 3. See *Re Yates' Settlement Trusts* [1954] 1 WLR 564. For adjournment of a preliminary enquiry or a summary trial, see the M.C.A. 1980, ss. 5, 10.

adjudication. Formal judgment or decision given by the court. In proceedings for bankruptcy an adjudication order declares the debtor bankrupt, so that he becomes subject to disabilities attaching to that status. It is usually made, eg, when creditors pass a resolution. It can be annulled in the court's discretion, when, eg, debtor has paid debts in full. See the B.A. 1914, s. 29. *See* BANKRUPTCY.

adjustment. Determining or settling of an amount entitled to be received by the assured under a policy of marine insurance. *See* AVERAGE.

Adler clause. Clause in a lease relating to a covenant (qv) against the assignment by a tenant without the landlord's consent, and containing the proviso ". . . that should tenant desire to assign or underlet . . . he shall before doing so offer in writing to landlord to surrender the lease . . . without any consideration, and the landlord may accept such offer at any time within 21 days from receipt thereof." See *Adler* v *Upper Grosvenor St Investment Ltd* [1957] 1 WLR 227; *Re Hennessy's Agreement* [1975] 1 All ER 60.

ad litem. For the suit. A *guardian ad litem* may be appointed by the court to defend an action on behalf of an infant (qv): Ch.A. 1975, s. 20; O. 80, rr. 2, 3; see the Child Care Act 1980, s. 7. A *grant ad litem* is made where representatives will not act and the estate must be represented in proceedings: *Re Simpson* [1936] P 40.

administer. Under the Medicines Act 1968, s. 130(9), to give to a person or animal, orally, by injection or by introduction into the body in any other way, or by external application, whether by direct contact with the body or not.

administration. 1. Process of managing affairs of a bankrupt by a trustee, or those of an absent person by an attorney or agent. 2. Process of collecting the assets of a deceased person, paying debts and distributing any surplus to those entitled. See the A.E.A. 1925, s. 34 and Sch 1.

administration action. Action to obtain administration of the estate of a deceased person. Personal representative or any other person interested in the estate may bring proceedings by originating summons or writ. See the S.C.A. 1981, s. 117.

administration bond. As a condition of granting administration to a person, the court may require one or two sureties to guarantee that they will make good any loss suffered by a person interested in the estate, following the breach of duties by administrator. See the A.E.A. 1971, s. 8.

administration, limited. *See* LIMITED ADMINISTRATION.

administration of assets. *See* ESTATES, ADMINISTRATION OF.

administration of estates. *See* ADMINISTRATION; ESTATES, ADMINISTRATION OF.

administration order. An order providing for the administration by the court of a debtor's estate. Any creditor, on proof of his debt, may be scheduled as a creditor of the debtor for the amount of his proof when the order has been made. See County C.A. 1959, s. 148, as amended. Order relating to bankruptcy (qv) may be replaced by a receiving order (qv): Insolvency Act 1976, s. 11.

administration, special. *See* LIMITED ADMINISTRATION.

administration suit. An action for the administration of the estate of a deceased person.

administrative tribunals. Tribunals outside the hierarchy of courts exercising jurisdiction conferred by Parliament, eg, Rent Tribunals. Chairmen are generally selected from a panel and are appointed by the Lord Chancellor: Tribunals & Inquiries Act 1971, s. 7. The Council on Tribunals reviews their working. They are controlled generally by the issue of prerogative orders, ie, certiorari, mandamus, prohibition (qqv).

administrator. One appointed by the court to manage the property of a deceased person in the absence of an executor (qv). (Fem: administratrix.) *See* GRANT.

administrator of an estate, duties of. To collect, get in and administer real and personal estate of the deceased; to exhibit on oath a full inventory of the estate and render an account of its administration to the court; to deliver up to the High Court, when required to do so, the grant of probate or administration: A.E.A. 1925, s. 25, as substituted by the A.E.A. 1971.

Admiralty Court. A part of the QBD, consisting of puisne judges (qv) of the High Court, assisted by nautical assessors (the Elder Brethren of Trinity House). See the S.C.A. 1981, ss. 6, 20–24; O. 75; and the C.J.J.A. 1982, s. 26. It has instant jurisdiction (concerning civil cases arising, eg, out of collisions) and prize jurisdiction (concerning seizure of enemy ships and cargoes).

admissibility, conditional. *See* CONDITIONAL ADMISSIBILITY.

admissibility, multiple. *See* MULTIPLE ADMISSIBILITY.

admissibility of evidence. Evidence is receivable by the court only if both relevant and admissible. In general, all evidence relevant to an issue is admissible; all that is irrelevant or insufficiently relevant ought to be excluded. See, eg, *Hollington* v *Hewthorn & Co Ltd* [1943] KB 587. Must be distinguished from relevance (qv), which is based on that which is logically probative whereas admissibility refers to that which is legally receivable whether logically probative or not. "[The terms relevance and admissibility] are frequently, and in many circumstances legitimately, used interchangeably; but I think it makes for clarity if they are kept separate, since some relevant evidence is inadmissible and some admissible evidence is irrelevant . . .": *per* Lord Simon in *DPP* v *Kilbourne* [1973] AC 729. *See* EVIDENCE.

admissions. 1. In civil proceedings, those facts (or part of a case) admitted, or taken to be admitted by parties to an action. An admission may be made in answer to interrogatories (qv) or by the pleadings (qv); or on special application made during proceedings. See O. 27; Civil Evidence Act 1968, s. 9. 2. In criminal proceedings, statements made voluntarily by the accused admitting the offence, eg, by plea of guilty or confession. See the C.J.A. 1967, s. 10 (provision for formal admissions at or before trial); *R* v *Best* [1909] 1 KB 692. 3. "Admissions by conduct" may be implied from a party's conduct. See, eg, *R* v *Cramp* (1880) 14 Cox CC 390. *See* ADMISSIONS OF FACT, JUDGMENT ON; CONFESSION.

admissions by privies. Statements by persons who were, at the time of their making, in privity with a party (eg, proprietor and predecessor in title, principal and agent). They may be used against that party as admissions. See, eg, *Woolway* v *Rowe* (1834) 1 A & E 114.

admissions of fact, judgment on. Where, by his pleadings, a party makes admissions of facts, any other party may make an application to the court for judgment on those admissions: see O. 27, r. 3.

adopted children register. A register maintained by the Registrar-General at the General Register Office in which entries relating to adoption orders (qv) are made. Any person is entitled to search an index of the register: Adoption Act 1976, s. 50.

adoption. 1. Incorporation of international law into municipal law, eg,

by custom. 2. Process, effected by a court order, whereby rights and duties of a parent in relation to a child are vested in some other person(s), ie, the adopter(s). Recognised only after the Adoption of Children Act 1926. Regulated by the Adoption Acts 1958–76 and the Ch.A. 1975. A person other than an adoption agency (qv) shall not make arrangements for the adoption of a child or place a child for adoption unless the proposed adopter is a relative of the child or he is acting in pursuance of a High Court order: 1976 Act, s. 11(1).

adoption agency. An organisation arranging adoption. Approval of agencies, granted for three years, rests with the Secretary of State. See the Ch.A. 1975, ss. 4–7; the Adoption Act 1976, s. 72(1); and the Adoption Agencies Regulations (1976) (SI 1976/1796).

adoption, freeing child for. Where on the application by an adoption agency, an authorised court is satisfied in the case of each parent or guardian of the child that he freely and with full understanding of what is involved, agrees generally and unconditionally to the making of an adoption order, or his agreement to the making of the order can be dispensed with, the court may make an order declaring the child free for adoption: Adoption Act 1976, s. 18(1).

adoption order. An order vesting parental rights and duties relating to a child in the adopters, made on their application by an authorised court: Adoption Act 1976, s. 12(1). It may be made by the Family Division, county court or magistrates' court. The court must give prime consideration to the child's long-term welfare before making an order: s. 6. An order is not generally made unless the child is free for adoption: s. 16(1). *See* PARENTAL RIGHTS AND DUTIES.

adoption order, British. "An adoption order, an order under s. 8 of the Ch.A. 1975, or any provision for the adoption of a child effected under the law of N Ireland or any British territory outside UK": Adoption Act 1976, s. 72(1).

adoption order, convention. An adoption order made by the High Court under the Adoption Act 1976, relating to the Hague Convention on the Adoption of Children (Cmnd 2613). See the D.P.A. 1978, s. 74.

adoption order, status conferred by. An adopted child is treated in law, where the adopters are a married couple, as if he had been born as a child of the marriage and, in any other case, as if he had been born to the adopter in wedlock, and as if he were not the child of any person other than the adopter(s): Adoption Act 1976, s. 39. The section prevents an adopted child from being illegitimate: s. 39(4).

adoption probationary period. Where the applicant or one of the applicants (for adopting a child) is a parent, step-parent or relative of the child, or the child was placed with the applicants by an adoption agency or in pursuance of a High Court order, an adoption order will not be made unless the child is at least 19 weeks old and at all times during the preceding 13 weeks had his home with the applicants or one of them: Ch.A. 1975, s. 9(1). See also the 1975 Act, ss. 9(2), 18(1), 87(3); and the Adoption Act 1976, s. 13.

adoption, removal of children pending. A parent or guardian who has agreed to the adoption of his child may not remove the child from the applicants while an adoption order is pending, without a court order: Adoption Act 1976, s. 27.

adoption service. A service established and maintained by a local authority to meet needs, in relation to the adoption of children who have been or may be adopted, their parents or guardians, persons who may have adopted or may adopt a child: Adoption Act 1976, s. 1.

adoption society. "A body of persons whose functions consist of or include the making of arrangements for the adoption of children": Adoption Act 1976, s. 72(1).

adoptive Acts. Acts which become effective in a local authority's area only after formal adoption by that authority. See, eg, the provisions relating to licensing systems in the Private Places of Entertainment (Licensing) Act 1967.

adoptive relationship. Relationship existing by virtue of the Adoption Act 1976, s. 39. A male adopter is known as the adoptive father, a female adopter as the adoptive mother: 1976 Act, s. 41.

adult. Person of full age (18). See *R v Tottenham Juvenile Court, ex p ARC* [1982] 2 WLR 945. *See* MAJORITY.

adulteration. An offence under, eg, the Food and Drugs Act 1955, resulting from the adding of a substance to food which renders it dangerous to health, if done with the intention that it should be sold in that state for human consumption.

adultery. An act of voluntary sexual intercourse (which need not be completed) between two persons not married to each other, but one or both of whom are married at the time of the act to a third person. See *Sapsford v Sapsford* [1954] 2 All ER 373. If the respondent has committed adultery and the petitioner finds it impossible to live with the respondent, it may be evidence of irretrievable breakdown of a marriage, which is now the sole ground for the presentation of a divorce petition: Mat.C.A. 1973, s. 1. Adultery by a wife which has not been condoned or connived at, is a bar to an application for maintenance under Mat.C.A. 1973, s. 27, as amended. See *Gray v Gray* [1976] Fam 324. The onus of proof is on the petitioner. Damages for adultery cannot now be claimed: Law Reform (Misc. Provs.) Act 1970.

adultery, proof of. Modes of proof include: confessions; respondent's previous convictions (see the Civil Evidence Act 1968, s. 11); finding of adultery and paternity in earlier civil proceedings; results of blood tests concerning paternity (see the F.L.R.A. 1969, s. 20(1)). The standard proof for adultery seems to be proof on the balance of probabilities.

ad valorem. In proportion to the value. In the case of an *ad valorem* tax, the amount paid is proportionate to the value of the article taxed.

advance freight. *See* FREIGHT.

advancement. 1. Power of advancement allows a trustee (qv) to apply capital for the advancement or benefit of any person entitled to capital of the trust property or any share in it: Tr.A. 1925, s. 32. 2. Presumption of advancement, ie, that a gift was intended, arises where a voluntary conveyance has been made to the wife or child of the donor or to a person to whom he stands *in loco parentis* (qv). See *Tucker* v *Burrow* (1865) 2 H & M 515; *Bennet* v *Bennet* (1879) 10 ChD 474. *See* PORTION.

adversary procedure. Accusatorial procedure (qv).

adverse occupation of residential premises. It is an offence for a person who is on premises as a trespasser, after having entered as such, to fail to leave on being required to do so by or on behalf of a displaced residential occupier of the premises or a protected intending occupier (ie, one who has in those premises a freehold interest or leasehold interest with not less than 21 years still to run who acquired the interest for money or money's worth, who requires the premises for his own occupation as a residence and is excluded by the trespasser): C.L.A. 1977, s. 7(1),(2). For defences available to the accused, see s. 7(6)–(8).

adverse possession. Refers to one person's ownership of land which is inconsistent with the right of another who claims to be the true owner. Minor acts of trespass do not constitute adverse possession: *Leigh* v *Jack* (1879) 5 Ex D 264. It is not necessary to establish inconvenience to the owner in order to establish adverse possession: *Treloar* v *Nute* [1976] 1 WLR 1295. See *Hyde* v *Pearce* [1982] 1 All ER 1029.

adverse witnesses. Witnesses who disappoint the party calling them, ie, they are unfavourable and hostile witnesses.

advertent and inadvertent negligence. *See* NEGLIGENCE, ADVERTENT.

advertisement. Public announcement or notice. Includes, under the C.C.A. 1974, s. 189(1) ''every form of advertising, whether in a publication, by television or radio, by display of notices, signs, labels, showcards or goods, by distribution of samples, circulars, catalogues, price lists or other material, by exhibition of pictures, models or films, or in any other way . . .''. Public advertisement of a reward for the return of stolen or lost goods ''to the effect that no questions will be asked'' is an offence under the Th.A. 1968, s. 23. See *Denham* v *Scott* [1983] Crim LR 558.

advertiser. In relation to an advertisement, this means any person indicated by the advertisement as willing to enter into transactions to which the advertisement relates: C.C.A. 1974, s. 189(1); S.I. 1980/54.

advice on evidence. Document prepared by counsel following the close of pleadings (qv), on instructions by a party's solicitor. It surveys the dispute, enumerates facts in issue and how they should be dealt with, and expresses an opinion concerning the possibility of success and the appropriateness of a settlement.

Advisory, Conciliation and Arbitration Service. A body set up under the E.P.A. 1975, s. 1, charged with a general duty of promoting the improvement of industrial relations, and encouraging the extension, development and reform of collective bargaining. It is controlled by a council, comprising a chairman and nine members. See *Grunwick Processing Laboratories Ltd* v *ACAS* [1978] 1 All ER 338.

Advisory Council on Misuse of Drugs. Statutory body set up under the Misuse of Drugs Act 1971, which keeps under review the situation regarding drugs that appear likely to be misused and which advises on the restriction of availability of such drugs. *See* DRUGS, CONTROLLED.

advocate. One who is professionally qualified and has the right to plead another's cause in court, eg, a barrister (qv) or solicitor (qv).

Advocate-General. An assistant to a judge of the Court of Justice of the European Communities. He is not a member of the Court, but advises, rather like *amicus curiae* (qv), making reasoned submissions on matters referred to it. Submissions are given orally before judgment is given. See the Treaty of Rome 1957, arts. 166, 167. *See* COURT OF JUSTICE OF THE EUROPEAN COMMUNITIES.

advowson. Incorporeal hereditaments (qv) to which the law of real property applies, consisting of the perpetual right to present to an ecclesiastical living. The owner of the right is known as the patron. See the Lim.A. 1980, s. 25.

aedificatum solo, solo cedit. That which is built upon land becomes part of the land. *See* FIXTURES.

aequitas est quasi aequalitas. Equity is, as it were, equality. See *Jones* v *Maynard* [1951] Ch 572.

affidavit. Written statement, sworn or affirmed (usually before a Commissioner for Oaths (qv)), in the name of the deponent. See O. 38, r. 2(3) (evidence given on affidavit). Statements on affidavit are not generally subjected to cross-examination (qv). Affidavits used in interlocutory matters may contain certain hearsay evidence: O. 41, r. 5(2). *See* EVIDENCE, HEARSAY.

affidavit of documents. When a party has received a list of documents (qv) he may give notice to the other party requiring verification by affidavit. See O. 24, r. 5.

affiliation order. An order of the magistrates' court adjudging, finding or declaring a person to be the father of a child and (usually) providing for the maintenance of the child. See the Affiliation Proceedings Act 1957; the Attachment of Earnings Act 1971; the Maintenance Orders (Reciprocal Enforcement) Act 1972, s. 21(1), and the M.C.A. 1980, s. 93; *Foy* v *Brooks* [1977] 1 WLR 160. Proceedings may be instituted by the mother, or local authority, or custodian of child (see the Ch.A. 1975, s. 45) and such an order can be enforced by committal. See the Child Care Act 1980, ss. 49, 50, Sch. 2; and the C.J.J.A. 1982, s. 5.

affinity. Relationship resulting from marriage, eg, between a wife and her husband's blood relations, as opposed to consanguinity, ie, relationship by blood.

affirm. 1. To confirm a judgment, as where an appellate court confirms the judgment of a court below it. 2. To make a solemn declaration instead of taking an oath (if one has no religious belief, or the taking of an oath is contrary to a religious belief). The usual form is "I . . . do solemnly, sincerely and truly declare and affirm that the evidence which I shall give shall be the truth, the whole truth and nothing but the truth." See the Oaths Act 1978, s. 6. 3. To declare with full knowledge of the facts an intention to proceed with a contract. Lapse of time may be evidence of affirmation. See *Leaf* v *International Galleries* [1950] 2 KB 86.

affirmanti non neganti incumbit probatio. The burden of proof is on him who affirms, not on him who denies.

affirmative pregnant. An assertion in a pleading, implying, or not excluding, some negative. *See* NEGATIVE PREGNANT.

affray. Unlawful fighting or a display of force (but without actual violence) in such a manner as to frighten reasonable persons. See *Button* v *DPP* [1966] AC 591. One person fighting unlawfully may properly be convicted of an affray: *Taylor* v *DPP* [1973] AC 964. See also *R* v *Sidhu* [1976] 63 Cr App R 24; *R* v *Crimlis* [1976] Crim LR 693.

affreightment. A contract of affreightment, in the form of a bill of lading (qv) or charterparty (qv), is an undertaking by a ship owner to carry goods for a person known as the *freighter*, in his ship for reward. *See* FREIGHT.

a fortiori [ratione]. For a stronger reason.

after-acquired property. A husband was entitled at common law absolutely on his marriage to the property belonging to his wife, including that which she acquired after marriage. The separate treatment of a married woman's property was introduced by the L.P.A. 1925, s. 170 (now repealed).

after care condition. Phrase used in relation to planning permission, referring to steps to be taken, after working of minerals, to bring land to the required standard for use in agriculture, forestry, or for amenity: see the T.C.P.A. 1971, s. 40A (inserted by the T.C.P.(Minerals)A. 1981, s. 5). *See* RESTORATION CONDITION.

A.-G. Attorney-General (qv).

age. "A person: is over or under a particular age if he has, or as the case may be has not, attained that age: is between two particular ages if he has attained the first but not the second": S.S.A. 1975, Sch. 20.

age, full. *See* FULL AGE.

agency. *See* AGENT.

agent. Generally one who is employed so as to bring his principal into contractual relationships with other persons. An agency can be created: by express agreement, verbally or in writing; by implication or conduct (see *Summers* v *Solomon* (1857) 7 E & B 879); by necessity, as when a person has been entrusted with another's property, the preservation of which requires certain actions, eg, feeding and stabling an animal (see *GN Rwy* v *Swaffield* (1874) LR 6 Ex 132). An agency may be terminated by operation of law or action of parties. *See* RATIFICATION.

agent and principal, duties of. A principal's duties are generally: to pay the agent his agreed remuneration; to indemnify the agent against expenses, liabilities and claims incurred in discharging the agency. An agent's duties are: to exercise his duties with appropriate care and skill; to perform those duties personally; to avoid conflict between his personal interests and those of the principal; to hand over to the principal all money due.

agent provocateur. "A person who entices another to commit an express breach of the law which he would not otherwise have committed and then proceeds to inform against him in respect of such an offence": *Royal Commission on Police Powers* 1928 (Cmd 3297), cited in *R* v *Mealey and Sheridan* (1975) 60 Cr App R 59. If a crime is procured by an *agent provocateur*, that is in itself no defence, but it may result in a lighter sentence. See *R* v *McEvilly* (1975) 60 Cr App R 150; *R*

v *Ameer and Lucas* [1977] Crim LR 105. *See* ENTRAPMENT.

agent, special. An agent employed to transact particular business only.

agent, universal. An agent appointed, usually by power of attorney (qv), with unlimited authority to act for his principal.

age of consent. *See* CONSENT, AGE OF.

age, pensionable. In the case of a man, 65; in the case of a woman, 60: S.S.A. 1975, s. 27(1). See the S.S.A. 1979, s. 4.

age, proof of. Procedure whereby a person's age is proved by: production of a birth certificate and evidence of identity; declaration of a deceased person against interest or in the course of duty; someone present at birth. In some cases, see, eg, the S.O.A. 1956, s. 28(3), there may be an "inference of age" from appearance.

aggravated assault. An assault (qv) such as that committed upon a woman, meriting a more severe punishment than that following a common assault. See the O.P.A. 1861, ss. 38, 43; the C.J.A. 1925 and 1967; the Police Act 1964, s. 51; and the Th.A. 1968, s. 8 (under which a person guilty of assault with intent to rob is liable to life imprisonment): *Holden* v *King* (1876) 35 LT 479.

aggravated burglary. *See* BURGLARY.

aggrieved person. "A man who has suffered a legal grievance, a man against whom a decision has been pronounced which has wrongfully deprived him of something, or wrongfully refused him something, or wrongfully affected his title to something": *per* James LJ in *Ex p Sidebotham* (1880) 14 Ch D 458.

agistment. The taking of another's animals to graze on one's pastures, for reward.

agnates. Relations by the father's side, eg, one's son, brother, sister. *See* COGNATES.

agreement. A consensus of minds, or evidence of such consensus, in spoken or written form, relating to anything done or to be done. "A declared concurrence of will of two or more persons whereby a change in their legal spheres is intended": Gareis. *See* CONTRACT.

agreement, closed-shop. *See* CLOSED-SHOP AGREEMENT.

agreement, conditional. An agreement, the operation of which is dependent on the occurrence of an uncertain event. See *Pym* v *Campbell* (1856) 6 E & B 370; *Hargreaves Transport Ltd* v *Lynch* [1969] 1 WLR 215.

agreement, modifying. An agreement varying or supplementing an earlier agreement: C.C.A. 1974, s. 82(2).

agreement, multiple. A term used under the C.C.A. 1974, s. 18, to refer to an agreement, the terms of which place a part of it within one category of agreement mentioned in the Act, and another part of it within a different category of agreement so mentioned, or within a category of agreement not so mentioned, or which place it or a part of it within two or more categories of agreement so mentioned.

agreement, non-commercial. A consumer credit agreement (qv) or a consumer hire agreement not made by the creditor or owner in the course of a business carried on by him: C.C.A. 1974, s. 189(1).

agreements, regulated. *See* REGULATED AGREEMENTS.

agricultural holding. "The aggregate of the agricultural land comprised in a contract of tenancy": Agricultural Holdings Act 1948, s. 1(1). "Agricultural land" is land used for agricultural purposes in relation to a trade or business. Security of tenure is conferred under ss. 2, 3; see also the Agricultural (Misc. Provs.) Act 1976, ss. 12, 16, 18. Notice period is generally one year and is operative only if, eg, consent is given by the Agricultural Land Tribunal and land is required for non-agricultural use. Rent may be fixed, in absence of agreement, by an arbitrator appointed under the 1948 Act, s. 5. See also the Agricultural Holdings (Notices to Quit) Act 1977. See *Wetherall* v *Smith* [1980] 2 All ER 530.

agriculture. This includes horticulture, fruit growing, seed growing, dairy farming, livestock breeding and keeping, forestry, the use of land as grazing land, meadow land, osier land, market gardens and nursery grounds and the preparation of land for agricultural uses: H.S.W.A. 1974, s. 53(1). See Agricultural Marketing Act 1983, s. 8.

aid or abet. "Aiding and abetting almost inevitably involves a situation in which the secondary party and the main offender are together at some stage discussing the plans which they may be making in respect of the alleged offence, and are in contact so that each knows what is passing through the mind of the other": *A.-G.'s Reference (No 1 of 1975)* [1975] 2 All ER 684. "Whosoever shall aid, abet, counsel or procure the commission of any misdemeanour at common law or by virtue of any Act passed or to be passed, shall be liable to be tried, indicted and punished as a principal offender": Accessories and Abettors Act 1861, s. 8. See also the M.C.A. 1980, s. 44; *R* v *Coney* (1882) 8 QBD 534; *Wilcox* v *Jeffrey* [1951] 1 All ER 464; *R* v *Jones and Mirrless* (1977) 65 Cr App R 250; *R* v *Dunnington* (*The Times*, 11.8.1983). *See* ABET; ACCESSORY; ACCOMPLICE; PROCURING AN OFFENCE.

aids. 1. Services due from a tenant to his lord, eg, ransom for an imprisoned lord. Abolished under the Tenures Abolition Act 1660. 2. A *grant in aid* may be made to a local authority by Parliament to support the revenue from rates. See the L.G.A. 1966 and 1974. *See* BLOCK GRANT.

air pollution. A local authority may require the occupier of any premises (except private dwellings) in its area to furnish information concerning the emission of pollutants and other substances into the air from those premises: Control of Pollution Act 1974, s. 80(1). See also the Clean Air Acts 1956 and 1958, imposing fines for the emission of dark smoke from buildings in certain areas.

air, right to flow of. The right can subsist as an easement (qv) if claimed in respect of some defined channel, eg, a ventilator. See *Harris* v *De Pinna* (1886) 33 Ch D 238; *Cable* v *Bryant* [1908] 1 Ch 259.

airspace, interference with. A possible trespass created by an intrusion into another's airspace. See the Civil Aviation Act 1949; *Kelsen v Imperial Tobacco Co* [1957] 2 QB 334; *Woollerton & Wilson Ltd v Richard Costain Ltd* [1970] 1 WLR 411. "In none of [the cases] is there an authoritative pronouncement that [in the phrase 'trespass to land'] 'land' means the whole of space from the centre of the earth to the heavens": *Commissioner for Rwys v Valuer-General* [1974] AC 328. See *Bernstein v Skyviews & General Ltd* [1977] 2 All ER 902—no right of privacy in airspace. See the Civil Aviation Act 1982, s. 77. *See* CUJUS EST SOLUM.

alcoholics, treatment centres for. *See* DETOXIFICATION CENTRES.

alderman. A senior member of municipal government. See the L.G.A. 1972, s. 249.

aleatory contract. A wagering contract. See *Ellesmere v Wallace* [1929] 2 Ch 1. *See* BET.

alias. (*Alias dictus* = otherwise called) Second, or assumed, name.

alibi. Elsewhere. Argument by an accused person alleging that at the supposed time of the commission of the offence he was elsewhere. He may not bring evidence to support an alibi, except with leave of the court, unless he has given particulars to the prosecution within seven days of the end of committal proceedings. See the C.J.A. 1967, s. 11; Practice Direction [1969] 1 WLR 603; *R v Jackson and Robertson* [1973] Crim LR 356; *R v Bonnick* (1977) 66 Cr App R 266; *R v Cooper* (1979) 69 Cr App R 229.

alien. At common law, one who was "born out of the allegiance of our sovereign Lord the King": Littleton. Under the B.N.A. 1981, s. 51(1), it means a person who is neither a Commonwealth citizen, nor a British protected person, nor a citizen of the Republic of Ireland. An *alien enemy* is the subject of a state with which this country is at war, or who resides voluntarily or carries on business in enemy, or enemy-occupied, territory. See *Sooracht's Case* [1943] AC 203. *See* NATURALISATION.

alienable. Capable of being transferred.

alienate. To exercise the power of disposing of or transferring property.

alienation. Power of disposing of or transferring an interest in property; the exercise of that power by an *alienor* to an *alienee*.

alienation, restraint on. Conditions attempting to fetter the right to dispose of or transfer freely an interest in possession in property. Generally void. See, eg, *Re Dugdale* (1888) 38 Ch D 176; *Caldy Manor Estate Ltd v Farrell* [1974] 3 All ER 753.

alieni juris. Of another's right. Term used to refer (in contrast to *sui juris* (qv)) to persons subject to the authority of another, eg, minors.

alimentary trust. A protective trust (qv).

alimony. "That allowance which a married woman sues for on separation from her husband": Cowel. Maintenance pending suit (qv) has replaced alimony pending suit; financial provision for a spouse has replaced an order for permanent alimony: see the Mat.C.A. 1973, Part II.

aliquis non debet esse judex in propria causa quia non potest esse judex et pars. No man should be a judge in his own cause, since he cannot act at the same time as judge and party. See, eg, the General Rate Act 1967, s. 106, authorising an exception to the rule.

aliter. Otherwise.

aliunde. From another place or person.

allegation. A statement of fact in proceedings made by a party who undertakes to prove it. *See* AVERMENT.

allegiance. "Such natural or legal obedience which every subject owes to his prince": *Termes de la Ley*. Allegiance may be due not only from subjects, but also from aliens resident in British territory or elsewhere where they retain British passports: *Joyce v DPP* [1946] AC 347. Breach of allegiance may amount to treason (qv).

allegiance, oath of. *See* OATH OF ALLEGIANCE.

all fours. Cases or judgments alike in all material respects are said to "run on all fours".

allocatur. It is allowed. Term referring to certificate of allowance of costs issued by taxing office. See O. 62, r. 22.

allocutus. Demand by court of a convicted person, asking whether he has cause to show why judgment should not be pronounced against him.

allodium. Land held in absolute ownership.

allotment, letter of. Notification to an applicant that shares in a company have been appropriated to him, usually by a resolution of the Board of Directors. See the Cos.A. 1948, ss. 47, 49–52; and the Cos.A. 1980, ss. 14, 16–18, 22–25, 28. Allotment signifies acceptance of an offer to take shares. There is no binding contract until an allotment is made and a letter has been posted, or has reached the allottee in another way. See *Dunlop* v *Higgins* (1848) 1 HLC 381; *Household Fire Insurance Co* v *Grant* (1879) 4 Ex D 216. *See* SHARE.

alteration. A material alteration (eg, of a date), which alters the sense or effect of an instrument, generally invalidates it. An alteration in a deed (qv) is presumed to have been made before or at the time of execution; an alteration in a will (qv) is presumed to have been made after the time of execution. See the W.A. 1837, s. 21; *Cooper* v *Bockett* (1846) 4 Moo PC.

alteration of share capital. A company may alter its capital if authorised by its articles (qv): Cos.A. 1948, s. 61. A resolution in a general meeting is needed and notice must be given to the Registrar. Shares may be *consolidated*, eg, by the amalgamation of smaller into larger, and *sub-divided*, or converted to stock. Nominal or authorised capital (qv) may be increased and unissued nominal capital cancelled. *See* SHARE.

alternative counts. *See* COUNTS, ALTERNATIVE.

alternative danger, principle of. Common law principle relating to tort, arising where the plaintiff has not necessarily contributed by negligence (qv) to his injuries if, as the result of the defendant's negligence, the plaintiff was placed in a dilemma and, in the agony of the moment, chose a wrong alternative. See, eg, *Jones* v *Boyce* (1816) 1 Stark 493.

alternative, pleading in the. Inclusion in pleadings (qv) of two or more inconsistent sets of material facts and the claiming of relief in the alternative.

alternative verdict. *See* VERDICT, ALTERNATIVE.

amalgamation. The combination of two or more companies into one company or into a unit controlled by one company. See Cos.A. 1948, ss. 206, 208. See *Re Savoy Hotel* [1981] Ch 351.

ambiguity. Uncertain meaning. 1. *Patent ambiguity* (eg, a blank space in a deed) is one apparent on the face of the instrument. It cannot generally be resolved by parol evidence (qv). See *Kell* v *Charmer* (1856) 23 Beav 195; *Watcham* v *A.-G. for E Africa* [1919] AC 533. 2. *Latent ambiguity* (eg, "my horse I leave to my nephew John," where the testator had two nephews of that name) is one not apparent on the face of the instrument. It may generally be resolved by parol evidence (qv). See *Doe d Gord* v *Needs* (1836) 2 M & W 129. For the rectification, etc, of wills see the A.J.A. 1982, ss. 20–22. *See* EQUIVOCATION.

ambulatory. Capable of being revoked. Thus, a man's will is ambulatory until the moment of his death. See *Vynior's Case* (1609) 8 Co Rep 81b.

ameliorating waste. Alterations which, in fact, improve land: *Doherty* v *Allman* (1877) 3 App Cas 709— injunction refused where tenant was converting dilapidated store houses into dwellings. *See* WASTE.

amendment. Correction of a defect in a writ or pleadings, or in criminal proceedings. "I know of no kind of error or mistake which, if not fraudulent or intended to overreach, the court ought not to correct, if it can be done without injustice to the other party": *Cropper* v *Smith* (1884) 26 Ch D 700. After service, a writ may be amended once without leave before the close of pleadings: O. 20, r. 3. Amendment at any stage on such terms as may be just is allowed under O. 20, r. 5.

amends, tender of. An offer of money

tendered in satisfaction of the alleged committing of a wrong. Where used as a defence, money tendered must be brought to court.

amenity. That which is conducive to comfort or convenience. "In relation to any place includes any view of or from that place": Petroleum (Consolidation) Act 1928, s. 23. For standard amenities relating to a dwelling, see, eg, the H.A. 1974, s. 89. See *FFF Estates* v *Hackney LBC* [1981] QB 503.

amenity, loss of. Also referred to as "loss of faculty" and "loss of enjoyment of life". Result of injuries depriving the plaintiff of some enjoyment. See *H. West & Son Ltd* v *Shephard* [1964] AC 326; *Povey* v *Governors of Rydal School* [1970] 1 All ER 841.

amenity, preservation of. Basis of provisions relating to buildings of special interest, trees, caravan sites, etc. See, eg, tree preservation orders: Town and Country Planning (Tree Preservation Order) Regulations 1969; designation of conservation areas (qv): Caravan Sites and Control of Development Act 1960.

a mensa et thoro. From board and bed. A decree in the ecclesiastical courts (qv), prior to the Mat.C.A. 1857, which had the effect of a judicial separation (qv).

amercement. Obsolete penalty (fine) once inflicted "at the mercy of" (*à merci*), ie, at the discretion of, the court. See *Re Nottingham Corporation* [1897] 2 QB 502.

amicus curiae. Friend of the court. A person who is not engaged in the case, but who brings to the court's attention a point which has apparently been overlooked. See *Morelle* v *Wakeling* [1955] 2 QB 379.

ammunition. Defined in the Firearms Act 1968, as ammunition for any firearm, and includes grenades, bombs and other like missiles, whether capable of use with a firearm or not, and "prohibited ammunition" (which includes any ammunition containing, or designed or adapted to contain, any noxious liquid, gas or other things: s. 5(1)(2)).

amnesty. An act of government by which certain past offences are pardoned.

analogy, use of. Use in legal argument of a principle based on two things resembling each other in one or more respects. ("A certain proposition is true of the one, therefore it is true of the other": J. S. Mill.)

ancestor. 1. One from whom a person is descended. 2. Before the L.P.A. 1925, a person from whom real property was inherited. See *Zetland* v *Lord Advocate* (1878) 3 App Cas 505; *Knowles* v *A.-G.* [1951] P 4.

ancient demesne. Tenure, abolished by the L.P.A. 1922, s. 128, whereby the land of tenants was passed by common law conveyance. See *Iveagh* v *Martin* [1961] 1 QB 232.

ancient document. A document 20 years old or more. "Ancient documents coming out of proper custody and purporting on the face of them to show exercise of ownership . . . may be given in evidence without proof of possession or payment of rent as being in themselves acts of ownership and proof of possession": *Malcolmson* v *O'Dea* (1863) 10 HLC 593. See the Evidence Act 1938, s. 4; *Bristow* v *Cormican* (1878) 3 App Cas 641. *See* DOCUMENT.

ancient lights. A right which arises "when the access and use of light . . . shall have been actually enjoyed . . . for the full period of 20 years without interruption . . . unless it shall appear that the same was enjoyed by some consent or agreement . . . by deed or writing": Prescription Act 1832, s. 3. See also the Rights of Light Act 1959 (giving a temporary extension of the period to 27 years).

ancient monument. Any scheduled monument or other monument, which, in the opinion of the Secretary of State is of public interest by reason of the historic, architectural, traditional, artistic or archaeological interests attaching to it: Ancient Monuments and Archaeological Areas Act 1979, s. 61(12), Schs 1, 2.

ancillary credit business. Business comprising or relating to: credit brokerage; debt adjusting; debt-counselling; debt-collecting; the operation of a credit reference agency: C.C.A. 1974, s. 145(1).

ancillary probate. *See* PROBATE, ANCILLARY.

ancillary relief. Phrase used, eg, under the Matrimonial Causes Rules 1977, r. 68, referring to an order for maintenance pending suit, financial provision order, property adjustment order, variation order, etc.

animal. Term which includes (*a*) any kind of mammal, except man, (*b*) any kind of four-footed beast, which is not a mammal, (*c*) fish, reptiles, crustaceans and other cold-blooded creatures not falling within (*a*) or (*b*) above: Animal Health Act 1981, s. 87. "Wild animals" are animals not normally domesticated in Britain: Zoo Licensing Act 1981, s. 21(1).

animals, classification of. Animals *domitae naturae* or *mansuetae naturae* (tame or domesticated, eg, horses); animals *ferae naturae* (of a wild nature), eg, monkeys. Under the Animals Act 1971, s. 2(2), liability arises, in the case of an animal of a non-dangerous species if: damage is of a kind which the animal, unless restrained, was likely to cause, or which if caused by the animal, was likely to be severe; likelihood of the danger or its severity is due to the animal's characteristics not likely to be found in animals of that species; those characteristics are known to its keeper, or his servant, or a member of the household under 16 years. See also the Dangerous Wild Animals Act 1976; *Wallace v Newton* [1982] 1 WLR 325. *See* DANGEROUS SPECIES; DANGEROUS WILD ANIMALS.

animals, dangerous. *See* DANGEROUS WILD ANIMALS.

animal, wild. "Any animal (other than a bird) which is or (before it was killed or taken) was living wild": Wildlife and Countryside Act 1981, s. 27(1).

animus. Intention. 1. *animus deserendi.* Intention of deserting. 2. *animus furandi.* Intention of stealing. 3. *animus manendi.* Intention of remaining. 4. *animus non revertendi.* Intention of not returning. 5. *animus possidendi.* Intention of possessing. 6. *animus quo.* Intention with which. 7. *animus*

revocandi. Intention of revoking. 8. *animus testandi.* Intention of making a will.

annoyance. "The expression 'annoyance' is wider than 'nuisance', and a thing that reasonably troubles the mind and pleasure—not of a fanciful person or of a skilled person who knows the truth, but of the ordinary sensible English inhabitant of a house, seems to me to be an 'annoyance', although it may not appear to amount to physical detriment to comfort": *Tod-Heatley v Benham* (1888) 40 Ch D 80. See also *Everett v Remington* [1892] 3 Ch 148; *Wood v Cooper* [1894] 3 Ch 671.

annual return. Document required under the Cos.A. 1948, s. 124(1), which must be filed annually with the Registrar of Companies. It must be filed within 42 days after the annual general meeting and must be accompanied by a copy of the auditors' report and balance sheet. It must contain particulars set out in the Cos.A. 1948, Sch. 6, Part I. Notice of receipt of the return by the Registrar must be published in the *London Gazette*. See the European Communities Act 1972, s. 9(3) and the Cos.A. 1976, ss. 1–11.

Annual Practice, The. *See* RULES OF THE SUPREME COURT.

annual value. Value placed on land or hereditaments (qv) for purposes of assessment of liability to local rates and income tax.

annuity. An annual payment of a sum of money as a personal obligation of the grantor or charged on personalty or a mixed fund. See *Hill v Gregory* [1912] 2KB 61. An annuity, which before January 1st, 1926, was capable of being registered in the register of annuities, is void against a creditor or purchaser of any interest in the land charged with the annuity, unless it is registered in the register of annuities or register of land charges: L.C.A. 1972, Sch. 1(4). The fact that an annuity is registered does not prevent it being overreached.

annul. To declare judicial proceedings or their outcome to be no longer of legal effect.

annulment. 1. Annulment of adjudication. The court may annul (see B.A. 1914, ss. 29, 31) an adjudication in bankruptcy (qv) where, eg: in its opinion the debtor should not have been judged bankrupt, or it is proved that the debts have been paid in full, or it approves a composition (qv) or scheme. The power is discretionary: *Re Taylor* [1901] 1 QB 744. See the Bankruptcy Rules 1952, r. 213. 2. Annulment of marriage. 3. Appeal for annulment. Under the Treaty of Rome, arts. 173, 174, the European Court of Justice (qv) may, on appeal, annul an action of the EEC Council or Commission (qv) because of the lack of jurisdiction, or violation of an essential procedural matter, or infringement of the Treaty, or misuse of powers.

annus, dies et vastum. Year, day and waste (qv).

answer. 1. Statement of defence (qv) delivered in reply to statement of claim (qv). See O. 26, r. 1 (in connection with interrogatories (qv)). 2. In proceedings for divorce, the defence of a respondent or co-respondent to a petition (qv).

antecedent negotiations. Defined, in relation to credit agreements, as including, eg, negotiations with a hirer or debtor conducted by the owner or creditor in relation to the making of a regulated agreement: C.C.A. 1974, s. 1.

antecedent rights. Rights existing, in their own sake, prior to the commission of a wrongful act, eg, one's right not to have reputation attacked unjustifiably. Contrasted with *remedial rights* (which arise from the infringement of a primary right), eg, rights to damages after events of this nature.

antecedents. Term used to refer, eg, to an offender's record and other history. Where, after the conviction of an offender, a police officer gives evidence of the offender's character and antecedents, he must confine himself to evidence of the previous convictions, home circumstances, etc, and matters in the offender's favour. See *R v Wilkins* (1977) 66 Cr App R 49; *R v Warrington Justices ex p*

Mooney (1980) 2 Cr App R (S) 40.

ante-date. Dating of a document before the date on which it was drawn up. See the B.Ex.A. 1882; s. 13(2).

ante litem motam. Before litigation commenced.

ante-natal care, time off for. Right of a pregnant employee not to be unreasonably refused time off during her working hours to receive ante-natal care: Employment Act 1980, s. 13.

anticipation, restraint on. Settlements of property on women were at one time accompanied by restraints on their assigning income before it became due. Restraints of this nature were abolished by the Law Reform (Married Women and Tortfeasors) Act 1935 and the Married Women (Restraint upon Anticipation) Act 1949.

anticipatory breach. Term referring to the repudiation (qv) of a contract before the time for performance. The other party may immediately treat the contract as though it were discharged and sue for damages. See *Hochster v De La Tour* (1835) 2 E & B 678; *Woodar Investments v Wimpey Ltd* [1980] 1 All ER 571. *See* BREACH OF CONTRACT.

Anton Piller order. High Court order to a defendant to permit the plaintiff to enter the defendant's premises to inspect, remove or make copies of the plaintiff's documents. The plaintiff must show that there is a danger of property or vital evidence being removed. Generally applicable to copyright cases: see *Anton Piller KG v Manufacturing Processes Ltd* [1976] Ch 55; *Yousif v Salama* [1980] 3 All ER 405; *Rank Film Distributors Ltd v Video Information Centre* [1982] AC 380; (order limited by possibility of self-incrimination); *Dunlop Holdings and Dunlop v Staravia* [1982] Com LR 3. See the S.C.A. 1981, s. 37; and *Practice Direction* [1982] 1 WLR 1375.

apology. In an action for libel (qv), an apology accompanied by payment of money into the court may be pleaded as a defence or in mitigation of damages. In a case of unintentional defamation, an offer of amends, comprising the published correction of a statement complained of and an apology, may be tendered. See the Libel Acts 1843 and 1845; the Defamation Act 1952; and O. 82, r. 7.

a posteriori. From effect to cause; from subsequent conclusions.

appeal. "The transference of a case from an inferior to a higher tribunal in the hope of reversing or modifying the decision of the former": *Edlesten* v *LCC* [1918] 1 KB 81. In general, the right of appeal must be given by statute.

Appeal Committee of House of Lords. *See* HOUSE OF LORDS, APPEAL COMMITTEE OF.

Appeal, Court of. *See* COURT OF APPEAL.

appeal, interlocutory. Appeal from an order made by a master which lies as of right, in general, to a judge in chambers: O. 58, r. 1. An appeal lies from the judge to the Court of Appeal, usually only by leave of a judge or the Court of Appeal, save, eg, where liberty of the subject is involved.

appeal, reopening of. Following the hearing and dismissal of an appeal by the Court of Appeal, or the abandonment of a notice of appeal, a reopening is not allowed (save in the case of a procedural defect in the hearings). The applicant may petition the Home Secretary, who can refer the case to the Court.

appeals, civil. Appeal lies: from a district registrar to a judge in chambers (O. 58); from a master in the QBD to a judge in chambers or the Court of Appeal (O. 58, rr. 1, 2); from the county court to the Court of Appeal; from the High Court to the Court of Appeal (O. 59); from the Court of Appeal to the House of Lords (Administration of Justice (Appeals) Act 1934, s. 1). See the S.C.A. 1981, s. 54(6).

appeals, criminal. Appeal lies: from courts of summary jurisdiction to the Crown Court (M.C.A. 1980, s. 108); from justices by way of case stated to the High Court (s. 111); in indictable cases, from the Crown Court to the Court of Appeal (Criminal Division) (Criminal Appeal Act 1966, s. 1; Criminal Appeal Act 1968, ss. 45,

52); from the Court of Appeal to the House of Lords. For right of prosecution to appeal on a point of law following acquittal on indictment, see C.J.A. 1972, s. 36(1). See also the C.L.A. 1977, s. 44; Statement of Lord Widgery CJ [1980] 1 WLR 270.

appearance, entering. Procedure, following service of a writ of summons, now abolished and replaced by acknowledgment of service and notice of intention to defend. See O. 12; S.I. 1979/1716.

appear, failure to. Failure of party to appear when an action is called. If neither party appears, the action can be struck off the list. If one party fails to appear, the judge may proceed with the trial. See O. 35, r. 1.

appellant. The person making an appeal.

appellate jurisdiction. Power of a court to hear an appeal.

appendant. Annexed to a hereditament (qv) by operation of law, eg, a common of pasture. Can generally be claimed by prescription (qv). *See* APPURTENANT.

appointed day. Date on which an Act is to become operative.

appointee. *See* APPOINTMENT, POWER OF.

appointment, excessive. Exercise of a power of appointment (qv) which is excessive in the circumstances, eg, where the appointor grants an interest greater than that authorised by the power, or where he appoints to persons who are outside the class of objects of the power. See *Re Boulton's ST* [1928] Ch 703; *Re Hay's ST* [1981] 3 All ER 786.

appointment, power of. The power given to a person, usually by trust or settlement, enabling him to dispose of an interest in property which is not his. If A confers on B the right to exercise a power of appointment, and B exercises it in favour of C, A is the *donor* of the power, B is the *donee* or *appointor*, C is the *appointee*, B's exercise of the power is the *appointment*. Powers may be: *public* (conferred by statute) and *private*; *general* (enabling the appointor to appoint in favour of any person) and *special* (enabling the appointment to be made only to members of a given class); *hybrid* (neither special nor general). See the L.P.A. 1925, s. 1(7) under which the exercise of a power creates an equitable interest. See *Re Rank's ST* [1979] 1 WLR 1242. *See* POWER.

appointor. *See* APPOINTMENT, POWER OF.

apportionment. Division into parts which are proportionate to interests and rights of parties. See the Apportionment Act 1870; and the L.P.A. 1925, s. 140. Where a duty arises to convert assets of a hazardous and wasting nature in the interests of a remainderman, trustees must apportion between capital and income ("equitable apportionment"). See *Howe* v *Lord Dartmouth* (1802) 7 Ves 137. *See* REMAINDER.

apprehension or prosecution, impeding. *See* IMPEDING APPREHENSION OR PROSECUTION.

apprentice. A person bound by contract to serve and learn from a master who, in turn, undertakes to instruct him in a trade or profession. The contract must be in writing or by deed, and is usually signed also by the parent or guardian. It is binding on an infant (qv) if beneficial to him. See the Child Care Act 1980, s. 23; *Learoyd* v *Brook* [1891] 1 QB 431; *Dunk* v *George Waller & Son* [1970] 2 QB 163.

approach. In relation to a bridge or tunnel, means the highway giving access thereto, ie, the surface of that highway together with any embankment, retaining wall, or other work or substance supporting or protecting the surface: Highways Act 1980, s. 329(1).

approbate and reprobate. Phrase referring to a person who, taking a benefit under an instrument, must either accept or reject the instrument as a whole. *Qui approbat non reprobat* (qv). See *Codrington* v *Codrington* (1875) 45 LJ Ch 660.

appropriation. Allocation of a sum of money for expenditure. An "appropriation in aid" refers to a transaction whereby a government department receives money from a source other than the Exchequer and is allowed to set it off against expenses.

The annual Appropriation Act gives legal force to Parliament's decisions on the Government's estimates.

appropriation, dishonest. *See* DISHONEST.

appropriation of payments. *See* PAYMENTS, APPROPRIATION OF.

approval, sale on. Where goods are delivered to a buyer on approval, or sale and return, the property passes to the buyer when he adopts the transaction, eg, by signifying approval. If he does not signify approval or acceptance to the seller, the property passes to him if he retains the goods on the expiration of a fixed time or, if no time has been fixed, on the expiration of a reasonable time: S.G.A. 1979, s. 18. See *Poole* v *Smith's Car Sales Ltd* [1962] 1 WLR 744.

approved schools. Schools approved by the Home Secretary for young offenders. They were abolished by the C. & Y.P.A. 1969 and their place was taken by the system of community homes under the control of local authorities.

approved societies. Bodies formerly approved by the Minister of Health for the administration of national health insurance benefits.

approvement. Common-law right of a lord of the manor to enclose waste lands over which his tenants exercised pasture rights. Approvement of a common now requires the consent of the Secretary of State for the Environment, after a local inquiry. See the L.P.A. 1925, s. 194.

approximation of laws of EEC. Under the Treaty of Rome 1957, members of the EEC agree that the activities of the Community shall include "the approximation of laws of Member States to the extent required for the proper functioning of the Common Market": art. 3(*b*). *See* EEC.

appurtenant. Belonging to; necessary to the enjoyment of a thing. Annexed to a hereditament (qv) by an act of parties or statute, eg, a right of way (which can generally be claimed by express grant or prescription (qv)). "An appurtenant right must be related to the needs or use of the dominant tenement. For this reason an exclusive right to grazing, or taking timber, or fishing without limit, cannot exist as appurtenant to another property": *Anderson* v *Bostock* [1976] Ch 312.

a priori. From cause to effect; from previous assumptions.

aqua cedit solo. Water passes with the soil. Ownership of water generally goes with that of the soil below.

arbitration. The settling of a dispute by an arbitrator. Where arbitrators cannot agree they may appoint an "umpire". The decision of an arbitrator is known as an "award". Procedure on arbitration is based on the ordinary rules of English law. An award may be enforced, with leave of the High Court, as an order of the court. Where so directed by the High Court, an arbitrator or umpire must state, in the form of a special case for the opinion of the High Court, an award or question of law arising. See the Arbitration Acts 1950, 1975, 1979; O. 73; *Bremer Vulcan* v *S India Shipping Corp* [1981] AC 909; *Pioneer Shipping* v *BTP Tioxide Ltd* [1982] AC 724; *Paal Wilson & Co A/S* v *Partenreederei Hannah Blumenthal* [1982] 3 WLR 1149.

arbitration agreement. An agreement in writing, including an agreement contained in an exchange of letters or telegrams, to submit to arbitration present or future differences capable of settlement by arbitration: Arbitration Act 1975, s. 7(1). See *Surrendra Overseas Ltd* v *Government of Sri Lanka* [1977] 2 All ER 481.

arbitration agreement, domestic. An agreement that does not provide for arbitration in a foreign state, and to which the parties are neither nationals of nor habitually resident in a foreign state: Arbitration Act 1979, s. 3(7).

arbitration and interest. An arbitrator has jurisdiction to award interest for late payment: *Tehno-Impex* v *Gebr. van Weelde Scheepvaartkantoor BV* [1981] QB 648. See also the Arbitration Act 1950, s. 19 A (added by the A.J.A. 1982, s. 15, Sch 1, Part IV).

arbitration award, judicial review

of. The confirmation, variation, setting aside of the award, or its remission to the reconsideration of the arbitrator or umpire, by the High Court: Arbitration Act 1979, s. 1.

arbitration clause. "It embodies the agreement of both parties that, if any dispute arises with regard to the obligations which one party has undertaken to the other, such dispute shall be settled by a tribunal of their own constitution": *Heyman* v *Darwins Ltd* [1942] AC 356.

arbitration convention award. "An award made in pursuance of an arbitration agreement in the territory of a State, other than the UK, which is a party to the New York Convention [on the Recognition and Enforcement of Foreign Arbitral Awards 1958]": Arbitration Act 1975, s. 7(1).

arbitrations, statutory. Arbitration provided for by Acts of Parliament. See eg, the E.P.(C.)A. 1978.

arbitrator, quasi. *See* QUASI-ARBITRATOR.

arbitrators, appointment of. Appointment may be by: mutual consent of the parties to an arbitration agreement; nomination by a third person, eg, the president of a professional body; the court.

Archbishop. Head of the clergy in a province. His jurisdiction is within his diocese and throughout the province, in which he acts as superior ecclesiastical judge. The two Archbishops in England are Canterbury and York. See the Ecclesiastical Jurisdiction Measure 1963.

Arches, Court of. *See* COURT OF ARCHES.

Area Mental Health Review Tribunals. *See* MENTAL HEALTH REVIEW TRIBUNALS, AREA.

arguendo. In the course of argument.

argumentative affidavit. An affidavit including an indirect argument on the relation of the alleged facts to the essence of the matter in question. See O. 41, r. 5. *See* AFFIDAVIT.

armchair principle. A rule of construction (qv) applied to wills. "You may place yourself, so to speak, in [the testator's] armchair, and consider the circumstances by which he was surrounded when he made his will to assist you in arriving at his intention": *Boyes* v *Cook* (1880) 14 Ch D 53.

Armed Forces. Royal Navy, Royal Marines, regular army and regular air force, and any reserve or auxiliary force of those services called out on permanent service or called into actual service or embodied: Customs and Excise Management Act 1979, s. 1(1).

arm's length, at. 1. Out of reach of personal influence. 2. Conduct of negotiations in a strict, formal manner. See, eg, *Stanton* v *Drayton Commercial Investment Co* [1982] 3 WLR 214.

arraign. To bring the named accused to the bar of the court so that the indictment (qv) can be read to him and he can be asked to plead to it. Unless the defendant is mute, insane or refuses to plead, he must plead personally to the arraignment. "It is only after arraignment, which concludes with the plea of accused to the indictment, that it is known whether there will be a trial, and, if so, what manner of trial": *R* v *Vickers* [1975] 2 All ER 945. *See* PLEADINGS.

arrangement, deeds of. Under the Deeds of Arrangement Act 1914, which refers to arrangements between the debtor and assenting creditors before bankruptcy proceedings are instituted, registration is necessary, eg, where an assignment has been made for the benefit of creditors generally. A deed which is not registered within seven days of execution is generally rendered void as against the purchaser of any land relating to it or affected by it unless registered under the L.C.A. 1972, s. 7(2).

array. *See* CHALLENGE TO JURY.

arrears. Money remaining unpaid after the agreed time for payment.

arrest. To restrain and detain a person by lawful authority. "Whether or not a person has been arrested depends not on the legality of the arrest but on whether he has been deprived of his liberty to go where he pleases": *Spicer* v *Holt* [1977] AC 987. See C.L.A. 1967, s. 2; *Christie* v *Leachinsky* [1947] AC 573; *R* v *Inwood* [1973] 2 All ER 645; *R* v *Brown*

[1977] RTR 160; *Swales* v *Cox* [1981] 1 All ER 1115; *Wills* v *Bowley* [1982]3 WLR 10. *See* DETAIN; FALSE IMPRISONMENT.

arrestable offence. An offence for which the sentence is fixed by law or for which a person (not previously convicted) may under or by virtue of any enactment be sentenced to imprisonment for a term of five years, and any attempt to commit such an offence: C.L.A. 1967, s. 2(1), as amended. An offence may be declared by statute to be arrestable, although carrying a maximum period of less than five years' imprisonment: see, eg, the Th.A. 1968, s. 12(3). A person may arrest without warrant (qv) anyone who is or whom he with reasonable cause suspects to be in the act of committing an arrestable offence, and, where an arrestable offence has been committed, anyone who is or whom he with reasonable cause suspects to be guilty of the offence: C.L.A. 1967, s. 2(2)(3). A police officer may arrest without warrant anyone whom he with reasonable cause suspects to be guilty of committing or about to commit an arrestable offence. See the C.L.A. 1967.

arrest and warrant. Arrest may be made *with* a warrant (qv), ie, by order for arrest. Arrest *without* warrant ("summary arrest") is permissible in the exercise of the common law power of arrest (qv), in relation to arrestable offences (qv) or where otherwise authorised by statute (eg, the Town Police Clauses Act 1847, s. 28—see *Wills* v *Bowley* [1982] 3 WLR 10).

arrest, common law power of. Constables and private citizens have a power of arrest without warrant where: a breach of the peace (qv) was committed in front of the arresting person; the arrestor reasonably believed that a breach of the peace would be committed in the immediate future, although none had been committed; a breach of the peace had been committed and it was reasonably feared that it would be renewed: *R* v *Howell* [1982] QB 416. *See* ARREST; ARREST AND WARRANT.

arrested development of mind. This

may be classified as follows: 1. *Severe abnormality*, when the patient's state includes subnormality of intelligence and is of such a nature or degree that he is incapable of living an independent life or guarding himself against serious exploitation. 2. *Subnormality*, when the patient's state is one (not amounting to severe subnormality) including subnormality of intelligence and which requires or is susceptible to medical treatment or other special care. See the M.H.A. 1983.

arrest for questioning by police. *See* QUESTIONING, DETAINING BY POLICE FOR.

arrest, malicious. Arrest (in civil cases) effected maliciously and without reasonable cause.

arrest of judgment. The move by an accused person between conviction and sentence that judgment be not given because of defects in the indictment. It forms no bar to a new indictment. *See* INDICTMENT.

arrest or prosecute, discretion to. *See* DISCRETION TO ARREST OR PROSECUTE.

arrest, powers of private persons to. Very limited powers are available under some statutes and in the case of arrestable offences (qv). Following such an arrest, the person arrested must be taken before a police officer or magistrate as soon as reasonably practicable: *John Lewis & Co v Tims* [1952] AC 676.

arrest, resisting. Refusal to submit to arrest. "It is the corollary of the right of every citizen to be free from arrest that he should be entitled to resist arrest unless the arrest is lawful": *Christie* v *Leachinsky* [1947] AC 573. See also *R* v *Spencer* (1863) 3 F & F 857.

arrest, search upon. Common law power of a constable to search a person on arrest and to take into custody any article which he believes may be connected with the offence. See *R* v *O'Donnell* (1835) 7 C & P 138. *See* SEARCH, POWER OF.

arrived ship. "Before a ship can be said to have arrived at a port she must, if she cannot proceed immediately to a berth, have reached the position within the port where she is at the immediate and effective dis-

position of the charterer": *per* Lord Reid in *The Johanna Oldendorff* [1974] AC 479 (the so-called "Reid test"). See *The Aello* [1961] AC 135; *Federal Commerce and Navigation Co Ltd* v *Tradax Export SA* [1977] 2 All ER 849.

arson. The common law offence of arson (maliciously and voluntarily burning the dwelling house of another) was abolished under the Criminal Damage Act 1971, s. 11(1). By s. 1(3), offences committed under s. 1 are charged as arson. See *R* v *Aylesbury Crown Court, ex p Simmons* [1972] 3 All ER 574; *R* v *Denton* [1981] 1 WLR 1446; *R* v *Miller* (*The Times*, 18.3.1983).

articles. Clauses or rules in a document, eg, articles of partnership or clerkship (binding a person to serve as an articled clerk).

artificial insemination. Introduction of semen into the uterus by other than natural means. See *Slater* v *Slater* [1953] P 235—decree of nullity of marriage (qv) following a course of artificial insemination. See also *R.E.L.* v *E.L.* [1949] P 211; *A.* v *C.* (1978) 8 Fam Law 170. On the problem of a child born as a result of artificial insemination, see the Home Office Committee Report, 1960, para 80 (Cmnd 1105).

artificial person. A body, eg, a corporation (qv) recognised by law as having rights and duties. Known also as a "juristic person". See the I.A. 1978, s. 5, Sch. 1; *Lee* v *Lee's Air Farming Ltd* [1961] AC 12. *See* NATURAL PERSON.

art, words of. *See* WORDS OF ART.

ascertained goods. Goods identified and agreed upon when a contract is made. See the S.G.A. 1979, s. 16; *The Elafi* [1982] 1 All ER 208. *See* UNASCERTAINED GOODS.

asportation. Carrying away with a view to stealing. An essential feature of larceny (qv) in which the slightest removal sufficed: *R* v *Walsh* (1824) 1 Moo 14.

assault. A crime and a tort resulting from an act by which any person intentionally, or possibly recklessly, causes another to fear reasonably the immediate application to himself of unlawful physical violence: *Fagan* v

Metropolitan Police Commissioner [1969] 1 QB 439. Example: where X advances towards Y, shakes his fist, threatening to beat Y there and then, so that Y is put in fear of immediate violence. The term is often used to include battery, in which case it is an offence under the O.P.A. 1861. For assault as a tort see *Stephens* v *Myers* (1830) 4 C & P 349. It was held in *R* v *Venna* [1976] QB 421 that *mens rea* in assault may consist either of intent to apply physical force, or recklessness. See also *DPP* v *Majewski* [1977] AC 443. *See* BATTERY.

assault, consent and. *See* CONSENT AND ASSAULT.

assault, indecent. *See* INDECENT ASSAULT.

assay mark. *See* HALLMARKING.

Assembly. An institution of the EEC (qv), consisting of representatives of the peoples of member states, who are designated, at present, by their respective parliamentary bodies. See the Treaty of Rome, art. 137. It has advisory and supervisory powers and must be consulted in some cases as part of the process leading to the decisions of the Council of Ministers (qv). By motion of censure it may force the resignation of the Commission of EEC (qv): art. 144. Its recommendations and opinions are delivered in the form of resolutions.

assembly, unlawful. *See* UNLAWFUL ASSEMBLY.

assent. Agreement. "The instrument or act whereby a personal representative effectuates a testamentary disposition by transferring the subject-matter of the disposition to the person entitled to it": *Re King's Will Trusts* [1964] Ch 542. Executors and administrators (qqv) may transfer interests in realty and leaseholds (qqv) by means of an assent in writing: A.E.A. 1925, s. 36.

Assent, Royal. *See* ROYAL ASSENT.

assent, vesting. *See* VESTING ASSENT.

assessment. The act of determining or apportioning. Used in relation to damages (qv), liability to tax, etc.

assessors. Persons with specialist knowledge appointed to assist the court, eg, in Admiralty business. They generally take no part in mak-

ing decisions. See the S.C.A. 1981, s. 70; *The Savina* [1976] 2 Lloyd's R 26.

assets. Physical property or rights which have a value in monetary terms. 1. The assets of a business include: *current assets*, eg, stock, cash; *fixed assets*, eg, machinery, goodwill. Under the Cos.A. 1981, Sch. 1, fixed assets are defined as those intended for use on a continuing basis in the company's activities; current assets are those not intended for such use. 2. The assets of a deceased person consist of the property available for the payment of his debts and liabilities, and include, eg, his property, subject to the general power of appointment (qv) which he exercised by will; entailed property held by him: A.E.A. 1925, s. 32. See the Capital Gains Tax Act 1979, s. 19(1); *O'Brien* v *Benson's Holdings Ltd* [1979] STC 735.

assets, administration of. *See* ESTATES, ADMINISTRATION OF.

assets, distribution of. *See* LIQUIDATION, DISTRIBUTION OF ASSETS ON.

assets, family. *See* FAMILY ASSETS.

assets, marshalling of. *See* MARSHALLING.

assets, net. The aggregate of assets less the aggregate of liabilities: Cos.A. 1980, s. 87(4) (c).

assets, wasting. *See* WASTING ASSETS.

assign. 1. To transfer property to another by assignment. 2. An assignee (qv).

assignee. A person to whom an assignment is made.

assignment. 1. *Legal.* Under the L.P.A. 1925, s. 136, debts and other legal choses in action (qv) may be assigned. The assignment must be absolute, in writing, followed by express notice in writing to the debtor or trustee. 2. *Equitable.* An assignment which does not comply with requirements of a legal assignment. It need not be in writing if intention is clear. 3. *By operation of law.* A contract is assigned by operation of law, eg, on bankruptcy and on death. *See* NOVATION.

assignment of lease. *See* LEASE, ASSIGNMENT OF.

assignor. A person who transfers property to another by assignment.

assistance, writ of. Obsolete writ used by Court of Chancery to enforce order for possession of land. Replaced by writ of possession (see O. 46, r. 3).

assisting offenders. "Where a person has committed an arrestable offence, any other person who, knowing or believing him to be guilty of the offence or of some other offence, does without lawful authority or reasonable excuse any act with intent to impede his apprehension or prosecution shall be guilty of an offence": C.L.A. 1967, s. 4(1).

assize. 1. A statute or ordinance, eg, Assize of Clarendon 1166. (The term was derived from the *session* of King and Council.) 2. Assize Courts tried criminal cases under commissions of oyer and terminer (qv). They were abolished under the Courts Act 1971, s. 1.

assize, petty. Procedure introduced by Henry II, enabling justices in eyre to grant a remedy for loss of seisin (qv). Examples: mort d'ancestor; novel disseisin (qqv).

associated company. A company which, at a given time, has been in the control of another during the previous year, or where both companies are under the control of the same persons: Finance Act 1965. See the Cos.A. 1967, s. 4.

associated employers. Any two employers are treated as associated if one is a company of which the other (directly or indirectly) has control, or if both are companies of which a third person (directly or indirectly) has control: Redundancy Payments Act 1965, s. 48(4); E.P.(C.)A. 1978, s. 153(4); *Umar* v *Pliastar* [1981] ICR 727.

association, articles of. A document which regulates a company's internal affairs, consisting of regulations governing the rights of members *inter se* and the conduct of the company's business, eg, the appointment and powers of directors. Table A of the Cos.A. 1948 may be used as the articles of a company limited by shares. Articles are subject to the memorandum of association (qv) and cannot give any power not given by the memorandum. They can be altered by special resolution at a general meeting: Cos.A. 1948, s. 10(1). See also the Cos.A. 1967, s. 14; and the Cos.A. 1980, s. 2(4). *See* COMPANY.

association clause. A clause in a company's memorandum of association (qv) in which the subscribers declare that they wish to be formed into a company and agree to take the number of shares opposite their names.

association, memorandum of. A document (see the Cos.A. 1980, Sch. 1, Part 1) which regulates a company's external activities and which must be drawn up on the formation of a company. It states the company's name, objectives, registered office, domicile, amount of company's nominal capital, number and amount of shares, etc, in accordance with the provisions of the Cos.A. 1948 and 1980. It can be varied by special resolution: Cos.A. 1948, s. 5. See also the Cos.A. 1967, s. 46; and the European Communities Act 1972, s. 9. *See* COMPANY'S NAME.

assumpsit. He has undertaken. 1. "A voluntary promise made by word": *Termes de la Ley*. 2. A common law action for damages abolished by virtue of the J.A. 1925, brought for breach of contract not under seal. *See* INDEBITATUS ASSUMPSIT.

assurance. 1. "That which operates as a transfer of property": *Re Ray* [1896] 1 Ch 468. 2. A contract which guarantees payment of a sum on the happening of a specified event which must happen sooner or later, eg, death. *See* LIFE ASSURANCE.

assured tenancy. "A tenancy under which a dwelling-house is let as a separate dwelling is an assured tenancy and not a housing association tenancy (within the meaning of the Rent Act 1977, s. 86) nor a protected tenancy if it would, when created, have been a protected tenancy or, as the case may be, a housing association tenancy but for this section and the following conditions are satisfied —namely, that the interest of the landlord has, since the creation of the tenancy, belonged to an approved body, that the dwelling-house is, or forms part of, a building which was erected (and on which construction work first began) after the passing of this Act and before the tenant first occupied the dwelling-house under the tenancy, no part of it had been occupied by any person as his residence except under an assured tenancy": H.A. 1980, s. 56. See the Rent Act 1977, s. 16A.

asylum. 1. A refuge, a place of retreat and relative security. 2. An establishment for the detention and care of sufferers from mental disease: Mental Treatment Act 1930, s. 20(1). Now referred to as "mental hospital": See the M.H.A. 1959, s. 147(1); the M.H.A. 1983, Part II.

at sea. Phrase used, eg, relating to privileged wills (qv) by which a mariner or seaman "being at sea" may make an informal will. "At sea" has been given an extended meaning so as to include, eg, a Merchant Navy apprentice on leave between voyages and due to rejoin his ship— *In b Newland* [1952] P 71; an officer directing naval operations on a river —*In b Austen* (1853) 17 Jur 284. See also *In b Yates* [1919] P 93, and *In b Rapley (The Times, 17.3.1983).*

attachment. 1. Arrest under a writ of attachment, eg, because of disobedience relating to a court order. Generally replaced by punishment for contempt. See O. 52. 2. Enforcement of direction to pay money, by attachment of earnings order. See the Attachment of Earnings Act 1971 (amended by the A.J.A. 1982, ss. 53–54). A "consolidated attachment order" can be made under s. 17 for payment of two or more judgment debts. 3. Attachment of debts relates to procedure in garnishee proceedings (qv). See O. 49, r. 1, and the S.C.A. 1981, 2. 40.

attachment, foreign. *See* MAREVA INJUNCTION.

attainder. "When a man hath committed a felony or treason and judgment is pronounced upon him": Cowel. The property of one who was attaint was forfeited, but this was abolished under the Forfeiture Act 1870.

attempt, common law offence of. Performance of an act which may be regarded as a movement to the commission of an offence and which cannot reasonably be interpreted as having any other objective than the commission of the offence: *R v Button* [1900] 2 QB 597. Abolished under Criminal Attempts Act 1981, s. 6(1).

attempt, intention and. "In any case where (a) apart from this subsection a person's intention would not be regarded as having amounted to an intent to commit an offence; but (b) if the facts of the case had been as he believed them to be, his intention would be so regarded, then [for the purposes of s. 1(1) of this Act] he shall be regarded as having had an intent to commit that offence": Criminal Attempts Act 1981, s. 1(3).

attempt, statutory offence of. "If with intent to commit an offence to which this section applies, a person does an act which is more than merely preparatory to the commission of the offence, he is guilty of attempting to commit the offence": Criminal Attempts Act 1981, s. 1(1). Applies to any offence which, if completed, would be triable as an indictable offence (qv) except: conspiracy; aiding and abetting; assisting offenders or accepting consideration for not disclosing information about an arrestable offence: s. 1(4). A person may be guilty of attempting to commit an offence even though the facts are such that the commission of the offence is impossible: s. 1(2).

attendance. In relation to a "letting with board or attendance", which does not constitute a protected tenancy (qv), means "service personal to the tenant provided by the landlord in accordance with his covenant for the benefit or convenience of the individual tenant for his use or enjoyment of the demised premises": *Palser* v *Grinling* [1948] AC 291.

attendance allowance. Non-contributory benefit payable (under the S.S.A. 1975 provisions) to those so disabled that they require constant attendance (which must be certified by an Attendance Allowance Board).

attendance centre. A place at which offenders under 21 may be required to attend and be given under supervision, appropriate occupation or instruction, in pursuance of an order made under the C.&Y.P.A. 1969, s. 15(2A)(4); P.C.C.A. 1973, s. 6(3)(c); or the C.J.A. 1982, s. 17: C.J.A. 1982, s. 16. For discharge and variation of an order, see s. 18. See Home Office Circular No. 80/1982; S.I. 1983/621.

attestation. The signature of a document by one who is not a party to it, but who is the witness to the signature of another. The W.A. 1837 requires the attestation of two witnesses. See *Re Colling* [1972] 1 WLR 1440; Law Revision Report 1980 (Cmnd 7902); and the A.J.A. 1982, s. 17. *See* WILL, VALIDITY OF.

Att.-Gen. Attorney-General (qv).

attorney. One appointed by another to act in his place. *See* POWER OF ATTORNEY.

Attorney-General. The chief law officer of the Crown and head of the English Bar. His duties include representing the Crown in legal proceedings and conducting some Crown prosecutions. He may stay proceedings by *nolle prosequi* (qv). He may be a member of the cabinet. His consent is necessary in some cases before prosecution: see, eg, the Official Secrets Act 1911, s. 8. "As the guardian of the public interest, the Attorney-General has a special duty in regard to the enforcement of the law . . . it is his duty to represent the public interest with complete objectivity and detachment": *A.-G. (ex rel McWhirter)* v *IBA* [1973] QB 629. See also *Gouriet* v *Union of Post Office Workers* [1978] AC 435.

Attorney-General and relator actions. Where the A.-G. has refused his consent to relator proceedings in the civil courts, a private citizen who asserts that the public interest is involved by threat of a breach of the criminal law has no right to go to the civil courts for a remedy either by way of injunction or a declaration: *Gouriet* v *Union of Post Office Workers* [1978] AC 435. "That it is the exclusive right of the Attorney-General to represent the public interest . . . is not technical, nor procedural, not fictional. It is constitutional": *per* Lord Wilberforce. *See* RELATOR.

Attorney-General's Reference. The A.-G. may refer to the Court of Appeal (Criminal Division) points of law, following an acquittal after trial in the Crown Court: see the C.J.A. 1972, s. 36(1). (The Court of Appeal may refer the point to the House of Lords if it appears that the House should consider it: s. 36(3).) "We hope to see this procedure used extensively for short but important points which require a quick ruling of this court before a potentially false decision of law has too wide a circulation in the courts": *per* Lord Widgery CJ (see *Re A.-G.'s Ref (No. 1 of 1975)* [1975] QB 773).

attorney, grants to. *See* GRANTS TO ATTORNEY.

attorney, power of. *See* POWER OF ATTORNEY.

attornment. 1. The acknowledgment of one person that he holds goods on behalf of another: S.G.A. 1979, s. 45(3). 2. Agreement of an estate owner to become the tenant of one who has acquired the estate next in reversion or remainder. See *Portman Building Society* v *Young* [1951] 1 All ER 191; *Regent Oil Co* v *J. Gregory Ltd* [1966] Ch 402.

auction. Public sale of property by an auctioneer to the highest bidder. See, eg, Sale of Land by Auction Act 1867; S.G.A. 1979, s. 57. An *auctioneer* is one who is licensed to conduct sales by auction. A contract comes into existence as the result of an auctioneer's acts, when a bid is accepted and his hammer falls (or in other customary manner) and a bidder may retract his bid until that event. See *Bristol Car Auctions* v *Wright* [1972] 1 WLR 1519; *Chelmsford Auctions* v *Poole* [1973] QB 542. *See* MOCK AUCTION.

auctioneer's obligations. Stated in *Benton* v *Campbell, Parker & Co* [1925] 2 KB 410, as: warranting his authority to sell; warranting that he knows of no defect in his principal's title; undertaking to give quiet possession against the price received by him; undertaking that possession will be undisturbed by the principal or himself.

audi alteram partem. Hear the other side. It is a principle of natural justice

(qv) that no man should be condemned unheard. See, eg, *Local Government Board* v *Aldridge* [1915] AC
120; *Ridge* v *Baldwin* [1964] AC 40.

audience, right of. Right to appear
and conduct proceedings in court.
Solicitors' rights are confined to
magistrates' courts, county courts,
some proceedings in the Crown
Court, certain tribunals, the High
Court and Divisional Court (concerning bankruptcy matters). See the
S.C.A. 1981, s. 83. Barristers have
the right relating to almost all judicial
proceedings and an exclusive right
relating to the House of Lords, Judicial Committee of Privy Council,
Court of Appeal and High Court
(save where solicitors have a concurrent right).

audit. Detailed inspection of accounts,
usually by a person not employed
within the organisation. For the audit
of accounts of local authorities see the
L.G.A. 1972, ss. 154–167.

audita querela. Complaint having been
heard. A writ, probably first authorised in 1336, now obsolete, given
on application so as to provide a
remedy where a matter relating to
defence had arisen since the date on
which judgment had been given.

**Audit Commission for Local Auth-
orities in England and Wales.** Body
of 13–17 members, appointed by the
Secretary of State under the Local
Government Finance Act 1982, s. 11,
with the tasks of preparing a code of
audit practice, prescribing a scale of
fees, etc. See the 1982 Act, Part III,
Sch. 3.

auditor. A member of a recognised
body of accountants who examines
accounts. An auditor's report must
be attached to a company's balance
sheet: Cos.A. 1948, s. 156. It must
be read at the general meeting and
must be available for inspection by
any member: Cos.A. 1967, s. 14(2).
Appointment and duties of auditors
must be in accordance with the
Cos.A. 1948, s. 161, the Cos.A.
1967, s. 14, the Cos.A. 1976, ss.
13–20, and the Cos.A. 1981, Sch. 3.
An auditor's duties are to prepare
reports for company members; to
acquaint himself with his duties

under statute; to exercise reasonable
care. See *Secretary of State for Trade and
Industry* v *Hart* [1982] 1 All ER 817.
For local government auditors, see
the Local Government Finance Act
1982, s. 36(1). *See* COMPANY.

authenticate. To make valid and
effective by proof or by appropriate
formalities as required by law.

authorised capital. The total amount
of capital which a company is authorised by its memorandum of association (qv) to issue. Known also as
"nominal" or "registered" capital.
See COMPANY; ISSUED CAPITAL.

authorised securities. Securities in
which trustees may invest under the
Tr.A. 1925 (as amended). *See* INVEST-
MENT, TRUSTEES' POWERS OF.

authority. 1. Judicial decision or opinion expressed by an author of repute
used as grounds of a statement of
law. 2. Rights bestowed by one person on another allowing performance
of an act. 3. A body exercising
powers, eg, a local authority (qv).

automatism. "An act done by the
muscles without any control by the
mind, such as a spasm, a reflex
action or a convulsion, or an act done
by a person who is not conscious of
what he is doing, such as an act done
whilst suffering from concussion or
whilst sleepwalking": *Bratty* v *A.-G.
for N Ireland* [1963] AC 386. Actions
resulting from a state of automatism
are involuntary and, as such, not
generally punishable. Where automatism is due to mental disease, the
defence is known as "insane automatism" and the M'Naghten Rules
(qv) apply; in such a case the burden
of proof is on the accused. See *Kay* v
Butterworth (1945) 89 SJ 381; *R* v
Quick [1973] QB 910; *R* v *Isitt* [1978]
Crim LR 159; *Roberts* v *Ramsbottom*
[1980] 1 All ER 7 (unsuccessful defence to negligence); *Moses* v *Winder*
[1981] RTR 37; and *R* v *Bailey* [1983]
1 WLR 760.

autonomic legislation. Legislation by
a body which has independent power
to legislate for its own members, eg,
the Law Society, General Medical
Council.

autopsy. *See* POST-MORTEM.

autrefois acquit. Formerly acquitted.

A plea in bar that the accused has been acquitted previously of the same offence. "The test to establish the plea is (1) that defendant had been previously acquitted of the same offence, or (2) that he could have been convicted at the previous trial of the offence with which he is subsequently charged, or that the two offences are substantially the same . . .": *Re Wilson* [1948] 1 WWR 680. See *R v Thomas* [1950] KB 26; *R v Griffiths* (1981) 72 Cr App R 307. *See* NEMO DEBET BIS VEXARI.

autrefois convict. Formerly convicted. A plea in bar that the accused has been previously tried and convicted for the same offence. The offence with which he is charged must be the same, or practically the same, offence as that with which he was previously charged. See *Connelly v DPP* [1964] AC 1254 (in which plea was considered extensively by the House of Lords); *Iremonger v Vissenga* [1976] Crim LR 524.

autre vie. The life of another. A tenant *pur autre vie* is a tenant for the life of another, as where A grants land to B "during the life of C". A tenancy of this nature exists only in equity. *See* CESTUI QUE VIE.

available market. Phrase used in the S.G.A. 1979 s. 50(3), providing that where there is an available market for goods, the measure of damage for breach of contract is prima facie the difference between the contract price and the market price at the date of the breach. See *Thompson Ltd v Robinson Ltd* [1955] Ch 177; *Lazenby Garages Ltd v Wright* [1976] 1 WLR 459.

available on request. A reference in a written contract to its being subject to "the general conditions available on request", suffices to incorporate into that contract the terms contained in a current edition of those conditions. See *Smith v S Wales Switchgear* [1978] 1 All ER 18.

average. Derived from *averia* (damage). Used in contracts for carriage of goods by sea to refer to apportionment of loss. 1. *General average loss* is caused by an act which occurs where an extraordinary sacrifice is voluntarily and reasonably made so as to preserve property, eg, jettison of cargo. The loss is borne rateably by all those interested: Marine Insurance Act 1906, s. 66. See *Castle Insurance Ltd v HK Islands Shipping* (*The Times*, 26.7.1983). 2. *Particular average* arises where the property is damaged by an accident not suffered for the general benefit, eg, loss of a ship's boat. The loss remains where it falls.

averment. Allegation or affirmation made in pleadings (qv).

a vinculo matrimonii. From the bond of matrimony. A decree for the dissolution of a marriage, formerly pronounced by the ecclesiastical court. *See* DIVORCE.

avoidance. Setting aside; making null or void.

avoidance and evasion of tax. *See* TAX EVASION AND AVOIDANCE.

avulsion. Removal, by the sudden and perceptible action of water, of soil from one person's land and its deposit on another's. Ownership of such soil does not change, as is general in the case of accretion (qv).

award. *See* ARBITRATION.

B

B. Baron (judge of the Court of Exchequer (qv)).

backed for bail. A warrant issued by a magistrate can be endorsed with a direction that the person named shall, on arrest, be released on bail (qv) on specified terms. See the M.C.A. 1980, s. 117; and the C.L.A. 1977, s. 38. *See* WARRANT.

bad. Wrong in law; unsound; void.

bad debt. A debt which, seemingly, cannot be recovered. *See* the Finance Act 1978, s. 12.

bail. *Bailler* = to deliver. Release of a person arrested on his giving security or accepting specified conditions. A person arrested may be granted bail under a duty to surrender to custody (qv). No recognisance for his surrender to custody may be taken from him: Bail Act 1976, s. 3. He may be required to provide a surety to secure his surrender: ss. 3, 8. On withholding of bail he may apply to the Crown Court or High Court: s. 5(6); Practice Direction, 16.8.81. See also the C.J.A. 1967; the Courts Act 1971; the P.C.C.A. 1973; and the M.C.A. 1980. Bail need not be granted if the court is satisfied that there are substantial grounds for believing that the defendant, if released, would fail to surrender to custody, or would commit an offence while on bail or interfere with witnesses: 1976 Act, Sch 1, para 2. See the S.C.A. 1981, s. 81 (as amended by the C.J.A. 1982, s. 29) for the High Court's powers to grant bail.

bail, continuous. Direction by the magistrates' court, where the accused is remanded on bail, with or without sureties, instructing him to appear at every time and place to which the proceedings may be adjourned from time to time: Bail Act 1976; M.C.A. 1980, s. 128(4).

bailee. *See* BAILMENT.

bailee, unconscious. Where a defendant becomes possessed of goods belonging to a plaintiff through a third party's mistake, and the defendant believes that the goods were his, or is not aware that they belonged to anyone but himself, he can be described properly as an unconscious bailee, and before dealing with the goods he has a duty to use a sufficient standard of care in all the circumstances to ascertain that they were his own: *AUX Ltd* v *EGM Solders Ltd* (*The Times*, 7.7.1982).

bailiff. Originally "an officer that belongeth to a manor, to order the husbandry": *Termes de la Ley*. Now a person employed by a sheriff (qv) to serve and execute writs (qv) and processes. See the Courts Act 1971, s. 22.

bail in criminal proceedings. "Bail grantable in or in connection with proceedings for an offence to a person who is accused or convicted of the offence, or bail grantable in connection with an offence to a person who is under arrest for the offence or for whose arrest for the offence a warrant (endorsed for bail) is being issued": Bail Act 1976, s. 1(1). For bail on a murder charge, see *Court of Appeal Note* [1982]1 All ER 403.

bailment. The delivery of goods by one person (the "bailor") to another (the "bailee") so that they might be used for some specified purpose, upon a condition that they shall be redelivered by the bailee to, or in accordance with the specified directions of, the bailor, or kept until he reclaims them. Examples: deposit of goods in a railway luggage office; pawning of goods. The bailee is under a duty to take reasonable care of the goods and to return them in accordance with the terms of the contract of bailment. See *Coggs* v *Barnard* (1703) 2 Ld Ray 909; *Lee Cooper Ltd* v *Jeakins & Sons Ltd* [1967] 2 QB 1; *Port Swettenham Authority* v *Wu* [1979] AC 580.

bailor. *See* BAILMENT.

bail with sureties. Granting of bail

on condition that the person provides one or more sureties for the purpose of seeing that he surrenders to custody (qv): Bail Act 1976, s. 8(1). It is an offence to agree to indemnify sureties in criminal proceedings: s. 9(1). In considering the suitability of a proposed surety, regard is had to his character, financial resources, proximity to the accused: s. 8(2).

balance. "What remains after something has been taken out of a fund": *Re Burke Irwin's Trusts* (1918) 1 IR 350.

balance of probabilities. Concept in the law of evidence relating to the standard of proof whereby the party upon whom the legal burden of proof rests is entitled to a verdict in his favour if he has established some preponderance of probability in his favour. See *Hornal* v *Neuberger Products* [1957] 1 QB 247. *See* STANDARDS OF PROOF.

balance sheet. A statement showing assets and liabilities of a business at a given date. A company's balance sheet must give a true and fair picture of the company at the end of the financial year. See the Cos.A. 1948, s. 149. It must comply with requirements of the Cos.A. 1948, Sch 8, Part I, as amended by the Cos.A. 1981. *See* COMPANY ACCOUNTS, PUBLICATION OF.

ballot. A system of voting involving secret votes. See, eg, the Representation of the People Act 1983; and the Employment Act 1982, s. 3 (ballots for approval of union membership agreements).

banishment. Expulsion from the king's realm. See, eg, 39 Eliz I c.4, under which "dangerous rogues" might be banished.

bank. Financial institution engaged in the accepting of deposits of money, granting of credit (by loan, overdraft, etc) and other transactions such as the discounting of bills, dealing in foreign exchange, etc. See the Cos.A. 1948, s. 429; and the Cos.A. 1967, s. 119 (now repealed); *United Dominions Trust Ltd* v *Kirkwood* [1966] 2 QB 431.

banker. One engaged in the business of banking. "The relation between a banker and a customer who pays money into the bank is the ordinary relation between debtor and creditor, with a superadded obligation, arising out of the custom of bankers to honour the customer's drafts": *Joachimson* v *Swiss Bank Corporation* [1921] 3 KB 110.

bankers' books. Under the Bankers' Books Evidence Act 1879, s. 3, a copy of an entry in a banker's book may be received as prima facie evidence of such an entry and of the transactions and accounts recorded therein. See *Williams* v *Summerfield* [1972] 2 QB 513—permission granted to the police to inspect the bank accounts of an accused person. See the Banking Act 1972, Sch. 6, Part I; O. 38, r. 13; *Barker* v *Wilson* [1980] 2 All ER 81; and *R* v *Dadson* [1983], Crim LR 540. *See* EVIDENCE.

bankers' draft. *See* DRAFT.

bank holiday break. A bank holiday not included in the Christmas or Easter break and the period commencing with the last weekday before that bank holiday and ending with the next weekday which is not a bank holiday: L.G.A. 1972, s. 270(2).

bank holidays. In England and Wales, Easter Monday, the last Monday in August, December 26th (if not a Sunday), December 27th in a year during which December 25th or 26th is a Sunday, any other day so proclaimed: Banking and Financial Dealings Act 1971.

banking business. No person may use any name or describe himself so as to indicate that he is a bank or is carrying on a banking business, other than the Bank of England, other EEC central banks, recognised and trustee savings banks, the Central Trustee Savings Bank and the Post Office: Banking Act 1979, s. 36(1). See S.I. 1980/347. *See* BANKS, RECOGNISED.

banking instrument. Any cheque or other instrument to which the Cheques Act 1957, s. 4, applies; any document issued by a public officer intended to enable a person to obtain payment from a government department of a sum mentioned in the document; any bill of exchange or promissory note, postal order, money order, credit transfer, credit advice or debit advice: British Telecommunications Act 1981, s. 67(4).

bankruptcy. Compulsory administration of the estate of an insolvent person (known as a "bankrupt") by the court for the benefit of his creditors. See the B.A. 1914; the Bankruptcy (Amendment) Act 1926; the Insolvency Act 1976; and the Bankruptcy Rules 1952. The objects of bankruptcy are: to enquire into the reasons for a debtor's insolvency; to free him from his debts; to secure a fair distribution of property among creditors. Proceedings begin with the presentation of a petition, followed by a public examination (qv), meeting of the creditors, order of adjudication (order of discharge (qv) where appropriate). See S.I. 1983/775.

bankruptcy, acts of. Enumerated in the B.A. 1914, s. 1, thus: if a debtor (D) makes a conveyance or assignment of his property to a trustee for the benefit of creditors generally; if D makes a fraudulent conveyance, gift, delivery or transfer of his property or any part thereof; if D makes any conveyance or transfer of his property or creates a charge thereon which would be void as a fraudulent preference if he were adjudged bankrupt; if, with intent to delay creditors, D leaves England, or begins to keep house; if execution against D has been levied by the seizure of goods and goods have been sold by a sheriff or held by him for 21 days; if D files a declaration of . inability to pay debts or presents a bankruptcy petition against himself; if D fails to comply with a bankruptcy notice; if D gives notice to a creditor that he has suspended the payment of debts. Where D fails to make a payment required under an administration order under the County C.A. 1959, Part VII, a receiving order (qv) may be made against him, which is deemed to constitute an act of bankruptcy: Insolvency Act 1976, s. 11.

bankruptcy, debtor in. *See* DEBTOR IN BANKRUPTCY.

bankruptcy notice. Notice served by a judgment creditor (qv) on a debtor requiring him to pay the debt. Noncompliance within ten days of service is an act of bankruptcy (qv): Insolvency Act 1976, s. 4.

bankruptcy order, criminal. *See* CRIMINAL BANKRUPTCY ORDER.

bankruptcy petition. Petition presented by creditors, or the debtor, asking the court to make a receiving order. It must prove, eg, that the debt due to a creditor or creditors is at least £200 (Insolvency Act 1976, s. 1) and that the creditors have not consented to the act of bankruptcy. A sealed copy of the creditors' petition is served on the debtor.

bankruptcy, trustee in. Generally appointed by an ordinary resolution of creditors, or by a committee of inspection. The certificate of appointment issued to the trustee is advertised in the *London Gazette*. The trustee is empowered: to sell the bankrupt's property or transfer it to purchasers; to give receipts for money; to prove and draw dividends in respect of debts due to the bankrupt (see the B.A. 1914, s. 55); to summon meetings; to apply to the court for directions, etc.

bankrupt, discharge of. *See* ORDER OF DISCHARGE.

bankrupt, undischarged. One who has not received a discharge from bankruptcy. He is guilty of an offence if he obtains credit to the extent of £50 or upwards without stating that he is an undischarged bankrupt: B.A. 1914, s. 155, as amended by the Insolvency Act 1976, s. 1.

banks, recognised. Institutions recognised by the Bank of England, under the Banking Act 1979, s. 3, as enjoying a high reputation and standing in the financial community, carrying on its business with integrity, prudence and professional skill, and providing in the UK a specialised banking service or a wide range of banking services (including current or deposit account facilities, overdraft or loan facilities, foreign exchange services, financial advice): Banking Act 1979, Sch 2.

banns. Proclamation in church in the form of a public notice of an intended marriage. Banns must be published on three Sundays preceding the marriage. See the Marriage Act 1949, ss. 5–14; *Chard* v *Chard* [1956] P 259.

bar. 1. An impediment, as in bars to divorce (qv). 2. A line in the House of Commons beyond which non-members may not cross during sittings. 3. A place in court where a prisoner is stationed, or where barristers speak for their clients. 4. The English Bar is the professional body of barristers. 5. The profession of barrister.

Bar Council. The General Council of the Bar, created in 1894. Most of its functions were taken over in 1974 by the Senate of the Inns of Court and the Bar (qv). It is concerned with maintaining the standards of the Bar and with improvements in its services. It may make its own bye-laws and rules (for which judicial sanction is not required): *In re T.* (*The Times*, 20.5.1981).

bare licensee. One who has been given permission to enter a place for his own purposes, so as not to be a trespasser. Example: X grants a gratuitous permission to Y to walk across X's meadow. Known also as a "mere licensee". See *Berg Homes* v *Grey* (1979) 253 EG 473. *See* LICENCE.

bare site value. Price to be paid as compensation for compulsory purchase of, eg, an unfit house, is the value of the site cleared of buildings and available for development. See the H.A. 1969, ss. 67, 68, Schs. 4, 5. See *Davy* v *Leeds Corporation* [1965] 1 All ER 753; *Saghir* v *City of Birmingham DC* (1980) 255 EG 795.

bare trust. A trust (qv) which requires the trustee to act as a mere repository of the trust property, with no active duties to perform, as where X devises property to Y in trust for Z. Y's only duty is to convey the legal estate (qv) to Z. Y is a "bare trustee". For a definition of property held on a bare trust see the Development Land Tax Act 1976, s. 28(1). See *Christie* v *Ovington* (1875) 1 Ch D 279.

bargain. Agreement, contract (qv).

bargain and sale. A popular method of conveyancing in the sixteenth century, later abolished under the L.P.A. 1925, s. 51. V, the vendor, contracted to sell land to P, the pur-

chaser, and to receive the purchase price. V was said to have "bargained and sold" the fee simple (qv) to P, and V was considered seised to the use of P. Under the Statute of Uses 1535 P was considered to have the legal estate. This method was used to convey a legal estate without public formalities.

bargain, unconscionable. A catching bargain (qv).

bar, pleas in. When the indictment (qv) is put to the defendant, he can raise pleas alleging some reason why he should not be tried and maintaining that there should be an enquiry forthwith into that reason. Examples: *autrefois acquit* (qv); *autrefois convict* (qv).

barratry. 1. Common law offence (common barratry) committed by one who frequently incited or maintained quarrels at law. Abolished under the C.L.A. 1967. 2. Wrongs which prejudice a shipowner or charterer committed wilfully by the master or crew of a ship. See *The Salem* [1982] 2 All ER 1057; *Shell International* v *Gibbs* [1983] 2 WLR 371.

barring of entailed interest. Procedure whereby a tenant in tail puts and end to the fee tail (qv). A tenant in tail in possession, if of full age, may execute a deed which, in effect, converts entail into fee simple (qv): Fines and Recoveries Act 1833, s. 15. A tenant in tail whose interest is in remainder may, if of full age, convert entail into fee simple with the consent of protector of settlement (qv). A tenant in tail, of full age, whose interest is in remainder may, without the protector's consent, partially bar the entail (thus creating a base fee). The L.P.A. 1925, s. 176, allows the devise or bequest of entails under specified conditions, so that, in effect, the beneficiary takes the fee simple absolute. Interests in tail after possibility (qv) and entails awarded by an Act of Parliament forbidding disentailment may not be barred. See also the Lim.A. 1980, s. 27. *See* BASE FEE.

barrister. A person called to the Bar by an Inn of Court (qv). His function is primarily that of an advocate and he has exclusive right of audience in certain types of judicial proceedings. He may not sue for fees, which are deemed to be in the nature of an honorarium: *Wells* v *Wells* [1914] P 157. He is immune from actions for negligence. "If a barrister is to be able to do his duty fearlessly and independently he must not be subject to the threat of an action for negligence": *Rondel* v *Worsley* [1969] 1 AC 191. See, for cases of claims in negligence in pre-trial work, *Saif Ali* v *Sydney Mitchell & Co* [1980] AC 198. For suspension in cases of misconduct, see *Re H.* [1981] 3 All ER 205.

barrister's duty to the court. "He has a duty to the court which is paramount. It is a mistake to suppose that he is the mouthpiece of his client to say what he wants: or his tool to do what he directs. He is none of these things. He owes allegiance to a higher cause . . . the cause of truth and justice . . . He must disregard the most specific instructions of his client if they conflict with his duty to the court": *per* Lord Denning in *Rondel* v *Worsley* [1969] 1 AC 191.

barrister's fees. There is no contractual relationship between an instructing solicitor and a barrister, so that payment of fees is a "matter of honour", not a legal obligation. (The barrister, however, may refer a defaulting solicitor to the Law Society.) "A counsel can maintain no action for his fees, which are given not as a salary, but as a mere gratuity which a counsellor cannot demand without doing wrong to his reputation": Blackstone. *See* HONORARIUM.

barrister's professional obligation. "A barrister cannot pick or choose his clients. He is bound to accept a brief from any man who comes before the courts. No matter how great a rascal he may be. No matter how given to complaining. No matter how undeserving or unpopular his cause. The barrister must defend him to the end": *per* Lord Denning in *Rondel* v *Worsley* [1969] 1 AC 191.

barter. The practice of exchanging goods or services: see *La Neuville* v *Nourse* (1913) 3 Camp 351. See Law Commission Working Paper No 71, 1977. For part-barter,

see *Simpson* v *Connolly* [1953] 1 WLR 911.

bar, trial at. Obsolescent phrase, referring to trial before a full court, rather than before a single judge. See *Dixon* v *Board of Trade* (1886) 18 QBD 43.

base fee. "That estate in fee simple into which an estate in tail is converted where the issues in tail are barred, but persons claiming estates by way of remainder or otherwise are not barred": Fines and Recoveries Act 1833, s. 1. A base fee may be converted into fee simple absolute (qv) in the following ways: 1. Fresh disentailing deed. 2. Owner of base fee in possession may enlarge it into fee simple by will. 3. Union of base fee with remainder in fee. 4. Lapse of time: Lim.A. 1980, s. 27. *See* BARRING OF ENTAILED INTEREST.

basic norm. *See* LAW, PURE THEORY OF.

bastard. An illegitimate child, ie, one born out of lawful wedlock. Property rights of an illegitimate child have now been modified. See, eg, the F.L.R.A. 1969, ss. 14, 15 and Sch 1, Part III (right of illegitimate child to succeed on the intestacy of a parent, and in relation to reference to children in disposition of property). "Whatever may have been the position in the past, the general attitude towards illegitimacy has changed and the legal incidents of being born a bastard are now almost non-existent": *S.* v *S.* [1972] AC 24. See Law Comm Report No. 118, 1973 (recommending the removal of all legal disadvantages affecting an illegitimate child). *See* LEGITIMACY.

battered wife. "A woman who has suffered serious or repeated physical injury from the man with whom she lives": from Minutes of Evidence of the Select Committee on Violence in Marriage, 1974. *See* INJUNCTIONS, MATRIMONIAL.

battery. A crime and a tort involving the actual, intended (or negligent) and direct use of unlawful physical force on a person without his consent. It includes even the slightest force; no actual harm need result. Consent, self-defence, lawful and reasonable chastisement may be defences. In common usage "assault" (qv) is often a synonym for battery; in law they are distinct. See *R* v *Day* (1845) 9 JP 212; *Kenlin* v *Gardiner* [1967] 2 QB 510; *Fagan* v *Metropolitan Police Commissioner* [1969] 1 QB 439.

battle, trial by. Norman procedure, in essence an appeal to the "God of battles" to bring victory to the rightful party. The plaintiff and defendant, or their "champions", fought, the outcome being considered as a divine judgment. Abolished in 1819 after an attempt to claim procedure was made in *Ashford* v *Thornton* (1818) 1 B & Ald 405.

bawdy house. Brothel (qv).

beach. The foreshore (qv). It includes land above the high-water mark which is in apparent continuity with the beach at high-water mark, or which possesses a character more akin to the foreshore than the hinterland: *Tito* v *Waddell* (*No. 2*) [1977] Ch 106.

bearer. *See* BILL OF EXCHANGE.

bearer shares. Shares (qv) for which no register of ownership is kept by the issuing company. They must pass physically from seller to buyer and are usually lodged with a bank.

Beddoe order. Leave granted to trustees by the court so as to enable them to sue or defend and to be reimbursed out of the trust estate: *Re Beddoe* [1893] 1 Ch 547; *Midland Bank Trust Co* v *Green* [1980] Ch 590.

begin, right to. *See* RIGHT TO BEGIN.

behaviour, breakdown of marriage and. "Behaviour is something more than a mere state of affairs or a state of mind . . . [it is] action or conduct by the one which affects the other. Such conduct may take the form of an act or omission . . . and, in my view, it must have some reference to the marriage": *per* Baker J in *Katz* v *Katz* [1972] 3 All ER 219. See the Mat.C.A. 1973.

bench. Used in a collective sense to refer to the judges or magistrates in a court. A barrister who becomes a judge is said to be "raised to the bench".

Benchers. The governing body of each of the Inns of Court (qv). They are judges or senior members of the Bar (qv) and have control over the admis-

sion of students and calls to the Bar. Appeal from their decisions is to the Lord Chancellor and judges of the High Court who sit as "visitors" (qv).

bench warrant. Order for the immediate arrest of a person issued by a court, eg, for failure to appear on breach of the condition of bail (qv). *See* WARRANT.

benefice. The office of rector or vicar, with cure of souls, including the office of vicar in a team ministry established under the Pastoral Measure 1968, but does not include any office in a Royal Peculiar nor the office of deacon or provost of a parish church cathedral: Incumbents (Vacation of Benefices) Measure 1977, s. 19.

beneficial freehold owner. One who, holding the fee simple absolute (qv) in law and equity, is the "sole owner" of land.

beneficial interest. The equitable interest of a beneficiary (qv). Thus, if land is held by X in trust for Y, X has the legal estate, Y has the beneficial interest. See Companies (Beneficial Interests) Act 1983.

beneficiary. 1. One entitled for his own benefit, ie, for whose benefit property is held (eg, by a trustee). Known also as *cestui que trust* (qv). 2. One who receives a gift under a will.

beneficiary, remedies of. Rights of a beneficiary arising where a trustee departs from the terms of a trust (qv) or where he is in breach of some duty imposed on him by statute or equity, including an order for an account; injunction; damages; tracing order. *See* TRACING TRUST PROPERTY.

benefit of clergy. Privilege exempting clergymen from the criminal process. A "criminous cleric" was brought before the King's court, tried by a church court and handed back to the King's court for punishment: Constitutions of Clarendon 1164. In 1352 the privilege was allowed to secular clerks, the test being literacy (usually a test of ability to read the so-called "neck verse"—the first verse of Psalm LI—"Have mercy upon me, O God"). Abolished by the C.L.A. 1827 and the Felony Act 1841.

benefits under social security legis-

lation. *See* CONTRIBUTORY BENEFITS; NON-CONTRIBUTORY BENEFITS.

benevolent society. A society established for a benevolent or charitable purpose, under the Friendly Societies Act 1974.

Benjamin order. Where personal representatives (qv) may experience delay in winding up and distributing an estate because they are not sure whether a missing beneficiary (qv) is alive or not, the court may make an order authorising distribution on the assumption that, eg, the beneficiary is dead: *Re Benjamin* [1902] 1 Ch 723. See *Re Eleanor Taylor's Estate* [1969] 2 Ch 245.

bequeath. To dispose of personal property by will.

bequest. A gift by will of personal property, known also as a "legacy" (qv).

bereavement, damages for. A claim for damages for bereavement, under the Fatal Accidents Act 1976, may be brought for the benefit of the wife or husband of the deceased: s. 1A (inserted by the A.J.A. 1982, s. 3). The right of a person to claim under s. 1A does not survive for the benefit of his estate on his death: Law Reform (Misc. Provs.) Act 1934, s. 1A (inserted by the A.J.A. 1982, s. 4).

besetting. *See* WATCHING AND BESETTING.

best evidence rule. "The judges and sages of the law have laid it down that there is but one general rule of evidence, the best that the nature of the case will allow": *Omychund* v *Barker* (1745) 1 Atk 21. The rule requires in effect, that the best or most direct evidence of a fact should be adduced, or its absence accounted for. Example: the best evidence of the existence of the contents of a letter is its production in court. See *R* v *Francis* (1874) LR 2 CCR 128; *Garton* v *Hunter* [1969] 2 QB 37. The rule no longer applies as the court admits all relevant evidence: *Kajala* v *Noble* (1982) 75 Cr App R 149. *See* EVIDENCE.

bestiality. The offence of buggery (qv) committed with a beast.

bet. Something staked on the outcome of a contingency. Used as synonym for wager. See, eg, the Betting, Gaming and Lotteries Acts 1963–1980; the Lotteries and Amusements Act 1976; and the Betting and Gaming Duties Act 1981. It does not include a stake hazarded in the course of gaming: Gaming Act 1968, s. 53, Sch 2. *See* LOTTERY.

betterment. 1. An increase in the value of real property because of beneficial public works nearby. 2. Prospective developmental value of land.

beyond reasonable doubt. *See* PROOF BEYOND REASONABLE DOUBT.

beyond the seas. Outside the UK, Channel Islands and the Isle of Man. The defendant's absence "beyond the seas" no longer prevents time running for purposes of limitation of actions (qv).

bias. Lacking impartiality. "Its proper significance is to denote a departure from the standard of even-handed justice which the law requires from those who occupy judicial office": *Franklin* v *Minister of Town and Country Planning* [1948] AC 87.

bias, rule against. An implied requirement of natural justice (qv), namely, that no man shall be a judge in his own cause. See, eg, *Metropolitan Properties Ltd* v *Lannon* [1969] 1 QB 577; *Herring* v *Templeman* [1973] 3 All ER 569.

bid. To make an offer for some thing which is being sold by auction (qv). A bid may generally be retracted before acceptance: S.G.A. 1979, s. 57(2). Where a sale is subject to a reserve price and bids fail to reach that level, the highest bid can be treated as a "provisional bid" which may be accepted later if the seller agrees: *Willis & Son* v *British Car Auctions* [1978] 1 WLR 438.

bigamy. The offence committed by a married person who "shall marry any other person during the life of the former husband or wife, whether the second marriage shall have taken place in England or Ireland or elsewhere": O.P.A. 1861, s. 57. See the C.L.A. 1977, Sch 2. To prove bigamy, the prosecution must show: proof of the first marriage of the accused; its validity; its subsistence at the date of the second marriage (qv); proof of a second marriage by the accused with some person other than the lawful spouse. See *R* v *Curgerwen* (1865) 1 LR 1 CCR 1; *R* v *Allen* (1872) LR 1 CCR 367; *R* v *Tolson* (1889) 23 QBD 168.

bilateral discharge. Applies to executory contract. Discharge may take the form of: extinction of the contract; extinction and substitution of a new agreement; partial dissolution of the contract, eg, by modification of terms. *See* CONTRACT.

bill. 1. Bill in Parliament. A draft Act which is discussed by Parliament and is known as an Act (qv) when it has received the Royal Assent (qv). It may be *private* (eg, referring to a particular person or town) or *public* (relating to the whole country). 2. An account delivered to a debtor by a creditor. 3. Formerly, a written petition complaining of a wrong, eg, a bill in equity, seeking redress—the forerunner of the writ (qv). 4. A written instrument, eg, bill of exchange (qv).

Bill, blocking of. Process whereby consideration of a Bill set down for discussion by the Commons at a time reserved for unopposed business is prevented by a member's call of "Object!"

bill of costs. Statement of account furnished by a solicitor to his client, relating to work done on his client's behalf. See *Bartletts de Reya* v *Byrne* (1983) (*The Times*, 14.1.1983). *See* COSTS.

bill of exchange. An unconditional order in writing, addressed by one person to another, signed by the person giving it, requiring the person to whom it is addressed to pay on demand, or at a fixed or determinable future time, a sum certain in money to or to the order of a specified person or to bearer: B.Ex.A. 1882, s. 3(1). Person who gives the order to pay is the "drawer"; person to whom the order to pay is given is the "drawee"; person to whom the payment is to be made is the "payee".

bill of exchange, discharge of. A bill of exchange is discharged when all the rights and liabilities attaching to it are nullified, in one of the following ways: by payment in due course; by renunciation; by cancellation; by

material alteration; by delivery up. See the B.Ex.A. 1882, ss. 59, 61–64.

bill of indictment. A bill which charges a person with an indictable offence and is signed by an officer of the court, can become an indictment (qv). It may be preferred by direction or with the consent of a High Court judge, or by direction of the Court of Appeal, or under an order made by virtue of the Perjury Act 1911, s. 9, or where a person is committed for trial by examining magistrates. See the A.J. (Misc. Provs.) A. 1933, s. 2; the Indictments (Procedure) Rules 1971, r. 4; *R* v *Thompson* [1975] 2 All ER 1028; and *R* v *Raymond* [1981] 2 ER 246.

bill of lading. Document used in foreign trade, signed by the shipowner, master or other agent, stating that goods have been shipped on a named ship, and setting out the terms on which they have been delivered to and received by the shipowner. It acts as a document of title to the goods and is evidence of the contract for their carriage. It is not a fully negotiable instrument (qv). Where the bill relates to carriage of goods from a British port, certain terms are implied under the Carriage of Goods by Sea Act 1971; eg, that care has been taken to ensure the ship's sea-worthiness at the beginning of a voyage and that the goods will be loaded carefully. See the Bills of Lading Act 1855; *Vita Food Products* v *Unus Shipping Co* [1939] AC 277; and *The El Amria* [1982] 2 Ll R 28.

Bill of Middlesex. Legal fiction abolished under the Uniformity of Process Act 1832, involving a writ of *latitat* (qv).

Bill of Rights. An Act of 1689, providing that suspension of laws was illegal, that subjects had a right to petition the King, that parliamentary elections ought to be free, that debates in Parliament ought to be free, that excessive fines ought not to be imposed "nor cruel and unusual punishment inflicted", etc.

bill of sale. A document "given with respect to transfer of chattels used in cases where possession is not intended to be given": *Johnson* v *Diprose* [1893]

1 QB 512. It must be registered within seven days of making. An *absolute bill* is governed by the Bills of Sale Act 1878; a *conditional bill* (eg, by way of security) is governed by the Bills of Sale Amendment Act 1882. The term includes, eg, assignments, transfers; it does not include assignment for the benefit of creditors, transfer of goods in the ordinary course of trade. See also the Bills of Sale Acts 1890 and 1891; and *NV Slavenburg's Bank* v *Intercontinental Natal Resources* [1980] 1 All ER 955.

Bill, passage through Parliament. Stages are generally as follows: introduction into the Commons (unless Bill commences in the Lords); first reading (purely formal, not accompanied by debate); second reading (most important stage, calling for full debate); committee stage (in which Bill is considered in close detail); report stage (often purely formal); third reading (often without debate); consideration of Lords' amendments; Royal Assent (qv).

bill procedure, voluntary. Procedure whereby the prosecution applies to the judge for leave to prefer a bill of indictment (qv) against an accused person, eg, after refusal by the magistrates to commit. See the Indictments (Procedure) Rules 1971.

bills in a set. Bills of exchange executed in duplicate, triplicate, etc. Payment of one part of a set discharges the other parts also: B.Ex.A. 1882, s. 71.

bind over. To require a person to enter into a bond or recognisance to perform or abstain from performing an act. See the M.C.A. 1980, s. 115; *R* v *Hendon Justices ex p Gorchein* [1973] 1 WLR 1502; *R* v *London Magistrates' Court ex p Brown* [1974] Crim LR 313; and *Shaw* v *Hamilton* [1982] 2 All ER 718.

bird, wild. "Any bird of a kind which is ordinarily resident in or is a visitor to Great Britain in a wild state (but does not include poultry, or, except in ss. 5, 16, any game bird)": Wildlife and Countryside Act 1981, s. 27(1). See *Robinson* v *Kenworthy* (*The Times*, 13.5.1982).

birth. Act of commencing existence separate from one's mother. *See* ABORTION.

birth, attendance by persons at. A person other than a registered midwife or registered medical practitioner may not attend a woman in childbirth: Nurses, Midwives and Health Visitors Act 1979, s. 17(1).

birth, citizenship by. *See* CITIZENSHIP, BRITISH, ACQUISITION BY BIRTH.

birth, concealment of. "If any woman shall be delivered of a child, every person who shall by any secret disposition of the dead body of the said child, whether such child died before, at, or after its birth, endeavour to conceal the birth thereof, shall be guilty of a misdemeanour": O.P.A. 1861, s. 60. See *R* v *Berriman* (1854) 6 Cox 388; *R* v *Opie* (1860) 8 Cox 332.

birth, proof of. Process of proving a person's birth by: production of the birth certificate; evidence of someone present at the birth; declaration of the deceased person against interest or in the course of duty. See the Civil Evidence Act 1968; the Births and Deaths Registration Act 1953; and the Ch. A. 1975, s. 93.

birth, registration of. Procedure, which must be completed within 42 days of birth, consisting of furnishing the following particulars: date, place of birth, name, surname and sex of child; name, surname, place of birth and occupation of father; name, surname, maiden surname, surname at marriage, place of birth of mother; mother's usual address; name, surname, qualification, address and signature of informant; registrar's signature. See Births and Deaths Registration Act 1953; the National Health Service Act 1977, s. 124; S.I. 1982/955 and 1123.

blacking of goods. Refusal of employees, who are taking industrial action, to handle or work on materials supplied by the employer so as to evade the effects of that action. See the Employment Act 1980, s. 17.

blackleg. One who continues, or attempts to continue, his work while his colleagues are on strike (qv).

blackmail. Originally payment for immunity from raids, levied by freebooters in the north of England. Now an offence under the Th.A. 1968, s. 21(1): "A person is guilty of blackmail if, with a view to gain for himself or another or with intent to cause loss to another, he makes any unwarranted demand with menaces and for this purpose a demand with menaces is unwarranted unless the person making it does so in the belief (*a*) that he had reasonable grounds for making the demand *and* (*b*) that the use of menaces is a proper means of reinforcing the demand." See *R* v *Harvey* (1980) 72 Cr App R 139; and *R* v *Cutbill* (1982) 4 Cr App R (S) 1.

blank transfer. Transfer of shares executed without the transferee's name being filled in on the document of transfer. See the Finance Act 1963, s. 67. *See* SHARE.

blasphemy. The offence of denying, in a scandalous way, Christianity, the Bible, the Book of Common Prayer. The Blasphemy Act 1697 was repealed by the C.L.A. 1967. It remains a common law offence. See *Bowman* v *Secular Society Ltd* [1917] AC 406; *R* v *Gott* (1922) 16 Cr App R 87. On a charge of blasphemous libel an intention to blaspheme is not required; the offence is committed by an insulting, immoderate, vilifying or offensive reference to God or Christianity: *R* v *Lemon* [1979] AC 617.

blight notice. Notice served on a prospective land-acquiring authority, in the case of a proposed land development plan, stating that the owner has genuinely and unsuccessfully attempted to sell the land for a reasonable price on the open market, and requiring the authority to purchase it. The authority must serve any counter-notice within two months. See the T.C.P.A. 1971, ss. 193–195 (as amended by the L.G.P.L.A. 1980, s. 147); *Mancini* v *Coventry CC* (1982) 44 P & CR 114.

blind person. One without the faculty of seeing. A person "unable to perform any work for which eyesight is essential": Residential Homes Act 1980, s. 10(1). A blind person cannot witness a will for the purposes of the W.A. 1837, s. 7: *Re Gibson* [1949] P 434. *See* DISABLED PERSON.

B list. *See* A AND B LISTS.

block grant. Central government aid to local authorities, based on the difference between an authority's total expenditure and an assumed contribution from rates. See the L.G.P.L.A. 1980, as amended by the Local Government Finance Act 1982, Part II.

blood relationship. The connection between persons descended from one or more common ancestors. Persons are said to be of the *whole blood* to one another if descended from the same pair of ancestors (eg, X and Y, brothers, who have the same father and mother); of the *half blood* to one another if descended from only one common ancestor (eg, X and Y, who have the same father but different mothers).

blood tests. 1. In some civil proceedings relating to paternity, the court may direct that a blood test be made to ascertain whether a party to the proceedings is or is not thereby excluded from being the father. (The tests relate to the presence of blood group substances or antigens or genetically-controlled serum components, eg, haptoglobins.) See the F.L.R.A. 1969, Part 3; the Blood Tests (Evidence of Paternity) Regulations 1971; *W.* v *W.* (*No 4*) [1964] P 67; and O 112. 2. A person arrested under the Road Traffic Act 1972, ss. 6–12 (as substituted by the Transport Act 1981, Sch 8) may be obliged to provide a specimen of blood for a laboratory test. *See* PATERNITY, DECLARATION OF.

blue book. Government publication, eg, a report of a Royal Commission. *See* PARLIAMENTARY PAPERS.

blue chip. Colloquial term referring to a well-established company's shares which have a high status as investments. See *Re Kolb's Will Trusts* [1962] Ch 531.

blue pencil test. Phrase referring to severance of contract (qv). "Severance can be effected when the part severed can be removed by running a blue pencil through it" without affecting the remaining part: *Attwood* v *Lamont* [1960] 3 KB 571; *Goldsoll* v *Goldman* [1915] 1 Ch 292; *Ronbar*

Enterprises Ltd v *Green* [1954] 1 WLR 815.

board meeting. Meetings of directors of a company (qv) held for the despatch of business. Questions are decided by majority vote; the chairman has a casting vote. See Table A, arts. 98–106; *Barron* v *Potter* [1914] 1 Ch 895.

Board of Trade. *See* TRADE, DEPARTMENT OF.

bocland. Bookland. Land which, in pre-Norman Conquest times, was held by charter, handbook, or other written title.

bodily harm, grievous. "Another term of art in English criminal law of respectable pedigree but uncertain meaning": *Hyam* v *DPP* [1974] 2 All ER 41. Formerly interpreted to mean "some harm sufficiently serious to interfere with the victim's health or comfort": *R* v *Ashman* (1858) 1 F & F 88. In *DPP* v *Smith* [1961] AC 290 it was stated that there is "no warrant for giving the words 'grievous bodily harm' a meaning other than that which the words convey in their ordinary and natural meaning. 'Bodily harm' needs no explanation, and 'grievous' means no more and no less than 'really serious'." See also *R* v *Miller* [1951] VLR 346; *R* v *Belfon* [1976] 3 All ER 46; *R* v *Salisbury* [1976] VR 62; *R* v *Wilson* (*The Times*, 7.2.1983); and *R* v *Jenkins* (1983) (*The Times*, 26.2.1983). *See* MALICE; WOUNDING.

body corporate. "A succession or collection of persons having in the estimation of the law an existence and rights and duties distinct from those of the individual persons who form it from time to time": Co Litt 250a. Examples: a company registered under the Cos.A. 1948; a local authority (qv); a body controlled by royal charter. *See* CORPORATION.

bomb hoax. It is an offence to place any article in any place or dispatch any article by post, rail or other means with the intention of inducing in some person a belief that it is likely to explode or ignite and cause personal injury or damage to property: C.L.A. 1977, s. 51(1). It is an offence to communicate information which is known to be false with the intention of inducing in a person a false belief that a bomb or other thing liable to explode or ignite is present in any place or location: s. 51(2).

bona fide. In good faith; honestly.

bona fide **holder for value.** *See* HOLDER IN DUE COURSE.

bona vacantia. Ownerless goods. 1. Goods found with no apparent owner. In general they are deemed to belong to the first finder, except in the case of shipwrecks, treasure trove (which belongs to the Crown), etc. 2. Under the A.E.A. 1925, the residuary estate of an intestate goes, in default of any person taking an absolute interest, to the Crown, Duchy of Lancaster or Cornwall, as *bona vacantia*. The Crown or Duchy may provide for the dependants of the intestate and for other persons for whom he might reasonably have been expected to make provision. See also the Inheritance (Provision for Family and Dependants) Act 1975, s. 24; and the Cos.A. 1981, s. 108.

bond. 1. Agreement under seal whereby a person (the "obligor") binds himself to another (the "obligee") to perform or refrain from an action. It may be a "simple bond"—without condition, or a "common money bond"—given to secure payment of money. It binds the obligor's real and personal estate: L.P.A. 1925, s. 80. 2. An interest-bearing document based on a long-term debt, usually issued by corporations.

bond, performance. Bond payable "on demand without proof or condition": *Edward Owen Ltd* v *Barclays Bank* [1978] QB 159.

bonus. That which is received over and above what is expected, eg, a gratuity, an additional dividend.

bonus shares. A company deciding to finance expansion from reserves comprising undistributed profits may bring its issued capital (qv) into line with the capital it employs by issuing bonus shares to existing shareholders to the value of the additional capital. See the Cos.A. 1948, s. 52.

books of account. Documents and other records which must be prepared and kept by a company, including, eg, a balance sheet (qv), profit and loss account, auditors' report, directors' report. Accounts must be kept in a manner likely to be adopted by prudent businessmen: *Hinds* v *Buenos Aires Grand National Tramway Co* [1906] 2 Ch 654. See the Cos.A. 1948, s. 147; Cos.A. 1981, Sch. 1.

books, partnership. See PARTNERSHIP BOOKS, INSPECTION OF.

books, statutory. See STATUTORY BOOKS.

borough. In early times a fortified town or castle. Later, a town or city incorporated by charter, with a corporation consisting of a mayor, aldermen and councillors. The title is no longer generally used. See the L.G.A. 1972.

borough, county. See COUNTY BOROUGH.

borough court. Court of record for a borough. Abolished, from April 1974, under L.G.A. 1972.

borough English. Ancient mode of descent by which land in, eg, Surrey, Sussex and localities of Nottingham, descended to the youngest son. Abolished under the A.E.A. 1925.

borough quarter sessions. Court presided over by a Recorder (qv) and held four times a year. It had civil, criminal, original and appellate jurisdiction which passed to the Crown Court (qv) by virtue of the Courts Act 1971.

Borstal institutions. Offenders aged 15 and under 21, convicted of an offence punishable with imprisonment, were sent from six months to two years to a Borstal institution (patterned originally on a reformatory opened at Borstal, Rochester, under the Prevention of Crime Act 1908) where detention was accompanied by training and instruction. Sentences of this nature were abolished by the C.J.A. 1982, s. 1(3).

bote. 1. (Anglo-Saxon) graduated compensation for injury. 2. (Anglo-Saxon) contributions by landowners, eg, brycg-bot—for repair of bridges, burh-bot—for repair of fortresses. See ESTOVERS.

bottomry. Obsolete term, meaning pledge of a ship and freight so as to secure a loan which allows a ship to continue its voyage.

boundaries, offences committed on. Where an offence is committed on the boundary between areas, or within five hundred yards of such a boundary, or in a harbour or river lying between such areas, the offence may be treated as having been committed in any of those areas: M.C.A. 1980, s. 3(1).

boundary. That which indicates or fixes some limit, eg, a fence, wall. See *Lee* v *Barrey* [1957] 1 All ER 191.

boundary commissions. Bodies set up under the House of Commons (Redistribution of Seats) Acts 1949 and 1958, one each for England, Scotland, N Ireland and Wales. They report to the Home Secretary on suggested electoral boundaries. See *R* v *Boundary Commission for England ex p Foot and Others* [1983] 2 WLR 458.

boycott. To engage in an organised refusal to deal with a person or body, eg, a manufacturer or supplier. See *Quinn* v *Leathem* [1901] AC 495.

Brandeis brief. Phrase referring to an American mode of presenting evidence, derived from the technique first employed in *Muller* v *Oregon* (1908) 208 US 412 by Louis D. Brandeis (who later became an associate justice of the US Supreme Court), utilising a short statement of legal argument as a preface to a wide range of material based on committee reports, social statistics, factory inspectors' reports, etc.

brawling. Noisy quarrelling. Originally used with reference to the creation of a disturbance on consecrated ground.

breach. The infringing or violation of a right, duty or law.

breach, anticipatory. See ANTICIPATORY BREACH.

breach of close. Unlawful entry on another's land.

breach of confidence. See CONFIDENCE, BREACH OF.

breach of contract. The refusal or failure by a party to a contract to fulfil an obligation imposed on him under that contract, resulting from, eg, repudiation of liability before completion, or conduct preventing proper performance. The contract is discharged where the breach results in the innocent party treating it as rescinded and where it has the effect of "depriving the party who has further undertakings still to perform of substantially the whole benefit which it was the intention of the parties as expressed in the contract as the consideration for performing those undertakings": *Hong Kong Fir Shipping Co* v *Kawasaki Kisem Kaisha* [1962] 2 QB 26. See *Photo Production* v *Securicor* [1980] AC 827 (discussion by the HL of the nature of fundamental breach).

breach of privilege. Actions which constitute a contempt of a parliamentary privilege (qv).

breach of promise of marriage. Failure to fulfil a promise to marry. Action for breach was abolished by the Law Reform (Misc. Provs.) Act 1970, s. 1(1). *See* ENGAGEMENT TO MARRY.

breach of statutory duty. *See* STATUTORY DUTY, BREACH OF.

breach of the peace. Offence committed whenever harm is actually done, or is likely to be done to a person, or in his presence to his property, or wherever a person is in fear of being so harmed through assault, affray, riot, unlawful assembly or other disturbance: *R* v *Howell* [1982] 1 QB 416. See *Albert* v *Lavin* [1982] AC 546.

breach of trust. The result of some improper act or omission relating to the administration of a trust or the interests of the beneficiaries (qv) arising under it. It may arise from failure to carry out the trustee's general duties or some abuse of his powers. A trustee is generally liable for any loss caused directly or indirectly to the trust property and to the beneficiaries' interests as result of the breach. For the court's power to relieve a trustee from the consequences of a breach of trust see the Tr.A. 1925, s. 61; see also the Lim.A. 1980, s. 21; and *Bartlett* v *Barclays Bank Trust Co. (Nos. 1 and 2)* [1980] Ch. 515. *See* TRUST.

breakdown of marriage. A court

hearing a petition for divorce should not hold that the marriage has broken down irretrievably unless satisfied by the petitioner of one or more of the following: that the respondent has committed adultery and the petitioner finds it intolerable to live with the respondent; that the respondent has behaved in such a way that the petitioner cannot reasonably be expected to live with the respondent; that the respondent has deserted the petitioner for a continuous period of two years immediately prior to the presentation of the petition; that the parties to the marriage have lived apart for at least two years immediately preceding the presentation of petition and that the respondent consents to the grant of a decree; that the parties have lived apart for a continuous period of at least five years immediately preceding the petition: Mat.C.A. 1973, s. 1(2).

breaking and entering. Term referring to the felony of burglary committed by one who, in the night, broke and entered a dwelling-house with intent to commit any felony therein: Larceny Act 1916, s. 25, repealed by the Th.A. 1968. *See* BURGLARY.

breathalyser. Device consisting of a measuring bag or some other device (eg, Alcolmeter), used in the administration of a breath test to a motorist by a constable who has reasonable cause to suspect him of having alcohol in his body or having committed a road traffic offence while his vehicle was in motion. See the Road Traffic Act 1972. ss. 6 *et seq.* (as substituted by the Transport Act 1981, Sch 8).

breath test. A constable in uniform may require a person to provide a specimen of breath for a breath test if he has reasonable cause to suspect him of having alcohol in his body while driving or attempting to drive or in charge of a motor vehicle on a road or other public place, or if the person has been driving, attempting to drive or in charge of a motor vehicle, or if he is reasonably believed to have been involved in an accident: Road Traffic Act 1972, s. 7(1) (as substituted by the Transport Act

1981, Sch 8). See also the Road Traffic Act 1972, s. 12(2) (as so substituted); *Corp* v *Dalton* [1983] RTR 160.

brevi manu. As the result of direct action; by a short cut.

brewster sessions. Annual meeting of licensing justices to consider applications for licences, renewals, etc, relating to the sale of alcoholic liquor. Must be held within the first two weeks of February: Licensing Act 1964, Sch 1. *See* LICENSING OF PREMISES.

bribery. The offence of taking, or bestowing, or promising, a price, reward or favour intended to influence the judgment or conduct of a public official. In its legal sense it implies corruption: *Gardner* v *Robertson*, 1921 SC 132. See the Public Bodies Corrupt Practices Act 1889; the Representation of the People Act 1949, s. 99; *R* v *Smith* [1960] 2 QB 423; and *Cheung Chee Kwong* v *The Queen* [1979] 1 WLR 1454. *See* CORRUPTION.

bridging loan. Generally a short-term advance made by a bank to a customer pending the receipt by the customer of funds from some other source. See the C.C.A. 1974, s. 58(2) (*b*).

bridleway. Highway over which the public have right of way on foot, on horseback or leading a horse, with or without a right to drive animals along the highway: Highways Act 1980, s. 329(1).

Bridlington Agreement. Inter-union rules, agreed by the TUC at Bridlington in 1939, relating to the transfer of members from one union to another, spheres of influence, poaching of members. See the Royal Commission on Trade Unions 1968 (Cmnd 3623), paras 686–691; *Spring* v *National Amalgamated Stevedores and Dockers Society* [1956] 1 WLR 585; and *Cheall* v *APEX* [1983] 2 WLR 679. *See* TRADE UNION.

brief. Written instructions to a barrister (qv) from a solicitor (qv) relating to the representing of a client in legal proceedings. Usually includes a narrative of the facts, copies of documents, etc.

Bristol Tolzey Court. Originally a court of the bailiffs of the Bristol Hundred, later amalgamated with the Court of the Lord Steward. Its sessions were held, until its abolition by the Courts Act 1971, under a charter granted by Queen Anne in 1710.

British Commonwealth. *See* COMMONWEALTH.

British dependent territories citizenship. *See* CITIZENSHIP, BRITISH DEPENDENT TERRITORIES.

British Empire. Term, now in disuse, referring to those lands over which Britain possessed sovereignty. *See* COMMONWEALTH.

British overseas citizen. *See* CITIZEN, BRITISH OVERSEAS.

British possession. Any part of Her Majesty's dominions outside the UK; and where parts of such dominions are under both a central and a local legislature, all parts under the central legislature are deemed, for the purposes of this definition, to be one British possession: I.A. 1978, Sch 1.

British protected person. One who is a member of any class of persons declared to be British protected persons by an Order in Council under s. 38, or by virtue of the Solomon Islands Act 1978: B.N.A. 1981, s. 50(1). Applies to former protectorates, protected states or UK trust territories. The status is not transmissible.

British protectorates. Territories which, although not colonies and not part of HM Dominions, were governed in internal and external affairs by Britain. See S.I. 1982/1070.

broadcasting. The act of making public by means of radio or television transmission. A broadcast programme is publication in permanent form for purposes of defamation (qv) under the Defamation Act 1952.

Broadmoor. An institution, classified as a "special hospital" (qv) providing treatment for patients (formerly known as criminal lunatics) with dangerous, violent or criminal propensities, under conditions of special security. See the M.H.A. 1959, ss. 97–99; and the M.H.A. 1983, Part III.

brokage, marriage. Contract by which one person undertakes, in consideration for a money payment, to procure a marriage for another. Generally illegal and void: *Hermann v Charlesworth* [1905] 2 KB 123.

brokerage. Payment or commission earned by a broker. Sum paid to a person by a company (qv) under authority in the articles for placing shares (qv). See *Andreae v Zinc Mines of Great Britain* [1918] 2 KB 454.

broker, insurance. *See* INSURANCE BROKER.

brothel. "A place resorted to by persons of both sexes for the purpose of prostitution": *Singleton v Ellison* [1895] 1 QB 607. Under the S.O.A. 1956, ss. 33, 36, it is an offence to keep or manage a brothel or knowingly to permit the whole or part of premises to be used for the purposes of habitual prostitution. See *Donovan v Gavin* [1965] 2 All ER 611; *Kelly v Purvis* [1983] 2 WLR 299. See also the S.O.A. 1967, s. 6.

brutum fulmen. An empty threat.

budget. An estimate of government expenditure and revenue for the ensuing financial year presented to Parliament by the Chancellor of the Exchequer (qv), usually every April. Budget proposals are embodied in a Finance Bill.

buggery. "It is an offence for a person to commit buggery with another person or animal": S.O.A. 1956, s. 12(1). The act consists of sexual intercourse *per anum* by a man with a man or woman or sexual intercourse *per anum* or *per vaginam* by a man or woman with an animal. (There is no such offence as "rape *per anum*": *R v Gaston* (1981) 73 Cr App R 164.) Under the S.O.A. 1967, s. 1, it is not an offence for a man to commit buggery with another man provided that the parties consent, that they have attained the age of 21 and that the act was done in private. See *R v Angel* [1968] Crim LR 342; *R v Stewart* [1973] Crim LR 319.

bugging. Electronic surveillance (qv).

building. "Its ordinary and natural meaning is, a block of brick or stone work covered in by a roof": *Moir v Williams* [1892] 1 QB 264. See *Windsor Hotel v Allan* [1981] JPL 274. *See* MESSUAGE.

building lease. 1. One made partly in consideration of some person erecting new or additional buildings or improving or repairing buildings: S.L.A. 1925, s. 44. A building lease for 999 years may be made by a mortgagor or mortgagee in possession or tenant for life (qv): L.P.A. 1925, s. 99; S.L.A. 1925, s. 41. 2. Lease made by a landlord generally for 99 years, at a rent known as "ground rent", the lessee covenanting to erect buildings.

building scheme. Where land is developed, as in the case of a building scheme, eg, for a housing estate, the developer can require the purchaser of a plot to enter into a restrictive covenant (qv) so as to maintain the character of the estate. See *Elliston v Reacher* [1908] 2 Ch 374; *Baxter v Four Oak Properties Ltd* [1965] Ch 876; *Gilbert v Spoor* [1982] 2 WLR 183.

building society. A body established for the purpose of raising by subscriptions from members a stock or fund for making loans to members out of the society's funds upon security of freehold or leasehold estates by way of mortgages. See the Building Societies Acts 1874 and 1962. *See* MORTGAGE.

building society mortgage. Mortgage created where the mortgagor is a member of a building society, so that the society's rules are part of the mortgage conditions. The society will not generally advance money on a second mortgage unless the first has been in the society's favour. See the Building Societies Act 1962.

Bullock order. Where the plaintiff joins two defendants in the alternative because he is unsure as to which one is liable, he may be able to obtain an order against the unsuccessful defendant to pay the costs (qv) of the successful defendant: *Bullock v London General Omnibus Co* [1907] 1 KB 264. The plaintiff is not entitled to such an order as of right. See O. 15, r. 4.

burden of adducing evidence. The onus on the plaintiff or prosecutor of adducing sufficient evidence (qv) to satisfy the court that a hearing ought to continue. Known also as "evidential burden".

burden of proof. The obligation of proving facts. Used in a number of senses, eg: *general burden* (proving a case); *specific burden* (proving an individual issue); *evidential burden* (adducing sufficient evidence in support of a disputed fact) (see *Jayasena* v *R* [1970] AC 618). In general, the burden lies on the party who substantially asserts the affirmative of the issue (ie, the plaintiff or prosecution). It may shift when the plaintiff or prosecution establishes a prima facie case. See the Prevention of Corruption Act 1916, s. 2; *Woolmington* v *DPP* [1935] AC 462; and *R* v *Edwards* [1975] QB 27. *See* PROOF.

burden of proof, shifting of. Phrase used in the law of evidence to indicate the moving of the burden of proof (ie, the obligation to prove facts) from one side to the other, as where, eg, there exists a disputable presumption of law in favour of one party (so that his adversary must rebut it) or where the subject-matter of one party's allegation is peculiarly within the opponent's knowledge (so that the latter must rebut the allegation). See, eg, *R* v *Turner* (1816) 5 M & S; *Redpath* v *Redpath* [1959] 1 All ER 650. *See* EVIDENCE.

burglary. *Burge-breche* = breach of a borough. Under the Larceny Act 1916, an offence committed by breaking and entering in the night with intent to commit a felony. Under the Th.A. 1968, s. 9(1), a person is guilty of burglary if "he enters any building or part of a building as a trespasser and with intent to commit any such offence as is mentioned in sub-s. (2) [stealing, inflicting grievous bodily harm, etc.]; or, having entered any building or part of a building as a trespasser he steals or attempts to steal anything in the building or that part of it or inflicts or attempts to inflict on any person therein any grievous bodily harm." "Aggravated burglary" is committed by one who commits burglary and has with him any firearm or imitation firearm, weapon of offence or explosive: s. 10(1). See the C.L.A. 1977, Sch 2. See *R* v *Jones* [1976] 1 WLR 672; *Rv Walkington* [1979] 2 All ER 716; and *R* v *Gregory* [1982] Crim LR 229.

burial, prevention of. It is an offence against public order to prevent the proper burial (or cremation) of a human body without lawful excuse: *R* v *Hunter* [1974] QB 95; *R* v *Swindell* (*The Times*, 9.10.1981).

business. Includes any trade (qv), profession or vocation: Counter-Inflation Act 1973, s. 21(1). Under the Fair Trading Act 1973, s. 137(2), it includes a professional practice and any other undertaking carried on for gain or reward or which is an undertaking in the course of which goods or services are supplied otherwise than free of charge.

business liability. Term used in the Unfair Contract Terms Act 1977, s. 1(3) to refer to liability for breach of obligations or duties arising from things done or to be done by a person in the course of a business (whether his own business or another's) or from the occupation of premises used for the occupier's business purposes.

business, special. *See* SPECIAL BUSINESS.

business tenancy. A tenancy comprising property occupied by a tenant for the purposes of a business carried on by him or for those and other purposes. Security of tenure and rent are affected by the Landlord and Tenant Act 1954, Part II, as amended. See also the Rent Act 1977, s. 24; and *O'May* v *City of London Real Property Co* [1982] 1 All ER 660.

business travel. Travelling which a person is necessarily obliged to do in the performance of the duties of his employment: Finance Act 1976, s. 72(5) (*c*).

buyer. Under the S.G.A. 1979, s. 61(1), is "a person who buys or agrees to buy goods".

bye-law. "An ordinance affecting the public or some portion of the public imposed by some authority clothed with statutory powers, ordering something to be done or not to be done and accompanied by some sanction or penalty for its non-observance . . . it has the force of law within the sphere of its legitimate operation": *Kruse* v *Johnson* [1898] 2 QB 91. It may be declared invalid if, eg, not made in the manner prescribed by statute, or if repugnant to the law of the land, or unreasonable. See the L.G.A. 1972, ss. 235(1), 236.

C

C. 1. Chancellor (qv). 2. Abbreviation for Command Papers. *See* COMMAND PAPERS, NUMBERING OF; PARLIAMENTARY PAPERS.

c. *Circa* = about, approximately.

C.A. Court of Appeal (qv).

Cabinet. A group of ministers selected by and presided over by the Prime Minister (qv), collectively responsible for the general character and policy of legislation, consisting of the political heads of government departments and others. Cabinet ministers are also members of the Privy Council (qv). *See* MINISTERIAL RESPONSIBILITY.

call. 1. As in "call to the Bar"—the ceremony in the Inns of Court whereby students who have passed the appropriate examinations and kept terms are admitted as barristers (qv). 2. As in "call" made by a company (qv) whereby directors are empowered to ask shareholders for instalments of payment for shares. Calls cannot be made until the minimum subscription has been allotted. 3. As in "call on contributories" whereby a company or its liquidator makes a demand on those liable to contribute to the payment of debts. *See* A AND B LISTS.

calling the jury. Announcement of the persons who have been selected to form a jury. See the Juries Act 1974, s. 11. *See* JURY.

camera, in. *See* IN CAMERA.

cancellation. The act of nullifying or invalidating an instrument, eg, by striking out signatures or removing a seal. The act must be accompanied by the intention to cancel.

cancellation, delivery up of documents for. An equitable remedy whereby a void document is delivered up and cancelled, eg, lest some person be deceived by it, as where a guarantee was procured by misrepresentation (see *Cooper* v *Joel* (1859) 1 De G F & J 240), or a conveyance had been forged (see *Peake* v *Highfield* (1826) 1 Russ 559).

cannabis. Hallucinogenic drug obtained from hemp (*cannabis sativa*). "'Cannabis' (except in the expression 'cannabis resin') means any plant of the genus *Cannabis* or any part of any such plant (by whatever name designated) except that it does not include cannabis resin or any of the following products after separation from the resin of the plant, namely (*a*) mature stalk of any such plant, (*b*) fibre produced from mature stalk of any such plant, and (*c*) seed of any such plant": C.L.A. 1977, s. 52, substituted for the Misuse of Drugs Act 1971, s. 37(1). A controlled drug (Class B) under the 1971 Act. It is an offence under the 1971 Act to import, export, have in one's possession, produce or supply (except by authorisation) the drug or to cultivate any plant of the genus *Cannabis*. See *Taylor* v *Chief Constable of Kent* [1981] 1 WLR 606; *R* v *Boyesen* [1982] AC 768.

canon. Generally, a rule of *canon law,* ie, a codified Roman ecclesiastical system of law. *Canon law* also refers to the law of the Church of England. (Canon law does not bind the laity: *Middleton* v *Croft* (1736) 2 Ark 690.)

canonical disability. Impotence (qv).

canvassing. 1. Soliciting votes from, eg, electors. 2. Where one individual visits another off trade premises in order to obtain the entry of another into a regulated agreement (qv): C.C.A. 1974, s. 48. Canvassing for debtor–creditor agreements (qv) off trade premises is illegal: s. 49(1).

capacity of child in criminal law. *See* DOLI CAPAX.

capacity to contract. The legal competency, power or fitness to enter and be bound by a contract. Thus, an infant (qv) generally lacks contractual capacity, save where he binds himself by contract for necessaries or for other matters relating to his benefit. See *Doyle* v *White City Stadium* [1935] 1 KB 110; *Chaplin* v *Leslie Frewin Ltd* [1966] Ch 71. *See* CONTRACT.

capax doli. *See* DOLI CAPAX.

capias. That you take. Name of a group of writs, eg, *capias ad responden-dum* (issued for the arrest of a defendant against whom an indictment had been found); *capias in withernam* (*wither* = against: *nam* = *seizure*) (writ issued in case of replevin (qv) where goods had been removed to an unknown place, and the taking of other goods to the same value was authorised).

capital. 1. In commercial usage, the capital of a business is its net worth, ie, the value of its assets less the amount owing to its creditors. 2. In company law, it refers to, eg, authorised, issued or paid-up capital (qv).

capital allowances. Allowances available to persons carrying on a trade, profession, vocation or employment who have incurred capital expenditure on certain types of asset (including machinery and plant (qv)) for the purpose of their business. See, eg, the Capital Allowances Act 1968; and the Finance Act 1983, chap II.

capital, alteration of. *See* ALTERATION OF CAPITAL.

capital clause. Clause in memorandum of association (qv) setting out company's authorised capital (qv), number and denomination of shares. In the case of a public company (qv) the clause must state an amount not less than the authorised minimum: Cos.A. 1980, ss. 3(2), 85(1).

capital gains tax. Tax introduced by the Finance Act 1965, levied on the gains made on the disposal of assets. See the Capital Gains Tax Act 1979; and the Finance Act 1983, ss. 10–29. See *Aberdeen Construction Group Ltd* v *IRC* [1978] 1 All ER 963.

capital interest, qualifying. "Means, in relation to any body corporate, an interest in shares comprised in the equity share capital of that body corporate of a class carrying rights to vote in all circumstances at general meetings of that body corporate": Cos. A. 1981, Sch 6. For "equity share capital", see s. 154(5).

capitalisation. In relation to profits of a company (qv), means applying profits in wholly or partly paying up unissued shares in the company to be allotted to members as fully or partly-paid bonus shares, or transferring profits to capital redemption reserve fund: Cos. A. 1980, s. 45(3).

capitalisation, ex. *See* EX CAPITALIS-ATION.

capital, loan. Any debenture stock or funded debt issued by a corporate body or other body formed or established in the UK or any capital raised by such a body, being capital which is borrowed, or has the character of borrowed money, whether in the form of stock or any other form and stock or marketable securities issued by the government of a Commonwealth country outside the UK: Finance Act 1976, s. 126(5).

capital money. 1. Money that is paid to trustees of a settlement in the exercise of a statutory power, eg, mortgage of land for purposes authorised by the S.L.A. 1925, sale of land or heirlooms under the S.L.A. 1925, s. 67(2). 2. Money that should be treated as capital, eg, that paid under a fire insurance policy which the tenant for life (qv) was obliged to maintain. See the S.L.A. 1925, s. 81. *See* SETTLEMENT.

capital punishment. Death by hanging. Now a punishment only for high treason (qv) and piracy with violence (qv). Capital punishment for murder was abolished by the Murder (Abolition of Death Penalty) Act 1965, and a sentence of life imprisonment substituted. "Capital murder", punishable by death, was a certain type of murder under the Homicide Act 1957, s. 5, eg, murder done in the cause or furtherance of theft. The category disappeared following the 1965 Act. See the Armed Forces Act 1981, s. 17.

capital redemption reserve. Made up of amounts equal to nominal value of shares cancelled as a result of the company redeeming or purchasing its own shares out of distributable profits: see the Cos. A. 1981, ss. 45, 46, 53.

capital, reduction of. *See* REDUCTION OF CAPITAL.

capital reserve. Non-distributable funds retained in a business. "Statutory capital reserves'' include share premium account and capital redemption reserve fund (qv). See the Cos. A. 1948, ss. 56, 58.

capital, serious loss of. When the net assets of a public company (qv) fall to one half or less of called-up share capital, the directors, not later than 28 days from the day at which the loss became known to a director, must call an extraordinary general meeting (qv) on a date not less than 56 days from that date to consider action to be taken: Cos. A. 1980, s. 34(1).

capital, share. See SHARE CAPITAL.

capital transfer tax. Tax charged at progressive rates, cumulatively, on the value of property transferred by chargeable transfers and made by a person in his lifetime. Introduced under the Finance Act 1975, Part III. "Chargeable transfers" are transfers of value (other than exempt transfers) made after 26th March 1974. A "transfer of value" is "any disposition made by a person as a result of which the value of his estate immediately after the disposition is less than it would be but for the disposition; and the amount by which it is less is the value transferred by the transfer": s. 20(2). See the Finance Act 1981, ss. 92–104.

caption. 1. Arrest. 2. Heading of a legal instrument.

car. See MOTOR CAR.

caravan. A structure capable of being moved by towing or being transported on a motor vehicle or a trailer and designed or adapted for human habitation. See the Caravan Sites Act 1968, s. 13; the L.G.P.L.A. 1980, ss. 70, 173; *R* v *Welwyn Hatfield DC ex p Brinkley* (1982) 80 LGR 727; and the Mobile Homes Act 1983.

care. The degree of attention or diligence that may fairly and properly be expected in given circumstances.

care and control. "Care" includes protecting and guidance; "control" includes discipline: C. & Y.P.A. 1969, s. 70(1). See *Re S.* [1977] 3 All ER 582.

care, duty of. See DUTY OF CARE.

care for safety, duty of. Duty of an occupier of premises ("the common duty of care") owed to all his visitors,

except trespassers, under the Occupiers' Liability Act 1957, s. 2. Under the Defective Premises Act 1972, s. 7, a landlord has a duty of taking reasonable care to see that persons who might be affected by defects in the premises he has let are reasonably safe from danger or injury.

careless and inconsiderate driving. It is an offence to drive a motor vehicle on a road without due care and attention, or without reasonable consideration for other persons using the road: Road Traffic Act, 1972, s. 3. See also the Road Traffic Act 1974, Sch 5. See *Taylor* v *Rogers* (1960) 124 JP 217.

care proceedings. A procedure involving children and young persons, based on the C. & Y.P.A. 1969, which to some extent replaces criminal proceedings in respect of juveniles with "care proceedings". A local authority or authorised person who believes that there are grounds for considering the advisability of a care order (eg, that the juvenile has committed an offence) may bring the juvenile before a juvenile court (qv). The court may order a parent or guardian to enter into a recognisance to take proper care of the juvenile. A "care order" can be made, committing the juvenile to the care of a local authority (qv): 1969 Act, s. 1. See the C. & Y.P.A. 1969, s. 20 A (added by the C.J.A. 1982, s. 22).

care, removal of child from. It is an offence under the Ch.A. 1975, s. 53, for a parent whose child has been received into care to remove the child from care without either the consent of the local authority or without giving 28 days' notice of that intention.

care, restriction of liberty of children in. In general, a child in the care of a local authority may not be placed in accommodation for restricting liberty unless he has a history of absconding and if he absconds it is likely that his welfare will be at risk, or if kept in other accommodation he is likely to injure himself: Child Care Act 1980, s. 21A, (as substituted by the C.J.A. 1982, s. 25(1)).

care, servant's contractual duty of. "The servant owes a contractual duty of care to his master, and a breach of that duty founds an action for damages for breach of contract": *per* Ackner LJ in *Janata Bank v Ahmed* [1981] IRLR 457.

cargo. 1. Anything carried or to be carried in a ship or other vessel: Docks and Harbours Act 1966, s. 58(1). See *National Dock Labour Board v John Bland & Co* [1971] 2 All ER 779. 2. Goods which are, or are to be, or have been loaded in a ship, excluding a passenger's personal baggage carried on board by him, and including anything taken on board a ship from the sea or sea-bed with a view to its being discharged to shore: Dock Work Regulation Act 1976, Sch 4, Part I.

carnal knowledge. Phrase used in early statutes to mean sexual intercourse. See now the S.O.A. 1956, s. 44.

carriage of goods by air, liability relating to. In general, a carrier is liable without proof of breach of contract or negligence on his part. Only the actual consignor and consignee have claims in respect of damage to goods. See the Carriage by Air Act 1961; the Carriage by Air (Supplementary Provs.) Act 1962; the Carriage by Air and Road Act 1979; and *Rustenberg Platinum Mines v S African Airways* [1977] 1 Ll R 564.

carriageway. Way constituting or comprised in a highway (qv), being a way (other than a cycle track) over which the public have a right of way for the passage of vehicles: Highways Act 1980, s. 329(1).

carrier, common. One who, by profession, undertakes for money payment the carrying of goods for those who employ him. His duties include the receiving and carrying of goods of the type he professes to carry; the carrying of goods by a reasonable route; delivery without unreasonable delay . He may be sued for damages if he wrongfully refuses to carry goods. See the Carriers Acts 1830 and 1865; *Belfast Ropework Co v Bushell* [1918] 1 KB 210; *Rosenthal v LCC* (1924) 131 LT 563.

carrier, common, liability for safety of goods. Generally, liability, as an insurer of goods, for loss or damage except where caused by act of God (qv), act of Queen's enemies, consignor's fault, goods' inherent vice.

carrier, private. A carrier who is not a common carrier (qv), ie, who is never bound to carry. He is liable for any loss caused by his negligence. See *Barnfield v Goole and Sheffield Transport Co* [1910] 2 KB 94; *James Buchanan & Co v Hay's Transport Services* [1972] 2 Ll R 535.

carriers by sea and inland waterways. Classified as common carriers (qv); public carriers (ie, those who are not common carriers: known also as "private carriers"); carriers who carry incidentally to their main business: *Liver Alkali Co v Johnson* (1874) LR 9 Ex 338; *Consolidated Tea Co v Oliver's Wharf* [1910] 2 KB 395.

carrier's lien. Common law lien under which a carrier is entitled to keep possession of goods until he is paid freight owing to him for their carriage: *Skinner v Upshaw* (1702) 2 Ld Raym 752.

carte blanche. White card (used for the granting of permission relating to some act). Generally involves the grant of an unlimited authority.

case. An action or trial.

case stated. A statement of the facts in a case submitted, eg, by magistrates for the opinion of a higher court (such as the Divisional Court). Application for statement can be made by the defendant, prosecutor or a "person aggrieved" (although not a party). Application must identify the point of law on which opinion is sought. See the M.C.A. 1980, s. 111; the S.C.A. 1981, s. 28; S.I. 1982/1109; and *R v Croydon Justices ex p Lefor Holdings* [1981] 1 All ER 520.

cash. Term applied to ready money of the current coin of the realm, including notes of the Bank of England. Under the C.C.A. 1974, s. 189(1), it includes money in any form.

cash on delivery. *See* C.O.D.

casual ejector. The nominal defendant (known as "Richard Roe") in an action of ejectment (qv). (This type of action was abolished by the Common Law Procedure Act 1852).

casus belli. Occasion of war. An event which is used to justify a war.

casus omissus. A case not provided for by the law. See, eg, *R* v *Munks* [1964] 1 QB 304; *Fisher* v *Bell* [1961] 1 QB 394.

catching bargain. An entrapping or unconscionable bargain, eg, a loan made on extortionate terms to one who has an expectancy (eg, an expectant heir). See the C.C.A. 1974, s. 137; *Nevill* v *Snelling* (1880) 15 Ch D 679; *Cresswell* v *Potter* [1978] 1 WLR 255. *See* UNCONSCIONABLE TRANSACTION.

cattle. "Bulls, cows, steers, heifers and calves": Animal Health Act 1981, s. 89(1).

cattle trespass. Damage done by cattle trespassing on land of their owner's neighbour. Was actionable *per se*, without proof of damage. See now the Animals Act 1971, s. 4. *See* STRAYING LIVESTOCK.

causa causans. The immediate cause. "The real effective cause of damage": *Pandorf* v *Hamilton* (1886) 17 QBD 675.

causa proxima et non remota spectatur. It is the immediate, not the remote, cause that should be considered. The *causa proxima* "is the cause proximate in efficiency, not necessarily in time": *Leyland Shipping Co* v *Norwich Union* [1918] AC 350.

causa remota. Remote cause; one operating indirectly through intervention of other causes. See *R* v *Jordan* (1956) 40 Cr App R 152; *R* v *Blaue* [1975] 1 WLR 1411; *R* v *Malcherek* [1981] 1 WLR 690. *See* NOVUS ACTUS INTERVENIENS.

causation. The relation of cause and effect. Where an *actus reus* (qv) is so defined that the occurrence of stated consequences is required (eg, that the *actus reus* of the accused caused a death), the conduct of the accused which is alleged to have been the cause of those consequences has to be proved. See, eg, *R* v *Jordan* (1956) 40 Cr App R 153; *R* v *Blaue* [1975] 1 WLR 1411; *R* v *Malcherek* [1981] 1 WLR 690. *See* NOVUS ACTUS INTERVENIENS.

cause. 1. A suit or action. 2. That which produces or contributes to some event. "If a man intending to secure a particular result does an act which brings that about, he causes that result": *Alphacell Ltd* v *Woodward* [1972] 2 All ER 475.

cause of action. The facts out of which arises a right to sue. "Every fact which is material to be proved to entitle the plaintiff to succeed, every fact which the defendant would have a right to traverse": *Cooke* v *Gill* (1873) LR 8 CP 107. See *Sparham–Souter* v *Town & Country Developments* [1976] QB 858.

causes, concurrent. *See* CONCURRENT CAUSES.

caution. 1. A warning. 2. Any person interested in registered land (qv) may lodge a caution with the Registrar against any dealing with that land. Entry of dealing with such land may not then be made on the register unless the cautioner has received notice. See the L.R.A. 1925, ss. 53, 54; *Elias* v *Mitchell* [1972] Ch 652; and *Clearbrook Property Holdings* v *Verrier* [1974] 1 WLR 243. 3. A police caution, used when it has been decided not to bring a prosecution, is a formal statement (oral or written) informing an offender that if he is reported for another offence, the circumstances in which the caution was issued may be taken into consideration. (The procedure has no statutory basis.)

c.a.v. *Cur. adv. vult.* (qv).

caveat. Warning, usually in the form of an entry in a register intended to prevent some action being taken without notice being given to person issuing the warning (the *caveator*). See, eg, the S.C.A. 1981, s. 108, allowing a caveat against a grant of probate (qv) or administration to be entered in the principal registry or district probate registry: L.R.A. 1925, s. 30.

caveat emptor. Let the buyer beware. In general, the buyer is expected to look to his own interests. See, however, the S.G.A. 1979, ss. 13, 14. *See* CONDITION; WARRANTY.

caveat venditor. Let the seller beware.

C.B. Chief Baron of the Exchequer.

Cd. Abbreviation for Command

Papers. *See* COMMAND PAPERS, NUMBER-ING OF; PARLIAMENTARY PAPERS.

Central Criminal Court. Established by the Central Criminal Court Act 1834 as an assize court, exercising criminal jurisdiction in the Greater London area. Popularly known as the "Old Bailey". Abolished by the Courts Act 1971, but it has been retained in name, so that when the Crown Court (qv) sits in London it is known as the Central Criminal Court: S.C.A. 1981, s. 8(3). The Lord Mayor of London and any City Alderman may sit as a judge with a High Court or circuit judge, or recorder. Appeal lies to Court of Appeal (Criminal Division).

Central Office of the Supreme Court. Departments which carry out the administrative business of the Supreme Court; they include those of the Masters' Secretary and Queen's Remembrancer, Action, Filing and Records, Crown Office and Associates, Supreme Court Taxing Office. See the S.C.A. 1981, s. 96 and O. 63.

certainties, the three. Phrase applied to the necessary conditions for the creation of a valid private trust, stated by Lord Eldon in *Wright* v *Atkyns* (1823) Turn & R 143 and by Lord Langdale in *Knight* v *Knight* (1840) 3 Beav 148 thus: "...the words must be imperative...the subject must be certain...the object or persons intended to have the benefit must be certain."

certificate, land. A certificate under seal of the Land Registry given to a registered proprietor (qv) as his document of title. It records details of the registered land (qv), eg, charges, incumbrances, class of title. The certificate is retained by the Land Registry if a charge on the land is registered or protected by mortgage caution (qv): L.R.A. 1925, s. 65.

certificate of incorporation. *See* INCORPORATION, CERTIFICATE OF.

certificate of shares. Document enabling a shareholder to show a good prima facie title to his shares. See the Cos. A. 1948, s. 81. The shareholder has a right to a certificate which should be prepared and ready for delivery within two months of the allotment of shares or their transfer. See also the Forgery and Counterfeiting Act 1981, s. 5(6).

certificate to commence business. A trading certificate (qv).

Certification Officer. Appointed by the Secretary of State under the E.P.A. 1975, s. 7, having as his principal duty the certification that a trade union applying to him is or is not independent. *See* TRADE UNION, INDEPENDENT.

certiorari. To be fully informed of. Originally a writ from the High Court to an inferior court commanding proceedings to be removed to a superior court "that conscionable justice may be therein administered": *Termes de la Ley*. Abolished under the A.J. (Misc. Provs.) A. 1938, s. 7, which replaced it with an order of certiorari. Used, eg, to review and to quash decisions of tribunals. See the S.C.A. 1981, s. 29; *R* v *Aston University Senate, ex p Roffey* [1969] 2 QB 538; and *R* v *Sheffield Crown Court ex p Brownlow* [1980] QB 530.

certum est quod certum reddi potest. That which can be made certain is to be treated as certain. See, eg, *Duncombe* v *Brighton Club and Norfolk Hotel Company* (1875) LR 10 QB 371.

cessante ratione legis, cessat ipsa lex. With the reason of the law ceasing, the law itself ceases. See *Miliangos* v *George Frank Ltd* [1976] AC 443.

cessate grant. When a grant limited as to time has been made and has ceased to have effect at the end of that time, a subsequent grant is known as a *cessate* or *supplemental* grant. It is, in effect, a renewal of the entire original grant. *See* GRANT.

cesser. 1. A ceasing (usually of liability). Thus, a "cesser clause" in a charterparty (qv) states that the charterer's liability ceases when the cargo has been landed. 2. "Provision for cesser on redemption" is a clause in a mortgage (qv) providing for the ending of a term of years when the loan is repaid. See the L.P.A. 1925, s. 116. 3. "Cesser of interest" refers to the determination of an interest which may then pass to another.

cestui que trust. Shortened form of *cestui à que trust* ("he for whom is the trust"). The beneficiary (qv). Plural: *cestuis que trust*. *See* TRUST.

cestui que use. Shortened form of *cestui à qui oes le feoffment fut fait.* One to whose use property was conveyed. Thus, X conveyed land to Y to the use of Z and his heirs. Z was known as *cestui que use*. *See* TRUST; USE.

cestui que vie. Shortened form of *cestui à que vie* (he for whose life...). He for whose life a grant of land is made. Thus, where X is a tenant "for the life of Y", Y is *cestui que vie*. *See* AUTRE VIE.

ceteris paribus. Other things being equal.

cf. Compare.

chain of representation. An executor of a sole or last surviving executor of a testator is the executor of that testator. So long as the chain is unbroken, the last executor in the chain is the executor of every preceding testator. The chain is broken by failure to obtain probate or to appoint an executor, or by an intestacy. See the A.E.A. 1925, s. 7. *See* EXECUTOR.

chain of title. Successive conveyances from the original source to the present owner. *See* TITLE DEEDS.

challenge to jury. Procedure whereby, before a jury is sworn, the defendant may challenge the members. See the Juries Act 1974, s. 12. Challenges may be: 1. *Peremptory,* ie, without the defendant disclosing the cause. (The Crown may also challenge without disclosing the cause.) Up to three peremptory challenges may be made, (see the C.L.A. 1977, s. 43). 2. *For cause,* ie: *to the array,* by which the defendant challenges the whole panel summoned; *to the separate polls,* by which he challenges individual jurors. See *R* v *Brandreth* (1817) 32 St Tr 755; *R* v *Harrington* (1976) 64 Cr App R 1. *See* JURY.

chambers. Usually, the offices of a judge in which application by way of summons may be heard, or the offices of counsel.

champerty. *Campi partitio* = dividing of land. An offence, abolished under the C.L.A. 1967, resulting from a person's maintenance (qv) of another

in an action, on condition that the subject-matter of the action was to be shared by them.

Chancellor. 1. Lord High Chancellor (known as the Lord Chancellor). Appointed by the Crown on the Prime Minister's advice. He is the principal legal dignitary, a member of the Cabinet (qv) and Speaker of the House of Lords, presiding at judicial proceedings on appeal. The Lord Chancellor (Tenure of Office and Discharge of Ecclesiastical Functions) Act 1974 makes it possible for a Roman Catholic to hold the office. 2. Chancellor of the Exchequer, political head of the Treasury (qv) and responsible for control of national revenue and expenditure. A member of the Cabinet (qv). He presents the annual budget (qv) to Parliament.

chance-medley. *Chance medlée* = mingled chance. The killing of an aggressor in self-defence upon some sudden affray. It was considered excusable (as opposed to justifiable) homicide. "The doctrine has no longer any place in the law of homicide": *R* v *Semini* [1949] 1 KB 405.

Chancery, Court of. *See* COURT OF CHANCERY.

Chancery Division. A division of the High Court of Justice, consisting of the Lord Chancellor (qv), a vice-chancellor, and other puisne judges (qv). Matters over which it has jurisdiction include administration of estates, execution of trusts, contested probate and (under the Patents Act 1977, s. 96(1)) patents. A single judge of the Division may hear appeals, eg, from the Commissioner of Inland Revenue. See the S.C.A. 1981, s. 5, Sch 1.

Chancery Masters. Deputies of the judges of the Chancery Division. *See* MASTERS OF THE SUPREME COURT.

change of voyage. Takes place "where after the commencement of the risk, the destination of the ship is voluntarily changed from the destination contemplated by the policy": Marine Insurance Act 1906, s. 45(1).

character, evidence as to. Evidence as to the character of a party (ie, reputation, disposition) may be given in the following circumstances: 1. *In criminal cases.* Evidence of the good character of the accused can always be given in chief or cross-examination (qv). Evidence of bad character may be given with leave of the judge to rebut the evidence of the good character of the accused, or if he has attacked the character of any witness for the prosecution. Evidence of character may be given after conviction. See *Lowery* v *R* [1974] AC 85. See the Criminal Evidence Act 1898, s. 1(f) (iii) (as amended by the Criminal Evidence Act 1979, s. 1). 2. *In civil cases.* Evidence of good character may not be given (except in rebuttal) so as to aggravate damages. Evidence of the plaintiff's bad character is admissible, eg, where his character is in issue (eg, in defamation). *See* EVIDENCE.

charge. 1. A criminal accusation. 2. Judge's instruction to a jury. 3. Expenses. 4. An incumbrance, eg, on land, which secures payment of money. Charges over land capable of subsisting at law are, under the L.P.A. 1925, s. 1(2), eg, charges by way of legal mortgage. Other charges take effect as equitable interests. See the L.C.A. 1972. 5. A fixed charge is a charge on specific property. A floating charge may be created by a company to secure debentures. The floating charge "is ambulatory and hovers over the property until some event occurs which causes it to settle and crystallise into a specific charge": *Barker* v *Eynon* [1974] 1 All ER 900. See the A.J.A. 1977, s. 7(1).

charge, acceptance of. Police procedure whereby an arresting officer gives details of circumstances of an arrest to a superior officer, leaving it to him to decide whether further action should be taken.

charge by way of legal mortgage. A mortgage may be created by a charge by deed expressed to be by way of legal mortgage: L.P.A. 1925, s. 85(1). The mortgagee has the same protection, powers and remedies as if he had taken a lease of a fee simple (qv). See *Regent Oil Co* v *J.A. Gregory Ltd* [1966] Ch 402. *See* MORTGAGE.

charge, general equitable. *See* EQUITABLE CHARGE, GENERAL.

charge sheet. Document, which should be signed by the accusers wherever possible, on which the officer on duty at a police station records the names of those given into custody, the names of the accusers and the accusations.

charges, joinder of. *See* JOINDER OF CHARGES.

Charges Register. *See* REGISTER AT LAND REGISTRY.

charging clause. Clause authorising a solicitor who is a trustee (qv) to charge for his professional services: see *Re Royce's WT* [1959] Ch. 626.

charging order. A judgment creditor (qv) can apply on affidavit (qv) for an order imposing a charge on the debtor's land, securities, or funds in court. See the Charging Orders Act 1979, s. 1. He may also apply by summons for an order charging a partnership interest: Partnership Act 1890, s. 23. See O. 50; O. 81, r. 10; and *National Westminster Bank* v *Stockman* [1981] 1 WLR 67 (an order may be made over a beneficial interest in proceeds of land held under a trust for sale (qv)). *See* JUDGMENTS, ENFORCEMENT OF.

charitable trust. A trust by the terms of which the income is to be applied exclusively for purposes of a charitable nature. Trusts of this kind were named in the preamble to the Statute of Charitable Uses 1601 as trusts for the relief of poverty, the advancement of education, the advancement of religion, other purposes beneficial to the community. *See* CHARITY; TRUST.

Charities, Central Register of. Set up under the Charities Act 1960 and kept by the Charity Commissioners: to provide a permanent central record of property devoted to charity; to provide information to the public concerning charities; to provide an authoritative means of determining whether an organisation is charitable in law or not. Registration is generally compulsory: s. 4(6). There are some exceptions in the case of, eg, "exempt charities", "excepted charities", very small charities with no permanent endowment, places of religious worship registered under the Places of Worship Registration Act 1855.

charity. "Any institution, corporate or not, which is established for charitable purposes and is subject to the control of the High Court in the exercise of the court's jurisdiction with respect to charities": Charities Act 1960, s. 45(1). See *Re Hummeltenberg* [1923] 1 Ch 237; *Oxfam* v *City of Birmingham DC* [1975] 2 All ER 289; and *IRC* v *Helen Slater Charitable Trust Ltd.* [1982] Ch 49.

Charity Commissioners. A statutory body (see the Charities Act 1960) which administers charities, secures the effective use of charity property and investigates abuses, removing trustees from office where necessary.

charity shops. Shops used wholly or mainly for the sale of goods donated to a charity, the proceeds of which (after deduction of expenses) are applied for the purposes of a charity: Rating (Charity Shops) Act 1976. They are entitled to rate relief under the General Rate Act 1967, s. 40.

charter. 1. Written instrument executed between parties, eg, a deed (qv). 2. Instrument from the Crown granting rights and privileges. 3. A constitution, eg, the Charter of the United Nations Organisation.

charterparty. A document by which a shipowner lets his ship to a charterer for the purpose of carrying a cargo, or undertakes that his ship will carry a cargo. It must be in writing, with or without seal. A *charterparty by way of demise* is one by which master and crew are the charterer's servants for the duration of the charterparty: *Baumwoll* v *Furness* [1893] AC 8. See, eg, *Aries Tanker Corporation* v *Total Transport Ltd* [1977] 1 WLR 185.

chattels. Generally property other than freeholds (qv), ie, personal property. 1. *Chattels real.* "Interests issuing out of or annexed to real estates, of which they have one quality, viz, immobility, which denotes them real, but want the other, viz, a sufficient, legal indeterminate duration, and this want it is that constitutes them chattels": Blackstone. Example: leaseholds (qv). 2. *Chattels personal.*

Pure personalty, eg, choses in possession (qv), choses in action (qv).

cheat. "A deceitful device for defrauding another of his known right contrary to the plain rules of common honesty": 1 Hawk PC. "To cheat and defraud is to act with deliberate dishonesty as to the prejudice of another person's proprietary right": *R* v *Sinclair* [1968] 3 All ER 241. The common law offence was abolished by the Th.A. 1968, s. 32, except for offences relating to public revenue. Under the Th.A. 1968, s. 25(5) "cheat" means an offence under s. 15, ie, dishonestly obtaining property belonging to another with the intention of permanently depriving the other of it: *R* v *Rashid* [1977] 1 WLR 298; *R* v *Doukas* [1978] 1 WLR 372.

cheque. A bill of exchange (qv) drawn on a banker, payable on demand: B.Ex.A. 1882, s. 73. A *crossed cheque* is one crossed with two parallel lines between which is written, eg, the name of a bank, or the words "and company" (often abbreviated), the purpose being to provide security against fraud by ensuring the cheque is paid only into a banking account. See *R* v *Davies* [1982] 1 All ER 513; *Aziz* v *Knightsbridge Gaming Ltd* (*The Times* 6.7.1982). For "cheque voucher", see the Finance Act 1982, s. 44(5).

cheque card. Card issued by a bank and presented with a cheque to a supplier of goods or services who, as a result, is assured of payment by that bank. The drawer of the cheque represents that he has authority from the bank to use the card so as to oblige the bank to honour the cheque; where he has no such authority he may be guilty of obtaining a pecuniary advantage by deception, contrary to the Th.A. 1968, s. 16(1): *R* v *Charles* [1977] AC 177.

cheque, countermand of payment. Revocation by drawer of the authority to pay a cheque. Must be written and unequivocal: see the B.Ex.A. 1882, s. 75; *Barclays Bank* v *W.J. Simms* [1979] 3 All ER 522 (there is no reason in principle why a bank cannot recover money paid under a stopped cheque).

cheque, issue of. A cheque is "issued" at the time of its first delivery, complete in form, to the person who takes it as a holder: B.Ex.A. 1882. s. 3.

cheque, overdue. Cheque which has been in circulation for an unreasonable time. Can only be negotiated subject to any defect of title; is not, therefore, a negotiable instrument. See the B.Ex.A. 1882, s. 36(2)(3).

cheque, post-dated. Cheque dated subsequently to actual date on which drawn, and issued before the date it bears. See the B.Ex.A. 1882, s. 13(2); *Royal Bank of Scotland* v *Tottenham* (1894) 71 LT 168.

cheque, stale. Cheque which is "out of date", ie, one bearing a date twelve (or, in some cases, six) months prior to presentation. See *London County Banking Co* v *Groome* (1881) 8 QBD 288.

chief rent. A type of perpetual rent-charge (qv), known also as "fee farm rent", occurring where a vendor, on the sale of a fee simple (qv), in lieu of taking the purchase money in a lump sum, reserves to himself a rent payable to himself and his heirs in perpetuity.

child. Under the C. & Y.P.A. 1933, s. 14, a person under 14. Under the Ch.A. 1975, s. 107(1) and the Child Care Act 1980, s. 11(4), a person under 18. In the Mat.C.A. 1973, s. 52(1) it includes, in relation to one or both of the parties to a marriage, an illegitimate or adopted child of that party or of both parties. See also the Inheritance (Provision for Family and Dependants) Act 1975, s. 25(1). For the trial of an information against a child, see the M.C.A. 1980, ss. 24, 29 (authorising the (exceptional) trial of a juvenile (qv) otherwise than in a juvenile court (qv)).

child benefit. Cash benefit payable (tax-free) to the person responsible for a child (and replacing family allowances), ie, one under 16, or under 19 if receiving full-time education. See the Child Benefit Act 1975.

child destruction. "Any person who with intent to destroy the life of a child capable of being born alive, by any wilful act causes a child to die before it has an existence independent of its mother, shall be guilty of" child destruction: Infant Life (Preservation) Act 1929, s. 1(1). The section does not apply where the act was done in good faith for the purpose of preserving the mother's life. See, however, the Abortion Act 1967, s. 5. *See* ABORTION; UNBORN PERSONS, KILLING OF.

child of the family. In relation to the parties to a marriage, this means, under the D.P.A. 1978, s. 88(2), a child of both of those parties or any other child, not boarded out with those parties, who has been treated by them as a child of their family. See also *Snow* v *Snow* [1971] 3 All ER 833; and *Re M.* (1980) 10 Fam L 184.

child, protected. *See* PROTECTED CHILD.

child, removal of. When making an interim or final custodianship order relating to a child (under the Ch.A. 1975, s. 34(4)), the court may make an order restricting or prohibiting removal of child out of England and Wales without leave of the court: D.P.A. 1978, s. 70.

children. Refers, in general, to descendants of the first degree. See *Re Coley* [1901] 1 Ch 40.

children, employment of. Under the C. & Y.P.A. 1933–63, a child may not be employed if under 13, before 7 am or after 7 pm, or before the close of school on a school-day, or for more than two hours on any school-day or Sunday, or when he may be required to carry, lift or move anything so heavy as to be likely to cause injury. See also the Children (Performances) Regulations 1968, and the Employment of Children Act 1973 (under which local education authorities continue to supervise details of proposed employment, etc: s. 2).

children, indecency with. *See* GROSS INDECENCY.

children, indecent photographs of. It is an offence for a person to take, or permit to be taken, any indecent photograph of a person under the age of 16, or to distribute or show such a photograph, or to have such a photograph in his possession with a view to its being distributed or shown by himself or others, or to advertise that he distributes, shows or intends to show such a photograph: Protection of Children Act 1978, s. 1(1). For defences, see s. 1(4); for rights of entry, search and seizure, see s. 4.

children, interrogation of. *See* INTERROGATION OF CHILDREN.

children, promotion of welfare of. It is the duty of local authorities to make available such advice, guidance and assistance as may promote the welfare of children by diminishing the need to receive children into or keep them in care or to bring them before a juvenile court: Child Care Act 1980, s. 1(1). Under s. 2, it is the duty of local authorities to receive into care orphans, deserted children, etc, where it is necessary in their interests. See the Ch.A. 1975; the Children's Homes Act 1982; and *Lewisham LBC* v *M* [1981] 1 WLR 1248.

children's evidence. *See* EVIDENCE, YOUNG CHILDREN'S SWORN.

child stealing. The offence of unlawfully, either by force or fraud, leading or taking away or decoying or enticing away or detaining any child under the age of 14: O.P.A. 1861, s. 56. See *R* v *Whitfield* (1975) 61 Cr App R 209; and *R* v *Austin* [1981] 1 All ER 334.

Chiltern Hundreds. The voluntary retirement of an MP is not permitted. He retires, in effect, by accepting an office of profit under the Crown, ie, the nominal office of "Steward or Bailiff of Her Majesty's three Chiltern Hundreds of Stoke, Desborough and Burnham"—a sinecure office with only nominal duties and fees. See the House of Commons Disqualification Act 1975, s. 4, *See* HUNDRED; OFFICE OF PROFIT.

chirograph. A deed written on a sheet of paper which was then divided, with "chirographum" (ie, "autograph") written in capital letters between the division. A part was given to each party. An indented cutting was known as an "indenture" (qv).

Chivalry, Court of. *See* COURT OF CHIVALRY.

chose. A thing. 1. A *chose in action* is "when any man hath cause, or may bring an action for some duty due to him": *Termes de la Ley*. Example: debts, copyright. See *R* v *Kohn* (1979) 69 Cr App R 395 (theft of chose in action). 2. A *chose in possession* is a movable chattel, the right in which can be enforced by taking physical possession. Example: one's goods.

Church of England. The established church of which the Sovereign must always be a member. Organised into dioceses (43) grouped into two provinces (Canterbury and York). Dioceses are subdivided into 14,300 parishes. The central governing body is the General Synod. Doctrine is governed by the Thirty-nine Articles (see 13 Eliz 1 c 12).

c.i.f. Cost, insurance, freight. If a merchant, M, agrees to sell goods "at £x per unit c.i.f. Liverpool Docks", the sum includes the price of the goods, insurance premium and freight payable to Liverpool Docks. M is obliged to make out an invoice, to ship at the docks the goods described in the contract, to procure a contract of affreightment and arrange for insurance, and to send the appropriate documents to the buyer. See *Groom* v *Barber* [1915] 1 KB 316; *Johnson* v *Taylor Bros & Co* [1920] AC 155; and *The Elafi* [1982] 1 All ER 208.

cinematograph exhibition. Defined, for the purposes of the Obscene Publications Act 1959, s. 2, as amended by the C.L.A. 1977, s. 53(4), as "an exhibition of moving pictures produced on a screen by means which include the projection of light". *See* FILM.

circuit judges. Judges appointed by the Queen on recommendation of the Lord Chancellor from barristers of at least 10 years' standing, or Recorders of at least three years' standing (see the Courts Act 1971, s. 16), who are employed in the circuits, or groups of centres, which they visit. Each circuit has a presiding judge appointed by the Lord Chancellor. See the S.C.A. 1981, s. 8.

circuit system. The country is divided into circuits for the purpose of hearing criminal and civil cases: S Eastern, Midland and Oxford,

Northern, North-Eastern, Western, Wales and Chester. Circuit committees were set up in 1972, under the Courts Act 1971, s. 30, to advise the Lord Chancellor on such questions "as he may from time to time refer to them".

circuity of action. Course of proceedings longer than is necessary. May provide grounds for dismissal of an action: *Post Office* v *Hampshire CC* [1980] QB 124.

circulars, government. Communications published by government departments to local authorities, etc, relating to statements of government policy. They have been held to constitute delegated legislation: *Jackson, Stansfield & Sons* v *Butterworth* [1948] 2 All ER 558.

circumstantial evidence. *See* EVIDENCE, CIRCUMSTANTIAL.

citation. 1. Summons giving notice to a person to appear before the court. 2. Notice issued by an executor applying for probate (qv) in solemn form, calling upon persons to appear and show why probate should not be granted. 3. The referring to a decided case of legal authority in support of an argument.

citation of Act. *See* STATUTE, CITATION OF.

citizen, British Overseas. A citizen of the UK and Colonies who did not become a British citizen or a British Dependent Territories citizen when the B.N.A. 1981 came into operation, becomes a British Overseas citizen: s. 26.

citizen's arrest. Colloquialism referring to an individual person's power to arrest another where an arrestable offence (qv) has been committed and he suspects, with reasonable cause, that the other is guilty of committing the offence: C.L.A. 1967, s. 2(3). A private citizen also has the power to arrest in trying to prevent or stop a breach of the peace (qv). *See* ARREST, COMMON LAW POWER OF.

citizenship, British, acquisition by birth or adoption. After commencement of the B.N.A. 1981, a person born in the UK is a British citizen if at the time of his birth his father or mother is a British citizen, or settled in Britain, or if he is a foundling, or if he is born in the UK and one of his parents subsequently becomes settled here or if he becomes registered as a British citizen, or if he is adopted in the UK and the adopter is a British citizen: s. 1.

citizenship, British, acquisition by descent. A child born overseas is a British citizen if, at his birth, one of his parents is British (though not by descent) or is employed overseas in the service of the British Government or the EEC: B.N.A. 1981, s. 2. For classes of persons regarded as British citizens by descent, see s. 14.

citizenship, British, acquisition by registration. British Dependent Territories citizens, or British Overseas citizens, or British subjects or British protected persons may apply for registration as British citizens after satisfying certain residential period and other requirements (five years' presence in the UK, etc.). See ss. 4, 5, 7, 8 (registration by virtue of marriage), 9, 10.

citizenship, British, acquisition by registration of minor. The Secretary of State may register any minor as a British citizen on application. A minor born abroad may be registered as a British citizen, within 12 months of his birth, or, where he is stateless, and one of his parents is a British citizen by descent and a grandparent was a British citizen otherwise than by descent: B.N.A. 1981, s. 3. See also s. 32.

citizenship, British, automatic acquisition of. British citizenship is acquired automatically by all those citizens of the UK and Colonies who had the right of abode (see the Immigration Act 1971, s. 2) in the UK at the commencement of the B.N.A. 1981: s. 11. For exceptions, see s. 11(2).

citizenship, British, Dependent Territories. Status bestowed under the B.N.A. 1981, Part II, in certain circumstances on those living in the dependent territories, eg, Bermuda, Falkland Islands, Gibraltar, Hong Kong. See the B.N.A. 1981, Sch 6.

citizenship, British, registration by virtue of marriage. For five years, the right to register as a British citizen which is held by wives of citizens of the UK and Colonies, provided the marriage subsists, is preserved: B.N.A. 1981, s. 8.

citizenship, British, renunciation and resumption of. Under the B.N.A. 1981, s. 12, a person may renounce his citizenship if he has, or expects to acquire, another nationality or citizenship. Under s. 13, he may resume citizenship (on one occasion only) if he is of full capacity and the renunciation was necessary to enable him to retain or acquire some other citizenship or nationality.

citizenship, Commonwealth. Every person who, under the B.N.A. 1981, is a British citizen, or British Overseas citizen, or a British subject or a citizen of a country listed in Sch 3, has the status of Commonwealth citizen: s. 37.

citizenship, deprivation of. *See* DEPRIVATION OF CITIZENSHIP.

city. A town holding a royal charter, which is or has been the see of a bishop, or which has been created a city by the Sovereign on recommendation of Home Secretary. "City" is used also to refer to London's financial institutions (see the Wilson Report 1980, Cmnd. 7937).

City of London. An area of London, of 670 acres, with its own administrative government consisting of a Lord Mayor, Court of Aldermen, common councillors and the city companies.

civil. Opposite sense of, eg, criminal (as in a civil action) or military.

civil commotion. A serious riot, falling short of attempted insurrection. "The disturbances must have sufficient cohesion to prevent them from being the work of a mindless mob": *per* Mustill J in *Spinney's Ltd* v *Royal Insurance Co*. [1980] 1 Ll R 406.

civil debt, sum enforceable as. Any sum recoverable summarily as a civil debt which is adjudged to be paid by order of a magistrates' court, or any sum expressed by statute to be so enforceable: M.C.A. 1980, s. 150(1). A sum recoverable on complaint for an affiliation order and a sum that may be adjudged to be paid by a summary

conviction cannot be recovered summarily as civil debts: M.C.A. 1980, s. 58(2).

civilian. 1. One who is versed in the civil law (qv). 2. One who is not a member of the military forces.

civil law. 1. Used to refer to "the law each people has settled for itself, peculiar to the State itself": Justinian's *Institutes*. 2. Used also to refer to the entire *corpus* of Roman Law.

Civil List. An annual appropriation charged on the Consolidated Fund (qv), received by the Crown for purposes of maintaining the royal household, etc.

Civil List pensions. Pensions granted by the Crown to persons who "have just claims on the royal beneficence or who by their personal services to the Crown or by the performance of duties to the public or by their useful discoveries in science and attainments in literature and the arts have merited the gracious consideration of their sovereign and the gratitude of their country".

civil remedy. A remedy available to a private individual as the outcome of civil proceedings, eg, damages, compensation, order of specific performance, injunction, declarations as to rights, orders of mandamus, prohibition, certiorari (qqv).

Civil Service. The body of servants of the Crown (other than, eg, those holding political or judicial office or HM Forces) who serve in an established capacity and are paid wholly and directly out of money voted by Parliament. Managed by the Civil Service Department, which was created in 1968.

civil wrong. A tort (qv).

C.J. Chief Justice.

C.J.C.P. Chief Justice of the Court of Common Pleas (qv).

C.J.K.B. Chief Justice of the Court of King's Bench.

claim. 1. The demand or assertion of a right. 2. A privilege (qv).

claim of privilege *See* PRIVILEGE, CLAIM OF.

claims, small. *See* SMALL CLAIMS.

claim, statement of. *See* STATEMENT OF CLAIM.

clameur de haro. An ancient form of

outcry after felons or trespassers. Apparently survives in the Channel Islands. (For a report of its wording and use in Guernsey, see *The Times*, 5.8.1983.)

class gift. A gift is said to be to a class of persons when it is "to all those who shall come within a certain category or description defined by a general or collective formula, and who, if they take at all, are to take one divisible subject in certain proportionate shares": *Pearks* v *Moseley* (1880) 5 App Cas 714. Example: "to all my sons who shall live to the age of 30". It is contingent until the identity of every member is ascertained. See the P. & A.A. 1964, s. 4; *Andrews* v *Partington* (1791) 3 Bro CC 401; *Re Chapman's ST* [1977] 1 WLR 1163; and *Re Clifford's ST* [1980] 1 All ER 1013.

class rights. Rights attached to different classes of share (qv), concerning, eg, voting, dividends, as set out in a memorandum and articles of association (qqv) or terms of share issue. See the Cos.A. 1980, s. 33; European Communities Act 1972, s. 9(3) (as amended by the Cos. A. 1980, Sch 3, para 45); Cos.A. 1981, s. 102. For variation of class rights, see the Cos.A. 1980, s. 32.

clause. A subdivision of a document; an individual section of a Parliamentary Bill.

clausum fregit, quare. Wherefore he broke into the close. Term used with reference to trespass to land (qv). In its developed form it was a writ, *c.* 1245, giving a lessee an action for damages against a party who had ejected him.

clean hands. Phrase used in a maxim of equity: he who comes into equity must come with clean hands, ie, the plaintiff must have a clear conscience as regards the past. See *Gill* v *Lewis* [1956] 2 QB 1; *Overton* v *Banister* (1844) 8 Jur 906.

clearance area. Term used in the H.A. 1957 and 1974 to refer to an area made the subject of a declaration by the local authority (qv) if satisfied that, eg, the houses in the area are unfit for human habitation and ought to be demolished and that alternative accommodation can be made available for those who will be displaced, and that the authority has sufficient resources for this purpose. See now the H.A. 1974, Part IV; *Wahiwala* v *Secretary of State for the Environment* [1976] JPL 366; *Elliot* v *London Borough of Southwark* [1976] 2 All ER 781.

clear days. Generally, days reckoned exclusively of those on which anything is begun and terminated.

Clerk of the House. The chief of the permanent officers of the House of Commons, appointed by the Queen on the Prime Minister's advice. He is responsible for the Clerk's Department. In the House of Lords, a similar official is known as the Clerk of the Parliaments.

clerks, judges'. *See* JUDGES' CLERKS.

clerks, principal. *See* PRINCIPAL CLERKS.

clerk to the justices. *See* MAGISTRATES' CLERK.

client. In relation to contentious business (qv), any person who as principal or on behalf of another person retains or employs a solicitor, and any person who is liable to pay a solicitor's costs. In relation to non-contentious business, any person who as principal or on behalf of another has express or implied power to retain or employ, and does retain or employ, a solicitor, and any person liable to pay a solicitor's costs: Solicitors Act 1974, s. 87.

client account. A current or deposit account in the name of a solicitor at a bank in the title of which account the word "client" appears: Solicitors Accounts Rules 1975.

clogging the equity of redemption. No agreement which clogs the equity, ie, which makes a mortgage irredeemable, will be recognised by the courts. See *Biggs* v *Hoddinott* [1898] 2 Ch 307; *Kreglinger* v *New Patagonia Meat Co* [1914] AC 25; *Lewis* v *Frank Love Ltd* [1961] 1 WLR 261. *See* MORTGAGE.

close. 1. Enclosed land. 2. Termination of proceedings, as in "close of pleadings" (qv).

close company. A company which, for purposes of corporation tax, is considered as under the control of five or fewer participators or by any number of participators who are directors. The term does not apply to a company not resident in the UK. A "participator" is, eg, one who owns share capital and has voting rights in the company, or a loan creditor of the company (except where the loan arises in the ordinary course of banking). See the Income and Corporation Taxes Act 1970, ss. 283, 302. *See* COMPANY.

closed-shop agreement. An agreement whereby employers agree to employ only union members. Based on "union membership agreements" (see the T.U.L.R.A. 1974, s. 30(1) as amended by the T.U.L.R. (Amendment) A. 1976), which are agreements between independent trade unions and one or more employers' associations or one or more employers, relating to employees of an identifiable class, having the effect in practice of requiring the employees of the class to which the agreements relate (whether or not there is a condition to that effect in their contract of employment) to be or become members of the unions which are parties to those agreements. See also the Employment Act 1982, s. 3.

closing order. Order made under the H.A. 1957, for closing part or whole of a building which is unfit for human habitation: ss. 17, 18. Refers also to a local authority order relating to shops' closing hours (see the Shops Act 1950).

closing speeches. Speeches by each side before the summing up. Generally, the prosecuting counsel speaks first; the defence usually has the right to the final word to the jury: Criminal Procedure (Right of Reply) Act 1964.

closure. The ending of a debate (as in Parliament) by the carrying of the motion "that the question be now put".

club. A voluntary association of a number of persons meeting together for recreational or social purposes. Members are generally liable only to the extent of their subscriptions to a common fund. The remedy for wrongful expulsion is a declaration or injunction (qv). See *Lee* v *Showmen's Guild of Great Britain* [1952] 2 QB 329;

Dockers' Labour Club v *Race Relations Board* [1976] AC 285; and *Re GKN Bolts and Nuts Work Club* [1982] 1 WLR 774.

Cmd. Abbreviation for Command Papers. *See* COMMAND PAPERS, NUMBERING OF; PARLIAMENTARY PAPERS.

Cmnd. Abbreviation for Command Papers. *See* COMMAND PAPERS, NUMBERING OF; PARLIAMENTARY PAPERS.

co. Abbreviation of "company" (qv). See *Banque De L'Indochine, etc* v *Euroseas Group Finance Co* [1981] 3 All ER 198.

coastal waters. In relation to the UK, Channel Islands and Isle of Man, so much of the waters adjoining the countries respectively as is within the fishery limits of the British Isles and, in relation to any other country, so much of the waters adjoining that country as is within the distance to which provisions of the law of that country corresponding to the provisions of the 1934 Act extend: Whaling Industry (Regulation) Act 1934, s. 17; Fishery Limits Act 1964, s. 3(3).

C.O.D. Cash on delivery. Term indicating that payment must be made at the time the goods are received by the purchaser from the carrier. See the Post Office Act 1969, s. 7 (as amended).

code. A systematical collection, in comprehensive form, of laws, eg, the Code of Hammurabi (eighteenth century BC), the *Code Napoléon* (1804).

Code of Industrial Relations Practice. Guidance for the purpose of promoting the improvement of industrial relations issued by the Secretary of State after consultation with ACAS (qv): Employment Act 1980, s. 3. See also the E.P.A. 1975, s. 6, Sch 17.

code of practice. Rules for practical guidance with respect to the requirements of some statute. See, eg, the Highway Code (qv). Failure to observe a code does not generally render a person liable to proceedings, but it may be admissible in evidence.

code of practice on disciplinary procedures. Code prepared by the Advisory, Conciliation and Arbitration Service (qv), which gives practical guidance on the drawing up of disciplinary rules and procedures. It recommends, *inter alia,* that all employees should be given a copy of the employer's rules on procedures, that full investigation of a case should precede disciplinary action.

codicil. "An addition or supplement added into a will or testament after the finishing of it, for the supply of something which the testator had forgotten, or to help some defect in the will": *Termes de la Ley.* It must be executed with all the formalities appropriate to the execution of a will. *See* TESTAMENT; WILL.

codifying statute. An Act which codifies the whole of case and statute law on a particular matter, eg, the O.P.A. 1861 and the B.Ex.A. 1882. For the interpretation of a codifying statute see *Bank of England* v *Vagliano Bros* [1891] AC 107. *See* CONSOLIDATION ACT.

coercion. The use of physical or moral force in an attempt to interfere with the exercise of free choice. See, eg, the C.J.A. 1925, s. 47; *Hodges* v *Webb* [1920] 2 Ch. 70; and *R* v *Richman* [1982] Crim LR 507. *See* DURESS; UNDUE INFLUENCE.

cognates. Those related on the mother's side. *See* AGNATES.

cognisance, judicial. Judicial notice (qv).

cohabitation. Living together as or as if husband and wife. Cohabitation for a period exceeding six months after the grant of a decree nisi in a suit based on adultery is apparently a bar to a decree absolute: *Biggs* v *Biggs* [1977] Fam. 1. See the Mat. C.A. 1973, ss. 1(5), 2(1), 9(1); and *Foley* v *Foley* [1981] Fam 160.

cohabitation rules. "Where two persons are cohabiting as man and wife, their requirements and resources shall, unless there are exceptional circumstances be aggregated and treated as the man's": Supplementary Benefits Act 1976, Sch 1 para 3(1) (*b*). "Where...the requirements and resources of any person fall to be aggregated with, and to be treated as, those of another person, that other person only shall be entitled to benefit": 1976 Act, s. 1(2).

collateral. 1. Belonging to the common ancestral stock, although not in direct line of descent. 2. Security given additionally to the main security. 3. Collateral contracts exist where there is one contract, the consideration for which is the making of some other contract, eg, "If you will make this contract we have discussed, then I will give you £1,000." See *Heilbut, Symons & Co* v *Buckleton* [1913] AC 20; *Shanklin Pier Ltd* v *Detel Products* [1951] 2 KB 854; *Strongman Ltd* v *Sincock* [1955] 2 QB 525.

collective bargaining. Negotiations relating to the conditions and terms of employment carried on between trade unions and employers or their associations. A "collective agreement" is one resulting from such bargaining. It may be written, oral, formal or informal. It is not intended to be legally enforceable unless in writing and containing a provision to that effect. See the T.U.L.R.A. 1974, s. 18. *See* TRADE UNION.

collective resale price maintenance, prohibition of. *See* RESALE PRICE MAINTENANCE, COLLECTIVE, PROHIBITION OF.

collective responsibility. Doctrine at the basis of the constitutional convention that the Cabinet (qv) is collectively responsible to Parliament for the conduct of the Executive.

collusion. Agreement, usually secret, for some deceitful or unlawful, purpose. Collusion in the presentation of a petition for divorce (qv) is no longer a bar to divorce. See the Mat. C.A. 1973, s. 19 (as amended).

collusive action. *See* COMMON RECOVERY.

colony. "Any part of Her Majesty's dominions outside the British Islands except: (a) countries having fully responsible status within the Commonwealth; (b) territories for whose external relations a country other than the UK is responsible; (c) associated states": I.A. 1978, Sch 1.

colore officii. By virtue of one's office. See *Steele* v *Williams* (1853) 8 Exch 625.

colourable. Term used, eg, in the C.C.A. 1974, s. 138(4) (*c*) ("colourable small agreement"), to indicate that which is pretended, or plausible.

Command Papers. *See* PARLIAMENTARY PAPERS.

Command Papers, numbering of. The five series are as follows: 1833–69 (number, with no prefix, eg, "3989"); 1870–99 (numbered with prefix "C", eg, "C 3550"); 1900–18 (numbered with prefix "Cd", eg, "Cd 9005"); 1919–56 (numbered with prefix "Cmd", eg, "Cmd 8778"); 1957 to date (numbered, with prefix "Cmnd", eg, "Cmnd 3456").

Commercial Court. Puisne judges (qv) of the High Court who hear actions in the Commercial list "arising out of the ordinary transactions of merchants and traders; amongst others, those relating to construction of mercantile documents, export or import of merchandise, affreightment, insurance, banking and mercantile agency and mercantile usages". See O. 72. Procedure is generally more flexible than in other courts and some strict rules of evidence may be relaxed. See the S.C.A. 1981, s. 6.

commission. 1. Remuneration paid to an agent. 2. Formal authority to exercise a power. 3. A body directed to perform a duty, the members of which are known as "commissioners". Thus, a Commission of the Peace was appointed by the Crown, consisting of persons who were to act as justices of the peace (qv) in certain districts. 4. Examination on oath under terms of O. 39, eg, where a witness is ill or likely to be abroad at the time of the hearing.

Commissioners for Oaths. Solicitors who administer oaths, eg, to those making affidavits (qv). See the Commissioners for Oaths Act 1889; and the Solicitors Act 1974, s. 81, under which solicitors holding practising certificates have powers of a Commissioner for Oaths.

Commission for Racial Equality. *See* RACIAL EQUALITY, COMMISSION FOR.

Commission of EEC. Body consisting of nationals of member states appointed by common accord of their governments with the task of ensuring the proper functioning and developing of the common market: Treaty of Rome 1972, art. 155. The Commission watches over the application of EEC legislation, formulates and recommends views and delivers opinions.

Commission of Review. Ecclesiastical body consisting of three Lords of Appeal in Ordinary and two Lords Spiritual to whom appeal lies from a Commission of Convocation which has tried a non-doctrinal offence by a bishop or archbishop, or a matter tried by the Court of Ecclesiastical Causes Reserved (which tries matters relating to ritual doctrine and ceremonial of the church).

Commissions for local administration. *See* LOCAL ADMINISTRATION, COMMISSIONS FOR.

committal for sentence. Procedure whereby magistrates, who are of the opinion that a greater punishment should be inflicted on an offender than they are empowered to impose, commit the offender to the Crown Court (qv) for sentence. Matters relating to sentence must be left to the Crown Court. See the M.C.A. 1980, ss. 37, 38; and the P.C.C.A. 1973, ss. 8, 16(3), 17(2), 24(2) (relating to probation, conditional discharge, community service orders, suspended sentences).

committal for trial. The sending of a person for trial following a preliminary investigation before magistrates. The court may exercise the option of committing without consideration of all the evidence before it if made up of written statements in the form required by the M.C.A. 1980, s. 102 and if defendant is legally represented. The procedure is known as "a short committal" or "a committal". See the I.A. 1978, Sch 1.

committal in civil proceedings. Method of enforcing a judgment by committal to prison, available, eg, in cases of disobedience of an order of the court. See the A.J.A. 1970, s. 11; O. 45; *Heatons Transport Ltd* v *TGWU* [1973] AC 15; *Re Barrell Enterprises* [1973] 1 WLR 19. The disobedience, which must amount to contempt of court, must be more than casual, accidental and unintentional. *See* CONTEMPT OF COURT.

committal proceedings. Proceedings before a magistrates' court acting as examining justices: M.C.A. 1980, s. 150(1).

committal proceedings, reporting of. Written reporting or broadcasting of committal proceedings is generally forbidden, except in relation to, eg, names of parties, counsel, solicitors, witnesses, etc: see the M.C.A. 1980, s. 8. The accused may apply for the restriction to be lifted: s. 2. If, in the case of two or more accused, one objects to the making of an order lifting the restriction, the court must hear representations and may make an order only if satisfied that it is in the interests of justice so do so: s. 2A (inserted by the C.J. (Amendment) A. 1981, s. 1(2)).

committee of inspection. 1. A group of creditors and contributories appointed to act with the liquidator (qv) on the winding-up of a company (qv). See the Cos.A. 1948, s. 295. 2. Committee representing creditors, formed to superintend the administration of a bankrupt's property by the trustee: B.A. 1914, s. 20. The committee should meet at least once a month.

Committee of Privileges. *See* PRIVILEGES, COMMITTEE OF.

Committee of Supply. A committee of the whole House of Commons (qv) which considers and discusses estimates of expenditure for the ensuing financial year and votes on supplies. *See* BUDGET; CONSOLIDATED FUND.

Committee of the whole House. Formed by the House of Commons (qv) or Lords (qv) resolving members into a committee, presided over by the Chairman of Committees, to consider a specific matter referred to it by the House.

Committee of Ways and Means. Committee of the whole House of Commons (qv) which discusses new taxes and ways and means of raising supplies. Resolutions are embodied in the annual Finance Acts and Consolidated Fund Acts. *See* BUDGET; CONSOLIDATED FUND.

committee, select. Committee ap-

pointed by a House of Parliament, usually on the motion of a government whip, to take evidence on some subject and to report to the House.

commit to custody. To commit to prison or, where any enactment authorises or requires committal to some other place of detention instead of committal to prison, to that other place: M.C.A. 1980, s. 150(1).

commodity organisations, international. *See* INTERNATIONAL COMMODITY ORGANISATION.

common. Land subject to rights of common. *See* COMMON, RIGHT OF.

common assault. An assault (qv) which is not of an aggravated nature. Punishable under the O.P.A. 1861, s. 42. See *R* v *Beasley* (1981) 73 Cr App R 44. *See* AGGRAVATED ASSAULT.

common calling. Phrase used formerly to refer to the occupation exercised by a surgeon, smith, farrier, common carrier, innkeeper, in relation to an action under *assumpsit* (qv) for damages resulting from injury due to alleged incompetence. See, eg, *Bretherton* v *Wood* (1823) 3 B & B 54; *Jackson* v *Mayfair Window Cleaning Co* [1952] 1 All ER 215.

common carrier. *See* CARRIER, COMMON.

common employment. At common law a master was not liable for the negligent harm resulting from the action of one of his servants towards a fellow-servant engaged in a common employment at the time of the accident. See *Radcliffe* v *Ribble Motor Services Ltd* [1939] AC 215. The doctrine was abolished by Law Reform (Personal Injuries) Act 1948, s. 1(1).

common fund basis of costs. Assessment of costs (qv) related to the payment by a party to proceedings or out of any fund other than a fund which the party to whom the costs are to be paid holds as trustee (qv) or personal representative. There will be allowed, on this basis, "all such costs as were necessary or proper for the attainment of justice or for enforcing or defending the rights of the party whose costs are being taxed": O. 62, r. 28(2). See *Layzell* v *British Portland Cement* [1961] 1 WLR 577. *See* TAXATION OF COSTS.

common informer. *See* INFORMER.

common land. Land subject to rights of common and wasteland of a manor not subject to such rights. See the Commons Registration Act 1965; and *Baxendale* v *Instow Parish Church* [1982] Ch 14. *See* COMMON, RIGHT OF.

common law. "The common sense of the community, crystallised and formulated by our forefathers." Blackstone speaks of "the chief cornerstone of the laws of England which is general and immemorial custom, or common law, from time to time declared in the decisions of the courts of justice; which decisions are preserved among our public records, explained in our reports, and digested for general use in the authoritative writings of the venerable sages of the law." The phrase apparently came into use at the end of the thirteenth century, when reference is found in the Year Books (qv) to *"la commune ley"*.

common law, declaratory theory of. *See* DECLARATORY THEORY OF COMMON LAW.

common-law market. *See* MARKET.

common-law marriage. Colloquialism "'...inaccurate but expressive'': *per* Bridge LJ in *Dyson Holdings* v *Fox* [1975] 3 All ER 1030) referring to the relationship arising out of cohabitation as man and wife, based on an informal agreement to form a marriage relationship, but without any religious or civil ceremony. *See* MARRIAGE.

Common Market. Term used as a synonym for the EEC (qv) which, under the Treaty of Rome 1957, art. 2, has as a task the promotion of a harmonious development of economic activities throughout the Community by establishing a common market and approximating the economic policies of member states.

common ownership enterprise. A body which is certified as having no share capital, limited by guarantee and a bona fide co-operative society or one registered under the Industrial and Provident Societies Acts 1965–1975 and controlled by a majority of the people working for the body and those working for its subsidiaries:

Industrial Common Ownership Act 1976, s. 2(1). See the Finance Act 1981, s. 25.

Common Pleas, Court of. *See* COURT OF COMMON PLEAS.

common recovery. Mode of barring estate tail (qv) by a collusive action, abolished by the Fines and Recoveries Act 1833. Process comprised the following steps: (1) Friendly plaintiff, A, brings action against tenant in tail, B; (2) B conveys life estate to "tenant to the praecipe" (qv), C; (3) C vouches B to warranty; (4) B vouches the common vouchee (a court official), D, on fiction that D had conveyed land to B with warranty of title; (5) D admits fiction and leaves court; (6) Judgment is given against D, so that the land is held to belong to A, and D must give land of equal value to C; (7) No land is given by D, and B's land goes to A under the judgment, the land now being rid of the estate tail; (8) A conveys land back to B in fee simple. *See* FEE TAIL.

common, right of. A *profit à prendre* (qv), ie, a right to take something off the land of another. Classified as: appendant, appurtenant, in gross, *pur cause de vicinage* (qv), or, according to the subject-matter, as a common of pasture, turbary, etc. Rights of common must be registered with a local authority. See the Commons Registration Act 1965; *Central Electricity Board* v *Clwyd CC* [1976] 1 WLR 151; *Re Yately Common* [1977] 1 All ER 505.

Common Serjeant. Formerly a judicial officer of the City of London, who sat in Central Criminal Court (qv). Now a circuit judge *ex officio*. See the Courts Act 1971, Sch 2.

Commons, House of. *See* HOUSE OF COMMONS.

commons, registration of. Registration with county councils of persons claiming to be or established as owners of common land in England and Wales. See the Commons Registration Act 1965; *New Windsor Corporation* v *Mellor* [1975] Ch 380.

common, tenancy in. A tenancy in which tenants held in undivided shares and there was no right of survivorship (qv). Existed where, eg, land was limited to two or more persons and words of severance (qv) were used, eg, "to X and Y in equal moieties". After 1925 a legal estate may not be held under tenancy in common. Under the L.P.A. 1925, s. 34, where a legal estate has been limited to tenants in common it vests in them as joint tenants upon the statutory trusts for sale. The tenancy in common continues in equity "for giving effect to the rights of persons interested in the land": L.P.A. 1925, s. 35.

Commonwealth. 1. The period from the execution of Charles I (1649) to the restoration of the monarchy (1660). 2. The Commonwealth of Nations (or British Commonwealth), ie, a group of independent nations (the UK and nations once part of the British Empire) recognising the British monarch as Head of the Commonwealth.

Commonwealth citizen. A person who is a British citizen, British Dependent Territories citizen, British Overseas citizen, or British subject, or who is a citizen of a country listed in Sch 3: B.N.A. 1981, s. 37(1).

Commonwealth Development Corporation. Statutory body comprising chairman, deputy chairman, and 4–10 members appointed by the Minister of Overseas Development, to assist overseas countries in the development of their economies by, eg, investigating and formulating projects for promotion or expansion of agricultural and industrial enterprise: Commonwealth Development Corporation Act 1978, ss. 1–3. See also the Commonwealth Development Corporation Act 1982.

commorientes. Persons dying together on the same occasion at the same time. Under the L.P.A. 1925, s. 184, they are presumed for purposes affecting title to property, to have died in order of seniority. The statutory presumption does not apply in the case of intestate spouses. See the A.E.A. 1925, s. 46(3); the Finance Act 1969, Sch 17, Part II; and the Intestates' Estates Act 1952, s. 1(4).

communication, privileged. See PRIVILEGED COMMUNICATION.

communis error facit jus. Common error may make law. See *Baker* v *Bolton* (1808) 1 Camp 493; and the Fatal Accidents Act 1976.

communities. Divisions of districts in Wales. Basically they resemble English parishes but community councils need not meet more than once a year. See the L.G.A. 1972.

Communities, European. See EUROPEAN COMMUNITIES.

Community, European Economic. See EEC.

community homes. Homes for the accommodation and maintenance of children in the care of local authorities: Child Care Act 1980, s. 32.

Community law. The directly applicable law of the EEC treaty and instruments made by the institutions of EEC. It operates as a separate system side by side with English law but, in the event of a conflict, it takes precedence over domestic law. "No provisions of municipal law of whatever nature they may be, prevail over Community law": *Internationale Handelsgesellschaft* v *EVSt* [1972] CMLR 255. In general, community law becomes part of the law of the UK if it is, in its nature, and under the EEC treaties, self-executing, or is the subject of a separate enactment by Act of Parliament, or is implemented, under the European Communities Act 1972, s. 2(2), by statutory instrument. See COMMUNITY LAW, SOURCES OF; COURT OF JUSTICE OF THE EUROPEAN COMMUNITIES.

Community law, sources of. Sources of EEC law are: the treaties with their annexes and protocols; conventions between member states; administrative acts; judicial legislation of the Court of Justice of the European Communities (qv).

Community legislation, forms of. The Council and Commission of the EEC (qv) may: (1) make *regulations*, which have a general application and are binding in their entirety and directly applicable in all member states; (2) issue *directives,* which are binding, only as to the result to be achieved, on member states; (3) take *decisions* binding in their entirety upon those to whom they are addressed; (4) make *recommendations* or deliver *opinions,* which have no binding force. See Treaty of Rome 1957, art. 189; *Van Duyn* v *Home Office* (No 2) [1975] 3 All ER 190; *R* v *Goldstein* [1983] 1 WLR 157.

Community legislation, interpretation of. "Beyond doubt the English courts must follow the same principles as the European Court ...No longer must [the English courts] examine the words in meticulous detail. No longer must they argue about the precise grammatical sense. They must look to the purpose or intent...They must divine the spirit of the Treaty and gain inspiration from it": *H.P. Bulmer Ltd* v *J. Bollinger S.A.* [1974] Ch 401. "Any question as to the meaning and effect of any Community instrument shall be treated as a question of law and, if not referred to the European Court, be for determination as such in accordance with the principles laid down by a relevant decision of the European Court": European Communities Act 1972, s. 3(1).

community service order. In the case of a person who has attained the age of 16 and has been convicted of an offence punishable with imprisonment, a court may make an order requiring him to perform unpaid work, within 12 months, for a specified number of hours (40–120, and, in some cases, 240). Breach of the order may be punished by fine, revocation of order and punishment for original offence. See the P.C.C.A. 1973, ss. 14–17 (as amended by the C.J.A. 1982, s. 68, Sch 12); *R* v *Evans* [1977] 1 All ER 228; *R* v *Afzad* [1981] Crim LR 705; *R* v *Lawrence* [1982] Crim LR 377.

commutative contract. Contract (qv) based on each party giving and receiving an equivalent.

commutative justice. *See* JUSTICE, COMMUTATIVE, DISTRIBUTIVE AND CORRECTIVE.

commute. To substitute one punishment for another.

Companies Court. Collective title given to those judges of the Chancery Division (qv) nominated by the Lord Chancellor, who have jurisdiction in relation to certain matters derived from the operation of companies. Thus, they have jurisdiction to wind up any company (qv) registered in England: Cos.A. 1948, s. 211 (f). See *Practice Direction,* 3rd March 1977.

companies register. Register based on the Cos.A. 1948, recording charges created by companies on or after January 1st 1970, other than floating charges (qv). Must be registered at the Land Charges Registry if they are to bind any purchaser. If they are to bind liquidators and creditors they must be registered within 21 days of creation. See the Cos.A. 1948, s. 95; the L.C.A. 1972, s. 3; *Property Discount Corp* v *Lyon Group* [1981] 1 All ER 379.

company. An association of persons formed for the purposes of an undertaking or business carried on in the name of the association. May be classified as *chartered companies* (formed by the grant of a charter from the Crown), *statutory companies* (formed under an Act of Parliament), *registered companies* (formed under the Cos.A.), or as *public companies* limited by shares or by guarantee or unlimited. See the Cos.A. 1967–81. *See* LIMITED LIABILITY.

company accounts. Accounts prepared under the Cos.A. 1976, s. 1, which must be prepared in accordance with Sch 8. The balance sheet must give a true and fair picture of the state of affairs of the company at the end of its financial year: Cos.A. 1948, s. 149 (inserted by Cos.A. 1981, s. 1(1)).

company accounts, publication of. A company (qv) "shall be regarded as publishing any balance sheet or other account if it publishes, issues or circulates it or otherwise makes it available for public inspection in a manner calculated to invite members of the public generally, or any class of members of the public, to read it": Cos.A. 1981, s. 21(3).

company, associated. *See* ASSOCIATED COMPANY.

company books. *See* STATUTORY BOOKS.

company, British. A company incorporated under the laws of Great Britain, over which a Commonwealth citizen has control, or two or more Commonwealth citizens are together in a position to exercise control, or over which such a company, or two or more such companies, or such a company and a Commonwealth citizen are together in a position to exercise control: National Film Corporation Act 1981, s. 9(3). *See* COMPANY; COMPANY, CONTROL OF.

company, control of. The power of a person to secure by means of the holding of shares or possession of voting power in or in relation to that company or any other body corporate, or by virtue of powers conferred by the articles of association (qv), that the affairs of the company are conducted in accordance with the wishes of that person: National Film Corporation Act 1981, s. 9(3).

company, dormant. *See* DORMANT COMPANY.

company, family. *See* FAMILY COMPANY.

company, group. "In relation to any company, means any body corporate which is that company's subsidiary or holding company, or a subsidiary of that company's holding company": Cos.A. 1981, Part VI.

company, holding. *See* HOLDING COMPANY.

company, investigation of. The Department of Trade is empowered to investigate the affairs of a company (qv) (see the Cos.A. 1948, ss. 164–168; the Cos.A. 1967, ss. 39, 42; and the Cos.A. 1980, s. 75(2)); the ownership of a company (see the Cos.A. 1948, ss. 172, 175); the share dealings of a company (see the Cos.A. 1967, ss. 25, 27, 31(2), 32(1)); the books and papers of a company (see the Cos.A. 1967, ss. 109, 110, 114).

company, investment. *See* INVESTMENT COMPANY.

company, limited. *See* LIMITED COMPANY.

company limited by guarantee. *See* GUARANTEE, COMPANY LIMITED BY.

company, medium-sized. Under the Cos.A. 1981, s. 8(3), a company is treated as medium-sized if the amount of its turnover does not

exceed £5,750,000, the balance sheet total does not exceed £2,800,000, and the average number of employees does not exceed 250.

company meetings. *See* MEETINGS, COMPANY.

company, members of a. *See* MEMBERS OF A COMPANY.

company name, alteration of. Name may be altered by special resolution with written consent of Secretary of State: Cos.A. 1981, s. 24. The Secretary of State may direct a change in name if, eg, the name has been gained by deception: s. 24(3).

company name, approval of. Under the Cos.A. 1981, ss. 22–27 the Secretary of State for Trade is empowered to refuse registration of a company by a name which he considers undesirable, eg, if it is too like the name of an existing company, or suggests Royal patronage, or includes unjustifiably words such as "National".

company, officers of a. Term which includes directors, managers and secretary. Auditors and company solicitors may be included.

company, oversea. *See* OVERSEA COMPANY.

company, participator in. *See* CLOSE COMPANY.

company, private. *See* PRIVATE COMPANY.

company, public. *See* PUBLIC COMPANY.

company, quoted. A company (qv) which satisfies the conditions that its shares or some class thereof are listed in the Official List of the Exchange and are dealt in on the Stock Exchange regularly from time to time. See the Finance Act 1980, Part VII.

company register of members. *See* REGISTER OF MEMBERS.

company, registration of. Procedure whereby a company is registered by the Registrar of Companies on delivery of documents including a memorandum of association, printed articles of association, a statement in prescribed form of names of intended first director(s) and first secretary, statement of capital and statutory declaration by the solicitor engaged in the formation of the company, or by a named director or secretary, of compliance with the requirements of the Acts relating to registration. See the Cos.A. 1948, s. 12; the Cos.A. 1976, ss. 21, 23; and the Cos.A. 1980, s. 3(5).

company, related. "In relation to any company, means any body corporate (other than one which is a group company (qv) in relation to that company) in which that company holds on a long-term basis a qualifying capital interest (qv) for the purpose of securing a contribution to that company's own activities by the exercise of any control or influence arising from that interest": Cos.A. 1981, Sch 1, Part VI.

company, re-registration of. Under the Cos.A. 1980, a private company may be re-registered as a public company, a public company as a private company, an unlimited company as a public company, an old public company (qv) as a public or private company. See ss. 5–8, 10, 11.

company return. *See* ANNUAL RETURN.

company's common seal. Required in the case of deeds, share certificates and warrants, contracts which would necessitate a deed if entered into by a private person. See the Cos.A. 1948, ss. 35(1), 81, 83, Table A, art. 113. A company's official seal is a facsimile of the common seal, with the addition on its face of the name of the territory in which it is to be used.

company secretary. Person appointed, usually at a board meeting, by the directors of a company. See the Cos.A. 1948, s. 177. He can act as agent for the company and is an officer of the company. A sole director may not be the secretary: s. 177(1). For qualifications see the Cos.A. 1980, s. 79. See, eg, *Panorama Developments Ltd* v *Fidelis Furnishing Fabrics Ltd* [1971] 2 QB 711.

company, sham. *See* LIFTING THE VEIL.

company, small. Under the Cos.A. 1981, s. 8(2), a company is treated as small if the amount of turnover does not exceed £1,400,000, the balance sheet total does not exceed £700,000, and the average number of employees does not exceed 50.

company's name. If a company is a public company, its name must end

with the words "public limited company" (PLC): Cos.A. 1980, s. 2(2). If a private company, with the word "limited": Cos.A. 1948, s. 2(1). May be abbreviated to "Ltd.": Cos.A. 1980, s. 78. See *Ewing* v *Buttercup Margarine Co. Ltd* [1917] 2 Ch 1; European Communities Act 1972, s. 9(7)(c). For the power to dispense with "Ltd" in the case of a private company, see the Cos.A. 1980, s. 88(1) and Sch 3, para 5. For trading under a misleading name, see the Cos.A. 1980, s. 76. See also the Cos.A. 1981, Part II.

company's profits. *See* PROFITS, COMPANY'S.

company, statutory. *See* STATUTORY COMPANY.

company union. A union, membership of which is confined specifically to a firm's employees.

company, unlimited. *See* UNLIMITED COMPANY.

company, unregistered. *See* UNREGISTERED COMPANY.

compellability of witnesses. *See* WITNESSES, COMPELLABLE.

compensation. Payment for loss or injury sustained, eg, as under the Criminal Damage Act 1971, s. 8 (compensation for destruction or damaging property of another). See also the M.C.A. 1980, s. 40, the Land Compensation Acts 1961 and 1973; the L.G.P.L.A. 1980, Part XIII; and the P.C.C.A. 1973 s. 35 (as amended by the C.J.A. 1982, s. 67) (under which a convicted person may be required to pay compensation for injury, loss or damage resulting from that offence or any other offence taken into consideration by the court in determining sentence). An element of interest may be included: *R* v *Schofield* [1978] 2 All ER 705. See *R* v *Wylie* [1974] Crim LR 608; *Quigley* v *Stokes* [1977] 1 WLR 434; *R* v *Donovan* [1982] RTR 126; *R* v *Amey* [1983] 1 WLR 345.

Compensation Board, Criminal Injuries. *See* CRIMINAL INJURIES COMPENSATION BOARD.

competence of witnesses. *See* WITNESSES, COMPETENCE OF.

competition, distortion of. The Treaty of Rome 1957, art. 85, prohibits as incompatible with the Common Market (qv) all agreements and practices which have as their object or effect the prevention, restriction or distortion of competition within the Common Market. See, eg, *Application des Gaz S.A.* v *Falks Veritas Ltd* [1974] Ch. 381; *Camera Care Ltd* v *EEC Commission* [1980] 1 CMLR 334. *See* EEC.

competition for prizes. A competition where, eg, the allocation of prizes depends on the outcome of sporting events and competitors have to forecast that outcome. See the Pool Competitions Act 1971, s. 7(2). Generally unlawful if conducted in or through any newspaper, or in connection with any trade or business or sale of articles: Lotteries and Amusements Act 1976, s. 14(1).

competition law. That part of the law dealing with matters such as those arising from monopolies and mergers, restrictive trading agreements, resale price maintenance, and agreements involving distortion of competition affected by EEC rules.

competitive practices, anti-. A person engages in an anti-competitive practice if, in the course of business, he pursues a course of conduct which, of itself or when taken together with a course of conduct pursued by persons associated with him, has or is intended to have or is likely to have the effect of restricting, distorting or preventing competition in connection with the production, supply or acquisition of goods in the UK, or the supply or securing of services in the UK: Competition Act 1980, s. 2(1). See S.I. 1980/979. For exemptions, see the 1980 Act, s. 2(2)–(5).

complainant. One who makes a complaint (qv). "In relation to a person accused of a rape offence or an accusation alleging a rape offence, means the woman against whom the offence is alleged to have been committed". S.O. (Amendment) A. 1976, s. 4(6). Anonymity of complainants in rape offence cases is assured by s. 4(1).

complaint. 1. The initiating step in civil proceedings in the magistrates' courts: see the M.C.A. 1980, Part II.

2. Allegation against a person. A complaint in a sexual case—the fact that it was made and its particulars—may be corroborative of the complainant's credibility or absence of consent. The complaint in such a case must have been made at the first reasonable opportunity after the offence and must not have been made merely in answer to questions of a leading or threatening nature: *R* v *Osborne* [1905] 1 KB 551. See *R* v *Camelleri* [1922] 2 KB 122.

complaint, hearing of. Procedure before a magistrates' court (qv) in which the substance of a complaint is stated to the defendant, the court hears the evidence and the parties, and makes the order for which the complaint is made or dismisses the complaint: M.C.A. 1980, s. 53. For the procedure in the event of non-appearance of the parties, see ss. 55–57.

completely constituted trust. A trust which has been perfectly created, in that the settlor has done everything in his power necessary to transfer his interest in the trust property to a trustee for the benefit of the intended beneficiaries, or has declared himself a trustee of that property. See *Letts* v *I.R.C.* [1956] 3 All ER 588. *See* TRUST.

completion. Final stages in, eg, a contract for the sale of land, effected by delivery up of the land with good title, acceptance of title and payment of agreed price. See the Statutory Conditions of Sale 1925.

completion notice. Notice served by a local planning authority, announcing that planning permission (qv) will be ineffective if a development is not completed within a specified period (of not less than one year): T.C.P.A. 1971, s. 44.

composition. 1. Sum of money accepted by creditors in satisfaction of debts. Can be registered under the Deeds of Arrangement Act 1914. 2. The ingredients of which a product is made, the proportions and degrees of strength, purity, etc. See the Medicines Act 1968, s. 132.

compos mentis. Of sound mind.

compound. 1. To settle or adjust by

agreement, eg, by accepting a composition (qv). 2. Compounding a felony, ie, the offence of agreeing for consideration not to prosecute or impede a prosecution, was abolished effectively by the C.L.A. 1967. 3. Compounding an arrestable offence (qv), ie, accepting or agreeing to accept consideration for not disclosing information which might be of material assistance in prosecuting an offender, is generally an offence under the C.L.A. 1967, s. 5(1).

compound settlement. The settlement formed by a series of separate instruments, eg, as in the case of the original settlement, disentailing instrument and resettlement. See the S.L.A. 1925, s. 30(3). *See* SETTLEMENT.

compromise. Settlement out of court of claims in dispute. "The word implies some element of accommodation on each side. It is not apt to describe total surrender. A claimant who abandons his claim is not compromising it": *Re NFU Development Trust Ltd* [1973] 1 All ER 135.

comptroller. Controller. One who examines accounts relating to public money. The Comptroller and Auditor-General is the head of the Exchequer and Audit Department. See the I.A. 1978, Sch 1; and the National Audit Act 1983, s. 1.

compulsion. *See* DURESS.

compulsory purchase order. An order for the purchase of land made in accordance with the statutory procedure: see, eg, the Highways Act 1980, ss. 257–259; the Acquisition of Land Act 1981; S.I. 1982/6; and the Civil Aviation Act 1982, s. 49. The acquiring authority makes an order in draft which is submitted to the confirming authority (usually the Minister), objections are heard by an inspector and the order is confirmed, modified or rejected. Disputes may be heard by the High Court. See the L.G.P.L.A. 1980, s. 91.

compulsory references. Procedure, regulated by the S.C.A. 1981, s. 68 and O. 36, concerning cases in which the powers of the High Court are exercised by an official referee (qv), eg, reference of an issue of fact for report or enquiry.

compulsory winding-up by the court. Procedure whereby a company (qv) is wound up if, eg, it has passed a special resolution to wind up, or it is unable to pay its debts or it has failed to commence operations within a year of incorporation or the court believes it equitable that it should be wound up. See the Cos.A. 1948, s. 222.

compurgation. Procedure whereby an accused person made a sworn denial of the accusation and brought together 12 persons who swore on oath to the validity of his statement. See *King* v *Williams* (1824) 2 B & C 538. Abolished by the Civil Procedure Act 1833.

computer. Any device for storing and processing information: Civil Evidence Act 1968, s. 5. For the use of computers, etc. for certain company records, see the Stock Exchange (Completion of Bargains) Act 1976, s. 3. For the use of computers relating to bank accounts see *Momm* v *Barclays Bank International Ltd* [1976] 3 All ER 588. See *R* v *Pettigrew* (1980) 71 Cr App R 39; *R* v *Wood* (1983) 76 Cr App R 23. *See* PRIVACY.

computer documents, statements in. Under the Civil Evidence Act 1968, s. 5, statements contained in documents produced by computers are admissible of a fact stated therein of which direct oral evidence would have been admissible if, eg, throughout the material time the computer had been operating properly and had been supplied with information of the kind contained in the statement. *See* EVIDENCE.

concealed fraud. In the case of land, this means "designed fraud by which a party knowing to whom the right belongs, conceals the circumstances giving that right, and, by means of such concealment, enables himself to enter and hold": *Petre* v *Petre* (1853) 1 Drew 397. The deliberate destruction of another's title deeds is an example. In such a case time does not run until the plaintiff has discovered, or could with reasonable diligence have discovered, the fraud: Lim. A. 1980, s. 32(1).

concealment. 1. Suppression of, or

neglect to communicate, a material fact. If fraudulent, it may provide grounds for rescission of contract. 2. Concealment of a valuable security, dishonestly and with a view to gain or with intent to cause loss to another, is an offence under the Th.A. 1968, s. 20(1). See *R v Kanwar* [1982] 2 All ER 523 (concealing stolen goods).

concealment of birth. *See* BIRTH, CONCEALMENT OF.

concert parties. Colloquialism describing groups of persons acting in concert to acquire a company's shares. See the Cos.A. 1981, s. 67. Members of such groups must keep one another informed of their existing interests, acquisitions and disposals of shares in the company: s. 68.

conciliation. Settlement of a dispute outside the courts by reference to a third party. See, eg, the E.P. (C.) A 1978, s. 133; and *Practice Direction (Family Division)* [1982] 1 WLR 1420.

conclusive evidence. *See* EVIDENCE, CONCLUSIVE.

concurrent and consecutive sentences. Following the conviction of the defendant of several offences, the court may impose separate sentences to be served at the same time (concurrently) or to follow on another (consecutively). See *R v March* [1970] 1 WLR 998; *R v Dick* [1972] Crim LR 58. *See* SENTENCE.

concurrent causes. Two or more events which are causative in relation to a plaintiff's injury so that both are considered proximate. See *Baker v Willoughby* [1970] AC 467; *Rouse v Squires* [1973] QB 889.

concurrent interests. Interests in land held at one and the same time, by two or more persons, eg, grant of land "to X and Y in fee simple".

concurrent lease. A lease (qv) created out of a reversion on an existing lease and existing concurrently with another lease.

concurrent tortfeasors. Persons who, having committed a tort (qv) are each answerable in full for the entire damage caused to the plaintiff.

concurrent writs. Writs in duplicate, or those issued, eg, for service on two or more defendants in an action or for service on a person whose whereabouts are unknown. See O. 6, r. 6.

condition. The declaration of circumstances essential to the occurrence of an event, eg, the exercise of a right. 1. "Conditions in deed" are those which are actual and expressed; "conditions in law" are implied. 2. A *condition precedent* is one which delays the vesting of a right until the occurrence of a particular event; a *condition subsequent* is one which provides for the defeat of an interest on the occurrence or non-occurrence of a particular event; a *condition concurrent* is one under which performance by one party is rendered dependent on performance by the other at the same time. See, eg, *Re Da Costa* [1912] 1 Ch 377; *Wynne v Fletcher* (1857) 24 Bear 430. 3. A condition in a contract for the sale of goods is a stipulation, the breach of which may give rise to a right to treat the contract as repudiated: S.G.A. 1979, s. 11(3). See *Wickman Machine Tool Sales Ltd v Schuler AG* [1972] 2 All ER 1173.

conditional acceptance. *See* ACCEPTANCE, CONDITIONAL.

conditional admissibility. Phrase referring to evidence, the relevance of which may be conditional on the giving of later evidence. Evidence so admitted is said to have been admitted *de bene esse* (qv).

conditional agreement. *See* AGREEMENT, CONDITIONAL.

conditional appearance. Procedure indicating appearance (after issue of writ) under protest. Now replaced, under RSC (Writ and Appearance) 1979; see O. 12, rr. 7, 8. *See* SERVICE, ACKNOWLEDGMENT OF.

conditional discharge. Where the court considers it inappropriate to pass sentence or make a probation order, having regard to the circumstances including the nature of the offence and the character of the offender, it may discharge the offender subject to a condition that he does not commit a further offence for a period fixed by the court (usually between 1–3 years). He may be sentenced for the original offence if he commits another offence during the fixed period. See the P.C.C.A. 1973, s. 7 as amended by the C.L.A. 1977, s.

57(2); *R* v *Wright* [1977] Crim LR 236.

conditional fee. A fee simple with an attached condition, eg, grant of land "to A in fee simple on condition that he shall not marry X, Y or Z". *See* FEE SIMPLE ABSOLUTE IN POSSESSION.

conditional interest. An interest on condition subsequent. *See* CONDITION.

conditional sale agreement. Agreement for the sale of goods or land under which the whole or part of the purchase price is payable in instalments, and the property in the goods or land is to remain in the seller until the conditions of the agreement are fulfilled. See the C.C.A. 1974, s. 189(1); and the S.G.A. 1979, s. 25(2).

conditional will. A will executed with the intention that it shall be rendered operative only on the occurrence of a specified event. See *Re Spratt* [1897] P 28; *Re Govier* [1950] P 237.

condition concurrent. *See* CONDITION.

condition precedent. *See* CONDITION.

conditions of sale. Terms upon which land is to be sold. In the case of a contract by correspondence, the L.P.A. 1925, s. 46 provides that it shall be governed, subject to contrary intention expressed, by the Statutory Form of Conditions of Sale.

condition subsequent. *See* CONDITION.

condominium. Joint sovereignty exerted over territory (eg, Andorra, administered by Spain and France).

condonation. Pardon or forgiveness. Specifically, forgiveness of a matrimonial offence and restoration of the offending spouse. No longer an absolute bar to divorce, but it may be material in hearings by magistrates. *See* DIVORCE, BARS TO.

conduct, unreasonable. *See* UNREASONABLE CONDUCT.

conference. 1. Procedure used to resolve disagreement between the Houses of Parliament, each House being represented by appointed "managers". 2. Discussion between counsel, solicitor and, in some cases, client.

confessing error. Agreement by a successful party to an action that a judgment should be reversed, following the allegation by the other party of an error in law or fact.

confession. An admission by the accused which amounts to guilt in a criminal case, made out of, or in, court (where it is termed a "plea of guilty"). "A confession well proved is the best evidence that can be produced": *per* Erle J in *R* v *Baldrey* (1852) 1 Den CC 430. Generally admissible only against the person who made it and it must be made voluntarily, ie, without a promise or hope of forgiveness or threat of punishment held out by a person in authority (eg, prosecutor, police officer, magistrate). A confession made to, but not induced by, a person in authority is admissible. See *R* v *Isequilla* [1975] 1 WLR 716; *DPP* v *Ping Lin* [1975] 3 All ER 175; and *R* v *Rennie* [1982] 1 WLR 64. *See* PERSON IN AUTHORITY.

confession and avoidance. The admission by a party of the truth of an allegation ("confession") but, at the same time, an allegation of other facts which apparently alter or nullify the effects ("avoidance"), eg, where the defendant agrees that he struck the plaintiff, but did so only in selfdefence. See, eg, *Lush* v *Russell* (1850) 5 Ex 203; O. 18, r. 8(1).

confession of defence. Where the defendant alleges a ground of defence which has arisen after the commencement of the action and the plaintiff delivers confession of that defence.

confidence, breach of. Equitable doctrine whereby the donee of confidential information relating, eg, to a business, and which requires protection, is under a duty not to use that information to the donor's detriment. See *Prince Albert* v *Strange* (1841) 1 Mac & G 25; *Littlewoods Organisation Ltd* v *Harris* [1977] 1 WLR 1492; Younger Committee on Privacy 1972.

confidential communication. A communication which is privileged as being protected from disclosure in evidence given in proceedings, eg, a communication between a party and solicitor made during those proceedings. "He who has received information in confidence shall not take advantage of it": *Seager* v *Copydex* [1967] 1 WLR 923. An injunction (qv) may be available to restrain a person from utilising a confidence reposed in him. See *Waugh* v *BR Board* [1980] AC 521. *See* PRIVILEGE.

confinement. 1. Imprisonment. 2. Labour resulting in the issue of a living child, or labour after 28 weeks of pregnancy resulting in the issue of a child, alive or dead: S.S.A. 1975, s. 23(1).

confiscate. To deprive of property by seizure.

conflict of laws. *See* PRIVATE INTERNATIONAL LAW.

confusion of goods. The intermixing of goods of the same type, belonging to two or more owners, so that identification of the separate parts cannot be made.

congenital disabilities, civil liability relating to. Under the Congenital Disabilities (Civil Liability) Act 1967 a child has a cause of action if born disabled as the result of a tortious act done to one of his parents before the child's birth or conception: s. 1. "Disabled" refers to the child being born with any deformity, disease or abnormality, including predisposition to physical or mental defect in the future: s. 4(1). See *McKay* v *Essex Area Health Authority* [1982] QB 1166.

conjugal rights, restitution of. Prior to 1971 a spouse could petition for a decree which, in effect, ordered a deserting spouse to return to cohabitation. Abolished under the Matrimonial Proceedings and Property Act 1970, s. 20.

connected persons. Persons who are considered, under the Cos.A. 1980, to be "connected with a director": s. 64. They include a director's spouse, child, company or partner with which he is associated, persons acting as trustees of a trust under which the beneficiaries include the director or other connected persons. For connected persons in relation to capital gains tax, see the Capital Gains Tax Act 1979, s. 63.

connivance. Passive consent or co-operation in relation to a wrong-doing. Specifically, permission for, or acquiescence in, a respondent's adultery. As such it was an absolute bar to divorce. Abolished by the Divorce

Reform Act 1969. See *Crewe* v *Crewe* (1800) 3 Hag Ecc 123; *Mudge* v *Mudge* [1950] P 173.

consanguinity. *See* AFFINITY.

consensus ad idem. *See* AD IDEM.

consent. Compliance with or deliberate approval of a course of action. It is not generally binding if obtained by coercion, fraud or undue influence (qv). See, eg, the F.L.R.A. 1969, s. 8; *Hegarty* v *Shine* (1878) 14 Cox CC 145; and *R* v *Williams* [1923] 1 KB 340.

consent, age of. Usually refers to the age at which a person is legally competent to consent to sexual intercourse. Raised from 12 to 13 in 1875, and to 16 in 1885. See *Report of Advisory Committee on Sexual Offences* (1921, Cmnd 8216).

consent and assault. Consent is generally a defence to a charge of assault (qv), but this is subject to considerations of public policy. In the absence of some good reason, eg, properly conducted games, assault cannot be rendered lawful by consent if it caused, or was intended to cause, actual bodily harm. See *A.-G's Ref (No. 6 of 1980)* [1981] QB 715.

consent judgment. O. 42, r. 5A, makes it possible for parties to an action in the Queen's Bench Division, who are legally represented, to consent to a judgment which will (*inter alia*) embody their settlement of the dispute.

conservation areas. Areas of social, architectural or historic interest, the character or appearance of which it is desirable to preserve or enhance, and designated as conservation areas by a local planning authority: T.C.P.A. 1971, s. 277, amended by the Town and Country Amenities Act 1974, s. 1(1). It is an offence to cause a "listed building" which forms part of such an area to be demolished or altered so that its character is affected, without obtaining consent: 1974 Act, ss. 55, 56.

consideration. That which is actually given or accepted in return for a promise. "Some right, interest, profit or benefit accruing to one party, or some forbearance, detriment, loss, or responsibility given, suffered or undertaken by the other'': *Currie* v *Misa* (1875) LR 10 Ex 153. Example: X receives £50 for which he promises to deliver goods to Y, the £50 is the consideration for the promise to deliver the goods. Consideration is *executed* when the act constituting the consideration is performed; it is said to be *executory* when it is in the form of promises to be performed at a future date. Consideration is required for all simple contracts. It must be legal; it must not be past; it must move from the promisee. See, eg, *Roscorla* v *Thomas* (1842) 3 QB 234; *Shadwell* v *Shadwell* (1860) 9 CB(NS) 159; *Dunlop Tyre Co* v *Selfridge & Co* [1915] AC 847. For consideration for a bill of exchange (qv), see the B.Ex.A. 1882, s. 27.

consideration, good. *See* GOOD CONSIDERATION.

consideration, past. Consideration which is wholly executed and finished before a promise is made. Example: X does some service for Y and, subsequently, Y promises X that, in consideration of that service, he will pay X a sum of money. There is no consideration to support Y's promise and it cannot be sued on. See *Re McArdle* [1951] Ch 669.

consistory court. A court held by a diocesan bishop and presided over by a chancellor for the trial of ecclesiastical causes arising within his diocese. Appeal is to the Court of Arches (qv), or Court of Ecclesiastical Causes Reserved or Chancery Court of York.

Consolidated Fund. The general account, established in 1786, into which government receipts are paid and out of which payments are made in the form of standing charges, known as Consolidated Fund services. It is represented by the account kept at the Bank of England by the Government.

Consolidation Act. An Act which repeals or re-enacts or collects in a single statute previous enactments and amendments relating to a topic. Acts of this nature may be passed without customary debate in Parliament: Consolidation of Enactments (Procedure) Act 1949. Examples:

Legal Aid Act 1974; Solicitors Act 1974. Differs from codification, which systematises statutes and case law. *See* CODIFYING STATUTE.

consolidation of actions. A number of pending actions relating to the same subject-matter tried together by order of the court. See O. 4, r. 10; *Healey* v *Waddington & Sons Ltd* [1954] 1 WLR 688.

consolidation of mortgages. Where one person creates at least two separate mortgages in favour of one mortgagee, that mortgagee has a right to require that the mortgagor, on seeking to exercise his equitable right to redeem one of the properties, shall redeem both of the properties or neither of them: *Jennings* v *Jordan* (1880) 6 App Cas 698. It is allowed only where the legal date for redemption (qv) has passed (for both mortgages) and where the right to consolidate has been reserved by at least one of the mortgages and where the equities of redemption are vested in one person and the mortgages in another, or where that position has existed at some time in the past. See the L.P.A. 1925, s. 93; *Pledge* v *White* [1896] AC 187. *See* MORTGAGE.

consortium. 1. A business combination. 2. Right of one spouse to companionship and affection of the other. See *Lawrence* v *Biddle* [1966] 2 QB 504. See the A.J.A. 1982, s. 2, for the abolition of certain claims for loss of services.

conspiracy. The statutory offence is created by C.L.A. 1977, s. 1(1) (substituted by the Criminal Attempts Act 1981, s. 5(1)): "If a person agrees with any other person or persons that a course of conduct shall be pursued which, if the agreement is carried out in accordance with their intentions, either (a) will necessarily amount to or involve the commission of any offence or offences by one or more of the parties to the agreement, or (b) would do so but for the existence of facts which render any of the offences impossible, he is guilty of conspiracy to commit the offence or offences in question.''

conspiracy at common law. ''The crime of conspiracy is the creation of the common law and peculiar to it'': *DPP* v *Doot and Others* [1973] 1 All ER 940. The offence of conspiracy at common law was abolished under the C.L.A. 1977, except in relation to conspiracy to defraud and in so far as it may be committed by entering into an agreement to engage in conduct which tends to corrupt public morals or outrages public decency but would not amount to or involve the commission of an offence if carried out by a single person otherwise than in pursuance of an agreement: s. 5.

conspiracy, exemptions from liability for. A person is not guilty of conspiracy to commit any offence if he is an intended victim of that offence: C.L.A. 1977, s. 2(1). A person is not guilty of conspiracy to commit any offence(s) if the only other person or persons with whom he agrees are (both initially and at all times during the currency of the agreement) persons of any one or more of the following descriptions: his spouse; a person under the age of criminal responsibility (see the C. & Y.P.A. 1933, s. 50); and an intended victim of that offence or of each of those offences: C.L.A. 1977, s. 2. See *R* v *Longman* (1980) 72 Cr App R 121.

conspiracy, restrictions on institutions of proceedings for. Under the C.L.A. 1977, s. 4(1), proceedings may not be instituted except by or with the consent of the DPP (qv) if the offence or each of the offences in question is a summary offence. Consent of the A-G (qv) may be required under s. 4(2).

conspiracy, tort of. Combination of two or more persons, without lawful justification, so as to cause wilful damage to another, or the agreement to perform an unlawful act with resulting damage. See *Crofter Hand Woven Harris Tweed Co* v *Veitch* [1842] AC 435.

constable. An officer of the law whose task it is to help in maintaining the peace and bringing to justice those who infringe it.

constat. It follows. It is clear beyond argument.

constituency. One of the 650 basic, separate electoral units in the UK in which eligible persons elect a Member of Parliament.

constitution. 1. The manner in which a state or other body is organised. 2. The body of fundamental doctrines and rules of a nation from which stem the duties and powers of the government and the duties and rights of the people. ''That assemblage of laws, institutions and customs... according to which the community hath agreed to be governed'': Bolingbroke. The UK's constitution is based on statute, common law and convention. See Royal Commission on the Constitution 1973 (Cmnd 5460).

construction. The process of construing (ie, discovering and applying the meaning of) written instruments, eg, by resolving ambiguities and other uncertainties. Often used synonymously with ''interpretation'': *Chatenay* v *Brazilian Submarine Telegraph Co* [1891] 1 QB 79. See *Franklin* v *A.-G.* [1974] QB 185.

construction, rules of. Decisions of the courts relating to the interpretation of documents: eg, the meaning of a document must be sought for in the document itself (*Simpson* v *Foxon* [1907] P 54); the intention may prevail over the words used (*Lloyd* v *Lloyd* (1837) 2 My & Cr 192); words are to be taken in their literal meaning (*Wallis* v *Smith* (1882) 21 Ch D 243); a deed is to be construed as a whole (*East Ham Corporation* v *Sunley* [1965] 1 WLR 30).

constructive. Not directly expressed; inferred.

constructive desertion. Conduct of a respondent equivalent to the expulsion of a petitioner from the matrimonial home with the intention of ending consortium (qv). See *Marsden* v *Marsden* [1968] P 544; *Price* v *Price* [1970] 1 WLR 993. It is conduct equivalent to ''driving the other spouse away'': *Boyd* v *Boyd* [1938] 4 All ER 181. Examples: husband's adultery; husband's accusing wife of immorality and telling her to go; treasonable activities of wife resulting in her conviction (*Ingram* v *Ingram* [1956] P 390). It may be an indication of irretrievable breakdown of marriage and grounds for proceedings leading to, eg, separation and maintenance. *See* DESERTION; DIVORCE.

constructive dismissal. Indirect dismissal as where, eg, employer unilaterally changes terms of relationship so that employee has virtually no choice but to resign. See the E.P. (C.)A. 1978, s. 55. See, eg, *Western Excavating* v *Sharp* [1978] 1 All ER 715.

constructive fraud. Equity considers as fraud those transactions which lead the court to the belief "that it is unconscientious for a person to avail himself of the legal advantage which he has obtained": *Torrance* v *Bolton* (1872) 8 Ch App 118. Equity will set aside, eg, inequitable dealings with the weak, poor and ignorant (see *Baker* v *Monk* (1864) De G J & S 388; *Miller* v *Cook* (1870) 40 LJ Ch 11; the L.P.A. 1925, s. 174); appointments made by the exercise of a special power (qv) for a corrupt or foreign purpose (see *Re Dick* [1953] Ch 343; and the L.P.A. 1925, s. 157).

constructive malice. Malice proved indirectly from attendant circumstances when the state of mind of the accused cannot be proved. Abolished with reference to homicide by the Homicide Act 1957, s. 1(1), the marginal note to which reads "Abolition of constructive malice": "Where a person kills another in the course or furtherance of some other offence, the killing shall not amount to murder unless done with the same malice aforethought (express or implied) as is required for a killing to amount to murder when not done in the course or furtherance of another offence... A killing done in the course or for the purpose of resisting or avoiding or preventing a lawful arrest, or of effecting or assisting an escape or rescue from legal custody shall be treated as a killing in the course or furtherance of an offence."

constructive manslaughter. *See* MANSLAUGHTER, CONSTRUCTIVE.

constructive notice. Where a purchaser fails to make a reasonable investigation he will be deemed to have had notice of what would have been discovered had he made the normal and customary enquiries. See the L.P.A. 1925, s. 199; and the L.P.A. 1969, ss. 24, 25. See *Peto* v *Hammond* (1861) 30 Beav 495; *Walker* v *Linom* [1907] 2 Ch 104.

constructive total loss. Where the subject-matter insured is reasonably abandoned because the actual total loss appears unavoidable, or the expenditure to prevent actual total loss would exceed the value of the subject-matter if it were saved. Example: the sinking of a vessel so that the cost of raising it will be greater than its value if recovered. See the Marine Insurance Act 1906, s. 60(1); *Assicurazioni Generali* v *Bessie Morris SS Co* [1892] 1 QB 571.

constructive trust. A trust imposed by equity, irrespective of the express or presumed intentions of the parties, in the interest of conscience and justice, as where X, an agent acting on behalf of his principal, Y, makes a profit directly out of his work and X is held to be a constructive trustee for that profit to Y. See *Keech* v *Sandford* (1726) Sel Cas Ch 261; *Competitive Insurance Co Ltd* v *Davies Investments Ltd* [1975] 1 WLR 1240; *Peffer* v *Rigg* [1977] 1 WLR 285. *See* TRUST.

construe. To discover and apply the meaning of a written instrument. *See* CONSTRUCTION.

consumer. A person to or for whom goods or services are, or are sought to be, supplied in the course of a business carried on by the supplier and who does not receive them in the course of a business carried on by him: C.C.A. 1974.

consumer credit agreement. A personal credit agreement (qv) under which the creditor provides the debtor with credit not exceeding £5,000: C.C.A. 1974, s. 8(2). It is a regulated agreement (qv) under the Act. The agreement may be of the following types: *restricted use* (credit facilities used for stipulated purposes only); *unrestricted use* (debtor is free to use the credit in any way he wishes); *debtor–creditor–supplier* (credit supplied by supplier himself or an independent creditor); *debtor–creditor* (credit provided with no agent between supplier and creditor). See S.I. 1980/52.

consumer credit business. A business relating to the provision of credit under consumer credit agreements (qv) which are regulated agreements (qv): C.C.A. 1974, s. 189(1).

consumer credit register. Known also as the "public register". Kept by the Director-General of Fair Trading (qv) under the C.C.A. 1974, s. 35(1), relating, eg, to applications for issue, variation and renewal of licences required to carry on a consumer credit business or consumer hire business.

consumer, dealing as. A party to a contract "deals as consumer" in relation to another party if he neither makes the contract in the course of a business nor holds himself out as doing so, and the other party does make the contract in the course of a business and in the case of a contract governed by the law of sale of goods or hire-purchase, or by s. 7 [of this Act], the goods passing under or in pursuance of the contract are of a type ordinarily supplied for private use or consumption: Unfair Contract Terms Act 1977, s. 12(1).

consumer goods, guarantee of. In the case of goods of a type ordinarily supplied for private use or consumption, where loss or damage arises from the goods proving defective while in consumer use (ie, while a person is using them or has them in his possession for use, otherwise than exclusively for the purposes of a business) and results from the negligence of a person concerned in the manufacture or distribution of the goods, liability for the loss or damage cannot be excluded or restricted by reference to any contract term or notice contained in or operating by reference to a guarantee of the goods: Unfair Contract Terms Act 1977, s. 5. This section does not apply as between parties to a contract under which, or in pursuance of which, possession or ownership of the goods passed: s. 5(3).

consumer hire agreement. Agreement based on a bailment of goods for a period of not more than three months, requiring payment of not more than £5,000, which is not a hire purchase agreement: C.C.A. 1974, s. 15(1).

consumer hire business. A business relating to the bailment of goods under consumer hire agreements (qv) which are regulated agreements (qv): C.C.A. 1974, s. 189(1).

consumer protection. Legislation designed to protect the economic and other interests of consumers. Examples: the Trade Descriptions Acts 1968 and 1972; the Fair Trading Act 1973; the C.C.A. 1974; the Consumer Safety Act 1978; and S.I. 1982/523.

Consumer Protection Advisory Committee. Body, consisting of 15 members, appointed by the Secretary of State. On reference made to them, they report to the Director-General of Fair Trading (qv) concerning matters relating to "consumer trade practices" (qv) under the Fair Trading Act 1973.

consumer safety. *See* SAFETY OF GOODS.

consumer sale. A sale of goods by a seller in the course of business where the goods are of a type ordinarily bought for consumption or private use and sold to a person who does not buy or hold himself out as buying them in the course of business. See the Unfair Contract Terms Act 1977.

consumer trade practice. Phrase used in the Fair Trading Act 1973 to mean any practice carried on in connection with the supply of goods or services to consumers, relating, eg, to terms and conditions of supply, promotion, methods of salesmanship, packing of goods, methods of demanding or securing payment.

consummation of a marriage. The completion of a marital union by ordinary and complete sexual intercourse. See *W.* v *W.* (*otherwise K.*) [1967] 3 All ER 178. Incapacity of either party, or wilful refusal, to consummate, makes a marriage voidable. See the Mat.C.A. 1973, s. 12 (*a*), (*b*); *Baxter* v *Baxter* [1948] AC 274; *Cackett* v *Cackett* [1950] P 253.

contemporanea expositio. Contemporaneous interpretation. The reading of a document as it would have been read at the time of making. "In the construction of ancient deeds and grants, there is no better way of construing them than by usage: *contemporanea expositio* is the best way to go by": *A.-G.* v *Parker* (1747) 3 Atk 576. See, however, *Campbell College* v *Valuation Commissioners for N. Ireland* [1964] 2 All ER 705.

contempt of court and strict liability rule. The "strict liability rule" means the rule of law whereby conduct may be treated as a contempt of court as tending to interfere with the course of justice in legal proceedings, regardless of intent to do so: see the Contempt of Court Act 1981, s. 1. It applies only to publications (eg, by speech, writing, or broadcasts addressed to the public at large) if it creates a substantial risk that the course of justice will be seriously impeded or prejudiced, and if the proceedings in question are "active", eg, when a warrant for arrest has been issued: s. 2, Sch 1. See *Home Office* v *Harman* [1982] 2 WLR 338.

contempt of court, defences. These include innocent publication or distribution, contemporary report published in good faith, part of discussion of public affairs: Contempt of Court Act 1981, ss. 3–5. See *R* v *Horsham Justices ex p Farquharson* [1982] QB 762; *A.-G.* v *David English* [1982] 3 WLR 278.

contempt of the House. An act or omission which brings into contempt the authority of a House of Parliament, or which directly obstructs its proceedings. In effect, a breach of parliamentary privilege (qv).

contentious business. Business before a court or arbitrator, not being business which falls within the definition of non-contentious or common form probate business which was contained in the J.A. 1925, s. 175(1), ie, in general, business of a lawyer where there is a contest between the parties: Solicitors Act 1974, s. 87(1).

contentious probate business. Comprises actions to revoke a grant previously made in solemn form, actions relating to applications for administration ("interest actions")

and actions as to the validity of wills. These actions are usually brought in the Chancery Division and begin with issue of a writ of summons out of Chancery Chambers (see O. 76). *See* PROBATE.

context. Parts of, eg, a document connected with a particular passage or sentence. "The real question which we have to decide is what does the word mean in the context in which we find it here, both in the immediate context of the subsection in which the word occurs and in the general context of the Act": *Re Bidie* [1948] 2 All ER 995. See also *Abrahams* v *Cavey* [1968] 1 QB 479.

continental shelf. The seabed and subsoil of the submarine areas adjacent to the coast, but outside the seaward limits of the territorial waters, of that country: Finance Act 1967, s. 2(2). See the Continental Shelf Act 1964, as amended; and the Continental Shelf (Protection of Installations) Order 1976.

continental shelf, foreign sector of. An area which is outside the territorial waters (qv) of any state and within which rights are exercisable by a state other than the UK with respect to the sea bed and subsoil and their natural resources: Oil and Gas (Enterprise) Act 1982, s. 28(1).

contingency. Something related to a possible future and uncertain event.

contingent legacy. A legacy (qv) bequeathed on an expressed contingency, eg, that the legatee shall marry.

contingent remainder. A remainder is contingent if the grantee is unascertained or if the title depends on the occurrence of a designated event. Example, a grant "to X for life, remainder in tail to his first son who shall attain the age of 21". See *Chinn* v *Collins* [1981] AC 533. *See* REMAINDER.

continuous bail. *See* BAIL, CONTINUOUS.

continuous employment. See the E.P.(C.) A. 1978, s. 151 and the Employment Act 1982, s. 20, Sch 2.

contra. Against; opposite.

contraband. 1. Goods, the import or export of which is forbidden. 2. Specifically, goods which, in time of war, may not be supplied by a neutral to a belligerent without risk of seizure.

contra bonos mores. Against morals. "Whatever is *contra bonos mores et decorum,* the principles of our law prohibit, and the King's court as the general censor and guardian of the public manners, is bound to restrain and punish": *Jones* v *Randall* (1744) 1 Cowp 17. See also *Shaw* v *DPP* [1962] AC 220; *Knuller* v *DPP* [1973] AC 435.

contract. A legally binding agreement. "Contracts when entered into freely and voluntarily shall be held sacred and shall be enforced by courts of justice": *Printing and Numerical Registering Co* v *Sampson* (1875) LR 19 Eq 462. *Contracts under seal,* known also as *deeds or specialty contracts,* must be in writing, signed, sealed and delivered. *Simple contracts* include oral contracts and contracts which require some writing. *Implied contracts* arise from the assumed intentions of the parties. *Contracts of record* arise from obligations imposed by a court of record (qv). Contract generally involves: (1) offer and unqualified acceptance; (2) *consensus ad idem* (qv); (3) intention to create legal relations; (4) genuineness of consent; (5) contractual capacity of the parties; (6) legality of object; (7) possibility of performance; (8) certainty of terms; (9) valuable consideration.

contract, bilateral. Contract in which the parties must fulfil reciprocal obligations to each other. *See* UNILATERAL CONTRACT.

contract, breach of. *See* BREACH OF CONTRACT.

contract, discharge of. *See* DISCHARGE.

contract, divisible. *See* DIVISIBLE CONTRACT.

contract, formal. *See* FORMAL CONTRACT.

contract, incapacitation and. A party who incapacitates himself, by his own act or default, from performing his obligations under a contract, is regarded as having refused to perform them. "To say 'I would like to but cannot', negatives intent to perform as much as 'I will not' ": *per*

Devlin J in *Universal Carriers* v *Citati* [1957] 2 QB 401.

contracting out. Removing oneself from an obligation. Thus, a trade union member may contract out of the obligation to contribute to his union's political fund (qv). See the Trade Union Act 1913; the E.P.A. 1975, s. 118; and *Birch* v *NUR* [1950] Ch 602. For contracting out of a credit agreement, see the C.C.A. 1974, s. 173(1).

contract, international supply. *See* INTERNATIONAL SUPPLY CONTRACT.

contract, measure of damages in. *See* MEASURE OF DAMAGES IN CONTRACT.

contract, naked. *See* NUDUM PACTUM.

contract of employment. A contract of service (or apprenticeship) which may arise from an agreement expressed in writing, orally or from conduct. Under the E.P. (C.) A. 1978, s. 1, employers must give a written statement (usually within 13 weeks of the beginning of employment) to employees relating to, eg, scale of remuneration, terms and conditions of work, hours of work, holiday pay, grievance procedures, length of notice (but this does not amount to a contract).

contract of record. Judgments and recognisances (qqv) enrolled in the records of proceedings of a court of record.

contract of sale. Includes an agreement to sell as well as a sale: S.G.A. 1979, s. 61(1). Price is generally one of the essentials of sale so that there may be no contract of sale if it remains "to be agreed" by the parties.

contract of service. A contract, written or oral, express or implied, to execute personally any work or labour. It usually implies a relationship of "master and servant". It has been held to exist where M (the master) has the power of selection of S (his servant), where M pays S wages, where M has the right to control S's method of work, where M has the right to suspend or dismiss S: *Short* v *Henderson* (1946) 62 TLR 427. Whether or not a contract is "of services" is to be judged by an objective test: *Davis* v *New England College* *of Arundel* [1977] ICR 6. See *Simmons v Heath Laundry Co* [1910] 1 KB 543; *Doggett* v *Waterloo Taxicab Co* [1910] 2 KB 336. *See* INTEGRATION TEST.

contract, open. *See* OPEN CONTRACT.

contractor. *See* INDEPENDENT CONTRACTOR.

contract, restricted. *See* RESTRICTED CONTRACT.

contracts, collateral. *See* COLLATERAL.

contract, severance of. *See* SEVERANCE.

contracts required to be in writing. The group of contracts which are valid only if written, including bills of exchange, marine insurance, bills of sale, acknowledgment of statute-barred debts, certain contracts relating to hire-purchase.

contracts, standard form. *See* STANDARD FORM CONTRACTS.

contract terms, unfair. *See* UNFAIR CONTRACT TERMS.

contractual liability, avoidance of. As between contracting parties (where one of them deals as consumer or on the other's written standard terms of business), then as against that party, the other cannot by reference to any contract term, when himself in breach of contract, exclude or restrict any liability of his in respect of the breach, or claim to be entitled to render a contractual performance substantially different from that which was reasonably expected of him, or, in respect of the whole or any part of his contractual obligation, to render no performance at all except in so far as the contract term satisfies the requirement of reasonableness: Unfair Contract Terms Act 1977, s. 3.

contract under seal. A contract expressed in a document to which the maker's seal is attached and which is delivered as "his deed". Generally, the following must be made under seal: contracts made without consideration (qv); conveyance of a legal estate (qv) in land or any interest in land, including leases for more than three years, etc.

contract, unenforceable. *See* UNENFORCEABLE CONTRACT.

contract, unilateral. *See* UNILATERAL CONTRACT.

contract, vicarious performance of. *See* VICARIOUS PERFORMANCE OF CONTRACT.

contract, wagering. *See* WAGERING CONTRACT.

contra proferentem rule. *See* VERBA CHARTARUM.

contribution. 1. Payment imposed on, or made by, some person. 2. Payment of the share of an individual relating to a loss for which several persons are jointly liable, eg, joint tortfeasors (qv). See the Civil Liability (Contribution) Act 1978; and O. 16, r. 10 (offer of contribution before trial of an action).

contributory. One who is liable to contribute to the assets of a company in the event of a winding-up (qv). See the Cos.A. 1948, s. 213; and the Cos.A. 1981, s. 58.

contributory benefits. Benefits under the S.S.A. 1975 and 1979, as amended, including benefits for unemployment, sickness, invalidity, maternity, widows, retirement pensions, death grant.

contributory mortgage. A mortgage in which the mortgage money is contributed by two or more persons in separate amounts. *See* MORTGAGE.

contributory negligence. "A man's carelessness in looking after his own safety." A defence established where it is proved that an injured party failed to take reasonable care of himself, thus contributing to his own injury: *Nance* v *British Columbia Electric Rwy* [1951] AC 601. Under the Law Reform (Contributory Negligence) Act 1945 a claim in respect of damage is reduced to such extent as the court thinks just and equitable having regard to the claimant's share in responsibility for damage. "Damage" includes loss of life and personal injury. See the Animals Act 1971, s. 10; the Fatal Accidents Act 1976, s. 5; and *Harrison* v *British Railways* [1981] 3 All ER 679. *See* NEGLIGENCE.

controlled drugs. *See* DRUGS, CONTROLLED.

controlled trust. Means, in relation to a solicitor, a trust of which he is a sole trustee or co-trustee with one or more of his partners or employees: Solicitors Act 1974, s. 87(1). *See* TRUST.

controller. Means, in relation to a body corporate (qv) a person in accordance with whose instructions any director is accustomed to act or who, alone with any associate, is entitled to exercise or control the exercise of, one-third or more of the voting power at a general meeting of the body corporate: C.C.A. 1974, s. 189(1). See also the Banking Act 1979, s. 49(3); and the Estate Agents Act 1979, s. 31(5).

controlling director. A director of a company, the directors of which have a controlling interest therein, who is the beneficial owner of, or who is able either directly or through the medium of other companies or by any other indirect means to control more than 5 per cent of the ordinary share capital of the company. See the Finance Act 1970, s. 26(1).

contumacious. Stubbornly contemptuous of the court.

convenience, flag of. The national flag flown by a merchant ship registered in a country other than that of its nominal owners.

convention. 1. A treaty between states. In interpreting a statute designed to enact a convention, the court may look at it in the event of an ambiguity: *The Banco* [1971] P 137. 2. Agreed usage or practice. 3. A convention of the constitution is one of the "rules for determining the mode in which the discretionary powers of the Crown (or of ministers or servants of the Crown) ought to be exercised": Dicey. Conventions are understandings, tacitly agreed, resulting from long practice by which the conduct of the Crown and Parliament is regulated in the absence of formal legal rules. Examples: the party with a majority in the Commons is entitled to have its leader made Prime Minister (qv); the Cabinet is collectively responsible to Parliament for the conduct of the Executive; lay peers do not participate in judicial proceedings in the House of Lords.

convention award, arbitration. *See* ARBITRATION CONVENTION AWARD.

convention, estoppel by. *See* ESTOPPEL.

conversion. 1. In criminal law, "fraudulent conversion" to one's use or benefit was formerly an offence under the Larceny Act 1916, s. 20. See now the Th.A. 1968, s. 1. 2. In equity, conversion is a notional change, under certain conditions, of land into money, or money into land, which arises as soon as the duty to convert arises. Example: P gives personalty on trust to Q to purchase land and hold it for R—the personalty is notionally considered as realty. See *Fletcher* v *Ashburner* (1779) 1 Bro CC 497; *Irani Finance Ltd* v *Singh* [1971] Ch. 59. *See* RECONVERSION.

conversion, tort of. An act in relation to a person's goods which constitutes a serious and unjustifiable denial of his title to them. See, eg: *Belvoir Finance Co Ltd* v *Stapleton* [1971] 1 QB 210; *Union Transport Finance Ltd* v *British Car Auctions Ltd* [1978] 2 All ER 385. An action lies in conversion for loss or destruction of goods which a bailee has allowed to happen in breach of his duty to his bailor (that is to say, it lies in a case which is not otherwise conversion, but would have been detinue (qv) before detinue was abolished): Torts (Interference with Goods) Act 1977, s. 2. Contributory negligence (qv) is no defence (except for certain bank cases under the Banking Act 1979, s. 47) in proceedings founded on conversion: 1977 Act, s. 11(1). *See* BAILMENT.

convert, duty to. A trustee's responsibility to convert, imposed by statute (see the A.E.A. 1925, s. 3), or by the trust instrument, or the rule in *Howe* v *Lord Dartmouth* (1802) 7 Ves 137, under which, where there is in a will a residuary bequest of personal estate which is to be enjoyed by persons in possession, and there is no intention on the part of the settlor that the property is to be enjoyed *in specie,* then the trustees are under a duty to convert all the property of a wasting, hazardous, reversionary or unauthorised character into authorised investments.

conveyance. 1. Transfer of ownership of property. 2. The instrument effecting the transfer. 3. Under the L.P.A. 1925, s. 205(1), includes "mortgage, charge, lease, asset, vesting declaration, disclaimer, release and every other assurance of property or of an interest therein by any instrument, except a will''. See also the L.C.A. 1972, s. 17(1). 2 Under the Th.A. 1968, s. 12(1) it is an offence to take a conveyance (ie, one constructed or adapted for the carriage of persons by land, water or air) for one's own or another's use without having the consent of the owner or other lawful authority. See *R* v *Clotworthy* [1981] RTR 477; *R* v *Stokes* [1983] RTR 59.

conveyance, deed of. *See* DEED.

conveyance, voluntary. *See* VOLUNTARY DISPOSITION.

conviction. Defined under the Bail Act 1976, s. 2(1) as: a finding of guilt; a finding that a person is not guilty by reason of insanity; a finding under the M.C.A. 1980, s. 30 that the person in question did the act or made the omission charged; a conviction of an offence for which an order is made placing the offender on probation or discharging him absolutely or conditionally. (When children and young persons are dealt with summarily, the words ''conviction'' and ''sentence'' must be replaced by ''finding of guilt'' and ''an order made''.)

conviction, proof of. The establishing of the fact of a person's conviction. Certified copies of extracts from court records are admissible (see the Evidence Act 1851, s. 13; the Criminal Procedure Act 1865, s. 6; and the Prevention of Crimes Act 1871, s. 18). Fingerprints (qv) or palm prints may suffice under the C.J.A. 1948.

convictions, evidence of previous. *See* PREVIOUS CONVICTIONS, EVIDENCE OF.

Convocation. Assembly of the clergy for each province, comprising an upper house (archbishop, bishops, suffragan bishops) and lower house (deans, archdeacons, pastors). Has a maximum life of five years.

cooling-off period. Period during which a regulated agreement (qv) may be cancelled by a debtor or hirer: see the C.C.A. 1974, ss. 67–74.

co-operative enterprise. A body to which the Secretary of State has given a certificate stating that he is satisfied that it is in substance a co-operative association and that it is controlled by a majority of the people working for it and of those working for its subsidiaries: Industrial Common Ownership Act 1976, s. 2(2).

co-ownership of real property. Subsists, as in a joint tenancy (qv) and a tenancy in common (qv), where two or more persons enjoy concurrent interests in the same property. *See also* COPARCENARY.

coparcenary. Where two or more persons together constituted a single heir, eg, tenant in tail (qv) who has died intestate and left female heirs only. The heirs (coparceners) held in undivided shares. Abolished, save in the case of a tenant in tail who dies without having barred the entail, by the A.E.A. 1925, s. 45(1). *See* BARRING OF ENTAILED INTEREST.

copyhold. Tenure at the will of the lord of the manor. Converted into socage tenure (qv) as from 1st January 1926: L.P.A. 1922, s. 128. See also the L.P.A. 1925; and the L.P. (Amendment) A. 1926.

copy of the file. Term used in the C.C.A. 1974, s. 158(5), referring to a transcript of information (kept, eg, on computer) reduced into plain English.

copyright. Copyright in a work is defined as ''the exclusive right…to do, and to authorise other persons to do, certain acts in relation to that work'': Copyright Act 1956, s. 1(1). Such acts include, eg, reproducing the work in any material form, performing it in public, broadcasting it. Usually it continues for the holder's lifetime, plus 50 years from the end of the calendar year in which he dies. An injunction is the usual remedy to restrain a breach. See also the Design Copyright Act 1968; the Performers' Protection Act 1963; the Universal Copyright Convention 1974; the Competition Act 1980, s. 30; the Copyright Act 1956 (Amend.) Act 1982; and *Infabrics* v *Jaytex* [1982] AC 1.

copyright, Crown. *See* CROWN COPYRIGHT.

coram. In the presence of, eg, *coram*

judice (in the presence of the judge, ie, before the court).

co-respondent. Generally refers to an alleged adulterer charged in a husband's petition for divorce or judicial separation and made, jointly with the wife, respondent to the suit. See the Mat.C.A. 1973, s. 49(1). *See* DIVORCE.

coroner. A person appointed under the Coroners Acts 1887–1980 from barristers, solicitors and registered medical practitioners of at least five years' standing. He has jurisdiction over treasure trove and, principally, inquests into deaths of persons dying within his district where there is, eg, reasonable cause for suspecting violent or unnatural death. He is not obliged to hold an inquest to view the body: Coroners Act 1980, s. 1. In some cases he must summon a jury whose verdict is termed an "inquisition" (qv). See also the C.L.A. 1977, s. 56, Sch 10; *R v HM Coroner (Hammersmith)* [1980] QB 21; *R v W Yorks Coroner ex p Smith* [1982] 3 WLR 920; S.I. 1980/557; the A.J.A. 1982, s. 62; and the Coroners' Juries Act 1983.

corporate body. *See* BODY CORPORATE.

corporate veil. *See* LIFTING THE VEIL.

corporation. A body of persons associated for some purpose and considered as having rights and duties and the capacity of succession. A *corporation aggregate* is made up of groups of persons, eg, incorporated companies. A *corporation sole* consists of one person and his successors, eg, a bishop. A corporation is domiciled in its place of incorporation: *Gasque v IRC* [1940] 2 KB 80. See the M.C.A. 1980, s. 46, Sch 3; and the C.J.J.A. 1982, s. 42. *See* BODY CORPORATE.

corporation, public. *See* PUBLIC CORPORATION.

corporation, statutory. *See* PUBLIC CORPORATION.

corporation tax. Tax paid on profits by companies and unincorporated associations other than partnerships. See the Taxes Management Act 1970, ss. 10, 11, 29–43, 60–69; and the Finance Act 1983, ss. 11–13.

corporeal hereditaments. Visible, tangible property, eg, houses, goods. *See* HEREDITAMENTS.

corpus delicti. The body of an offence, ie, the aggregation of fundamental facts constituting an offence.

corrective justice. *See* JUSTICE, DISTRIBUTIVE AND CORRECTIVE.

correspondent. "In relation to a letter or other communication, means the sender or the addressee": British Telecommunications Act 1981, s. 66(5). *See* LETTER; SENDER.

corroboration. Independent, admissible evidence tending to confirm that the principal evidence is true. "Perhaps the best synonym is 'support'": *DPP v Hester* [1972] 3 All ER 1056. In a criminal case it must confirm that the crime has been committed and that the accused committed it. It is required, usually, in some civil cases, eg, affiliation proceedings, and in some criminal cases involving, eg, perjury, unsworn evidence of children, evidence of an accomplice, some sexual offences. See *R v Hook* (1858) Dears & B 606; *R v Campbell* [1956] 2 QB 432; *Alli v Alli* [1965] 3 All ER 480; *DPP v Kilbourne* [1973] AC 729.

corruption. Generally refers to an inducement by means of an improper consideration to violate some duty. See the Prevention of Corruption Act 1916; *Report on Standards of Conduct in Public Life* 1976 (Cmnd 6534); *R v Pottinger* [1974] Crim LR 675; *DPP v Manners* [1977] 2 WLR 178; *R v Williams* [1981] Crim LR 188; and the Representation of the People Act 1983, ss. 158–160; *See* BRIBERY.

corruption of public morals. The term "suggests conduct which a jury might find to be destructive of the very fabric of society": *Knuller Ltd v DPP* [1972] 2 All ER 898.

costs. The expenses relating to an action. See, generally, the S.C.A. 1981, s. 51, and O. 62. Includes "fees, charges, disbursements, expenses and remuneration": O. 62, r. 1. Each party must pay his solicitor's costs and the unsuccessful party may be ordered to pay costs to his opponent. Costs are usually in the discretion of the court and may be dealt with by the court at any stage of the proceedings: O. 62, r. 4. See, eg, the Costs in Criminal Cases Act

1973; the Solicitors Act 1974, s. 87(1); and the Litigants in Person (Costs and Expenses) Act 1975. For magistrates' powers to award costs see the M.C.A. 1980, s. 64. *See* TAXATION OF COSTS.

costs, common fund basis of. *See* COMMON FUND BASIS OF COSTS.

costs, discretion in relation to. Element of latitude allowed to the court in dealing with the questions of costs. There should be taken into account: offer of contribution (qv); payment into court (qv) and amount of such payment (see O. 62, r. 5). The discretion "must be exercised judicially and the judge ought not to exercise it against the successful party, except for some reason connected with the case": *Donald Campbell & Co Ltd* v *Pollak* [1927] AC 732.

costs follow the event. Phrase referring to success in litigation generally being followed by the award of costs to the successful party.

costs in any event. Order made by the court suggesting its disapproval of a party's conduct, eg, where that party has refused to disclose relevant documents. The party is ordered to pay costs of the application whether or not he eventually wins the case. Costs of this kind are payable only after the actual case has been determined.

costs in Crown Court. *See* CROWN COURT, COSTS IN.

costs in the cause. "Means that the costs of...interlocutory proceedings are to be awarded according to the final award of costs in the action": *Stratford & Son Ltd* v *Lindley (No. 2)* [1969] 1 WLR 1547.

costs, party and party. *See* PARTY AND PARTY COSTS.

costs, recovery of. An action cannot be brought to recover costs due to a solicitor until one month after the delivery of a bill signed by the solicitor or a partner in the firm: Solicitors Act 1974, ss. 69 (as amended), 70.

costs reserved. Order in interlocutory proceedings whereby the master leaves to the trial judge the decision as to payment of costs.

costs, security for. *See* SECURITY FOR COSTS.

costs, taxation of. *See* TAXATION OF COSTS.

costs, trustees', basis. *See* TRUSTEES' COSTS BASIS.

costs, with. *See* WITH COSTS.

Council of Legal Education. Body responsible to the Senate of the Inns of Court and the Bar (qv) for the examinations and prescribed courses leading to call to the Bar (qv).

Council of Ministers. The body of representatives of the member states of the EEC, made up of government delegates. Its task is to ensure coordination of the general economic policies of member states: Treaty of Rome 1957, art. 145. The office of President is held by each member of the Council in turn. It meets when convened by the President or at the request of a member, or of the Commission of EEC (qv). *See* EEC.

Council on Tribunals. Body of 10–15 independent persons appointed by the Lord Chancellor and Secretary of State to keep under review the constitution and working of tribunals (qv). See Tribunals and Inquiries Act 1971, Sch 1 (as amended).

councils, county. Elected bodies for defined areas within the local government system comprising councillors (elected for four years) presided over by chairmen. They are responsible for, eg, lighting, highways, planning, police and fire services. See the L.G.A. 1972.

councils, district. Bodies corporate set up to administer local government in the divisions of counties known as districts (qv). See the L.G.A. 1972, Part IX; and the L.G. (Misc. Provs.) A. 1976, Part I.

councils, principal. Councils of the "principal areas", ie, areas of counties, districts, London boroughs, and Greater London. See the L.G.A. 1972.

councils, wages. *See* WAGES COUNCILS.

counsel. A practising barrister (qv).

counsel's duty in course of a trial. Prosecuting counsel "ought not to struggle for the verdict against the prisoner, but they ought to bear themselves rather in the character of ministers of justice assisting in the administration of justice": *per* Avery

J in *R* v *Banks* [1916] 2 KB 62. Defence counsel should present the defence of the accused "fearlessly and without regard to his personal interests": see *R* v *McFadden and Cunningham* (1976) 62 Cr App R 187.

counterclaim. A cross-action (qv) which is not a defence, but, in effect, the defendant's statement of claim. If claim and counterclaim are of an entirely different nature and cannot be tried together conveniently, the court may order that the counter-claim be tried separately. It must always claim relief against the plaintiff: *Furness* v *Booth* (1876) 4 Ch D 587. See O. 9; S.I. 1981/1687; *Fleming* v *Loe* [1901] 2 Ch 594; *The Gniezno* [1968] P 418.

counterclaim, discontinuance of. Procedure under O. 21, r. 3, whereby notice of discontinuance is served upon the plaintiff with leave (applied for by summons or motion or notice under O. 25, r. 7) or without leave if served within 14 days of service of the plaintiff's defence to the counter-claim, or within 14 days of expiration of the time intended for service if no defence was served.

counterfeit. A thing is a counterfeit of a currency note or of a protected coin (qv) if it is not a currency note or protected coin, but resembles them (whether on one side only or both) to such an extent that they are reasonably capable of passing for currency notes or protected coins, or if it is a currency note or protected coin which has been so altered that it is reasonably capable of passing for a currency note or protected coin of some other description: Forgery and Counterfeiting Act 1981, s. 28(1).

counterfeiting. It is an offence for a person to make a counterfeit of a currency note or of a protected coin (qv) intending that he or another shall pass or tender it as genuine: Forgery and Counterfeiting Act 1981, s. 14(1). It is an offence to make a counterfeit of a currency note or of a protected coin without lawful excuse or authority: s. 14(2). *See* COUNTERFEIT.

counterfeit notes. It is an offence to have in one's custody counterfeit notes and coins intending to pass or tender them as genuine; to have in one's custody and control things intended to be used for the purpose of counterfeiting; to import or export counterfeit notes or coins without Treasury consent: Forgery and Counterfeiting Act 1981, ss. 16–21.

counter-offer. *See* OFFER, COUNTER-.

counties palatine. The counties of Chester, Durham, Lancaster. Courts of these counties exercised chancery jurisdiction until their abolition by the Courts Act 1971, s. 41.

counts. The sections of an indictment (qv) containing separate allegations and charges. "Every count in an indictment is equivalent to a separate indictment; the prisoner can be tried on one or all of the counts": *R* v *Boyle* [1954] 2 QB 292.

counts, alternative. Separate clauses in an indictment (qv) each charging a separate offence, where the charges are based on the same facts or form part of a series of offences of the same or a similar nature. See the Indictment Rules 1971.

counts, general. Counts (qv) which are too general and insufficient may be quashed.

counts, separate. Where more than one offence is charged in an indictment (qv) each must generally be stated in a separate count (ie, section) and each must be numbered separately. A count which charges more than one offence may be void for duplicity: *R* v *Molloy* [1921] 2 KB 364. See *R* v *Wilson* (1979) 69 Cr App R 83; *Anderton* v *Cooper* (1980) 72 Cr App R 232.

county. Territorial division. See the L.G.A. 1972. England is divided into Greater London, metropolitan counties (six) and non-metropolitan counties (39). Wales has eight counties.

county borough. Former administrative division (of at least 50,000 inhabitants). Abolished following the L.G.A. 1972.

county councils. *See* COUNCILS, COUNTY.

county court actions. *See* ACTIONS, COUNTY COURT.

county court registrar. *See* REGISTRAR, COUNTY COURT.

county courts. The main civil courts, established by the County Courts Act

1846. Their jurisdiction is statutory and covers: actions founded on contract and tort where the amount claimed is not more than £5,000 (currently); equity matters, eg, trusts and mortgages where the amount does not exceed £30,000; actions for the recovery of land. All judges of the Supreme Court, circuit judges and recorders are empowered to sit in county courts. Rules of procedure are printed in the Green Book. Trial by jury may be ordered in an exceptional case. Each court sits at least once a month. Registrars, appointed by the Lord Chancellor from solicitors of at least seven years' standing, deal with matters relating to interlocutory hearings. See the County C.A. 1959 (as amended); the Courts Act 1971; the County Courts Jurisdiction Order 1981; A.J.A. 1977, ss. 10(3), 14; the I.A. 1978, Sch 1; the H.A. 1980, Part IV; the County Court Rules 1981; and the A.J.A. 1982, Part V.

county courts, choice of. In general, a plaintiff must commence proceedings in the court for the district in which the defendant resides or carries on business or in the court for the district where the cause of action arose wholly or in part. See the County Court Rules 1981, O. 2, r. 1(1); O. 16, r. 4.

county quarter sessions. County and borough sessions held at least four times a year to hear the less serious offences tried on indictment. Their jurisdiction was civil, criminal, original and appellate. Abolished under the Courts Act 1971.

coupon, insurance. See INSURANCE COUPON.

course of duty, declaration in. See DECLARATION IN COURSE OF DUTY.

course of employment. The scope of a person's employment. Thus, a wrong committed falls within the scope of employment if expressly or impliedly authorised by the master or if necessarily incidental to something which the person who has committed the wrong is employed to do. See *Vandyke* v *Fender* [1970] 2 All ER 336; *Heatons Transport Ltd* v *TGWU* [1973] AC 15; *Kooragang Investments* v

Richardson & Wrench [1982] AC 482.

court. 1. Residence of the Sovereign. 2. Formal assembly of a Sovereign's councillors. 3. The place where justice is administered. 4. Persons assembled under the authority of the law for the purpose of administering justice, ie, the judge or judges. See also the C.J.J.A. 1982, s. 50.

Court, Admiralty. See ADMIRALTY COURT.

court, attributes of. Created by the state; conducts its procedure in accordance with rules of natural justice; procedure includes public hearing, reception of oral evidence, hearing of argument, oral examination and cross-examination of witnesses; has before it at least two parties, one of whom may be the Crown; and arrives at a decision concerned with legal rights which is final and binding for so long as it stands: *per* Eveleigh L J in *A.-G.* v *BBC* [1981] AC 303.

Court, Borough. See BOROUGH COURT.

Court, Companies. See COMPANIES COURT.

Court, Consistory. See CONSISTORY COURT.

Court, Crown. See CROWN COURT.

Court for Consideration of Crown Cases Reserved. Established in 1888 so as to decide questions of law reserved for consideration by a judge or magistrate. Superseded by the Court of Criminal Appeal (qv).

court-house, petty sessional. A courthouse or place at which justices are accustomed to assemble for holding special or petty sessions (qv) (or for the time being appointed as a substitute place) or at which a stipendiary magistrate (qv) is authorised to do alone any act authorised to be done by more than one justice of the peace: M.C.A. 1980, s. 150(1).

Court of Appeal. It consists of the Lord Chancellor, Lord Chief Justice, Master of the Rolls, President of the Family Division, former Lord Chancellors, Lords of Appeal in Ordinary, Lords Justices of Appeal. There are two divisions: (1) *Criminal division.* Successor of the Court of Criminal Appeal (qv) which was created in 1907. It hears, eg, appeals by persons convicted on indictment, or against sentence from the Crown Court (qv). Appeal is from the Criminal division to the House of Lords. (2) *Civil division*. Hears, eg, appeals from the High Court, county courts, various tribunals. Appeal is usually by way of re-hearing. Appeal is from the Civil division to the House of Lords. See the S.C.A. 1981, ss. 2, 3, 15–18, 53; O. 59, r. 3; O. 114. *See* APPEAL.

Court of Appeal, reception of fresh evidence by. "First, it must be shown that the evidence could not have been obtained with reasonable diligence for use at the trial; secondly, the evidence must be such that, if given, it would probably have an important influence on the result of the case, though it need not be decisive; thirdly, the evidence must be such as is presumably to be believed, or, in other words, it must be apparently credible though it need not be incontrovertible": *per* Denning L J in *Ladd* v *Marshall* [1954] 1 WLR 1489. See *Skone* v *Skone* [1971] 1 WLR 812.

Court of Arches. Ecclesiastical court which has the jurisdiction of the former Provincial Court of Archbishop and hears appeals from the consistory court (qv).

Court of Chancery. Originally a court of equity consisting of Lord Chancellor, Master of the Rolls and vice-chancellors. Merged in the Supreme Court of Judicature by the J.A. 1873 and became known as the Chancery Division (qv).

Court of Chivalry. Ancient feudal court, presided over by the Earl Marshal, which decided disputes concerning, eg, the right to use armorial bearings. Last sat in 1955: *Manchester Corporation* v *Manchester Palace of Varieties (Ltd)* [1955] P 133.

Court of Common Pleas. Also known as the Court of Common Bench. A part of Curia Regis (qv) having extensive jurisdiction in civil actions, other than those concerning royal rights. It followed the King in his travels through the realm, before Magna Carta (qv). Transferred to the High Court by the J.A. 1873.

Court of Criminal Appeal. Created in 1907 by the Criminal Appeal Act

1907. Consisted of the Lord Chief Justice and judges of the QBD. It heard appeals from, eg, quarter sessions, assizes, the Central Criminal Court. Abolished by the Criminal Appeal Act 1966. *See* COURT OF APPEAL.

Court of Ecclesiastical Causes Reserved. Court composed of five judges, including two who have held high judicial office and three diocesan bishops, exercising jurisdiction over clergy in matters relating to ritual and doctrine. Petition lies to a Commission of Review (qv).

Court of Exchequer. 1. A division of Curia Regis (qv) with jurisdiction relating principally to public revenue matters. Jurisdiction was transferred to the High Court of Justice, Exchequer Division, under the J.A. 1873. 2. A Court of Exchequer Chamber was set up in 1830 to hear appeals from all common law courts. Jurisdiction passed to the Court of Appeal (qv).

Court of Faculties. An office administered by the Archbishop and responsible for the granting of faculties. See the Public Worship Regulation Act 1874. *See* FACULTY.

court of first instance. Court in which proceedings are initiated.

Court of High Commission. *See* HIGH COMMISSION, COURT OF.

Court of Human Rights, European. *See* EUROPEAN COURT OF HUMAN RIGHTS.

Court of Justice, International. *See* INTERNATIONAL COURT OF JUSTICE.

Court of Justice of the European Communities. Institution set up under the Treaty of Rome to ensure that in interpretation and application of the Treaty the law is observed. It consists of judges from each member state, assisted by three Advocates-General (qv). It sits in Luxembourg, expressing itself in judgments when called upon to do so in proceedings initiated by member states, institutions of the EEC and natural or legal persons. On all matters of Community law (qv), courts of the UK defer to relevant decisions of the Court of Justice. See the Treaty of Rome 1957; *Van Duyn* v *Home Office* [1974] 3 All ER 178; O. 114. *See* COMMUNITY LAW, SOURCES OF; EEC.

Court of Justice of the European Communities, references to. See O. 114. The following principles relating to references from English courts were set out in *H.P. Bulmer Ltd v J. Bollinger SA* [1974] Ch 401: (1) only questions of Community law may be referred; (2) questions will not be referred if a decision is not needed to enable the English court to give judgment; (3) questions will not be referred if free from doubt and generally clear; (4) points will not be referred if already decided by the Court of Justice; (5) all circumstances, including, eg, time, interests of justice, must be taken into account. See the EEC Treaty, art. 177. For actions heard directly by the Court, see arts. 173, 175, 178, 215.

Court of King's (Queen's) Bench. Superior court of common law having concurrent jurisdiction in civil actions with the Court of Common Pleas (qv), and criminal jurisdiction. It heard pleas of the Crown, ie, matters relating to wrongs committed against the peace of the King. Merged in the Supreme Court by the J.A. 1873.

court of last resort. A court from which there can be no appeal.

Court of Passage, Liverpool. *See* LIVERPOOL COURT OF PASSAGE.

Court of Pie Poudre. *Pieds poudrés* = dusty feet (probably reference to feet of litigants). Also known as the Piepowder Court. Originally a court of record with jurisdiction in commercial matters arising out of fairs and markets. Survived in the Bristol Tolzey Court (qv) until 1971.

Court of Probate. Usually the Family Division of the High Court. *See* PROBATE.

Court of Protection. Administers the property of mentally disordered persons (within the meaning of the M.H.A. 1983), and consists of a master and other officers. Where the property is of small value, the power of administration may be exercised by the High Court. See the Court of Protection Rules 1982; *Re T.B.* [1967] Ch 247; *Re W.* [1971] Ch 123; and M.H.A. 1983, s. 93.

court of record. Phrase used to refer to a court, the records of which are maintained and preserved, and which may punish for contempt of court (qv). See, eg, the S.C.A. 1981, s. 15(1).

Court of Requests. 1. A court of equity which grew out of the jurisdiction of the King's Council, concerned, in particular, with petitions from the poor. It was suspended in 1642. See *Stepney v Flood* (1598) Cro Eliz 646. 2. Courts of Requests, or of Conscience, were set up to hear small causes. Abolished by the County C.A. 1846.

Court of Session. The supreme civil court of Scotland.

court of summary jurisdiction. Obsolescent expression, now superseded by the term, "magistrates' court" (qv).

Court of Tynwald. *See* TYNWALD, COURT OF.

Court, Patents. *See* PATENTS COURT.

court, payment into. *See* PAYMENT INTO COURT.

court, requesting. *See* REQUESTING COURT.

Court, Rules of. *See* RULES OF COURT.

court, sale by the. *See* SALE BY THE COURT.

courts, county. *See* COUNTY COURTS.

courts' decisions, statement of reasons for. In general there is no duty to state a reason for a judicial decision: see, eg, *Davies v Price* [1958] 1 WLR 434. A statutory duty to state a reason exists by virtue of, eg, the Tribunals and Inquiries Act 1971. See also *R v Medical Appeal Tribunal, ex p Gilmore* [1957] 1 QB 574; *Re Poyser* [1964] QB 467; *Padfield v Minister of Agriculture* [1968] AC 997. There is an increase in circumstances where reasons must be given; see, eg, the C.J.A. 1982, s. 2.

Courts, Divisional. *See* DIVISIONAL COURTS.

courts, domestic. *See* DOMESTIC COURTS.

Courts Fund Office. *See* MONEY LODGED IN COURT.

courts, inferior. *See* INFERIOR COURTS.

courts, juvenile. *See* JUVENILE COURTS.

courts, magistrates'. *See* MAGISTRATES' COURTS.

courts-martial. Courts governed by

the Army and Air Force Acts 1955, the Naval Discipline Act 1957, and the Armed Forces Acts 1971, 1976 and 1981, exercising jurisdiction over members of HM Forces. Murder, manslaughter, rape and treason committed within the UK are tried by the ordinary criminal courts. Trial at a court-martial is generally preceded by an inquiry and takes place before 3–5 officers assisted by a judge-advocate. A finding of guilt must be confirmed by a superior officer. A Courts-Martial Appeal Court was created in 1951; appeal lies from it to the House of Lords. See the Courts-martial (Appeals) Act 1968; the A.J.A. 1977, s. 5; the S.C.A. 1981, s. 145; and the A.J.A. 1982, Sch 8.

courts of civil jurisdiction. These include county courts, the Queen's Bench Division, the Chancery Division, the Family Division, the Court of Appeal (Civil Division) and the House of Lords.

courts of criminal jurisdiction. These include magistrates' courts, the Crown Court, the Divisional Courts, the Court of Appeal (Criminal Division) and the House of Lords.

courts of special jurisdiction. Courts exercising a jurisdiction within specialised fields, eg, courts-martial, ecclesiastical courts.

Courts of the Staple. *See* STAPLE.

courts palatine. *See* PALATINE COURTS.

Courts, prize. *See* PRIZE COURTS.

courts, superior. *See* SUPERIOR COURTS.

court, suit of. *See* SUIT OF COURT.

Court, Supreme. *See* SUPREME COURT.

court, ward of. *See* WARD OF COURT.

covenant. A promise usually contained in a deed. No technical words are necessary to constitute a covenant: *Lant* v *Norris* (1757) 1 Burr 287. It will be implied only where it is apparently necessary to carry out the intention of the deed.

covenant running with the land. A covenant which ran with (or "touched and concerned") land was one which had direct reference to the land, eg, to renew a lease, to repair property, not to build on adjoining land. A covenant of this nature may be enforced if the entire interest in the land is transferred and there is

privity of contract (qv) between the parties. See *Williams* v *Earle* (1868) LR 3 QB 739; *Weg Motors* v *Hales* [1961] Ch 176.

covenants, implied. Covenants (qv) which, although not stated directly, arise in certain types of conveyance. Example: in a conveyance as beneficial owner, implied covenants include a good right to convey, quiet enjoyment, freedom from incumbrances. See the L.P.A. 1925, ss. 76, 77, Sch 2.

covenants, restrictive. *See* RESTRICTIVE COVENANTS.

covenants, usual. Where the phrase is contained in a lease it refers, generally, to convenants to pay rent, to pay the tenant's taxes and rates, to keep and deliver up premises in repair, to allow the lessor to enter and view the state of repairs: *Hampshire* v *Wickens* (1878) 7 Ch D 555. The list, however, is not closed: *Flexman* v *Corbett* [1930] 1 Ch 672. See *Chester* v *Buckingham Travel Ltd* [1981] 1 WLR 96.

cover note. Document issued by insurer to insured, covering risks until the issue of a policy. See *Mackie* v *European Assurance Society* (1869) 21 LT 102.

coverture. Legal status of a woman during marriage (ie, under the authority (cover) of her husband).

credit. 1. Usually an agreed period of time given by a seller to a buyer for payment for goods. As used in the C.C.A. 1974, the word covers all types of loan and financial accommodation, no matter the form in which made. "Running account credit" refers in the Act to facilities under a personal credit agreement, eg, an overdraft or shop budget. "Fixed sum credit" refers to a hire-purchase agreement, or a loan of a fixed amount. "Credit brokerage" is used in the Act to refer to the introduction of individuals desiring to obtain credit or goods on hire to persons who carry on a consumer credit or hire business. See also the S.G.A. 1979, s. 61. "Credit bargain" is any personal credit agreement (qv). 2. A "witness's credit" is his credibility.

credit business, ancillary. *See* ANCIL-LARY CREDIT BUSINESS.

credit card. *See* CREDIT TOKEN.

credit, cross-examination as to. Cross-examination (qv) of a witness designed to discredit him by showing, eg, that his character or background is such that he ought not to be believed. Generally, cross-examination *as to credit* relates to the character of the witness, cross-examination *as to credibility* may be concerned with attributes likely to affect his credibility, (eg, some physical characteristic). See, eg, *Maxwell* v *DPP* [1935] AC 309; *Toohey* v *Metropolitan Police Commissioner* [1965] AC 595. *See* EVIDENCE; CREDIT, RE-ESTABLISHING.

credit limit. Term used under the C.C.A. 1974, s. 10(2) in relation to running account credit to refer to the maximum debit balance which, under a personal credit agreement (qv), is allowed to stand on that account during a period, disregarding a term of the agreement allowing that maximum to be exceeded temporarily.

creditor. One to whom a debt is owing. 1. A secured creditor is one who holds a mortgage (qv) or charge on the debtor's property. An unsecured creditor holds no such charge. 2. A judgment creditor is one in whose favour a judgment for a sum of money has been entered against a debtor. 3. Under the C.C.A. 1974, s. 189(1) a creditor is a person providing credit under a consumer credit agreement or the person to whom his rights and duties under the agreement have passed by assignment or operation of law.

creditors' meeting. Meeting called by the official receiver (qv) to consider a debtor's statement of affairs (qv) within 14 days of the receiving order.

creditors' resolutions. In bankruptcy proceedings, resolutions may be *ordinary*, ie, decided by a majority in value of creditors present personally or by proxy, or *special*, ie, decided by a majority in number and three-fourths in value of the creditors present personally or by proxy. See the B.A. 1914, s. 167.

credit, re-establishing. Attempted restoration of a witness's reputation for veracity after it has been attacked, by cross-examining an attacking witness as to his means of knowledge, by general evidence that the attacking witness is unworthy of credit, or by general evidence that the witness attacked is worthy of credit.

credit reference agency. A business set up to supply information it has collected on a consumer's financial standing. Under the C.C.A. 1974 a consumer is entitled to obtain from a creditor details of any agency from which information was sought. The agency is also obliged to give the consumer a copy of any file kept about him. A consumer can ask the agency to remove any offending entry. See the C.C.A. 1974, ss. 145(8), 189(1); and S.I. 1977/329.

credit, restricted-use. *See* RESTRICTED-USE CREDIT AGREEMENT.

credit sale agreement. "An agreement for the sale of goods, under which the purchase price or part of it is payable by instalments, but which is not a conditional sale agreement": C.C.A. 1974, s. 189.

credits, irrevocable. *See* IRREVOCABLE CREDITS.

credit token. Defined under the C.C.A. 1974, s. 14, as "a card, cheque, voucher, coupon, stamp, form, booklet, or other document or thing" whereby a creditor undertakes, on its production, that he or a third party will supply goods, services or cash. Under s. 51 it is an offence to give a person a credit token if he has not asked for it in writing. A credit token agreement is a regulated agreement (qv) under the C.C.A. 1974, s. 14(2). See the Finance Act 1982, s. 45; and *R* v *Lambie* [1981] 2 All ER 776.

credit, total charge for. The true cost to the debtor of credit provided or to be provided under an actual or prospective consumer credit agreement (qv): C.C.A. 1974, s. 20(1).

credit union. Society registered under the Industrial and Provident Societies Act 1965, having as its objects the promotion of thrift among members, the creation of sources of credit for members, etc.: Credit Unions Act 1979.

cremation. The burning of a dead body in a crematorium. See the Cremation Acts 1902 and 1952; the Human Tissue Act 1961, s. 3; and the Cremation Regulations, S.I. 1965/1146.

crime. Any act or omission resulting from human conduct which is considered in itself or in its outcome to be harmful and which the State wishes to prevent, which renders the person responsible liable to some kind of punishment as the result of proceedings which are usually initiated on behalf of the State and which are designed to ascertain the nature, extent and legal consequence of that person's responsibility. In *Board of Trade* v *Owen* [1957] AC 602, the House of Lords adopted as a definition that given in Halsbury's *Laws of England:* a crime is an unlawful act or default which is an offence against the public and renders the person guilty of the act liable to legal punishment.

crimen laesae majestatis. The crime of "injured majesty", eg, treason (qv).

criminal. 1. One indicted for a crime (qv) and found guilty. 2. Pertaining to a crime, or the character of a crime.

Criminal Appeal, Court of. *See* COURT OF CRIMINAL APPEAL.

criminal bankruptcy order. Where a person is convicted of an offence before the Crown Court (qv), the court may, in addition to dealing with him in any other way, make a criminal bankruptcy order against him. The court must be satisfied that as a result of the offence, loss or damage (not attributable to personal injury) has been suffered by persons whose identity is known to the court and that the amount of the loss or damage exceeds a specified amount. No appeal lies against the making of such an order. A person specified in the order as having suffered loss or damage is treated as a creditor for a debt of that amount provable in the bankruptcy (qv). See the P.C.C.A. 1973, ss. 39–41 and Sch 2, Parts I–III; *DPP* v *Anderson* [1978] 2 All ER 512; *R* v *Reilly* [1982] 3 WLR 149.

criminal conversation. Common law action, abolished in 1857, by which a husband could recover damages against an adulterer.

criminal damage. The offence of destroying or damaging any property belonging to another, intentionally or recklessly and without lawful excuse: Criminal Damage Act 1971, s. 1(1). It is also an offence to threaten without lawful excuse, to destroy or damage property, or to possess anything with intent to destroy or damage property without lawful excuse: ss. 2, 3. See *R* v *Caldwell* [1982] AC 341; and *M* v *Oxford* [1981] RTR 246.

criminal information. Proceedings in the QBD at the suit of the Crown without any previous indictment commenced by the Attorney-General *ex officio* or at the suit of a relator (qv). Generally abolished under the A.J. (Misc. Provs.) A. 1938, s. 12 and the C.L.A. 1967, s. 6.

Criminal Injuries Compensation Board. Set up in 1964 to consider applications for *ex gratia* payments of compensation to victims of crimes of violence. Compensation is assessed on the basis of common law damages. For assessment guidelines see 14th Report of Board 1979 (Cmnd 7396), paras. 21–26. The Board consists of a chairman and eight legally qualified members appointed by the Home Secretary. Application is made by the injured party, or, if he is dead, the spouse or dependants. *See* COMPENSATION.

criminal jurisdiction, courts of. *See* COURTS OF CRIMINAL JURISDICTION.

Criminal Law Revision Committee. Committee of judges and lawyers established in 1959 to advise the Home Secretary on aspects of criminal law and to consider revisions.

criminal libel. *See* LIBEL.

criminal lunatic. Phrase used under the Criminal Lunatics Act 1884, s. 16, replaced by "Broadmoor patient" under the C.J.A. 1948, s. 62(2). *See* BROADMOOR.

criminal proceedings, furnishing of information by prosecutor in. Power to make rules under the Justices of the Peace Act 1979 includes the power to make rules requiring the prosecutor to secure that the accused or his representative is furnished with, or can obtain, advance information concerning the prescribed class of facts and matters of which the prosecutor proposes to adduce evidence: C.L.A. 1977, s. 48(1) (as amended); this provision has yet to be brought into force.

criminal violence. Considered in the context of the Criminal Injuries Compensation Scheme as a crime involving the commission of violence to another person: *R v Criminal Injuries Compensation Board, ex p Clowes* [1977] 3 All ER 854.

cross-action. An action brought by X against Y in reference to a transaction on the basis of which Y has brought an action against X. See *Davies v Hedges* (1871) LR 6 QB 687.

cross-appeals. Appeal against judgment by both parties to a case. See O. 59.

cross-examination. A stage in the examination of a witness (qv) designed to elicit information concerning facts in issue favourable to the party on whose behalf it is conducted, and to throw doubt on the accuracy of evidence given against that party. Known also as "cross-examination to the issue". Counsel may ask in cross-examination leading questions (qv) and questions designed to test knowledge, memory or to elicit existence of bias or previous contradictory statements. *See* CREDIT, CROSS-EXAMINATION AS TO.

cross-holdings. Situation in which two companies own shares in each other. Lawful unless the companies constitute a "group", ie, a relationship of holding and subsidiary to each other. See the Cos.A. 1948, s. 27. *See* SUBSIDIARY COMPANY; HOLDING COMPANY.

cross-offers. *See* OFFERS, CROSS.

Crown. The monarch, or monarchy (qv). Title to the Crown derives from the Act of Settlement 1701 and common law rules of descent. For the domicile and seat of the Crown, see the C.J.J.A. 1982, s. 46. *See* SOVEREIGN.

Crown Agents. The Crown Agents for Oversea Governments and Administrations. They provide commercial, financial and professional services for governments of independent countries, overseas public bodies and international bodies. See the Crown Agents Act 1979; and the Crown Agents (Additional Powers) Order 1981, S.I. 1981/1160.

Crown, Commonwealth and. The Crown is not single and indivisible, but separate in respect of each self-governing territory within the Commonwealth: *R v Secretary of State ex p Indian Association of Alberta* [1982] 2 WLR 641.

Crown copyright. Copyright in respect of publications of government departments, local authorities, etc: Copyright Act 1956, s. 39.

Crown Court. Created by the Courts Act 1971 as part of the Supreme Court and a superior court of record. Its jurisdiction is exercised by any High Court judge, circuit judge or recorder (qqv), or a judge of the High Court, circuit judge or recorder sitting with not more than four JPs: S.C.A. 1981, s. 8. It sits regularly at 90 centres. "There is one Crown Court which is indivisible": *R v Slatter* [1975] 1 WLR 1084. It may hear appeals from magistrates' courts and may sentence persons committed for sentencing by those courts. Appeal lies to the Court of Appeal: see the Criminal Appeal Act 1968, ss. 45, 52.

Crown Court, appeal to. The defendant may appeal against conviction in a magistrates' court. He may appeal only against sentence if he pleaded guilty, or against conviction and sentence if he pleaded not guilty. See the M.C.A. 1980, s. 108. Proceedings involve a complete rehearing of the case. See the S.C.A. 1981, s. 48.

Crown Court rules. Rules relating to procedure and practice in the Crown Court (qv), made by the Crown Court Rule Committee. See the S.C.A. 1981, s. 86; and S.I. 1982/1109.

Crown interest. An estate or interest "belonging to Her Majesty in right of the Crown or belonging to a government department or held in trust for Her Majesty for the purposes of a government department'': H.S.W.A. 1974, s. 72(9).

Crown, liabilities in tort of. ''The Crown shall be subject to all those liabilities in tort to which, if it were a private person of full age and capacity, it would be subject in respect of torts committed by its servants or agents or for any breach of those duties which a master owes to his servants or agents at common law or in respect of any breach of the duties attaching at common law to the ownership, occupation, possession or control of property'': Crown Proceedings Act 1947, s. 2. A Crown servant, for whose acts the Crown is liable, is defined in s. 2(5) as an officer appointed directly or indirectly by the Crown who is paid out of the Consolidated Fund (qv) or moneys provided by Parliament, or any other fund certified by the Treasury for the purposes of the Act. See O. 42; and O. 77.

Crown Office, Master of. *See* MASTER OF CROWN OFFICE.

Crown privilege. The principle of exclusion of evidence, the disclosure of which would be prejudicial to the interest of the Crown. Even where neither party raises objections, the judge may exclude that evidence. See the Crown Proceedings Act 1947; *Duncan* v *Cammell Laird & Co* [1942] AC 624; *Conway* v *Rimmer* [1968] AC 910; *Burmah Oil Co* v *Bank of England* [1980] AC 1090. *See* PRIVILEGE.

Crown prosecutor. Independent official who would head locally-based prosecuting solicitors' departments: suggested in Report of Royal Commission on Criminal Procedure 1981 (Cmnd 8092).

Crown road. ''A road other than a highway to which the public has access by permission granted by the appropriate Crown authority or otherwise granted by or on behalf of the Crown'': Transport Act 1968, s. 149(5) (*b*). See *Kellett* v *Daisy* [1977] RTR 396. *See* ROAD.

Crown servant. An individual who holds office under, or is employed by, the Crown: Cos.A. 1980, s. 72(5).

Crown servants, dismissal of.

''Any appointment as a Crown servant, however subordinate, is terminable at will unless it is expressly otherwise provided by statute'': *Kodeeswaran* v *A.-G. of Ceylon* [1970] AC 1111. See the T.U.L.R.A. 1974, Sch 1, para 33.

Crown service. The service of the Crown, whether within HM dominions or elsewhere: B.N.A. 1981, s. 50(1).

cruelty. Behaviour which when considered in the context of the hearing of a petition for divorce indicates that the respondent has behaved in such a way that the petitioner cannot reasonably be expected to live with the respondent, ie, that the marriage has broken down irretrievably. See the Mat.C.A. 1973, s. 1(2) (*b*). Cruelty has no artificial meaning in relation to proceedings for divorce, but it must be constituted by ''grave and weighty matters''. See *Le Brocq* v *Le Brocq* [1964] 1 WLR 1085. *See* DIVORCE.

cujus est solum ejus est usque ad coelum et ad inferos. Whose is the soil, his it is even to the heaven and the depths of the earth. Exceptions to this general presumption, as a result of which the owner of the soil has a restricted freedom, include, eg, rights of others over his land, statutory restrictions on the use of his land, limitation of the right to the ownership of minerals. See *Mitchell* v *Moseley* [1914] 1 Ch 438; *Woollerton & Wilson Ltd* v *Richard Costain Ltd* [1979] 1 All ER 483; and *Bernstein* v *Skyviews Ltd* [1978] QB 479.

culpable. 1. Involving the breach of a legal duty. 2. Blameworthy.

cum. With.

cum div. 1. Reference to a quotation relating to stocks and shares showing that the price includes dividends and interest accrued to date. 2. A transfer *cum div.* refers to a transfer of shares near the time of the declaration of the dividend by which the transferor is to obtain benefit of that dividend (as contrasted with a transfer *ex div.* (qv)).

cum testamento annexo. See GRANT OF REPRESENTATION.

cumulative legacy. *See* LEGACY, CUMULATIVE.

cur. adv. vult. *Curia advisari vult.* The court wishes to be advised. An abbreviation used in law reports indicating that the court has not given judgment immediately, but has deliberated further.

curator bonis. Trustee appointed to take care of the property and affairs of, eg, absent persons. Not recognised in English law: *Kamouh* v *Associated Electrical Industries* [1980] QB 177.

Curia Regis. The King's Court. The term was applied after the Norman Conquest to a body of the King's tenants-in-chief who assisted in the centralisation and administration of judicial power. It later developed into the King's Council, "the mother of the common law courts". Its last full meeting was in 1640.

current. As applied to legislation, means "for the time being in force."

curtain clauses. Those provisions of the land legislation of 1925 by which certain equitable interests (qv) are placed "behind a legal curtain", ie, those equities are transferred from land to the purchase money or to rents and profits where the land is leased. See the S.L.A. 1925, s. 110(2).

curtesy. A right to tenure "by the curtesy of England" possessed by a widower, giving him a life estate in the land of his deceased wife. The right existed only where the land had not been disposed of by the wife *inter vivos* or under a will, where the wife had been seised in deed and had been entitled to a freehold estate of inheritance (other than as a joint tenant) and where a child capable of succeeding to the land had been born alive. This concept has application now only to an entailed interest. See the A.E.A. 1925, s. 45(1); and the L.P.A. 1925, s. 130(4).

curtilage. Garden, field or yard included within an area surrounding a dwelling-house.

custodianship order. An alternative to adoption, vesting legal custody of a child in the applicant, who is then known as the child's custodian: Ch.A. 1975, s. 33. Those who may apply for an order include relatives or step-parents of the child, foster-parents and any person who applies with the consent of a person having legal custody of the child. The child's parents cannot apply. *See* ADOPTION.

custodian trustee. Office created by the Public Trustee Act 1906. For greater security, trust property can be vested in a custodian trustee who has custody of all securities and documents of title relating to the property and who pays or receives all sums payable to or out of income or capital of the property. Among those who may act as custodian trustee are the Treasury Solicitor (qv) and trust corporations (qv). *See* TRUST.

custody. 1. Control of some thing or person and possession (actual or constructive) in accordance with a law or duty. 2. Confinement or imprisonment of a person.

custody, commit to. *See* COMMIT TO CUSTODY.

custody disputes. Proceedings relating to disputes between parents of a child, a parent and a third party, persons not related to the child (eg, local authority and foster parents). "Where in any proceedings before any court...the custody or upbringing of a minor...is in question, the court in deciding that question shall regard the welfare of the minor as the first and paramount consideration": Guardianship of Minors Act 1971, s. 1; D.P.A. 1978, ss. 2, 6, 7, 15.

custody of child, actual. A person has custody of a child if he has actual possession of his person, whether or not that possession is shared with one or more other persons: Ch.A. 1975, s. 87(1). See the Guardianship of Minors Act 1971.

custody of child, legal. "As respects a child, so much of the parental rights and duties as relate to the person of the child (including the place and manner in which his time is spent)": Ch.A. 1975, s. 86. See also the D.P.A. 1978, s. 36.

custody, split orders for. Orders by the court in which, eg, custody of a child is awarded to both parties, but care and control (qv) is awarded to one. See the Guardianship of Minors

Act 1971, s. 9, as amended; the Mat.C.A. 1973, s. 23; the Guardianship Act 1973, s. 1; and *Cossey* v *Cossey* (1980) 11 Fam L 56.

custody, surrender to. Means "in relation to a person released on bail, surrendering himself into the custody of the court or of the constable (according to the requirements of the grant of bail) at the time and place for the time being appointed for him to do so": Bail Act 1976, s. 2(2). *See* BAIL.

custom. Long established practice considered as unwritten law. In order that a practice might be considered as a valid custom it should have been exercised from time immemorial (qv); have been exercised continuously; have been observed as of right; be reasonable; be contrary neither to statute and common law; be not inconsistent with other accepted customs. Existence of a custom may be proved: by direct evidence by a witness of his personal knowledge of its existence; by a witness testifying to its exercise; by evidence of a comparable custom in a similar trade or locality. See *Mills* v *Mayor of Colchester* (1867) LR 2 CP 567; and *North and South Trust Co* v *Berkeley* [1971] 1 All ER 980.

customary tenure. Tenure based on the custom of a manor, ie, copyhold (qv).

customs duties. Taxes on imports and exports, collected and administered by the Commissioners of Customs and Excise. See, eg, Customs and Excise Management Act 1979; Finance Act 1983, Part I.

cycling, reckless. *See* RECKLESS CYCLING.

cy-près doctrine. *Si près* = so near, as near. A charitable trust (qv) which by its terms is impossible initially or is impracticable, or becomes so subsequently, will not necessarily fail; the court may apply the trust property cy-près by means of a scheme (qv) to some other charitable purpose which resembles the original purpose as nearly as possible. See the Charities Act 1960, s. 14; *Moggridge* v *Thackwell* (1802) 7 Ves 36; *Re Lysaght* [1966] Ch 191; and *Re Woodhams* [1981] 1 WLR 493. *See* TRUST.

D

daily. Means, generally, every day including Sunday. See, eg, *LCC* v *Metropolitan Gas Co* [1903] 2 Ch 532.

damage. Loss or harm, physical or economic, resulting from a wrongful act or default and generally leading to the award of a measure of compensation. Includes the death of, or injury to, any person, including the impairment of physical or mental condition: Animals Act 1971, s. 11.

damage, criminal. *See* CRIMINAL DAMAGE.

damage feasant. Doing damage. Usually applied to animals belonging to X which are wrongfully on Y's land and are doing damage to it. Seizure by Y of X's animals is known as distress damage feasant (qv) which generally suspends the alternative remedy of damages: *Boden* v *Roscoe* [1894] 1 QB 608. Abolished in relation to animals: Animals Act 1971, s. 7 (which substituted a right of detention and sale).

damages. The court's estimated compensation in money for detriment or injury sustained by the plaintiff in contract or tort. Damages may be *general* or *special*. They can be classified as: (1) *nominal*, where no actual damage has been suffered; (2) *contemptuous*, where the amount awarded is derisory (see *Dering* v *Uris* [1964] 2 QB 669); (3) *substantial*, representing compensation for loss actually sustained; (4) *exemplary*, or *vindictive*, or *punitive*, given so as to punish the defendant; (5) *liquidated*, based on the pre-estimate for anticipated breach of contract; (6) *unliquidated*, dependent on the circumstances of the case. See *Rookes* v *Barnard* [1964] AC 1129; *Cassell & Co Ltd* v *Broome* [1972] 1 All ER 801; *Jobling* v *Associated Dairies* [1982] AC 794; and the S.G.A. 1979, Part VI. *See* GENERAL AND SPECIAL DAMAGES; MEASURE OF DAMAGES.

damages and supervening event. In assessing the quantum of damages, account is to be taken of the effects of a supervening, although unrelated, condition or illness: *Jobling* v *Associated Dairies* [1982] AC 794. *See* SUPERVENING EVENT.

damages, exemplary, justification of. "There are certain categories of case in which an award of exemplary damages can serve a useful purpose in vindicating the strength of the law, and thus affording a practical justification for admitting into the civil law a principle which ought logically to belong to the criminal": *Rookes* v *Barnard* [1964] AC 1129.

damages, measure of in contract. *See* MEASURE OF DAMAGES IN CONTRACT.

damages, mitigation of. *See* MITIGATION.

damages, multiple. *See* MULTIPLE DAMAGES.

damages, provisional assessment of. See the S.C.A. 1981, s. 32A (added by the A.J.A. 1982, s. 6) for the power to make a provisional evaluation of damages.

damnosa haereditas. A burdensome inheritance.

damnum absque injuria. Also *damnum sine injuria.* Damage without wrong, ie, damage or loss for which no action can be maintained.

danger, alternative, principle of. *See* ALTERNATIVE DANGER, PRINCIPLE OF.

dangerous machinery. "A part of machinery is dangerous if it is a possible cause of injury to anybody acting in a way in which a human being may be reasonably expected to act in circumstances which may be reasonably expected to occur": *Walker* v *Bletchley Flettons Ltd* [1937] 1 All ER 170. See the Factories Act 1961, s. 14 (under which such machinery must be securely fenced); *Wearing* v *Pirelli* [1977] 1 WLR 48 (employers may be liable under the Factories Act 1961, s. 14(1) where an injury is caused by dangerous machinery even though the injured person did not come into contact with it); and *Mirza* v *Ford Motor Co* [1981] ICR 757.

dangerous species. A species not commonly domesticated in the UK, and whose fully grown animals normally have such characteristics that they are likely, unless restrained, to cause severe damage or that any damage they may cause is likely to be severe: Animals Act 1971, s. 6(2). Where damage is caused by an animal of this type, the keeper is liable: s. 2(1). See the Dangerous Wild Animals Act 1976; and *Cummings v Granger* [1975] 1 WLR 1330. *See* DANGEROUS WILD ANIMALS.

dangerous things, liability relating to. Things likely to do mischief and the resulting liability were considered in *Rylands v Fletcher* (1868) LR 1 Ex 265, in which it was stated that "the person who for his own purposes brings on his lands and collects and keeps there anything likely to do mischief if it escapes, must keep it in at his peril, and, if he does not do so, is prima facie answerable for all the damage which is the natural consequence of its escape". Exceptions to this rule of strict liability include the plaintiff's default or consent; *vis major* (qv); act of God (qv); and the act of a stranger. See *Read v Lyons* [1947] AC 156; and *British Celanese Ltd v A. H. Hunt Ltd* [1969] 1 WLR 959.

dangerous wild animals. Animals enumerated in the Dangerous Wild Animals Act 1976, including, wild dog, wolf, baboon, alligator, crocodile, cobra, lion, tiger, leopard, panther, viper, adder, chimpanzee. No person may keep any dangerous wild animal except under the authority of a licence granted by a local authority: s. 1. The list was revised by the Dangerous Wild Animals Act 1976 (Modification) Order 1981, S.I. 1981/1173.

darrein presentment, assize of. Last presentation. An action, abolished under the Real Property Limitation Act 1833, relating to the presentation by someone other than the person who had last presented (or his heir) of a parson to a church or benefice (qv).

day. A period of 24 hours, from midnight to midnight. "The law maketh no fraction of a day": Coke. See *Re Shurey* [1918] 1 Ch 266. For "time of day", see the I.A. 1978, s. 9.

day certain. Fixed or appointed day.

days, clear. *See* CLEAR DAYS.

days of grace. The days immediately following the day on which a payment becomes due, allowed for payment to be made. Usually three days in the case of a bill of exchange (qv).

day training centre. Premises at which persons may be required to attend by a probation order containing an instruction under the P.C.C.A. 1973, s. 4. See *Cullen v Rogers* [1982] 1 WLR 729. The court's powers have been extended by the C.J.A. 1982, s. 65, Sch 11. *See* PROBATION.

day, year and waste. A right of the Crown, now abolished, to the profits of land of a person convicted of treason or felony, and the right to commit waste (qv).

D.C. Divisional Court (qv).

dead rent. Rent which must be paid under a mining lease even though the mine is not worked.

dealer. "A person carrying on a business of selling goods, whether by wholesale or by retail": Resale Prices Act 1976, s. 24(1).

dealer, motor. A person carrying on the business of selling or supplying mechanically propelled vehicles: Vehicles (Excise) Act 1971, s. 38(1).

death. Cessation of the life processes. Not defined by statute. (Note, however, an American definition: "A person will be considered medically and legally dead if, in the opinion of a physician, based on ordinary standards of medical practice, there is the absence of spontaneous brain function . . .": *Kansas Statutes* 1971.) See, eg, the Human Tissue Act 1961; *Report of the Committee on Death Certification* (Cmnd 4810); *Report on Transplantation Problems* (Cmnd 4106); [1976] 2 BMJ 1187.

death duties. Estate duty paid on property which passed at death. Replaced by capital transfer tax (qv).

death penalty. *See* CAPITAL PUNISHMENT.

death, presumption of. *See* PRESUMPTION OF DEATH.

death, proof of. Procedure whereby

death is established in evidence: by the production of the death certificate and proof of identity; by presumption ·of death (qv); by someone who has identified the corpse; by someone present at its occurrence.

death, registration of. Procedure, which must be completed within five days (or four days if the registrar has been notified in writing of the death), consisting of the furnishing of the following particulars: date and place of death; name, surname, sex, date, place of birth, address and occupation of the deceased; cause of death; name, surname, qualifications, address and signature of informant; signature of registrar; date of registration. See the Births and Deaths Registration Act 1953.

death, survival of causes of action on. In general, on the death of a person, all causes of action subsisting against or vested in him, survive against, or for the benefit of, his estate (save causes of action for defamation). Exemplary damages will not be awarded in favour of a deceased plaintiff's estate. See the Law Reform (Misc. Provs.) Act 1934, s. 1; and the Law Reform (Misc. Provs.) Act 1970.

de bene esse. Of well-being. Used in relation to that which is done subject to some possible future exception. Example: the taking of evidence for future use (see O.39, r.1). *See* DEPOSITION.

debenture. Document under a company's seal acknowledging indebtedness for a capital sum, undertaking to repay on an ascertainable date and to pay interest at a fixed rate. Debentures are not part of a company's capital. They rank first for capital and interest and are usually secured by a charge (qv) on company assets. Debenture holders are creditors of the company. Power to issue debentures is usually stated in express terms in the memorandum of association (qv). *Mortgage debentures* give the holder security by way of charge on company's property; *naked debentures* are simply undertakings to repay. See the Cos. A. 1948, s. 455.

debenture stock. An obligation or

debt due from a company and secured by trust deed.

de bonis asportatis. Of goods carried away. A writ of trespass (qv) in relation to chattels wrongfully taken.

de bonis non administratis. Of goods not administrable. Grant made where an administrator, with or without a will annexed, dies, or where an administrator cannot be found: *Re Loveday* [1900] P 154. In effect, a grant limited to unadministered property when a previous grant has ceased prematurely. *See* GRANT.

de bonis propriis. From one's own goods. Refers to a judgment against, eg, an executor, to be satisfied "out of his own pocket".

debt. A sum that one person is bound to pay to another. "Debt normally has one or other of two meanings: it can mean an obligation to pay money or it can mean a sum of money owed": *DPP* v *Turner* [1973] 3 All ER 124. A *specialty debt* is created by deed; a debt of *record* is, eg, a judgment debt.

debt-adjusting. Under the C.C.A. 1974, ss. 145(5), 189(1), the activities carried on by a person who acts as an intermediary between an individual and the creditor with a view to the discharge of a debt due.

debt-collecting. Under the C.C.A. 1974, ss. 145(7), 189(1), the taking of a step to procure payment of debts due under regulated and exempt credit or hire agreements (qqv).

debt-counselling. Under the C.C.A. 1974, ss. 145(6), 189(1), the giving of advice to debtors or hirers about the liquidation of debts due under regulated and exempt credit or hire agreements.

debt, imprisonment for. Generally abolished under the Debtors Act 1869. See also the A.J.A. 1970, s. 11.

debtor. One who owes a debt. Under the C.C.A. 1974, s. 189(1), it means "the individual receiving credit under a consumer credit agreement or the person to whom his rights and duties under the agreement have passed by assignment or operation of law, and in relation to a prospective consumer credit agreement (qv) includes the prospective debtor.''

debtor–creditor agreement. Under the C.C.A. 1974, s. 13, a regulated consumer credit agreement (qv) is a restricted use credit agreement falling within s. 11(1) (*b*) of the Act, but not made by a creditor under pre-existing arrangements, or in contemplation of future arrangements, between himself and the supplier, or a restricted-use agreement within s. 11(1) (*c*), or an unrestricted-use credit agreement, which is not made by a creditor under pre-existing arrangements between himself and a person (the "supplier") other than the debtor in the knowledge that the credit is to be used to finance a transaction between the debtor and supplier.

debtor–creditor–supplier agreement. Agreement, under the C.C.A. 1974, s. 12, whereby a creditor and supplier are the same person, or have a business link.

debtor in bankruptcy. Any person who at the time when an act of bankruptcy (qv) was done or suffered by him was personally present in England, or ordinarily resided, or had a place there, or was carrying on business in England (personally or by an agent) or was a member of a firm carrying on business there: B.A. 1914, s. 1(2).

debtor, judgment. *See* JUDGMENT DEBTOR.

debtors, harassment of. *See* HARASSMENT OF DEBTORS.

debt, writ of. Writ created in the twelfth century, brought on obligations such as debt acknowledged by deed under seal. Became virtually obsolete in the fifteenth century.

decedent. A deceased person.

deceit. A tort arising from a false statement of fact made by one person, knowingly or recklessly, with the intent that it shall be acted on by another who, as a result, suffers damage. See the Misrepresentation Act 1967, s. 2(1); *Derry* v *Peek* (1889) 14 App Cas 337; *Bradford Building Society* v *Borders* [1941] 2 All ER 205. *See* DECEIVE.

deceit, writ of. Writ, which originated in the thirteenth century, used against one who had utilised legal proceedings in order to deceive another. See *Bailey* v *Merrell* (1616) 3 Bulstr. Abolished by the Real Property Limitation Act 1833, s. 36.

deceive. To induce a person to believe that a thing is true which is false, or a thing is false which is true, contrary to that which the person practising such deceit knows or believes to be the case. See *Re London & Globe Finance Corpn Ltd* [1903] 1 Ch 728; *Welham* v *DPP* [1961] AC 103.

deception, evasion of liability by. Where a person by any deception dishonestly secures the remission of the whole or part of any existing liability to make a payment, whether his own liability or another's, or with intent to make permanent default in whole or part on any existing liability to make a payment, or with intent to let another do so, dishonestly induces the creditor or any person claiming payment on behalf of the creditor to wait for payment (whether or not the due date for payment is deferred) or to forgo payment; or dishonestly obtains any exemption from or abatement of liability to make a payment; he shall be guilty of an offence: Th.A. 1978, s. 2. See *R* v *Holt & Lee* [1981] 1 WLR 1000.

deception, obtaining property by. It is an offence under the Th.A. 1968 dishonestly to obtain property by deception or to obtain a pecuniary advantage by deception: ss. 15, 16. Deception means, in this context, "any deception (whether deliberate or reckless) by words or conduct as to fact or as to law, including a deception as to the present intentions of the person using the deception or any other person": s. 15 (4). See *R* v *Charles* [1977] AC 177; *Levene* v *Pearcey* [1976] Crim LR 63; *R* v *Davies* [1982] 1 All ER 513; *R* v *Waites* [1982] Crim LR 369. *See* PECUNIARY ADVANTAGE.

deception, obtaining services by. A person who by any deception dishonestly obtains services from another is guilty of an offence: Th.A. 1978, s. 1(1). It is an obtaining of services where the other is induced to confer a benefit by doing some act, or causing or permitting some act to be done, on the understanding that the benefit has been or will be paid for: s.

1(2). (This replaces the Th.A. 1968, s. 16(2)(*a*).)

decision, judicial. See JUDICIAL DECISION, REQUISITES OF.

decisions of EEC. See COMMUNITY LEGISLATION, FORMS OF.

declaration. 1. A statement of claims in proceedings. 2. A decision of the court. 3. A discretionary remedy declaring the position in law based on given facts: *Vine* v *National Dock Labour Board* [1957] AC 488. See O. 15, r. 16; and *Imperial Tobacco* v *A.-G.* [1981] AC 718. 4. A formal statement, eg, to assert a right. 5. A statement or testimony made by a witness not under oath. 6. A declaration of trust is an acknowledgment by a person that he holds property in trust (qv) for another. It may be implied from conduct. See *Gee* v *Liddell* (1866) 35 Beav 621. 7. A statutory declaration is one made before a Commissioner for Oaths (qv) in prescribed form. See the Statutory Declarations Act 1835; and the Th.A. 1968, s. 27(4).

declaration against interest. Statements of a deceased person are generally admissible as evidence if against his proprietary or pecuniary interests. See *Ward* v *H. S. Pitt & Co* [1913] 2 KB 130.

declaration concerning pedigree. An exception to the hearsay rule, whereby an oral or written statement of a deceased person relating to the pedigree of a relative, which is the subject of dispute, is admissible in evidence. The declarant must be a blood relation, or the spouse of a blood relation, of the person whose pedigree is in dispute. See the Civil Evidence Act 1968, s. 9; and *Johnson* v *Lawson* (1824) 2 Bing 86.

declaration concerning public or general rights. An exception to the hearsay rule, whereby an oral or written statement by a deceased person concerning the reputed existence of a right, public or general, is admissible in evidence provided it was made before the proceedings had commenced and the declarant had competent knowledge. See, eg, *R* v *Bedfordshire (Inhabitants)* (1855) 4 E & B 535. *See* EVIDENCE, HEARSAY.

declaration in course of duty. An exception to the hearsay rule, whereby a written or oral statement of a deceased person made in pursuance of a duty to act and record those acts, and made contemporaneously with those acts, may be admissible in evidence. See, eg, *Price* v *Torrington* (1703) 1 Salk 285. *See* EVIDENCE, HEARSAY.

declaration of intention. In relation to contract, this means merely that an offer will be made or invited in the future. It does not imply that an offer is made now. See *Harris* v *Nickerson* (1873) LR 8 QB 286.

declaration judgment. A judgment which merely states the court's opinion on a question of law, or declares the rights, existing or future, of the parties. It does not generally carry an order for enforcement. Action for declaration may be commenced by writ or originating summons. See O. 15, r. 16.

declaratory theory of common law. The theory "that every case was governed by a relevant rule of law, existing somewhere and discoverable somehow, provided sufficient learning and intellectual rigour were brought to bear": *Jones* v *Secretary of State for Social Services* [1972] AC 944. *See* COMMON LAW; JUS DICERE.

decree. 1. A law. 2. A judgment or order of the court. 3. In relation to dissolution of marriage, *decree absolute* is the decree which finally dissolves the marriage. It may be issued after six weeks from the day following the grant of a *decree nisi (nisi* = unless)— a type of conditional decree requiring something further to be done to make it absolute. (The period may be shortened for some substantial reason.) Recession of decree nisi may be granted if the petitioner misled respondent about some relevant matter. See the Mat.C.A. 1973, ss. 1(5), 10(1); and the Matrimonial Causes Rules 1977, rr. 66–67.

decrees absolute, central index of. Index of decrees absolute kept at the Divorce Registry. Any person is entitled to require a search to be made therein and to be furnished with a certificate of the result of the search: Matrimonial Causes Rules 1977, r. 67(3).

decrees nisi, rescission by consent. Orders of the court made by application of either party to a judge, where, after a decree nisi is pronounced but before it is made absolute, a reconciliation has been effected between the petitioner and respondent: Matrimonial Causes Rules 1977, r. 64(1).

dedication of way. The creation of a public right of way by "dedication and acceptance". It may be established at common law on proof of dedication by the owner to the public and of acceptance by the public, usually shown by user: *Cubitt* v *Lady Maxse* (1873) LR 8 CP 704. Under the Highways Act 1980, s. 31, the way is deemed to have been dedicated on proof of 20 years' enjoyment of way over land as of right and without physical obstruction.

dedimus. Dedimus potestatem. We have given the power. Writ conferring power on justices to administer oaths, or on commissioners.

de donis conditionalibus. The Statute of Westminster II 1285 provided that a grant of an estate "to X and the heirs of his body" would create a fee tail (qv) which descended on the death of the tenant in tail to his lineal heirs. The fee ceased to exist if the issue of the original tenant died out.

deed. An instrument signed, sealed, in writing (which includes print), executed and delivered, relating to a bargain, contract, transfer, etc. A *deed poll* is a declaration of a party's intention, eg, to alter his name. A *deed of conveyance* comprises: exordium (commencement); recitals; testatum; parcels; general words; habendum; tenendum; reddendum; conditions; powers; covenants; testimonium (qqv).

deed of gift. A deed which effects the transfer of property by way of gift.

deeds of arrangement. *See* ARRANGEMENT, DEEDS OF.

deemed. Supposed. "Sometimes the word is used to impose for the purpose of a statute an artificial construction of a word or phrase that would otherwise not prevail. Some-times it is used to put beyond doubt a particular construction that might otherwise be uncertain. Sometimes it is used to give a comprehensive description that includes what is obvious, what is uncertain and what is, in the ordinary sense, impossible": *St. Alwyn* v *A.-G. (No. 2)* [1952] AC 15. See *Barclays Bank* v *IRC* [1961] AC 509.

de facto. In fact; in reality.

defamation. The publishing of a statement which tends to lower a person in the estimation of right-thinking members of society. It may be actionable without proof of special damage where it involves, eg, imputation of a criminal offence punishable with imprisonment. Defences may be based on justification (or truth), privilege (absolute or qualified), fair comment (qqv). See the Defamation Act 1952; O. 82; *Youssoupoff* v *Metro-Goldwyn-Mayer Pictures Ltd* (1934) 50 TLR 581; and *Sim* v *Stretch* [1936] 2 All ER 1237. *See* LIBEL; SLANDER.

defamation, unintentional. *See* UNINTENTIONAL DEFAMATION.

default. Failure to do something required by law, eg, non-appearance in court on the required day. Judgment in default may be given against a party by reason of non-acknowledgment of service within the time limit (14 days from service of the writ). A default judgment may be *interlocutory* (ie, final as to liability, but leaving the amount due to the plaintiff to be assessed) or *final* (as to liability and quantum). The procedure is not generally available (unless leave is obtained) in cases relating to: hire-purchase and conditional sale agreement (see O. 83); mortgage actions commenced by writ (see O. 88, r. 7); tort actions between spouses during the subsistence of the marriage (see O. 89, r. 2); cases against the Crown (see O. 77, r. 9). See O. 13, O. 14. For imprisonment for default of payment of fines see the M.C.A. 1980, s. 82 and the P.C.C.A. 1973, s. 31 (as amended by the C.J.A. 1982, s. 69).

default notice. Term used under the C.C.A. 1974, s. 87, relating to a debtor's breach of agreement, whereby he must be issued with a default notice in the prescribed form if the creditor wishes to terminate the agreement, to recover possession or to enforce a security. Under s. 88(1) the notice must specify: the nature of the alleged breach; the action required to remedy it; the date before which that action is to be taken; the sum payable as compensation for breach.

default of acknowledgment of service. *See* DEFAULT.

default summons. Procedure by which a debt may be recovered in the county court (qv).

default, wilful. *See* WILFUL DEFAULT.

defeasance. Ending of an interest in property in accordance with conditions stipulated in a separate instrument relating to a deed.

defeasible. Capable of being annulled.

defect. Irregularity or fault. "Lack or absence of something essential to completeness": *Tate* v *Latham* (1897) 66 LJQB 351. A *patent defect* is one that ought to be discovered by ordinary vigilance. A *latent defect* is one that could not be discovered by reasonable examination. See *Ashburner* v *Sewell* [1891] 3 Ch 405.

defective. One suffering from severe subnormality, arrested or incomplete development of mind so that he is incapable of living an independent life: M.H.A. 1959. See M.H.A. 1983, Part I.

defective equipment, liability for. Under the Employers' Liability (Defective Equipment) Act 1969 an employer may be liable for defective equipment and liable in damages to an employee injured by it.

defective goods. *See* FITNESS FOR PURPOSE.

defective premises, liability for. Under the Defective Premises Act 1972 there is a duty to build premises properly and that duty is not abated by the subsequent disposal (including letting, assignment or surrender of the tenancy) of those premises by the person who owes that duty. "Premises" in the 1972 Act means the whole premises, land and buildings, unless there is clear language to restrict its meaning: *Smith* v *Bradford Metropolitan Council* (1982) 44 P & CR 171.

defective products. *See* PRODUCTS LIABILITY.

defectum sanguinis. Failure of issue. *See* ESCHEAT.

defence. Generally, the defendant's opposing or denying the truth of the prosecutor's or plaintiff's case. For service of a defence, see O. 18, r. 2. *See* STATEMENT OF DEFENCE.

defence, withdrawal of. *See* WITHDRAWAL OF DEFENCE.

defendant. Includes any person served with a writ of summons or process, or served with notice of, or entitled to attend, any proceedings. Applied generally to person charged with offences.

defendant, compelling appearance of. Appearance may be compelled by summons, warrant for arrest and arrest without warrant. See the Magistrates' Courts Rules 1981, rr. 94–98; and the M.C.A. 1980, s. 1.

defend, leave to. *See* LEAVE TO DEFEND.

deferred debts. Debts deferred under statute until those with priority are paid in full. See, eg, the B.A. 1914, s. 36.

deferred shares. Shares, now rarely issued, carrying a right to all, or a substantial proportion of, profits after ordinary shares have received a dividend. Known also as "founders' shares". The number of such shares must usually be stated in the prospectus (qv): Cos.A. 1948, s. 38.

deferring of sentence. Under the P.C.C.A. 1973, s. 1, the Crown Court (qv) or magistrates' court (qv) can defer passing sentence on an offender (with his consent) to enable the court, in determining his sentence, to consider any change in his circumstances or conduct after conviction (qv). See also the C.J.A. 1982, s. 63; *R* v *Fairhead* [1975] 2 All ER 737; and *R* v *Crosby* [1975] Crim LR 246.

defraud. "To deprive a person dishonestly of something which is his or of something to which he is or would or might but for the perpetration of the fraud be entitled": *Scott* v *Metropolitan Police Commissioner* [1974] 3 All ER 1032. See *R* v *Allsop* (1976) 64 Cr App R 29.

de jure. By right; by lawful title.

delay. *See* LACHES.

del credere agent. *Del credere* = of belief; of trust. An agent who receives a higher rate of commission than that which is usual, in return for a guarantee that his principal will receive due payment for goods sold. See, eg, *Harburg India Rubber Comb Co* v *Martin* [1902] 1 KB 778.

delegated legislation. Legislation made by some person or body (eg, a minister or local authority) under authority delegated by Parliament under statute. It may take the form of statutory Orders in Council (qv), departmental orders, regulations, rules. Known also as "subordinate legislation". Parliamentary control is exercised under, eg, the Statutory Orders (Special Procedure) Acts 1945 and 1965, the Laying of Documents before Parliament (Interpretation) Act 1948, and by the Joint Scrutinising Committee of the Commons.

delegated legislation, invalidation of. Procedure whereby courts declare legislation void as *ultra vires* the authorising statute. See, eg, *Hoffman-La Roche & Co* v *Secretary of State for Trade* [1974] 2 All ER 1128.

delegated legislation, justification of. Stated in the *Report on Ministers' Powers* 1932, to be: pressure on Parliament's time; technicality of much legislation; ease of modification in light of experience; the need for occasional arbitrary and swift action in administrative matters.

delegated legislation, publication of. It is the duty of the Queen's Printer of Acts of Parliament (ie, Stationery Office Controller) to print and sell copies of statutory instruments: Statutory Instruments Act 1946, s. 2. Exceptions: local instruments; those the publication of which is certified by the minister as unnecessary or undesirable. See *Simmonds* v *Newell* [1953] 2 All ER 38.

delegation. The investing of one person with appropriate and sufficient authority to act for another.

delegation, principle of. An aspect of vicarious and strict liability (qqv). "When an absolute offence has been created by Parliament, then the person on whom a duty is thrown is responsible, whether he has delegated or whether he has acted through a servant; he is absolutely liable regardless of any intent or knowledge or *mens rea*. The principle of delegation comes into play, and only comes into play, in cases where, though the statute uses words which import knowledge or intent such as in this case 'knowingly' or in some other cases 'permitting' or 'suffering' and the like, cases to which knowledge is inherent, nevertheless it has been held that a man cannot get out of the responsibilities which have been put on him by delegating those responsibilities to another": *R* v *Winson* [1968] 1 All ER 197. See also *Vane* v *Yiannopoulos* [1964] 3 All ER 820; *Howker* v *Robinson* [1972] 2 All ER 786. *See* MENS REA.

delegatus non potest delegare. A delegate cannot delegate. A trustee (qv), however, may appoint an agent, subject to the terms of the trust instrument, to carry out trust business: Tr.A. 1925, ss. 23, 25. "The law is not that trustees cannot delegate: it is that trustees cannot delegate unless they have authority to do so": *Pilkington* v *IRC* [1962] 3 All ER 622. See also the L.P.A. 1925, ss. 29, 30; and the Powers of Attorney Act 1971, s. 9.

delict. A wrongful act.

deliverable state. *See* GOODS, DELIVERABLE STATE.

delivery. The voluntary transfer of possession, ie, the putting of property into the legal possession of another. It may be actual or constructive, eg, by symbolic delivery (of a bill of lading).

delivery of a deed. Usually performed by the person executing the deed placing his finger on the seal, saying at the same time: "I deliver this as my act and deed." In essence it is "an act done so as to evince an intention to be bound": *Vincent* v *Premo Enterprises Ltd* [1969] 2 All ER 941. "After a deed is written and sealed, if it be not delivered, all the rest is to no purpose": *Termes de la Ley*. See *D'Silva* v *Lister House Development Ltd* [1971] Ch 17. *See* DEED.

delivery of goods. Whether it is for the buyer to take possession of the goods or for the seller to send them to the buyer is a question depending in each case on the contract, express or implied, between the parties: S.G.A. 1979, s. 29(1).

delivery, writ of. Writ of execution enforcing a judgment for delivery of goods by directing the sheriff (qv) to seize goods and deliver to the plaintiff, or for recovery of their assessed value. See O. 45, r. 4. A writ of *specific delivery* directs the seizure of goods stated in the writ, but with no alternative for payment of assessed value. *See* JUDGMENTS, ENFORCEMENT OF.

delusion. Continuing self-deception relating to some matter, in spite of evidence to the contrary. 1. In the case of a testator (qv), where the delusion does not result in the impairing of his understanding and where it relates to matters which do not involve his property, he may make a valid will: *Smee* v *Smee* (1879) 28 WR 703. See also *Banks* v *Goodfellow* (1870) LR 5 QBD 549. 2. For criminal acts committed under an insane delusion, see the M'Naghten Rules (qv).

demanding with menaces. *See* BLACKMAIL.

demand, liquidated. *See* LIQUIDATED DEMAND.

demesne. A term used in old land law to signify the lands of a manor which the lord occupied.

demesne, ancient. *See* ANCIENT DEMESNE.

de minimis non curat lex. The law does not concern itself with trifles. The so-called *de minimis principle* refers, eg, to circumstances in which the police tend to refrain from prosecuting: *Delaroy-Hall* v *Tadman* [1969] 2 QB 208; *R* v *Anderson* [1972] RTR 113; *R* v *Carver* [1978] QB 472.

demise. 1. Transference, on the death of a monarch, of the royal dignity. 2. Transfer by grant of a lease (qv) of lands. 3. Death.

demonstrative legacy. A gift, in its nature general, directed to be satisfied or paid out of a specified fund or specified part of the testator's property. Example: "£1,000 out of my account with Barclays". See *Re Webster* [1937] 1 All ER 602. *See* LEGACY.

demur. To deliver a plea by demurrer, ie, an allegation that a pleading shows no good cause of action. Now virtually obsolete. See O. 18; *R* v *Deputy Chairman of Inner London QS, ex p Metropolitan Police Commissioner* [1969] 3 All ER 1537. *See* PLEADINGS.

demurrage. An agreed sum to be paid by the charterer to the shipowner as liquidated damages (qv) for any delay beyond a time stipulated in the contract. See *Dias Compania Naviera SA* v *Dreyfus* [1978] 1 All ER 724; *The Sea Pioneer* [1982] Lloyd's Rep 13.

demurrer. *See* DEMUR.

denizen. An alien who had obtained letters patent from the Sovereign ("letters of denization") which gave him the status of a British citizen.

de novo. Anew.

deodand. *Deo dandum* = that must be given to God. Any inanimate instrument by which a killing had been effected, which was forfeit to the Crown. Abolished in 1846.

department, government. An administrative body which gives effect to government policy, usually headed by a departmental minister (qv) or permanent official. Examples: Ministry of Defence, Department of Education and Science.

departure. A party's pleading containing an allegation of fact, or raising a new ground or claim, inconsistent with a previous pleading of his. See O. 18, r. 10(1); *Herbert* v *Vaughan* [1972] 1 WLR 1128.

dependant. One who relies for his support on another. Within the meaning of the Inheritance (Provision for Family and Dependants) Act 1975, those who may apply for financial provision from the deceased's estate are: wife or husband, or former wife or husband who has not remarried, or child of the deceased; any person (not being a child of the deceased) who, in the case of any marriage to which the deceased was at any time a party, was treated by the deceased as a child of the family in relation to that marriage; any other person who immediately before the death of the deceased was being maintained, either wholly or partly by the deceased: s. 1.

See *Re Beaumont* [1980] Ch 444; and *Re Coventry* [1980] Ch 461.

dependent relative revocation. Where the revocation of a will is relative to another will and is intended to be dependent upon the fact of that other will being valid, then unless that other will takes effect, the revocation is ineffective. Example: the testator (qv) destroys his will with the intention of making another one, but then fails to make another will. The original will is considered as unrevoked. See *Dixon* v *Solicitor to the Treasury* [1905] P 42; *Re Allen* (1962) 106 SJ 115; *Re Jones* [1976] Ch 200; *Re Carey* (1977) 121 SJ 173; and the *Law Reform Committee* 1980, Cmnd 7902. *See* REVOCATION OF WILL.

dependent territory. Any territory outside the British Isles for whose external relations the Government of the UK are responsible. For the list see the B.N.A. 1981, Sch 6.

deponent. One who gives evidence by deposition (qv) on affidavit (qv).

deportation. Expulsion from a country. "The taking of the person in question from the country from which he is deported to some other place": *R* v *Secretary of State for Foreign Affairs, ex p Greenberg* [1947] 2 All ER 550.

deportation from the UK. Non-patrials only are liable to be removed from the UK under the following circumstances: where over 17, following conviction for an offence punishable with imprisonment where the court recommends deportation; where another member of their family is to be deported; where the Home Secretary deems deportation conducive to the public good; where they have remained beyond the time limit on a stay or failed to comply with a condition of admission. The court's recommendation for deportation of an offender from any EEC country is subject to EEC restrictions on interference with free movement of workers: *R* v *Bouchereau* [1978] 2 WLR 251. See the Immigration Act 1971, s. 3; EEC Directive 64/221, art 3(1); the C.J.A. 1982, s. 64, Sch 10; *R* v *Secretary of State for Home Department ex p Hosenball* [1977] 1 WLR 766; and *R* v *Nazari* [1980] 1 WLR 1366.

deportation, right of appeal against. Procedure whereby the person against whom the deportation order has been made exercises the right of appeal, in the first instance, to the adjudicators appointed by the Home Secretary. If dissatisfied with the adjudication, the appellant or Home Secretary may appeal to the Immigrants Appeal Tribunal. See the Immigration Act 1971, ss. 12–22; and *R* v *Home Secretary ex p Santillo* [1981] QB 778.

depose. To make a deposition (qv) or a statement on oath.

deposit. 1. A sum of money paid on terms under which it will be repaid, with or without interest or a premium, and either on demand or at a time or in circumstances agreed by or on behalf of the person making the payment and the person receiving it, and which are not referable to the provision of property or the giving of security: Banking Act 1979, s. 1(4). 2. Payment made in a contract for sale of land, so as to bind a bargain. See the L.P.A. 1925, s. 49(2); *Howe* v *Smith* (1884) 27 Ch D 89; *Barrington* v *Lee* [1971] 3 All ER 1231. 3. Use of title deeds as security for a loan (which creates an equitable charge (qv)). 4. In a contract for sale of goods, "a guarantee that the purchaser means business": *Soper* v *Arnold* (1889) 61 LT 702. 5. Any sum payable by a debtor or hirer by way of deposit or down payment: C.C.A. 1974, s. 189(1).

deposition. A statement made on oath before a magistrate or other official of the court by a witness. 1. In civil cases, depositions *de bene esse* (qv) may be read at the trial by consent or if the witness is dead or unable to attend because of sickness. See O. 39. 2. In criminal cases, depositions may be read, eg, if the witness is insane, or too ill to attend. In the case of certain types of offences against children, the child's deposition may be read if signed by an examining magistrate or if the court is satisfied that the child's attendance would involve serious risk to health. See the M.C.A. 1980, ss. 103, 105; the Magistrates' Courts

Rules 1981, rr. 7, 33. See also the Civil Evidence Act 1972, s. 1. *See* EVIDENCE.

deposit-taking business. Business in the course of which money received by way of deposit (qv) is lent to others or any other activity of the business is financed out of the capital of or interest on money received by way of deposit. In general, no person may accept a deposit in the course of carrying on a business which is a deposit-taking business (exceptions include the Bank of England, recognised banks (qv), licensed institutions): Banking Act 1979, ss. 1, 2. For the minimum criteria, see Sch 2.

deprave. To corrupt. "If someone is made or kept morally bad or worse by something they are depraved by it": *R* v *Sumner* [1977] Crim LR 362. See the Obscene Publications Act 1959. *See* OBSCENITY.

depravity, exceptional. Conduct on the part of the respondent which, under the Mat.C.A. 1973, s. 3, may allow the presentation of a petition for divorce before the expiration of a period of three years from date of marriage. It involves conduct which may establish in any subsequent divorce suit, irretrievable breakdown of the marriage. See, eg, *Bowman* v *Bowman* [1949] 2 All ER 128; *W.* v *W.* [1967] P 291; *C.* v *C.* [1980] Fam 23 (for the suggestion that the concept is archaic); and *Fay* v *Fay* [1982] 3 WLR 206 (the depravity must be something out of the ordinary).

deprivation of citizenship. Procedure whereby the Secretary of State may remove the status of British and British Dependent Territories citizenship from those registered or naturalised as such if he is satisfied that the registration or naturalisation was obtained by fraud, false representation or concealment of a material fact, or if he is satisfied of their disloyalty, disaffection or where the person has served a year's imprisonment within five years of registration or naturalisation: B.N.A. 1981, s. 40. See S.I. 1982/987.

deprivation of property, order for. Where a person is convicted of an offence punishable with not less than two years' imprisonment and the court is satisfied that the property in his possession or control at the time of his apprehension had been used to commit or facilitate the commission of the offence or was intended by him to be used for that purpose, an order depriving him of that property may be made: P.C.C.A. 1973, s. 43. See *R* v *Hinde* [1977] RTR 328; *R* v *Khan* [1982] 1 WLR 1403 (the order cannot be made to deprive a convicted person of any interest in real property).

derelict. A thing voluntarily abandoned or thrown away by its owner.

derivative action. A company's action, the right to which is derived from the company, brought by minority shareholder(s). It is an exception to the rule that the proper plaintiff in respect of a wrong alleged to be done to a company is, prima facie, the company. See *Foss* v *Harbottle* (1843) 2 Hare 461; *Edwards* v *Halliwell* [1950] 2 All ER 1064; and *Prudential Assurance* v *Newman Industries* [1982] Ch 204.

derivative deed. One deed of settlement or conveyance (qv) related to another document of settlement or conveyance, which enlarges, confirms or otherwise alters it.

derivative trust. A sub-trust (qv).

derogate. To annul or restrict the strength of an obligation or right. "No man may derogate from his own grant": *Wheeldon* v *Burrows* (1879) 12 Ch D 31.

descendant. A person descended from an ancestor (qv). See *Re Eyton* [1876] WN 142. Generally used to refer to lineal descendants only.

descent. Devolution (qv) of an estate by inheritance and not by will. Prior to their abolition by the A.E.A. 1925, s. 45, the rules were: descent was traced from the last purchaser (qv); priority of males, so that the eldest took to exclusion of others in the same degree; lineal descendants of purchaser represented him; lineal ancestors took after lineal descendants; paternal were preferred to maternal ancestors.

descent, citizenship by. *See* CITIZENSHIP, BRITISH, ACQUISITION BY DESCENT.

description, sale by. Refers to a

specific article sold as an article which corresponds to a description, or to articles to be identified by reference to a certain description. There is an implied condition (qv) that, where there is a sale of goods, they shall correspond with their descriptions: S.G.A. 1979, ss. 13, 14. See *Jones* v *Clarke* (1858) 2 H & N 725; *Varley* v *Whipp* [1900] 1QB 513.

desertion. 1. Continual absence from cohabitation (qv), which may be a ground for a decree of divorce or judicial separation (qv). "Separation without consent and just cause": *Pheasant* v *Pheasant* [1972] 1 All ER 587. It is a withdrawal not from a place but a state of things: *Mummery* v *Mummery* [1942] P 107. Characterised by the fact that the common life and common home have ceased to exist: *Walker* v *Walker* [1952] 2 All ER 138. Cessation of cohabitation and the respondent's intention permanently to desert the petitioner must be proved. Desertion for a period of two years may be proof of irretrievable breakdown of marriage. See the Mat.C.A. 1973, s. 1(2) (*c*). 2. Improper absence from one's place of duty with HM Forces, with the intention of remaining permanently absent. See the Armed Forces Act 1976; and the Reserve Forces Act 1980, s. 73, Sch 5.

desertion, constructive. *See* CONSTRUCTIVE DESERTION.

desertion, mutual. *See* MUTUAL DESERTION.

designs, registered. Designs protected under the Registered Designs Acts 1949–61. For purposes of the Act a design means "features of shape, configuration, pattern or ornament applied to an article by any industrial process or means, being features which in the finished article appeal to and are judged solely by the eye, but does not include a method or principle of construction or features of shape or configuration which are dictated solely by the function which the article to be made . . . has to perform": s. 1(3). See also the Design Copyright Act 1968.

de son tort. *See* EXECUTOR DE SON TORT; TRUSTEE DE SON TORT.

desuetude. Disuse. The doctrine of desuetude, whereby an obsolete statute ceases to have force, has no place in English law.

detain. To hold or retain as though in custody. While every arrest involves a deprivation of liberty, the converse is not necessarily true in that arrest can only be effected in the exercise of an asserted authority: *R* v *Brown* [1977] RTR 160. *See* ARREST.

detainer, forcible. *See* FORCIBLE DETAINER.

detaining for questioning, arrest and. *See* QUESTIONING, DETAINING BY POLICE FOR.

detention centres. Places of detention (for 3–6 months) for male offenders aged 14 and under 21 who have been convicted of an offence punishable with imprisonment. See C.J.A. 1982, ss. 4–5 for their replacement by youth custody establishments.

detention for short periods. Detention for a period not exceeding four days, ordered by a magistrates' court having the power to impose imprisonment, in police cells, etc. (as certified by the Secretary of State): M.C.A. 1980, s. 134.

determinable fee. A fee (qv) which may determine by an event, stated in express terms, before completion of the period for which it could continue. An instrument under which a determinable fee is created constitutes a settlement (qv): S.L.A. 1925, s. 1. See *Hopper* v *Liverpool Corporation* (1944) 88 SJ 213.

determinable interests. Interests which are terminable on the happening of specified contingencies. See, eg, *Re Leach* [1912] 2 Ch 422.

determine. To come, or to bring, to an end.

detinue. An action by which the plaintiff sought the return of an unlawfully detained chattel. Judgment for the plaintiff was that he recovered either the chattel or its value, and damages for detention. See O. 13, r. 3; and *General & Finance Facilities Ltd* v *Cooks Cars Ltd* [1963] 2 All ER 314. Abolished under the Torts (Interference with Goods) Act 1977, s. 2(1).

detoxification centres. Name given to treatment centres for alcoholics: C.J.A. 1972, s. 34. A constable is empowered to take a drunken offender to such a centre "and while a person is being so taken he shall be deemed to be in lawful custody". See Home Office Circular 111/1976.

detriment. 1. Injury, damage or loss suffered. 2. In the law of contract, means that the promisee, in return for a promise, has foregone a legal right which he might otherwise have exercised.

devastavit. He has wasted. A personal representative (qv) who misapplies or mismanages the assets of a deceased person is answerable for that waste, which is said to constitute a *devastavit*. Examples: acting fraudulently in paying legacies out of the correct order or conveying an estate to the personal representative's own use. See *De Cordova* v *De Cordova* (1879) 4 App Cas 692; *Re Parry* [1969] 2 All ER 512.

development. Concept of planning law, defined by the T.C.P.A. 1971 as "the carrying out of building, engineering, mining or other operations in, on, over or under land, or the making of any material change in the use of any buildings or other land": s. 22. See also the Town and Country Planning (Use Classes) Order 1972, listing 18 "use classes", changes within which are not classed as "development". See the Town and Country Planning (Minerals) Act 1981, s. 1. *See* PLANNING PERMISSION.

development land. "If the Secretary of State directs an authority to do so, it shall make an assessment of land which is in its area and which is in its opinion available and suitable for development for residential purposes": L.G.P.L.A. 1980, s. 116(1).

development land tax. Tax on realised development value (qv) accruing to a person on the disposal of an interest in land in the UK: Development Land Tax Act 1976, s. 1. See the Finance Act 1981, ss. 129–133.

development operations. Bodies established by the Secretary of State under the New Towns Act 1981, s. 3, to secure the laying out and development of new towns. For powers, see s. 4.

development, permitted. Categories of development (qv) for which individual applications for permission are not necessary, eg, certain developments within the curtilage (qv) of a dwelling house: see the Town and Country Planning General Development Order 1977, art. 3.

development value, realised. *See* REALISED DEVELOPMENT VALUE.

deviation. Departure from the norm, or from the method of performance agreed in a contract. See *Lilley* v *Doubleday* (1881) 7 QBD 510; *Edwards* v *Newland* [1950] KB 534.

deviation of ships. Where a ship deviates from a voyage contemplated by the voyage policy, or goes past the destination, the insurer is discharged from liability as from the time of deviation, except, eg, where the deviation was caused by circumstances beyond control of the ship's master, or where it was necessary for the ship's safety. See the Carriage of Goods by Sea Act 1971; and *Internationale Guano* v *Macandrew & Co* [1909] 2 KB 360.

devilling. Generally, the handing over of a brief (qv) by one barrister to another so that the latter can conduct the case.

devise. A gift of real property by will made by a devisor to a devisee. May be *general*, eg, "all my realty to X", or *specific*, eg, "Blackacre to Y", or *residuary*, eg, "all the rest of my real property to Z": *Re Wilson* [1967] Ch 53.

devolution. 1. The passing of property or rights from one person to another, eg, on death. 2. The transfer, or delegation, of powers and authority held by the central government to local or regional authorities. See Cmnd 5460 and 6585.

dictionary in interpretation of statutes, use of. A dictionary may be used by the court to ascertain words to which no particular legal interpretation attaches. See, eg, *R* v *Peters* (1866) 16 QBD 636 (Dr Johnson's definition of "credit"); *Re Ripon Housing Confirmation Order* [1939] 2

KB 838 (meaning of "park"); and *Gravesham BC* v *Wilson* (1983) (*The Times*, 3.3.1983) (meaning of "commodious").

dictum. An observation by a judge on a matter arising during the hearing of a case. *See* OBITER DICTUM.

digest. 1. A collection of rules of law, eg, the *Digest of Justinian*, published in AD 533. 2. A précis of cases, in the form of head-notes or main points, arranged in alphabetical order.

dilapidation. 1. Repairs needing to be made to premises at the end of a tenancy (qv). 2. A state of disrepair, relating to land and buildings, where legal liability is imposed on those responsible.

dilatory motion. A motion intended to postpone consideration of the business in hand.

dilatory plea. Plea by the defendant (qv) to the jurisdiction of the court, showing some reasons for abating the action or showing that the case does not fall within the court's jurisdiction. Generally obsolete.

diminished responsibility. Where a person kills or is party to the killing of another, he will not be convicted of murder if suffering from such abnormality of mind (whether arising from a condition of arrested or retarded development of mind or any inherent causes or induced by disease or injury) as substantially impaired his mental responsibility for his acts and omissions in doing or being a party to the killing. Such a person is liable to be convicted of manslaughter: Homicide Act 1957, s. 2. See the Criminal Procedure (Insanity) Act 1964; *R* v *Byrne* [1960] 2 QB 396; *R* v *Turnbull* (1977) 65 Cr App R 242; *R* v *Vinagre* (1979) 69 Cr App R 104; and *R* v *Dix* (1982) 74 Cr App R 306.

diplomatic privilege. The right extended to a foreign diplomat, or to certain members of his staff, whose government does not waive privilege, not to be prosecuted in an English criminal court. See the Diplomatic Privileges Act 1964; the European Communities Act 1972, s. 4; and the State Immunity Act 1978, ss. 16–20; *Dickinson* v *Del Solar* [1930] 1 KB 376; *R* v *Madan* [1961] 2 QB 1; and

Sengupta v *Republic of India* [1983] ICR 221. *See* PRIVILEGE.

direct evidence. *See* EVIDENCE, DIRECT.

direct examination. Examination-in-chief (qv).

directions, summons for. A summons, marking the end of preliminaries to an action, taken out by the plaintiff within one month of the close of pleadings (qv), for directions relating to, eg, discovery and inspection of documents (qv), so that all matters which must or can be dealt with on interlocutory application and have not been dealt with may be disposed of. See O. 25; *Nagy* v *Co-operative Press* [1949] 2 KB 188.

direction to jury. An instruction to the jury (qv) on a relevant point of law to be applied to the facts they are considering, given by the judge.

directives of EEC. *See* COMMUNITY LEGISLATION, FORMS OF.

direct labour organisation. Workers directly employed by local authorities to enable them to carry out statutory functions, eg, the maintenance of roads and housing: L.G.P.L.A. 1980, Part III.

director. Defined by the Finance Act 1976, s. 72(8) as: in relation to a company whose affairs are managed by a board of directors or similar body, a member of that board or similar body; in relation to a company whose affairs are managed by a single director or similar person, that director or person; in relation to a company whose affairs are managed by the members themselves, a member of that company. Defined in the Cos.A. 1948, s. 455 as "any person occupying the position of director by whatever name called." A director is a trustee (qv) for the company but not for individual shareholders, and an agent for the company. A *register of directors* must be kept at a company's registered office and changes must be published. A *board of directors* is appointed, in accordance with articles of association (qv), by shareholders to run a company. See the Cos.A. 1948, s. 200; the European Communities Act 1972, s. 9; the Cos.A. 1976, ss. 21, 31–32; and the Banking Act 1979, s. 49(2).

director, controlling. See CONTROLLING DIRECTOR.

director, full-time working. "A director who is required to devote substantially the whole of his time to the service of the company in a managerial or technical capacity": Finance Act 1976, s, 72(9).

Director General of Fair Trading. Appointed under the Fair Trading Act 1973. General functions are: to keep under review commercial activities in the UK relating to the supply of goods and services to the consumer; collecting and receiving information about activities and practices that may adversely affect consumers' economic and other interests; reviewing commercial activities relating to monopoly situations; making recommendations to the Secretary of State on these matters. Under the C.C.A. 1974, s. 1, he has the duty to administer the licensing system set up under that Act and generally to superintend the workings of the Act. See also the Competition Act 1980, ss. 9, 21–41. See FAIR TRADING, PROCEEDINGS RELATED TO.

director, managing. See MANAGING DIRECTOR.

Director of Public Prosecutions. An officer (barrister or solicitor of at least 10 years' standing) who works under the general supervision of the Attorney-General (qv). He undertakes proceedings in cases of murder or other cases appearing to him to be of importance, considers reports on complaints against the police referred to him and may appear for the Crown in a criminal appeal. Some statutes require his consent to a prosecution: eg, the S.O.A. 1967, s. 8; and the Th.A. 1968, s. 30. See the Prosecution of Offences Act 1979; and *Raymond* v *A.-G.* [1982] QB 839.

director, persons connected with. See CONNECTED PERSONS.

directors' duty of care. Directors have a fiduciary duty to the company and a duty of care, but are not liable for mere errors of judgment. See *Marzetti's Case* [1880] WN 50; and *Re City Equitable Fire Insurance Co Ltd* [1925] Ch 407. In the performance of their functions they should have

regard to the interests of the company employees as well as the interests of company members: Cos.A. 1980, s. 46(1).

director, shadow. "A person in accordance with whose directions or instructions the directors of a company are accustomed to act": Cos.A. 1980, s. 63. He is to be treated as a director for the purposes of the 1980 Act, Part IV, unless the directors act on his directions or instructions only when given in a professional capacity.

directors' interests, register of. Under the Cos.A. 1967, s. 29(1),(4), a company must keep a register recording information relating to notification by a director of any matter related to listed shares or debentures. Substantial contracts with directors must be disclosed in accounts: Cos.A. 1980, s. 54. For excluded transactions, see s. 58.

directors, loans to. With some few exceptions, a company may not make a loan to its directors or the directors of its holding company or enter into a guarantee for a loan made by another person to any of its directors: Cos.A. 1980, s. 49(1)(a).

directors' report. Report to be attached to a company's balance sheet (qv), stating, eg, dividend recommendation, changes in fixed assets, and giving a "fair review of the development of the business of the company and its subsidiaries". See the Cos.A. 1967, s. 16; and Cos.A. 1981, s. 15. See COMPANY.

directors, service. Directors employed by the company in some capacity. Remuneration may be governed by Table A, art. 76. See the Cos.A. 1967, s. 26 (as amended by the Cos.A. 1981, s. 61).

disability, person under. Phrase applied to, eg, an infant (qv) or mental patient (qv), ie, one who lacks some legal capacity or qualification.

disabled person. One who is blind, deaf or dumb or who is substantially and permanently handicapped by illness, injury or congenital deformity or any other disability for the time being prescribed for the purposes of the National Assistance Act 1948, s. 29(1): Residential Homes Act 1980,

s. 10(1). See the Disabled Persons (Employment) Acts 1948–58, imposing on those employing a substantial number of persons a duty to employ a quota of registered disabled persons; the Disabled Persons Act 1981, imposing a duty on highway authorities to have regard to needs of the disabled in executing highway works; and the Inland Revenue Statement of Practice SP 10/81, in which "disability" includes continuing incapacity to perform duties arising from culmination of process of deteriorating physical or mental illness.

disablement benefit. Benefit payable under the S.S.A. 1975 where an employee suffers, as the result of an accident, any loss of mental or physical faculty amounting to at least 1 per cent assessment. Payable, after three days from the accident, for 156 days after the time during which the employee cannot work. Assessment of under 20 per cent results in entitlement to *disablement gratuity*; 20 per cent or over results in entitlement to *disablement pension*.

disabling statute. A statute which deprives persons or bodies of legal rights or qualifications.

disaffection, incitement to. It is an offence, maliciously and advisedly to endeavour to seduce any member of the Forces from his duty or allegiance to the Crown: Incitement to Disaffection Act 1934. See also the Police Act 1964, s. 53.

disbar. To expel a barrister (qv) from his Inn of Court (qv).

discharge. Generally, a release from an obligation. 1. Discharge of contract refers to the freeing of parties from their mutual obligations by performance, express agreement, breach, or under the doctrine of frustration (qqv). 2. Release of a prisoner. 3. Release of a surety (qv) from liability. 4. Conditional or unconditional discharge (qv), ie, freeing of a person found guilty of an offence. See the P.C.C.A. 1973, s. 7. 5. Freeing of a bankrupt from debts and liabilities, by order of discharge. See the B.A. 1914, s. 26; the Insolvency Act 1976, s. 7; and *Re Reed* [1979] 2

All ER 22. 6. Dismissal of a jury on their having given a verdict. 7. Nullifying of rights and liabilities on a bill of exchange (qv).

discharge and modification of restrictive covenants. See RESTRICTIVE COVENANTS, DISCHARGE AND MODIFICATION OF.

disciplinary procedures, code of. See CODE OF PRACTICE ON DISCIPLINARY PROCEDURES.

disclaimer. Denial or disavowal of a claim; renunciation of title or interest. 1. A power (qv) may be disclaimed by deed: L.P.A. 1925, s. 156. 2. Where two gifts are made by a testator (qv), if one is onerous and the other beneficial, the beneficiary can disclaim the former: *Re Loom* [1910] 2 Ch 230. 3. A trustee in bankruptcy may disclaim unprofitable contracts, land burdened with very onerous covenants, etc. See the B.A. 1914, s. 54; and the A.E.A. 1925, s. 23.

disclosure, non-. Failure to perform a duty to make known relevant material information. See *Hill* v *Harris* [1965] 2 QB 601; and *Williams & Glyn's Bank Ltd* v *Boland* [1981] AC 487. *See* INSURANCE.

disclosure of documents. See DISCOVERY AND INSPECTION OF DOCUMENTS.

discontinuance, notice of. The voluntary ending of an action by the plaintiff giving written notice to the defendant, in proceedings commenced by a writ of summons. See O. 21.

discontinuance of action. See WITHDRAWAL OF DEFENCE.

discontinuance of counterclaim. See COUNTERCLAIM, DISCONTINUANCE OF.

discount. 1. Deduction from the catalogue price often allowed, eg, by a wholesaler to a retailer (known as a "trade discount"). 2. Inducement offered by a creditor to a debtor to pay swiftly (known as a "cash discount"). 3. Procedure whereby a bill of exchange (qv) is acquired for a sum less than its face value.

discount, issue of shares at a. Lawful only by way of underwriting commission (Cos.A. 1948, s. 53), or, in the case of a private company (qv) in exchange for over-valued consideration. See the Cos.A. 1980, s. 21.

discovery and inspection of documents. Disclosure by a party of the relevant documents in the action which are in his custody or possession. See the S.C.A. 1981, ss. 33–35. A party may require inspection of any document referred to in the other party's pleadings: O. 24, r. 10. In an action commenced by writ, discovery without order must be made by exchanging lists of documents within 14 days of the close of proceedings: O. 24, r. 2. Discovery by order follows where a party is not satisfied with the opponent's list, or where a party fails to comply with a rule of discovery without order: O. 24, r. 3; County Court Rules 1981, O. 14. See also *Norwich Pharmacal Co* v *Customs and Excise Commissioners* [1974] AC 133; *British Steel Corp* v *Granada TV* [1981] 1 All ER 417; and *Air Canada* v *Secretary of State for Trade* [1983] 1 All ER 161. *See* DOCUMENTS, LIST OF.

discovery, failure to make. Failure of a party to make a discovery of documents (qv) or to produce them for inspection when required. The master may then make an appropriate order for production for inspection under O. 24, r. 11. See *Chipchase* v *Rosemund* [1965] 1 WLR 153.

discretionary trust. A trust under which trustees are allowed discretion to pay or apply income for beneficiaries, but no beneficiary is able to claim of right that any part or all of the income is to be paid to him or applied in any way for his benefit. Example: land is conveyed to trustees upon trust to apply rent and profits "for the benefit of X in the absolute discretion of the trustees". See, eg, *Gartside* v *IRC* [1968] 1 All ER 121. *See* TRUST.

discretion, judicial. The power, residing in the court, of deciding a question where latitude of judgment is allowed. A discretionary remedy is, therefore, one which may or may not be granted. "A person entrusted with a discretion must direct himself properly in law. He must call his own attention to the matters which he is bound to consider. He must exclude from his consideration matters which are irrelevant to the matter that he has to consider": *Associated Picture Houses Ltd* v *Wednesbury Corporation* [1947] 2 All ER 680. See also *R* v *Metropolitan Police Commissioner, ex p Blackburn (No 3)* [1973] QB 241 (relating to police discretion); *R* v *Sang* [1980] AC 402.

discretion, judicial, relating to admissibility of evidence. "In every criminal case the judge has a discretion to disallow the evidence even if in law relevant, and, therefore, admissible, if admissibility would operate unfairly against the defendant": *Callis* v *Gunn* [1964] 1 QB 495. See the Civil Evidence Act 1968, s. 8; O. 38, r. 29; *Noor* v *Mahomed* [1949] AC 182. *See* EXCLUSIONARY RULES.

discretion statement. Statement made by a party to a matrimonial cause, praying that the court's discretion should be exercised notwithstanding the party's adultery. Not required after 1st January 1971.

discretion to arrest or prosecute. "It is for the Commissioner of Police or the Chief Constable . . . to decide in any particular case whether enquiries should be pursued, or whether an arrest should be made, or a prosecution brought": *per* Lord Denning in *R* v *Chief Constable of Devon and Cornwall ex p CEGB* [1982] QB 458.

discrimination. The according of some differential treatment to persons or bodies in the same position, eg, sex discrimination, racial discrimination. Discrimination on grounds of nationality is prohibited under the Treaty of Rome 1957, art. 7.

discrimination, racial. Discrimination by one person against another so that, on racial grounds (colour, race, nationality, ethnic or national origins), he treats the other less favourably than he treats or would treat others, or applies to that other a requirement which he applies or would apply equally to persons not of the same racial group as that other but which is such that the proportion of persons who can comply with it is considerably smaller than the proportion of persons not of that racial group who can comply with it and which he cannot show to be justifiable and which is to the detriment of that other because he cannot comply with it: Race Relations Act 1976, s. 1. Unlawful in the employment and other fields, under the 1976 Act. See also *Mandala* v *Lee* [1983] 2 WLR 260.

discrimination, sex. Unfavourable treatment, direct or indirect, of a person because of sex or marital status. May be unlawful under the Sex Discrimination Act, 1975, eg, when taking on staff or affording access to promotion. See, eg, *Jones* v *St John's College* [1979] ICR 848; and *Garland* v *BR Engineering Ltd* [1982] 2 WLR 918. *See* EQUAL PAY.

disease. Includes injury, ailment or adverse condition whether of body or mind: Medicines Act 1968, s. 132(1).

diseases, prescribed. The Secretary of State is empowered to prescribe a disease in relation to persons insured if satisfied that it ought to be treated as a risk of their occupation. See the National Insurance (Industrial Injuries) Act 1965 (as amended); the Pneumoconiosis etc. (Workers' Compensation) Act 1979, s. 1(3); S.I. 1979/1726; and the Industrial Diseases (Notification) Act 1981.

disentailing deed *See* BARRING OF ENTAILED INTEREST.

disentailment. Mode of barring of an entailed interest (qv) by deed, known as a disentailing assurance, so that the rights of the tenant's issue and of persons whose estates should take effect after the determination or in defeasance of the entailed interests are defeated. Interests ranking prior to entailed interests cannot be defeated in this way. See the L.P.A. 1925, s. 133.

disfranchise. To deprive of a right.

disherison. Debarring from an inheritance, ie, disinheriting.

dishonest. Lacking intentionally in an element of truth or probity. The "dishonest appropriatation" of property is an essential element in the offence of theft: Th.A. 1968, s. 1(1). Appropriation is not to be regarded as dishonest if, eg, a person appropriates property in the belief that he

has in law the right to deprive another of it: s. 2(1).

dishonest suppression of documents. *See* SUPPRESSION OF DOCUMENTS, DISHONEST.

dishonesty, proper test for. The test is a dual one: did the accused act dishonestly by the standards of "ordinary decent people" and, if so, must he have realised that his acts were by those standards dishonest. An accused can be convicted only if the answer to both questions is affirmative. See *R* v *Ghosh* [1982] QB 1053. See also *R* v *Morris* [1983] 2 WLR 768.

dishonour of bill. Refusal by the drawee of a bill of exchange (qv) to accept it, or failure to pay after acceptance. See the B.Ex.A. 1882, s. 47; and the A.J.A. 1977, s. 4.

dismissal, constructive. *See* CONSTRUCTIVE DISMISSAL.

dismissal, fair. *See* FAIR DISMISSAL.

dismissal from employment. Means, under the E.P.(C.)A. 1978, s. 55; the termination of an employee's contract of employment by the employer with or without notice; where under that contract an employee is employed for a fixed term, the expiry of that term without its renewal under the same contract; termination of a contract by an employee, with or without notice, in circumstances such that he is entitled to terminate it without notice by reason of the employer's conduct.

dismissal of action. Result of a successful application to the court by the defendant requesting that an action be dismissed, eg, because of default in service of a statement of claim: O. 19, r. 1. Generally the plaintiff must be guilty of inexcusable, inordinate and prejudicial delay: *Allen* v *McAlpine & Sons Ltd* [1968] 1 All ER 543. See *Dutton* v *Spink and Beeching (Sales) Ltd* [1977] 1 All ER 287; *Pryer* v *Smith* [1977] 1 All ER 218. For dismissal for want of prosecution, see *Birkett* v *James* [1977] 2 All ER 801; *Joyce* v *Joyce* [1979] 1 All ER 175.

dismissal procedures agreement. "An agreement in writing with respect to procedures relating to dismissal made by or on behalf of one or more independent trade unions and one or more employers or employers' associations". E.P.(C.)A. 1978, s. 153(1).

dismissal statement. A written statement, to which an employee with at least 26 weeks of continuous service is entitled, giving reasons for dismissal: E.P.(C.)A. 1978, s. 53. A complaint to a tribunal may be made if the statement is refused or is untrue.

dismissal, summary. See SUMMARY DISMISSAL.

dismissal, unfair. Dismissal, where, eg, the employee was or proposed to become a member of an independent union, or had taken part in its activities, or where he refused to join a union (where there is a union membership agreement (qv)) because of a genuine objection on grounds of conscience or deeply-held personal conviction. In general, the determination of whether dismissal is fair or unfair is related to the question of whether in the circumstances the employer had acted reasonably or not: s. 57(3); Employment Act 1980, s. 6; Employment Act 1982, ss. 2–9, Sch 3. See *Woods* v *WM Car Services Ltd* [1982] ICR 693.

dismissal, unfair, right arising from. In general, an employee has the right not to be unfairly dismissed by his employer: E.P.(C.)A. 1978, s. 54(1). The statutory right does not apply in the case of dismissal of an employee who has not served the firm for two years, or where during that period the number of employees in the firm had not exceeded 20, and he was informed in writing of the effect of this section at the time of engagement: see the 1978 Act, ss. 64, 141–149; and the Employment Act 1980, s. 8(1). For waiver of rights, see the 1978 Act, s. 142(1) and the 1980 Act, s. 8(2).

disorderly house. 1. A brothel (qv). See the S.O.A. 1956, ss. 33–36. 2. A house in which performances or exhibitions are given which amount to an outrage of common decency, which tend to corrupt or deprave (qv) or are calculated to injure the public interest so as to call for condemnation or punishment. See *R* v *Quinn* [1962] 2 QB 245; *R* v *Payne* [1980] Crim LR 595; and *R* v *Tan* [1983] 2 All ER 12.

disparagement of goods. See SLANDER OF TITLE.

dispensing power. The right to exempt from statute law, exercised by the Crown under the Tudor and Stuart dynasties. Effectively ended by the Bill of Rights 1689 (qv).

dispensing with service. Procedure whereby a registrar may by order dispense with the service of a copy of the petition for divorce on the respondent: Matrimonial Causes Rules 1977, r. 14(11).

disposal notification areas. Areas so declared by a local authority under the Community Land Act 1975, s. 23(2). The authority may exercise its powers for the purpose of obtaining information about disposals of development land (qv) in those areas by sale, lease, exchange, etc: s. 23(1).

disposal of premises. Includes a letting, assignment or surrender of a tenancy of the premises and the creation by contract of any other right to occupy the premises: Defective Premises Act 1972, s. 6(1).

disposal of uncollected goods. The bailee may give the bailor written notice (by delivery to the bailor), by post, by leaving it at his proper address, specifying goods, stating that they are ready for delivery and specifying the amount payable by the bailor in respect of the goods: Torts (Interference with Goods) Act 1977, Sch 1. If the bailee has given notice and has failed to trace the bailor, he is entitled to sell the goods: s. 12(3). See BAILMENT.

disposition. 1. The passing of property, whether by act of parties or act of the law: *Northumberland* v *A.-G.* [1905] AC 406. See the L.P.A. 1925, s. 15(1) (c); Legitimacy Act 1976, s. 10(1). 2. Term used in the law of evidence to indicate a person's general tendencies to think or act in a particular way. It may be proved by evidence of character, previous convictions, conduct on other occasions. See *Makin* v *A.-G. for NS Wales* [1894] AC 57; *Selvey* v *DPP* [1970] AC 304;

Boardman v *DPP* [1974] 3 All ER 887.

disposition, voluntary. *See* VOLUNTARY DISPOSITION.

dispossess. To oust from land. See the H.A. 1964, ss. 73–91, as amended by the L.G.P.L.A. 1980; and S.I. 1981/781. *See* OUSTER.

dispute. A conflict of claims or rights. Whenever one party to a contract requests something from the other party under the terms of their contract and that request is not complied with, there is a dispute: *Ellerine Bros Ltd* v *Klinger* [1982] 2 All ER 737.

dispute, trade. *See* TRADE DISPUTE.

disqualification. Deprivation of a right, power or privilege. Thus, where a person is convicted of certain driving offences, he may be ordered by the court to be disqualified from driving for a period. See the Transport Act 1981, s. 19, and the Road Traffic Act 1972, Sch 4 (as amended). See *R* v *Cooper* [1983] RTR 183.

disseisin. The wrongful putting out of a person seised of a freehold. *See* SEISIN.

dissentiente. Generally abbreviated to *diss.* Delivering a dissenting judgment.

dissolution. Breaking up; bringing to an end. 1. Dissolution of Parliament means bringing the life of an existing Parliament to an end, eg, proroguing Parliament, which is then dissolved by proclamation of the Queen. 2. Dissolution of a marriage, eg, by decree of divorce (qv). 3. Dissolution of a company by legal process resulting from, eg, its being struck off the register: Cos.A. 1948, s. 353.

distinguishing a case. Where the court has been invited to follow a previous decision, but feels that there are important points of difference between that decision and the case on which it was based and the case it is considering, the case is said to have been "distinguished".

distrain. To levy a distress (qv).

distress. The seizing of a personal chattel (qv) from a debtor or wrongdoer so as to obtain payment for a debt or satisfaction for a wrong committed. See the M.C.A. 1980, ss. 76–78. Chattels may be privileged from distress *absolutely* (fixtures, goods of a third party, etc) or *conditionally* (eg, beasts of the plough: Agricultural Holdings Act 1948). See S.I. 1980/26.

distress damage feasant. A form of self-help taking the form of the seizure by X of a chattel or animal belonging to Y which is wrongfully on X's land and damaging it. See *Burt* v *Moore* (1973) 5 TR 329; *Sorrell* v *Paget* [1950] 1 KB 152. Abolished in relation to animals by the Animals Act 1971, which creates a general right to detain and sell, after 14 days, trespassing livestock not under control: s. 7.

distribution. The division of property of an intestate among the next of kin. See the A.E.A. 1925, ss. 33, 46, 47; the Intestates' Estates Act 1952; Family Provision Act 1966; the F.L.R.A. 1969; and the Inheritance (Provision for Family and Dependants) Act 1975.

distribution of company assets. Distribution of company assets, in cash or otherwise to members except when made by way of issue of fully or partly-paid bonus shares, redemption of preference shares from the proceeds of fresh issue, reduction of share capital by reducing or writing off members' liability in respect of unpaid share capital, distribution or winding up: Cos.A. 1980, s. 45(2). For restrictions, see ss. 39, 40(1). See also the Cos.A. 1980, s. 43A (distributions in kind) (inserted by the Cos.A. 1981, s. 85).

distribution of company assets on liquidation, order of. The order is generally: secured creditors with fixed charges; liquidation costs; preferential creditors; secured creditors with floating charges; unsecured creditors; debts due to company members as members; repayment of capital to members; division of surplus assets among members.

distributive justice. *See* JUSTICE, DISTRIBUTIVE AND CORRECTIVE.

district councils. *See* COUNCILS, DISTRICT.

district registrars. County court registrars appointed by Lord Chancellor to act as district registrars of the High Court: S.C.A. 1981, s. 100.

district registry. Registries in England and Wales which function as branch offices of the Supreme Court, allowing proceedings to be commenced in many parts of the country by writ of summons. See the S.C.A. 1981, s. 99.

districts. The six metropolitan counties in England are divided into 36 metropolitan districts; the 39 non-metropolitan districts are divided into 296 districts; Wales has 37 districts; Scotland has 53 (based on nine regions).

distringas. That you distrain. Writ commanding sheriff (qv) to distrain on a person. A *distringas notice* was issued so as to prevent the transfer of shares in a company (qv); it was replaced later by a stop notice. See O. 50, rr. 11–15. *See* DISTRAIN.

disturbance. Interference with the existence or exercise of a right by, eg, "trespass or nuisance, or in any other substantial manner": *Fitzgerald v Forbank* [1897] 2 Ch 96.

dividend. 1. Amount payable to a bankrupt's creditors after payment of expenses and preferential debts. 2. A part of a company's net profit distributed among shareholders in proportion to their shareholdings. Must, generally, be paid out of profits. *See* PROFITS AVAILABLE FOR DISTRIBUTION.

dividend, interim. *See* INTERIM DIVIDEND.

Divine Right of Kings. "The State of monarchy is the supremest theory upon earth; for kings are not only God's lieutenants upon earth and sit upon God's throne, but even by God himself they are called gods . . . Kings are justly called gods for that they exercise a manner or resemblance of divine power on earth . . . it is seditious in subjects to dispute what a king may do in the height of his power . . .": James I, in a speech to Parliament, March 1610.

divine service, tenure by. Tenure involving fealty and obligation to say a mass at regular intervals. Abolished in 1660.

divisible contract. A contract in which the parties intend that their promises are to be independent of each other: *Taylor* v *Webb* [1937] 2 KB 283. An *entire* (or *indivisible*) contract is one in which there is agreement, implicit or explicit, that neither party may demand performance until he is ready to fulfil, or has fulfilled, his promise. See *Law Commission Working Paper* No 65, 1976. *See* CONTRACT.

division. Parliamentary procedure, whereby members separate into groups to record their votes.

Divisional Courts. Term applied collectively to the Queen's Bench Divisional Court, the Chancery Divisional Court and the Family Divisional Court. The Queen's Bench Divisional Court hears appeals on points of law by way of case stated from decisions of magistrates or from the Crown Court, hears appeals by solicitors from decisions of the Solicitors' Disciplinary Tribunal and exercises supervisory jurisdiction over inferior courts and tribunals. It consists of 2–3 judges. The Chancery Divisional Court consists of 1–2 judges and hears appeals from county courts concerning, eg, land registration matters and bankruptcy and appeals from the Commissioners of Inland Revenue. The Family Divisional Court usually consists of two judges and hears appeals from decisions of the Crown Court, county court and magistrates in matters of family law, eg, under the Guardianship of Minors Act 1971, affiliation, adoption and maintenance orders. See the S.C.A. 1981, s. 66.

Divisions of the High Court. These are the Chancery Division, Queen's Bench Division and Family Division. See the S.C.A. 1981, s. 5(1).

divorce. Dissolution of marriage on the ground of its irretrievable breakdown (qv). Proceedings commence with the filing of a petition, in the prescribed form, which sets out the facts on which the petitioner relies as proof of irretrievable breakdown of marriage, and which concludes with a prayer "that the said marriage may be dissolved". See the Mat.C.A. 1973, s. 1(1); and the Matrimonial Causes Rules 1977 (SI 1977/344).

divorce and judicial separation,

special procedure for. Procedure allowed, as from April 1977, under the Matrimonial Causes Rules 1977, whereby, if a petition is based on either adultery or desertion or two years' separation, etc, and it is undefended and there are no children of the family, the petitioner can apply to put the case in the Special Procedure List. If the registrar agrees, evidence is considered and, if he finds the facts proved, he will announce a day for the pronouncement of the decree in open court. The parties need not attend. See Practice Note, 15.6.77.

divorce, bars to. The Divorce Reform Act 1969 abolished most existing bars (eg, connivance, condonation) to divorce. The defence now available to the respondent is that no irretrievable breakdown of marriage (qv) has taken place. A decree nisi may be refused where the respondent would be caused grave financial hardship (see the Mat.C.A. 1973, s. 1(2) (*e*)) or other hardship (see *Reiterbund* v *Reiterbund* [1975] 1 All ER 280). Decree absolute will not be made until the court has considered the position of the children of the family: Mat.C.A. 1973, s. 41. See the Matrimonial Causes Rules 1977. *See* QUEEN'S PROCTOR.

divorce by mutual consent. Term applied to a decree of divorce after two years of separation immediately preceding the presentation of the petition, where the respondent consents to the grant of a decree: Mat.C.A. 1973, s. 1(2) (*d*).

divorce, ground for. The sole ground, after 1st January 1971, is the irretrievable breakdown of marriage (qv): Mat.C.A. 1973, s. 1(1).

divorce, petition for. Statement by the petitioner setting out the facts relating to the breakdown of marriage (qv) and praying for relief by way of dissolution of the marriage. No petition for divorce can be presented to the court within three years from the date of marriage except where a judge allows that the case is one of exceptional hardship suffered by the petitioner or of exceptional depravity (qv) on part of the respondent. See

the Mat.C.A. 1973, ss. 3, 4 as amended by the D.P.A. 1978, s. 62; the Matrimonial Causes Rules 1977, r. 5; *Law Commission Report* 1982, No 116 (recommending replacement of "three year" by "one year" rule).

Divorce Registry. The Principal Registry of the Family Division of the High Court of Justice.

divorce towns. Those towns at which sittings of the High Court are authorised to be held outside the Royal Courts of Justice for the purpose of hearing matrimonial proceedings. See the Matrimonial Causes Rules 1977, r. 2(2); and S.I. 1978/1759 (divorce county courts).

dock brief. Name of the procedure whereby a prisoner, on trial on indictment, could directly instruct from the dock and for a nominal fee any barrister sitting robed in the court. The process is largely obsolete.

Doctors' Commons. The sixteenth-century headquarters of the doctors of civil law, on the south side of St Paul's Churchyard, London. The College of Doctors of Law was dissolved in 1857.

document. A paper which can be relied upon as proof, or in support, of something. Under the Civil Evidence Act 1968, s. 10, a document is defined as, in addition to a document in written form: "(*a*) any plan, map, graph or drawing; (*b*) any photograph; (*c*) any disc, tape, soundtrack or other device in which sounds or other data (not being visual images) are embodied so as to be capable (with or without the aid of some other equipment) of being reproduced therefrom; and (*d*) any film, negative, tape or other device in which one or more visual images are embodied so as to be capable (as aforesaid) of being reproduced therefrom." See *Grant* v *Southwestern and Country Properties* [1974] 2 All ER 465 (tape recording of information held to be a document which could be produced for inspection within O. 24, r. 10(1)).

document, ancient. *See* ANCIENT DOCUMENT.

documentary evidence. Documents produced with the intention that they be inspected by judge and jury. *See* EVIDENCE.

document, intention of a. *See* INTENTION OF A DOCUMENT.

document, private, proof of execution of. Procedure involving: proof of handwriting; or proof of attestation (qv); or a presumption that a document produced from proper custody, which is not less than 20 years old, is validly executed. See the Evidence Act 1938, s. 4.

document, public. *See* PUBLIC DOCUMENT.

documents, affidavit of. *See* AFFIDAVIT OF DOCUMENTS.

documents, discovery of. *See* DISCOVERY AND INSPECTION OF DOCUMENTS.

documents, dishonest suppression of. *See* SUPPRESSION OF DOCUMENTS, DISHONEST.

document, secondary evidence of. Exceptions to the general rule that the original of a document must be put in evidence include the following cases: where the original is lost or destroyed; where the original is in possession of a third party who justifiably declines to produce it; where production of the original is highly inconvenient; where the document is a public document (qv); where (in civil proceedings) a party has failed to comply with a notice to produce, so that the party serving notice can put a copy of the document in evidence. *See* EVIDENCE, SECONDARY.

documents, inspection of. *See* DISCOVERY AND INSPECTION OF DOCUMENTS.

documents, list of. List of documents to be served by one party on the other, drawn up in accordance with O. 24. Documents are enumerated and identified by short descriptions. There is a further enumeration of documents which the party objects to producing. Other documents which have been in the party's possession, but which are no longer so, are also listed. See also O. 27, r. 4.

Doe, John. Name of the fictitious plaintiff formerly used in the action of ejectment (qv). See the comments of Donaldson L J in *Barrett* v *French* [1981] 1 WLR 848.

dogs injuring livestock. *See* LIVESTOCK.

dogs, killing or injuring of. *See* LIVESTOCK, PROTECTION OF.

doli capax. Capable of fraud or deceit. Phrase used to signify that a young person is old enough, or sufficiently intelligent, to be responsible in law for the wrongful acts of which he is accused. There is a conclusive presumption that a child under 10 is *doli incapax* (ie, incapable of crime). Between 10–14, he may be shown to be capable of discriminating between good and evil and, therefore, may be held responsible for his actions (the maxim is *malitia supplet aetatem—* malice supplements age). See *R* v *B* [1979] 1 WLR 1185 (where evidence of previous convictions was held admissible).

domain. 1. Concept involving absolute right to and authority over property. 2. Territory over which authority is exercised.

domain, eminent. *See* EMINENT DOMAIN.

Domesday Book. A record of William the Conqueror's "description of England", carried out in 1081–86 by panels of commissioners who based their survey of the lands of England on the accounts of the estates of the King and his tenants-in-chief (qv).

domestic agreements. Agreements made within the course of family life. They are considered as not normally made in contemplation of the creation of a legal relationship. See, eg, *Balfour* v *Balfour* [1919] 2 KB 571; *Pettitt* v *Pettitt* [1970] AC 777.

domestic animal. *See* ANIMAL.

domestic arbitration agreement. *See* ARBITRATION AGREEMENT, DOMESTIC.

domestic courts. Magistrates' courts sitting so as to hear domestic proceedings. Must consist of not more than three justices, who are members of a domestic court panel, including a man and a woman: M.C.A. 1980, s. 66(1). "Domestic proceedings" means proceedings under the enactments specified in the M.C.A. 1980, s. 65, eg, those relating to affiliation proceedings, maintenance orders, guardianship of minors. For the exclusion of persons other than the parties, etc, from such proceedings, see s. 69(2)–(6).

domestic premises. Premises occupied as a private dwelling-house, including any garden, yard, garage, outhouse or other appurtenance of such premises not used in common by the occupants of more than one such dwelling. See the H.S.W.A. 1974, s. 53(1) (as amended).

domestic proceedings, newspaper reports of. Save for proceedings under the Adoption Acts (which are protected under other provisions), it is an offence to publish particulars other than names, addresses and occupations of parties and witnesses, grounds of the application, submissions and points of law and the court's decision: M.C.A. 1980, s. 71.

domestic tribunals. Disciplinary committees exercising judicial or quasi-judicial functions, eg, disciplinary committee of the Law Society (see the Solicitors Act 1974, s. 46). The High Court exercises a supervisory jurisdiction over these tribunals (qv).

domestic violence. *See* INJUNCTIONS, MATRIMONIAL.

domicile. Generally, the country where a person has his permanent home: *Whicker v Hume* (1858) 7 HL Cas 124. Under the C.J.J.A. 1982, s. 41(1), "an individual is domiciled in the UK if and only if he is resident in the UK and the nature and circumstances of his residence indicate that he has a substantial connection with the UK." A person's *domicile of origin* is that which he receives at birth (usually the domicile of his father); this is preserved until he acquires another. A *domicile of choice* is acquired by a person establishing his residence in a chosen country, intending to remain there permanently. No person can be without a domicile or have more than one at the same time: *Udny v Udny* (1869) LR 1 Sc App 441. Under the Domicile and Matrimonial Proceedings Act 1973, a wife's "domicile of dependence" was abolished and her domicile is ascertained by reference to the same factors as in the case of any other individual capable of having an independent domicile: s. 1(2). See *Bell v Kennedy* (1868) Ld Raym 307; *IRC v Bullock* [1976] 3 All ER 353; and *IRC v Duchess of Portland* [1982] Ch 314.

dominant tenement. Land to which

there is attached the benefit of a right. Example: X owns Blackacre and grants to Y, his neighbour, owner of Whiteacre, a right to use a footpath over Blackacre. Whiteacre is the *dominant tenement*; Blackacre is the *servient tenement*.

dominion register. A company (qv) with a share capital whose objects involve business in a part of HM dominions (qv) outside Great Britain may keep there a register of members resident there: Cos.A. 1948, s. 119. A duplicate must be kept at the place where the principal register is kept: s. 120(3).

Dominions. Name formerly applied to the British Commonwealth countries of, eg, Australia, Canada, New Zealand. These countries, former dependencies of the UK, had, generally, complete self-government, usually modelled on the UK. See the Statute of Westminster 1931, s. 1; *Manuel v A.-G.* [1982] 3 WLR 821.

dominium. Ownership. (In its original sense, single and indivisible.)

domitae naturae. *See* ANIMALS.

domus sua cuique est tutissimum refugium. To every person his house is his surest refuge. See *Seymayne's Case* (1605) 5 Co Rep 91.

donatio mortis causa. A gift of property by a donor in anticipation of his death. (Plural: *donationes mortis causa.*) To be effective: the property must be capable of passing by *donatio*; death in the near future must be contemplated by the donor; *donatio* must have been made conditional on the donor's death; delivery is essential. See *Re Beaumont* [1902] 1 Ch 889; *Wilkes v Allington* [1931] 2 Ch 104; *Re Craven* [1937] Ch 423.

donee. One to whom a gift is made.

donor. One who gives.

doom. Anglo-Saxon term for judgment.

dormant company. A company is treated as dormant for any period during which it does not enter into any significant accounting transaction, ie, which it would be obliged by law to enter in its accounting records, other than receipt of issue price for subscribers' shares. See the Cos.A. 1981, s. 12.

dormant partner. A "sleeping partner'', ie, a member of a partnership (qv) who does not play an active part in the running of the business.

dotards. Dead or decayed trees, that cannot be used as timber. A tenant for life (qv) may, in general, cut dotards and all the trees which are not timber: *Re Harker's Will Trusts* [1938] Ch 323.

double insurance. *See* INSURANCE, DOUBLE.

double jeopardy. Possibility of repeated prosecution for the same offence. *See* AUTREFOIS ACQUIT. See also *R v Police Complaints Board ex p Madden* (1983) 127 SJ 85.

double portions, rule against. A child is generally prohibited from taking both a sum paid to him as a portion and a legacy which has been bequeathed to him as a portion. The general principle is: ''Equity leans against double portions.'' See *Pym v Lockyer* (1841) 5 My & Cr 29; *Fowkes v Pascoe* (1875) 10 Ch App 343. *See* PORTION.

double possibility. A rule, abolished by the L.P.A. 1925, s. 161, whereby a limitation, after a life interest to an unborn child or other issue of an unborn person, was prohibited. See *Lord Stafford's Case* (1609) 8 Co Rep 73a.

double probate. A grant of probate made to an executor (qv) to whom power has been reserved to prove at a later date, or on the happening of a specified event, and who has proved. Example: an executor who was an infant (qv) and who has later attained his majority. See *Re Griffin* (1910) 54 SJ 378. *See* GRANT; PROBATE.

double renvoi. *See* RENVOI.

doubt, reasonable. *See* REASONABLE DOUBT.

dower. The right of a widow to a life interest in the realty of her deceased husband. Abolished by the L.P.A. 1925 and the A.E.A. 1925, s. 45.

DPP. Abbreviation for Director of Public Prosecutions (qv).

draft. 1. An order for the payment of a sum of money. (A ''banker's draft'' is a draft drawn by a bank upon itself, eg, by a branch or head office or on another branch. See, eg, *Bank of Montreal* v *Dominion Gresham Guarantee Co* [1930] AC 659.) 2. A rough copy of a document.

driver. One who is in charge of a vehicle and, if a separate person acts as a steersman, the term includes that person as well as any other person in charge of the vehicle or engaged in the driving of it. See the Road Traffic Act 1972, s. 96(1). The essence of ''driving'' is the use of the driver's control in order to direct the movement of the motor vehicle however the movement is produced: *Burgoyne* v *Phillips* [1983] RTR 49.

driving, faulty. *See* FAULTY DRIVING.

driving licence. Authority to drive a motor vehicle. An applicant for a licence must be physically fit and pass a driving test (unless he already possesses a licence). It is an offence to drive on a road without holding a licence. See the Road Traffic Act 1972, ss. 84, 87, 87A, 91, 92; and the Road Traffic Act 1974, Sch 3; and S.I. 1981/52. See *Tynan* v *Jones* [1975] RTR 465.

driving, reckless. A person who drives a motor vehicle on a road recklessly is guilty of an offence: Road Traffic Act 1972, s. 2, (substituted by the C.L.A. 1977, s. 50(1)). A person who causes the death of another by driving a motor vehicle on a road recklessly is guilty of an offence: Road Traffic Act 1972, s. 1(1) (substituted by the C.L.A. 1977, s. 50(1)). (The offences of ''dangerous driving'' and ''causing death by dangerous driving'' have been abolished.) The offence of causing death by reckless driving can still be manslaughter: *In re Gail Anne Jennings* [1982] AC 624.

driving, reckless, conviction of. Juries must convict of reckless driving if satisfied that accused was driving a vehicle in such a way as to create an obvious and serious risk of causing physical injury to another road user or of doing substantial damage to property and that the accused either gave no thought to the possibility of there being such a risk, or, having realised that there was some risk involved, had nonetheless taken that risk: *R v Lawrence* [1982] AC 510.

driving test order. An order under the Road Traffic Act 1972, s. 97(7) disqualifying an offender from driving until he passes a test showing his competence to drive. See *R* v *Guilfoyle* (1973) 137 JP 568; *R* v *Donelly* [1975] 1 All ER 785.

driving while unfit. It is an offence to drive a vehicle if unfit through drink or drugs: Road Traffic Act 1972, s. 5(1). For attempts, see *Kelly* v *Hogan* [1982] RTR 352.

driving with alcohol concentration above prescribed limit. If a person drives or attempts to drive a motor vehicle on a road or other public place or is in charge of a motor vehicle on a road or other public place after consuming so much alcohol that the proportion of it in his breath, blood or urine exceeds the prescribed limit (qv), he is guilty of an offence: Road Traffic Act 1972, s.6 (as substituted by the Transport Act 1981, Sch 8). *See* BREATH TEST.

drugs, controlled. Drugs, classified by the Misuse of Drugs Act 1971 as: Class A (cocaine, LSD, opium, etc); Class B (amphetamine, cannabis, etc); Class C (benzphetamine, pemoline, etc). Classification affects the maximum penalties for the offence of having possession of a controlled drug. It is an offence for one who is an occupier of premises or concerned in their management to knowingly permit the smoking of opium or cannabis (qv) on those premises: s. 8. For "preparation" containing a drug, see Sch 2, Part 1, para 1; and *R* v *Stevens* [1981] Crim LR 568. For guidelines on sentencing offenders, see *R* v *Aramah*, [1983] Crim LR 271. *See* POSSESSION, UNLAWFUL, OF DRUGS.

drunkard, habitual. *See* HABITUAL DRUNKARD.

drunkenness. *See* INTOXICATION.

dry rent. Known also as rent seck. A rent not supported by a right of distress (qv). Ceased to exist after the Landlord and Tenant Act 1730. See *Cundiff* v *Fitzsimmons* [1911] 1 KB 513.

dubitante. Doubting. A word found in the law reports indicating that a judge is doubting the correctness of some proposition relating to the decision he has to take.

duces tecum. Bring with you. A subpoena ordering a person to attend a trial and to bring with him documents or other things to be produced in evidence. See O. 38. rr. 14–19. *See* SUBPOENA.

due. Owed, eg, as a debt. A debt is due when it is payable.

due care. Adequate caution in all the circumstances obtaining at a given time. See *Milkins* v *Roberts* [1949] SASR 251.

due course, payment in. *See* PAYMENT IN DUE COURSE.

due process of law. The regular course of the law through the courts.

dum bene se gesserit. So long as he shall conduct himself well. Phrase used in relation to offices, the tenure of which depends on the holder's conducting himself well, as in the case of a judge. *See* DURANTE BENE PLACITO NOSTRO.

dum casta vixerit. As long as she shall live chaste. See *Cobham* v *Tomlinson* (1672) T Jo 6 for use of this clause in a deed of separation. See also *P.* v *P.* [1957] NZLR 854.

dum sola. While single.

duplicated offences. Where an act or omission constitutes an offence under two or more Acts, or both under an Act and at common law, the offender shall, unless the contrary intention appears, be liable to prosecution and punishment under either or any of those Acts or at common law, but shall not be liable to be punished more than once for the same offence: I.A. 1978, s. 18.

duplicity, void for. *See* COUNTS, SEPARATE.

durante absentia. During absence. Administration (qv) is granted *durante absentia* when an executor is out of the realm.

durante bene placito nostro. During our (ie, the Crown's) good pleasure. Phrase used to describe the tenure of offices of judges during, eg, the reigns of James I and Charles I. Independence of judges was assured by the Act of Settlement 1701.

durante minore aetate. During minority. See the Non-Contentious Probate Rules 1954, rr. 31, 33.

durante viduitate. During widowhood.

duress. 1. Restraint by force, eg, imprisonment. 2. Actual violence or threats of violence to the person. Known also as *duress per minas* (by threats). A contract obtained by duress is voidable. "Duress, whatever form it takes, is a coercion of will so as to vitiate consent": *per* Lord Scarman in *Pao On v Lau Yiu Long* [1980] AC 614; *Kaufman v Gerson* [1904] 1 KB 591; *Alexander Barton v Alexander Ewan Armstrong* [1976] AC 104. 3. Duress as plea in charge of murder—in *Lynch v DPP for N Ireland* [1975] AC 653 it was held that on a charge of murder, it was open to a person accused as principal *in the second degree* to plead duress. See also *Abbot v R* [1976] 3 All ER 140; and *R v Graham* [1982] 1 WLR 294. See Law Commission Report No. 83, 1977. For duress vitiating a marriage, see *Szechter v Szechter* [1971] P 286. *See* UNDUE INFLUENCE.

duress, economic. Recovery of money paid under duress, other than to the person, is not limited to duress to goods; it can include economic duress where that is constituted by a threat to break a contract, even though there is good consideration for that further contract: *North Ocean Shipping Co v Hyundai Construction Co* [1978] 3 All ER 1170; *Pao On v Lau Yiu Long* [1980] AC 614; *Alec Lobb Garages v Total Oil GB* [1983] 1 WLR 87.

duress of goods. Where X is in a strong bargaining position by being in possession of Y's goods by virtue of a legal right (eg, by way of pawn), and Y is in a weak position because he needs the goods urgently, so that X demands from Y more than is justly due and Y pays. "Such a transaction is voidable. [Y] can recover the excess": *per* Lord Denning MR in *Lloyds Bank v Bundy* [1975] QB 326.

during Her Majesty's pleasure. Following a verdict of "not guilty by reason of insanity" the offender may be ordered by the court to be detained in a specified hospital during Her Majesty's pleasure. See the Criminal Procedure (Insanity) Act 1964, s. 1; M.H.A. 1983, s. 46.

Dutch auction. An auction (qv) at which property is offered at a relatively high price, then at a price which is gradually lowered, until an offer is made which is accepted. See the Mock Auction Act 1961, s. 3.

duties, absolute. *See* ABSOLUTE DUTIES.

duty. 1. An act that is due by legal or moral obligation. 2. The correlative of a right. 3. Payment levied on, eg, imports and exports.

duty of care. "You must take reasonable care to avoid acts or omissions which you can reasonably foresee would be likely to injure your neighbour. Who, then, in law is my neighbour? The answer seems to be—persons who are so closely and directly affected by my act that I ought reasonably to have them in contemplation as being affected when I am directing my mind to the acts or omissions which are called in question": *per* Lord Atkin in *Donoghue v Stevenson* [1932] AC 562. See *Junior Books Ltd v Veitchi Ltd* [1982] 3 WLR 477, where the House of Lords decided that the duty of care extended to financial loss.

duty of care, directors'. *See* DIRECTORS' DUTY OF CARE.

duty solicitors. Solicitors on duty on a rota basis at magistrates' courts who provide services to defendants appearing without representation. See the Legal Aid Act 1982, s. 1.

dwelling. "A building or part of a building occupied or intended to be occupied as a separate dwelling, together with any yard, garden, outhouses and appurtenances belonging to or usually enjoyed with that building or part": H.A. 1974, s. 29(1). See also the H.A. 1980, s. 3(2); and *Batey v Watefield* [1982] 1 All ER 611.

dying declaration. As an exception to the rule that hearsay is not admissible, the oral or written declaration of a dying person may be admissible evidence of the cause of his death in a trial for his manslaughter or murder if he would have been a competent witness had he lived, and if he had been in settled hopeless expectation of death at the time of making the declaration. "The principle on which this species of evidence is admitted is, that they are declarations made in extremity, when the party is at the point of death, and when every hope of this world is gone; when every motive to falsehood is silenced, and the mind is induced by the most powerful considerations to speak the truth: a situation so solemn and so awful is considered by law as creating an obligation equal to that which is imposed by a positive oath administered in a court of justice'': *R* v *Woodcock* (1789) 1 Leach 500. See also *R* v *Errington* (1838) 2 Lew CC 148; and *Nembhard* v *R* [1981] 1 WLR 1515. *See* EVIDENCE.

dying without issue. Construed, when used in a will (qv), to mean a want or failure of issue in the lifetime or at the time of the death of the stated person, and not an indefinite failure of his issue, unless a contrary intention shall appear by the will: W.A. 1837, s. 29. *See* ISSUE.

E

earned income. Income arising in respect of remuneration for any office or employment or in respect of a pension, superannuation, deferred pay, compensation for loss of office, income from property forming part of emoluments of any office or employment of profit, and income charged under Schedules A, B, D, derived from the carrying on of a trade, profession or vocation. See the Income and Corporation Taxes Act 1970.

earnest. Something of value, eg, a nominal sum, given to a seller by a buyer so as to bind a bargain.

earnings. Sums payable to a person by way of wages or salary (including fees, bonus, overtime pay, commission) and by way of pension, but not, eg, a disablement pension: A.J.A. 1970, s. 54. "Any remuneration or profit derived from an employment": S.S.A. 1975, s. 3(1).

easement. A right capable of forming the subject-matter of a grant which is appurtenant to the land of one person and exercisable over the land of another. Example: A, the owner of Blackacre, grants B, owner of adjoining Whiteacre, the right to walk across Blackacre. The right of way granted to B is in the *nature of an easement*; Blackacre is the *servient tenement*; Whiteacre is the *dominant tenement*; A is the *servient owner*; B is the *dominant owner*. An easement is *affirmative* (eg, as where A must allow B to perform a certain act); it is *negative* where the servient owner can be compelled by the dominant owner not to perform certain acts. See the L.P.A. 1925, s. 62.

easement, right as. A right is an easement only where it has the following qualities: there must be a dominant and servient tenement (qqv); the tenements must be owned by different persons; the easement must have some natural connection with the estate as being for its benefit; the

right must lie in grant. See *Moody* v *Steggles* (1879) 12 Ch D 261; *Mulliner* v *Midland Rwy Co* (1879) 11 Ch D 611; *Nickerson* v *Barraclough* [1981] Ch 426; and *Marchant* v *Capital and Counties Property* (1982) 263 EG 661.

eavesdropping. A public nuisance, abolished by the C.L.A. 1967, s. 13, committed when a person stood under windows "to hear news and carry it to others to make strife and debate among neighbours": *Termes de la Ley.*

ecclesiastical building. A building owned by the ecclesiastical authorities, as freehold or leasehold (qv), having some other ecclesiastic attribute marking it out as ecclesiastical: *A.-G.* v *Trustees of Howard United Reformed Church* [1974] 3 All ER 273. See the New Towns Act 1981, s. 80(1) (definition of "ecclesiastical property").

Ecclesiastical Causes Reserved, Court of. See COURT OF ECCLESIASTICAL CAUSES RESERVED.

ecclesiastical courts. These include: consistory courts (in each diocese); the Provincial Courts (Arches Court Court of York). Appeal is to the Judicial Committee of the Privy Council (qv). Consistory courts impose penalties such as rebuke, disqualification from preferment. *See* COMMISSION OF REVIEW; CONVOCATION; COURT OF ECCLESIASTICAL CAUSES RESERVED.

economic duress. *See* DURESS, ECONOMIC.

edict. An official proclamation of a rule or law.

EEC. European Economic Community, consisting, in 1983, of Belgium, France, Federal Republic of Germany, Italy, Luxembourg, the Netherlands (all original members), Britain, Irish Republic, Denmark and Greece. The Treaty of Accession was signed by the original member states in January 1972. The EEC was created by the Treaty of Rome 1957.

Its aims include the harmonious development of economic activities, an increase in stability and an accelerated raising of the standard of living: Treaty of Rome 1957, art. 2. The objects of the EEC are to be attained through the establishment of a common market. *See* COMMON MARKET; COMMUNITY LAW.

effects. Generally, a person's property. *See Mitchell* v *Mitchell* (1820) 5 Madd 69.

egg-shell skull principle. A defendant must take his victim as he finds him. "If a man is negligently run over or otherwise negligently injured in his body, it is no answer to the sufferer's claim for damages that he would have suffered less injury, or no injury at all, if he had not had an unusually thin skull or an unusually weak heart": *per* Kennedy J in *Dulieu* v *White* [1901] 2 KB 669.

ei qui affirmat non ei qui negat incumbit probatio. The burden of proof lies upon the person who affirms, not upon the person who denies. ". . . An ancient rule founded on considerations of good sense and it should not be departed from without strong reasons": *Joseph Constantine Steamship Line Ltd* v *Imperial Smelting Corp* [1942] AC 154. *See* BURDEN OF PROOF.

ejectione firmae, de. Writ of ejectment, introduced in 1500, which commenced an action against one who had been ejected *firma sua* (from his term).

ejectment. Remedy available originally to leaseholders, and later to freeholders, wrongfully dispossessed. A person claiming a freehold was held, by a fiction (qv) to have leased to a fictitious person, John Doe (qv) who was held to have been ejected by the casual ejector, the fictitious Richard Roe. The person in possession admitted to the fiction and relied on his real title as the basis of his defence. The title of the action was, eg, *Doe d. Smith* v *Jones* (ie, Doe, on the demise of *Smith* v *Jones*). Abolished under the Common Law Procedure Act 1852.

ejusdem generis. Of the same kind or nature. Rule of construction whereby if particular words forming a genus or kind are followed by general words, the general words are constructed *ejusdem generis*, ie, are held to be intended to describe only other things of the same kind as those enumerated by the particular words. Example: "To A I leave my coats, suits, hats and other wearing apparel"; "other wearing apparel" would include shirts but not the testator's fob watch. The rule does not apply where a contrary intention is shown, or where the particular words exhaust the genus. *See Re Miller* (1889) 61 LT 365; *Le Cras* v *Perpetual Trustee Co* [1967] 3 All ER 915. *See* CONSTRUCTION, RULES OF.

Elder Brethren. *See* ADMIRALTY COURT.

election. 1. Procedure whereby a constituency returns a member to Parliament. See the Representation of the People Acts 1949, 1969, 1977 and 1983. 2. The equitable doctrine whereby he who takes a benefit under an instrument must accept or reject the instrument as a whole. Example: A, under his will, gives B £50,000 and gives C Blackacre, which belongs to B. B must elect. He may either take the £50,000 and allow C to take Blackacre, or he may retain Blackacre and claim the £50,000, but in such a case he will be obliged to compensate C by paying him the value of Blackacre out of the £50,000. *See Cooper* v *Cooper* (1874) 44 LJ Ch 6; *Re Gordon's Will Trusts* [1978] Ch 145; and *Barclays Ltd* v *Bluff* [1981] 3 All ER 232.

elections, parliamentary. There are two types of election: (1) general elections, held following the dissolution of Parliament and the summoning of a new one by the Sovereign; and (2) by-elections, held when a vacancy occurs in the House of Commons (qv) following the resignation or death of a member or his election to the House of Lords (qv). *See* PARLIAMENT.

elector. 1. One whose name is shown on the register to be used at an election, excluding those shown on that register as below voting age on polling day: Representation of the People Act 1983, s. 1. 2. One who, taking a benefit under an instrument, either accepts or rejects the instrument as a whole.

electors, registration of. A person is entitled to be registered as an elector if he will attain voting age (ie, 18 or over) before the end of the 12 months following the day by which the register is required to be published. See the Representation of the People Acts 1949, and 1983, s. 12. Aliens, convicted persons in prison, peers (other than Irish peers) are among those who cannot be registered because of disqualification.

electricity, dishonest abstraction of. The dishonest use without due authority or dishonestly causing to be wasted or diverted, any electricity. An offence under the Th.A. 1968, s. 13. See *Low* v *Blease* [1975] Crim LR 513 (electricity held not to be "property" within the Th.A. 1968, s. 4); *Boggeln* v *Williams* [1978] 1 WLR 873; *R* v *Hodkinson* [1981] 1 All Er 628.

electronic surveillance. The use of concealed microphones, etc, to intercept communications. Evidence obtained in this way is generally admissible. See the Post Office Act 1969, s. 77, Sch 5; *R* v *Mills* [1962] 3 All ER 298; *R* v *Stewart* [1970] 1 All ER 689.

eleemosynary corporation. *Eleemosyna* = alms. A corporation organised for charitable purposes, usually for the distribution of alms in the name of the founder. See *Re Armitage's Will Trusts* [1972] 1 All ER 78.

elegit. He has chosen. Writ of execution allowing a judgment creditor (qv) to enter into possession of the debtor's land and hold it until the debt is satisfied. Ended by the A.J.A. 1956 and replaced by an order creating a charge over land or over an interest in the land. *See* the Charging Orders Act 1979; O. 50; *Irani Finance Ltd* v *Singh* [1971] Ch 59. Abolished by the S.C.A. 1981, s. 141.

emancipation. The act of setting free from the power and control of another.

embezzlement. Offence committed by a clerk or servant who fraudulently appropriated to his own use property delivered to or taken into possession by him on account of his master or employer. See the Larceny Act 1916, s. 17. No longer a separate offence under the Th.A. 1968.

emblements. *Emblaer* = to sow a field. The profits from sown lands. A lessee (qv) or his personal representatives may enter, after the determination of the lease, so as to reap certain cultivated crops which he has sown. See *Graves* v *Weld* (1833) 110 ER 731.

embody. A document is said to embody a provision if the provision is set out either in the document itself or in another document referred to in the document: C.C.A. 1974, s. 189(1).

embracery. The obsolescent common law offence of perverting the course of justice by attempting to influence or instruct a juror by corrupt means. See *R* v *Owen* [1976] 1 WLR 840.

emergency powers. Powers conferred by statutes such as the Emergency Powers Acts 1920 and 1964, allowing the Crown to issue a proclamation of a state of emergency whenever it appears, eg, that action is threatened or has been taken, calculated to deprive the community or any substantial portion of it of the essentials of life. The proclamation is in force for one month only, but may be renewed.

eminent domain. The right and inherent power of the state (apparently unknown to the common law) to appropriate private property within its boundaries to public use.

emolument. Some profit or advantage, ie, anything by which a person is benefited: *R* v *Postmaster General* (1878) 3 QBD 428. In the case of a company director (qv), fees and percentages paid by way of expenses allowances are included: Cos.A. 1948, s. 196. See also the Cos.A. 1967, ss. 6, 7. Includes "any allowances, privileges or benefits, whether obtained legally or by customary practice": Iron and Steel Act 1975, s. 37(1). See *Brumby* v *Milner* [1976] 1 WLR 1096.

emphyteusis. Term used in Roman law referring to a grant of rights of ownership over land in perpetuity subject to payment of a yearly rent and forfeiture in certain circumstances.

employed earner. One who is gainfully employed in Great Britain under a contract of service or in an office with emoluments chargeable to income tax under Sch E. *See* INCOME TAX.

employee. An individual who has entered into or works under a contract of employment: E.P. (C.) A. 1978, s. 153(1). The test of whether a person is or is not an employee may be answered by reference to the question: "Was the contract a contract of services within the meaning which an ordinary person would give to these words?": *Cassidy v Minister of Health* [1951] 2 KB 348. See *Ready Mixed Concrete Ltd v Mopni* [1968] 2 QB 497; *Market Investigations Ltd v Ministry of Social Security* [1969] 2 QB 173.

employee and order to work. No court may compel any employee to do any work or attend at any place for the performance of any work by way of an order for specific performance (qv) or an injunction (qv): T.U.L.R.A. 1974, s. 16.

employee's duties. Generally: to obey a lawful order within the terms of the contract (see *Turner v Mason* (1845) 14 M & W 112); to serve faithfully (ie, to co-operate with his employer); to perform his duties with proper care and diligence and indemnify his employer in appropriate cases (see *Lister v Romford Ice and Cold Storage Co Ltd* [1957] AC 555).

employees' inventions, right to. An invention made by an employee shall be taken to belong to his employer for purposes of this Act and all other purposes if it was made in the course of the employee's normal duties or duties outside his normal duties but specifically assigned to him and the circumstances were such that an invention might reasonably be expected to result from the carrying out of his duties, or it was made in the course of the employee's duties and, at the time of making the invention, because of the nature of his duties and the particular responsibilities arising from the nature of those duties, he had a special obligation to further the interest of the employer's undertaking: Patents Act 1977, s. 39(1).

employer. The master of a servant. A person by whom an employee is or was employed, a person for whom one or more workers work, or have worked or normally seek to work: T.U.L.R.A. 1974, s. 30(1). *See* MASTER AND SERVANT; SERVANT; WORKER.

employer and employee. *See* MASTER AND SERVANT.

employers, associated. *See* ASSOCIATED EMPLOYERS.

employers' association. An organisation (whether permanent or temporary) which consists wholly or mainly of employers or individual proprietors of one or more descriptions and is an organisation whose principal purposes include the regulation of relations between employers of that description or those descriptions and workers or trade unions or consists wholly or mainly of constituent or affiliated organisations which fulfil these conditions. See the T.U.L.R.A. 1974, s. 28(2).

employer's duties. Generally: to provide "a reasonable amount of work to enable [the employee] to earn that which the parties must be taken to have contemplated" (*Bauman v Hulton Press* [1952] 2 All ER 1121); to indemnify the employee against liabilities and losses properly incurred in the performance of his work; to provide adequate material and a proper system and effective supervision (see *Wilsons and Clyde Coal Co v English* [1938] AC 57; *Speed v Thomas Swift and Co Ltd* [1943] KB 557).

employer's liability. The liability of an employer to pay damages to employees for personal injuries sustained in the course of employment. In general, an accident arising out of the course of employment will be deemed, in the absence of evidence to the contrary, to have arisen out of that employment.

employment. Usually taken to include business, profession, vocation, trade, etc.

Employment Appeal Tribunal. Body set up under the E.P.A. 1975, s. 87, Sch 6, consisting of judges of the High Court and Court of Appeal, Court of Session and lay members, to hear appeals on questions of law relating to decisions of tribunals on, eg, the Redundancy Payments Act 1965, the Equal Pay Act 1970, the Sex Discrimination Act 1975, the E.P.A. 1975. Appeal on a point of law lies to the Court of Appeal (qv): E.P.A. 1975, s. 88(4). For rules of procedure see *Practice Direction,* [1981] 1 WLR 323.

employment, common. *See* COMMON EMPLOYMENT.

employment, course of. *See* COURSE OF EMPLOYMENT.

enabling statute. 1. A statute which makes legal that which was illegal. 2. A statute giving obligatory or discretionary powers.

enacting words. The introductory part of a statute, stating the authority by which it was made, which runs: "Be it enacted by the Queen's most Excellent Majesty, by and with the advice and consent of the Lords Spiritual and Temporal, in this present Parliament assembled, and by the authority of the same, as follows . . .".

enactment. An Act of Parliament (qv) or part of an Act. Includes any by-law or regulation having effect under an enactment: Education (Work Experience) Act 1973, s. 1(4). *See* LEGISLATIVE HISTORY OF AN ENACTMENT.

en autre droit. In the right of another person

enceinte. Pregnant.

enclosure. Also "inclosure". The discharge of land from all rights of common. Procedure is now regulated by the Commons Acts 1876 and 1879 and requires approval of application by the Secretary for the Environment. See the Highways Act 1980, s. 45(12).

encourage. To urge to a course of action; to incite. "There can be no incitement of anyone whether by words or written matter unless the incitement reaches the man whom it is said is being incited": *Wilson* v *Danny*

Quastel Ltd [1965] 2 All ER 541. See INCITEMENT.

encroachment. Unlawfully entering upon another's rights or possessions. See *Ankerson* v *Connelly* [1907] 1 Ch 678.

encumbrance. A liability which burdens property, eg, a lease, mortgage, easement, restrictive covenant, rent-charge (qqv). One who has the right to enforce an encumbrance is known as an "encumbrancer". See the L.P.A. 1925, s. 205(1)(vii).

encumbrance, freedom from. Warranty, under the S.G.A. 1979, s. 12(2) (*a*), "that the goods are free and will remain free, until the time when the property is to pass, from any charge or encumbrance not disclosed or known to the buyer before the contract is made".

endangered species. Certain animals and plants specified in the Endangered Species (Import and Export) Act 1976, Schs 1–3 (as amended) the import and export of which are generally restricted.

endorsement. 1. A signature, usually on the reverse side of a document, generally operating as a transfer of rights arising from the document. An *endorsement in blank* is a simple signature usually rendering a bill of exchange (qv) payable to bearer. A *special endorsement* specifies the name of the person to whom or to whose order the bill is to be made payable. A *conditional endorsement* transfers the property in a bill subject to the fulfilment of a stipulated condition. A *restrictive endorsement* prohibits further negotiation (eg, "pay X only"). See the B.Ex.A. 1882, s. 32. 2. Endorsement of a driving licence is a procedure whereby a person convicted of certain offences will have particulars of the conviction noted on that licence. See the Road Traffic Act 1972, s. 101; and the Transport Act 1981, s. 19.

endorsement of claim. A writ must be endorsed either with a full statement of claim (known formerly as "special endorsement") or a short statement of the nature of the claim or remedy or relief required. The writ must be endorsed with a claim for fixed costs where the claim is for a debt or liquidated demand (qv), and with the plaintiff's address and, where appropriate, his solicitor's name and address. Claims for interest must be specifically pleaded (O. 18, r. 8(4)). See O. 6, r. 2. *See* WRIT.

endorsement of service. Particulars of time, place and method of service endorsed on a writ within three days after personal or substituted service has been made. See O. 10, r. 1.

endorsement of writ, formal. A writ must be endorsed with the plaintiff's address, solicitor's name and address, etc. A writ lacking the appropriate formal endorsements will not be issued until they have been completed.

endowment. 1. Giving of dower (qv). 2. Provision for a charity (qv).

enemy. States and persons engaged in armed operations against Her Majesty's forces. See the Army Act 1955, s. 225.

energy conservation and control. Powers exercised by the Secretary of State under the Energy Act 1976, regulating or prohibiting the production, supply, acquisition or use of crude liquid petroleum, natural gas, petroleum products, other substances used for fuel, and electricity.

enfeoff. To invest a person with a freehold estate by feoffment (qv).

enforcement notice. Notice served under the T.C.P.A. 1971, s. 87, by a local planning authority on the owner and occupier of land on which there has been a breach of planning control, ie, where development (qv) has taken place without permission, or in disregard of the limitations of such permission. The notice specifies the breach and the steps required to remedy it and states a time for compliance. Appeal is to the Secretary of State. See *Button v Jenkins* [1975] 3 All ER 585; *LTSS Print Services Ltd v London Borough of Hackney* [1975] 1 All ER 374.

enforcement of judgments. *See* JUDGMENTS, ENFORCEMENT OF.

enfranchise. 1. The conferring of a right to vote at an election. 2. The conferring on a constituency of a right to return a member to Parliament. 3. The conversion of copyhold land into socage (qv).

enfranchisement of tenancy. Process whereby a tenant is entitled to acquire a freehold or extended long lease. The tenant must hold a tenancy exceeding 21 years at a rent less than two-thirds of the rateable value of the premises: Leasehold Reform Acts 1967 and 1979. See the H.A. 1980, Sch 21.

engage. 1. To engage to do something has the same force as "to covenant" (qv). 2. To be engaged in an occupation is to be occupied therein. It "connotes such a degree of employment as occupies the whole or at least a substantial part of the [employee's] time": *Buntine v Hume* [1943] VLR 123.

engagement to marry. Under common law this was considered as a contract, the breaking of which could lead to an action for breach of promise (qv). The action was abolished under the Law Reform (Misc. Provs.) Act 1970. (The engagement ring is presumed to be an absolute gift.) See also the Matrimonial Proceedings and Property Act 1970, s. 37.

Englishry, presentment of. In the Norman era, proof (usually by inquest and declaration by a dead person's four nearest relatives) that a slain person was English. This meant that a heavy fine on the community (known as *murdrum = morth*, a secret killing) was avoided. Abolished in 1340.

engross. 1. To prepare the text of a document. An engrossment is a deed prior to its execution. 2. To buy up, eg, corn, so as to sell it at a higher price (an offence abolished in 1843).

enjoyment. The taking of the benefit of some right. "The amenity or advantage of using": *per* Stirling J in *Smith v Baxter* [1900] 2 Ch 138.

enlarge. 1. To free. 2. To extend a period of time, eg, in which a person may appeal. 3. A mortgagee (qv) who has obtained title to the land free from the mortgage by remaining in possession for 12 years may enlarge the term of years into a fee simple (qv) by deed: L.P.A. 1925, ss. 88, 153.

enlistment, foreign. *See* FOREIGN ENLISTMENT.

enquiry, writ of. In a common law action, after a judgment of default was given for the plaintiff, the sheriff (qv) would enquire, with a jury of 12 persons, into the damages sustained by the plaintiff. The procedure commenced by a writ.

enrolment. The registration or recording on an official record of an act. See the S.C.A. 1981, s. 133.

entailed interest. *See* FEE TAIL.

enter. 1. To record in an account. 2. To go on land so as to assert some right. 3. The entrance of any part of the offender's body or of an instrument for removing any goods, into a house, during commission of the offence of burglary (qv).

entering appearance. See APPEARANCE, ENTERING.

entering judgment. *See* JUDGMENT, ENTERING.

enterprise entity. Doctrine in EEC law whereby a parent company and its subsidiary are treated as one economic unity if, eg, the latter has no autonomy and there is no competition between them: *Christiani & Nielson N.V.* [1969] CMLR D36.

enterprise zones. Designated areas in which some fiscal and administrative burdens may be removed, eg, exemption from rates of industrial buildings, development land tax: see the L.G.P.L.A. 1980, Part XVIII, Sch 32; and the Finance Act 1980, s. 74.

enticement of spouse. *See* CONSORTIUM.

entire contract. *See* DIVISIBLE CONTRACT.

entireties, tenancy by. *See* TENANCY BY ENTIRETIES.

entrapment. The enticing of a person into the commission of a crime so that he may be prosecuted. English law has no such doctrine of defence: *R v McEvilly* (1975) 60 Cr App R 59. Offences must not be created so as to trap criminals: *Sneddon* v *Stevenson* [1967] 2 All ER 1277. See also *R v Willis* [1976] Crim LR 127; *R v Sang* [1980] AC 402. See Law Commission Report No 83, 1977. *See* AGENT PROVOCATEUR.

entry, forcible. *See* FORCIBLE ENTRY.

entry into possession. Right of a legal mortgagee to enter into possession of the mortgaged property. An action for possession of a dwelling-house can be adjourned by the court, or the possession order suspended or postponed if it appears that the mortgagor is likely, within a reasonable period, to pay any sums due under the mortgage or to remedy a default consisting of a breach of any other obligation. See the A.J.A. 1970, ss. 36–39, as amended by the A.J.A. 1973, s. 7; *Four Maids Ltd* v *Dudley Marshall Ltd* [1957] 2 All ER 35. *See* MORTGAGE.

entry, violence for securing. It is an offence for a person who unlawfully uses or threatens violence to secure entry into premises for himself or some other person, provided that there is someone present on the premises who is opposed to the entry and the person using or threatening violence knows that that is the case: C.L.A. 1977, s. 6(1). For defences, see s. 6(3).

entry without warrant. *See* WARRANT, ENTRY WITHOUT.

entry, writ of. Writ by which the party claiming possession to the land disproved the possessor's title by showing, eg, that he had entered unlawfully. Abolished in 1834.

enure. Also "inure". To take effect.

en ventre sa mère. In his mother's womb. Refers to unborn child.

E. & O.E. Errors and omissions excepted.

eo instanti. At that instant.

eo nomine. By, or in, that name.

epitome of title. *See* ABSTRACT AND EPITOME OF TITLE.

equality clause. A provision relating to terms of a contract under which a woman is employed, having the effect that, where she is employed on like work with a man in the same employment or on work rated as equivalent with that of a man in the same employment, her contract is to be treated as modified, if necessary, so that it is no less favourable than that of the man or so that it includes any terms corresponding to those benefiting the man. See the Equal Pay Act 1970, s. 1; and the Sex Discrimination Act 1975, s. 8.

Equal Opportunities Commission. Body of 8–15 persons set up under the Sex Discrimination Act 1975, s. 53, to work towards the elimination of discrimination and to promote equality of opportunity between men and women generally and to review working of the 1975 Act and the Equal Pay Act 1970. *See* DISCRIMINATION, SEX.

equal pay. Under the Equal Pay Act 1970, it was provided that, as from the end of 1975, women doing the same or broadly similar work to men would qualify for equal pay and conditions of employment. The Treaty of Rome 1957, art. 119, calls for member states to apply the principle that men and women shall receive equal pay for equal work. The principle may be invoked before national courts: *Defresne* v *Sabena* [1981] 1 All ER 122; *EEC Commission* v *The UK* (1982) 61/81.

equitable. 1. Fair and just. 2. In accordance with rules of equity (qv). 3. In accordance with the practice and procedure of the courts of equity.

equitable apportionment. *See* APPORTIONMENT.

equitable assignment. *See* ASSIGNMENT.

equitable charge, general. An equitable charge which is not secured by a deposit of documents relating to the legal estate affected, and does not arise or affect an interest arising under a trust for sale or a settlement, and is not a charge given by way of indemnity against rents, and is not included in any other class of land charge: L.C.A. 1972, s. 2. Example: an equitable mortgage not protected by the deposit of title deeds. Registrable under Class C as a land charge: s. 2(4) (*i*). *See* LAND CHARGES.

equitable easement. "Any easement right or privilege over or affecting land created or arising after the commencement of this Act and being merely an equitable interest": L.C.A. 1972, s. 2. Registrable as a land charge under Class C. Example:

an easement for the grantee's life. See *Shiloh Spinners Ltd* v *Harding* [1973] AC 691. *See* EASEMENT.

equitable estate or interest. An estate interest or charge in or over land which is not a legal estate and which takes effect as an equitable interest or right. See the L.P.A. 1925, s. 1(3).

equitable estoppel. *See* ESTOPPEL.

equitable execution. Procedure whereby equitable relief is obtained by the appointment of a receiver (qv) or by injunction (qv). See O. 51 (receiver) and O. 29, r. 1 (injunction).

equitable interests. Interests, the recognition and protection of which were originally within the province of the courts of equity. See, eg, the L.P.A. 1925, s. 1(1)–(3). *See* EQUITABLE RIGHTS.

equitable lease. A lease which does not satisfy the necessary requirements for a legal lease but is, nevertheless, valid in equity. There must be a valid contract to create a lease and the contract must be specifically enforceable. See *Walsh* v *Lonsdale* (1882) 21 Ch D 9; *Warmington* v *Miller* [1973] QB 877. *See* LEASE.

equitable lien. *See* LIEN.

equitable mortgage. A mortgage which transfers an equitable interest only, either because the mortgagor's interest is equitable, or because the conveyance or other mode of transfer is equitable. It may be created, eg, by deposit of the title deeds, agreement to create a legal mortgage (qv), creation of an equitable charge (ie, where property is charged with payment of the debt, but there is no transfer of possession or ownership of the property). *See* MORTGAGE.

equitable presumptions. Presumptions raised in equity in certain cases, eg, as where a testator bequeaths two legacies to the same person under the same will (so that if the legacies are of unequal amounts, both will be payable). See *Hurst* v *Beech* (1820) 2 Madd 351; *Re Davies* [1957] 1 WLR 922.

equitable remedies. Those remedies principally evolved by equity, eg, specific performance, rescission, delivery up and cancellation of documents, injunctions, account, receivers.

equitable rights. 1. Those rights originally recognised and enforced only in the courts of equity. 2. Those rights which are good against all persons save the *bona fide* purchaser of a legal estate for value without notice, and those who claim under such a person. (In contrast, legal rights are "good against the whole world".)

equitable waste. The malicious or wanton destruction of property by a lessee (qv), eg, stripping a house of its doors. So-called because it could be remedied before the J.A. 1873 only in a court of equity. A tenant who commits waste of this nature can be restrained by an injunction and ordered to rehabilitate the premises. See *Vane* v *Lord Barnard* (1716) 2 Vern 738. *See* WASTE.

equity. *Aequus* = fair. 1. Impartiality. 2. "Any body of rules existing by the side of the original civil law, founded on distinct principles and claiming incidentally to supersede the civil law in virtue of a superior sanctity inherent in those principles": Maine. 3. A system of doctrines and procedures which developed side by side with the common law and statute law, having originated in the doctrines and procedures evolved by the Court of Chancery in its attempts to remedy some of the defects of common law. 4. A right to enforce an equitable remedy. 5. The issued share capital of a company: Cos.A. 1948, s. 154(5). For "equity security", see the Cos.A. 1980, s. 17(11).

equity and law, conflict of. *See* LAW AND EQUITY, CONFLICT OF.

equity and law, fusion of. *See* LAW AND EQUITY, FUSION OF.

equity, maxims of. Aphorisms purporting to state some of the fundamental principles of equity. A collection was made by Richard Francis in *Maxims of Equity* (1725). They include: equity acts *in personam*; equity follows the law; equity acts on the conscience; equity aids the vigilant; equity looks to the intent rather than the form; he who comes to equity must come with clean hands, etc.

equity, nature of. "Now equity is no part of the law, but a moral virtue, which qualifies, moderates and reforms the rigour, hardness and edge of the law, and is an universal truth; it does also assist the law where it is defective and weak in the constitution (which is the life of the law) and defends the law from crafty evasions . . . and this is the office of equity, to support and protect the common law from shifts and crafty contrivances against the justice of the law. Equity therefore does not destroy the law, nor create it, but assists it": *per* Lord Cowper in *Dudley* v *Dudley* (1705) Prec Ch 241.

equity of redemption. As soon as a mortgage is created, the mortgagor acquires a contractual (ie, legal) right to redeem on the contractual date of redemption and an equitable right to redeem after that date has passed; these rights comprise the mortgagor's *equity of redemption*. The right of redemption is inviolable and may not be restricted unduly. See *Biggs* v *Hoddinott* [1898] 2 Ch 307; *Kreglinger* v *New Patagonia Meat Co Ltd* [1914] AC 25; *Knightsbridge Estates Trust Ltd* v *Byrne* [1939] Ch 441. *See* MORTGAGE; REDEMPTION.

equity's darling. Name given to a *bona fide* purchaser for value without notice of a legal estate, who was protected in equity. See, eg, *Pilcher* v *Rawlins* (1872) 7 Ch App 259.

equity share capital. *See* SHARE CAPITAL, EQUITY.

equivocation. An ambiguity in a document, eg, where a person is described in terms which could apply equally to another. Example: "Blackacre to my nephew John", where the testator has two nephews named John. Evidence of the testator's intention may be admissible in explanation. See the A.J.A. 1982, ss. 20–22; and *Richardson* v *Watson* (1833) 4 B & Ad 787. *See* AMBIGUITY.

error. 1. "A fault in a judgment, or in the process or proceeding to judgment or in execution upon the same": *Termes de la Ley*. 2. Writ of error was used to instruct an inferior court (qv) to send records of proceedings for review by a superior court (qv). Abolished in civil cases by the J.A. 1875 and in criminal cases by the Criminal Appeal Act 1907.

error, jurisdictional. *See* JURISDICTIONAL ERROR.

error of law on the face of the record. An error which may be ascertained without recourse to any evidence other than examination of the record of the proceedings. The record "must contain at least the document which initiates the proceedings, the pleadings, if any, and the adjudication; but not the evidence, nor the reasons, unless the tribunal chooses to incorporate them": *R v Northumberland Compensation Appeal Tribunal, ex p Shaw* [1952] 1 KB 338.

escape. The common law offence committed by one who, being lawfully confined in connection with a criminal offence, breaks out of any place in which he is confined with the intention of escaping from custody. See the Prison Act 1952, as amended by the C.J.A. 1961, by which it is an offence to aid the escape of a prisoner.

escape of dangerous things. *See* DANGEROUS THINGS, LIABILITY RELATING TO.

escheat. Procedure whereby land reverted on the extinction of a tenancy (qv). 1. *Escheat propter delictum tenentis* (for the tenant's crime), ie, where the tenant was convicted and sentenced to death, the land reverted to the lord. 2. *Escheat propter defectum sanguinis* (for failure of blood), ie, where the tenant died without an heir, the land escheated to the lord. Abolished under the Inheritance Act 1833, s. 10 and the A.E.A. 1925, s. 45(1).

escrow. A deed or bond delivered to a person who is not a party to it, to be held by that party until conditions are performed, after which it is delivered and becomes absolute. See *Beesly v Hallwood Estates* [1961] Ch 105; *Terrapin International v IRC* [1976] 2 All ER 461; and *Alan Estates Ltd v WG Stores Ltd* [1982] Ch 511.

espionage, industrial. The obtaining of industrial intelligence by illegal

means. See *Cranleigh Precision Engineering v Bryant* [1964] 3 All ER 289; and *Ansell Rubber v Allied Rubber* [1967] VR 37.

essence of a contract. The essential conditions, the very basis, of a contract, without which no agreement would have been entered into. See the S.G.A. 1979, s. 10. *See* CONDITION; CONTRACT.

essoin. *Sonium* = care, worry. An excuse for not making an appearance in an action in court on an appointed day. See the Law Terms Act 1830, s. 6.

established use certificate. Certificate granted by a local planning authority stating that the use of land is "established" if begun: before the beginning of 1964 without planning consent and has continued since the end of 1963; or before the beginning of 1964 under planning permission subject to conditions which have not been complied with since the end of 1963; or after the end of 1963 following a change of use not requiring consent and there has been no change requiring consent since the end of 1963: T.C.P.A. 1971, ss. 94, 95. See *Broxbourne CC v Secretary of State* [1979] 2 All ER 13.

establishment, right of. The right to take up and pursue activities as self-employed persons and to set up and manage undertakings in the member states of the EEC: Treaty of Rome 1957, art. 52. See Directive 75/363; and *Patrick v Ministry of Cultural Affairs* [1977] 2 CMLR 523. *See* E.E.C.

estate. 1. An area of land. 2. An expression in land law which applies to the period of time for which a tenant (qv) was entitled to hold the land. "All estates are but times of their continuances": Bacon. Common law recognised the following estates: (1) freehold (ie, estates whose duration is not known)—estate in fee simple, estate in fee tail, estate for life, estate *pur autre vie*; (2) less than freehold (ie, where the duration is certain)—leaseholds for a fixed term of years, tenancies from year to year.

estate agency work. Things done by a person in the course of a business pursuant to the instructions of a client who wishes to dispose of or acquire an interest in land, relating to introductions of third persons to the client and the disposal or acquisition of that interest: Estate Agents Act 1979, s. 1(1). The Director General of Fair Trading (qv) is empowered under s. 3(1) to make orders prohibiting unfit persons from doing estate agency work. See SI 1981/1517.

estate contract. Contracts by estate owners or persons entitled at the date of contract to have a legal estate conveyed to them, to convey or create a legal estate, including a contract conferring valid options to purchase. A Class C charge under the L.C.A. 1972. See *Georgiades* v *Edward Wolfe & Co* [1965] Ch. 487; *Barrett* v *Hilton Developments Ltd* [1974] Ch 237.

estate duty. Tax on the value of property passing on death. Abolished under the Finance Act 1975, s. 49.

estate, future. *See* FUTURE INTEREST.

estate, net. *See* NET ESTATE.

estate owner. The owner of a legal estate, ie, the person in whom there is vested the fee simple absolute in possession (qv) in the case of a freehold or the term of years absolute (qv) in the case of a leasehold.

estate, real. *See* REAL ESTATE.

estate rentcharge. *See* RENTCHARGE.

estates, administration of. Procedure relating to assets of a deceased person, whereby they are collected, debts are paid and the surplus distributed to those beneficially entitled. Order of the application of assets (in the case of a solvent estate and subject to the testator's directions) is: property undisposed of by will; property not specifically devised or bequeathed but included in residuary gift; property specifically appropriated for payment of debts; property charged with payment of debts; fund retained to meet legacies; property specifically devised or bequeathed; property appointed under will by general power. See the A.E.A. 1925, s. 34(1), Sch 1, Part II. Funeral, testamentary and administration expenses have priority: A.E.A. 1925, Part I, Sch 1.

estates, legal. Estates capable of subsisting at law (qv).

estates of the realm. Originally, clergy, baronage, commons. The term is now applied to the Lords Spiritual and Temporal, ie, the House of Lords (qv) and the Commons, ie, the House of Commons (qv).

estates subsisting at law. Under the L.P.A. 1925, s. 1, the only estates in land capable of subsisting or of being conveyed or created at law, ie, "legal estates" are, as from 1st January 1926: an estate in fee simple absolute in possession (qv); a term of years absolute (qv). All other estates take effect as equitable interests (qv).

estimates. Annual statements of the government's proposals for public expenditure relating to the financial year (qv).

estoppel. A rule of evidence preventing a person from denying the truth of a statement he has made previously, or the existence of facts in which he has led another to believe. 1. *Estoppel in pais* (or by conduct). Thus, a tenant who has accepted a lease (qv) cannot dispute the lessor's title. 2. *Estoppel by deed*. A party to a deed "is estopped in a court of law from saying that the facts stated in the deed are not truly stated": *Baker* v *Dewey* (1823) 1 B & C 704. 3. *Estoppel by record*. A person cannot deny the facts upon which the judgment against him has been given. 4. *Equitable estoppel*. (i) Under the doctrine of *promissory estoppel*, where X, by words or conduct makes to Y an unambiguous representation by promise or asurance concerning his (X's) future actions, intended to affect the legal relationship between X and Y, and Y alters his position in reliance on it, X will not be allowed to act inconsistently with that representation. (ii) *Proprietary estoppel*. X may be estopped from denying Y's rights in X's property, eg, where Y has incurred expenditure in the property. For "estoppel by convention", see *Amalgamated Investments* v *Texas Commerce Bank Ltd* [1982] QB 84. See *E. R. Ives Investments Ltd* v *High* [1967] 2 QB 379; *Dillwyn* v *Llewelyn* (1862) 31 LJ Ch 658; *Brikom Investments* v *Carr* [1979] 2 All ER 753; *Greasley* v *Cooke*

[1980] 1 WLR 1306; and *Taylor Fashions* v *Liverpool Victoria Trustee Ltd* [1981] 1 All ER 897.

estoppel, issue. *See* ISSUE ESTOPPEL.

estoppel, licence by. *See* LICENCE BY ESTOPPEL.

estoppel, partnership by. *See* PARTNERSHIP BY ESTOPPEL.

estovers. *Estovoir* = to be necessary. Rights of a lessee (qv) to woodland timber for certain necessary or immediate repairs, eg, hay bote (or "bot") (for repair of fences), house bote (for repair of a dwelling). Common of estovers is the right to take necessary wood from another's land. *See* BOTE.

estrays. Valuable domestic animals found wandering away from their enclosure or home, without any known owner. They are considered, after a year and a day, to belong to the Crown.

estreat. A true copy of a record, relating to recognisances and fines. The estreat of a recognisance (qv) involved enforcing the record of a recognisance which had become forfeited.

et al. 1. *Et alibi* = and elsewhere. 2. *Et alii*, or *et aliae*, or *et alia* = and others.

et seq. *Et sequentes*. And those which follow.

European Communities. They comprise: the European Economic Community (EEC) (qv) (set up in 1957); the European Coal and Steel Community (set up 1951); the European Atomic Energy Authority (Euratom) (set up in 1957). See the European Communities Act 1972, s. 1.

European Communities, Court of Justice of the. *See* COURT OF JUSTICE OF THE EUROPEAN COMMUNITIES.

European Convention on Human Rights. *See* HUMAN RIGHTS, EUROPEAN CONVENTION ON.

European Court. Name given to the Court of Justice of the European Communities (qv).

European Court of Human Rights. The judicial body of the Council of Europe which can hear cases involving basic rights and freedoms. There is no obligation binding member states to accept its jurisdiction. It consists of a number of judges equal to the number of members of the Council. See *Convention on Human Rights* 1950; *Rules of Procedure* 1959.

European Economic Community. *See* EEC.

European Economic Community law. *See* COMMUNITY LAW.

European Parliament. Name given to the Assembly of EEC (qv).

euthanasia. Term applied to the (illegal) practice of painlessly putting to death those suffering from incurable diseases. *See* MERCY KILLING.

evasion of liability by deception. *See* DECEPTION, EVASION OF LIABILITY BY.

eviction. 1. The recovery of lands from possession of another by the course of law. 2. Dispossession of a tenant (qv) by his landlord. 3. Dispossession by virtue of paramount title.

eviction of occupier, unlawful. It is an offence to unlawfully deprive or attempt to unlawfully deprive residential occupier (qv) of any premises of his occupation of the premises or any part thereof unless the accused can show that he reasonably believed that the residential occupier had ceased to reside therein: Protection from Eviction Act 1977, s. 1(2). See *R* v *Davidson–Acres* [1980] Crim LR 50. Where premises have been let as a dwelling under a non-statutorily protected tenancy (qv) and the tenancy has come to an end but the occupier continues residence, it is unlawful for recovery to be enforced other than through the court: s. 3(1). *See* HARASSMENT OF OCCUPIER.

evidence. Testimony and production of documents and things relating to the facts into which the court enquires and the methods and rules relating to the establishing of those facts before the court. "That which demonstrates, makes clear, or ascertains the truth of the very fact or point in issue": Blackstone. The law of evidence comprises those rules which govern the presentation of facts and proof in proceedings before a court. Evidence may be classified as: direct and circumstantial; primary and secondary; conclusive and inconclusive.

evidence, admissibility of. *See* ADMISSIBILITY OF EVIDENCE.

evidence, advice on. *See* ADVICE ON EVIDENCE.

evidence as to character. *See* CHARACTER, EVIDENCE AS TO.

evidence, best. *See* BEST EVIDENCE RULE.

evidence, burden of adducing. *See* BURDEN OF ADDUCING EVIDENCE.

evidence, circumstantial. Evidence of facts not in issue from which can be inferred a fact in issue, eg, evidence that skid-marks made by the defendant's motor cycle were on the wrong side of the road. See, eg, *R v Exall* (1886) 4 F & F 922.

evidence, conclusive. Evidence which must be taken by the court as sufficient proof of a fact, ie, evidence which may not be disputed. Example: a certificate of incorporation of a company (qv) is conclusive evidence of its registration: Cos.A. 1980, s. 3(4).

evidenced in writing. Some contracts are unenforceable unless evidenced in writing, eg, contracts of guarantee (Statute of Frauds 1677), contracts for the sale and other disposition of land (L.P.A. 1925, s. 40). The phrase means that the writing must contain, eg, the signature of the party to be charged, names or other identification of the parties, description of the subject-matter and price. *See* CONTRACT.

evidence, direct. Used in two senses. (1). Testimony, as contrasted with hearsay, ie, an assertion by a witness offered as proof of the truth of a fact he asserts. (2). Statement by a witness that he perceived with one of his senses a fact in issue. Example: production of a document constituting a fact in issue, when its existence is disputed.

evidence, documentary. *See* DOCUMENTARY EVIDENCE.

evidence, exclusion of. *See* DISCRETION, JUDICIAL, RELATING TO ADMISSIBILITY OF EVIDENCE; EXCLUSIONARY RULES.

evidence, extrinsic. Evidence of statements of circumstances or facts not referred to in a document which may explain or vary its meaning. Not generally admissible except in the case of, eg, parol evidence to contra-dict express terms of a document, parol evidence to supplement the omitted terms of a private formal document, to show the real nature of a transaction, to explain a latent ambiguity (qv). See the Civil Evidence Act 1968, s. 1(1); the A.J.A. 1982, s. 21 (wills); *Doe d Gord v Needs* (1836) 2 M & W 129; *Kell v Charmer* (1856) 23 Beav 195; *Henderson v Arthur* [1907] 1 KB 10; *Re Van Lessen* [1955] 1 WLR 1326.

evidence, first-hand and second-hand hearsay. Statement made by X which is proved by producing a document wherein X made it, or by oral evidence of Y who heard X making the statement, is first-hand evidence. Where a witness, Y, states on oath that X told him that Z had made a statement, that hearsay statement is second-hand evidence.

evidence, hearsay. The oral or written statements of one who is not called as a witness which are narrated to the court by a witness or through a document, for the purpose of establishing the truth of what was asserted. Such evidence is generally inadmissible. Exceptions to the rule include: statutory exceptions; declarations of deceased persons (in very restricted circumstances); evidence given in former trials; depositions by witnesses; informal admissions and confessions. First-hand hearsay evidence (qv) was made admissible in civil proceedings by the Civil Evidence Act 1968, s. 2(1) (see also ss. 4, 5). See *Law Reform Committee 13th Report* 1966 (Cmnd 2964); the Civil Evidence Acts 1968 and 1972; O. 38; *Sparks v R* [1964] AC 964; *R v Patel* [1981] 3 All ER 94.

evidence, hearsay, common law exceptions applicable to criminal cases. These include: admissions and confessions; statements concerning the maker's physical condition, emotion or state of mind; statements relating to an event in issue; statements accompanying and explaining some relevant act; statements in former proceedings; statements by deceased persons; statements in public documents.

evidence, hearsay, statutory excep-

tions applicable to criminal cases. These include: the Criminal Evidence Act 1965; the C.J.A. 1967, s. 9; and the Th.A. 1968, s. 27(4).

evidence in civil proceedings, hearsay. Statements other than those made by a person while giving oral evidence in civil proceedings which are tendered as evidence of the facts stated therein. Under the Civil Evidence Act 1968, ss. 1, 2, such evidence is admitted in civil proceedings by agreement of the parties, or under the rules of the court, or under the Act or any other statute.

evidence, indirect. Hearsay or circumstantial evidence.

evidence in rebuttal. May be given, subject to the control of the judge, to counter what has been said in cross-examination relating to a fact in issue.

evidence, insufficient. Evidence which is so weak that a reasonable man would be unable to decide the issue in favour of the party on whose behalf it is adduced. See, eg, *Hawkins v Powells Tillery Steam Coal Co* [1911] 1 KB 988.

evidence, intrinsic. Evidence from within a document, needing no external matter to explain it.

evidence, irrelevant. *See* IRRELEVANT EVIDENCE.

evidence, judicial. The testimony, admissible hearsay, things, facts, documents, acceptable to a court as evidence of facts in issue. Divided into testimonial, circumstantial and real evidence (qqv).

evidence obtained illegally. Evidence obtained by some tort or criminal act or by an infringement of rules relating to police investigation. Such evidence is not automatically excluded. See *R v Barker* [1941] 2 KB 381; *Ghani v Jones* [1970] 1 QB 693.

evidence obtained illegally, admissibility of. "It matters not how you get it, if you steal it even, it would be admissible in evidence": *R v Leathem* (1861) 8 Cox CC 498. See *Kuruma v R* [1955] AC 197; *King v R* [1969] 1 AC 304; and *R v Sang* [1980] AC 402. See, however, *ITC Film Distributors v Video Exchange* [1982] 2 All ER 241, and the S.C.A. 1981, s. 72.

evidence of disposition. *See* DISPOSITION.

evidence of opinion. *See* OPINIONS IN EVIDENCE.

evidence of previous convictions. *See* PREVIOUS CONVICTIONS, EVIDENCE OF.

evidence of system. *See* SYSTEM, EVIDENCE OF.

evidence, oral. That given in court by word of mouth. It may be testimony (ie, what the witness perceived through his senses) or hearsay (qv).

evidence, original. May mean "direct evidence", or proof of some fact by first-hand means. Example: the production of a letter containing a libel is evidence of the words constituting that libel.

evidence, parol. 1. Testimony given by word of mouth of witness. 2. Extrinsic evidence (qv).

evidence, power to receive fresh. Power of the Court of Appeal (qv) to receive fresh evidence which is admissible and likely to be credible. See, eg, *R v Lomas* [1969] 1 All ER 920; *R v Melville* [1976] 1 All ER 395.

evidence, presumptive. Prima facie evidence (qv).

evidence, prima facie. "In its usual sense is used to mean prima facie proof of an issue, the burden of proving which is upon the party giving that evidence. In the absence of further evidence from the other side, the prima facie proof becomes conclusive proof and the party giving it discharges his onus": *R v Jacobson and Levy* [1931] App D 466. Example: a share certificate is prima facie evidence of a member's title: Cos.A. 1948, s. 81.

evidence, primary. Evidence which by its nature does not suggest that better evidence might be available. Example: the original of a document.

evidence, real. Known also as "demonstrative" and "objective" evidence. That which is afforded by production and inspection of material objects. Examples: an exhibit (qv) of goods alleged to have been stolen by the accused; a person's physical appearance (eg, his wounds); a view (qv); a witness's demeanour. *See* INSPECTION BY JUDGE.

evidence, relevant. *See* RELEVANT EVIDENCE.

evidence rule, parol. *See* PAROL EVIDENCE RULE.

evidence, secondary. That evidence which suggests the existence of better evidence and which might be rejected if that better evidence is available. Example: the copy of a document. Where an original document is destroyed, secondary evidence of its contents may be given. See Civil Evidence Act 1968; O. 38, r. 3. *See* DOCUMENT, SECONDARY EVIDENCE OF.

evidence, second-hand. Hearsay evidence (qv).

evidence, similar facts. Evidence which is adduced in an attempt to suggest, through its striking similarity, that there is an underlying link between the matters with which it purports to deal—which relate essentially to occasions other than those specifically in question—and the matter presently before the court. Its admissibility depends on its logical, probative value. See *R* v *Kilbourne* [1973] AC 729; *Boardman* v *DPP* [1975] AC 421; *R* v *Scarrott* [1977] 3 WLR 629; and *R* v *Barrington* [1981] 1 WLR 419.

evidence, testimonial. Assertions offered as proof of the truth of that which is being asserted. It includes a testimony (ie, an account by a witness of what he perceived with his senses) and hearsay (qv).

evidence, unsworn. Evidence not given on oath or by affirmation. In the case of children, corroboration (qv) (which must be sworn) may be required where proof of the offence rests on a child's unsworn testimony. An accused person might formerly have made an unsworn statement (qv) (see the Criminal Evidence Act 1898, s. 1(h)) but, generally, he could not be cross-examined on it. The "right" to make such a statement was abolished by the C.J.A. 1982, s. 72.

evidence, weighing of. "It is certainly a maxim that all evidence is to be weighed according to the proof which it was in the power of one side to have produced, and in the power of the other to have contradicted": *Blatch* v *Archer* (1774) 1 Cowp 63.

evidence, young children's sworn. Two matters should be considered when deciding whether a child should give sworn evidence: first, whether the child has sufficient appreciation of the particular nature of the case; second, whether the child realises that the oath involves more than the ordinary duty of telling the truth in ordinary day-to-day life: *per* May LJ in *R* v *Campbell* [1983] Crim LR 174. See *R* v *Hayes* [1977] 1 WLR 234; *R* v *Lal Khan* (1981) 73 Cr App R 190.

evidential facts. *See* FACTS, RELEVANT.

ex abundanti cautela. From an excess of caution. See, eg, *R* v *Thompson* [1982] QB 647.

examination. Interrogation on oath.

examination-in-chief. Known also as "direct examination". The object of examination-in-chief is to put the witness's story before the court so as to obtain a testimony in support of the version of the facts for which the party calling the witness is contending. It is conducted by the witness's own counsel. In general, it may not be based on leading questions (qv), save, eg, where the matter is merely introductory or where it has already been put in evidence by the other side, or where the judge considers the witness hostile (qv) and gives leave. *See* EVIDENCE.

examination of goods, buyer's right. Where goods are delivered to the buyer, and he has not previously examined them, he is not deemed to have accepted them until he has had a reasonable opportunity of examining them for the purpose of ascertaining whether they are in conformity with the contract: S.G.A. 1979, s. 34(1).

examiners. Barristers appointed by the Lord Chancellor to take evidence out of court: see O. 39.

examining justices. Magistrates who conduct a preliminary investigation of a charge made against a prisoner so as to determine whether there is sufficient evidence to justify a committal of the accused. The functions of examining justices may be discharged by a single justice: M.C.A. 1980, s. 4(1).

examples in statutes, use of. A recent

innovation in the drafting of statutes, whereby the schedule of an Act contains examples illustrating applications of the terminology and provisions of the Act. See, eg, the C.C.A. 1974, s. 188(1), Sch 2.

ex capitalisation. Term relating to the issue of new shares as a capitalisation issue (qv) so that the price is adjusted proportionately on the day of issue of the shares.

excepted perils. Term used in contracts of carriage to which the Hague Rules do not apply, whereby a carrier's liability is excluded for loss or damage to goods caused by: act of God (qv); act of the Queen's enemies; restraint of princes and rulers; perils of the seas; fire; barratry; piracy; robbery and theft; collisions, strandings and other accidents of navigation.

exception. 1. An objection taken to an answer, or some other challenge to it. 2. A clause in a deed preventing some thing passing which might otherwise pass under the deed. See *Suisse Atlantique Société* v *NV Rotterdamsche Kolen Centrale* [1967] 1 AC 361.

exceptional depravity. *See* DEPRAVITY, EXCEPTIONAL.

excess clause. Clause in an insurance policy providing that the insured is to bear the first amount of any loss. See *Hobbs* v *Marlowe* [1978] AC 16. *See* INSURANCE.

excess vote. The amount required to make good a government department's excess expenditure approved by a vote of the Committee of Supply.

exchange. 1. Reciprocal transfer of ownership or possession. 2. A place for the business transactions of dealer and brokers, eg, London Stock Exchange. 3. A transfer of settlement land for other land. An exchange of settled land or any part of it or easements may be made for other land or easements: S.L.A. 1925, s. 38 (iii).

exchange, bill of. *See* BILL OF EXCHANGE.

exchange contracts. Contracts, within art. VIII of s. 2(b), Bretton Woods Agreement Order in Council 1946, by which the currency of one country is exchanged for that of another. See *Wilson, Smithett & Cope*

Ltd v *Terruzzi* [1976] QB 683; and *United City Merchants Ltd* v *Royal Bank of Canada* [1982] QB 208.

exchange, investment. *See* INVESTMENT EXCHANGE.

Exchequer. The government department which receives and has the care of the national revenues. *See* CHANCELLOR.

Exchequer, Court of. *See* COURT OF EXCHEQUER.

excise. Tax levied on goods produced in the UK.

exclusionary rules of evidence. "I would hold that there has now developed a general rule of practice whereby in a trial by jury, the judge has a discretion to exclude evidence which, though technically admissible, would probably have a prejudicial influence on the minds of the jury, which would be out of proportion to its true evidential value": *per* Lord Diplock in *R* v *Sang* [1980] AC 402. *See* EVIDENCE.

exclusion clause. "One which excludes or modifies an obligation, whether primary, general secondary or anticipatory secondary, that would otherwise arise under the contract by implication of law": *per* Lord Diplock in *Photo Productions Ltd* v *Securicor Transport Ltd* [1980] AC 827. See the S.G.A. 1979, s. 55; and *George Mitchell* v *Finney Lock Seeds* [1983] 3 WLR 163.

exclusion clauses, restriction of. Under the Unfair Contract Terms Act 1977: liability for death resulting from negligence cannot be excluded or restricted by contractual terms (s. 2(1)); liability for loss or damage resulting from negligence cannot be excluded or restricted by a term which fails to satisfy a reasonableness test (s. 2(2)); a consumer cannot, by contract, be made to indemnify another person in respect of liability that may be incurred by that other for breach of contract or negligence except where the contract satisfies the reasonableness test (s. 4); liability for loss or damage from negligent manufacture of consumer goods (qv) cannot be restricted or excluded in a guarantee (s. 5).

exclusion order. 1. An order under the Prevention of Terrorism (Temporary Provisions) Act 1976, Part II, whereby the Secretary of State excludes from the UK persons whom he is satisfied are or have been concerned in the commission, preparation or instigation of acts of terrorism (qv) or who attempt to enter the country for such a purpose. 2. Order under the D.P.A. 1978, s. 16, instructing the respondent to leave the matrimonial home and/or prohibiting him from entering it. 3. Order prohibiting a convicted person from entering licensed premises: see the Licensed Premises (Exclusion of Certain Persons) Act 1980.

ex contractu. Arising out of a contract.

excusable homicide. 1. Homicide in reasonable self-defence of person or property. See the C.L.A. 1967, s. 3; *Palmer* v *R* [1971] AC 814. 2. Homicide by misadventure. See *R* v *Bruce* (1847) 2 Cox CC 262. *See* HOMICIDE; MURDER.

ex debito justitiae. Arising as a matter of right. A remedy available to the applicant as of right (in contrast to a discretionary remedy).

ex div. Ex dividend. Stock Exchange quotation relating to stocks and shares, stating that the price does not include dividends or interest accrued to date. *See* CUM DIV.

ex dolo malo non oritur actio. A right of action cannot arise out of fraud.

exeat. Let him go. Permission to leave. *See* NE EXEAT REGNO.

executed. That which is done or completed, as in, eg, *executed consideration* (qv). Thus, an *executed trust* is one in which the settlor has declared and perfected in the trust instrument the limitations of the estate of the trustees and the beneficiaries so that no further instrument is needed to define those interests. See *Egerton* v *Brownlow* (1853) 4 HL Cas 1. An *executed agreement*, under the C.C.A. 1974, s. 189(1) is a document signed by or on behalf of the parties, embodying the terms of a regulated agreement (qv) or such of them as have been reduced to writing.

execution. 1. The signing of a deed or other instrument in a manner which gives it a legally valid form. 2. The

carrying out of a court's sentence of death. 3. Enforcing the rights of a judgment creditor (qv). 4. Carrying out of the terms of a trust (qv).

execution of wills. No will is valid unless in writing and signed in order to give effect to it by the testator or by some other person in his presence and by his direction; and the signature must be made or acknowledged by the testator in the presence of two or more witnesses present at the same time, and each witness must attest and subscribe the will in the presence of the testator but not necessarily in the presence of any other witness: W.A. 1837, s. 9 (as substituted by the A.J.A. 1982, s. 17). *See* WILL.

execution, stay of. *See* STAY OF EXECUTION.

execution, writ of. Procedure relating to the enforcing of judgments by, eg, a writ of sequestration (qv). The writ will issue: after a praecipe (qv) is filed; after judgment upon which the writ is to issue is produced; after the officer authorised to seal the writ is satisfied that the period specified for payment has expired. See O. 46.

executive. The branch of government which carries out the general policy determined by the Cabinet (qv). It includes departments of state, local authorities.

executor. One appointed by a will (qv) to administer the testator's property and to carry out provisions of that will. In general the office can be exercised only by the person so appointed: *Re Skinner* [1958] 3 All ER 273. If an infant (qv) is appointed, however, probate will not be issued until he reaches the age of 18. An executor who is appointed by implication is known as an executor "according to the tenor [of the will]".

executor de son tort. Executor "in his own wrong". One who is not an executor, either by express or implied appointment, and who has not obtained a grant of administration, and intermeddles with the goods of the deceased or carries out an act which is characteristic of the office of executor. He may be sued by the rightful executor, administrator, creditor or beneficiary (qqv). See the A.E.A. 1925, ss. 28, 55(1) (xi); *New York Breweries Co Ltd* v *A.-G.* [1899] AC 62; *IRC* v *Stype Investments* [1981] 2 All ER 394; and *Re Clore* [1982] Ch 456.

executor, duties of. Principal duties include: getting in the assets of the deceased; paying funeral expenses; paying legacies; accounting for residual estate: *Re Adamson* (1875) LR 3 P & D 253.

executor's year. The period of one year from the death of the deceased in which the executor (qv) must complete the administration of the assets. Generally, until the end of that period, he is not bound to distribute the estate of deceased: A.E.A. 1925, s. 44. See *Brooke* v *Lewis* (1822) 6 Madd 358.

executory. That which remains to be done, as in executory consideration (qv). Thus, an executory trust is an agreement or covenant for the execution of a trust instrument, the terms of which are not defined precisely, at some future time, or directions on the basis of which the trustee is expected to prepare a final settlement at a future date. See *Miles* v *Harford* (1879) 12 Ch D 691.

executory interest. A future interest in land or personal property, except reversions (qv) or remainders (qv).

executrix. Feminine form of executor (qv).

exemplary damages. *See* DAMAGES.

exempli gratia. Generally abbreviated to eg. For example.

exemption clauses. Clauses in an agreement seeking to exempt the parties from general liability or excluding or modifying their liability in certain contingencies. *See* EXCLUSION CLAUSES.

exempt private company. A company which complied with the Cos.A. 1948, s. 28 (eg, it restricted the right of transfer of its shares). After curtailment of its privileges by the Cos.A. 1976, s. 2, the class disappeared under the Cos.A. 1980. *See* COMPANY.

ex gratia. As of favour. As in *ex gratia* payment—a payment not compelled by any legal right. See *Edwards* v *Skyways Ltd* [1964] 1 WLR 349.

exhibit. Something produced to be viewed by a judge or jury, or shown to a witness who is giving evidence, or an object referred to in an affidavit (qv). *See* EVIDENCE, REAL.

exhumation. Disinterring of a buried corpse. An unlawful act unless authorised. See the Coroners Act 1980, s. 4.

exile. Long voluntary absence, or expulsion from, one's native land. For the so-called "exile order", see *R* v *Hodges* (1967) 51 Cr App R 361; and *R* v *Williams* [1982] 1 WLR 1398.

ex lege, **right.** *See* RIGHT EX LEGE.

ex nudo pacto non oritur actio. A right of action cannot arise out of a bare pact, ie, an agreement made without consideration (qv). *See* CONTRACT.

ex officio. By virtue of office. *Ex officio information* is a criminal information (qv) filed by the Attorney-General (qv) on behalf of the Crown.

exonerate. 1. To clear of an accusation. 2. To relieve from a liability.

ex parte. On behalf of. 1. An *ex parte* injunction (qv) is granted after hearing only one party and in a case of great urgency. See *Bates* v *Lord Hailsham of Marylebone* [1972] 1 WLR 1373. 2. "*Ex p Jones*" in the title of a case indicates the name of the party on whose application the hearing has taken place.

ex parte **inspection order.** *See* INSPECTION ORDER, EX PARTE.

expatriation. 1. The voluntary act of renouncing allegiance to one's own country so as to take up residence permanently in a foreign country. 2. The act of forcing a person to leave his native country, eg, by exile.

expectancy, interest in. *See* INTEREST IN EXPECTANCY.

expectant heir. One who has a vested remainder or contingent remainder in property, or one who has a hope of succeeding to property. Catching bargains (qv) with expectant heirs may be set aside by the court: *Benyon* v *Cook* (1875) LR 10 Ch 391. *See* REMAINDER.

expectation of life, loss of. In an action for damages for personal injuries, no damages are recoverable in respect of any loss of expectation of life caused to the injured person by the injuries, but account is taken of any suffering caused by awareness of reduction in expectation of life: A.J.A. 1982, s. 1.

expenses, living. *See* LIVING EXPENSES.

expert opinion. Expert opinion is admissible evidence when the subject is one "upon which competency to form an opinion can only be acquired by a course of special study or experience": *R* v *Kusmack* (1955) 20 CR 365. The expert's duty is to "furnish the judge or jury with the necessary scientific criteria for testing the accuracy of their conclusions so as to enable the judge or jury to form their own independent judgment by the application of these criteria to the facts proved in evidence": *Davie* v *Edinburgh Magistrates*, 1953 SC 34. See the Civil Evidence Act 1972, s. 3 (admissibility of expert's opinion on matter in issue in civil proceedings); O. 40; *Joyce* v *Yeomans* [1981] 1 WLR 549; *R* v *Abadom* [1983] 1 WLR 126; and S.I. 1980/1010. *See* EVIDENCE.

Expiring Laws Continuance Acts. Acts passed to continue other Acts which would have expired otherwise.

explosive. "Any article manufactured for the purpose of producing a practical effect by explosion, or intended by the person having it with him for that purpose": Th.A. 1968, s. 10(1)(*c*). See the O.P.A. 1861, ss. 28–30; Explosive Substances Act 1883; *R* v *Byrne* (1975) 63 Cr App R 33; *R* v *Wheatley* [1979] 1 WLR 144; and *R* v *Bouch* [1982] 3 WLR 673 (petrol bomb as "explosive substance").

expose. 1. To display, eg, food for sale. An offence if unfit for human consumption. See the Food and Drugs Act 1955. 2. It is an offence (known as "indecent exposure") for a person wilfully and obscenely to expose his penis with intent to insult a female: Vagrancy Act 1824, s. 4. See *Ford* v *Falcone* [1971] 1 WLR 809; *Evans* v *Ewels* [1971] 1 WLR 671.

ex post facto. By a subsequent act. An *ex post facto* statute has a retrospective effect.

express. Distinctly stated, rather than implied.

expressio unius personae vel rei est exclusio alterius. The express mention of one person or thing is the exclusion of another. The rule does not operate where an expression was incomplete due to accident. See, eg, *Colquhoun* v *Brooks* (1887) 19 QBD 400; *Mills* v *United Counties Bank* [1911] 1 Ch 669; *London & Harrogate Securities Ltd* v *Pitts* [1976] 1 WLR 264; *Dean* v *Wiesengrund* [1955] 2 QB 120; *D.* v *NSPCC* [1977] 1 All ER 589.

express term. An express statement of undertakings and promises contained in a contract or other written instrument.

express trust. A trust created as the result of a settlor's expressed intention, eg, as where A conveys property to B on trust for C. In general, an express declaration will suffice for the creation of an express trust, eg, by will, deed, writing not under seal, spoken word. *See* TRUST.

expressum facit cessare tacitum. That which is expressed puts an end to that which is silent; ie, if something can be expressed, there is no room for implication. Where there is an express mention of certain things, anything of the same class not mentioned is excluded. See *Hare* v *Horton* (1833) 5 B & A 715; *R* v *Caledonian Rwy* (1850) 16 QB 19.

expropriation. The act, usually of a state, in enforcing the compulsory surrender of private property for the state's purposes, without compensation. For recognition of the validity of a foreign government's expropriation, see, eg, *A/S Tallinna Laevauhisus* v *Tallinna Shipping Co* (1946) 80 Ll Rep 99. *See* EMINENT DOMAIN.

ex proprio motu. Of his own motion. Term applied to an action taken by the court on its own initiative.

ex rel. Ex relatione. From a narrative. Applied to a person's report of proceedings usually not as the result of his having been present, but compiled from information given by another.

ex rights. Term relating to the issue of new shares to shareholders (qv) in proportion to their existing holdings, in which the price has been adjusted by deducting the value of the right to subscribe. *See* RIGHTS ISSUE.

extended sentence. Under the C.J.A. 1967, s. 37 (as re-enacted in the P.C.C.A. 1973, ss. 28, 29) a court may impose an extended sentence where an offender was convicted on indictment of an offence punishable with imprisonment for two years or more if the court is satisfied by reason of his previous conduct and the likelihood of his committing further offences that it is expedient to protect the public from him for a substantial time. See *R* v *Johnson* [1976] 1 WLR 426.

extinguishment. An obligation or right is extinguished when it ceases its existence, eg, as when a debt is paid, or an easement (qv) ends by express or implied release (qv), or by unity in the same owner of the fee simple (qv) of the dominant tenement and the servient tenement (qqv).

extortion. The obtaining of some benefit by intimidation or physical force applied to another. The unwarranted demanding of money by threats may be blackmail (qv).

extortionate. Oppressive. Under the C.C.A. 1974, ss. 137–140, a credit bargain is considered extortionate (and may be reopened by the court) if the debtor, or relatives, are required to make grossly extortionate payments or payments which contravene in gross fashion the ordinary principles of fair dealing. If a debtor alleges that a credit bargain is extortionate, the onus of proving the contrary is on the creditor: s. 171(7). See *Ketley* v *Scott* [1981] ICR 241.

extradition. The surrendering by one state, at the request of another, of a person accused of a crime under the laws of the requesting state. It is usually regulated by reciprocal extradition treaties between states. Extradition may be barred unless for an offence punishable in the surrendering state. See the Extradition Acts 1870–1935; the Fugitive Offenders Act 1967; the Suppression of

Terrorism Act 1978, s. 3; the Taking of Hostages Act 1982, ss. 3, 4; *R* v *Governor of Pentonville Prison ex p Singh* [1981] 1 WLR 1031; and *Govt of the USA* v *Jennings* [1982] 3 WLR 450. *See* POLITICAL OFFENCE.

extraordinary meeting. Meeting of a company (qv) called, eg, before the next ordinary meeting. The holders of not less than one-tenth of paid-up capital carrying voting rights can compel the directors to call such a meeting. See the Cos.A. 1948, s. 132.

extraordinary resolution. Resolution (qv) passed by a three-quarters majority at a general meeting of which notice declaring an intention to propose the resolution as an extraordinary resolution has been given. It may be used, eg, to wind up a company voluntarily. See the Cos.A. 1948, s. 141; and the Cos.A. 1980, s. 32.

extra-territoriality. Doctrine of international law under which some persons (eg, ambassadors) are considered to be outside the territory of the state in which they are living so as to carry out their duties. In effect, therefore, they are not within the jurisdiction of that state. *See* DIPLOMATIC PRIVILEGE.

extrinsic. Lying outside; derived from some external source.

extrinsic evidence. *See* EVIDENCE, EXTRINSIC.

ex turpi causa non oritur actio. A right of action will not arise from a base cause. Thus, an illegal contract is generally unenforceable. See, eg, *Beresford* v *Royal Insurance Co Ltd* [1938] AC 586; and *R* v *Chief National Insurance Commissioner ex p Connor* [1981] 1 All ER 166.

eye witness. One who has seen that to which he testifies.

eyre. *Eyre* = a hearing. A court of itinerant justices, established in 1176. A King's Justice acting under the commission *ad omnia placita* presided over each eyre. The last eyre was held in the reign of Richard II.

F

fact. 1. That which has actual existence. 2. A circumstance or incident relating to a case which is being heard. In general, questions of fact are decided by the jury; questions of law are for the judge. See *Metropolitan Rwy* v *Jackson* (1887) 3 App Cas 193.

factor. A mercantile agent who in the course of his business has authority to sell or buy goods, to consign goods for the purpose of sale, or to raise money on the security of goods: see the S.G.A. 1979, s. 26. See Factors Act 1889; *Hayman* v *Flewker* (1863) 13 CB NS 519; *Rolls Razor* v *Cox* [1967] 1 QB 522.

factory. Premises in which persons are employed in manual labour in any process for or incidental to, purposes, such as, the making of any article or any part of an article, the altering, repairing, ornamenting, cleaning, demolition of any article, the adapting for sale of any article. See the Factories Act 1961, s. 175; and the H.S.W.A. 1974.

facts, evidential. *See* FACTS, RELEVANT.

facts, inferential. Facts established indirectly by conclusions drawn from the evidence.

facts in issue, main. Those facts which must be proved by the party making an allegation (ie, by the plaintiff or prosecutor) in order to succeed, and the facts that the defendant must prove in order to establish his defence. "Whenever there is a plea of not guilty, everything is in issue": *R* v *Sims* [1946] 1 All ER 697. *See* EVIDENCE.

facts in issue, subordinate or collateral. Facts affecting the admissibility of evidence and the credibility of witnesses.

facts, investitive. Facts which invest persons with particular rights, eg, a breach of contract investing the plaintiff with the right to claim damages. "Divestitive facts" modify or extinguish rights, as in the case of payment of a debt.

facts, means of proof of. Generally: testimony of witnesses; real evidence; documentary evidence.

facts, notorious. *See* NOTORIOUS FACTS.

facts, primary. "Primary facts are facts which are observed by witnesses and proved by oral testimony, or facts proved by the production of a thing itself, such as original documents. Their determination is essentially a question of fact for the tribunal of fact, and the only question of law that can arise on them is whether there was any evidence to support the finding. The conclusions from primary facts are, however, inferences deduced by a process of reasoning from them": *British Launderers' Research Association* v *Hendon Rating Authority* [1949] 1 KB 462.

facts, probative. Facts which have a natural and logical tendency to prove or disprove a fact in issue.

facts, relevant. Facts from which facts in issue may be inferred. Known also as "evidential facts".

facts, similar. *See* SIMILAR FACTS.

facts which can be established by other means than proof. The following do not generally require affirmative proof: formal admissions (see the C.J.A. 1967, s. 10); facts judicially noted; presumptions (qv).

factum. An act or deed.

factum probandum. Plural: *facta probanda.* Principal fact; fact in issue. A fact which has to be proved. *See* EVIDENCE.

factum probans. Plural: *facta probantia.* Evidentiary fact; fact related to the issue. Fact given in evidence intended to prove those other facts which are in issue. May be proved by testimony, documents, other things, admissible hearsay, other evidentiary facts.

Faculties, Court of. *See* COURT OF FACULTIES.

faculty. A term used in ecclesiastical law to denote a special licence granted to a person to do that which was not allowed by common law, eg, to marry without publication of banns (qv). See the Faculty Jurisdiction Measure 1964; the Faculty Jurisdiction Rules 1967; *Re Holy Innocents, Fallowfield* [1982] 3WLR 666.

fair. 1. "A concourse of buyers and sellers for the purchase and sale of commodities pursuant to a franchise with an optional addition of provision for amusement": *Wyld* v *Silver* [1963] 1 QB 169. See the Fairs Act 1871. 2. Reasonable, impartial.

fair comment. Defence to an action for defamation (qv), in which the defendant shows that words complained of were not actuated by malice and were comment, were fair (in the sense of "honest") and amounted to comment on a matter of public interest. The defence will not extend to a misstatement of fact. See the Defamation Act 1952, s. 6; *Kemsley* v *Foot* [1952] AC 355; *London Artists Ltd* v *Littler* [1969] 2 KB 375.

fair dismissal. Dismissal from employment on the following grounds: capability or qualifications for the job; conduct; redundancy (see Redundancy Payments Act 1965); where continued employment of an employee results in a contravention of law; other substantial reasons, as where an employee fails to join a union specified in a union membership agreement approved by ballot. See the Employment Act 1982, s. 3. *See* DISMISSAL.

fair rent. That fixed under the Rent Acts of 1974 and 1977, when regard is had "to all the circumstances (other than personal circumstances) and in particular to the age, character, locality and state of repair of the dwelling-house, and if any furniture is provided for use under the tenancy, to [its] quantity, quality and condition". See *Palmer* v *Peabody Trust* [1975] QB 604. For certificates of fair rent issued to landlords, see the Rent Act 1977, s. 69, Sch 12. See, eg, *R* v *Rent Officer for Camden ex p Ebiri* [1982] 1 All ER 950.

fair trading, proceedings relating to. Under the Fair Trading Act 1973, where a firm fails to give an assurance to the Director General of Fair Trading (qv) that an unfair consumer practice or one detrimental to the interests of consumers will cease, the Director General can take proceedings against that firm in the Restrictive Practices Court (qv). *See* UNFAIR CONSUMER PRACTICE.

fair wages resolution. A resolution of the House of Commons (1891, 1909, 1946) urging, *inter alia*, that contractors with the public service should provide wages and conditions of work not less favourable than those established for the industry and trade in the district where the work is carried on, and that they should recognise the freedom of their employees to belong to trade unions. It is generally incorporated into all contracts between government departments and their contractors. See *Simpson* v *Kodak* [1948] 2 KB 184.

fair wear and tear. Where a repairing covenant exempts the covenantor from liability for fair (or "reasonable") wear and tear, "the tenant is bound to do such repairs as may be required to prevent the consequences flowing originally from wear and tear from producing others which wear and tear would not directly produce": *Haskell* v *Marlow* [1928] 2 KB 45. *See* WEAR AND TEAR.

falsa demonstratio non nocet cum de corpore constat. A false description does not vitiate a document when the thing is described with certainty. Thus, in *Pratt* v *Mathew* (1856) 22 Beav 328, the testator (qv) made a gift as follows: "to my wife, Caroline". He had a wife, Mary, but lived with Caroline with whom he had contracted a void marriage. It was held that the word "wife" did not affect the validity of the gift to Caroline. See also *Eastwood* v *Ashton* [1915] AC 900; *Maxted* v *Plymouth Corporation* [1957] CLY 243.

false. Untrue, or designedly incorrect and intended to deceive. A statement, although literally true, may be false if it is used so as to convey a false impression: see, eg, *R* v *Kylsant* [1932] 1 KB 442.

false accounting. *See* ACCOUNTING, FALSE.

false imprisonment. The direct,

intentional (or negligent) infliction of some bodily restraint which is neither expressedly nor impliedly authorised by law. A common law offence and a tort. See *Herring* v *Boyle* (1834) 1 Cr M & R 377; *Hussien* v *Chong Fook Kam* [1970] AC 943; *John Lewis & Co* v *Tims* [1952] AC 676.

false instrument. *See* INSTRUMENT, FALSE.

false judgment, writ of. A writ which was available to correct errors in an inferior court (qv).

false personation. It is an offence to personate another in certain circumstances, eg, for the purpose of voting at an election or where the other person is a juryman. See Representation of the People Act 1983, s. 60. *See* PERSONATION.

false plea. Known also as a "sham plea". A plea, obviously absurd or merely frivolous, entered only to delay the course of an action. See O. 18, r. 19.

false pretence. Phrase relating originally to an offence under the Larceny Act 1916, s. 32. Now relates to the offence of obtaining property by deception under the Th.A. 1968. *See* DECEPTION, OBTAINING PROPERTY BY.

false statement. *See* PERJURY.

false trade description. A trade description which is false or misleading to a material degree applied by a person to goods in the course of a trade or business: Trade Descriptions Act 1968. Any person who in the course of a trade or business applies a false trade description to goods or supplies or offers to supply any goods to which a false trade description is applied, is guilty of an offence: s. 1(1). See *Holloway* v *Cross* [1981] 1 All ER 1012. *See* TRADE DESCRIPTION.

falsification of accounts. *See* ACCOUNTING, FALSE.

falsify. 1. To alter a document, eg, by obliteration, with intent to deceive. 2. To show that some matter, eg, an item in an account, is false.

family. Social unit, usually consisting of a male and female adult living in one household and caring for their children. For an extended definition in relation to social security, see the Family Income Supplements Act 1970, s. 1(1) (as amended by the

S.S.A. 1980, s. 7(1)). See *Price* v *Gould* (1930) 46 TLR 411; and *Brook* v *Wollams* [1949] 2 KB 388.

family allowances. Allowances paid to families with two or more children below the specified age limits; phased out under the Child Benefit Act 1975. *See* CHILD BENEFIT.

family arrangement. An arrangement between members of a family for the benefit of the family as a whole.

family assets. Term which refers "to those things which are acquired by one or other or both of the parties, with the intention that there should be continuing provision for them and their children during their joint lives, and used for the benefit of the family as a whole": *Wachtel* v *Wachtel* [1973] 1 All ER 829. See also *Armstrong* v *Armstrong* [1974] 118 SJ 579; *Jones* v *Jones* [1976] Fam 8.

family company. Means, for the purpose of claiming relief from capital gains tax (qv), a company in which not less than 25 per cent of the voting rights are held by the person claiming relief or 10 per cent by himself and 75 per cent by his family, including himself. ("'Family" means here the person's spouse, and the brother, sister, ancestor or lineal descendant of that person or spouse.) See the Capital Gains Tax Act 1979.

Family Division. Formerly, the Probate, Divorce and Admiralty Division, renamed under the A.J.A. 1970, s. 1. A Division of the High Court consisting of a President and other judges. Its original jurisdiction includes hearing defended matrimonial cases, adoption, guardianship of minors; its appellate jurisdiction includes hearing appeals from magistrates' courts and county courts (relating to guardianship) and the Crown Court (eg, affiliation proceedings). See now the S.C.A. 1981, s. 5, Sch 1.

family income supplement. Benefit payable to a family with low incomes where the head of the family is in, or normally engaged in, remunerative work and there is at least one dependent child.

family name. *See* SURNAME.

family provision. The provision for a family which can be ordered by the court out of the net estate of the deceased. See the Inheritance (Provision for Family and Dependants) Act 1975; Family Provision Intestate Succession Order 1981/225; *Re Coventry* [1979] 2 All ER 408. *See* DEPENDANT.

farming. "Carrying on of activities appropriate to land recognisable as farm land. It must at least include the raising of beasts, the cultivation of land and the growing of crops": *Lowe v Ashmore Ltd* [1971] 1 All ER 1057. *See* FARM LAND.

farm land. Land in the UK wholly or mainly occupied for the purposes of husbandry, excluding a dwelling or domestic office and market garden land: Income and Corporation Taxes Act 1970, s. 526(5).

fatal accident, right of action relating to. "If death is caused by any wrongful act, neglect or default which is such as would (if death had not ensued) have entitled the person injured to maintain an action and recover damages in respect thereof, the person who would have been liable if death had not ensued shall be liable to an action for damages, notwithstanding the death of the person injured": Fatal Accidents Act 1976, s. 1(1). An action shall be for the benefit of, eg, the wife or husband, parent or grandparent, child or grandchild, issue of a brother, sister, uncle, aunt, of the deceased: s. 1(2). See the Lim.A. 1980, s. 33; and the A.J.A. 1982, s. 3. *See* BEREAVEMENT, DAMAGES FOR.

faulty driving. "Fault involves a failure; a falling below the care or skill of a competent and experienced driver, in relation to the manner of the driving and to the relevant circumstances of the case": *R v Gosney* [1971] 3 All ER 220.

fealty. Fidelity. The tie, based on oath, which bound a vassal to his lord.

fee. *Feodum* = a fief. Originally a benefice granted to a man and his heirs in return for services. Used in land law to indicate that an estate (qv) is capable of being inherited.

feeble minded. Extremely sub-normal in intelligence. See the M.H.A. 1959; and the M.H.A. 1983, Part I.

fee farm rent. *See* CHIEF RENT.

fee simple absolute in possession. One of the two estates in land which, after 1925, are capable of subsisting or being conveyed or created at law. *Fee* denotes an estate of inheritance. *Simple* denotes a fee which can pass to the general heirs of the tenant. *Absolute* means that the estate is not subject to determination by an event other than that which is implied in the words of limitation. *In possession* denotes an estate that is immediate, ie, neither in reversion nor in remainder. In effect, absolute ownership of land. See L.P.A. 1925, s. 1(1).

fee simple conditional. A conditional fee (qv).

fee tail. *Feodum talliatum* = a fee cut down. An entailed interest. Refers to land descending neither to an ancestor nor to a collateral relative, but only to the lineal descendants of the first tenant in tail. The estate endures for as long as the original tenant or his lineal descendants survive. Under the L.P.A. 1925, an entailed interest exists only as an equitable interest behind a trust. Types of fee tail include: fee tail male general; fee tail female general; special tail (where the heir may be selected only from descendants of a specified spouse).

felo de se. Felon of himself. Term which was used to refer to one who committed suicide (*felonia de se*). *See* SUICIDE.

felony. An offence which had been made such by statute or which, at common law, carried on conviction the penalties of death and forfeiture of property (abolished in 1870). All other offences were misdemeanours (qv). Under the C.L.A. 1967, s. 1, all distinctions between felony and misdemeanour were abolished; indictable offences are now regulated by those rules applying to misdemeanours.

felony, appeal of. Ancient procedure whereby the defendant could call for trial by battle (qv). Obsolescent by the sixteenth century and abolished in 1819.

feme covert. A married woman.

feme sole. An unmarried woman, eg, spinster, widow, divorced woman.

fence. Any type of barrier, eg, hedge, bank, wall, cattle grid: Animals Act 1971, s. 11. Right to have a fence maintained by an adjoining owner may be an easement (qv): *Crow* v *Ward* [1971] 1 QB 77. See the L.P.A. 1925, s. 194; the Highways Act 1980, s. 165(1); and *Lawrence* v *Jenkins* (1973) LR 8 QB 274.

feodum. A fee (qv).

feoffee. One to whom a feoffment (qv) was made.

feoffee to uses. One to whom a feoffment (qv) was made to the use of another person. *See* USE.

feoffment. A conveyance, in feudal times, with livery of seisin (qv). Abolished in 1845.

feoffor. One who made a feoffment (qv).

ferae naturae. *See* ANIMALS, CLASSIFICATION OF.

fermor. One who held "by lease for life or lives or for years, by deed or without deed": Coke. See Statute of Marlbridge 1267, s. 2; *Woodhouse* v *Walker* (1880) 5 QBD 404.

feudal system. A political and social system brought to England by the Normans in 1066, based on duties and rights resting essentially on land ownership and tenure. It was characterised by a hierarchy dominated by a King and Lords from whom vassals held land in fief and to whom they owed services, some of which continued until abolished under the Tenures Abolition Act 1660.

fiat. Let it be done. A command, endorsement, sanction, eg, a warrant of a judge.

fiat justitia, ruat coelum. Let justice be done, though the heavens fall.

fiction. "Any assumption which conceals, or affects to conceal, the fact that a rule of law has undergone alteration, its letter remaining unchanged, its operation being modified": Maine. Used to extend the courts' jurisdiction and to increase the scope of available remedies, Example: action of ejectment (qv).

fidelity guarantee insurance. Insurance taken out by an employer as indemnification against misappropriation by an employee. All the material facts must be disclosed in such a case: *London General Omnibus Co* v *Holloway* [1912] 2 KB 77.

fiduciary. Involving trust or confidence, eg, as describing the relationship between a trustee (qv) and beneficiary (qv). In general, where a fiduciary relationship between parties to a transaction exists, undue influence (qv) leading to some agreements, such as contract, may be presumed. See, eg, *Lancashire Loans Ltd* v *Black* [1934] 1 KB 380 (mother and daughter); *Allcard* v *Skinner* (1887) 36 Ch D (member of religious order and her Superior).

fieri facias. Abbreviated to *fi.fa.* Cause to be made. Writ directed to sheriff (qv) of the county in which is situated property to be seized so as to enforce a judgment for payment of money. Sheriff is commanded to cause to be made out of debtor's property a sum of money sufficient to satisfy judgment debt, plus interest and costs of execution. Goods exempted from seizure include, eg, goods belonging to a third person, fixtures attached to a freehold. See the S.C.A. 1981, s. 138; O. 45, O. 47; *Practice Direction* [1982] 1 WLR 2; and *The Observer Ltd* v *Gordon* [1983] Com LR 105. *See* JUDGMENTS, ENFORCEMENT OF.

fieri feci. I have caused to be made. The report of a sheriff (qv) after enforcement of a writ of execution.

fi.fa. *See* FIERI FACIAS.

fifteens. Term used in the Statute of Charitable Uses 1601, meaning a tax which was levied on movable property.

file. Term used in the C.C.A. 1974 to refer to all the information about an individual which is kept by a credit reference agency (qv).

filius nullius. A son of no man. A bastard (qv).

film. Any record, however made, of a sequence of visual images, which is a record capable of being used as a means of showing that sequence as a moving picture: Film Levy Finance Act 1981, s. 9(1).

finality clause. Clause in a statute

providing, eg, "the decision of the Minister shall be final." "Parliament only gives the impression of finality to the decisions of a tribunal on condition that they are reached in accordance with the law": *per* Denning LJ in *R* v *Medical Appeal Tribunal ex p Gilmore* [1957] 1 QB 574.

final judgment. Judgment awarded when an action is ended.

final process. Writ of execution relating to a judgment.

Finance Bill. Introduced following a budget (qv) so as to give effect to its proposals.

financial provision, enforcement of orders for. Enforcement by the High Court by means of garnishee, charging and attachment of earnings orders; writs of *fieri facias* (qv) and sequestration; judgment summons (Debtors Act 1869); appointment of receiver. See *Levermore* v *Levermore* [1980] 1 WLR 1277.

financial provision for children of the family. The court may make orders under the M.C.A. 1973, s. 23, concerning lump sums, secured or unsecured periodical payments, transfer or settlement of property and variation of nuptial settlements. The duration of orders is determined by s. 29; for the guidelines for determining applications, see s. 25(2). *See* CHILD OF THE FAMILY.

financial provision order during marriage. Either party to a marriage may apply for an order on the ground that the other party has failed to provide reasonable maintenance for the applicant, or has failed to provide, or to make a proper contribution towards, reasonable maintenance for any child of the family, or has behaved in such a way that the applicant cannot reasonably be expected to live with the respondent, or has deserted the applicant: D.P.A. 1978, s. 1. See the M.C.A. 1980, ss. 59–61 for the basic procedures in a magistrates' court.

financial provision, reasonable. Term used in the Inheritance (Provision for Family and Dependants) Act 1975 to refer to such provision as it would be reasonable in all the circumstances of the case for a husband or wife to receive, whether or not that provision is required by his or her maintenance: s. 1(2). The court is empowered to make an order for reasonable financial provision out of the deceased's estate: s. 2.

financial relief. Term relating to orders, eg, for maintenance pending a suit in divorce proceedings. See the Mat.C.A. 1973, s. 37; and the Matrimonial Causes Rules 1977, r. 2(2).

financial year. Usually refers to the period of 12 months ending on 31st March: I.A. 1978. *See* FISCAL YEAR.

finding is keeping. Popular misconception that finder of chattel acquires title as against all other persons, including the rightful owner. See the Th.A. 1968, ss. 1, 2; *Armoury* v *Delamirie* (1721) 1 Stra 505; *Bridges* v *Hawkesworth* (1851) 21 LJ QB 75; and *Parker* v *British Airways Board* [1982] 2 WLR 503.

findings. The conclusions of an enquiry.

finding, theft by, immunity from. "A person's appropriation of property belonging to another is not to be regarded as dishonest . . . if he appropriates the property in the belief that the person to whom the property belongs cannot be discovered by taking reasonable steps": Th.A. 1968, s. 2(c).

fine. *Finis* = end. 1. Monetary penalty payable on conviction. See the M.C.A. 1980, s. 150(1); the P.C.C.A. 1973, ss. 30–32; and the C.L.A. 1977, Sch 6. For fines on young offenders, see the M.C.A. 1980, s. 81 (orders requiring defaulters' parents to enter recognisances (qv) to ensure payment). For imprisonment in default, see *Forrest* v *Brighton Justices* [1981] AC 1038. For the relevance of means in the assessment of a fine, see the M.C.A. 1980, s. 35; *R* v *Fairbairn* [1981] Crim LR 190. See also the C.J.A. 1982, ss. 26, 37 (standard scale of fines). 2. Process used in conveyance by entry on court rolls. A writ was issued, followed by agreement of parties (*finalis concordia*) which was recorded on the rolls. Abolished in 1833. 3. Lump sum payment, a premium for the grant or renewal of a lease: L.P.A. 1925, s. 205(1) (xxiii). See *Binion* v *Evans* [1972] Ch 359. 4. Money paid in early times by a tenant to his lord when land was alienated.

fineness. In relation to a precious metal, the number of parts by the weight of that metal in one thousand parts by the weight of the alloy: Hallmarking Act 1973, s. 22(1).

fine order, transfer of. Transfer of an order making payment enforceable in the petty sessions area in which a person is residing, other than that for which the court acted: M.C.A. 1980, s. 89(1).

fine, payment in instalments of. A magistrates' court may order payment of a fine by instalments: M.C.A. 1980, s. 85. Variation of an order is allowed under s. 85A (added by the C.J.A. 1982, s. 51(1)).

fine, remission of. Power of a court to remit whole or part of a fine imposed by a magistrates' court, after enquiry into an offender's means, if the court thinks it just to do so, having regard to any change in his circumstances since the conviction: M.C.A. 1980, s. 85.

fingerprints. Impressions made by ridges at the end of the thumb and fingers, used as a means of identification. Under the C.J.A. 1948, s. 39, proof of previous convictions by reference to fingerprints was admissible. See also the M.C.A. 1980, s. 49 (allowing prints to be taken of persons over 14 appearing to answer to a summons for an offence punishable with imprisonment); *George* v *Coombe* [1978] Crim LR 47; and *R* v *Jones* [1978] RTR 137.

firearm. Defined under the Firearms Act 1968 as "a lethal barrelled weapon of any description from which any shot, bullet or other missile can be discharged, and includes any prohibited weapon, whether it is such a lethal weapon or not". It is an offence to purchase, acquire or possess such a weapon without a certificate. An imitation firearm is any object having the appearance of a firearm whether or not it is capable of

discharging a missile. It includes an air rifle: *Seamark* v *Prouse* [1980] 1 WLR 698. See the Th.A. 1968, s. 10(1) (*a*); the Criminal Damage Act 1971, s. 3; the Firearms Act 1982 (applying the provisions of the 1968 Act to imitation firearms readily convertible into firearms); *R* v *Howells* [1977] QB 614; *R* v *Hussain* [1981] 1 WLR 416; and *R* v *Pannell* [1982] Crim LR 752.

firearms, imitation, convertible. An imitation firearm is regarded as readily convertible into a firearm to which the Firearms Act 1968, s. 1, applies if it can be converted without any special skill on the part of the person converting it in the construction or adaptation of firearms of any description, and the work of conversion does not require special equipment or tools other than such as are in common use by persons carrying out construction and maintenance work in their own homes: Firearms Act 1982, s. 1(6).

fire damage, insured property and. Such damage is said to exist "where there has been ignition of insured property which was not intended to be ignited, or when insured property has been damaged otherwise than by ignition, as a direct consequence of the ignition of other property not intended to be ignited": *Harris* v *Poland* [1941] 1 KB 462.

fire damage, responsibility for. In general, the owner of a house in which a fire begins by accident, and not by negligence, is not responsible for damage caused to others. See the Fire Prevention (Metropolis) Act 1744, s. 86; *Musgrove* v *Pandelis* [1919] 2 KB 43; *Goldman* v *Hargrave* [1962] 2 All ER 989.

fire ordeal. *See* ORDEAL, TRIAL BY.

first instance, court of. *See* COURT OF FIRST INSTANCE.

First Lord of the Treasury. *See* TREASURY, FIRST LORD OF THE.

fiscal year. The financial year, reckoned, eg, for income tax purposes, as from 6th April in one year to 5th April in the following year.

fishery. Known also as "piscary". A right of fishing. 1. *A several fishery.* Exclusive right of fishing vested in the owner of the soil. 2. *A free fishery.* Exclusive right to fish. It may be a *Royal fishery*, ie, exclusive right of the Crown, or a right granted to a subject. 3. *A public or common fishery.* Right to fish in another's waters, in common with the owner of the soil.

fishing interrogatories. *See* INTERROGATORIES, FISHING.

fishing licence. Licence to fish (eg, for trout, salmon, freshwater fish) granted by a water authority. See the Salmon and Freshwater Fisheries Act 1975.

fish, Royal. Whale and sturgeon thrown ashore or caught near to the coast are considered the property of the Sovereign. See the Wild Creatures and Forest Laws Act 1971, s. 1.

fit for habitation. *See* HABITATION, FIT FOR.

fitness for purpose. Where goods are sold in the course of a business, and the buyer expressly or impliedly makes known to the seller any particular purpose for which the goods are being bought, there is an implied condition that they are fit for that purpose: S.G.A. 1979, s. 14(3). See *Baldry* v *Marshall* [1925] 1 KB 260; *Teheran-Europe Co* v *Belton* [1968] 2 QB 545; and *Lambert* v *Lewis* [1982] AC 225.

fixed charge. *See* CHARGE.

fixed penalty notice. Notice (which may be affixed to a stationary vehicle) offering the opportunity of the discharge of any liability to conviction of the offence to which the notice relates by payment of a fixed penalty: Transport Act 1982, s. 27, Sch 1.

fixed sum credit. *See* CREDIT.

fixed term. Expression relating to a lease (qv) for a fixed period. "In my opinion a 'fixed term' is one which cannot be unfixed by notice. To be a 'fixed term', the parties must be bound for the term stated in the agreement and unable to determine it on either side": *per* Lord Denning in *BBC* v *Ioannou* [1975] 2 All ER 999.

fixtures. Chattels affixed to land or to a building so that they are part thereof. Generally the degree of annexation required is such that the chattel must be connected to the land or to a building on the land in some substantial way. See *Hulme* v *Brigham* [1943] KB 152; *Jordan* v *May* [1947] KB 427; *Simmons* v *Midford* [1969] 2 Ch 415; *NZ Govt Property Corp* v *HM & S Ltd* [1981] 1 All ER 759; and *Hamp* v *Bygrave* (1983) (*The Times*, 6.1.1983).

flagrante delicto. Literally: while the crime is flagrant. In the very act of committing an offence.

flat. A separate self-contained dwelling which forms part of a building: *Murgatroyd* v *Tresarden* [1947] KB 316. "Any dwelling house which is not a house is a flat": H.A. 1980, s. 3(3). See Sch 19, para 16.

flats, purpose-built block of. A building which contains two or more flats, and for this purpose "flat" means a dwelling-house which forms part only of a building and is separated horizontally from another dwelling-house which forms part of the same building: Rent Act 1977, Sch 2, para 4.

floating charge. *See* CHARGE.

flood. Term used in, eg, insurance policies to mean a large and temporary movement of water having an element of violence and suddenness: *Young* v *Sun Alliance and London Insurance Ltd* [1976] 3 All ER 561.

flotsam. Wreckage of a cargo floating on the sea. It may go to the Crown if unclaimed.

f.o.b. Free on board. A price quoted f.o.b. includes carriage from the supplier's premises to the port of despatch and placing the goods on board ship.

folcland. Folkland. Term used in Anglo-Saxon times to describe land held by customary law without written title. It could not be alienated without the consent of those who had some interest in it.

following trust property. There is a right to follow trust property, recognised by common law and equity, where that property is in the hands of some person (eg, as the result of a disposition of trust property in breach of trust) and is in an identifiable form. Under common law, property was considered identifiable only if not mixed with other property. *See* TRUST.

food. "The word must be interpreted

in its primary sense—namely as something taken into the system as nourishment, and not merely as a stimulant": *Hinde* v *Allmand* (1918) 87 LJ KB 893. See the Food and Drugs Act 1955, s. 135, in which the term includes drink and other products of a like nature and substances used as ingredients in the preparation of food and drink. See the Agricultural Marketing Act 1983, s. 8; and *Meah* v *Roberts* [1977] 1 WLR 1187.

footpath. Highway over which the public have a right of way on foot only, not being a footway (ie, a way comprised in a highway which also comprises a carriageway (qv), being a way over which the public has a right of way on foot only): Highways Act 1980, s. 329(1).

forbearance. Refraining from enforcing, eg, a debt. Generally a forbearance to sue may be adequate consideration (qv). See *Alliance Bank* v *Broom* (1864) 2 D & S 289.

forbidden degrees. *See* RELATIONSHIPS, PROHIBITED DEGREES OF.

force. Violence, generally of an unlawful nature.

force majeure. An event that can generally be neither anticipated nor reduced to control, eg, an industrial strike which leads to loss of profits. See *Czarnikow Ltd* v *Centrala Handlu* [1978] 1 All ER 81; and *Bunge AG* v *Fuga AG* [1980] 2 Lloyd's Rep 513.

force, reasonable. *See* REASONABLE FORCE.

forcible detainer. 1. Refusal to restore the goods of one who has tendered amends, the remedy for which was trover (qv). 2. The offence of detaining land by violence or threats, after having entered peacefully. See *R* v *Mountford* [1972] 2 QB 28. Generally abolished under the C.L.A. 1977, s. 13.

forcible entry. The crime (tort) of entering land in a violent manner, in order to take possession thereof. It is immaterial whether those concerned had or had not a right to enter. See *Grove* v *E Gas Board* [1951] 2 TLR 1128; *McPhail* v *Persons Unknown* [1973] Ch 447. Generally abolished under the C.L.A. 1977, s. 13. *See* ENTRY, VIOLENCE FOR SECURING.

foreclose down. *See* REDEEM UP, FORECLOSE DOWN.

foreclosure. The forfeiture by a mortgagor of his equity of redemption (qv). The mortgagee's right to foreclose arises after the date for redemption has passed, or on the breach of a term in the mortgage, eg, failure to pay interest. It is carried out by order of the court and all those interested in the equity of redemption must be made parties to the action. See *Brighty* v *Norton* (1862) 3 B & S 305; See the L.P.A. 1925, ss. 88, 89, 91; the Lim.A. 1980, s. 29; and *Twentieth Century Banking Corporation* v *Wilkinson* [1977] Ch 99. *See* MORTGAGE.

foreign agreement. An agreement of which the proper law (qv) is the law of a country outside the UK: C.C.A. 1974, s. 145.

foreign bill. *See* INLAND BILL.

foreign country. A country other than the UK, a dependent territory, the Republic of Ireland, or a country mentioned in Sch 3: B.N.A. 1981, s. 50(1).

foreign currency. Any currency other than sterling, including special drawing rights: Industry Act 1980, Sch 1. Foreign currency liabilities are liabilities which are measured in a foreign currency, whether or not they are to be discharged in a foreign currency. See *Miliangos* v *George Frank Ltd* [1976] All ER 446.

foreign enlistment. It is an offence for a British subject to accept a commission or engagement in the military service of a foreign state at war with any foreign state at peace with this country, or to induce a British subject to commit this action: Foreign Enlistment Act 1870, s. 4. *See* MERCENARY.

foreigners, interrogation of. *See* INTERROGATION OF FOREIGNERS.

foreign judgments, enforcement of. In the case of contract, a foreign judgment is enforceable in an English court if the foreign court is competent, judgment is for a definite sum and is final and conclusive. "In actions *in personam* there are five cases in which the courts of this country will enforce a foreign judgment: (1) where defendant is a subject of the foreign country in which judgment has been obtained; (2) where he was resident in the foreign country when the action began; (3) where plaintiff has selected the forum in which he afterwards sues; (4) where defendant has voluntarily appeared; (5) where defendant has contracted to submit himself to the forum in which judgment was obtained'': *Emanuel* v *Syman* [1908] 1 KB 302. See the Foreign Judgments (Reciprocal Enforcement) Act 1933; the European Communities (Enforcement of Community Judgments) Order 1972; the Protection of Trading Interests Act 1980; and O. 71. See also the C.J.J.A. 1982.

foreign judgments, registration of. Judgments given in the superior courts of Commonwealth or foreign countries which accord reciprocity of treatment to judgments given in the superior courts of the UK can be registered and enforced if the Foreign Judgments (Reciprocal Enforcement) Act 1933 has been extended to the country in which judgment was obtained.

foreign law. All law except English law. Thus, the law of Scotland, of the Republic of Ireland, comes under the heading of ''foreign law''. What the rule of the particular foreign law which applies in a case states, is determined by the judge after considering, where appropriate, the evidence of expert witnesses. See the Civil Evidence Act 1972, s. 4(1); *In b Dhost Aly Khan* (1880) 6 PD 6; *Saxby* v *Fulton* [1909] 2 KB 208 (judicial notice of foreign law).

foreign law, exclusion of. The withholding of recognition from a foreign law or judgment because, eg, it is repugnant to English law. See *Government of India* v *Taylor* [1955] 1 All ER 292; *Oppenheimer* v *Cattermole* [1973] Ch 264.

foreman of jury. Member of a jury (qv) who is chosen as its chairman and announces its verdict.

forensic. Relating to legal matters. Forensic medicine (known also as ''medical jurisprudence'') deals with medical facts used in the interpretation of legal problems. See,

eg, *R* v *Powell* [1980] Crim LR 39.

foreshore. Includes ''the shore and bed of the sea and of every channel, creek, bay, estuary and navigable river as far up it as the tide flows'': Salmon and Freshwater Fisheries Act 1975, s. 41(1). See *Baxendale* v *Instow PC* [1982] Ch 14. *See* BEACH.

foresight. Looking forward to some event. In determining whether a person has committed an offence, the court is not bound to infer that he intended or foresaw a result of his actions by reason only of it being a natural and probable consequence of those actions, but shall decide whether he did intend or foresee that result by reference to all the evidence, drawing such inferences from the evidence as appear proper in the circumstances: C.J.A. 1967, s. 8.

forestry. Includes the felling of trees and the extraction and primary conversion of trees within the wood or forest in which they were grown, and the use of land or woodlands ancillary to the use of land for other agricultural purposes: H.S.W.A. 1974, s. 53(1). See also the Forestry Act 1979; and the T.C.P.(Minerals)A. 1981, s. 5.

forfeiture. 1. A punishment whereby the offender lost all his interests in his property. Thus, the goods and chattels of a felon were, prior to the Forfeiture Act 1870, s. 1, forfeited to the Crown. 2. The P.C.C.A. 1973, s. 43, empowers the court to deprive an offender of property used, or intended to be used, for purposes of crime. See also the Misuse of Drugs Act 1971, s. 27; and *R* v *Cuthbertson* [1981] AC 470. 3. In a lease (qv) a forfeiture clause reserves to the lessor a right of re-entry, upon which the lease is forfeited. See the L.P.A. 1925, s. 146; and the Protection from Eviction Act 1977; s. 2.

forfeiture of benefit under will. ''A man shall not slay his benefactor and thereby take the bounty.'' See *Re Crippen* [1911] P 108; and *Re Hall* [1914] P 1. See now the Forfeiture Act 1982, giving the court a discretion to modify the rule in respect of certain forfeited property rights in given circumstances in respect of one who has unlawfully killed another. Murderers are excluded from the operation of the Act: s. 5.

forfeiture of shares. Shares may be forfeited (i.e. taken away from company members) by resolution of the board of directors if such a power is given in the articles of association (qv). The object of forfeiture must be for the company's benefit. Shares may be forfeited, eg, where a member fails to pay a call properly made on him. See Table A, arts. 33–39; *Re Esparto Trading Co* (1879) 12 Ch D 191. *See* COMPANY; SHARE.

forgery. "A person is guilty of forgery if he makes a false instrument, with the intention that he or another shall use it to induce somebody to accept it as genuine, and by reason of so accepting it to do or not to do some act to his own or any other person's prejudice": Forgery and Counterfeiting Act 1981, s. 1. *See* INSTRUMENT, FALSE.

formal contract. Term applied to a contract, eg, for the sale of land, comprising particulars (describing property); special conditions (relating to sale in question); general conditions (standardised and incorporated into contract by reference to, eg, "national conditions of sale"). *See* CONTRACT.

formedon. A writ, abolished under the Real Property Limitation Act 1833, used by a person claiming land under a gift in tail in possession of one with no title to it.

forthwith. Immediately, or, more generally, when used in a statute, within a reasonable time. See *Hillingdon LBC v Cutler* [1968] Crim LR 109.

fortune telling. It is an offence to purport to "exercise powers of telepathy, clairvoyance or other similar powers". See the Vagrancy Act 1824, s. 4 (amended by the Fraudulent Mediums Act 1951, s. 2(b)); *R v Martin* [1981] Crim LR 109.

forum. 1. A judicial assembly. 2. Country in which jurisdiction is exercised. If, eg, X is sued in England on a contract made in Italy, England is the forum, and the *lex fori* (qv) is the law of England.

forum non conveniens. Doctrine

whereby the court refuses to exercise its right of jurisdiction because, for the convenience of parties and in the interests of justice, an action should be brought elsewhere. See *MacShannon v Rockware Glass Ltd* [1978] AC 795.

forum rei. The court of the country in which the subject-matter of the action is situated.

foster-child. A child below the upper limit of the compulsory school-leaving age whose care and maintenance are undertaken by some person who is not a guardian or relative: Foster Children Act 1980, s. 1(1). A child is not a foster-child under the 1980 Act if, eg, he is in the care of a person in premises in which any parent, adult relative or guardian of his is residing, or in a home maintained by a public or local authority. See the Adoption Act 1976, Sch. 3.

foster-parent. One who, while having the day-to-day care of a child does not possess any parental rights (which remain vested in, eg, the natural parents, legal guardian, local authority). For disqualifications, see the Foster Children Act 1980, s. 7.

founders' shares. *See* DEFERRED SHARES.

four corners. Phrase used to indicate that which is contained on the face of a written instrument, so that to look at its "four corners" is to construe it as a whole, without referring to one part more than another.

four-day order. Supplemental order, based on O. 42, by which, if a time within which an act to be done is not specified, four days will be given for compliance.

four unities, the. *See* JOINT TENANCY.

fractionem diei non recipit lex. The law does not recognise any fraction of a day. (There are some few exceptions to this general rule, eg, in cases of necessity.)

franchise. 1. The right of voting in a parliamentary or local election. 2. A privilege belonging to the Crown, or by virtue of a grant, expressed or implied, to a subject. Example: the right to hold markets. Known also as a "liberty". See the Wild Creatures and Forest Laws Act 1971, s. 1; *Iveagh v Martin* [1961] 1 QB 232.

franchise clause. Clause in an insurance policy relieving the insurer from total liability in respect of losses below a standard percentage or other figure. See *Stewart* v *Merchants' Marine Insurance Co* (1885) 16 QBD 619.

frankalmoign. Free alms. Type of land tenure originating in the Anglo-Saxon era, when lands were granted to the church in return for prayers for the grantor's soul. Abolished under the A.E.A. 1925, Sch. 2.

fraud at common law. Intentional deceit. A false representation by the defendant of an existing fact, made knowingly, or without belief in its truth, or recklessly, careless whether it be true or false, with the intention that the plaintiff should act on it, and which results in damage to the plaintiff. " 'Fraud' in my opinion, is a term that should be reserved for something dishonest and morally wrong"; *per* Wills J in *Ex p Watson* (1888) 21 QBD 301. See *Horsfall* v *Thomas* (1862) 10 WR 650; *Redgrave* v *Hurd* (1881) 20 Ch D 1.

fraud, concealed. *See* CONCEALED FRAUD.

fraud, constructive. *See* CONSTRUCTIVE FRAUD.

fraud on a power. "The term . . . merely means that the power has been exercised for a purpose, or with an intention, beyond the scope of or not justified by the instrument creating the power"; *Vatcher* v *Paull* [1915] AC 372. Example: an appointment made for a corrupt purpose (see *Lord Hinchinbroke* v *Seymour* (1789) 1 Bro CC 385). *See* APPOINTMENT, POWER OF.

fraud on minority. *See* MINORITY SHAREHOLDERS, OPPRESSION OF.

frauds relating to theft. Under the Th.A. 1968, the following offences relating to fraud exist: obtaining property by deception, s. 15; obtaining a pecuniary advantage by deception, s. 16; false accounting, s. 17; false statements by company directors, s. 19; dishonest suppression of documents, s. 20(1); dishonest procuring by deception of the execution of a valuable security, s. 20(2). Each is an arrestable offence (qv).

fraudulent conversion. *See* CONVERSION.

fraudulent conveyance. 1. "Every conveyance of property made . . . with intent to defraud creditors shall be voidable at the instance of any person thereby prejudiced"; L.P.A. 1925, s. 172(1). See, eg, *Cadogan* v *Cadogan* [1977] 1 All ER 200. The section does not apply in the case of an estate (qv) or interest in property conveyed for valuable consideration (qv) and in good faith. A voluntary disposition of land made with intent to defraud a subsequent purchaser is voidable at the instance of the purchaser: L.P.A. 1925, s. 173. 2. Under the B.A. 1914, s. 1, a fraudulent conveyance by a debtor may constitute an act of bankruptcy (qv).

fraudulent mediums. *See* WITCHCRAFT.

fraudulent misrepresentation. *See* MISREPRESENTATION, FRAUDULENT.

fraudulent preference. A conveyance or transfer of a debtor's property intended to give a creditor or surety any preference over other creditors and made by a person insolvent at the time. It constitutes an act of bankruptcy (qv) and if the debtor is subsequently adjudged bankrupt on a petition presented within six months, is void against the trustee in bankruptcy: B.A. 1914, s. 44. See *Re Matthews* [1982] 1 All ER 338.

fraudulent trading. Trading by a company (qv) with intent to defraud creditors or other persons. See the Cos.A. 1981, s. 96. See also *R* v *Cox and Hedges* (1982) 75 C.App.R. 291.

freebench. Dower to which the widow of a copyholder was entitled by special custom. Abolished under the L.P.A. 1922, Sch 12 in relation to enfranchised land. *See* DOWER.

freehold. An estate of an uncertain maximum duration. Originally an estate held by a "free man". *See* ESTATE.

freeing for adoption. Process of relinquishment of rights whereby a child is freed for the purposes of adoption: Ch.A. 1975, s. 14.

free movement. Phrase used in the Treaty of Rome 1957, which set up the EEC (qv), referring to the movement of persons, services and capital within the EEC, which is to be without limitations. See *R* v *Saunders* [1979] 2 All ER 267.

freight. A consideration paid to a carrier for the carriage of goods. *Lump sum freight* is paid by the charterer as a lump sum for the use of a ship. *Pro rata freight* is the amount recoverable by a carrier when the owner of goods agrees to take delivery at a port short of the agreed destination. *Advance freight* is payable before delivery of goods.

frequenting. Term used in relation to a suspected person (qv), to suggest visiting a place repeatedly. It involves the notion of more than mere physical presence and something which is to some degree continuous: *Nakhla v The Queen* [1976] AC 1. See the Vagrancy Act 1824, s. 4.

friendly society. A society registered by the Chief Registrar of Friendly Societies as a friendly society under the Friendly Societies Acts 1974 and 1981, being a society which, as part of its ordinary business, provides benefits during sickness or other infirmity, or in old age, or in widowhood, or for orphans: S.S.A. 1975, Sch. 20.

fringe benefits. Benefits granted by an employer to an employee which do not enter into his basic wage. See the Finance Act 1976, ss; 60–72.

frivolous action. *See* VEXATIOUS ACTION.

front bench. The two benches occupied in the House of Commons (qv) by ministers of the government and the principal members of the opposition.

fructus industriales. That which is the produce of "labour and industry". Example: corn, as compared with *fructus naturales* (crops which grow naturally). See *Marshall v Green* (1875) 1 CPD 35.

frustration of contract. Where there is an event or change of circumstances so fundamental as to strike at the root of a contract as a whole and beyond what was contemplated by the parties, that contract is considered frustrated. Under the Law Reform (Frustrated Contracts) Act 1943, all sums payable under a frustrated contract are recoverable and sums payable cease to be payable. The Act does not apply to a contract containing a provision to meet a case of frustration, to a contract of insurance or carriage of goods by sea, or to a contract not governed by English law. See *Fibrosa Case* [1943] AC 32; *Morgan v Manser* [1948] 1 KB 184; *BP Exploration Comp v Hunt (No. 2)* [1982] 2 WLR 253. For frustration of a lease, see *National Carriers v Panalpina* [1981] AC 675. *See* CONTRACT.

frustration, self-induced. Frustration of a contract due to one's own conduct or to the conduct of those for whom one is responsible: *Bank Line Ltd v Arthur Capel & Co* [1919] AC 435. See *The Eugenia* [1964] 2 QB 226.

fugitive offender. One who, found in the UK and accused of a relevant offence (non-political) in a designated Commonwealth country or dependency, may be arrested and returned to that country under the Fugitive Offenders Act 1967. See the Taking of Hostages Act 1982, s. 4; *Fernandez v Government of Singapore* [1971] 2 All ER 691; *Union of India v Narang and Others* [1977] 2 All ER 463; and S.I. 1979/1712.

full age. Age of majority: 18 since the F.L.R.A. 1969, s. 1. See INFANT.

functus officio. Having discharged his duty. Refers to one who has exercised his authority and brought it to an end in a particular case. Thus, a judge who has convicted a person charged with an offence is *functus officio*. See *Re VGM Holdings* [1941] 3 All ER 417.

funds, payment into court. *See* PAYMENT INTO COURT.

funeral expenses. Reasonable expenses involved in burying a deceased person must be paid out of his estate prior to any other duty or debt: *R v Wade* (1818) 5 Pr 621.

fungibles. Movable goods which are ordinarily dealt with by number, measurement or weight. "Fungible assets" are assets of a company "substantially indistinguishable one from another": Cos.A. 1981, Sch 1.

furniture. "For articles to be furniture . . . I do not think it is essential that they shall be movable, and though, of course, articles of furniture are commonly movable, I do not think they pass out of the popular meaning of furniture because they are fixed by a nail or a screw to a wall or floor": per Stamp J in *F. Austin Ltd* v *Commissioners of Customs & Excise* [1968] 2 All ER 13. See also *Gray* v *Fidler* [1943] 2 All ER 289.

future goods. *See* GOODS.

future interest. An interest limited so that it confers a right to the enjoy-ment of property at some time in the future. Example: grant "to A for his life and then to the first of his sons who shall attain the age of 21"—in the case of the first of A's sons, the interest takes effect in the future.

future lease. An existing lease carry-ing the right to possession at a speci-fied time in the future. *See* LEASE.

G

gage. A pledge. Something given as security for some act. In the twelfth century the *vivum vadium* (living pledge) allowed a mortgagee to take possession of land rents and profits in discharge of principal and interest. The *mortuum vadium* (dead pledge) allowed him to take rents and profits in discharge of the interest only.

gain. ''The most appropriate definition to be found in a dictionary may be 'increase in resources or business advantages resulting from business transactions or deaings' '': *Re Riverton Sheep Dip* (1943) SASR 344. See *Armour* v *Liverpool Corpn* [1939] Ch 422.

game. Animals *ferae naturae* hunted for sport or food, including hares, pheasants, partridges, grouse, heath or moor game, woodcock, etc. See the Game Laws (Amendment) Act 1960, by which a constable may arrest a person trespassing in pursuit of game. See also the Wild Creatures and Forest Laws Act 1971. *See* ANIMAL; POACHING.

game licence. Licence necessary for the killing of and dealing in game. See the Game Licences Act 1860; and the Post Office Act 1969, ss. 12, 134.

gaming. Known also as ''gambling''. ''The playing of a game of chance for winnings in money or money's worth, whether any person playing the game is at risk of losing any money or money's worth or not'': Gaming Act 1968, s. 52. The 1968 Act prohibited gaming in public bars and wherever a charge is made. It also prohibits gaming involving playing or staking against a bank or where the chances are unequal. Commercial gaming may be permitted under licence. See the Betting, Gaming and Lotteries Act 1963; the Lotteries and Amusements Act 1976; the Gaming (Amendment) Act 1982. (For a definition of ''gaming machine'', see the Betting and Gaming Duties Act 1981, s. 25.)

gaming contracts. Contracts which are wagers upon a game, eg, a horse race. Generally, they involve ''the playing of a game of chance for winnings in money or money's worth'': Betting, Gaming and Lotteries Act 1963. Generally null and void; no action can be brought to recover money relating to a wager. Securities given for gaming contracts are, in effect, given for an illegal consideration (qv) and are void as between the parties. See the Gaming Act 1968; *Carlton Hall Club* v *Lawrence* [1929] 2 KB 153; *C.H.T.* v *Ward* [1963] 3 All ER 835.

gaol delivery. A commission authorising judges and commissioners of assize (qv) to try all those who were in prison when they arrived at a circuit town. It was effectively abolished under the Courts Act 1971.

garnishee. One who has been warned by a court order that a debt is to be paid to some person who has obtained a garnishee order against his creditor, and not to that creditor. See O. 49; *Llewellyn* v *Carrickford* [1970] 1 WLR 1124.

garnishee proceedings. Proceedings enabling a judgment creditor (qv) to have assigned to him the benefit of any debt owned by the garnishee (qv) to the judgment debtor (qv). Example: A owes B £1,000 and C owes A £1,000. B may commence proceedings to obtain a garnishee order so that C will pay the £1,000 directly to B. Where proceedings fail, the courts have a wide discretion as to costs and may order the judgment debtor to pay them: *Wright & Son* v *Westoby* [1972] 3 All ER 1078. See O. 49. See also *Choice Investments Ltd* v *Jeromnimon* [1981] QB 149. *See* JUDGMENTS, ENFORCEMENT OF.

gavelkind. *Gafolcund* = yielding a rent. Socage tenures (qv) in Kent, held under unique conditions, eg, land could be alienated by a tenant at the age of 15, could be devised and was not liable to escheat (qv) for felony (qv). Abolished by the A.E.A. 1925, s. 45(1) (a). See also the L.P.A. 1922, Sch 12.

Gazette. *See* LONDON GAZETTE.

gazump. Colloquial term used to refer to a situation in which the vendor of a house "subject to contract" (qv) withdraws from the bargain, or threatens to do so, in the expectation of receiving a higher price elsewhere. See Law Commission Report 1975, No. 65.

G.D.O. General Development Order (qv).

general agent. One authorised to act generally in his principal's business affairs. *See* AGENT.

general and special damages. For purpose of procedure, damages may be divided thus: 1. General damages, such as will be presumed to have resulted from the defendant's acts. They may include, eg, damages for pain, inconvenience and generally need not be specifically pleaded. 2. Special damages, such as will not be presumed, eg, loss of earnings, medical expenses. These must be pleaded specifically and proved. *See* DAMAGES.

general average. *See* AVERAGE.

General Council of the Bar. *See* BAR COUNCIL.

General Development Order. A Town and Country Planning and General Development Order which gives permission for certain specified classes of development (qv).

general devise. *See* DEVISE.

general equitable charge. *See* EQUITABLE CHARGE, GENERAL.

generalia specialibus non derogant. General things do not derogate from special things. See, eg, *The Vera Cruz* (1884) 10 App Cas 59; *Harlow* v *Minister of Transport* [1951] 2 KB 98.

generalia verba sunt generaliter intelligenda. General words are to be understood generally.

generalibus specialia derogant. Special things derogate from general things.

general improvement area. A predominantly residential area, so declared by a local authority (under, eg, the H.A. 1969 and 1974), in which it is considered that living conditions should be improved and

that the improvement should be carried out or assisted by the authority.

general issue. A plea by the defendant who traversed or denied allegations in their entirety, eg, "never indebted" in an action of debt. No longer admissible in a civil action, save where in accordance with the requirements of statute. See O. 18.

general legacy. A bequest which does not identify specifically the thing bequeathed. Example: "a horse to X and a gold watch to Y". The subject-matter of a general legacy need not form part of the testator's assets at the time of his death: *Bothamley* v *Sherson* (1875) LR 20 Eq 304. *See* LEGACY.

general lien. A right to retain possession of another's goods until all claims against that other are satisfied. It exists, eg, in the case of bankers and solicitors. See *Halesowen Presswork & Assemblies Ltd* v *Westminster Bank Ltd* [1971] 1 QB 1. *See* LIEN.

general occupant. If X, a tenant *pur autre vie* (qv), died during Y's lifetime and Y was the *cestui que vie* (qv), and the grant was "to X during the life of Y", the land went, on X's death, to the person who first took possession —the so-called *general occupant*. If the grant were "to X and his heirs during the lifetime of Y", the land went, on the death of X, to his heir—the so-called *special occupant*. Abolished under the A.E.A. 1925, s. 45.

general power. *See* APPOINTMENT, POWER OF.

general verdict. A finding of the point in issue, generally; eg, a verdict of guilty, or one of not guilty. *See* SPECIAL VERDICT.

general warrant. Warrant in which neither the persons nor the premises to be searched were named. Declared illegal in *Wilkes* v *Wood* (1765) 19 St Tr 1153. "By the law of England every invasion of private property be it ever so minute is a trespass. No man can set foot on my ground without my licence . . . he is bound to show by way of justification that some positive law has empowered or excused him": *Entick* v *Carrington* (1675) 19 St Tr 1030. See, however,

Elias v *Pasmore* [1934]2 KB 164. *See* WARRANT.

general words. Words which were necessary in a conveyance (qv) to convey rights and easements (qv). Under the L.P.A. 1925, s. 62, such words are implied, if no contrary intention is expressed.

Geneva Conventions. A group of international treaties signed in Geneva in 1864–1949, aimed at the amelioration of the effects of war on combatants and non-combatants. See the Geneva Conventions Act 1957.

genocide. The offence committed by one who, with intent to destroy a national, ethnic, racial or religious group, kills or causes serious bodily or mental harm to members of the group, inflicts on the group conditions of life intended to physically destroy it, or forcibly transfers children of that group to another group. See the Genocide Act 1969.

gentlemen's agreement. Colloquial term used to describe an agreement resting on the honour of the parties. It is not usually enforceable at law.

gestation. The time between conception and birth (around 267 days for man). See *Hadlum* v *Hadlum* [1949] P 197; *Preston-Jones* v *Preston-Jones* [1951] AC 391.

gift. A gratuitous transfer of the ownership of property: Blackstone.

gift, imperfect. A gift which has not been completely constituted. An apparently imperfect transfer may be effective: if the conditions for a *donatio mortis causa* (qv) are satisfied; under the rule in *Strong* v *Bird* (1874) LR 18 Eq 315; by statute, eg, the L.P.A. 1925, ss. 1, 19 and the S.L.A. 1925, ss. 4, 9, 27; under the doctrine of equitable estoppel (qv).

gift *inter vivos*. A gratuitous grant or transfer of property between living persons. Validity of the gift necessitates the intention to give and appropriate acts to make the intention effective. See, eg, *Thomas* v *Times Book Club Co Ltd* [1966] 2 All ER 241; *Dewar* v *Dewar* [1975] 2 All ER 728.

gift over. Phrase signifying a gift which comes into existence when a particular preceding estate (qv) is determined.

gilt-edged. Term referring to Stock Exchange securities considered to carry a minimum of risk. Generally used of UK government stocks. For a list, see, eg, the Capital Gains Tax Act 1979, Sch 1, Part II.

gipsies. Described in the Caravan Sites Act 1968 as "persons of nomadic habit of life, whatever their race or origin". They are prohibited under the Highways Act 1980 from encamping on highways. Local authorities have the duty under the 1968 Act to provide adequate accommodation for gipsies residing in or resorting to their area. See the L.G.P.L.A. 1980, s. 70; *R* v *Sheffield CC ex p Mansfield* (1978) 37 P & CR 1 and *Page Motors* v *Epsom BC* (1982) 80 LGR 337.

glebae adscriptitii. Villeins who could not be removed from the land they held so long as they carried out the services they owed. *See* VILLEIN TENURE.

glebe. 1. A plot of cultivated land. 2. Land belonging to a church or ecclesiastical benefice (qv). See *Oakley* v *Boston* [1976] QB 270.

glebe building. A building, wall or fence which the incumbent of a benefice (qv) is obliged to maintain in repair, but not a parsonage house: Repair of Benefice Buildings Measure 1972, s. 31.

God's penny. A small, nominal sum paid as an earnest (qv) on the striking of a bargain.

going equipped for stealing. "A person is guilty of an offence if, when not at his place of abode, he has with him any article for use in the course of or in connection with any burglary, theft or cheat": Th.A. 1968, s. 25(1). See *R* v *Bundy* [1977] 1 WLR 914; *R* v *Doukas* [1978] 1 WLR 372.

going public. Procedure whereby a private company becomes a public company by offering its shares for sale through the Stock Exchange. *See* COMPANY.

gold coin clause. Agreement in international trade that a sum of money shall be paid in gold coins.

golden handshake. Phrase referring to payment (usually of considerable value) made *ex gratia* (qv) or as compensation for loss of office. See the Finance Act 1981, s. 31.

golden rule. Rule for construing a

statute: *Mattison* v *Hart* (1854) 14 CB 385. "The grammatical and ordinary sense of the words is to be adhered to unless that would lead to an absurdity or some repugnancy or inconsistency with the rest of the instrument, in which case the grammatical and ordinary sense of the words may be modified so as to avoid such absurdity, repugnancy or inconsistency, but no further": *Grey* v *Pearson* (1857) 6 HLC 61. See *Federal Steam Navigation Co* v *Department of Trade and Industry* [1974] 2 All ER 97.

good behaviour. A person may be ordered by a magistrate (qv) to keep the peace, or to be of good behaviour and may also be ordered to enter into recognisances (qv). If he fails to be of good behaviour for that period the recognisances may be estreated and he becomes liable to be sentenced for the original offence. See the M.C.A. 1980, ss. 115, 116.

good consideration. Consideration founded on generosity, natural affection or normal duty. It is not regarded as "valuable consideration" (eg, money, money's worth) so that, eg, a settlement merely supported by good consideration is regarded as "voluntary". Because equity will not assist a volunteer, should A promise B that he will create a trust and should he fail to do so, B cannot compel performance if he has not given valuable consideration. See the L.P.A. 1925, s. 172(3); *Re D'Angibau* (1880) 15 Ch D 228; *Re Cook's Settlement Trusts* [1965] Ch 902; and *Midland Bank Trust Co* v *Green* [1981] AC 513. *See* CONSIDERATION.

good faith. "The words, in my opinion, mean 'honestly'. A claim is not made honestly if made with the intention of committing a criminal offence, or of facilitating the commission of a future offence": *per* Phillimore LJ in *Central Estates Ltd* v *Woolgar* [1971] 3 All ER 647. See the B.Ex.A. 1882, s. 90.

good leasehold title. A title under the L.R.A. 1925, whereby no guarantee as to the lessor's right to validly grant the lease is given, but in other respects the title is effectively equivalent to absolute leasehold title.

good repair. Such a state of repair as will satisfy a respectable occupant using the premises fairly. See *Dashwood* v *Magniac* [1891] 3 Ch 306.

goods. Under the S.G.A. 1979, all chattels personal, other than things in action and money: s. 61. In effect, therefore, all things in possession, save money used as currency of the realm. "Future goods" are those to be manufactured or acquired by the seller following the making of the contract of sale. "Specific goods" are those "identified and agreed upon at the time a contract of sale is made": s. 61.

goods, deliverable state. Goods "in such a state that the buyer would under the contract be bound to take delivery of them": S.G.A. 1979, s. 61(5).

goods, delivery of. *See* DELIVERY OF GOODS.

goods, duress of. *See* DURESS OF GOODS.

goods, hire of, contract for. "A contract under which one person bails or agrees to bail goods to another by way of hire, other than an excepted contract": Supply of Goods and Services Act 1982, s. 6(1). "Excepted contract" refers to a hire-purchase agreement or a contract under which goods are bailed in exchange for trading stamps on their redemption: s. 6(2). For implied terms, see ss. 7–10.

goods, protected. *See* PROTECTED GOODS.

goods, quality of. *See* QUALITY.

goods, safety of. *See* SAFETY OF GOODS.

goods, slander of. *See* SLANDER OF GOODS.

goods, title to, transfer of. *See* TITLE TO GOODS, TRANSFER OF.

goods, transfer of, contract for. "A contract under which one person transfers or agrees to transfer to another the property in goods, other than an excepted contract": Supply of Goods and Services Act 1982, s. 1(1). "Excepted contract" refers to a contract of sale of goods, a hire-purchase agreement, a contract under which property is transferred on redemption of trading stamps, a contract intended to operate by way of mortgage, pledge, charge or other security: s. 1(2). For implied terms and warranties, see ss. 2–5.

goods, trespass to. *See* TRESPASS TO GOODS.

goods, wrongful interference with. See INTERFERENCE WITH GOODS, WRONGFUL.

goodwill. An intangible asset resulting from a right to the advantages of a business derived from its past reputation. "It is the attractive force which brings in custom": *Inland Revenue* v *Muller* [1901] AC 224. "The whole advantage, wherever it may be, of the reputation and connection of the firm which may have been built up by years of honest work or gained by lavish expenditure of money": *Trego* v *Hunt* [1896] AC 7. See the Cos.A. 1981, Sch 1, para 21.

go-slow. A form of industrial action by workers, taking the form of working more slowly than usual. Known also as "working to rule", ie, reducing output by paying exaggerated attention to rules relating to working conditions. See *Secretary of State for Employment* v *ASLEF (No. 2)* [1972] 2 QB 455.

government. 1. The exercise of authority. 2. The institutions, customs and laws through which government functions. 3. Her Majesty's Government, ie, a body of ministers responsible for the administration of the nation's affairs.

grand assize. Introduced by Henry II as an alternative to trial by battle (qv). The plaintiff alleged in his writ of right that he had been dispossessed wrongfully. Twelve knights were called to deliver to the justices of assize a verdict as to whether the plaintiff's allegation of title was, in fact, truthful. Abolished by the Civil Procedure Act 1833. See ASSIZE.

grand jury. See JURY, GRAND.

grand larceny. The offence of stealing goods worth more than twelve pence. *Petty larceny* referred to stealing goods below that value. The distinction was abolished in 1827.

grand serjeanty. A tenure originating in services rendered to the King by his courtiers and followers, eg, officers of the King's household. The tenure enjoyed by the great nobles of the realm was *grand serjeanty*; the tenure involving only minor services was *petty serjeanty*. Grand serjeanty became the equivalent of knight service (qv); petty serjeanty, the equivalent of socage (qv).

grant. 1. Transfer of property under written instrument without immediate delivery. 2. The allocation of rights, etc, to persons.

grant, block. See BLOCK GRANT; AIDS.

grant in aid. See AIDS.

grant of representation. 1. Probate (qv). 2. *Cum testamento annexo*, made when the deceased left a valid will which has not been proved by an executor (qv). See the S.C.A. 1981, s. 119. 3. Simple administration, when deceased died wholly intestate.

grants, special and limited. 1. Grants of representation may be limited as to property, eg, where the testator (qv) has expressly limited the powers of his executor; in the case of grants as to specific settled land; grants *caeterorum* (where a grant has been made to a portion of the estate and it is necessary to apply for administration of the rest of the estate); *de bonis non administratis* (qv). 2. Grants may be limited as to time, eg, until the will be found; for the use of infants (qv); during mental incapacity; *ad litem* (qv); *ad colligenda bona* (qv).

grants to attorney. When an executor or administrator entitled to a grant resides outside England and the grant is limited until that person shall obtain a grant, it may be made to the lawfully constituted attorney of the person entitled for his use and benefit: Non-Contentious Probate Rules 1954, r. 30(1).

gratis. Without recompense or charge; free.

gratuitous. Given freely, ie, without legal consideration.

grave hardship. In the case of divorce (qv) based on five years living apart, the respondent can object to the granting of a decree by showing that dissolving the marriage would result in "grave financial or other hardship to him": Mat.C.A. 1973, s. 5(1). "Grave" is given its ordinary meaning and hardship is to be determined objectively, according to the standard of sensible people. See *Reiterbund* v *Reiterbund* [1975] Fam 99; and *Rukat* v *Rukat* [1975] Fam 63.

Gray's Inn. One of the four Inns of Court (qv). The site of the Inn was let by the Dean of St Paul's to Reginald de Grey, chief justice of Chester, in the thirteenth century. The Inn began to function as a legal institution *c.* 1320.

Great Britain. *See* UNITED KINGDOM.

great seal of the realm. The seal, in custody of the Lord Chancellor, held through the Clerk of Crown in Chancery, used for the sealing of treaties, summoning of Parliament, etc. See the S.C.A. 1981, s. 129.

Green Book. *See* COUNTY COURTS.

green paper. *See* PARLIAMENTARY PAPERS.

green, village. *See* VILLAGE GREEN.

grievance proceedings. Arrangements, usually involving some adjudicatory process, by which an employee in dispute with his employer may seek a settlement. See, eg, the Industrial Relations Code of Practice 1972, paras 120–125.

grievous bodily harm. *See* BODILY HARM, GRIEVOUS.

gross. Entire; exclusive of deductions. The term "in gross" means, when referring to a right, that it is not appendant (qv) or otherwise annexed to land.

gross indecency. 1. It is an offence for a man to commit an act of gross indecency [a term not defined by statute: but see the Wolfenden Committee Report 1957, Cmnd 247, p. 38] with another man in public or private, to be a party to the commission of such an act or to procure its commission. See the S.O.A. 1956, s. 13; *R* v *Hall* [1963] 2 All ER 1075; *R* v *Preece, R* v *Howells* [1977] QB 370. The term is used in practice to refer to a sexual act, other than buggery (qv), between males. 2. It is an offence for a person to commit an act of gross indecency with or towards a child under the age of 14 or to incite such a child to do such an act with him or any other person. See Indecency with Children Act 1960; *R* v *Speck* [1977] 2 All ER 859.

gross negligence. Used colloquially to refer to negligence characterised by total indifference to the rights of others and the consequences of one's act. "The use of the expression 'gross negligence' is always misleading. Except in the one case when the law relating to manslaughter is being considered, the words 'gross negligence' should never be used in connection with any matter to which the common law relates because negligence is a breach of duty, and, if there is a duty and there has been a breach of it which causes loss, it matters not whether it is a venial breach or a serious breach": *Pentecost* v *London District Auditor* [1951] 2 KB 759.

gross negligence, killing by. In a case of alleged killing by gross negligence, the facts must be such "that in the opinion of the jury, the negligence of the accused went beyond a mere matter of compensation between subjects and showed such disregard for the life and safety of others as to amount to a crime against the State and conduct deserving of punishment": *R* v *Bateman* (1925) 133 LT 730. See *Andrews* v *DPP* [1937] 2 All ER 552; *R* v *Lamb* [1967] 2 QB 981. *See* NEGLIGENCE.

gross value of premises. Phrase used in the Rent Acts to mean letting value of premises by the year, assuming that the cost of insurance and repairs is carried by the landlord.

ground rent. *See* BUILDING LEASE.

group accounts. Accounts laid in general meeting before a company which has subsidiaries: Cos.A. 1948, s. 150. They must consist of a consolidated balance sheet and profit and loss account (see s. 151(1)) and must comply with requirements of the Cos.A. 1948, Sch 8. See also the Cos.A. 1981, s. 2.

group company. *See* COMPANY, GROUP.

guarantee. A collateral engagement to answer for the debt, default or miscarriage of another person. To be enforceable, such a promise must be evidenced in writing: Statute of Frauds 1677, s. 4. "Miscarriage" refers here to "that species of wrongful act for the consequences of which the law would make the party civilly responsible": *Kirkham* v *Marter* (1819) 2 B & A 613. See the Export Guarantees and Overseas Investment Act 1978, s. 15(1); Cos.A. 1980, s. 63(1).

guarantee, company limited by. Company (qv) formed, eg, for charitable or educational purposes. If it has share capital, a member is liable up to the amount unpaid on his shares and also up to the amount of guarantee; but if it has no share capital, he is liable only up to the amount of the guarantee. See Table D; and the Cos.A. 1980, Sch 1, Part II. A company limited by guarantee is prohibited from having a share capital unless it had a share capital before the 1980 Act came into force: Cos.A. 1980, s. 1(2).

guarantee payments. Payments made by an employer to an employee who has more than four weeks' service and who is laid off: E.P.(C.)A. 1978, ss. 12–18 (as modified by the Employment Act 1980, s. 14). Employees hired for a period of less than 12 weeks are generally excluded. Amount of payment is regulated by a formula set out in s. 14(2).

guarantor. One who promises to answer for another; a surety (qv).

guardian. One appointed to take care of another person, his affairs and property. "A person appointed by deed or will in accordance with the provisions of the Guardianship of Infants Acts 1886 and 1925 or the Guardianship of Minors Act 1971 and the Guardianship Act 1973, or by a court of competent jurisdiction to be guardian of the child": Adoption Act 1976, s. 72(1).

guardian *ad litem*. *See* AD LITEM.

guillotine. A parliamentary pro-

cedure, whereby a period for debate on the stages of a Bill is fixed by an "allocation of time order", at the end of which debate is stopped. First used in 1887. Known also as "closure by compartments".

guilty. 1. Confession by the defendant that he has committed the offence with which he is charged. He may, for example, plead guilty to one count in an indictment, but not guilty to another. See *Machent* v *Quinn* [1970] 2 All ER 255. A plea of guilty made under pressure upon counsel from the trial judge is not a proper plea, so that the ensuing trial is a nullity; *R* v *Inns* (1975) 60 Cr App R 231. 2. A finding after the trial that the accused has committed the offence upon which the jury may find that verdict (eg, not guilty of murder, but guilty of manslaughter). For changing guilty pleas, see *S* v *Recorder of Manchester* [1969] 3 All ER 1230. For a mistaken plea of guilty, see *R* v *Phillips* [1982] 1 All ER 245. *See* NOT GUILTY.

guilty knowledge. That awareness by virtue of which a person's act or omission is rendered criminal in nature. In *Roper* v *Taylor's Central Garages (Exeter) Ltd* [1951] 2 TLR 284, it was categorised as (1) actual knowledge, which could be inferred from the accused's conduct; (2) knowlege in the eye of the law, where the accused has deliberately refrained from making enquiries; (3) constructive knowledge.

guilty mind. *See* MENS REA.

guilty, plea by post of. *See* POST, PLEA OF GUILTY BY.

H

habeas corpus. That you have the body. A prerogative writ used to command a person who is detaining another in custody to produce the body of that person before the court. "The King is at all times entitled to have an account why the liberty of his subjects is restrained": Blackstone. The writ *habeas corpus ad subjiciendum* commands a person to produce the detainee, with details of the day and cause of his caption and detention, to do, submit to and receive what shall be directed by the court. The QBD has jurisdiction to issue the writ. See the Habeas Corpus Acts 1679 (qv), 1816 and 1862. The Acts have been suspended on occasions, such as in time of war. See the A.J.A. 1960, s. 14; O. 54, r. 9; *R v Home Secretary, ex p Lees* [1941] 1 KB 72; and *Re Sherman and Apps* [1981] 2 All ER 612.

Habeas Corpus Act 1679. "An Act for the better securing the liberty of the subject and for prevention of imprisonment beyond the seas." Among its provisions were: that an unconvicted prisoner could demand from a judge a writ of habeas corpus (qv), that no person once delivered by habeas corpus should be recommitted for the same offence and that no inhabitant of England should be sent to imprisonment out of England.

habendum. To have. The clause in a conveyance (qv) which defines the extent of the purchaser's interest or estate (eg, "to hold unto the purchaser in fee simple").

habitation, fit for. Phrase referring to an undertaking by a landlord that premises are or will be rendered fit for habitation. There is no general implied undertaking of this nature by a landlord. Exceptions include: furnished houses (see *Collins v Hopkins* [1923] 2 KB 617); houses at a low rental (see the H.A. 1957, s. 6); covenants relating to the letting of dwelling-houses after October 1961 for periods of less than seven years (see also the H.A. 1961). Note the duty to build dwellings properly and of care for safety (Defective Premises Act 1972).

habit, presumption from. The fact that a person was in the habit of acting in a certain way may be relevant to the issue of whether he acted in that way on the occasion which forms the basis of the court's enquiry. See *Joy v Phillips, Mill & Co Ltd* [1916] 1 KB 849—evidence was admitted of a boy's practice of teasing a horse, in an action resulting from his death caused by a kick from the horse. *See* EVIDENCE.

habitual criminal. Under the Prevention of Crime Act 1908, where the court had sentenced to penal servitude a person convicted of felony who had at least three previous serious convictions since the age of 16, he could be pronounced a habitual criminal. See, eg, *R v Norman* [1924] 2 KB 315. The expression was replaced, under the C.J.A. 1948 by "persistent offender" (qv). See the P.C.C.A. 1973, ss. 28, 29.

habitual drunkard. A person who, not being mentally disordered, is at times, because of habitual intemperate drinking of intoxicants, dangerous to others or incapable of managing himself or his affairs. See the Habitual Drunkards Act 1879 (repealed in 1976). *See* INTOXICATION.

habitual residence. The residence required to establish domicile (qv) without the *animus* (qv) necessary for the purpose of domicile. See *Cruse v Chittum* [1974] 2 All ER 940 (habitual residence was said to involve "a regular physical presence which must endure for some time").

Hague Conventions. Agreements signed at the Hague Peace Conference in 1899 and 1907 relating to, eg, the definition of a state of belligerency, and the use of gas in warfare.

Hague Rules, application to goods of. Article I of the 1924 Rules, as amended in 1968, defines goods to which the Rules apply, as including: "goods, wares, merchandise and articles of every kind whatsoever, except live animals and cargo which by the contract of carriage is stated as being carried on deck and is so carried". Carriage of goods "covers the period from the time when the goods are loaded on to the time when they are discharged from the ship". See *The Hollandia* [1982] 3 WLR 1111.

Hague Rules on bills of lading. Rules agreed in 1924 relating to the carriage of goods by sea, as amended by the Brussels Protocol 1968, eg, that a bill of lading shall be conclusive evidence when transferred to a third party acting in good faith. *See* BILL OF LADING.

half blood. *See* BLOOD RELATIONSHIP.

half-secret trust. Situation created where a will or other instrument discloses the existence of a trust, but not its terms, eg, as where property is left to X "on the trusts I have discussed with him". Thus, where a sealed letter handed by the testator (qv) to the trustee (qv) is marked "not to be opened until after my death" and the trustee knows that it contains terms of a trust which he agrees to carry out, such a communication suffices to create a half-secret trust. See *Re Keen* [1937] Ch 326; *Re Bateman's Will Trusts* [1970] 3 All ER 817.

hallmarking. The marking of articles of precious metal (eg, gold, silver, platinum) by a sponsor's mark (indicating manufacturer or sponsor) or assay mark (indicating standard of fineness and place where assay took place). See the Hallmarking Act 1973; and *Barge* v *Graham Brown Ltd* [1981] 3 All ER 360.

handcuffing. Process of fastening a person's wrists by a chain or bar. Justifiable only where necessary so as to prevent escape or in cases of a violent breach of the peace (qv). See *Wright* v *Court* (1825) 4 B & C 596; *R* v *Taylor* (1895) 59 JP 393.

handling. "A person handles stolen goods if (otherwise than in the course of the stealing) knowing or believing them to be stolen goods he dishon-estly receives the goods, or dishonestly undertakes or assists in their retention, removal, disposal or realisation by or for the benefit of another person, or if he arranges to do so": Th.A. 1968, s. 22(1). See *A.-G.'s Ref (No. 4 of 1979)* [1981] 1 All ER 1193; *R* v *Bloxham* [1982] 2 WLR 392; *R* v *Kanwar* [1982] 2 All ER 528; and *R* v *Sanders* (1982) 75 Cr App R 84.

handwriting, proof of. Types of relevant evidence include: direct evidence, eg, testimony of the person whose writing has to be proved; opinion, eg, by a handwriting expert; comparison (see, eg, *Cobbett* v *Kilminster* (1865) 4 F & F 490). See also *R* v *Silverlock* [1894] 2 QB 766; *R* v *Tilley* [1961] 3 All ER 406. *See* EVIDENCE.

hanging. Execution by the gallows, abolished in relation to murder by the Murder (Abolition of Death Penalty) Act 1965. *See* CAPITAL PUNISHMENT.

hanging, drawing and quartering. Formerly the penalty for treason. The sentence was ". . . that the offender be dragged to the gallows; that he be hanged by the neck and then cut down alive; that his entrails be taken out and burned while he is yet alive; that his head be cut off; that his body be divided into four parts and that his head and quarters be at the King's disposal." Abolished in 1870. The last offender to suffer the full penalty was Francis Towneley, a Jacobite, executed in 1746 on Kennington Common.

Hansard. Colloquial name for the *Official Report of Parliamentary Debates*, usually published daily, so-called after Luke Hansard, printer to the Commons. *Hansard* may never be referred to in construing a statute: *Davis* v *Johnson* [1979] AC 264. See also *Hadmor Productions* v *Hamilton* [1982] 1 All ER 1042.

harassment of debtors. It is an offence for a person, with the object of coercing another to pay money claimed from the other as a debt due under a contract, to harass the other with demands for payments which are calculated to subject him or members of his family or household to alarm, distress or humiliation, or to falsely represent that criminal proceedings lie for failure to pay the money claimed: A.J.A. 1970, s. 40. See *R* v *Bokhari* [1974] Crim LR 559.

harassment of occupier. It is an offence to do acts calculated to interfere with the peace or comfort of a residential occupier or member of his household or to persistently withdraw or withhold services reasonably required for occupation with intent to cause the occupier to give up occupation or refrain from exercising any right or pursuing any remedy in respect of the premises: Protection from Eviction Act 1977, s. 1(3). See *R* v *Pheeko* [1981] 1 WLR 1117 (not an absolute offence).

harbour. Port, estuary, haven, dock or other place containing waters and in respect of which some body is empowered by an enactment to make charges in respect of vessels entering or using facilities therein: Prevention of Oil Pollution Act 1971, s. 8.

harbouring. Providing shelter, with the object of concealing. At one time it was an offence to harbour a thief or reputed thief, under the Prevention of Crimes Act 1871 (now repealed). The action which could be brought for harbouring a wife or child (which provided a method of seeking damages from the person with whom a spouse was committing adultery) was abolished under the Law Reform (Misc. Provs.) Act 1970. For harbouring a child required to return to a local authority, see the Child Care Act 1980, s. 14.

harbouring an employee. Where an employee had left his employment in breach of contract and was then employed by another who was aware of that breach, or became aware of it later, and yet continued the employment, that other person might have been liable in damages to the original employer. See *Wilkins Bros Ltd* v *Weaver* [1915] 2 Ch 322; *Jones Bros Ltd* v *Stevens* [1955] 1 QB 275.

hardship. "The word 'hardship' is not a word of art . . . in my judgment the ordinary sensible man would take the view that there are two aspects of 'hardship'—that which the sufferor

from the hardship thinks he is suffering and that which a reasonable bystander with knowledge of all the facts would think he was suffering": *per* Lawton J in *Rukat* v *Rukat* [1975] 1 All ER 343.

harmonisation of laws. Phrase used to refer to the adjustment of legislation by member states of the EEC (qv) in a given area of social and economic policy.

hay bote. *See* ESTOVERS.

headings. Words prefixed to sections of a statute, regarded as preambles (qv). Reference to headings may be made so as to assist in resolving an ambiguity. See *R* v *Hare* [1934] 1 KB 354; *Qualter Hall & Co Ltd* v *Board of Trade* [1962] Ch 273; *DPP* v *Schildkamp* [1971] AC 1.

head lease. A lease (qv) from which lesser interests (ie, sub-leases) have been created.

head note. Summary of points decided in a case, placed at the head of a law report.

Health Services, National. The health services established in England and Wales and in Scotland respectively in pursuance of s. 1 of the National Health Service Act 1946 (for England and Wales) and the National Health Service (Scotland) Act 1947. See now the Health Service Act 1980.

hearing. The trial of a cause or action.

hearsay evidence. *See* EVIDENCE, HEARSAY.

heir. One who succeeds by descent (qv). Under the L.P.A. 1925, s. 132, a limitation of property in favour of the heir (special or general) which, prior to the Act, would have conferred on the heir an estate by purchase, confers a corresponding equitable interest (qv) on the person who would have answered the description of heir before the Act.

heir apparent. A person who, if he survives his ancestor, will be his heir. He is not the heir until after the death of the ancestor, since *nemo est heres viventis* (qv).

heirloom. "Any piece of household stuff which, by custom of some countries, having belonged to a house for certain descents, goes with the house, after the death of the owner, unto the heir and not to the executors": *Termes de la Ley.* The tenant for life can sell heirlooms, the money arising from the sale being capital money: S.L.A. 1925, s. 67.

heir presumptive. One who would be the heir (eg, an eldest son) if his ancestor were to die immediately.

heirs of the body. Words of limitation in a conveyance which comprehends "all the posterity of the donee in succession": *Re Woodward Estate* [1945] 1 WWR 722. *See* LIMITATION, WORDS OF.

helping the police with their enquiries. Euphemism for questioning by the police at a police station of those suspected of involvement in an offence, without their being arrested. See *R v Lemsatef* [1977] 1 WLR 812. *See* QUESTIONING, DETAINING BY POLICE FOR.

hereditaments. 1. Real property which devolved on an heir (qv) on an intestacy (qv). Classified as: *incorporeal* (rights of property, eg, easements); *corporeal* (physical objects, eg, land, buildings). 2. "Property which is or may become liable to a rate, being a unit of such property which is, or would fall to be, shown as a separate item in the valuation list": General Rate Act 1967, s. 115(1).

heresy. Deliberate and overt denial of some accepted dogma of the church. A capital offence until 1677. See the Ecclesiastical Jurisdiction Measure 1963; *Noble v Voysey* (1871) LR 3 PC 357.

heriot. A feudal duty, whereby, on the death of the tenant, the lord took horses and arms and, later, the best beast or chattel. See *Western v Bailey* [1896] 2 QB 234. *See* FEUDAL SYSTEM.

Her Majesty's pleasure, during. *See* DURING HER MAJESTY'S PLEASURE.

hide of land. An old English unit of area of land. Used in the Domesday Book (qv) to mean a unit of *c.* 120 acres.

High Commission, Court of. Originated in 1583 in commissions granted for enforcing the state's religious policies. Its judges were ecclesiastical lawyers and doctors of civil law. Could fine, imprison, excommunicate. See *Chancey's Case* (1611) 12 Co Rep 82. Abolished in 1641 by an Act referring to it as having caused "great and unsufferable wrong and oppression of the King's subjects".

High Court, the. Consists of the Lord Chancellor, Lord Chief Justice, President of the Family Division, Vice-Chancellor, and up to eighty puisne judges. Its divisions are the Chancery Div., the Queen's Bench Div. and the Family Div: S.C.A. 1981, ss. 4, 5. The Patents Court is part of the Chancery Div.; the Admiralty Court and Commercial Court are part of the Queen's Bench Div: s. 6. For the general jurisdiction, see ss. 19, 25–31. For the distribution of business, see s. 61, Sch 1.

high seas. The seas lying more than 5 km beyond the coast of a country. The criminal law of England extends to all British ships upon the high seas (*Oteri v The Queen* [1976] 1 WLR 1272) and to acts of British subjects when passengers on foreign ships on the high seas (*R v Kelly* [1982] AC 665).

high treason. Formerly treason which was not *petit treason* (ie, the killing of a master by his servant). In effect, treason against the Sovereign. *Petit treason* was abolished in 1828. High treason is now known merely as "treason". *See* TREASON.

high water mark. The line of the seashore to which the waters rise at the point of high tide.

highway. A road or way either on land or water (eg, path, bridge) used by the public for passing and repassing as a matter of right. It may exist by statute, dedication (qv) or prescription (qv). See the Highways Act 1980; *Dawes v Hawkins* (1860) 8 CB 848; *A.-G. v Shonleigh Nominees Ltd* [1974] 1 WLR 305.

Highway Code. A standard of conduct for road users, issued by the Secretary of State for the Environment. Failure to observe the Code does not, in itself, render a person liable to criminal proceedings; it may, however, be taken into account in such proceedings (Road Traffic Act 1972, s. 37 (as substituted by the Transport Act 1981, s. 60)). See *R v*

Chadwick [1975] Crim LR 105.

highway, nuisance in relation to. "Any wrongful act or omission upon or near a highway, whereby the public are prevented from freely, safely and conveniently passing along the highway": *Jacobs* v *Lee* [1950] AC 361. See the Highways Act 1980; *Hubbard* v *Pitt* [1976] QB 142; *Haydon* v *Kent CC* [1978] QB 343.

highway, obstruction of. 1. If a person's land abuts on the highway he can maintain an action of trespass against a person who uses the highway in an unreasonable manner, eg, by obstruction. See *Harrison* v *Duke of Rutland* [1893] 1 QB 142. 2. The obstruction of a highway is an offence. See the Highways Act 1980, s. 137; *R* v *Moule* [1964] Crim LR 303; *Dixon* v *Atfield* [1975] 1 WLR 1171; *Lewis* v *Dickson* [1976] RTR 431.

hijacking. The offence of unlawfully seizing by force or threats of any kind the control of an aircraft in flight: Aviation Security Act 1982, s. 1(1).

Himalaya clause. Clause in a contract of carriage referring to the protection of the carrier's servants, sub-contractors and agents. So-called because of an action arising from injuries to a passenger on the *SS Himalaya: Adler* v *Dickson* [1955] 1 QB 158.

hire. Payment for the temporary use of something, eg, a good, or a person's labour power. In a contract of hire there is an implied warranty (qv) that the goods hired are as fit for the purpose of their hiring as skill and care can make them. Under the C.C.A. 1974, a hirer is the bailee of goods under a consumer hire agreement (qv) or the person to whom the hirer's rights and duties under the agreement have passed by assignment (qv) or operation of law.

hire or reward, for. "The probable explanation of the composite phrase is that the words 'for hire' were used because they were the most familiar words to describe remuneration for carriage in some vehicles, and the words 'or reward' were added since 'reward' is a wider word and apt to cover some forms of remuneration or some arrangements for which the words 'for hire' might not be appropriate": *per* Lord Pearson in *Albert* v *Motor Insurers' Bureau* [1971] 2 All ER 1345.

hire purchase agreement. An agreement, other than a conditional sale agreement (qv), under which goods are bailed in return for periodical payments by the bailee and the property in the goods passes to the bailee if the terms of the agreement are not complied with and the bailee exercises his option to purchase or some other specified event occurs: C.C.A. 1974, s. 189(1).

historic buildings. See LISTED BUILDINGS.

H.L. House of Lords (qv).

HMSO. Her Majesty's Stationery Office, controlled by the Queen's Printer of Acts of Parliament and responsible for supplying official publications. Copyright of all government documents vests in the Controller of the Office. See S.I. 1980/456.

holder. The holder of a bill is the payee or endorsee who is in possession of it, or the bearer thereof: B.Ex.A. 1882, s. 2. *See* BILL OF EXCHANGE.

holder for value. Holder of a bill of exchange (qv) for which value has been given at some time (not necessarily by the holder himself).

holder in due course. A holder who has taken a bill which is regular and complete on the face of it under the following conditions: that he became the holder before it was overdue and without notice of its having been previously dishonoured (if that were so); that he took it in good faith and for value; that at the time the bill was negotiated he had no notice of defective title of the negotiator. See the B.Ex.A. 1882, s. 29(1). *See* BILL OF EXCHANGE.

holding charge. A minor charge made pending the investigation of a more serious charge. See, eg, *Christie* v *Leachinsky* [1947] AC 573.

holding company. A company (qv) whose business consists wholly or mainly in the holding of shares or securities of one or more companies which are its 75 per cent subsidiaries: Finance Act 1980, s. 37(12).

holding out. A course of action which persuades others to believe in a party's possessing an authority which, in fact, does not exist. A person who acts in this way may be stopped from denying the truth of his representations if others have acted on them. See the Partnership Act 1890, ss. 3, 14; *Smith* v *Bailey* [1891] 2 QB 403; *Bevan* v *National Bank Ltd* (1906) 23 TLR 65; and *Tower Cabinet Ltd* v *Ingram* [1949] 1 All ER 1033.

holding over. The continuation in possession of land by a tenant (qv) after the expiration of the tenancy agreement. The tenant may become liable to an action for possession and double rent and damages.

holiday lettings. The letting of property for a holiday under terms allowing its recovery at the end of that period. Not a protected tenancy (qv): see the Rent Act 1977, s. 9. ("Holiday" was considered in *Buchmann* v *May* [1978] 2 All ER 993, to be "a period of cessation from work or a period of recreation.")

holograph. A document, such as a will or deed, written in the testator's or grantor's own hand. See *Re Kanani* (1978) 122 SJ 611; Law Reform Committee Report, 1980 (Cmnd 7902).

homage. The ritual acknowledgment by a feudal vassal of the bond of tenure between himself and his lord. It included the act of kneeling (a symbolic surrender), the lord's clasping his hands (acceptance of surrender), and an oath of fealty. *See* FEUDAL SYSTEM.

homeless person. One who, under the Housing (Homeless Persons) Act 1977, has no accommodation which he, together with others of his family, is entitled to occupy, or who has accommodation but cannot secure entry to it or whose occupation may lead to violence from others residing therein: s. 1. Under s. 2 he has a "priority need for accommodation" when the housing authority is satisfied that, eg, he has dependent children residing with him. See *Lewis* v *Devon DC* [1981] 1 All ER 27.

home loss. Term used in the Land Compensation Act 1973 whereby compensation is made available for the loss of a house acquired by a local authority for demolition, and for injury sustained through the loss of a house.

Home Secretary. The minister in charge of the Home Office, which deals, in general, with the domestic functions in England and Wales not specifically assigned to other departments of state. He exercises some prerogative powers of the Crown, including the prerogative of mercy (qv). He is concerned, specifically, with the administration of justice, the prison service, treatment of offenders, community relations, immigration and naturalisation procedures, supervision of the control of firearms and dangerous drugs.

homeworker. Person who contracts with another for the execution of work to be done in a place not under the control or management of that other and who does not normally make use of the service of more than two persons in the carrying out of contracts for the execution of work with statutory minimum remuneration: Wages Councils Act 1979, s. 28. For employment status see *Nethermere Ltd* v *Taverna* [1983] IRLR 103.

homicide. The killing of a human being by a human being. May be categorised as lawful (eg, committed in the execution of justice) or unlawful, or as justifiable (qv), excusable (qv) or criminal (ie, a killing, neither justifiable nor excusable, such as murder, manslaughter, infanticide). *See* INFANTICIDE; MANSLAUGHTER; MURDER.

homosexual conduct. Sexual activity with a member of one's own sex. Buggery (qv) or gross indecency (qv) with another man is no longer an offence if both parties have attained the age of 21, if both have consented and the act is done in private: S.O.A. 1967. The Act does not legalise homosexual acts punishable under the statutes relating to discipline in the Armed Forces. A consenting partner who is under 21 is guilty of an offence. Proceedings may require the consent of the DPP (qv). Lesbianism (qv) is not an offence. See *R v Angel* [1968] Crim LR 342.

honeste vivere. Phrase used by the Roman jurist Ulpian and adopted in Justinian's *Institutes* (AD 533) in a summary of the basic precepts of the law, thus: *honeste vivere, alterum non laedere, suum cuique tribuere* (to live honestly, not to harm another and to give every man his due).

honorarium. A voluntary, or honorary, payment or reward, often given as compensation for services in circumstances in which payment cannot be enforced at law or in which custom and propriety might not allow a fee or fixed payment. *See* BARRISTER'S FEES.

honour clauses. Clauses in agreements indended as express declarations that transactions between the parties to which those agreements relate are not to be binding in law. The courts will generally give effect to such declarations. See, eg, *Appleson v Littlewood* [1939] 1 All ER 464; *Rose and Frank Co v Crompton* [1925] AC 445; *Edwards v Skyway* [1964] 1 WLR 349.

hospital order. An order by the magistrates' court (qv) or Crown Court (qv) authorising an offender's admission to, and detention in a specified hospital. See the M.H.A. 1983, s. 37; and the Courts Act 1971, ss. 56, 62. Applications for discharge are heard by Area Mental Health Review Tribunals (qv). See *R v Blackwood* (1974) 59 Cr App R 176.

hospital premises. Premises "used or to be used for the prevention, diagnosis or treatment of illness or for the reception of patients": Health Services Act 1976, s. 14(1). See also the M.H.A. 1983, s. 145(1).

hospital, special. *See* SPECIAL HOSPITAL.

hostage. 1. Person taken by a belligerent and held as security. 2. Person seized in the UK or elsewhere in order to compel a state, international governmental organisation or person to do or abstain from doing any act. One who threatens to kill, injure or continue to detain the hostage commits an offence under the Taking of Hostages Act 1982, s. 1(1).

hostel. "A building wherein is provided, for persons generally or for a class or classes of persons, residential accommodation (otherwise than in separate and self-contained sets of premises) and either board or facilities for the preparation of food adequate to the needs of those persons, or both": H.A. 1974, s. 129(1).

hostile witness. One who, in the opinion of the court, is hostile to the party calling him and is unwilling to tell the truth. With leave of the court that party may cross-examine him. See the Criminal Procedure Act 1865, s. 3; the Civil Evidence Act 1968, s. 3(1) (*a*); *R v Mann* (1972) 56 Cr App R 750; *R v Thompson* (1976) 64 Cr App R 96; *R v Pitt* [1982] 3 WLR 359. *See* WITNESS.

hotchpot. *Hocher* = to shake together. The bringing together of properties into a common lot so that equality of division may be assured. Thus, an advancement by a deceased person in his lifetime must be brought into account against the share which the child to whom the advancement has been made would receive under an intestacy (qv): see, eg, *Taylor v Taylor* (1875) LR 20 Eq 155; and *Re Osoba* [1978] 1 WLR 791.

hotel. "An establishment held out by the proprietor as offering food, drink and, if required, sleeping accommodation, without special contract, to any traveller presenting himself who appears able and willing to pay a reasonable sum for the services and facilities provided and who is in a fit state to be received": Hotel Proprietors Act 1956, s. 1(3). *See* INN.

hot pursuit. Doctrine whereby a state exercises a claim to pursue across its frontiers.

hours of darkness. The time between half-an-hour after sunset and half-an-hour before sunrise: Highways Act 1980, s. 329(1).

house. Defined, eg, under the Leasehold Reform Act 1967, s. 2, as including any building designed or adapted for living in and reasonably so called. It includes (see the H.A. 1957, s. 189) any part of a building which is occupied or intended to be occupied as a separate dwelling. See *Sovmots Investments v Secretary of State for Environment* [1977] QB 411; and

Tandon v *Trustees of Spurgeons Home* [1982] AC 755.

house bote. *See* ESTOVERS.

housebreaking. Breaking and entering (qv) a dwelling house or other building. *See* BURGLARY.

housebreaking implements, possession of. "A person shall be guilty of an offence if, when not at his place of abode, he has with him any article for use in the course of or in connection with any burglary, theft or cheat": Th.A. 1968, s. 25(1). See *R* v *Ellames* [1974] 3 All ER 130 (it was held that s. 25 was aimed at acts preparatory to a burglary, theft or cheat); *R* v *Bundy* [1977] 2 All ER 382. *See* BURGLARY.

house in multiple occupation. "A house which is occupied by persons who do not form a single household, exclusive of any part thereof which is occupied as a separate dwelling by persons who do form a single household": H.A. 1974, s. 129(1).

housekeeping allowances, savings from. "If any question arises as to the right of a husband or wife to money derived from any allowance made by the husband for the expenses of the matrimonial home or for similar purposes, or to any property acquired out of such money, the money or property shall, in the absence of any agreement between them to the contrary, be treated as belonging to the husband and wife in equal shares": Married Women's Property Act 1964, s. 1.

House, Leader of the. Member of the House of Commons who is responsible for the arrangement of government business in the House. He announces the business for the following week, usually every Thursday. The Leader of the Lords has similar functions.

House of Commons. The Lower House of Parliament. A representative assembly elected by universal adult suffrage, consisting of 650 members (523 for England, 38 for Wales, 72 for Scotland, 17 for N Ireland). Its chief officer is the Speaker, elected by members to preside over the House. Persons disqualified for membership include: aliens; persons under 21; holders of

certain judicial offices; civil servants; members of the police and regular armed forces; members of a legislature of a country outside the UK: House of Commons Disqualification Act 1975, s. 1(1). *See* PARLIAMENT.

House of Commons Commission. Body of Commissioners set up under the House of Commons (Administration) Act 1978, s. 1, consisting of the Speaker, Leader of the Commons, member of the Commons nominated by Leader of the Opposition, and three other members (none of whom may be a Minister), to appoint staff in the House and to determine their numbers and remuneration, etc.

House of Lords. The Upper House of Parliament. It consists of the *Lords Temporal* (ie, all hereditary peers and peeresses who have not disclaimed their peerages under the Peerage Act 1963, life peers and peeresses, Lords of Appeal in Ordinary) and the *Lords Spiritual* (Archbishops of Canterbury and York, Bishops of London, Winchester and Durham and 21 other bishops of the Church of England). The House is presided over by the Lord Chancellor. *See* PARLIAMENT.

House of Lords, Appeal Committee of. Committee set up by the House of Lords, consisting of Lords qualified under the Appellate Jurisdiction Acts 1876 and 1877 "which shall consider any petition or application for leave to appeal that may be referred to them and any matter relating thereto, or to causes depending, or formerly depending in [the Lords] and shall report thereon to the House": House of Lords Standing Order No 81(2) (*b*). The Committee may take decisions and give directions. It is chaired by the Lord Chancellor or senior Lord of Appeal in Ordinary.

House of Lords, jurisdiction of. The right of a peer to be tried "by his peers" was abolished by the C.J.A. 1948. The House has appellate jurisdiction. In civil cases it hears appeals from the Court of Appeal (qv) with leave of that Court or the Appeals Committee of the House. In criminal cases it hears appeals from the Court of Appeal if that Court certifies that a point of law of general public importance is involved and either the Court or the House gives leave to appeal because the point is one which ought to be considered by the House. The judges in the Lords are Lords of Appeal in Ordinary (qv) and peers who have held, or hold, high judicial office. Lay peers do not participate. The president is the Lord Chancellor. See the A.J.A. 1960, s. 1; and the Criminal Appeal Act 1968, s. 33.

House of Lords, petitions for leave to appeal to. Petitions are referred to the Appeal Committee (three Lords of Appeal) who will consider whether it appears competent to be received by the House and, if so, whether it should be referred for an oral hearing. The petition is then referred for an oral hearing if any member of the Committee considers that it is competent or expresses doubts as to whether it is incompetent, and considers that it is fit for oral hearing: *Practice Direction* [1979] 1 WLR 497.

house to house collections. Collections made from house to house for charitable purposes requiring a licence: House to House Collections Act 1939, s. 1. See also *Hankinson v Dowland* [1974] C.L.Y. 302; *Davison v Richards* [1976] Crim LR 46.

housing action areas. Areas in which a local authority considers living conditions to be unsatisfactory and can be dealt with most effectively in a period of 5 years so as to secure the improvement of housing conditions in the area as a whole: H.A. 1974, s. 26. See the H.A. 1980, Sch 13. *See* CLEARANCE AREA.

housing association. A society, body of trustees or company not trading for profit, established so as to construct, improve or manage houses: H.A. 1957, s. 189(1), as amended by the Rent Act 1977, s. 86(3). See also the H.A. 1980. s. 74; *Eton College v Bard* [1983] 3 WLR 231.

housing association tenancy. A tenancy arising where the interest of the landlord belongs to a housing association (qv) or housing trust (qv), or to the Housing Corporation (qv): Rent Act 1977, s. 86. For rent limits, see s. 88. See also the H.A. 1980, s. 56.

housing association tenancy, con-version into regular tenancy of. If a tenancy ceases to be one to which Part VI of the Rent Act 1977 applies and becomes a protected tenancy (qv), that tenancy shall be a regulated tenancy (qv) and the housing association which is the landlord shall give written notice to the tenant informing him that his tenancy is no longer excluded from protection under the Act Rent Act 1977, s. 92(1). See Sch 14.

housing benefits. Statutory rent and rates rebates schemes administered under the Social Security and Housing Benefits Act 1982, Part II.

Housing Corporation. An authority set up under the H.A. 1964, s. 1, with extended powers and functions under the H.A. 1974, s. 1, which is concerned with, eg, promotion and assistance of development of registered housing associations and unregistered building societies. See the H.A. 1980, ss. 120–132.

housing subsidy. Subsidy payable to local authorities, new town corporations and Development Board for Rural Wales: H.A. 1980, s. 96(1). The subsidy to local authorities is calculated by adding the base amount (see s. 98) to the housing costs differential (see s. 99) and subtracting the local contribution differential (see s. 100): s. 97. For the subsidy to other bodies, see s. 101.

housing trust. A corporation or body of persons which is required by the terms of its constituent instrument to devote its funds to the provision of houses for persons the majority of whom are members of the working classes, and other purposes incidental thereto, or is required to devote its funds to charitable purposes and in fact devotes them to the provision of houses: Rent Act 1977, s. 15(5).

hue and cry. Ancient procedure of pursuit of a felon, with cries and shouts of alarm. The neighbours of the person wronged by the felon were under a duty to assist in the pursuit. *See* CLAMEUR DE HARO.

human habitation, fitness for. Under the H.A. 1957, and 1969, a house may be deemed unfit for habitation if unreasonably defective in matters such as stability, water supply, drainage, sanitary conveniences, disposal of waste water.

Human Rights, European Convention on. Convention signed and ratified by members of the Council of Europe in November 1950 and in force since September 1953. Rights and freedoms it purports to protect include: right to life; freedom from torture and slavery; right to liberty and fair trial; freedom of thought and religion, etc. Under the Convention were created the Commission on Human Rights and the Court of Human Rights (qv). The Commission's function is conciliatory; it receives petitions alleging noncompliance with the Convention and initiates investigations. It meets *in camera* (qv). "The court can and should take the Convention into account. They should take it into account whenever interpreting a statute which affects the rights and liberties of the individual": per Lord Denning in *R v Secretary of State for the Home Department, ex p Bhajan Singh* [1975] 2 All ER 1081. See *Legislation on Human Rights with particular reference to the European Convention* (HMSO, July 1976); and *Ahmed v ILEA* [1978] QB 36.

Human Rights, European Court of. *See* EUROPEAN COURT OF HUMAN RIGHTS.

Human Rights, Universal Declaration of. Adopted by the United Nations Commission on Human Rights and by the General Assembly in 1948. Relates to rights such as life, liberty, security of a person, freedom from arbitrary arrest, right to a fair hearing, freedom of thought and religion, right to social security and to work, right to education.

human tissue, removal of. Under the Human Tissue Act 1961, the removal of parts of the body of a deceased person by a medical practitioner for therapeutic purposes, medical education or research, is permitted if that person has so requested in writing, or orally during his last illness in the presence of two or more witnesses.

hundred. A territorial division, known in Anglo-Saxon society, consisting of a group of adjoining townships. It may have consisted of an area taxed at one hundred hides or of one hundred households. Each hundred had its court, held once a month, presided over by the hundred *ealdor* (chief officer); its jurisdiction was based on custom. *See* HIDE OF LAND.

hung jury. *See* JURY, HUNG.

husband and wife. At common law were considered as "one person", so that, eg, the husband was entitled on marriage to chattels and choses in possession (qv) belonging to his wife. Statutes have vitiated the significance of this concept. Thus, eg, under the Th.A. 1968, s. 30(1), husbands and wives are liable in respect of offences which they commit against one another's property as if they were not married; under the Law Reform (Married Women and Tortfeasors) Act 1935, s. 1, a married woman is capable of acquiring, holding and alienating property as if a feme sole (qv). They can be guilty of the tort of conspiracy (qv): *Midland Bank Trust Co v Green (No. 3)* [1982] Ch 592. See also the Law Reform (Husband and Wife) Act 1962; the Matrimonial Proceedings and Property Act 1970; and O. 89.

hybrid Bill. A parliamentary Bill which though of general application, affects some local or private interests. A Bill of this nature is subject to special procedure; in general, it is treated like a private bill after its second reading.

hypothecation. The right of a ship's master, in case of necessity, to assign the ship or the ship and its cargo by bottomry bond undertaking to repay the principal and interest on the safe arrival of the ship. A *letter of hypothecation* is one addressed to a bank, giving details of a shipment of goods relating to a draft. In the event of dishonour of the draft, the bank is allowed to sell the goods. *See* BOTTOMRY.

hypothetical dispute. Issues based on mere supposition. In general, the courts will not adjudicate upon disputes of this kind: *Glasgow Navigation Co v Iron Ore Co* [1910] AC 293; *Re Bärnato* [1949] Ch 258. See O. 15, r. 16 for declaratory judgment powers; *Mellstrom v Garner* [1970] 2 All ER 9.

I

ibid, ib. *Ibidem.* In the same place; from the same source.

id certum est quod certum reddi potest. That is certain which can be made certain. See, eg, *Plant* v *Bourne* [1897] 2 Ch 281.

idem, id. The same.

identification parade. Procedure whereby persons, including an arrested suspect, are viewed by a witness for purposes of identification. See *Identification Parades* (Home Office Circular, 9/1969); *Identification Evidence* (Home Office Circulars, 127/1976, 109/1978); *R* v *Turnbull* [1977] QB 224; and *R* v *Holland* [1983] Crim LR 545.

identity, evidence of. 1. Primary evidence, eg, obtained by an identification parade (qv) before trial. 2. Secondary evidence, eg, by an identifying witness who swears that he identified the accused on a former occasion, and by another witness to say that he saw this. See *R* v *Christie* [1914] AC 545. 3. Circumstantial evidence, eg, the accused's fingerprints. See *R* v *Castleton* (1909) 3 Cr App R 74; *R* v *Davis* (1975) 62 Cr App R 194.

id est. Generally abbreviated to ie. That is.

idle and disorderly person. One who was found guilty of a relatively trivial offence under the Vagrancy Act 1824, eg, begging in a public place.

ignorantia juris neminem excusat. Ignorance of the law does not excuse. When mistake is pleaded as a defence, the mistake must be one of fact, not of law. "Every man of England is, in judgment of law, party to the making of an Act of Parliament, being present thereat by his representatives": Blackstone. "Every man must be taken to be cognisant of the law, otherwise there is no knowing of the extent to which the excuse of ignorance might be carried. It would be urged in almost every case": *R* v *Bailey* (1800) Russ & Ry 1.

See *R* v *Esop* (1836) 7 C & P 456; and *Secretary of State* v *Hart* [1982] 1 WLR 481.

illegal. In violation of a law or rule which has the force of law.

illegal contracts. Contracts which are forbidden by statute or are contrary to common law or public policy and are, therefore, generally void. Examples: a contract tending to injure the public service, eg, by the attempted sale of a public office or a contract to procure a title of honour (see *Parkinson* v *College of Ambulance* [1925] 2 KB 1); a contract to oust jurisdiction of court (see *Re Davstone Estate Ltd* [1969] 2 Ch 378); a contract in restraint of trade (see *Nordenfelt* v *Maxim Nordenfelt Gun Co Ltd* [1894] AC 535); a contract to commit a criminal offence or civil wrong (see *Napier* v *National Business Agency* [1951] 2 All ER 263). See CONTRACT.

illegal entrant. "A person unlawfully entering [the UK] or seeking to enter in breach of a deportation order or of the immigration laws": Immigration Act 1971, s. 33(1). His detention is lawful: Sch 2. See *Khawaja* v *Home Secretary* [1983] 1 All ER 765.

illegal practices. Term often applied specifically to offences of a corrupt nature committed at municipal or parliamentary elections, eg, a candidate's incurring expenditure beyond that permitted. See, eg, the Representation of the People Act 1983.

illegal trust. One which offends against statute or morality or public policy. In the case of an intentional creation of a trust for an illegal purpose, a resulting trust (qv) may be implied in favour of the settlor if the illegal purpose has not been executed. See *Ayerst* v *Jenkins* (1873) LR 16 Eq 275. See TRUST.

illegitimate child. See BASTARD.

illusory appointment. An appointment (qv), under which a merely nominal share was appointed to an object, which could be set aside: *Wilson* v *Piggott* (1974) 2 Ves Jun 35. Under the L.P.A. 1925, s. 158, no appointment is to be invalid merely on the ground that "an unsubstantial, illusory or nominal share only is appointed to or left unappointed to devolve upon any one or more of the objects of the power".

illusory trust. A conveyance by a debtor to trustees upon trust for creditors which can be revoked, in some circumstances, by the debtor, is an example. See *Bill* v *Cureton* (1835) 4 LJ Ch 98; *Johns* v *James* (1878) 8 Ch D 744. *See* TRUST.

immigration. Entering a country for purposes of permanent residence there. See the Immigration Act 1971, which confers the right of abode on, eg, citizens of the UK and colonies who are connected with Britain by birth. Power to refuse leave to enter the UK rests initially with immigration officers. The Secretary of State has power to give leave to remain in the UK: s. 4. See also *Bohar Singh Khera* v *Secretary of State* (1983) (*The Times,* 14.2.1983).

immoral contracts. Agreements founded on an immoral consideration (qv), eg, future illicit cohabitation. In general, they are void. See *Pearce* v *Brookes* (1866) LR 1 Ex 213; *Wilson* v *Carnley* [1908] 1 KB 729; *Fender* v *Mildmay* [1938] AC 11. *See* EX TURPI CAUSA NON ORITUR ACTIO.

immovables. Generally, land and property attached.

immunity. Freedom or exemption from some obligation or penalty. Thus, eg, a barrister (qv) has immunity from being sued in contract for professional negligence; no action lies against a judge in respect of words or actions arising in the exercise of his judicial office ("judicial immunity") (qv); no action lies in respect of words spoken in the course of an action by, eg, advocates or parties; no foreign sovereign may be impleaded in an action *in personam.* See *Astley* v *Younge* (1759) 2 Burr 807; *Anderson* v *Gorrie* [1895] 1 QB 668; *Sirros* v *Moore* [1975] QB 118; and *The Philippine Admiral* [1977] AC 373.

immunity, diplomatic. Diplomatic privilege (qv).

immunity from jurisdiction, state. A state is immune from the jurisdiction of the courts of the UK and courts shall give effect to that immunity, even though the state does not appear in the proceedings in question: State Immunity Act 1978, s. 1. Exemptions from immunity include, eg, where state submits to jurisdiction; in relation to contracts to be performed in UK; contracts of employment; liability for VAT, customs duties. See *I Congreso Del Partido* [1981] 3 WLR 328. *See* IMMUNITY, RESTRICTIVE.

immunity, restrictive. Doctrine suggesting that, in the interests of justice, it may be necessary to allow individuals engaging in commercial transactions with states to bring such transactions before the courts. See *Trendtex Trading Corp* v *Central Bank of Nigeria* [1977] QB 529. The doctrine is accepted as part of the law of England: *I Congreso Del Partido* [1981] 3 WLR 328.

immunity, vicarious. Principle that an agent performing a contract is entitled to any immunity conferred on his principal. It was enunciated in *Elder, Dempster & Co* v *Paterson, Zochonis & Co* [1929] AC 522, but rejected in *Scruttons Ltd* v *Midland Silicones Ltd* [1962] AC 446.

imparlance. Conference between parties relating to the settlement of a dispute or action.

impeachable of waste. Liability of a person, eg, tenant for life (qv) for waste. See, eg, *Re Ridge* (1885) 31 Ch D 504. *See* WASTE.

impeachment. The prosecution of an offender by the House of Commons (qv) before the House of Lords (qv). The jurisdiction was last exercised in 1806 (in the case of Viscount Melville, First Lord of the Admiralty, for alleged malversation in office).

impending apprehension or prosecution. "Where a person has committed an arrestable offence, any other person who, knowing or believing him to be guilty of the offence or of some other arrestable offence, does without lawful authority or reasonable excuse any act with intent to impede his apprehension or prosecution shall be guilty of an offence": C.L.A. 1967, s. 4. *See* ARRESTABLE OFFENCE.

imperfect gift. *See* GIFT, IMPERFECT.

imperfect trust. An executory trust. *See* EXECUTORY.

imperitia culpae adnumeratur. Want of skill is considered a fault. See *Phillips* v *William Whitely Ltd* [1938] 1 All ER 566; *Roe* v *Ministry of Health* [1954] 2 QB 66; *Mutual Life and Citizens' Assurance Co Ltd* v *Evatt* [1971] AC 793.

impersonation. False personation (qv) for some improper motive.

implead. To sue or prosecute.

implied condition. Where a buyer makes known to a seller, expressly or by implication, the purpose for which goods are required, in a manner showing that he relies on the seller's skill or judgment and the goods are of a description which it is in the course of the seller's business to supply, there is an implied condition that the goods are reasonably fit for the purpose: S.G.A. 1979, s. 14.

implied contract. A contract inferred from the conduct of parties or from some relationship existing between them. *See* CONTRACT; QUASI-CONTRACTS.

implied covenants. *See* COVENANTS, IMPLIED.

implied malice. 1. An intention (in a case of homicide) to do grievous bodily harm as compared with express malice, ie, an intention to kill. 2. Malice inferred from all the circumstances. *See* MALICE.

implied tenancy. *See* TENANCY, IMPLIED.

implied term. A term which will be implied (eg, from statute or custom) where it is necessary to carry out the presumed intention of the parties to a contract and is so obvious that the parties must have intended it to apply. Such a term will not override an express term (qv). See the Supply of Goods (Implied Terms) Act 1973; the Unfair Contract Terms Act 1977; *Liverpool CC* v *Irwin* [1977] AC 239; *Shell UK Ltd* v *Lostock Garage Ltd* [1977] 1 All ER 481.

implied trust. A trust which will be

enforced by the court as a result of surrounding circumstances, or the language of the parties, so that effect is given to their implied, but unexpressed, intentions. Example: X purchases property in the name of Y; there is a presumption in equity that X intended Y to hold that property in trust for him. See *Re Howes* (1905) 21 TLR 501. *See* TRUST.

importune. To make advances to another for an immoral purpose. It is an offence for a man persistently to solicit or importune in a public place for immoral purposes: S.O.A. 1956, s. 32. See *Field* v *Chapman* [1953] CLY 787; *R* v *Ford* [1977] 1 WLR 1083. It is an offence for a common prostitute to loiter or solicit in a street or public place for the purpose of prostitution (qv): Street Offences Act 1959, s. 1 (but imprisonment may not be imposed for it: C.J.A. 1982, s. 71(1)); *Behrendt* v *Burridge* [1976] 3 All ER 285. See *R* v *Gray* (1982) 74 Cr App R 324. *See* LOITER.

impossibility. That which is contrary to the law of nature, to some rule of law or to the very nature of some transaction.

impossibility of performance. Impossibility does not generally excuse from performance. Where, however, an event occurs which destroys the basis of the contract and which is not the fault of the parties, the contract is terminated. See *Taylor* v *Caldwell* (1863) 3 B & S 826; *Re Shipton* [1915] 3 KB 676. *See* FRUSTRATION OF CONTRACT.

impotence. The inability to have, or to permit, ordinary sexual intercourse. Impotence of either party to consummate a marriage is a ground for rendering the marriage voidable. See *R.E.L.* v *E.L.* [1949] 211; *S.* v *S.* [1956] P 1; *W.* v *W.* [1967] 3 All ER 178.

impound. To seize and retain in the custody of the law.

imprimatur. Let it be printed. A licence to publish, or print, a book.

imprisonment. The restraint of a person's liberty. A man is said to be a prisoner "so long as he hath not his liberty freely to go at all times to all places whither he will, without bail or mainprise or otherwise": *Termes de la Ley.*

imprisonment for life. *See* LIFE IM-PRISONMENT.

imprisonment, imposing of. "Means to pass a sentence of imprisonment, or fix a term of imprisonment for failure to pay any sum of money, or for want of sufficient distress to satisfy any sum of money, or for failure to do or abstain from doing anything required to be done or left undone": M.C.A. 1980, s. 150(1).

imprisonment of those not previously imprisoned. No court shall pass a sentence of imprisonment on a person of under 21 nor any person over 21 on whom such a sentence has not previously been passed unless of the opinion that no other method of dealing with him is appropriate, and information as to his character, physical and mental condition must be taken into account: P.C.C.A. 1973, s. 20(1).

imprisonment of young offenders. No court may pass a sentence of imprisonment on a person under 21 or commit him to prison for any reason: C.J.A. 1982, s. 1(1). This does not apply to one remanded in custody for trial or sentence: s. 1(2). *See* YOUTH CUSTODY SENTENCE.

improvement notice. 1. Notice served on a person, under the H.S.W.A. 1974, s. 21, by an inspector who is of the opinion that the person is contravening a provision in circumstances that make it likely that the contravention will continue or be repeated. The notice requires that the contravention shall be remedied. *See Belhaven Brewery Co* v *McLean* [1975] IRLR 370. See the C.L.A. 1977, Sch 1. 2. Notice served on a person having control of a dwelling, under the H.A. 1974, s. 88, by a local authority, relating to a lack of standard amenities. *See* PROHIBITION NOTICE.

improvements. Term used in the Rent Act 1977, Part IV, to refer to structural alterations, extensions or additions and the provision of additional fixtures or fittings, but not anything done by way of decoration or repair: s. 75(1).

imputations. Statements ascribing misconduct or fault to some person. It was established in *Selvey* v *DPP* [1970] AC 304 that the Criminal Evidence Act 1898, s. 1(f)(ii) permits cross-examination (qv) of an accused person as to his character when imputations on the character of the prosecutor and witnesses are cast so as to show their unreliability as witnesses, independently of the evidence they have given, and when the casting of such imputations is essential to allow the accused to establish a defence.

imputed notice. *See* NOTICE.

inadvertence. Carelessness; lack of proper attention.

in aequali jure melior est conditio possidentis. Where the parties have equal rights, the claim of the actual possessor is the stronger. See *Bailey* v *Barnes* [1894] 1 Ch 25.

inalienability, rule against. Known also as the "rule against perpetual trusts". The general principle is that property must not be rendered inalienable. See, eg, *Cocks* v *Manners* (1871) LR 12 Eq 574; *Re Wightwick's Will Trusts* [1950] Ch 260.

inalienable. Incapable of being transferred.

in alieno solo. On another's land.

in bonis. In the goods of. Abbreviated to *"In b.* Smith".

in camera. In a [judge's] private room, ie, private sittings. It refers to a case heard, not in open court, but in closed court or a judge's private room, eg, where the case relates to aspects of the Official Secrets Act 1920, or involves hearing evidence relating to sexual capacity. *See* OPEN JUSTICE.

incapable of self-support. "A person is incapable of self-support if, but only if, he is incapable of supporting himself by reason of physical or mental infirmity and is likely to remain so incapable for a prolonged period": S.S.A. 1975, Sch 20.

incapable of work. One who cannot work "by reason of some specific disease or bodily or mental disablement, or deemed in accordance with regulations to be so incapable": S.S.A. 1973, s. 99(1).

incapacitation and contract. *See* CONTRACT, INCAPACITATION AND.

incapacity. Lack of legal power, competence, because of, eg, infancy.

in capite. In chief. A tenant *in capite* held, under the feudal system (qv), immediately from the King. Tenure *in capite* was abolished in 1660.

incendiarism. Arson (qv).

incest. Sexual intercourse between persons who are within certain degrees of consanguinity. It is an offence under the S.O.A. 1956 for a man to have sexual intercourse with a woman whom he knows to be his granddaughter, daughter, sister or mother and for a woman of the age of 16 or over to permit a man whom she knows to be her grandfather, father, brother, or son to have intercourse with her by her consent: ss. 10, 11. See *R v Carmichael* [1940] 1 KB 630; *R v Whitehouse* [1977] QB 868; *R v Harrison* [1980] Crim LR 56; Working Party on Sexual Offences (1980).

incest, incitement to. It is an offence for a man to incite to have sexual intercourse with him a girl under the age of 16 whom he knows to be his granddaughter, daughter or sister: C.L.A. 1977, s. 54(1).

Inchmaree clause. Marine insurance policy clause covering damage to, or loss of, ship due to latent defect not discoverable by due diligence. See *Thomas & Mersey Marine Insurance Co v Hamilton, Fraser & Co* (1887) 12 App Cas 484. See *The Brentwood* [1973] 2 Lloyd's Rep 232.

inchoate. Begun, or in an early stage, but not complete. Inchoate offences (eg, incitement) are committed even though the substantive offences with which they are connected are not committed.

incident. Refers to an accompanying condition, eg, the incidents of tenure (such as homage) relating to the feudal system (qv).

incitement. The act of urging to a course of criminal action. It is a common law offence for one person to incite another to commit an offence. See the Incitement to Mutiny Act 1797; the Incitement to Disaffection Act 1934 (under which it is an offence, maliciously and advisedly to attempt to seduce a member of the armed forces from his duty or allegiance to the Crown); the Official Secrets Act 1920, s. 7 (under which it is an offence for a person to incite another to commit an offence under the Act); the Race Relations Act 1976, s. 20, amending the Public Order Act 1936; *R v Higgins* (1801) 2 East 5; *R v Curr* [1967] 2 QB 944; *R v Bodin* [1979] Crim LR 176; and *R v Fitzmaurice* [1982] 2 WLR 227. See also the M.C.A. 1980, s. 45.

inclosure. *See* ENCLOSURE.

inclusio unius est exclusio alterius. The inclusion of one is the exclusion of another.

income. The financial return from one's labour, business, land or capital. "The term 'income' means, as applied to a commercial business, the profits made in that business...the balance of gain over loss. It seems to me to be altogether straining the ordinary signification of the term 'income' to say that it means the volume of business. That is the 'turnover', not the 'income'": *Yates v Yates* (1913) 33 NZLR 281. For "assessable income" in relation to tax, see, eg, *R v Nagel* [1981] STI 529; *Wicks v Firth* [1981] STI 589.

income tax. An annual tax charged on all income originating in the UK and on all income arising abroad of persons resident in the UK. It is imposed for the year of assessment beginning in April. First levied as a temporary measure in 1799, it was repealed soon after the end of the Napoleonic wars and reintroduced in 1842. The tax is based on the following schedules: *A* (rents, rent charges, other receipts from land ownership); *B* (occupation of commercial woodlands); *C* (profits from public revenue dividends); *D* (trade, professional profits or gains); *E* (salaries, wages, annuities, etc); *F* (company dividends, etc.). See the annual Finance Acts; the Taxes Management Act 1970; and the Income and Corporation Taxes Act 1970.

income tax appeal tribunals. Bodies set up to hear disputes concerning the Inland Revenue relating to liability to tax, each consisting (in the case of General Commissioners of Income Tax) of local business and professional persons assisted by a qualified clerk, or (in the case of Special Commissioners) of barristers and members of the Inland Revenue Department. Appeal on a point of law lies to the High Court. See the Taxes Management Act 1970.

incompletely constituted trust. A trust which requires some further action by the settlor before it is perfectly created. See *Milroy* v *Lord* (1862) 4 De G & J 264; *Re Fry* [1946] 12 All ER 106. *See* TRUST.

in consimili casu, consimile debet esse remedium. In similar cases, the remedy should be similar.

in contemplation of death. "It is sufficient that [the donor of a gift made in contemplation of death] is suffering at the relevant time from an illness which may prove mortal; in such circumstances the gift is taken to be made 'in contemplation of death' and the implication is that it is conditional on death": *Dufficy* v *Mollica* [1968] 3 NSWR 751. *See* DONATIO MORTIS CAUSA.

incorporate. 1. To combine into a whole, eg, as where one document is taken to be part of another. 2. To admit to membership of a corporation. 3. To form into a corporation, eg, by Act of Parliament. An "unincorporated body" has, in general, no independent legal personality, unlike the incorporated association.

incorporation by reference. "If a testator, in a testamentary paper duly executed, refers to an existing unattested testamentary paper, the instrument so referred to becomes part of his will; in other words it is incorporated into it": *In b Smart* [1902] P 238. See *Re Schintz's Will Trusts* [1951] Ch 870; *Re Tyler* [1967] 1 WLR 1269. *See* WILL.

incorporation, certificate of. Issued by the Registrar of Companies after inspection of a company's documents, eg, memorandum and articles of association (qv), list of those who have consented to be directors. Issue incorporates members of the company into a *persona* at law, and is conclusive evidence that the require-

ments of the Cos.A. relating to registration have been complied with. See the Cos.A. 1980, ss. 3(4), (5), 13. Under the European Communities Act 1972, s. 9(3), the Registrar is obliged to publish a notice of issue of a certificate of incorporation in the *London Gazette. See* COMPANY.

incorporation, doctrine of. Doctrine that rules of international law are incorporated automatically into English law unless they are in conflict with an Act of Parliament, as contrasted with the doctrine of transformation (qv). See *Triquet* v *Bath* (1764) 3 Burr 1481. The doctrine was accepted as correct in *Trendtex Trading Corporation* v *Central Bank of Nigeria* [1977] QB 527.

incorporeal hereditaments. Rights of property to which the law of real property applies, eg, easements, profits. *See* HEREDITAMENTS.

incorrigible rogue. One who has been convicted of certain offences, or who has violently resisted arrest on a charge, under the Vagrancy Act 1824. See *R* v *Jackson* [1974] 2 All ER 211.

incriminate. 1. To charge with a crime. 2. To involve in the possibility of a prosecution. A person cannot generally be compelled to answer a question the answer to which would incriminate him. See the S.C.A. 1981, s. 72; *R* v *Boyes* (1861) 1 B & S 311; *Re Reynolds* (1882) 20 Ch D 294. For statutory exceptions to the rule see, eg, the Civil Evidence Act 1898, s. 1 (*e*); the Civil Evidence Act 1968, s. 14(1); and the Criminal Damage Act 1971, s. 9.

incumbent. One who holds an ecclesiastical benefice (qv). See the Incumbents (Vacation of Benefices) Measure 1977.

incumbrance. Encumbrance (qv).

indebitatus assumpsit. Being indebted he undertook. An action of *assumpsit* (qv) brought to recover a debt. The plaintiff alleged a debt, then a promise in consideration. Now obsolete.

indecency. "Indecency is not confined to sexual indecency; indeed it is difficult to find any limit short of saying that it includes anything which an ordinary decent man or woman would find to be shocking, disgusting and revolting": *Knuller Ltd* v *DPP* [1972] 2 All ER 898. *See* OBSCENITY.

indecency, gross. *See* GROSS INDECENCY.

indecency with children. *See* GROSS INDECENCY.

indecent assault. A hostile act accompanied with circumstances of indecency on the part of the accused. See the S.O.A. 1956, ss. 14, 15; and *Faulkner* v *Talbot* [1981] 3 All ER 468.

indecent assault on men. An offence under the S.O.A. 1956, s. 14. A boy under 16, or a man who is a defective, cannot in law give any consent which would prevent an act being an assault for the purposes of s. 14.

indecent assault on women. An offence under the S.O.A. 1956, s. 14. A girl under 16, or a woman who is a defective, cannot in law give any consent which would prevent an act being an assault for the purposes of s. 14.

indecent display. If indecent matter is publicly displayed (ie, displayed in or so as to be visible from any public place), the person making the display or causing or permitting the display is guilty of an offence: Indecent Displays (Control) Act 1981, s. 1(1), (2). "Public place" includes any place to which the public have access (whether on payment or otherwise); it does not include part of a shop which the public can enter only after passing an adequate warning notice: s. 1(3), (6). Certain specified matter is excluded from the Act, eg, that included in a TV broadcast, the display of an art gallery: s. 1(4).

indecent exposure. *See* EXPOSE.

indefeasible. That cannot be annulled or made void.

indemnifying measure. *See* ACT OF INDEMNITY.

indemnity. 1. Exemption from incurred penalties. See, eg, the Indemnity Act 1920; and the Charitable Trusts (Validation) Act 1954. 2. Compensation for injury or loss. See *W.H. Smith & Son* v *Clinton* (1908) 99 LT 840. 3. Indemnity insurance is based on the principle that the insured cannot recover more than his actual loss:

Darrell v *Tibbitts* (1880) 5 QBD 560. 4. Contract of indemnity is exemplified thus: X and Y enter a shop and Y says to the shopkeeper, "Let X have these goods, I will see you are paid" (see *Birkmyr* v *Darnell* (1704) 1 Salk 27). Such a contract need not be in writing, unlike a contract of guarantee.

indemnity clauses, unreasonable. "A person dealing as consumer cannot by reference to any contract term be made to indemnify another person (whether a party to the contract or not) in respect of liability that may be incurred by the other for negligence or breach of contract, except in so far as the contract term satisfies the requirement of reasonableness". Unfair Contract Terms: Act 1977, s. 4(1).

indenture. A deed (qv) made on paper which was cut or indented, so that its two parts ("counterparts") could be fitted together. Although a deed which purports to be an indenture is not in fact indented, it may have the same effect: L.P.A. 1925, s. 56.

independent contractor. One who by contract agrees to perform a particular task for another and who, in the execution of his work, is not under the control of the person for whom it is performed, and who may use his discretion as to the general mode of execution. In general, an employer is not liable for the torts of an independent contractor unless he has authorised them explicitly or implicitly. See *Performing Right Society* v *Mitchell* [1924] 1 KB 762; *Mersey Docks & Harbour Board* v *Coggins & Griffiths Ltd* [1947] AC 1; and *Rivers* v *Cutting* [1982] 1 WLR 1146.

independent trade union. *See* TRADE UNION, INDEPENDENT.

index map. *See* PUBLIC INDEX MAP.

index of minor interests. A record of minor interests (qv) protected by notice, inhibition, restriction or caution. Priority is determined in general by order of entry. See the L.R.A. 1925, s. 3.

indicia. Signs; marks; criteria.

indictable offence. An offence which, if committed by an adult, is triable on indictment (qv) whether it is exclusively so triable or triable either way: C.L.A. 1977, s. 64(1) (*a*). For procedure where trial on indictment appears more suitable, see the M.C.A. 1980, s. 21; and the S.C.A. 1981, s. 46. See also the I.A. 1978, Sch 1. *See* OFFENCES TRIABLE EITHER WAY.

indictment. A written or printed accusation of a crime. "A plain, brief and certain narrative of an offence committed": 2. Hale PC 169. Its form is determined by the provisions of the Indictments Act 1915 and the Indictment Rules 1971. It consists of three parts: the commencement (name of case and defendant, court of trial, statement that named person is charged with offence(s) which follow(s)); the statement of offence(s); and the particulars (eg, description of offence, date, place of offence, name of victim). *See* BILL OF INDICTMENT.

indictment, objection to. *See* OBJECTION TO INDICTMENT.

indictment, pleas to. *See* BAR, PLEAS IN; JURISDICTION, PLEA TO.

indirect evidence. *See* EVIDENCE, INDIRECT.

indisputability clause. Clause in an insurance policy which provides that the policy becomes indisputable after it has been in force for a particular time. It cannot preclude an insurer from alleging that a policy was obtained by fraud. See *Anstey* v *British Natural Petroleum Life Assurance Ltd* (1909) 99 LT 765; and *Anctil* v *Manufacturers' Life Insurance Co* [1899] AC 604. *See* INSURANCE.

individual. Generally, a natural person (qv). Under the C.C.A. 1974, s. 189, it includes a partnership or other incorporated body.

indivisible contract. *See* DIVISIBLE CONTRACT.

indorsement. Endorsement (qv).

inducement. 1. Persuasion by promise or threat to a course of action. 2. Introductory part of pleadings (qv). 3. Inducement or procuration leading to a breach of contract involves persuading an employee to break his contract. See *Lumley* v *Gye* (1853) 2 E & B 216 ("To draw a line between advice, persuasion, enticement and procurement is practically impossible in a court of justice").

inducement leading to confession. "In order to render a confession admissible in evidence it must be perfectly voluntary; and there is no doubt that any inducement in the nature of a promise or of a threat held out by a person in authority vitiates a confession": *R* v *Baldry* (1852) 2 Den 430. See *Judges' Rules* 1964; *R* v *Jarvis* (1867) LR 1 CC R 96; *R* v *Stanton* (1911) 6 Cr App R 198; *Customs and Excise Commissioners* v *Harz and Power* [1967] 1 All ER 177; *R* v *Zaveckas* [1970] 1 All ER 413; and *R* v *Challinor and Cross* (1983) 76 Cr App R 229. *See* CONFESSION.

industrial and provident society. A society registered under the Industrial and Provident Societies Acts 1965–78 which carries on an industry, business or trade specified in its rules, wholesale or retail, including dealings with land. See also the Income and Corporation Taxes Act 1970, s. 340.

industrial death benefit. Benefit payable under the S.S.A. 1975, (as amended) comprising: widow's pension on death of husband resulting from industrial accident (and, on her remarriage, a gratuity); widower's benefit if wife has died as the result of an industrial accident and he, having been maintained by her permanently, is incapable of supporting himself.

industrial development certificate. Certificate issued by the Secretary of State for the Environment, required before applying for planning permission to erect an industrial building or to alter the use of a building for industrial purposes. See the T.C.P.A. 1971, as amended.

industrial diseases benefits. Benefits payable under the S.S.A. 1975 to employers in respect of injuries and prescribed diseases (qv) arising from the nature of the employment. See the 1975 Act, ss. 76–78.

industrial dispute. A dispute between one or more employers or organisations of employers and one or more workers relating wholly or mainly to terms and conditions of work, engagement or non-engagement or suspension or termination of employment, allocation of work, etc. See the T.U.L.R.A. 1974, s. 29; and *USDAW* v *Sketchley* [1981] IRLR 291.

industrial espionage. *See* ESPIONAGE, INDUSTRIAL.

industrial injuries benefits. Benefits provided under the S.S.A. 1975, ss. 50–75, to employed earners (qv) suffering personal injuries caused by accidents arising out of and in the course of their employment, and to the relatives and spouses of those killed in such accidents and to employed earners suffering prescribed diseases due to the nature of their employment. "Accidents" include mishaps arising where the employee is, at the time of the accident, in breach of orders or statutes or where the cause is misconduct or negligence on the part of some other person. Benefits include: injury benefit (qv); disablement benefit (qv); industrial benefit; industrial death benefit (qv). Appeal relating to disablement is to a medical appeal tribunal, then to a commissioner or tribunal of commissioners. See also the S.S. (Misc. Provs.) A. 1977, ss. 9–11; and the S.S. and Housing Benefits Act 1982.

industrial practice, unfair. *See* UNFAIR INDUSTRIAL PRACTICE.

industrial premises. Premises used or designed or suitable for use for the carrying on of any such process or research (or ancillary premises used for those purposes) specified in the T.C.P.A. 1971, s. 66(1); Highways Act 1980, s. 203(3).

industrial tribunals. First established under the Industrial Training Act 1964. They have since developed, following other legislation (eg, E.P.(C.)A. 1978, s. 128), into bodies hearing complaints relating to unfair dismissal, redundancy payments, terms of employment. Each tribunal consists of a legally qualified chairman appointed by the Lord Chancellor, and two other persons. The tribunals sit in different parts of the country as and when required and may conduct proceedings in whatever manner is considered

suitable. For the rules of procedure, see S.I. 1980/884. Appeal lies to the Employment Appeal Tribunal (qv).

ineffective contract. Term applied to a case in which money has been paid by one party to another on the strength of a transaction which he believes is a contract, but which, in fact, is of no effect, as where there is a total failure of consideration. See, eg, *Wilkinson* v *Lloyd (1845) 7 QB 27; Rowland* v *Divall* [1923] 2 KB 500.

in esse. State of actual existence, as compared with *in posse* (qv).

inevitable accident. An unlooked for mishap which could not have been avoided by the exercise of reasonable care or skill. See *Stanley* v *Powell* [1891] 1 QB 86; *Jones* v *LCC* (1932) 48 TLR 577.

in extenso. At length. Used with reference to the detailed reporting of a case, rather than a summary.

in extremis. In one's last extremity; final illness.

infamous conduct. "If a medical man in the pursuit of his profession has done something with regard to it which would be reasonably regarded as disgraceful or dishonourable to his professional brethren of good repute and competency, then it is open to the General Medical Council, if that be shown, to say that he has been guilty of infamous conduct in a professional respect": *Allinson* v *General Medical Council* [1894] 1 QB 750. See also the Medical Act 1978; the Dentists Acts 1957 and 1973; *McEniff* v *General Dental Council* [1980] 1 All ER 461; and *Le Scroog* v *General Optical Council* [1982] 1 WLR 1238.

infant. Under the F.L.R.A. 1969, a person under the age of 18. Such a person may be described also as a "minor". For actions relating to a minor, see O. 80.

infanticide. The offence committed by a woman who by any wilful act or omission causes the death of her child, under the age of 12 months, when at the time of the act or omission the balance of her mind is disturbed by reason of her not having fully recovered from the effect of giving birth to the child or by reason of the effect of lactation consequent on the birth of the child. She is punished as if guilty of manslaughter (qv): Infanticide Act 1938, s. 1(1). See *R v Soanes* (1948) 32 Cr App R 136; *R v Scott* [1973] Crim LR 708.

infanti proximus. Next to infancy. Term derived from Roman law describing a child who can speak but who lacks *intellectus* and *judicium*, ie, understanding.

inferential facts. *See* FACTS, INFERENTIAL.

inferior courts. Those courts with a jurisdiction limited, geographically and in relation to the value of that which is in dispute and subject to the supervision of a superior court, eg, county courts, magistrates' courts (qqv) and valuation courts (see *A.-G. v BBC* [1981] AC 303). See also *Peart v Stewart* [1983] 2 WLR 451.

influence, undue. *See* UNDUE INFLUENCE.

in forma pauperis. In the character of a pauper. Procedure, now superseded by legal aid (qv), by which a poor person was assisted so as to take or defend proceedings in the High Court.

information. Statement by which a magistrate is informed of the offence for which a summons or warrant is required. In general, any person may lay an information, unless there is a statutory rule to the contrary. An information will suffice if it merely describes the alleged offence in ordinary, non-technical language. It is usually in writing and may be substantiated on oath and includes the name of the party charged, the offence (when and where committed). See the M.C.A. 1980, s. 1. *See* LAYING AN INFORMATION.

information agreement. Agreement under the Restrictive Trade Practices Act 1968, s. 5, for the finishing of information relating to prices charged, costs, processes of manufacture, etc.

information, criminal. *See* CRIMINAL INFORMATION.

information, disclosure of. There is a duty on an employer to disclose to authorised representatives of independent trade unions (qv), on request, information without which

they would be materially impeded in collective bargaining and information which it would be good industrial relations practice to disclose. See the E.P.A. 1975, s. 17. See the Employment Act 1982, s. 1.

informer. 1. One who brought an action, or informed, in a court so as to recover a penalty on a conviction. 2. One who informs the police of violations of the law. The police may not use informers in such a way that crimes result: *R v Birtles* [1969] 2 All ER 1131. See *R v Lowe* (1977) 66 Cr App R 122. 3. A "common informer" was one who sued for a penalty which went to the person informing of a breach. The procedure was abolished by the Common Informers Act 1951.

infra. Below.

infringement. Violation of or trespass on some right.

in gross. See GROSS.

ingross. Engross (qv).

inhabitant. One who resides, actually and permanently, in some given place and has his domicile (qv) there. The word refers generally to something more permanent than mere residence (qv).

inherent vice. A defect inherent in goods which causes damage to them, eg, fruit rotting because of some latent defect (see *Bradley v Fed Steam Navigation Co* (1927) 137 LT 266); couplings of a carriage breaking because of a defect in their construction (*Lister v Lancs and Yorks Rwy Co* [1903] 1 KB 878). A common carrier (qv) is not generally liable for damage resulting from inherent vice.

inheritance. That which descends to the heir (qv) on the death of the owner. The old canons of inheritance (largely abolished by the A.E.A. 1925) were the rules concerning descent of land the owner of which died intestate.

inhibition. An entry on the proprietorship register on application of any person interested, eg, as where a proprietor's land certificate has been stolen. It prohibits the registration or entry of any dealing with registered land until the occurrence of an event named in the prohibition. See the L.R.A. 1925, s. 57.

in invitum. Against a person's consent

or will. Used with reference to the force of a law, or its impact, irrespective of one's assent.

injunction. An order of the court directing a person to refrain from doing or continuing to do an act complained of, or restraining him from continuing an omission. Non-compliance is a contempt of court (qv). Classified thus: (1) *prohibitory* (forbidding continuation or omission of a wrongful act); (2) *mandatory* (restraining continuation of omission by direct performance of a positive act); (3) *interlocutory* (qv) (temporary injunction, intended to maintain the *status quo* until trial); (4) *perpetual* (granted after the hearing of an action); (5) *ex parte* (qv)—see O. 29; (6) *interim* (restraining the defendant until some specified date); (7) *quia timet* (qv). See the S.C.A. 1981, s. 37; and *Chief Constable of Kent* v *V* [1982] 3 WLR 462.

injunction, interlocutory, grant of. Principles were clarified in *American Cyanamid Co* v *Ethicon Ltd* [1975] AC 396. There is no rule requiring the plaintiff to establish a prima facie case. Rule is that the court must be satisfied that there is a serious, not frivolous, question for trial. Governing consideration is then the balance of convenience (although inadequacy of damages is of significance). Relative strength of the case of both parties is considered only as a last resort. See *Stratford & Son* v *Lindley* [1965] AC 269; *Hubbard* v *Pitt* [1976] QB 142; *Bryanston Finance Ltd* v *De Vries* [1976] Ch 63; *Losinka* v *Civil and Public Services Association* [1976] ICR 473.

injunction, Mareva. *See* MAREVA INJUNCTION.

injunctions, matrimonial. Injunctions available in the High Court (if ancillary to other matrimonial proceedings) and county court (qv) restraining the other party to a marriage from molesting the applicant or a child living with the applicant or excluding the other party from the matrimonial home (qv) or requiring the other party to permit the applicant to enter and remain in the matrimonial home. Available also in the case of a man and woman living in the same household as husband and wife: Domestic Violence and Matrimonial Proceedings Act 1976, s. 1. A court has the power to attach a power of arrest to an injunction made in divorce proceedings or under the 1976 Act: *Lewis* v *Lewis* [1978] 1 All ER 729. See *Davis* v *Johnson* [1979] AC 264; and *Hopper* v *Hopper* [1979] 1 All ER 181.

injuria. A legal wrong.

injuria non excusat injuriam. An injury received does not justify doing an injury.

injuria sine damno. Wrong without damage. Phrase used in the law of torts to refer to the violation of an interest which may constitute an actionable tort (qv) without proof of damage (ie, pecuniary loss).

injuries, personal, action for. "An action in which there is a claim for damages in respect of personal injuries to the plaintiff or any other person or in respect of a person's death; and 'personal injuries' includes any disease and any impairment of a person's physical or mental condition": O. 1, r. 4.

injurious affection. Land may be affected injuriously where part is taken from the owner by the state's exercise of compulsory purchasing powers and, in such a case, the owner may be entitled to compensation if, eg, the value of the remaining land has fallen. See the Land Compensation Act 1973, s. 44 (as amended).

injurious falsehood. A tort (qv), resulting from written or oral falsehoods, maliciously published, calculated in the ordinary course of things to produce, and, in the event, producing, actual damage: *Ratcliffe* v *Evans* [1892] 2 QB 524. Known, at one time, as "slander of title" (qv) and "slander of goods" (qv). The Defamation Act 1952, s. 3(1) refers to "slander of title, slander of goods or other malicious falsehood". See *Fielding* v *Variety Incorporated* [1967] 2 All ER 497.

injury. 1. The violation of the rights of another, or its results. 2. An actionable wrong. 3. "Any disease and any impairment of a person's physical or mental condition": Fatal Accidents Act 1976, s. 1(5).

injury benefit. Benefit payable under the S.S.A. 1975 in respect of any day of the period of 156 days from an injury as a result of which an employee is incapable of work.

injury, personal. Any disease and any impairment of a person's physical or mental condition: Lim.A. 1980, s. 38(1).

inland bill. A bill of exchange which is both drawn and payable within the British Isles or which is drawn within the British Isles upon some person resident therein. The term "foreign bill" is applied to any other bill. See the B.Ex.A. 1882, s. 4. *See* BILL OF EXCHANGE.

Inland Revenue, Commissioners of. The government body which administers the laws relating to taxation and advises the Chancellor of the Exchequer on relevant matters. See the Taxes Management Act 1970.

inland waters. *See* TERRITORIAL WATERS.

in lieu. In place of.

in limine. On the threshold; preliminary.

in loco parentis. In the place of a parent. Generally it refers to one who, although not the parent of a particular child, takes on himself parental offices and duties in relation to that child. See *Powys* v *Mansfield* (1837) 3 My & C 359; *Bennet* v *Bennet* (1879) 10 Ch D 474.

inn. At common law a house, the owner of which holds himself out as being willing to receive travellers who are willing to pay an appropriate price for accommodation. See now the Hotel Proprietors Act 1956. See also *Williams* v *Linnit* [1951] 1 KB 565. For limitation of an innkeeper's liability, see s. 2. *See* HOTEL.

Inner Temple. One of the Inns of Court (qv). It stands on land granted in perpetuity by James I in 1609.

inner urban areas, assistance for. Under the Inner Urban Areas Act 1978, if the Secretary of State is satisfied that special social need exists in any inner urban area in

Great Britain and that the causes could be alleviated by his exercising powers under the Act, he may by order specify a district including that area as a "designated district", empowered to make loans for the acquisition by any person of land within that district or the carrying out by any person of works on the land, intended to benefit the district.

innocence, presumption of. *See* PRESUMPTION OF INNOCENCE.

innocent misrepresentation. *See* MISREPRESENTATION.

innominate. Neither named nor classified. For innominate terms in a contract, see *Bunge Corporation (NY) v Tradax Export* [1981] 1 WLR 711.

in nomine. In the name of.

Inns of Chancery. Former seminaries associated with the Inns of Court (qv), which ceased to exist in the nineteenth century. They included Staple Inn, Lyon's Inn and Clement's Inn.

Inns of Court. Lincoln's Inn, Inner Temple, Middle Temple, and Gray's Inn (qqv), which have the exclusive right of call to the Bar (qv). Their members are benchers (qv), barristers (qv) and students.

innuendo. *Innuere* = to hint. A plea by the plaintiff in an action for defamation (qv) that, although the words are not defamatory in themselves, by reason of a conjunction of the words and some extrinsic statement, they have, in effect, a secondary defamatory meaning. See, eg, *Thomson* v *Chain Libraries* [1954] 1 WLR 999; *Grappelli* v *Derek Block (Holdings)* [1981] 1 WLR 822; and *Hayward* v *Thompson* [1982] QB 47.

inops consilii. Without (legal) advice.

in pais. In the country (as contrasted with "in court"). Refers to that which has taken place without legal proceedings. *Trial per pais* referred to trial by jury (ie, trial "by the country").

in pari causa possessor potior haberi debet. Where both parties have an equally strong claim, he who is in possession is in the stronger position.

in pari delicto potior est conditio

possidentis. Where both parties are equally in the wrong, the position of the possessor is the best.

in pari materia. In an analogous case.

in personam. Against a person. An expression used to indicate, eg, proceedings taken against some specific person (*actio in personam*), or rights available against specific persons (*jura in personam*). The maxim "Equity acts *in personam*" refers to the old procedure of the Court of Chancery which issued an order "upon a person" so that he was commanded to do or refrain from doing an act.

in posse. State of potential, not actual, existence (as compared with *in esse* (qv)).

inquest. *See* CORONER.

inquiry, preliminary. *See* PRELIMINARY INVESTIGATION.

inquiry, tribunals of. Bodies set up by Parliament to enquire into matters of urgent public importance. They may summon witnesses, take evidence on oath. Sittings are generally in public.

inquiry, writ of. Procedure, now abolished, by which, following a judgment in default, "twelve honest and lawful men" were asked on oath to estimate the damage sustained by the plaintiff.

inquisition. 1. Enquiry by a jury (qv). 2. Verdict of an inquest, consisting of three sections: caption (date, place of inquest, coroner, jury); verdict (finding of identity of deceased, time, place, probable cause of death); attestation (signatures of coroner, concurring jurors). *See* CORONER.

inquisitorial procedure. System in force in some continental countries under which the judge searches for facts, listens to witnesses, examines documents and orders that evidence be taken, after which he makes further investigations if he considers them necessary. *See* ACCUSATORIAL PROCEDURE.

in re. In the matter of.

in rem. Against a thing. An expression used to indicate, eg, an action taken against no specific person, but rather "against the world", eg, to assert a right of property against all persons

(an action *in rem*, relating to *jura in rem*). A judgment *in rem* is the judgment of "a court of competent jurisdiction determining the status of a person or thing, or the disposition of a thing (as distinct from a particular interest in it of a party to the litigation)": *Lazarus-Barlow* v *Regent Estates* [1949] 2 KB 465.

insanity. Generally, unsoundness of mind. Term used to refer to one whose state of mind prevents his knowing right from wrong so that he cannot be held responsible for his acts. See the M.H.A. 1983. Every person is presumed sane until the contrary has been proved. The burden of proving insanity is generally on the accused: *Woolmington* v *DPP* [1935] AC 462. *See* M'NAGHTEN RULES.

insanity, not guilty by reason of. *See* SPECIAL VERDICT.

inscribed stock. Stock for which a certificate of ownership is not issued.

insider dealing. Dealing by "insiders" in current, listed securities of a company, using confidential information likely to affect their market value. Generally it is prohibited: see the Cos.A. 1980, Part V. "Insiders" include a person who, within the preceding six months has been knowingly connected with the company and has unpublished, price-sensitive information relating to the securities, and any person who has contemplated a take-over involving the company and is in possession of such information: s. 68. Under s. 69, specified individuals (eg, some Crown servants) are prohibited from abusing information obtained in their official capacity. Prohibitions apply also to off-market deals (qv).

in situ. In its original or natural position.

insolvency. Inability to pay one's debts, because of lack of sufficient property. See the Insolvency Act 1976; and Cork Report 1982, Cmnd 8558.

Insolvency Services Account. Account kept by the Secretary of State with the Bank of England relating to sums standing to the credit of bankrupt estates or to liquidated companies: Insolvency Act 1976, s. 3.

in specie. In its own form.

inspection and investigation of a company. Procedure whereby the Department of Trade is empowered to inspect a company's papers and books, to investigate a company's affairs, membership, directors' interests in its shares or debentures. See, eg, the Cos.A. 1948, ss. 164(1), 172(3) as amended; and the Cos.A. 1967, s. 109. *See* COMPANY.

inspection by judge. Provision (see, eg, O. 35) whereby a judge may inspect a place or thing with respect to which a question has arisen in a cause or other matter. "I think that a view is part of the evidence just as much as an exhibit. It is real evidence": *per* Lord Denning in *Goold* v *Evans & Co* [1951] 2 TLR 1189. See *Buckingham* v *Daily News Ltd* [1956] 2 All ER 904; *Salsbury* v *Woodland* [1970] 1 QB 324; *Tito* v *Waddell* [1975] 3 All ER 997.

inspection of documents. *See* DISCOVERY AND INSPECTION OF DOCUMENTS.

inspection order, *ex parte.* Order *in personam* to permit inspection by the plaintiff, who fears that if notice is given to the defendant he may destroy relevant documents, or transfer them, thus preventing the effective discovery of documents (qv). See *EMI Ltd* v *Pandit* [1969] 1 All ER 418; *Anton Piller KG* v *Manufacturing Processes Ltd* [1976] FSR 129; *Universal Studios Inc* v *Mukhtar* [1976] 2 All ER 330. *See also* ANTON PILLER ORDER.

instalment. Portions into which a sum of money, or a debt, may be divided for payment at fixed intervals.

instalment deliveries. Unless otherwise agreed, the buyer of goods is not bound to accept delivery of them by instalments: S.G.A. 1979, s. 31(1).

instance, court of first. A court in which proceedings are started; as contrasted with, eg, the Court of Appeal (qv).

instant committal. Short committal. *See* COMMITTAL FOR TRIAL.

in statu quo. In the state or position in which something was or is.

instruct. To authorise an advocate to act, or to communicate information to him relating to proceedings.

instrument. A written document (such as a deed or will) executed formally, evidencing, eg, rights, duties.

instrument, banking. *See* BANKING INSTRUMENT.

instrument, false. Phrase used in the Forgery and Counterfeiting Act 1981, s. 1. An instrument is false if, eg, it purports to have been made in the form in which it is made by a person who did not in fact make it in that form: s. 9(1). "Instrument" includes any document, formal or informal, stamp sold by the Post Office, Inland Revenue stamp, disc, tape, soundtrack or similar device. *See* FORGERY.

insulting behaviour. A person who in any public place or public meeting uses insulting words or behaviour with intent to provoke a breach of the peace (qv) is guilty of an offence under the Public Order Act 1936, s. 5. See *Ward* v *Holman* [1964] 2 QB 580; *R* v *Davies* [1976] Crim LR 697; and *Parkin* v *Norman* [1982] 2 All ER 583.

insurable interest. An interest giving an insured person a right to enforce a contract of insurance. It exists if the insured person is liable to sustain some monetary loss, or if he may be claimed against following a loss to another. Examples: a father has not necessarily an insurable interest in his son's life (*Halford* v *Kymer* (1830) 10 B & C 724); a husband may insure his wife, and a wife her husband (*Griffiths* v *Fleming* [1909] 1 KB 805); a trustee may insure in respect of the interest of which he is trustee (*Tidswell* v *Ankerstein* (1792) Peake 151). See the Life Assurance Act 1774, s. 1.

insurance. Generally a contract (qv) of indemnity against a contingency. The *insurer* assumes the risks of the contingency in consideration of payment of a *premium*, so that the *insured*, who suffers the damage, will be compensated from a common insurance fund. It is a contract *uberrimae fidei* (qv), necessitating full disclosure of *all* facts affecting the risk. See *Lambert* v *Co-op Insurance Society Ltd* [1975] 2 Lloyd's Rep 485; and Insurance Law —Non-disclosure and Breach of

Warranty 1980 (Cmnd 8064). "Insurance" is used with reference to events which *may* happen (eg, fire on one's property), "assurance" (qv) is used to refer to events which *must* happen (eg, death). A contract of insurance may be not only for the payment of money, but for a benefit corresponding to such payment: *Department of Trade and Industry v St Christopher's Motorists Association* [1974] 1 WLR 99. See the Insurance Companies Act 1982; and the Policyholders Protection Act 1975.

insurance business. Divided, under the Insurance Companies Act 1982, s. 1(1) into "long term business" (meaning insurance business of the classes specified in Sch 1—life and annuity, tontines (qv), pension fund management, etc) and "general business" (meaning insurance business of the classes specified in Sch 2, Part I —accident, sickness, fire, damage to property, suretyship, etc). See the Insurance Companies Act 1982, s. 95.

insurance coupon. 1. Coupon which is intended to constitute a contract of insurance. 2. Coupon which is an undertaking to issue a policy of insurance to the holder on compliance with terms and conditions. See *General Accident Corporation v Robertson* [1909] AC 404.

insurance, double. Insurance by the insured of one risk on the same interest in the same property with more than one insurer. See *Millandon v W Marine Insurance Co* (1836) 9 La 27; and *Gale v Motor Union Insurance Co* [1928] 1 KB 359.

insurance, over-. Situation in which the aggregate of all the insurance exceeds the total value of the insured's interests.

intangible property. *See* TANGIBLE PROPERTY.

integration. The amalgamation of firms or other productive units.

integration test. "One feature, which seems to run through the instances is that, under a contract of service (qv), a man is employed as part of the business, and his work is done as an integral part of the business; whereas, under a contract for services, his work, although done for the business,

is not integrated into it, but is only necessary to it": *per* Denning LJ in *Stevenson, Jordan and Harrison v Macdonald & Evans* [1952] 1 TLR 101.

intellectual property. A group of rights, eg, patents, registered designs, copyright, trade marks, knowhow (qv). For the attitude of the EEC, see *Deutsche Gramaphon v Metro 78/70.*

intention. Refers in criminal law to a mental state in which a person foresees and wills those consequences which may possibly flow from his conduct. It may constitute the *mens rea* (qv) required for a crime. "A decision to bring about, in so far as it lies within the accused's power, [a particular consequence], no matter whether the accused desired that consequence of his act or not": *R v Mohan* [1975] 2 All ER 193. See also *Cunliffe v Goodman* [1950] 2 KB 237; *Lloyds Bank v Marcan* [1973] 2 All ER 359. *See* ACTUS NON FACIT REUM NISI MENS SIT REA.

intention of a document. The sense of a document, derived from a perusal and comprehension of its contents.

intention of Parliament. Phrase used in the interpretation of statutes (qv). "We do not sit here to pull the language of Parliament to pieces and make nonsense of it . . . We sit here to find out the intention of Parliament and of ministers and carry it out, and we do this better by filling in the gaps and making sense of the enactment than by opening it up to destructive analysis": *Magor and St Mellons RDC v Newport Corporation* [1950] 2 All ER 1226. This approach was rejected later by the House of Lords.

intent, wounding with. *See* WOUNDING WITH INTENT.

inter alia. Among other things.

inter alios. Among other persons.

intercourse, questions to spouses relating to. "The evidence of a husband or wife shall be admissible in any proceedings to prove that marital intercourse did or did not take place between them during any period": Mat.C.A. 1973, s. 48(1). In a criminal case neither husband nor wife is compellable to give evidence of these matters.

intercourse, sexual. *See* SEXUAL INTERCOURSE, PROOF OF.

interesse termini. Interest of a term. The legal, proprietary right, carrying with it a right of entry, which a lessee (qv) had before entering or taking possession of the land. Abolished under the L.P.A. 1925, s. 149(1) (2). See *Lewis* v *Baker* [1905] 1 Ch 46.

interest. 1. A right in property. "It extendeth to estates, rights and titles that a man hath of, in, to, or out of lands": Coke. 2. The return on capital invested ("the price of money"). 3. A share of control in, eg, a company (qv). 4. Concern in the outcome of an event.

interest action. Action brought to settle the right of contending claimants to obtain a grant of administration (qv). It is brought in the Chancery Division and is commenced by a writ of summons issued out of Chancery Chambers; see O. 76.

interest, declaration against. *See* DECLARATION AGAINST INTEREST.

interest, disclosure of. The duty of, eg, a member of a local authority to make known the fact that he has a direct or indirect pecuniary interest in a contract which is under discussion by the authority and to refrain from voting on it. See the L.G.A. 1972, ss. 94–98.

interest, future. *See* FUTURE INTEREST.

interest in expectancy. A reversionary interest. *See* REVERSION.

interest in possession. An interest which confers a right to present enjoyment of property. See the Finance Act 1975, Sch 5, para 6(2); *Pearson* v *IRC* [1980] Ch 1.

interest on debts and damages. The High Court and county courts (qqv) are empowered in proceedings for the recovery of a debt or damages to award simple interest at such rate as is thought fit: S.C.A. 1981, s. 35A (inserted by the A.J.A. 1982, Sch 1).

interest reipublicae ut sit finis litium. It concerns the State that litigation shall not be protracted.

interests, theory of. Theory, proposed by the American jurist, Pound (1870–1964), suggesting that the main problem for legislators is the balancing of individual, public and social interests. "Interests" were seen as demands, desires or expectations which human beings, individually or in groups, seek to satisfy.

interference with goods, wrongful. Conversion of goods (also called "trover" (qv)), trespass to goods, negligence so far as it results in damage to goods or to an interest in goods, any other tort so far as it results in damage to goods or to an interest in goods: Torts (Interference with Goods) Act 1977, s. 1. Relief given may take form of: order for delivery of the goods and payment of consequential damages; or an order for delivery, but giving the defendant the alternative of paying damages by reference to the value of the goods, together in either alternative with payment of any consequential damages; or damages: s. 3(1) (2). See *Brandeis Goldschmidt Ltd* v *Weston Transport Ltd* [1981] QB 864.

interference with subsisting contract. Tort (qv) committed by X who, without lawful justification, intentionally interferes with a contract between Y and Z by persuading Y to break his contract with Z or by committing a tortious act which prevents Y's performing the contract. See *Daily Mirror* v *Gardner* [1968] 2 QB 762; *Torquay Hotel Ltd* v *Cousins* [1969] 2 Ch 106.

interference with vehicles. *See* VEHICLE INTERFERENCE.

interfering with witnesses. It is an offence at common law to attempt to dissuade or prevent a witness from appearing at a hearing or giving evidence. See, eg, *Shaw* v *Shaw* (1861) 31 LJ PM & A 35.

interim. In the meantime.

interim dividend. A dividend declared at any time between two annual general meetings of a company (qv). It is not in the nature of a debt due from the company and cannot be sued for by a shareholder. See Table A, art. 115; and the Cos.A. 1980, s. 43(2) (*b*). *See* DIVIDEND.

interim order. An order issued pending further directions, eg, one made pending appeal.

interim payment. A payment on account of any damages, debt or other sum (excluding any costs) which a party may be held liable to pay to or for the benefit of another party to proceedings if a final judgment or order of the court in the proceedings is given or made in favour of that other party: S.C.A. 1981, s. 32(5). See O. 29, rr. 9–17.

interim relief. Granting of an interlocutory injunction (qv). See the A.J.A. 1969, s. 20; O. 29; *American Cyanamid Co* v *Ethicon* [1975] AC 396 (on interim payment of damages).

interim rent. When a landlord (qv) has given notice to terminate a tenancy, or a tenant has requested a new one, the landlord can apply to the court to determine an interim rent to be paid until commencement of new tenancy. See the Landlord and Tenant Act 1954, s. 24A; *English Exporters Ltd* v *Eldonwall Ltd* [1973] 1 All ER 726.

interlineation. Writing between (or on) the lines of a document. Under the W.A. 1837, s. 21, no interlineation in a will made after execution has effect except in so far as the words or effect of the will before interlineation shall not be apparent, unless it is executed as a will. See *In b Heath* [1892] P 253.

interlocutory. *Interloqui* = to speak between. Not final, (ie, during the course of an action). Examples: interlocutory injunction (qv) or interlocutory judgment or order (one which does not finally determine the rights of the parties).

interlocutory appeal. *See* APPEAL, INTERLOCUTORY.

interlocutory injunction. *See* INJUNCTION.

interlocutory proceedings. The preparatory stages of an action occurring between an originating summons or the issue of a writ and the trial of the resulting issues.

interlocutory relief, application for. Application is made: by motion (oral application to judge in open court); by summons (parties attending before a master or judge in chambers

on the date specified in the summons —the "return day"); *ex parte* on affidavit.

intermixture. The commingling of substances so that the parts can no longer be distinguished. See *Smith* v *Torr* (1862) 7 F & F 505; *Sandeman & Sons* v *Tyzack* [1913] AC 680.

international commodity organisation. Body whose purpose is to regulate trade in a commodity, whether as import or export, or to promote or study that trade or to promote research into that commodity or its uses or further development: International Organisation Act 1968, s. 4A 1(c) (substituted by the International Organisation Act 1981, s. 2).

International Court of Justice. Principal judicial organ of the United Nations Organisation which succeeded the Permanent Court of International Justice in 1946. Its seat is at The Hague and its function is to pass judgment on disputes between states. A state which has not accepted the court's jurisdiction cannot be sued without that state's consent. Disputes are decided in accordance with international law, or (with agreement of parties) *ex aequo et bono*, ie, on the foundation of a "fair solution". The body of judges is intended to represent "the main forces of civilisation and . . . the principal legal systems of the world".

international law. 1. The *corpus* of legal rules applying between sovereign states, known as *public international law*. 2. The body of rights and duties of citizens of different sovereign states towards one another, known as *private international law* (qv) or conflict of laws.

international supply contract. Phrase used in the Unfair Contract Terms Act 1977, s. 26, to refer to a contract made by parties whose places of business (or, if they have none, habitual residences) are in the territories of different states, if the goods to which the contract relates are, at the time of its conclusion, in the course of carriage, or will be carried from the territory of one state to that of another, or the acts constituting the offer and acceptance have been done in the territories of different states, or the contract provides for the goods to be delivered to the territory of a state other than that within whose territory those acts were done.

inter partes. Between the parties.

interpleader summons. Procedure whereby a person who is sued, or expects to be sued, by rival claimants takes out a summons which is served on the claimants, calling on them to appear before a master so as to stake their claims. The court may then order that the issue between the claimants be tried and will direct who shall be the plaintiff and defendant. A *stakeholder's interpleader* relates to, eg, a banker holding cash and faced with opposing claims. A *sheriff's interpleader* relates to goods seized under writ of *fi.fa.* (qv) and a claim by a third person that they belong to him. See O. 17, O. 58, r. 7.

interpretation clause. Part of an Act which provides that certain words and phrases used in that Act shall have certain meanings. See, eg, the L.P.A. 1925, s. 205; and the C.C.A. 1974, ss. 184–189. See *Savoy Hotel Co v LCC* [1900] 1 QB 665; *Carter v Bradbeer* [1975] 3 All ER 158.

interpretation of statutes. Where a statute's words are not clear or not certain, the courts may be called upon to interpret them. In this they are guided by rules, such as: (1) Literal rule—words of a statute in their original sense will prevail unless they would produce unintended consequences: *Corocraft v Pan Am Airways* [1969] 1 All ER 82. (2) Golden rule (qv)—manifest absurdity resulting from interpretation to be avoided: *Becke v Smith* (1836) 2 M & W. (3) Statute must be read as a whole. (4) There is a presumption against altering the law or ousting the courts' jurisdiction. (5) The court must adopt an interpretation which will correct the mischief which the statute was passed to remedy: *Heydon's Case* (1584) 3 Co Rep 7a. See Law Commission Paper No 21, 1969; the I.A. 1978, s. 6; *Maunsell v Olins* [1975] AC 373; and *In Re Energy Conversion*

Devices [1982] Com LR 219.

interpreter. One who translates the words of a witness. An accused who is unable to understand English properly is entitled to an interpreter's services: *R v Lee Kun* [1916] 1 KB 337. In civil proceedings the court has a discretion to allow the use of an interpreter: *Re Fuld* [1965] P 405. See *R v Attard* (1959) 43 Cr App R 90 (use of notes to refresh interpreter's memory).

interregnum. 1. Tenure of power while a throne is vacant. 2. Period during which a throne is vacant, eg, between the death of a monarch and accession of the successor.

interrogation. Questioning of suspects. *See* JUDGES' RULES.

interrogation of children. "As far as practicable, children (whether suspected of crime or not), should only be interviewed in the presence of a parent or guardian, or, in their absence, some person who is not a police officer and is of the same sex as the child": Home Office Circular 31/1964.

interrogation of foreigners. In the case of a foreigner making a statement in his native language, the interpreter should take it down in that language and the foreigner should sign the statement. An official English translation should be made and proved as an exhibit with the original statement: *Judges' Rules* 1964, Administrative Directions para 5.

interrogatories. Written questions answerable on oath relating to any matter relevant to an action, which a party may administer, with leave, to an opponent. See O. 26. Their purpose is to obtain admissions and to limit the scope of an opponent's case. They must be answered within the time prescribed. "The allowance or disallowance of interrogatories is a matter for discretion, and they should be allowed or disallowed on the merits of the particular case": *Heaton v Goldney* [1910] 1 KB 758. Answers to interrogatories are binding. See *Riddick v Thames Board Mills* [1977] QB 88.

interrogatories, fishing. Questions

posed which are not intended to further a genuine enquiry, but in order to elicit answers which may be used to support a case lacking in substance. See *Pankhurst* v *Hamilton* (1886) 2 TLR 682; *Brayley* v *Associated Newspapers Group* (*The Times*, 2.7.76); see also the County Court Rules 1981, O. 14, r. 11.

in terrorem. By way of terror. Threat or intimidation, eg, by way of a condition in a gift. Example: gift of property by X to Y, on condition that Y shall never marry Z. Conditions of this nature are usually void. See *Wilbeam* v *Ashton* (1807) 1 Camp 78—penalty (qv) held over a party to a contract *in terrorem.*

interruption. The breaking of continuity, eg, of enjoyment of some right. See, eg, the Prescription Act 1832, s. 4.

inter se. Among themselves.

intervener. One who intervenes in a suit (eg, relating to divorce) in his own, or the public's, interest. *See* QUEEN'S PROCTOR.

intervening cause. An independent cause coming between the original act or omission and an injury so that a result is produced which might not otherwise have occurred. *See* CAUSATION; NOVA CAUSA INTERVENIENS.

inter vivos. Between parties who are alive.

inter vivos, **gift.** *See* GIFT INTER VIVOS.

intestacy. State of dying intestate, ie, without having made a valid will (qv). A partial intestacy results from a will which disposes of only part of deceased's property. For administration and devolution see the A.E.A. 1925; the A.E.A. 1971; and the Intestates' Estates Act 1952.

intimidation. The act of frightening or coercing another into a course of action. See the S.O.A. 1956, s. 2 (offence of procuring a woman by threats or intimidation to have sexual intercourse); *A.-G.* v *Butterworth* [1963] 1 QB 696 (intimidation of juror or witness, which is treated as a contempt (qv)). The tort of intimidation arises where A threatens B so that B acts, or refrains from acting, to B's or C's detriment. See *Hardie & Lane Ltd* v *Chilton* [1928] 2 KB 306;

Rookes v *Barnard* [1964] AC 1129. See also the T.U.L.R.A. 1974, s. 13.

intoxicating liquor. Beer, cider, wine spirits, etc. See the Licensing Act 1964; *Hall* v *Hyder* [1966] 1 WLR 410 (in which it was stated that beer and lemonade shandy could be held to be "intoxicating liquor" if the beer, before the mixing, was of a strength requiring an excise licence).

intoxication. Condition of stupefaction induced by alcohol or a narcotic. Voluntary drunkenness may be a defence where it produces insanity within the M'Naghten Rules (qv) or where mistake is pleaded (see *R* v *Gamlen* (1858) 1 F & F 90), or where it negatives the existence of intent or some specific *mens rea* required. Self-intoxication is no defence to any crime, the definition of which does not require a specific intent. See *DPP* v *Beard* [1920] AC 479; *A.-G. for N Ireland* v *Gallagher* [1963] AC 359; *R* v *Lipman* [1970] 1 QB 152; *R* v *Caldwell* [1982] AC 341. *See* DIMINISHED RESPONSIBILITY.

intoxication, dangerous. *See* DANGEROUS INTOXICATION.

in transitu. During the passage. Right of stoppage *in transitu* is the right, under the S.G.A. 1979, ss. 44–46, to stop goods in transit, to resume and to retain possession until the price is paid. The right is available when the buyer becomes insolvent.

intra vires. Within its powers. Opposite of *ultra vires* (qv).

intrinsic. Essential to, or inherent in, something.

intrinsic evidence. *See* EVIDENCE, INTRINSIC.

inure. Enure (qv).

inventions, employees'. *See* EMPLOYEES' INVENTIONS, RIGHT TO.

inventory. An itemised list or catalogue. Under the A.E.A. 1925, s. 25(*a*), the personal representatives (qv) of a deceased person are under a duty to exhibit on oath a full inventory of the estate when required by court to do so.

in verbis non verba sed res et ratio quaerenda est. In interpreting words, one ought to look not only to the words but to the things and meaning behind them.

investigation of a company. See COMPANY, INVESTIGATION OF.

investigation, preliminary. See PRELIMINARY INVESTIGATION.

investitive facts. See FACTS, INVESTITIVE.

investment. "The verb 'to invest' when used in an investment clause may safely be said to include as one of its meanings 'to apply money in the purchase of some property from which interest or profit is expected and which property is purchased in order to be held for the sake of the income which it will yield'": *Re Wragg* [1919] 2 Ch 58. Generally, the term means the laying out of money with a view to earning an income from it, by way of interest, dividend, rent, etc.

investment company. A public company (qv) whose shares are listed on the Stock Exchange and which has complied with certain requirements, eg, its business must consist of investing its funds mainly in securities with the aim of spreading investment risk and giving members the benefit of the results of the management of its funds: Cos.A. 1980, s. 41.

investment exchange. An organisation which offers to deal in securities with a subscriber whose identity is not revealed to other subscribers and which records and confirms acceptance of its offers: Cos.A. 1980, s. 72(5).

investment, trustees' powers of. In general, a trustee (qv) may not lawfully invest trust funds upon securities (qv) other than those authorised by the settlement or statute. Under the Trustee Investment Act 1961, trustees may invest in three types of investment: narrower-range type not requiring advice (eg, National Savings Certificates); narrower-range type requiring advice (eg, debentures); wider-range type (eg, shares in building societies). Where trustees wish to invest in wider-range securities the trust fund must be divided into two parts: narrower-range part; wider-range part (of equal value at the time of the division): s. 2(1). See also the Finance Act 1982, s. 150.

invitation to treat. An offer to receive an offer. "According to the ordinary law of contract the display of an article with a price on it in the shop window is merely an invitation to treat. It is in no sense an offer for sale, the acceptance of which constitutes a contract": *per* Lord Parker in *Fisher* v *Bell* [1961] 1 QB 394. See *Pharmaceutical Society of Great Britain* v *Boots* [1953] 1 All ER 482; *Thornton* v *Shoe Lane Parking* [1971] 2 QB 163. See also *C. A. Norgren Co* v *Technomarketing* (1983) (*The Times*, 3.3.1983). See OFFER.

invitee. One who is present on property by the express or implied invitation of the owner or occupier, eg, a person "invited to the premises by the owner or occupier for purposes of business or of material interest": *Fairman* v *Perpetual Investment Building Society* [1923] AC 74. See the Occupiers' Liability Act 1957, s. 2.

involuntary conduct. A person's action in circumstances in which his mind was not in control of his bodily movement. Generally a defence to a charge, except, eg, where the accused had voluntarily consumed alcohol or drugs, or in the case of strict liability in criminal law (qv). "No act is punishable if it is done involuntarily": *Bratty* v *A.-G. for N Ireland* [1963] AC 386. See AUTOMATISM.

IOU. Abbreviation of phrase "I owe you", used as written acknowledgment of a debt. It is not a negotiable instrument, merely evidence of debt.

ipse autem rex non debet esse sub homine sed sub Deo et sub lege, quia lex facit regem. The King himself should not be subject to any man, but he should be subject to God and the law, for the law makes him King: Bracton.

ipse dixit. He himself said it. Used in relation to an assertion based only on the authority of the speaker or writer, but not proved. See, eg, *Creed* v *Scott* [1976] RTR 485.

ipsissima verba. The identical words.

ipso facto. By the law itself; by the nature of the case.

ipso jure. By the law itself; by operation of law.

irrebuttable presumptions. Those

inferences which may not be rebutted because evidence will not be admitted to contradict them. Known also as ''conclusive evidence''. Example: the presumption that everyone knows the law. *See* PRESUMPTION.

irrelevant evidence. Facts not in issue or not tending to prove facts in issue, eg, ''similar facts evidence'', ie, that a person has behaved in a certain way on other occasions. See, eg, *Makin v A.-G. for NS Wales* [1894] AC 57; *Harris v DPP* [1952] AC 694. *See* EVIDENCE.

irresistible impulse, defence of. The defence of a man's having committed an offence under an uncontrollable impulse is not accepted. ''. . . A fantastic theory . . . which if it were to become part of our criminal law, would be merely subversive'': *R v Kopsch* (1925) 19 Cr App R 50). See *A.-G. for S. Australia v Brown* [1960] AC 432; and *R v Smith* [1982] Crim LR 531. The defence of diminished responsibility (qv) may be considered, however, as based in part on irresistible impulse.

irretrievable breakdown of marriage. *See* BREAKDOWN OF MARRIAGE.

irrevocable. Incapable of being revoked. Thus, a will (qv) is not irrevocable unless the testator (qv) ceases to be of sound mind, thus losing testamentary capacity. See *Vynior's Case* (1609) 8 Co Rep 81b.

irrevocable credits. Procedure whereby a contract for the sale of goods to a foreign buyer provides for payment through the buyer's bank which notifies the creditor that he will be paid when he tenders the shipping documents to the bank. See *Guaranty Trust Co of NY v Hannay* [1918] 2 KB 623.

island company. ''An oversea company incorporated in the Channel Islands or the Isle of Man'': Cos.A. 1948, s. 416(4) (as substituted by the Cos.A. 1981, s. 109).

issue. 1. Offspring. A person's issue comprises his children, grandchildren and other lineal descendants. See *Re Hey's Settlement Trusts* [1945] Ch 294; *Re Manley's Will Trusts* [1976] 1 All ER 673. 2. The outcome of, eg, an action. 3. The matter in dispute. 4. A point in question. 5. Total amount of banknotes in circulation.

issued capital. That part of a company's nominal capital (qv) which has actually been issued to shareholders.

issue, dying without. *See* DYING WITHOUT ISSUE.

issue estoppel. ''Issue estoppel can be said to exist when there is a judicial establishment of a proposition of law or fact between parties to earlier litigation and when the same question arises in later litigation between the same parties. In the latter litigation the established proposition is treated as conclusive between the same parties'': *R v Hogan* [1974] 2 All ER 142. In *DPP v Humphrys* [1977] AC 1, the House of Lords held that issue estoppel was not part of the criminal law of England.

issues, separate, trials of. *See* TRIALS, SEPARATE, OF SEPARATE ISSUES.

itemised pay statement. *See* PAY STATEMENT, ITEMISED.

J

J. Justice. (Title of High Court judge.)

jactitation of marriage. *Jactare* = to boast. A petition for jactitation is available to a party when some person wrongly asserts or boasts that he is married to that party. See the S.C.A. 1981, s. 26; the Matrimonial Causes Rules 1977, r. 8(1); *Goldstone* v *Smith* (1922) 38 TLR 403.

Jason clause. Clause inserted in some contracts of affreightment where a dispute may be subject to the USA Harter Act 1893, under which a ship owner is not liable for faults in navigation if he has exercised due diligence in making the vessel seaworthy. See *The Jason* (1912) 225 US 32. For a revised clause, see *Drew Brown Ltd* v *Orient Trader* [1973] 2 Lloyd's Rep 174.

JCPC. Judicial Committee of the Privy Council (qv).

jetsam. Equipment or cargo of a ship which is cast overboard and sinks.

jettison. To throw overboard a ship's cargo or tackle so as to lighten it in an emergency. (The first reported case is *Morse's Case* (1609) 12 Coke R 63.) See *Milward* v *Hibbert* (1842) 3 QB 120.

John Doe. *See* DOE, JOHN.

joinder of causes of action. The joining in one action of several causes of action against the same defendant. Joinder is not necessarily final and severance may be ordered. See O. 15, r. 1; *Child* v *Stenning* (1877) 46 LJ Ch 523; *Bendir* v *Anson* [1936] 3 All ER 326.

joinder of charges. "Charges for any offences may be joined in the same indictment if those charges are founded on the same facts or form or are a part of a series of offences of the same or a similar character": Indictment Rules 1971, r. 9. See also *In re Clayton* [1983] 2 WLR 555.

joinder of documents. Phrase referring to the formation of, eg, a memorandum by two or more documents read together, so as to satisfy the Statute of Frauds 1677, s. 4, or the L.P.A. 1925, s. 40. See *Reading Trust Ltd* v *Spero* [1930] KB 492; *Timmins* v *Moreland Street Property Co* [1958] Ch 110; and *Smith* v *S Wales Switchgear* [1978] 1 All ER 18.

joinder of offenders. The joint indictment (qv) of two or more persons alleged to have joined in the commission of an offence. Only in a very exceptional case is it wise to order separate trials when two or more are jointly charged with participation in one criminal offence. See *R* v *Grondkowski* [1946] KB 369; *R* v *Moghal* [1977] Crim LR 373.

joinder of parties. The joining together (as plaintiffs or defendants) of two or more persons in a single action, eg, as where, if separate actions were brought by or against each of them, there would arise in all the actions some common question of fact or law. See O. 15, r. 4.

joint account clause. Statement inserted in a mortgage (qv) where two or more persons had lent money, declaring that on the death of one mortgagee, the survivor's receipt would suffice as a discharge for the money. See the L.P.A. 1925, s. 111.

joint heir. Co-heir. *See* HEIR.

joint industrial councils. Set up following *Report of the Committee on Relations between Employers and Employed* (1918) for the purpose of industry-wide bargaining. They consist of equal numbers of persons appointed by employers and employees. Wages councils (qv) may be converted by the Secretary of State into statutory joint industrial councils: Wages Councils Act 1979, ss. 10, 14, Schs 1, 2.

jointly and severally. Persons who are jointly and severally bound render themselves liable not only to a joint action against them, but also to separate actions against them individually.

joint mortgage. A mortgage made to

persons jointly. The mortgage money is considered as having been lent on joint account so that a survivor may give a good receipt. See the L.P.A. 1925, s. 111. *See* MORTGAGE.

joint obligation. A bond entered into jointly by two or more persons. All of those persons must sue, or be sued, upon the bond together. A release given to one will release all.

joint purchase. Where X and Y purchase property in Y's name there is generally a resulting trust (qv) in favour of X as a proportionate beneficiary (as to the money he advanced). See *Wray v Steele* (1814) 2 Ves & B 388; *Jones v Maynard* [1951] Ch 572.

jointress. A woman entitled to jointure (qv).

Joint Scrutiny Committee. A committee set up by Parliament (qv), comprising seven members from each House to consider statutory instruments in draft, schemes requiring approval by statutory instrument, etc. *See* STATUTORY INSTRUMENTS.

joint-stock company. Business unit based on the division of its capital into shares, its profits being distributed in proportion to number of shares held by investors.

joint tenancy. Existed where land was held by two or more persons under a grant without words which indicated that they were to hold separate and distinct shares (eg, "to X and Y in fee simple"). Each joint tenant was possessed of the property "by every part and by the whole". Possession was based on the "four unities" (qv) of possession, interest, time (of vesting) and title. Under the L.P.A. 1925, s. 36, joint tenants hold legal estate on trust for sale. Such a tenancy may be determined by: alienation to a stranger; acquisition by one tenant of a larger estate; agreed sale; partition; mutual agreement; any course of dealing suggesting that "the interests of all were mutually treated as constituting a tenancy in common": *Burgess v Rawnsley* [1975] Ch 429.

joint tortfeasors. Persons whose shares in the commission of a tort (qv) have resulted from concerted action in the furtherance of a common design. Examples: principal and agent; partners. Their liability is joint and several and the release under seal (or by way of accord and satisfaction (qv)) releases all (but this is not so in the case of concurrent tortfeasors (qv)). See *The Koursk* [1924] P 140; *Semtex v Gladstone* [1954] 1 WLR 945; and *Ronex Properties Ltd v John Laing Ltd* [1982] 3 WLR 875. See also the Civil Liability (Contribution) Act 1978 for the liability of tortfeasors *inter se.*

jointure. 1. A joint interest limited to husband and wife. 2. An estate (qv) settled on a wife, taken by her in place of dower (qv).

joint venture. A partnership of a temporary nature, eg, as where merchants in different countries join in an export transaction on their joint account. On completion of the venture the partnership comes to an end.

joint will. One document in which two or more persons incorporate their testamentary wishes. It takes effect as the separate wills of the persons who have made it. See *Re Duddell* [1932] 1 Ch 585. *See* WILL.

Journals. The authentic record of proceedings of the Lords and Commons, known as the *Journals of the House of Commons*, and the *Journals of the House of Lords*. They date from 1547 (Commons) and 1509 (Lords).

joy riding. A ride taken in a stolen vehicle. It is an offence to take a motor vehicle or other conveyance for one's own or another's use without the consent of the owner or other lawful authority, or knowing that it has been taken without authority to drive it or to allow oneself to be carried in it: Th.A. 1968, s. 12(1).

J.P. Justice of the Peace (qv).

judge. One with power to decide disputes and determine appropriate penalties, etc. In the UK, judges of the High Court, circuit judges and recorders (qqv) are recommended for appointment by the Lord Chancellor. Lords of Appeal in Ordinary, the Lord Chief Justice and the Master of the Rolls are recommended for appointment by the Prime Minister. See the S.C.A. 1981, s. 10. For the precedence of judges of the Supreme Court, see s. 13. A judge is generally appointed from practising barristers (qv). Superior judges are subject to the power of removal only by the Queen on an address presented by both Houses of Parliament (which must originate in the Commons). (The last time a judge was removed in this way was in 1830—Sir Jonah Barrington, an Irish Judge.) Their salaries and pensions are paid direct from the Consolidated Fund (qv). A judge is not liable in tort for any judicial act performed by him within his jurisdiction, or for acts, performed in good faith, in excess of that jurisdiction. See *Fray* v *Blackburn* (1863) 3 B & S 576; *Sirros* v *Moore* [1975] QB 118.

judge advocate. A barrister (qv) appointed by the Office of the Judge Advocate-General (or, in the case of the Navy, a legally qualified serving officer appointed by the convening authority) to sit in a court-martial involving more serious cases.

Judge Advocate-General's Department. This department advises the Secretary of State for Defence and the Defence Council on legal matters relating to the administration of military law, and reviews proceedings of courts-martial.

judge, qualities of. "Patience and gravity of hearing is an essential part of justice; and an over-speaking judge is no well-tuned cymbal": Bacon (*Of Judicature*).

judges' clerks. Clerks attached to the Lord Chief Justice, Master of the Rolls, President of Family Division, Vice-Chancellor, Lords Justices of Appeal and puisne judges of the High Court. They are appointed by the Lord Chancellor. See the S.C.A. 1981, s. 98.

judge's oath. Oath taken by judge on his appointment: "I do swear by Almighty God that . . . I will do right to all manner of people after the laws and usages of this Realm without fear or favour, affection or ill will." See the Promissory Oaths Act 1868; and the S.C.A. 1981, s. 10(4).

judge's order. An order made by a judge in chambers on a summons.

judges, presiding. *See* PRESIDING JUDGES.

Judges' Rules. Code of guidance for the police, last drawn up by the judges of the QBD in 1964, relating to questioning and charging; a slight revision was made in 1979. The rules do not have the force of law, nor does failure to comply with them necessarily render a confession inadmissible: *R* v *Prager* [1972] 1 WLR 260; *R* v *Osborne* [1973] QB 678. The rules include, eg, the "formal caution" given when a person is formally charged or told that he may be prosecuted: "Do you wish to say anything? You are not obliged to say anything unless you wish to do so, but whatever you say will be taken down in writing and may be given in evidence." Replacement by a statutory code of practice was suggested in Report of Commission on Criminal Procedure 1981 (Cmnd 8092).

judge, undue intervention of. "The judge's part . . . is to hearken to the evidence, only himself asking questions of witnesses when it is necessary to clear up any point that has been overlooked or left obscure; to see that the advocates behave themselves and keep to the rules laid down by law; to exclude irrelevancies and discourage repetition; to make sure by wise intervention that he follows the points that the advocates are making and can assess their work; and at the end to make up his mind where the truth lies. If he goes beyond this, he drops the mantle of a judge and assumes the role of an advocate: and the change does not become him well": *per* Lord Denning in *Jones* v *NCB* [1957] 2 QB 55. See *R* v *Winter* (1982) 74 Cr App R 16.

judgment. A formal decision made and pronounced by a court of law or other tribunal. It may include the reasoning leading to the decision. See the C.J.J.A. 1982, s. 18(2).

judgment by consent. Voluntary settlement of an action (qv). *See also* CONSENT JUDGMENT.

judgment creditor. *See* CREDITOR.

judgment debt. A sum payable under a judgment or order enforceable by a court (not being a magistrates' court (qv)); or order of a magistrates' court for payment of money recoverable summarily as a civil debt; or any order of any court which is enforceable as if it were for the payment of money so recoverable.

judgment debtor. One against whom judgment has been given for a sum of money, whose property may be taken in execution.

judgment, entering. Procedure whereby, after a judgment in an action has been given and drawn up, it is presented for entry and entered by an officer "in the book kept for the purpose": O. 42, r. 5(1). Party presenting judgment must produce an associate's certificate, pleadings, etc.

judgment in default. *See* DEFAULT.

judgment, mistakes in. *See* SLIP RULE.

judgment, reversal of. *See* REVERSAL OF JUDGMENT.

judgments, enforcement of. In the case of judgments for payment of money, they may be enforced: in the High Court (qv) under O. 45, r. 1, by writ of *fi.fa.* (qv), garnishee proceedings (qv), charging order, appointment of receiver, order of committal, writ of sequestration (qv); in the county court (qv) by judgment summons and order for attachment of earnings. In case of judgments for possession of land, enforcement may be by writ of possession. In case of judgments for delivery of goods, enforcement may be by writ of delivery. In case of judgments relating to performance of or abstention from some act, enforcement may be by order of committal or writ of sequestration. See also the C.J.J.A. 1982, s. 4.

judgment, summary. *See* SUMMARY JUDGMENT UNDER ORDER 14.

judgment summons. Procedure for enforcing judgments of the High Court and county court.

judicial act. An act resulting from the exercise of judicial power, eg, determination by the court of a question of rights. "No action lies for acts done or words spoken by a judge in the exercise of his judicial office, although his motive is malicious and the acts or words are not done or spoken in the honest exercise of his

office": *Anderson* v *Gorrie* [1895] 1 QB 668. *See* JUDICIAL IMMUNITY.

Judicial Committee of the Privy Council. Created by the Judicial Committee Act 1833, amended by the Appellate Jurisdiction Acts 1876–1947. Consists of the Lord Chancellor, Lord President, ex-Lord President and Lords of Appeal in Ordinary but can also include members of the Privy Council (qv) who have held high judicial office. Its jurisdiction includes: appeals from courts outside the UK; appeals from ecclesiastical courts (qv); appeals from medical tribunals. It does not deliver a judgment, but tenders advice to the Sovereign, who acts on the report and approves an appropriate Order in Council. It is not bound by its own previous decisions. Dissenting opinions may be delivered in open court: Judicial Committee (Dissenting Opinions) Order in Council 1966. Decisions are not binding on English courts, but are treated by them as persuasive. See, eg, *Thomas* v *The Queen* [1980] AC 125.

judicial control of jury. *See* JURY, JUDICIAL CONTROL OF.

judicial decision, requisites of. A judicial decision presupposes an existing dispute between two or more parties and involves: presentation of case by parties to dispute; ascertainment of fact by means of evidence adduced by parties; submission of legal arguments; decision which disposes of the whole matter by a finding on disputed facts and an application of law of the land to facts so found including, where necessary, ruling on any disputed question of law: Committee on Ministers' Powers 1932, Cmd 4060.

judicial decision, statement of reasons for. *See* COURTS' DECISIONS, STATEMENTS OF REASONS FOR.

judicial dicta. *See* OBITER DICTUM.

judicial discretion. *See* DISCRETION, JUDICIAL.

judicial evidence. *See* EVIDENCE, JUDICIAL.

judicial function, delegation of. In general, judicial functions may not be delegated: see *R* v *Gateshead Justices ex p Tesco* [1981] QB 470.

judicial immunity. "Every judge of the courts of this land—from the highest to the lowest—should be protected to the same degree, and liable to the same degree . . . Each should be protected from liability to damages when he is acting judicially. Each should be able to do his work in complete independence and free from fear . . . Nothing will make him liable except it be shown that he was not acting judicially, knowing that he had no jurisdiction to do it": *Sirros* v *Moore* [1975] QB 118. *See* IMMUNITY.

judicial independence. Practice in the UK whereby judges are freed from outside pressures. Secured by, eg, the charging of judges' salaries on the Consolidated Fund (qv), separation of judiciary from Parliament, security of tenure of office, judicial immunity (qv).

judicial notice. Known also as "judicial cognisance". Means "those facts which a judge can be called upon to receive and to act upon either from his general knowledge of them, or from enquiries to be made by himself for his own information from sources to which it is proper for him to refer": *Commonwealth Shipping Representative* v *P & O Branch Services* [1923] AC 191. Examples of such facts are: territorial and geographical divisions; matters of common and certain knowledge; law and custom. The doctrine may extend also to juries in relation to matters within their everyday experience and knowledge. See the I.A. 1978, s. 3; the B.A. 1914, s. 142; and the European Communities Act 1972, s. 3(2).

judicial precedent. *See* PRECEDENT.

judicial proceedings, reporting of. Publication of reports of proceedings, regulated by, eg, the Judicial Proceedings (Regulation of Reports) Act 1926; and the Domestic and Appellate Proceedings Act 1968. Reports of nullity cases and cases concerning children usually carry initials only of parties. See also the M.C.A. 1980, s. 69.

judicial review. Control exercised by courts over the procedure of subordinate bodies, which may result in grant of prerogative orders (qv) or declaration (qv) stating a person's rights. It is concerned not with the decision of which review is sought, but with the decision-making process: *R* v *Chief Constable of W Wales Police ex p Evans* [1982] 1 WLR 1155.

judicial review, application for. "No application for review shall be made unless leave of the Court has been obtained . . . The Court shall not grant leave unless it considers that the applicant has sufficient interest in the matter to which the application relates": O. 53, r. 3(1), (5). See the S.C.A. 1981, s. 31; *R* v *IRC ex p National Federation of Self Employed Ltd* [1982] AC 617; *R* v *Felixstowe Justices ex p Baldwin* (1981) 72 Cr App R 131; *Millbanks* v *Secretary of State for Home Affairs* (1982) (*The Times*, 26.11.1982).

judicial separation. Remedy based on a judicial decree under which it becomes no longer necessary for the petitioner to cohabit with the respondent. A petition may be presented by either party on grounds of, eg, the respondent's adultery and the petitioner's finding it intolerable to live with the respondent, desertion for a period of two years by the respondent. See the Mat.C.A. 1973, s. 17.

judicial trustee. "Any fit and proper person nominated for the purpose in the application [by a settlor, beneficiary or trustee (qqv)] may be appointed a judicial trustee, and, in the absence of such nomination, or if the court is not satisfied of the fitness of a person so nominated, an official of the court may be appointed": Judicial Trustees Act 1896, s. 1(3). See the A.J.A. 1982, s. 57. He must audit accounts annually, on request of a beneficiary (qv) or trustee, and, on appointment, exercises all the powers of any other trustee. *See* TRUST.

judicial writ. *See* WRIT.

judiciary. Term applied to the judges collectively.

judiciary, higher. Lords of Appeal in Ordinary, Judges of the Supreme Court of England and Wales, judges of the Court of Session and Judges of the Supreme Court of N Ireland: Judicial Pensions Act 1981, s. 1.

judicis est jus dicere, non dare. It is for the judge to administer, not to make, law.

judicium Dei. Judgment of God. Principle at the basis of trial by ordeal (qv).

judicium rusticum. Phrase used, in a derisive sense, to refer to rough justice. For the use of the phrase see *Tito* v *A.-G.* [1977] Ch 106.

junior barrister. 1. A barrister who is not a Queen's Counsel (qv). 2. The junior of two counsel appearing for a party.

jura in personam. Rights *in personam* (qv).

jura in rem. Rights *in rem* (qv).

jura in re propria. Rights over one's own property.

jura regalia. Royal rights.

jurat. *Jura* = to swear. 1. Certificate which is part of an affidavit (qv) stating where, when, before whom it was made. See O. 41. 2. Magistrate in the Channel Islands.

juridical. Relating to, or acting in, the administration of justice. "Juridical days" are those on which the courts are open.

jurimetrics. Term introduced into legal vocabulary by the American writer on jurisprudence, Lee Loevinger: "Jurimetrics is concerned with such matters as the quantitative analysis of judicial behaviour, the application of communication and information theory to legal expression, the use of mathematical logic in law, the retrieval of legal data by electronic and mechanical means, and the formulation of a calculus of legal predictability" (*Law and Contemporary Problems*, Duke University, USA).

jurisdiction. 1. Power of a court to hear and decide on a case. 2. Authority to legislate. 3. Territorial limits within which legal authority may be exercised. In the case of the English courts, held to comprise England, Wales, Berwick-on-Tweed and those parts of the sea claimed as territorial waters: *R* v *Kent Justices, ex p Lye* [1967] 2 QB 153. 4. The term "jurisdictional act" is used to mean a legislative, administrative or judicial measure of the Sovereign.

jurisdictional error. Error committed when, eg, an administrative agency acts beyond the jurisdiction conferred on it. See *Pearlman* v *Keepers and Governors of Harrow School* [1979] 1 All ER 365; and *Re Racal Communications Ltd* [1980] 2 All ER 634.

jurisdiction, ouster of. *See* OUSTER OF JURISDICTION.

jurisdiction, plea to. Plea (now virtually obsolete) that the court lacks jurisdiction to try the defendant.

jurisdiction, service out of the. Serving of a writ based on leave granted under O. 11. Application is made *ex parte* to a master in chambers, based on an affidavit (qv) showing grounds upon which it is made. See *The Hagen* [1908] P 189; *BP Exploration Co* v *Hunt* [1976] 3 All ER 879.

juris et de jure. Of law and from law. Term applied to irrebuttable presumptions (qv).

juris praecepta sunt haec. These are the precepts of the law [to live honestly, to hurt no person, to give every man his due]: Justinian's *Institutes. See* HONESTE VIVERE.

jurisprudence. The science or philosophy of law. "Recorded thinking about the source, nature, end and efficiency of law, substantive and adjective, and of legal institutions": Reuschlein (1951).

juristic act. *See* ACT, JURISTIC.

juristic person. *See* ARTIFICIAL PERSON.

juror. The member of a jury. Among those ineligible, disqualified or excused from service as jurors are: judges, barristers, police officers, clergy, the mentally ill, members of Parliament, members of HM Forces, doctors, etc. See the Juries Act 1974, Sch 1. *See* JURY.

jurors' book. List of those in each county who were qualified to serve as jurors. See now the Juries Act 1974, s. 3 (authorising the use of electoral registers).

juror's oath. "I swear by Almighty God that I will faithfully try the several issues joined between Our Sovereign Lady the Queen and the prisoner at the bar and give a true verdict according to the evidence": Practice Note [1957] 1 All ER 290.

jury. A body of persons selected according to the law and sworn to give a verdict on some matter according to the evidence. See the S.C.A. 1981, s. 69; and O. 33, r. 5. In general, the jury decides facts; the judge decides question of law. Picked from those registered as electors, aged 18–65, who have been resident in the UK for at least five years since the age of 13: Juries Act 1974, s. 1. Those ineligible include barristers and solicitors, clergy, mentally ill, etc. Those disqualified include those who have been sentenced in the UK to imprisonment for five years or more. "Whenever a man is on trial for serious crime, or when in a civil case a man's honour or integrity is at stake, or when one or other party must be deliberately lying, then trial by jury has no equal": *Ward* v *James* [1966] 1 QB 273. *See* CHALLENGE TO JURY.

jury, challenge to. *See* CHALLENGE TO JURY.

jury, foreman of. *See* FOREMAN OF JURY.

jury, grand. Originated in the Assize of Clarendon 1166. Comprised 12–23 persons before whom a bill of indictment had to be placed. Abolished under the C.J.A. 1948.

jury, hung. Jury unable to agree on any verdict.

jury, judicial control of. Ways in which a judge exercises control over a jury, as where, eg, he rules that there is no case to answer, or that there is insufficient evidence on an issue (so that the jury does not consider it), or by his summing up. See also the Criminal Appeal Act 1968, s. 2(1).

jury, petty. Twelve "good and lawful men" called by a sheriff (qv) to try issues of fact in a criminal charge.

jury, retirement of. *See* RETIREMENT OF JURY.

jury's deliberations, confidentiality of. It is a contempt of court to obtain, disclose or solicit a jury's deliberations, arguments or votes cast: Contempt of Court Act 1981, s. 8.

jury, special. Jury formerly drawn from a panel of persons with property of a certain rateable value. Abolished under the Courts Act 1971, s. 40(1).

jury, vetting. The checking of potential jurors so as to exclude those who might be disqualified. Held to be not unlawful: see *R* v *Mason* [1981] QB 881. See *R* v *Sheffield Crown Court ex p Brownlow* (1980) 71 Cr App R 157; and *A.-G.'s Guidelines* (2.8.1980).

jus. A right, deriving from a rule of law—a concept of Roman law. 1. *Jus naturale:* "what nature has taught all living things" (an ideal to which the law should seek to conform). 2. *Jus gentium:* the law of peoples, ie, law of universal application. 3. *Jus civile:* "the law each people has settled for itself". Used also to refer to the entire *corpus* of Roman Law.

jus accrescendi inter mercatores pro beneficio commercii locum non habet. For the benefit of commerce, the right of survivorship (qv) among merchants is not known.

jus dicere. To say what the law is. "Judges ought to remember that their office is *jus dicere* and not *jus dare*; to interpret law, and not to make law, or give law": Bacon (*Of Judicature*). "Whoever hath an absolute authority to interpret any written or spoken laws, it is he who is truly the law-giver to all intents and purposes and not the person who first wrote or spoke them": Bishop Hoadly, in a sermon before George I in 1717.

jus disponendi. The right of disposition.

jus in re aliena. A right over the property of another (eg, the right to enforce an encumbrance (qv)), as compared with *jus in re propria* (a right of the owner of a chattel).

jus mariti. A husband's right. The right to a wife's chattels acquired on marriage, prior to the Married Women's Property Act 1882.

jus pascendi. The right of grazing.

jus quaesitum tertio. Right on account of third parties. Refers to a contract which purports to confer rights on a third party. "Our law knows nothing of a *jus quaesitum tertio* arising by way of contract. Such a right may be conferred by way of property, as, for example, under a trust, but it cannot be conferred on a stranger to a contract as a right to enforce the contract *in personam*": *Dunlop Pneumatic Tyre Co*

Ltd v *Selfridge & Co Ltd* [1915] AC 847. See *Beswick* v *Beswick* [1968] AC 58. *See* CONTRACT.

jus soli. Law of the "place of one's birth". Principle that nationality by birth is determined by the country in which the birth takes place. It no longer applies in English law, following the B.N.A. 1981: see s. 1.

jus spatiandi et manendi. The right to stray and remain. May form an easement (qv), as in the right to use a garden. See *Re Ellenborough Park* [1956] Ch 131.

just and equitable. Phrase used, eg, in company law, relating to a petition to wind up a company when the court is of opinion that it is "just and equitable" that it should be wound up. Companies have been wound up under this head because of, eg, deadlock among members, the company's insolvency; or the company has misapplied funds. See the Cos.A. 1948, s. 222; *Ebrahimi* v *Westbourne Galleries Ltd* [1972] 2 All ER 492; *Re A & BC Chewing Gum Ltd* [1975] 1 WLR 579. *See* COMPANY.

jus tertii. Right of a third person. Defence set up by X who is apparently liable to Y and, on being sued by Y, asserts that the property or money claimed by Y belongs by paramount title to Z. In general, a wrongdoer may not set up *jus tertii* (but see the Torts (Interference with Goods) Act 1979, s. 8(1)). See *Armory* v *Delamirie* (1721) 1 Stra 505 (in relation to conversion (qv)); *Asher* v *Whitlock* (1865) LR 1 QB 1 (in relation to ejectment (qv)).

justice. 1. The basic value underlying a system of law, or the objective which that system seeks to attain. 2. The virtue which results in each person receiving his due: Justinian. 3. The impartial resolution of disputes arising from conflicting claims. 4. "Justice is the correct application of a law, as opposed to arbitrariness": Ross.

justice, commutative, distributive and corrective. Jurisprudential concept derived from Aristotle. *Commutative justice* is rendering every person the exact measure of his dues. *Distributive justice* is concerned essentially with the allocation of rights, duties and burdens among the members of a community so that equilibrium is ensured. ("It orders the equal treatment of those equal before the law": Friedmann.) *Corrective* (or "remedial") *justice* corrects disequilibrium in a community. (It "is usually administered by a court or other organ invested with judicial or quasi-judicial powers": Bodenheimer.)

justice, natural. The *corpus* of basic general principles to be followed in the adjudication of any matter. "Justice that is simple or elementary, as distinct from justice that is complex, sophisticated and technical": *John* v *Rees* [1970] Ch 345. "There must be due inquiry. The accused person must have notice of what he is accused. He must have an opportunity of being heard, and the decision must be honestly arrived at after he has had a full opportunity of being heard": *Leeson* v *General Medical Council* (1889) 43 Ch D 366. "It is to be implied, unless the contrary appears, that Parliament does not authorise by [an] Act the exercise of powers in breach of the principles of natural justice": *Fairmount Investments Ltd* v *Secretary of State for the Environment* [1976] 2 All ER 865. See *Local Government Board* v *Arlidge* [1915] AC 120; *Stevenson* v *United Road Transport Union* [1976] 3 All ER 28.

justice, open. *See* OPEN JUSTICE.

justice, perverting the course of. *See* PERVERTING THE COURSE OF JUSTICE.

justice, retributive. Theory of punishment based on a supposed moral link between wrong-doing and justice. Offenders, it is claimed, ought to be punished under the law in proportion to their guilt and the injury inflicted on their victims.

justices' clerks. *See* MAGISTRATES' CLERKS.

justices in eyre. Justices who travelled throughout the realm so as to try actions and investigate affairs in the counties. *See* EYRE.

justices of the peace. Lay magistrates appointed directly by the Lord Chancellor to the magistrates' courts which hear and determine charges relating to summary offences and those which may be tried on indictment without jury. Justices of the Peace may sit as examining justices to conduct preliminary enquiries. Originated in a royal proclamation of the late twelfth century, creating "knights of the peace" to aid the sheriff (qv) in the enforcement of law. Known later as *custodes pacis* (keepers of the peace) and, from *c*. 1360, as "justices of the peace". See the Justices of the Peace Act 1979. *See* MAGISTRATES' COURTS.

justifiable homicide. The killing of one person by another where no blame attaches to the killer, eg, as in the carrying out of an authorised death sentence. See *A.-G. for N Ireland's Reference (No 1 of 1975)* [1977] AC 105. *See* HOMICIDE.

justification. A defence which admits the plaintiff's allegations, but pleads that the events referred to were justifiable. Example: in libel (qv) the defendant admits that he published the words complained of, but pleads that they were true. The defendant must justify the precise imputation on which the plaintiff's allegation is founded. "Defendant has to prove not only that the facts are truly stated but also that any comments upon

them are correct": *Cooper* v *Lawson* (1838) 8 A & E 746. See the Defamation Act 1952, s. 5; O. 82; and *Harakas* v *Baltic Shipping Exchange* [1982] 1 WLR 958.

justifying bail. Proof of sufficiency of bail or of sureties in relation to their ownership of property. *See* BAIL.

juvenile courts. Magistrates' courts (qv) exercising jurisdiction over offences committed by, and other matters relating to children (under 14) and young persons (14–16). They consist of a chairman and other justices. At least one member of each court must be a woman. Proceedings are not generally open to the public, nor may the identity of the juvenile be published unless the court or Home Secretary so orders. See the C. & Y.P.A. 1969; the Magistrates' Courts (Children and Young Persons) Rules 1970; and the M.C.A. 1980, ss. 29, 146.

juvenile offenders. Term applied to children (under 14) and young persons (14–16). For the right to trial by jury see *R* v *Islington Juvenile Court, ex p Daley* [1982] 3 WLR (House of Lords decision on when a juvenile becomes an adult, with reference to the M.C.A. 1980, ss. 18(1), 24 (1)).

K

kangaroo closure. A form of closure of a debate in Parliament (qv) in which, on report and committee stage, the chairman "jumps over" some amendments, which are left undiscussed, to other amendments and clauses.

kangaroo court. A mock hearing in which elementary and generally accepted norms of justice are not observed.

K.B. King's Bench. *See* COURT OF KING'S BENCH.

K.C. King's Counsel.

keeping house. An act of bankruptcy (see B.A. 1914, s. 1(1) (*d*)) constituted by the failure of a debtor to meet a creditor who calls for payment, or by his keeping to his house so as to avoid his creditors. See *Dudley* v *Vaughan* (1808) 1 Camp 271. *See* BANKRUPTCY, ACTS OF.

keeping term. *See* TERM.

keeping the peace. In essence, being of good behaviour. A person can be bound over by a magistrate (qv) to keep the peace. See the M.C.A. 1980, ss. 115, 116; *Veater* v *G* [1981] 1 WLR 567.

kidnapping. The offence of stealing, carrying away or secreting of some person against his will or that of his guardians. The use of force or fraud is an essential element: *R* v *Hale* [1974] 1 All ER 1107. See *R* v *Reid* [1972] 1 QB 299; *R* v *Ogden* (1973) 58 Cr App R 457; *R* v *Wellard* [1978] 1 WLR 921.

kill. To cause the death of another by some act or omission. *See* HOMICIDE; MURDER.

killing, acquisition of property by. A beneficiary (qv) who, by some criminal act kills the testator, or next of kin who kills an intestate, will not be allowed to benefit from his crime. See *Cleaver* v *Mutual Reserve Fund Life Association Ltd* [1892] 1 QB 147; *Re Crippen* [1911] P 108; *Re Giles* [1972] Ch 544. See also the Forfeiture Act 1982.

kin. Relationship by blood.

King. *See* MONARCH; SOVEREIGN.

King can do no wrong. A rule of law, part of the so-called "prerogative of perfection", under which the Crown could not be sued at common law. The position was changed under the Crown Proceedings Act 1947.

King's (Queen's) Bench, Court of. *See* COURT OF KING'S (QUEEN'S) BENCH.

Kings, Divine Right of. *See* DIVINE RIGHT OF KINGS.

King's (Queen's) Peace. *See* PEACE OF THE KING.

knight service. A feudal tenure, based on military service to the Sovereign in return for the grant of land. Its incidents included homage (qv), aids, reliefs, ransom and wardship. Abolished under the Tenures Abolition Act 1660.

knock for knock. An agreement under which insurance agencies pay those they have insured, and do not insist on actions being brought by one party against the other. See *Hobbs* v *Marlowe* [1977] 2 All ER 241.

knock-out agreement. An agreement among bidders at an auction (qv) that some of them shall desist from bidding. Illegal when entered into by a dealer. See the Auctions (Bidding Agreements) Acts 1927 and 1969; *Rawlings* v *General Trading Co* [1920] 3 KB 30.

know-how. Knowledge of how to accomplish something. Expert skill. "Any industrial information and techniques likely to assist in the manufacture or processing of goods or materials . . .": Income and Corporation Taxes Act 1970, s. 386(7). "It indicates the way in which a skilled man does his job, and is an expression of his individual skill and experience": *Stevenson, Jordan and Harrison* v *Macdonald & Evans* [1952] 1 TLR 101. See also *Rolls-Royce* v *IRC* [1962] 1 WLR 425. An EEC Notice of 1968 states that obligations regarding an exchange of know-how are acceptable provided they are reciprocal and non-exclusive: [1968] CMLR D5.

knowledge. Awareness of, or acquaintance with, fact or truth. "The case of shutting the eyes is actual knowledge in the eyes of the law; . . . the legal conception of constructive knowledge, generally speaking, has no place in the criminal law": *per* Devlin J in *Roper* v *Taylor's Central Garage* [1951] 2 TLR 284. See *R* v *Hallam* [1957] 1 QB 569; and *Warner* v *Metropolitan Police Commissioner* [1969] 2 AC 256.

L

labour, direct. *See* DIRECT LABOUR ORGANISATIONS.

labour, manual. *See* MANUAL LABOUR.

laches. *Lasche* = indolent. Negligence and unreasonable delay in the assertion of a right will defeat equities. "A court of equity has always refused its aid to stale demands where a party has slept upon his rights and acquiesced for a great length of time. Nothing can call forth this court into activity but conscience, good faith and reasonable diligence": *Smith* v *Clay* (1767) Amb 645. See *Lindsay Petroleum Co* v *Hurd* (1874) 22 WR 492; *Wroth* v *Tyler* [1974] Ch 30.

Lady Day. A quarter-day (qv). 25th March.

laenland. Loanland. Anglo-Saxon land holding, specifically land which was leased without written charter, often involving incidents of tenure, eg, military service. Inheritable, but limited generally to "three lives", ie, three holders in succession.

laesae majestatis, crimen. See CRIMEN LAESAE MAJESTATIS.

lagan. Known also as *ligan*. Goods thrown into the sea, with an attached buoy, so that they can be found again.

land. 1. "Land in the legal signification comprehendeth any ground, soil or earth whatsoever, as meadows, pastures, woods, moor, waters, marshes, furzes and heath . . . It legally includeth also all castles, houses and other buildings": Coke. 2. "'Land' includes land of any tenure, and mines and minerals, whether or not held apart from the surface, buildings or parts of buildings (whether the division is horizontal, vertical, or made in any other way) and other corporeal hereditaments; also a manor, an advowson, and a rent and other incorporeal hereditaments, and an easement, right, privilege, or benefit in, over, or derived from land . . .": L.P.A. 1925, s. 205(1) (x). See the I.A. 1978, Sch 1.

land certificate. *See* CERTIFICATE, LAND.

land charges. Those rights and interests affecting land, eg, estate contracts (qv), restrictive covenants (qv), general equitable charges and easements (qv). See the L.C.A. 1972.

land charges, local. *See* LOCAL LAND CHARGES.

land charges, register of. A register kept in the Land Charges Department of the Land Registry, recording six classes of charge: (1) *Class A.* Rent, or annuities, or principal money payable by instalments, not created by deed, but by charge on land created pursuant to some person's application under the provisions of statute; (2) *Class B.* Statutory land charges arising automatically; (3) *Class C.* Puisne mortgages, limited owner's charges, estate contracts, general equitable charges; (4) *Class D.* Charge for capital transfer tax, restrictive covenants, equitable easements; (5) *Class E.* Annuities created before 1st January 1926 and not registered as annuities; (6) *Class F.* Those affecting land by virtue of the Matrimonial Homes Act 1967 and the Matrimonial Proceedings and Property Act 1970. See *Williams and Glyn's Bank* v *Boland* [1980] 2 All ER 408; Law Commission Report (1982, Cmnd 8638). See the L.C.A. 1972; and the Local Land Charges Act 1975.

land, compulsory purchase of. The acquisition of land, freehold or leasehold by an authority under statute, commencing with a compulsory purchase order, followed, where necessary, by the hearing of objections. The expropriated owner must be compensated by the acquiring authority for the land taken, by way of purchase price, for any damage directly consequent on the taking and for depreciation of land he retains. Basis of compensation may be "market value", ie, the amount which the land if sold in the open market by a willing seller might be expected to realise. See, eg, the Land Compensation Acts 1961 and 1973; and the Acquisition of Land Act 1981. *See* COMPULSORY PURCHASE ORDER.

land, development. *See* DEVELOPMENT LAND.

land holding, registration of public. The Secretary of State is empowered to compile a register of freehold and leasehold interests owned by specified public bodies in certain areas: L.G.P.L.A. 1980, Part X.

land improvement company. Company (qv) authorised by an Act of Parliament to execute, or make an advance of money for the execution of, improvements of land.

landlord. The owner or holder of land (qv) leased to another. Includes, under the Rent Act 1977, s. 152(1), "any person from time to time deriving title under the original landlord and also includes, in relation to any dwelling-house, any person other than the tenant who is, or but for Part VII of this Act would be, entitled to possession of the dwelling-house". See also the H.A. 1980, Sch 19, para 18.

landlord, provision of services by. Provision of "attendance, heating or lighting, the supply of hot water and any other privilege or facility connected with the occupancy of a dwelling, other than a privilege or facility requisite for the purposes of access, cold water supply or sanitary accommodation": Rent Act 1977, s. 19(8). See now the H.A. 1980, s. 136, Sch 19.

land planning control. System administered by a central authority (Department of Environment) and local planning authorities (ie, county, district councils (qqv)). The county planning authority formulates policy and general proposals which it submits to the Secretary of State, who appoints persons to examine proposals publicly. Local plans are then published. See the T.C.P.A. 1962 and 1971; the Inquiries Procedure Rules 1974; and the Acquisition of Land Act 1981, Part I.

land registration. System of registra-

tion of title based on the Land Registration Acts and Rules. Its purpose is the simplification of transfers of land. Title is entered in a central register and the time needed for effective transfer of title is reduced. The main parts of the register are: Property (eg, description of land); Proprietorship (eg, whether title is absolute); Charges (eg, mortgages, restrictive covenants). In a sense, title is guaranteed by the state. See the L.R.A. 1925, 1936, 1966; the L.C.A. 1972; the A.J.A. 1977, ss. 24, 25; and the A.J.A. 1982, s. 66.

Land Registry registers. Five registers are kept: pending actions; annuities; writs and orders affecting land; deeds of arrangement affecting land; land charges. See the L.C.A. 1972; and the Local Land Charges Act 1975. *See* LAND CHARGES REGISTER.

Lands Tribunal. Set up under the Lands Tribunal Act 1949. Consists of lawyers and valuers who hear disputes relating, eg, to compulsory purchase, assessment of compensation. Appeal lies to the Court of Appeal (qv) on a point of law by way of case stated, within 6 weeks of the decision by the Tribunal, and thence to the Lords. See the Land Compensation Act 1961, ss. 1–4; the L.P.A. 1969, s. 28; and S.I. 1981/105.

land tax. Tax on land and houses, based on valuation of estates. Abolished by the Finance Act 1963, s. 68.

lapse. Failure of a legacy (qv) or devise (qv) because of the death of the intended legatee or devisee before that of the testator. Doctrine of lapse does not apply: to beneficiaries under a secret trust (qv); in case of entailed interest if the devisee leaves descendants capable of inheriting who are living at the time of the testator's death (and this rule extends under the L.P.A. 1925, s. 130(1) to a similar bequest of personalty); in case of a legacy or devise to a child or other issue of the testator if the legatee or devisee leaves issue living at the time of the testator's death. See the W.A. 1837, ss. 32, 33 (as substituted by the A.J.A. 1982, s. 19).

lapse of offer. An offer is held to have lapsed: on the death either of the offeror or offeree before acceptance; where no time for acceptance is prescribed, by non-acceptance within a reasonable time; by non-acceptance within the time prescribed for acceptance by the offeror. *See* OFFER.

larceny. Theft, under the Larceny Act 1916, s. 1 (repealed by the Th.A. 1968). *Petty larceny* referred to stolen property with a value not exceeding 12 pence; *grand larceny* referred to stolen property with a value exceeding 12 pence. *See* THEFT.

la reyne le veult; la reyne s'avisera. See ROYAL ASSENT.

last opportunity, rule of. So-called rule which allowed a plaintiff to recover, in spite of his own negligence, if the circumstances were such that defendant could have avoided the accident and plaintiff could not. The doctrine is now "gone forever": *per* Lord Denning in *Lloyds Bank* v *Budd* [1982] RTR 80.

last resort, court of. *See* COURT OF LAST RESORT.

latent ambiguity. *See* AMBIGUITY.

latent defect. *See* DEFECT.

Latin jurisdiction, the. Name given in early times to the jurisdiction of the Court of Chancery based on petitions, where proceedings were recorded in Latin. (The Chancellor's equitable jurisdiction was known as "the English jurisdiction", because proceedings were recorded in English.)

latitat. He is hidden. Phrase relating to a writ commanding the sheriff of Middlesex to arrest the defendant and bring him before the court. If the defendant could not be found in Middlesex, the writ was issued to the sheriff of the county in which the defendant was alleged to be hiding, ordering his arrest. Abolished under the Uniformity of Process Act 1832.

law. 1. The written and unwritten body of rules largely derived from custom and formal enactment which are recognised as binding among those persons who constitute a community or state, so that they will be imposed upon and enforced among those persons by appropriate sanctions. 2. One of the rules of law (ie, "a law made by Parliament"). 3.

Jurisprudence (qv). 4. The general condition of a state in which laws are accepted and observed.

law and equity, conflict of. "Wherever there is any conflict or variance between the rules of equity and the rules of the common law . . . the rules of equity shall prevail": S.C.A. 1981, s. 49(1).

law and equity, fusion of. "The innate conservatism of English lawyers may have made them slow to recognise that by the Judicature Act 1873 the two systems of substantive and adjectival law formerly administered by courts of law and equity have surely mingled now": *per* Lord Diplock in *United Scientific Holdings Ltd* v *Burnley BC* [1978] AC 904.

law and fact. "Law is a principle; fact is an event. Law is conceived; fact is actual. Law is a rule of duty; fact is that which has been according to or in contravention of the rule": Black.

law, classification of. Division of law into categories, eg: (1) *Public law*— concerned with relationships of members of the community and the state, eg, constitutional law, criminal law; (2) *Private law*—derived from relationships of members of the community *inter se*, eg, contract, torts.

Law Commission. Permanent body established under the Law Commissions Act 1965, consisting of a chairman and four lawyers of high standing, whose duty it is to keep the law under review with a view to its systematic development and reform, including codification, elimination of anomalies, repeal of obsolete enactments, reduction in number of separate enactments. See also the A.J.A. 1982, s. 64.

law, evolution of. "Law is, of course, neither an unalterable fact of nature, nor a product of intellectual design, but the result of a process of evolution in which a system of rules developed in constant interaction with a changing order of human actions which is distinct from it": F. A. Hayek.

lawful. Warranted or authorised by, or not contrary to, nor forbidden by, the law. *See* LEGAL.

lawful homicide. Excusable or justifiable homicide (qqv).

Law Lords. Lord Chancellor, Lords of Appeal in Ordinary, ex-Lord Chancellors and other peers who have occupied the high ·judicial offices.

law merchant. That source of English law based on the settlement of disputes between merchants and their usages. "It is neither more nor less than the usages of merchants and traders in the different departments of trade, ratified by decisions of courts of law": *Goodwin* v *Robarts* (1875) LR 10 Ex 337. *See* USAGE.

law, natural. Phrase used in jurisprudence (qv) to refer to the so-called "law of nature", ie, a system of justice and its underlying principles, held to be common to all mankind. It may be distinguished from "positive law", ie, the legal rules adopted and enforced in formal fashion by the state.

law officers of the Crown. For England and Wales, the Attorney-General and Solicitor-General; for Scotland, the Lord Advocate and Solicitor-General for Scotland. See the Prosecution of Offenders Act 1979, s. 10.

law of nations. International law (qv).

law, positive. *See* LAW, NATURAL.

law, private and public. *See* PRIVATE LAW; PUBLIC LAW.

law, pure theory of. Theory, promulgated in 1911 by Kelsen, explaining law in terms free from all extraneous, non-legal factors. Law is a coercive order of human behaviour and is built from "legal norms" which are valid only if authorised by legal norms of a higher rank. The norms rest ultimately upon the force of a "basic norm" (*Grundnorm*) eg, that Parliament is sovereign. The basic norm is "a juristic presumption or postulate implicit in legal thinking".

Law Reform Committee. Consists of five judges, four practising barristers, two solicitors and three academic lawyers, appointed by the Lord Chancellor to consider changes which are desirable, having particular regard to judicial decisions.

Law Reports. Law reporting falls into three periods: (1) the Year Books (qv) *c*. 1270–1530; (2) the private reporters (Coke, Dyer, etc) *c*. 1535–1865; (3) the modern semi-official reports from 1865, undertaken by the Incorporated Council of Law Reporting for England and Wales (eg, *Weekly Notes*, up to 1952, and *Weekly Law Reports*, from 1953) and the modern private reports, including, eg, *All England Law Reports*, *Lloyd's Law Reports*. *See* Appendix.

law, rule of. 1. Government based on the general acceptance of the law. 2. A legal rule. 3. Concept outlined by Dicey (*Law of the Constitution*, 1885)— the regular law of the land predominates over and excludes the arbitrary exercise of power by the government, all people are equally subject to the law administered by the ordinary courts and that law is derived from individuals' rights as declared by the courts.

law sittings. *See* SITTINGS.

Law Society. The body which controls solicitors, constituted under the Royal Charter of 1845. It is governed by an elected Council and its objects are "promoting professional improvement and facilitating the acquisition of legal knowledge". Under the Solicitors Act 1974 it may make regulations concerning legal education and training and examinations. In order to practise as a solicitor a person must have been admitted as a solicitor, must be enrolled on the Society's Roll and must have a current practising certificate: Solicitors Act 1974, s. 1. *See* SOLICITOR.

law, sources of EEC. *See* COMMUNITY LAW, SOURCES OF.

law, sources of English. Generally held to include: common law; equity; legislation; custom; law merchant; canon law; Roman law; EEC law.

law, substantive and adjective. *Substantive law* comprises those rules which guide the courts in arriving at decisions. *Adjective law* (or rules of procedure) comprises those rules which determine the course of an action, eg, in which court a case is to be heard.

lawsuit. Contentious litigation.

law, wager of. *See* WAGER OF LAW.

lawyer. One who is a practitioner of the law. *See* LEGAL PROFESSION.

lay days. 1. Days during which a ship is delayed in port. 2. Days allowed by a charterparty (qv) for loading or unloading cargo. They begin to run against the charterer from the time he has notice that the vessel is ready to load: *Fairbridge* v *Pace* (1844) 1 C & K 317.

laying an information. Procedure whereby a magistrate is informed, eg, by a police officer, of a suspected offence. See the M.C.A. 1980, s. 1. "An information is . . . the statement by which the magistrate is informed of the offence for which the summons or warrant is required": *R* v *Hughes* (1879) 4 QBD 614. "No objection shall be allowed to any information . . . for any defect in it in substance or in form, or for any variance between it and the evidence adduced on behalf of the prosecutor or complainant": M.C.A. 1980, s. 123. See *R* v *Gateshead Justices ex p Tesco* [1981] QB 470. An information is laid when received by the office of the clerk to the justices: *R* v *Manchester Stipendiary Magistrate ex p Hill* [1982] 3 WLR 331 (House of Lords consideration of the M.C.A. 1980, s. 127). *See* INFORMATION.

lay magistrates. Unpaid magistrates, as compared with stipendiaries. *See* MAGISTRATES.

lay observer. Appointed to consider complaints made by members of the public concerning the Law Society's handling of complaints about solicitors. He issues an annual report. See the Solicitors Act 1974.

L.C. Lord Chancellor (qv).

L.C.J. Lord Chief Justice (qv).

leader. Leading counsel in a case.

Leader of HM Opposition. *See* OPPOSITION, LEADER OF HM.

Leader of the House. *See* HOUSE, LEADER OF THE.

lead evidence, to. To call or adduce evidence (qv).

leading case. An important case, eg, one which establishes principles so that it is often cited in court.

leading questions. Questions put to a witness (qv) which suggest the desired answer or put the answer into his mouth or, in the case of a disputed matter, permit the reply, "Yes" or "No". Example: "Did you see X at noon in Trafalgar Square on Saturday, 18th October last?" Not generally allowed save, eg, in examination-in-chief (qv), where the matter is only introductory and not material, or in the case of matter already put in evidence by the other side, or in cross-examination. *See* EVIDENCE.

leapfrog procedure. Procedure introduced by the A.J.A. 1969, s. 12, whereby an appeal in civil proceedings can go directly from the High Court (qv) or a Divisional Court (qv) to the House of Lords (qv) without prior appeal to the Court of Appeal (qv). A certificate must be granted by the trial judge after agreement of all parties, and the Lords must grant leave: s. 13. The judge must be satisfied that there is involved a point of law which is of general public importance relating to a matter of statutory construction or a matter in respect of which he feels bound by a previous decision of the Court of Appeal or the House of Lords. For the use of the procedure, see, eg, *Supplementary Benefits Commission* v *Jull* [1980] 3 All ER 65.

lease. A term of years (qv) (see *Re Land and Premises at Liss* [1971] Ch 986), or leasehold (qv), or the document used to bring into existence a term of years. Where L grants a lease to T, L is known as the *lessor*, or *landlord* (qv), and T is known as the *lessee*, or *tenant* (qv).

lease and release. Procedure formerly employed at common law for conveyancing. Vendor (V) bargained and sold land for one year (ie, as leasehold (qv)) to purchaser (P). V was then seised to P's use on the payment of the purchase price. P received legal estate, reversion (qv) remained in V. Then V extinguished his reversion on the next day by deed of release and, as a result, P's leasehold was transformed into fee simple (qv). Release was replaced by deed of grant under the Real Property Act 1845.

lease, assignment of. Disposal by lessee (qv) of his estate in land. Assignment of a legal term must be by deed if it is to be effective at law; an assignment of an informal nature for value may be valid in equity. See the L.P.A. 1925, ss. 52, 146(2); and *Old Grovebury Manor Farm* v *Seymour Plant Ltd (No 2)* [1979] 3 All ER 504. For unreasonable refusal by a landlord to consent to an assignment, see, eg, *Bromley Park Garden Estates Ltd* v *Moss* [1982] 1 WLR 1019.

lease, concurrent. *See* CONCURRENT LEASE.

lease, determination of. A lease may come to an end by: notice; expiry; surrender or merger; becoming a satisfied term (qv); forfeiture; enlargement; frustration.

lease, equitable. *See* EQUITABLE LEASE.

lease, forestry. A lease to the Minister of Agriculture, Fisheries and Food for any purpose for which he is authorised to acquire land. Rent may be nominal for the first 10 years, or variable according to the annual value of timber cut. See also the S.L.A. 1925, s. 48.

lease, future. *See* FUTURE LEASE.

leasehold. The interest, ie, term of years, created by a lease (qv), or agreement for lease. If created by lease it is a *legal leasehold estate*; if created by agreement for lease, it is, in effect, an *equitable lease*. Leasehold estates recognised at law are: term of years; periodic tenancy; tenancy at will; tenancy at sufferance. *See* ESTATE; FREEHOLD; TERM OF YEARS.

leasehold, enfranchisement of. *See* ENFRANCHISEMENT OF TENANCY.

leasehold ownership. That which exists where the tenant (or lessee) is granted exclusive possession of land by the landlord (or lessor) with the intention that he should hold it as the tenant only for a fixed period of time less than that held by the landlord.

leasehold valuation tribunals. Rent assessment committees set up to determine matters under the Leasehold Reform Act 1967, s. 21(1)–(3): H.A. 1980, s. 142, Sch 22.

lease, legal. *See* LEGAL LEASE.

lease, parol. *See* PAROL LEASE.

lease, perpetually renewable. *See* PERPETUALLY RENEWABLE LEASE.

lease, renewal of. Grant of a further term of years in relation to an expiring lease. A contract for renewal of a lease or sub-lease for a term exceeding 60 years from the end of the lease or sub-lease is void: L.P.A. 1922, Sch 15. See also the L.P.A. 1925, s. 149.

leasing scheme. Arrangement whereby houses are rented from a private landlord by some public body (eg, a local authority) which will then sublet to its own tenants. In general, the Rent Acts will not protect the subtenancy granted by the public body.

leave to defend. At the hearing of a summons under O. 14, the master may give the defendant unconditional leave to defend, or conditional leave on such terms as to giving security or time or mode of trial or otherwise as is thought fit.

leet. The jurisdictional district of the old local courts.

legacy. A gift of personal property by will (to a legatee). A legacy may be: (1) *specific* (gift of a specified thing, eg, "my gold wedding ring"); (2) *demonstrative* (qv); (3) *general* (qv); (4) *pecuniary* (sum of money, but an annuity is also included under the A.E.A. 1925, s. 55(1)); (5) *residuary* (ie, residue of personal estate). A legacy may fail because of, eg, disclaimer, lapse, ademption, uncertainty.

legacy, cumulative. Legacy additional to one previously given to the same legatee in the same or a subsequent instrument.

legacy, substitutional. Gift of personalty (qv) by a testator (qv) made in lieu of a previous gift where he indicates that he does not wish the legatee to take both gifts.

legal. 1. In accordance with forms of law. 2. According to common law (qv), but not equity (qv). *See* LAWFUL.

legal aid order. Order made by a court under the Legal Aid Acts 1974, 1982, granting legal aid, eg, where a person desires to appeal.

legal aid scheme. Scheme providing free legal aid to meet the cost of work usually done by a lawyer. Expenses are paid out of a legal aid fund drawn from the Exchequer grant, costs and damages recovered in litigation, and contributions by assisted persons. Free aid is available to persons whose disposable income and capital do not exceed a certain sum. An applicant must show that he has reasonable grounds for asserting or disputing a claim. In criminal proceedings a legal aid order may be made by the court if it appears to be in the interests of justice and the defendant requires financial help to meet the costs of the proceedings. Legal advice and assistance, short of bringing actions, is also available. See the Legal Aid Acts 1974 and 1982; *Megarity* v *Law Society* [1982] AC 81; and the Legal Aid in Criminal Proceedings (Costs) Regulations 1982 (S.I. 1982/1197).

legal assignment. *See* ASSIGNMENT.

legal custody of child. *See* CUSTODY OF CHILD, LEGAL.

legal easement. An easement created by statute, deed or prescription for an interest equivalent to an estate in fee simple absolute in possession (qv) or a term of years absolute (qv). Enforceable against "all the world", unlike the equitable easement (qv) which cannot be enforced against the bona fide purchaser for value of the legal estate without notice. *See* EASEMENT.

legal estates. Estates capable of subsisting at law (qv).

legal executives. Unadmitted staff employed by solicitors, eg, managing clerks. The Institute of Legal Executives is responsible for regulations relating to qualifications, etc. For right of audience in county courts of a Fellow of the Institute, see the County Courts (Right of Audience) Direction 1978.

legal fiction. *See* FICTION.

legality, presumption of. *See* OMNIA PRAESUMUNTUR.

legality, principle of. *See* NULLUM CRIMEN SINE LEGE.

legal lease. A leasehold estate for a term of years created, in general, by deed. See the L.P.A. 1925, ss. 1(1), 52(1), 54(2). See LEASE.

legal liability. *See* RESPONSIBILITY.

legal logic. 1. Process of legal reasoning. 2. Application of modes of formal logic to legal reasoning. "The life of the law has not been logic; it has been experience": Holmes, *The Common Law* 1881. "Causes . . . are not to be decided by natural reason but by the artificial reason and judgment of law": Coke, *Prohibitions del Roy* (1607) 12 Co Rep 63. Note, however, commencement of the judgment delivered by Romer LJ in *Ex p Mwenya* [1960] 1 QB 241, utilising the manner of formal logic. ("The essential contention of the Crown . . . may be expressed syllogistically as follows . . ."), and the judgment of Pearson LJ in *Hardy* v *Motor Insurers' Bureau* [1964] 2 QB 745. See *SCM (UK) Ltd* v *W. J. Whittall Ltd* [1970] 2 All ER 417. *See* LOGIC AND THE LAW.

legal memory. *See* TIME IMMEMORIAL.

legal mortgage. Mortgage created, in the case of freehold land by a demise for a term of years absolute with a provision for cesser on redemption, or by charge by deed expressed to be by way of legal mortgage; in the case of leasehold land, by sub-demise for a term of years absolute (qv) at least one day less than the mortgaged lease with a proviso for cesser on redemption, or by charge by deed expressed to be by way of legal mortgage. The legal mortgage operates so as to secure the repayment of a debt or the discharge of some other obligation. See the L.P.A. 1925, s. 85. *See* MORTGAGE.

legal personality. Those qualities or characteristics of an individual, eg, age, domicile, from which are derived his legal status and capacity.

legal positivism. *See* POSITIVISM, LEGAL.

legal profession. Solicitors and barristers—a division dating from the fourteenth century, unique to the British Commonwealth. *See* BARRISTER; SOLICITOR.

legal relations, intention to create. An essential element in the creation of a contract. Where the parties do not expressly deny the intention, it is a question of construction: *Balfour* v *Balfour* [1919] 2 KB 571. Where the parties expressly deny intention (as in the so-called gentlemen's agreement (qv)), the agreement will not generally be enforced: *Jones* v *Vernons Pools Ltd* [1938] 2 All ER 626. See also *Appleson* v *Littlewood Ltd* [1939] 1 All ER 464; *Edwards* v *Skyways* [1964] 1 WLR 349. *See* CONTRACT.

legal rights. Rights *in rem* (qv), ie, available "against the world at large", as compared with equitable rights (qv).

legal separation. *See* JUDICIAL SEPARATION.

legal tender. Money that can be offered in the final discharge of a debt and cannot be refused by the creditor. Unlimited legal tender is money that can be tendered up to any amount (eg, Bank of England notes).

legal year. The annual period of time constituted by the four sittings of the court (Michaelmas, Hilary, Easter, Trinity). *See* SITTINGS.

legatee. One to whom a legacy is left. *See* LEGACY.

legislation. 1. A body of statutes. 2. The making of laws. In the UK this takes three major forms: Acts of Parliament (qv); delegated legislation (qv); autonomic legislation, ie, by bodies such as the unions making their internal rules and regulations.

legislation, subordinate. Delegated legislation (qv).

legislative history of an enactment. Term used in statutory interpretation to refer to the general background relating to the passing of a Bill, eg, reports of committees, drafts of the Bill, parliamentary debates. The general rule is that no reference to these matters may be made where the meaning of the statute is plain without making recourse to it. See, eg, *Beswick* v *Beswick* [1968] AC 58; *Sagnata Investments* v *Norwich Corporation* [1971] 2 QB 614; *Black-Clawson Ltd* v *Papierwerke Waldhof-Aschaffenburg AG* [1975] 1 All ER 810.

legislature. The Queen in Council in Parliament, ie, Crown, Lords and Commons. The supreme authority in the realm. *See* PARLIAMENT.

legitimacy. Status of a child resulting from birth in lawful wedlock. See the Legitimacy Act 1976; the F.L.R.A. 1969; the Mat.C.A. 1973, s. 45; the Ch.A. 1975, Sch 1, Part III; and the Fatal Accidents Act 1976, s. 1(4).

legitimacy, declaration of. Under the Mat.C.A. 1973, s. 45, a British subject is able to apply to the court for a declaration that he is legitimate and that the marriage of his parents or grandparents was valid. See the Matrimonial Causes Rules 1977, r. 110; *Barritt* v *AG* [1971] 1 WLR 1713; *The Ampthill Peerage* [1977] AC 547; and *Veasey* v *A.-G.* (1981) 11 Fam Law 249.

legitimacy of children of void and voidable marriages. 1. *Voidable marriages*: if celebrated before 1st July 1971, a child, who would have been the legitimate child of the parties to the marriage if at the date of the decree of nullity it had been dissolved instead of being annulled, is deemed to be their legitimate child; if celebrated after that date, children conceived before the decree absolute are legitimate (see the Mat.C.A. 1973, s. 16). 2. *Void marriages*: children are legitimate if at the time of intercourse resulting in their birth (or time of celebration of marriage if later) both or either of parties reasonably believed the marriage was valid: Legitimacy Act 1976, s. 1. See *Sheward* v *A.-G.* [1964] 2 All ER 324.

legitimacy, presumption of. *See* PRESUMPTION OF LEGITIMACY.

legitimation. Legitimation of a child by subsequent marriage of its parents ("*per subsequens matrimonium*"). Where the parents of an illegitimate person marry one another, the marriage shall, if the father of the illegitimate person is at the date of the marriage domiciled in England and Wales, render that person, if living, legitimate from the date of the marriage: Legitimacy Act 1976, s. 2. See the Ch.A. 1975, s. 8(9).

leonina societas. A partnership (qv) in which one partner takes all the profits (ie, has "the lion's share") and another bears all the losses.

le roi le veult; le roi s'avisera. See ROYAL ASSENT.

lesbianism. Female homosexuality. Not an offence in law. See *Kerr* v *Kennedy* [1942] 1 KB 409 (an imputation of lesbianism held to be an imputation of unchastity, in relation to an action for slander (qv)); *Gardner* v

Gardner [1947] 1 All ER 630 (conduct of wife was ground for a divorce petition where the husband's health suffered, so that he could allege cruelty).

lessee. One to whom a lease is made. Includes also those who derive title under him: L.P.A. 1925, s. 205(1) (xxiii). Known also as "tenant" (qv). *See* LEASE.

lessor. One who makes a lease to another. *See* LEASE.

let or hindrance, without. Without any obstruction.

letter of attorney. Power of attorney (qv).

letter of credit. Document provided, eg, for the exporter by the importer, so that the exporter can draw his draft upon a bank. It usually states the period within which it can be drawn, the maximum amount, and refers to documents accompanying it. See *Power Curber Ltd v Nat Bank of Kuwait* [1981] 1 WLR 1233 (a letter of credit ranks as cash and must be honoured); and *R v Benstead* (1982) 75 Cr App R 276.

letter of hypothecation. *See* HYPOTH-ECATION.

letter of request. Letter issued to a foreign court asking a judge to take the evidence of some person within that court's jurisdiction. See O. 39, r. 2. Known also as a "rogatory letter". See *Re Westinghouse Electric Corporation* [1978] AC 547.

letter rogatory. *See* ROGATORY LETTER.

letters of administration. Document issued to an administrator (qv) granting his authority.

letters patent. Document bearing the Great Seal of the Realm, used, eg, for the opening of Parliament, Royal Assent.

levant and couchant. Rising and lying down. 1. The number of cattle capable of being maintained on land to which a common of pasture was annexed. See now the Commons Registration Act 1965. 2. Where cattle escape from X's land to Y's, because of Y's default, Y's landlord could not distrain them for rent until they had been on the land levant and couchant, ie, at least one night.

levari facias. Writ of execution (super-seded by the writ of *elegit* (qv)) commanding the sheriff (qv) to levy a judgment debt by seizing and selling the debtor's goods and taking rents and profits.

levy. 1. Imposition of assessment or tax. 2. Body of men raised by order.

lex causae. The law relating to the legal system governing a matter. See, eg, *Leroux v Brown* (1852) 12 CB 801.

lex domicilii. Law of the place of a person's domicile (qv).

lex fori. Law of the place in which a case is heard.

lex loci actus. Law of the place where an act is carried out.

lex loci celebrationis. Law of the place where a marriage is celebrated. See *Re Bethell* (1888) 38 ChD 220.

lex loci contractus. Law of the place where a contract is made. See *Bodley Head Ltd v Flegon* [1972] 1 WLR 680.

lex loci delicti commissi. Law of the place where a wrong was committed. See *Monro v American Cyanamid Corporation* [1944] 1 All ER 386. See also O. 11.

lex loci situs. Law of the place where the property in question is situated.

lex loci solutionis. Law of the place where the contract is to be performed, or payment made.

lex mercatoria. Law merchant (qv).

lex non scripta. Unwritten law; common law.

lex scripta. Written law; statute law.

lex talionis. Law of retaliation. "An eye for an eye, a tooth for a tooth." See *Exodus*, xxi, 24.

liability. 1. Legal obligation or duty. 2. Amount owed.

liability, business. *See* BUSINESS LIA-BILITY.

liability for manufactured products. "A manufacturer of products which he sells in such a form as to show that he intends them to reach the ultimate consumer in the form in which they left him with no reasonable possibility of intermediate examination, and with the knowledge that the absence of reasonable care in the preparation or putting up of the products will result in an injury to the consumer's life or property, owes a duty to the consumer to take that reasonable care": *Donoghue v Stevenson*

[1932] AC 562. See also the Consumer Safety Act 1978; *Vacwell Engineering Co* v *BDH Chemicals* [1971] 1 QB 88. *See* PRODUCTS LIABILITY.

liability, legal. *See* RESPONSIBILITY.

liability, strict, and criminal law. *See* STRICT LIABILITY IN CRIMINAL LAW.

liability, vicarious. The liability which arises because of one person's relationship to another. Thus, in tort (qv) a master is generally liable for the acts of his servant performed in the course of his employment. See, eg, *Lloyd* v *Grace, Smith & Co* [1912] AC 716; *Rose* v *Plenty* [1976] 1 All ER 97; and *Kooragang Investments* v *Richardson & Wrench Ltd* [1982] AC 462. In criminal law a master may be held liable for a servant's offences: see, eg, the Trade Descriptions Act 1968; *Ferguson* v *Weaving* [1951] 1 KB 814.

libel. The publication in permanent form of a statement which tends to expose a person to hatred, ridicule or contempt. The broadcasting of words by radio is treated as publication in permanent form: Defamation Act 1952, s. 1. Libel may be a crime as well as a tort if it tends to provoke a breach of the peace (qv), and is actionable *per se* without proof of special damage. See the Law of Libel (Amendment) Act 1888; *Hulton* v *London Express Newspaper* [1940] 2 KB 507; Law Commission Paper No 84 (1982); and *Desmond* v *Thorne* [1982] 3 All ER 268. *See* DEFAMATION.

liberty. 1. The necessary condition for freedom. 2. Absence of restraint. 3. The condition of government under the law. (But note: "Liberty is too imperfectly defined when it is said to be government by laws and not by men. If the laws are made by one man or a junta of men in a state, and not by common consent, a government by them does not differ from slavery": Richard Price, 1778.) 4. A franchise (qv).

licence. 1. Necessary authority to act granted by a competent authority. 2. In land law a licence is given by X to Y when X, the occupier of land, gives Y permission to perform an act which, in other circumstances, would be considered a trespass, eg, where X allows Y to reside in X's house as a lodger. A *bare licence* is gratuitous permission. A licence may be coupled with an interest, as where X sells standing timber to Y on condition that Y is to sever the timber; in this case the sale implies the grant of a licence to Y to enter X's land. See *Somma* v *Hazelhurst* [1978] 2 All ER 1011.

licence by estoppel. Where a licensee has been allowed by the licensor to act so that an estoppel emerges in his favour, the licensor is bound by it. See *Hussey* v *Palmer* [1972] 3 All ER 744; *Crabb* v *Aran DC* [1975] 3 All ER 865. *See* ESTOPPEL.

licence, release on. *See* RELEASE ON LICENCE.

licensed premises, exclusion from. The court is empowered to impose as an additional penalty on a person convicted of an offence involving violence or threatened violence on licensed premises, an exclusion order banning him from such premises for a period between three months and two years: Licensed Premises (Exclusion of Certain Persons) Act 1980. Under the Licensing Act 1964, s. 174, a licensee may refuse to admit or may expel persons who are drunk, violent, quarrelsome or disorderly.

licensee. 1. One who has permission, express or implied, to enter premises for his own purpose, but not for any business interest of the occupier. See the H.A. 1980, s. 48. 2. One granted a licence, under the Licensing Act 1964, for the sale of intoxicating liquor on the premises.

licensing of premises. The granting of justices' licences at the general annual licensing meeting, enabling intoxicating liquor to be sold on the premises. See the Licensing Act 1964, as amended by the Finance Act 1967, the L.G.A. 1972 and the Licensing (Amendment) Act 1981. *See* BREWSTER SESSIONS.

liege. One bound by allegiance and feudal service.

lie in grant. Phrase referring to property capable of passing by a deed of grant.

lie in livery. Phrase referring to property capable of passing by an act of physical delivery.

lien. *Ligare* = to bind. A right to hold and retain another's property until a claim is satisfied. 1. *Possessory lien.* Right to retain until a claim is met. Possession must be continuous, rightful and not for a particular purpose. It may be general or particular (qqv). 2. *Maritime lien.* Right specifically binding a ship or cargo for payment of claim arising under maritime law. It is not founded on possession. 3. *Equitable lien.* Charge on property conferred by law until claims have been satisfied. It is attached independently of possession and is binding on all who acquire the property with notice of the lien. 4. *Unpaid seller's lien.* Right of an unpaid seller of goods to retain possession of them until payment or tender of the price where, eg, the buyer becomes insolvent: S.G.A. 1979, ss. 41–43.

lien, vendor's. *See* VENDOR'S RIGHTS.

life annuity. Annual payment which continues during a life or lives. *See* ANNUITY.

life assurance. Contract (qv) based on agreement by the assurer to pay a given sum upon the happening of some event contingent upon the duration of life. A *whole life* policy secures a capital sum at death, whenever it may occur. An *endowment assurance policy* secures a capital sum on survival to a fixed date, or at an earlier death. A *last survivor assurance* secures a sum payable at the death of the last survivor of two or more lives. A *temporary assurance policy* secures a capital sum only if death takes place within a specified term. *See* ASSURANCE; INSURANCE.

life estate. An estate for the life of the tenant (eg, by express limitation, such as a grant "to X for life") or by operation of law (as in curtesy (qv)) or *autre vie* (qv). *See* ESTATE.

life imprisonment. Fixed penalty for murder. See the Murder (Abolition of Death Penalty) Act 1965. For some other offences, eg, manslaughter, it is the maximum penalty. Where imposed for murder, the court is empowered to declare the minimum term which ought to be served before release on licence, but this does not bind the Home Secretary (who con-

sults the Lord Chief Justice and trial judge before ordering such a release). Recommendation for a minimum term cannot be made except in the case of murder: *R* v *Flemming* [1973] 2 All ER 401. See Cmnd 7844, 1980.

life interest. An interest in property for one's life, or the life of another. See the Capital Gains Tax Act 1979, s. 55(4). *See* INTEREST.

life or lives in being. For purpose of the rule against perpetuities (qv), the common law rule was that the lives in being selected by the donor could be stated expressly or by implication and there is no restriction as to the number of lives selected: *Re Villar* [1928] Ch 471. All persons alive or conceived when the instrument creating interest becomes operative are eligible lives in being. Changes introduced by the P. & A.A. 1964 relate to so-called "statutory lives" in being (qv).

life peerage. Rank of peer or peeress created by the Crown (in the case of non-judicial peerages) under the Life Peerages Act 1958.

life policy. Instrument by which a payment of money is assured on death (except death by accident only) or the happening of a contingency dependent on human life or an instrument evidencing a contract subject to the payment of premiums for a term dependent on human life: Insurance Companies Act 1982, s. 96(1).

life tenant. *See* TENANT FOR LIFE.

lifting the veil. Phrase describing the process whereby the court may look behind the "curtain of corporate secrecy". Thus, although the court is bound by the principle of a company's being a separate legal person distinct from its members, it will look at the underlying economic reality, eg, as where the company has been engaged in fraudulent trading or where the company is a mere sham. See the Cos.A. 1948, ss. 31, 108(4), 166, 209; the Cos.A. 1976, s. 8(1); the Cos.A. 1980, s. 64(4) (*b*); and the Cos.A. 1981, s. 81. See *Smith, Stone and Knight* v *Birmingham Corporation* [1939] 4 All ER 116; *D.H.N. Food Distributors* v *Tower Hamlets London BC* [1976] 1 WLR 852; *Woolfson* v

Strathclyde RC (1979) 38 P & CR 521. *See* COMPANY.

light, easement of. The right that light flowing over adjoining land shall not be obstructed unreasonably. See *Colls v Home & Colonial Stores Ltd* [1904] AC 179; *Allen v Greenwood* [1980] Ch 119. There is no natural right to light—the easement exists only in relation to a window or skylight.

limitation of actions. Provision whereby, after a certain period of time stated by statute, actions cannot be brought. Generally: in the case of land, 12 years from the date of accrual of action; in the case of tort and simple contract, six years from the date of accrual of action (for contract under seal, 12 years from the date of accrual). See the Limitation Act 1980; and *Pirelli Ltd v Faber and Partners* [1983] 2 WLR 6.

limitation, words of. In land law, those words in an instrument which delimit the estate, ie, which indicate the size of the interest given. Example: land given "to X and his heirs", the words of limitation are "and his heirs", indicating X's quantum of interest, but giving nothing to the heirs by direct gift (in this case X is the "purchaser" (qv)). Strict words of limitation must be used to create a fee tail (qv). See *Shelley's Case* (1581) 1 Co Rep 93b; and the L.P.A. 1925, s. 131. *See* PURCHASE, WORDS OF.

limited administration. Administration of the assets of a deceased person which is limited, eg, in time (as where the person appointed sole executor is an infant (qv)), or pending legal proceedings or where the person nominated sole executor is of unsound mind. *See* ADMINISTRATION.

limited company. A public company (qv). It is considered to be a distinct being or *persona*: *Salomon v Salomon & Co Ltd* [1897] AC 22. Liability of each shareholder may be limited by shares or guarantee and the winding-up of the company, if insolvent, will not make members bankrupt (qv). Its powers are limited to those arising under the memorandum of association (qv). *See* COMPANY.

limited executor. One granted lim-ited probate, eg, as where a testator (qv) limits his will to specific property. *See* EXECUTOR.

limited liability. Principle by which, in the case of a company limited by shares, no shareholder will be called upon to pay more than the amount remaining unpaid on his shares. See the Cos.A. 1948, ss. 22, 31 (as amended by the Cos.A. 1980, s. 88(1)), 202.

limited owner. One who owns an interest in property which is less than the fee simple (qv).

limited owner's charge. An equitable charge acquired under statute by a tenant for life or a statutory owner. A Class C land charge (qv). *See* LAND CHARGES, REGISTER OF.

limited partnership. Consists of general partners (liable for the firm's debts and obligations) and limited partners (who, at the time of entry, contribute a sum as capital or property which is valued at a stated amount). It is not a legal entity distinct from the persons who compose the firm. See the Limited Partnerships Act 1907; the Cos.A. 1967; *Re Barnard* [1932] 1 Ch 269. *See* PARTNERSHIP.

Lincoln's Inn. One of the Inns of Court (qv). Its records commence in 1422, the Inn having been sited originally in Shoe Lane. Its name may be derived from that of the Earl of Lincoln who, in the reign of Edward II, brought professors of law to teach there.

lineal consanguinity. Relationship between ascendants and descendants, eg, grandfather and grandson.

lineal descent. Descent in direct line.

linked transaction. Term used in the C.C.A. 1974, s. 19(1), to refer to the debtor's entry into one transaction linked with another (eg, purchase of a deep freezer on credit and a later agreement to buy food for stocking purposes). Generally treated as a "regulated agreement" (qv).

liquidated damages. *See* DAMAGES.

liquidated demand. A demand in the nature of a debt, ie, a specific sum of money due and payable under or by virtue of a contract. Its amount must either be already ascertained or capable of being ascertained as a mere matter of arithmetic: O. 6, r. 2(1).

liquidation. The winding-up of a company by a liquidator (qv) whose duties include the getting in and realisation of its property, the payment of its debts and the distribution of any surplus among members. See the Cos.A. 1948, ss. 237–251, 303.

liquidation, voluntary. See VOLUNTARY WINDING-UP.

liquidator. One appointed to wind up a company. His task is not to carry on the company's business but to conduct its affairs so that it may be wound up as swiftly as possible. A corporate body may not be appointed as liquidator. The official receiver (qv) becomes the "provisional liquidator" when a winding-up order is made; he may become the permanent liquidator. See the Cos.A. 1948, s. 245; and the Insolvency Act 1976. A liquidator who institutes proceedings does so at his own risk and is personally liable for litigation costs: *Re Lanaghan Bros* [1977] 1 All ER 265.

lis. Action; suit; dispute.

lis alibi pendens. Suit pending elsewhere. Such a situation may provide grounds for staying an action. See, eg, *McHenry* v *Lewis* (1882) 22 ChD 397.

lis mota. A lawsuit which is anticipated, or which is existing.

lis pendens. See PENDENS LIS.

listed buildings. Buildings statutorily listed under the T.C.P.A. 1974, s. 54, as being of special architectural or historic interest. See S.I. 1977/228; *Amalgamated Investment & Property Co* v *John Walker & Sons Ltd* [1977] 1 WLR 164; the L.G.P.L.A. 1980, Sch 15; the Local Government and Planning (Amendment) Act 1981; and the National Heritage Act 1983. *See* PRESERVATION ORDER.

listed securities. In relation to a company, means any securities of the company listed on a recognised stock exchange (qv): Cos.A. 1980, s. 72(5).

list of documents. See DOCUMENTS, LIST OF.

list of members. A company's annual return must include a list of names and addresses of members, and of those who have ceased to be members

since the last return. See the Cos.A. 1948, Sch 6.

lite pendente. See PENDENTE LITE.

literal method. A method for the construction of a statute by the courts. Its basis is: that words are to be taken prima facie in their ordinary, literal or grammatical meaning; that they are to be taken to be used in the same sense they had when the statute was passed; that the same words carry the same meaning. But "the literal meaning of the words is never allowed to prevail where it would produce manifest absurdity or consequences which can never have been intended by the legislature": *Corocraft* v *Pan Am Airways* [1969] 1 QB 616. See *R* v *Inhabitants of Ramsgate* (1827) 6 B & C 712; and *Duport Steels* v *Sirs* [1980] 1 WLR 142.

litigant. See LITIGATION.

litigant, assistance by friend of. Every litigant in person is entitled to be accompanied in court by a friend to assist him in the conduct of his case. The friend "may take notes, may quietly make suggestions and give advice; but no one can demand to take part in the proceedings as an advocate, contrary to the regulations of the court as settled by discretion of the justices": *Collier* v *Hicks* (1831) 2 B & A 663, cited in *McKenzie* v *McKenzie* [1971] P 33.

litigant in person, costs of. Costs awarded to the litigant in person. He may recover under the Litigants in Person (Costs and Expenses) Act 1975, for work reasonably done in his leisure time, and earnings lost through taking time off from work, to prepare or conduct the case. He may charge only for work which would have been done by a solicitor had he been legally represented.

litigation. The taking of legal action by a party, who is known as a "litigant".

litis aestimatio. Measure of damages.

Liverpool Court of Passage. An ancient court exercising civil jurisdiction in Liverpool. Abolished under the Courts Act 1971.

Liverpool, Crown Court of. A court exercising the criminal jurisdiction of quarter sessions and assizes (qqv) within the area of its jurisdiction. Abolished under the Courts Act 1971.

livery of seisin. Part of the early procedure of conveying a freehold (qv), known as *feoffment of fee with livery of seisin* (abolished under the L.P.A. 1925, s. 51). It consisted of *livery in law* (symbolic delivery of property within sight of the land to be conveyed) or *livery of deed* (grantor stood on land to be conveyed and invited grantee to enter).

lives in being, statutory. *See* STATUTORY LIVES IN BEING.

livestock. Any creature kept for the production of food, wool, skins or fur, or for the purpose of its use in the carrying on of any agricultural activity: H.S.W.A. 1974, s. 53(1). "Cattle, horses, asses, mules, hinnies, sheep, pigs, goats and poultry, and also deer not in the wild state": Animals Act 1971, s. 11. The 1971 Act, s. 4, imposes liability on a person in possession of livestock which stray on to another's land and damage it or any property on it. Under s. 3, the keeper of a dog which causes damage by killing or injuring livestock is liable for the damage. See *Cresswell* v *BOC Ltd* [1980] 3 All ER 443.

livestock, protection of. It is a defence to an action for injuring or killing a dog to prove that it was done by a person entitled so to act for the protection of livestock and that notice was given at a police station within 48 hours: Animals Act 1971, s. 9.

living apart. In relation to divorce proceedings, this does not mean mere physical separation, but it involves a spouse's ceasing to recognise the marriage as subsisting: *Santos* v *Santos* [1972] 2 All ER 246. By the Mat.C.A. 1973, s. 2(6), husband and wife are treated as living apart unless they live in the same household with each other.

living expenses. The phrase is to be construed as meaning "expenses of living"; it is not limited to living expenses solely attributable to an individual person's expenditure. It includes expenses representing costs incurred for housing, food, clothing,

necessary travelling and the like, and encompasses all the usual costs associated with any individual's particular life style: *Nutbrown* v *Rosier and Another* (*The Times*, 1.3.1982).

living memory. "Time whereof the memory of man runneth not to the contrary."

living together. A man and his wife are not deemed to be living otherwise than together unless they are permanently living in separation either by agreement or under an order of the court, or one has deserted the other and the separation incident to the desertion has not come to an end. See *Piper* v *Piper* (1978) 8 Fam Law 263.

L.J. Lord Justice of Appeal (qv).

Lloyd's. Lloyd's of London. An incorporated society of private insurers constituting an international insurance market, based on the work of over 7,000 underwriters in competition with one another. *Lloyd's Register of Shipping* is based on a survey and classification of ships. See Insurance Companies Act 1982, s. 83. For power to suspend underwriters see *R* v *Committee of Lloyd's ex p Postgate* (1983) (*The Times*, 12.1.1983). *See* A1.

loan capital. *See* CAPITAL LOAN.

loan, quasi-. *See* QUASI-LOAN.

local administration, commissions for. Bodies, for England and Wales, set up under the L.G.A. 1974, s. 23(1), each including the Parliamentary Commissioner (qv), to investigate complaints of injustice in consequence of maladministration in local government. Each commission submits an annual report to its representative body, comprising representatives of authorities subject to the commissions' jurisdiction.

local authority. Body constituted for the administration of a local government unit. In relation to England and Wales, it means the Greater London Council, Common Council of the City of London, county councils, London borough councils, district councils. See the L.G.P.L.A. 1980, s. 20. Defined under the Finance Act 1974, s. 52(2) as "(*a*) any authority having power to make or determine a rate; (*b*) any authority having power to issue a precept, requisition or other demand for the payment of money to be raised out of a rate". *See* PRECEPT; RATE.

local government. Government on a local basis by elected committees, forming part of the UK's administrative system, based on pattern of elected bodies for defined areas with responsibility for the provision of services within those areas. See the L.G.A. 1972 and 1974.

Local Government Ombudsman. *See* OMBUDSMAN, LOCAL GOVERNMENT.

local land charges. Any charge acquired by a local authority which is binding on successive owners of the land affected; any prohibition or restriction on the use of land imposed by a local authority or minister or government department which is binding on successive owners of the land affected; any positive obligation affecting land enforceable by a minister, government department or local authority binding on successive owners of the land affected: Local Land Charges Act 1975, s. 1. See also the Local Land Charges Rules 1977 (S.I. 1977/985). Registers of local land charges are kept in London by London boroughs and the City of London, and in other areas by district councils.

local land charges register. Consists of twelve parts: part 1 includes general financial charges; part 2 includes specific financial charges; part 3 includes planning charges; part 4 is reserved for charges not registrable in the other parts; part 5 includes fenland ways maintenance charges; part 6 relates to land compensation charges; part 7 refers to New Towns charges; part 8 includes civil aviation charges; part 9 refers to open-cast coal charges; part 10 is reserved for listed buildings charges; part 11 is for light obstruction notices; part 12 is for drainage scheme charges. See S.I. 1977/985; and the I.A. 1978, Sch 1.

locatio conductio. A contract of bailment for hire, expressing letting and hiring.

locatio rei. The hiring of some thing. Bailment or letting of a thing to be used by the bailee for compensation to be paid by him.

loc. cit. Loco citato = in the place cited. At the passage [of a book] cited.

lock-out. The closing of a place of employment, or the suspension of work, or the refusal by an employer to continue to employ any number of persons employed by him, in consequence of a dispute.

loco parentis. See IN LOCO PARENTIS.

locum tenens. Holding an office. One who acts as a lawful substitute or deputy.

locus in quo. Place in which. Scene of the event.

locus regit actum. The place governs the act, ie, an act is governed by the law of the place where it is performed. See, eg, *R v Bham* [1966] 1 QB 159.

locus sigilli. Place of the seal. "L.S." may be used in a document to show where the seal should be. See *First National Securities Ltd v Jones* [1978] 2 All ER 221. *See* SEALING.

locus standi. Place to stand. A right to be heard, or the legal capacity to challenge some decision. See, eg, *R v Liverpool Corporation, ex p. Liverpool Taxi Operators' Association* [1972] QB 299; and *R v IRC ex p National Federation of Self Employed Ltd* [1982] AC 617. See O. 53, r. 3(5).

lodger. One who occupies part of a house, but whose occupation is under control of a landlord or his representative who resides in or retains possession of or dominion over that house: *Thompson v Ward* [1906] 1 KB 60. See the H.A. 1980, s. 35(1); and *Luganda v Service Hotels* [1969] 2 Ch 209.

logical plentitude, theory of. Theory in jurisprudence (qv) stating that law is an organic *corpus* of principles with an inherent power of expansion and adaptation to new circumstances.

logic and the law. "The purpose and value of logic to the law is to ensure that persons whose relevant circumstances are similar receive similar treatment. It is in other words to promote equity: to use it to defeat equity is to misuse it": *per* Lord Simon in *Rugby Water Board v Shaw-Fox* [1973] AC 202. *See* LEGAL LOGIC.

logic, legal. *See* LEGAL LOGIC.

loiter. To act in a way which suggests

that a person is idling in the street for an unlawful purpose. Loitering for purposes of prostitution is an offence: Street Offences Act 1959, s. 1.

London, City of. *See* CITY OF LONDON.

London Gazette. An official journal of the government, first published *c.* 1665. It contains, eg, proclamations, notices of receiving orders.

long tenancy. "A tenancy granted for a term of years certain exceeding 21 years, whether or not subsequently extended by act of the parties or by any enactment": Rent Act 1977, s. 152(1). See *Poland v Earl of Cadogan* [1980] 3 All ER 544.

long title. *See* TITLE, LONG.

long vacation. The former name for the period 1st August to 30th September during which the Supreme Court does not generally transact business except in urgent cases. See O. 64. The normal break has been reduced to the single month of August.

looting. 1. Sacking; plundering; robbing. 2. Stealing from any person killed, injured or detained during military operations or taking otherwise than for the public service any vehicle, equipment or stores abandoned by the enemy: Armed Forces Act 1971. See *R v Bailey* 4 Cr App R (S) 15.

lord. 1. Peer of the realm. 2. One of whom land is held by a tenant (qv).

Lord Advocate. The Crown's principal law officer in Scotland. He represents the Crown in legal proceedings and conducts Crown prosecutions.

Lord Chancellor. *See* CHANCELLOR.

Lord Chief Justice. Presides over the QBD and the Court of Appeal (Civil Division) and ranks next to the Lord Chancellor in the legal hierarchy. Appointed by the Sovereign upon recommendation of the Prime Minister. See the S.C.A. 1981, s. 10(2)(*a*).

Lord Lieutenant of the County. Office first created in the sixteenth century when the holder was commander of county militia and chief among county justices. Now appointed by the Crown on the advice of the Prime Minister. He recommends the appointment of magistrates.

Lord Privy Seal. Duties attaching to this office were abolished in 1884. The office remains and is filled by a member of the cabinet.

Lords, House of. *See* HOUSE OF LORDS.

Lords Justices of Appeal. Judges who sit in the Court of Appeal (qv), appointed by the Queen from judges of the High Court (qv) or barristers of at least 15 years' standing. See the S.C.A. 1981, s. 10.

Lords of Appeal in Ordinary. Senior members of the judiciary, usually appointed from the Court of Appeal (qv), who hear appeals in the House of Lords (qv). They have held other high judicial office for two years or have been practising barristers of at least 15 years' standing. See the Appellate Jurisdiction Acts 1876–1947.

Lords Spiritual. *See* HOUSE OF LORDS.

Lords Temporal. *See* HOUSE OF LORDS.

loss, liability in marine insurance for. An insurer will be liable for losses proximately caused by a peril which has been insured against. A *partial loss* is a loss other than a total loss. A *total loss* may be *actual* or *constructive*; *actual total loss* is where the subject-matter insured is destroyed or so damaged that it has ceased to be a thing of the kind insured against; *constructive total loss* is where the subject-matter insured has been abandoned because its actual total loss seems unavoidable. See *Asfar & Co v Blundell* [1896] 1 QB 123; *Andersen v Morten* [1908] AC 334.

loss of consortium and services. *See* PER QUOD CONSORTIUM ET SERVITIUM AMISIT.

lost capital. Where, eg, a £1 share in a company is represented by only 50p worth of assets, a company may write off the lost capital and pay dividends without regard to that loss: Cos.A. 1948, s. 66(1).

lost modern grant. Doctrine based on fiction (qv) whereby the court can presume from long user (ie, 20 years) that a grant of easements and profits has been made at some time after 1189, but that it has now been lost. User as of right must be shown, right claimed must be capable of being acquired by grant. Claim may be made only where a presumption at common law is not possible in the circumstances: *Tehidy Minerals v Norman* [1971] 2 QB 528.

lost years principle. Principle derived from *Oliver v Ashman* [1962] 2 QB 210 whereby courts were prevented from awarding to persons who had suffered injury or disease which shortened their lives damages for loss of what they might have earned during the "lost years". Overruled by House of Lords in *Pickett v British Rail Engineering Ltd* [1979] 1 All ER 774. See also *Skelton v Collins* (1966) 115 CLR 94; *Gammell v Wilson* [1981] 2 WLR 248; *Benson v Biggs Wall Ltd* [1982] 3 All ER 300; *Ashley v Vickers* (*The Times*, 18.1.1983). See now the A.J.A. 1982, s. 1.

lottery. A game of chance. Generally unlawful: Lotteries and Amusements Act 1976, s. 1. Exceptions: small lotteries incidental to "exempt entertainments" (eg, bazaars, sales of work, dances); private lotteries (eg, those in which the sale of tickets is restricted to members of one society); societies' lotteries (ie, promoted on behalf of a society concerned with athletics, charitable purposes, etc); local lotteries (ie, promoted by a local authority and registered with the Gaming Board). A lottery ticket "includes any document evidencing the claim of a person to participate in the chances of the lottery": 1976 Act, s. 23(1). See *Readers Digest Association v Williams* [1976] 3 All ER 737; *Imperial Tobacco Co v A.-G.* [1981] AC 718.

l.s. *Locus sigilli* (qv).

lucid interval. A temporary period of rational thought and behaviour between periods of insanity. A will made during such a period may be admitted to probate (qv). See *Chambers and Yatman v Queen's Proctor* (1840) 2 Curt 415, in which the deceased made a will during a lucid interval and killed himself, while insane, on the following day, and the will was admitted to probate.

lucri causa. For the purpose of gain.

lump. Term applied colloquially to "labour-only sub-contracting" whereby self-employed labourers are paid a lump sum (without deduction of tax) by an agent who is paid, in turn by a contractor. See the Finance Act 1975, ss. 68–81; *R v Lovett, R v Collins* (1975) 61 Cr App R 316; *Ferguson v John Dawson Ltd* [1976] 1 WLR 1213—man working on "lump" held to be an employee, entitled to recover damages against his employers for a breach of statutory duty as a result of which he was injured.

lump sum award. A once-for-all award of damages, comprising pecuniary loss incurred up to the trial and a final estimate of future pecuniary and non-pecuniary loss.

lump sum contract. Contract (qv) by which it is intended that complete performance shall take place before payment may be demanded. Failure to complete performance prevents any payment being recovered. See *Sumpter v Hedges* [1898] 1 QB 673; *Dakin & Co v Lee* [1916] 1 KB 566; *Hoenig v Isaacs* [1952] 1 All ER 176 (recovery of sum relating to faulty workmanship).

lump sum freight. *See* FREIGHT.

lunatic. An idiot or person of unsound mind: Lunacy Act 1890, s. 341. This term has now been replaced by "patient". See M.H.A. 1983, s. 145(1)

lunatic, criminal. *See* CRIMINAL LUNATIC.

M

machinery and plant. Expression relating to capital allowances, used in the Finance Act 1971 to refer to a deduction against income tax, based on expenditure on machinery and plant purchased for the purpose of one's trade. See *Munby* v *Furlong* [1977] 2 All ER 953. *See* PLANT.

machinery, dangerous. *See* DANGEROUS MACHINERY.

magistrates. Honorary (or lay) magistrates (as contrasted with stipendiary magistrates (qv)) are part-time justices of the peace (qv) appointed by the Crown on the advice of the Lord Chancellor. They may be removed from the commission by the Lord Chancellor without showing cause. At the age of 70 they are placed on the supplemental list and cease to be entitled to exercise any judicial function (see the A.J.A. 1973, s. 5; and the Justices of the Peace Act 1979, s. 8). They hear criminal and some few civil cases. Functions include: committing offenders for trial by judge and jury; trying offences summarily; sitting with judges of the Crown Court to hear appeals from magistrates' courts; licensing of premises selling intoxicating liquor; issue of betting and gaming licences; hearing applications for affiliation orders, custody of children, adoptions; maintenance of spouses and/or children. See the M.C.A. 1980.

magistrates' clerk. Usually a lawyer of not less than 5 years' standing, who advises magistrates at their request on law and procedure. Generally he should not go with magistrates when they retire to consider their verdict; should they require his advice after they have retired they may send for him, but he should return to the court when his advice has been given. See the Justices of the Peace Acts 1949, 1968 and 1979, ss. 25–30; and the M.C.A. 1980, s. 141.

magistrates' courts. Constituted by any justice or justices of the peace acting under common law or any enactment or by virtue of a commission: M.C.A. 1980, s. 148. Consists generally of 2–7 part-time, unpaid JPs who hear complaints and try certain cases summarily. A single justice may conduct a preliminary investigation. Jurisdiction, which is local, is civil and criminal, largely comprising matters relating to: summary offences; indictable offences triable summarily; indictable offences triable only on indictment; offences triable either way; certain civil debts; some affiliation and domestic proceedings. A stipendiary magistrate (qv) has, in effect, the powers of two lay justices. See the C.L.A. 1977, ss. 27–32, 41, 45–46; the Justices of the Peace Act 1979, ss. 19–20; and the Magistrates' Courts Act 1980, together with the Magistrates' Courts Rules 1981 (S.I. 1981/552).

magistrates' courts committees. Continued in operation by the Justices of the Peace Act 1979, s. 20, with functions relating to matters of an administrative nature arising under the Act: see s. 19(1).

magistrates' courts rule committee. Appointed by the Lord Chancellor (qv) to advise on procedure to be followed in magistrates' courts and by justices' clerks. It includes the Lord Chief Justice, President of Family Division, chief metropolitan stipendiary magistrate, and others (including a justices' clerk, practising barrister and solicitor): M.C.A. 1980, s. 144.

magistrates' courts, sittings of. A magistrates' court may sit on any day of the year, and in particular (if the court thinks fit) on Christmas Day, Good Friday or any Sunday: M.C.A. 1980, s. 153.

magistrates, ex-officio. Those who became magistrates by virtue of holding another office, eg, that of mayor.

Generally abolished under the Justices of the Peace Act 1968 and the A.J.A. 1973, save for High Court judges and the Lord Mayor and some aldermen in the City of London.

magistrates, restrictions on imprisonment by. In general, a magistrates' court has no power to impose imprisonment for less than five days, or more than six months in respect of any one offence: M.C.A. 1980, ss. 31, 132. The aggregate of consecutive terms of imprisonment may not generally exceed six months: s. 133(1). (For exceptional cases involving twelve months, see s. 133(2).)

magistrates, stipendiary. See STIPENDIARY MAGISTRATES.

Magna Carta. The Great Charter (of Liberties), dated 15th June 1215. A statement in 37 chapters by King John of concessions to church and freemen, comprising a preamble and 63 clauses. It enunciated a number of fundamental principles, eg, "to none will we sell, to none will we deny or delay right or justice".

mail, detaining or delaying. It is an offence for an officer of the Post Office wilfully to detain or delay contrary to his duty any postal packet or message (by telephone and telegraph) in the course of transmission by post. See the Telegraph Act 1863, s. 45; the Post Office Act 1953, s. 58; *Gouriet* v *Union of Post Office Workers* [1978] AC 435.

maim. To injure a person so that he is rendered less capable of defending himself. See the O.P.A. 1861.

mainly. Probably "more than half": *per* Lord Morton in *Fawcett Properties* v *Buckingham CC* [1961] AC 636.

mainprise. Writ, now obsolete, ordering a sheriff (qv) to take sureties (qv) for the appearance of an accused person. The sureties were known as "mainpernors".

main purpose rule. See REPUGNANCY.

main residence. A tenant who occupied more than one residence could exercise his rights under the Leasehold Reform Act 1967 only in relation to the house he occupied as his main residence: s. 1. Thus, one who owned a main residence abroad and the lease of a house in the UK would have no rights under the Act. Which of two houses is the main residence is a matter of fact and degree. See also the Finance Act 1965, s. 29; *Varty* v *Lynes* [1976] 1 WLR 1091.

maintain, failure to. Either party to a marriage may apply to the court for an order that the other party has failed to provide reasonable maintenance for the applicant or for any child of the family: Mat.C.A. 1973, s. 27 (amended by the D.P.A. 1978).

maintain, liability to. A man is liable to maintain his wife and children, and a woman is liable to maintain her husband and children: S.S.A. 1975, s. 17 (as set out in the S.S.A. 1980, Sch 2).

maintenance. 1. Intermeddling in an action. "A taking in hand, bearing up or upholding of quarrels and sides, to the disturbance of the common right": Coke. Criminal and tortious liability for maintenance was abolished by the C.L.A. 1967. 2. The supply of necessaries, eg, food, clothing. Trustees (qv) may be empowered by provisions in a settlement or under the Tr.A. 1925, to apply income of a trust fund towards the maintenance of a beneficiary (qv). See the Tr.A. 1925, s. 31. 3. Financial arrangements embodied in a maintenance agreement (qv).

maintenance after termination of marriage. The court may make orders under the Mat.C.A. 1973, ss. 23, 24, known as "financial provision orders" (for lump sums or secured or unsecured periodical payments) and "property adjustment orders" (for settlement or transfer of property, variation of ante- or post-nuptial settlements or reduction of interest in such settlements). For guidelines, see s. 25(1). See *Davis* v *Davis* [1967] P 185; and *Martin* v *Martin* [1978] Fam 12.

maintenance agreement. Agreement in writing made between parties to a marriage, relating to financial arrangements whether made during continuance or after dissolution of the marriage, or a separation agreement which contains no financial arrangements in a case where no other agreement in writing between the same parties contains such arrangements: Mat.C.A. 1973, ss. 34, 35; Inheritance (Provision for Family and Dependants) Act 1975. See *Minton* v *Minton* [1979] 1 All ER 79; and *Dipper* v *Dipper* [1980] 2 All ER 722.

maintenance agreement by deceased person. Under the Inheritance (Provision for Family and Dependants) Act 1975, s. 17(4), means: any agreement made, in writing or not, and whether before or after the commencement of the Act, by the deceased with any person with whom he entered into a marriage, being an agreement containing provisions governing rights and liabilities towards one another when living separately of the parties to that marriage (whether dissolved or annulled) in respect of the making or securing of payments or the disposition or use of any property, including any rights and liabilities with respect to maintenance or education of any child, whether or not a child of the deceased or a person treated by the deceased as a child of the family in relation to that marriage.

maintenance order. An order, including an affiliation order, or order consequent on an affiliation order, which provides for the periodical payment of sums of money towards the maintenance of any person, being a person whom the person liable to make payments under the order is liable to maintain, and an affiliation order, or order consequent upon an affiliation order, providing for payment by a person adjudged, found or declared to be a child's father of expenses incidental to, eg, the child's birth: Maintenance Orders (Reciprocal Enforcement) Act 1972, s. 21(1). See the D.P.A. 1978, s. 11, Sch 2; and the C.J.J.A. 1982, s. 37(1), Sch 11.

maintenance pending suit. Replaced "alimony (qv) pending suit". On petition for divorce, nullity or separation, the court may order either party to the marriage to make to the other periodical payments for his or her maintenance beginning not earlier than the date of the presen-

tation of the petition and ending with the date of determination of the suit: Mat.C.A. 1973, s. 22.

majority. 1. Full age, 18, under the F.L.R.A. 1969. 2. The greater number of those present, or voting, at an assembly or other meeting.

majority rule. 1. Basic principle of democratic organisation. 2. Principle whereby a company's shareholders exercise control of the company through the general meeting. Minority shareholders are protected by common law (see *Foss* v *Harbottle* (1843) 2 Hare 461) and the provisions of the Cos.A. 1948, s. 210. See also *Clemens* v *Clemens Bros and Another* [1976] 2 All ER 268.

majority verdict. *See* VERDICT, MAJORITY.

making off without payment. Offence under Th.A. 1978, s. 3, committed where a person who, knowing that payment on the spot for any goods supplied or service done is required or expected from him, dishonestly makes off without having paid as required or expected and with intent to avoid payment of the amount. "Payment on the spot" includes payment at the time of collecting goods on which work has been done or in respect of which service has been provided. Does not apply where supply of goods or provision of service is contrary to law or where service done is such that payment is not legally enforceable. Any person may arrest without warrant anyone who is, or whom he, with reasonable cause, suspects to be, committing or attempting to commit this offence: s. 3(4). See *R* v *McDavitt* [1981] Crim LR 843 (upheld in *R* v *Brooks* (1983) 76 Cr App R 66).

mala fides. Bad faith.

mala in se. Acts wrong in themselves (eg, murder).

mala praxis. A dereliction from professional duty resulting in injury, eg, as where a physician injures a patient as a result of neglect.

mala prohibita. Acts which are wrongs because they are prohibited by law, but which are not necessarily or obviously wrongs in themselves, eg, failure to make tax returns.

male issue. Male descendants in the male line only (unlike "male descendants" which may refer to male descendants of the propositus (qv) through males or females). See *Re Du Cros' Settlement Trusts* [1961] 3 All ER 193.

malfeasance. The commission of an unlawful act. *See* MISFEASANCE.

malice. 1. Generally refers to an attitude inherent in "a wrongful act done intentionally without just cause or excuse": *Bromage* v *Prosser* (1825) 4 B & C 247. 2. In relation to *mens rea* (qv) of murder, categorised as: (1) *express* (an intention to kill); (2) *implied* (qv) (an intention to do only grievous bodily harm (qv)); (3) *universal* (eg, as where X fires a gun into a crowd, not caring who is killed, and killing Y); (4) *transferred* (as where X, intending to kill Y, shoots at him, but kills Z, who, unknown to X, was standing near Y, so that X's malice is considered as having been "transferred" to Z: *R* v *Salisbury* (1553) 1 Plowd 100; *R* v *Monger* [1973] Crim LR 301); (5) *constructive* (qv). 3. A constituent of defamation (qv). The plaintiff must prove that words complained of were published maliciously, eg, in abuse of fair comment. See the Defamation Act 1952, s. 4(6).

malice aforethought. Term used in the context of the crime of murder to mean an intention on the part of the accused to kill or to cause grievous bodily harm (qv) to another. See the C.J.A. 1967, s. 8; *DPP* v *Smith* [1961] AC 290; and *R* v *Cunningham* [1982] AC 566.

malice prepense. Malice aforethought (qv).

malicious arrest. *See* ARREST, MALICIOUS.

malicious damage. An offence involving damage to property caused by acts done unlawfully and maliciously under the Malicious Damage Act 1861, repealed by the Criminal Damage Act 1971. See *R* v *Gittins* [1982] RTR 363. *See* CRIMINAL DAMAGE.

malicious falsehood. A false and malicious statement concerning a person, made to someone other than that person, relating to his property or business interests which damages his general material interests. "Malicious" involves some dishonest or other improper motive (but not carelessness). Known also as "slander of title" (qv). See the Defamation Act 1952, s. 3(1); *Ratcliffe* v *Evans* [1892] 2 QB 524; *Balden* v *Shorter* [1933] Ch 427; *Drummond-Jackson* v *BMA* [1970] 1 All ER 1094.

malicious prosecution. A tort (qv) in which the plaintiff proves: that he has sustained damage; that the defendant prosecuted him; that the prosecution ended in the plaintiff's favour; that the prosecution lacked any reasonable and probable cause; that the defendant acted maliciously (ie, with some other motive than desire to bring to justice a person whom the accuser believes to be guilty): *Brown* v *Hawkes* [1891] 2 QB 718. See also *Glinski* v *McIver* [1962] AC 726; and *Evans* v *London University Hospital Medical College* [1981] 1 WLR 184.

malicious prosecution, reasonable and probable cause in relation to. Definition approved by the House of Lords in *Herniman* v *Smith* [1938] AC 305 is: "An honest belief in the guilt of accused based upon full conviction, founded upon reasonable grounds, of the existence of a state of circumstances, which, assuming them to be true, would reasonably lead any ordinarily prudent and cautious man, placed in the position of the accuser, to the conclusion that the person charged was probably guilty of the crime imputed."

malicious wounding. Offence committed under the O.P.A. 1861, s. 20, by a person who unlawfully and maliciously wounds or inflicts any grievous bodily harm (qv) upon another either with or without any weapon or instrument. "Maliciously" requires an actual intention to do the particular kind of harm done or recklessness: *R* v *Cunningham* [1957] 2 QB 396. See *Flack* v *Hunt* (1979) 70 Cr App R 51. Known also as "unlawful wounding". *See* WOUNDING.

malingerer. One who falsely pretends to be suffering from sickness or disability, or who injures himself so as to render himself unfit for service, or causes himself to be injured by another with that intent, or who prolongs or aggravates any sickness or disability. See the Army Act 1955, s. 42(1).

malitia supplet aetatem *See* DOLI CAPAX.

malversation. Misbehaviour or corruption in an office or public trust.

man. A male adult person. In the Sex Discrimination Act 1975, s. 82(1) it is used to include a male "of any age".

manager, appointment of. Equitable remedy allowing the court to appoint a manager who is empowered to continue a business. Often the same person is appointed as receiver (qv) and manager. "Nothing is better settled than that this court does not assume the management of a business or undertaking except with a view to the winding-up and sale of the business or undertaking": *Gardner* v *London Chatham and Dover Rwy* (1887) 2 Ch App 201.

managing director. A director (qv) who has charge of the management of the company.

Manchester, Crown Court of. A court exercising the criminal jurisdiction of quarter sessions and assizes (qqv) within the area of its jurisdiction. Abolished under the Courts Act 1971.

mandamus. We command. Originally a writ from the High Court (qv) ordering performance of a public duty. Replaced by an order, under the A.J.A. 1938, s. 7. Used, eg, to direct the holding of municipal elections (*Re Barnes Corporation* [1933] 1 KB 668); to compel hearing of an appeal by an inferior tribunal (*The King* v *Housing Tribunal* [1920] 3 KB 334). See now the S.C.A. 1981, s. 29.

mandate. 1. A direction from a superior to an inferior court. 2. A contract of agency to perform a task for another person. 3. An order or injunction. 4. A commission granted by the League of Nations to a member state relating to the establishment of government over conquered territory, eg, the former German territories in Africa after the First World War.

mandatory injunction. *See* INJUNCTION.

mandavi ballivo. I have commanded the bailiff. Return to a writ (qv) in which a sheriff (qv) gives assurance that its execution has been committed to a bailiff.

man of straw. 1. One who is used to shield another, eg, in an action. 2. One of little means and, hence, not worth suing.

manor. A feudal unit, usually comprising the lord's manor house and the land he occupied and cultivated, together with land held by tenants and waste used for pasture. See the L.P.A. 1925, s. 205(1) (ix).

mansion house, principal. A lord's chief dwelling-house. A house usually occupied as a farmhouse or which, together with adjoining lands, does not exceed 25 acres, is not a principal mansion house within the meaning of the S.L.A. 1925, s. 65, and may not be disposed of without consent of trustees. See *Re Feversham Settled Estate* [1938] 2 All ER 210.

manslaughter. Generally unlawful homicide unaccompanied by malice aforethought (qv), eg, as where X kills Y as a result of grossly negligent conduct. May be classified as (1) *voluntary*, ie, as in the case of a killing which would have been murder, but is considered as manslaughter because the accused successfully pleads diminished responsibility (qv) or provocation; (2) *involuntary*, ie, as where the *actus reus* (qv) of homicide is unaccompanied by malice aforethought, resulting from an act performed with criminal negligence. See *R* v *Instan* [1893] 1 QB 450; *R* v *Bonnyman* (1942) 86 SJ 274; *R* v *Larkin* [1943] 1 All ER 217; *R* v *Stone and Dobinson* [1977] QB 354; *R* v *Dalby* [1982] 1 WLR 425; *A.-G.'s Ref (No. 4 of 1980)* [1981] 1 WLR 705; *R* v *Paget* [1983] Crim LR 274; and *R* v *Mitchell* (*The Times*, 24.2.1983). *See* NEGLECT.

manslaughter, constructive. Killing by an unlawful act likely to cause bodily harm which is not serious.

mansuetae naturae. Tame by nature. Term applied to animals, such as horses, dogs. *See* ANIMALS, CLASSIFICATION OF.

manual labour. Includes work done with the hands, even though it is highly skilled and technical: *Stone Lighting & Radio Ltd* v *Haygarth* [1968] AC 157.

Mareva injunction. Procedure based on foreign attachment whereby the court comes to a creditor's aid when the debtor (resident or non-resident) has absconded or is overseas but has assets in this country. See *Mareva Compania Naviera SA* v *International Bulk-Carriers SA* [1975] 2 Lloyd's Rep 509. For guidelines on creditor's applications, see *Third Chandris Shipping Corp* v *Unimarine SA* [1979] QB 645. See the S.C.A. 1981, s. 37; the C.J.J.A. 1982, s. 25; *Cretanor Maritime Co* v *Irish Marine Management* [1978] 1 WLR 966; and *The Theotokos* [1983] 2 All ER 65.

marginal notes. Notes printed in margins of Acts of Parliament, explanatory of the clauses. They do not form part of an Act (except in the case of certain private Acts). They may be considered by the court in a case of ambiguity. See *Chandler* v *DPP* [1964] AC 763; *DPP* v *Schildkamp* [1971] AC 1.

marine insurance contract. Contract (qv) whereby an insurer engages to indemnify the assured against those losses incident to a marine adventure. See the Marine Insurance Act 1906.

maritagium. 1. Right of a lord to give his infant ward in marriage. 2. An early mode of disposition of land, whereby a father, on the marriage of his daughter, conveyed land to her and the husband and the heirs of their bodies.

marital privileges. See PRIVILEGES, MARITAL.

maritime lien. See LIEN.

maritime perils. Perils arising from navigation of the sea, eg, fire, war, pirates, restraint of princes (qv), jettisons and other perils which may be designated by the insurance policy: see the Marine Insurance Act 1906, s. 3. The term "perils of the seas" does not include the ordinary action of wind and waves: see *Samuel & Co* v *Dumas* (1922) 13 Ll L Rep 503.

market. 1. Trading area in which

activities are held under common law by which "everyone was entitled to come into the market place to sell and buy without let or hindrance, moving about or walking to and fro": *R* v *Barnsley Metropolitan BC, ex p Hook* [1976] 3 All ER 452. 2. "A place to which sellers who have not found buyers take their goods in the hope of finding buyers, and to which buyers resort in the hope of finding the goods they want": *Scottish CWS Ltd* v *Ulster Farmers' Mart Co Ltd* [1959] 2 All ER 486.

market, available. See AVAILABLE MARKET.

Market, Common. See COMMON MARKET.

market overt. An "open public and legally constituted market". A market held on days prescribed by charter, custom or statute. It means, in the City of London (qv), every shop in which goods usually sold in that shop are exposed for sale. "The sale must not be in the night, but between the rising of the sun and the going down of the same": *Market Overt Case* (1596) 5 Co Rep 33b. Where goods are sold in market overt, the buyer obtains title provided they are bought in good faith and without notice of any defect or lack of title on part of the seller: S.G.A. 1979, s. 22(1). See *Clayton* v *Le Roy* [1911] 2 KB 1031; *Bishopgate Motor Finance Co* v *Transport Brakes Ltd* [1949] 1 KB 322; *Reid* v *Commissioner of Police of Metropolis* [1973] QB 551.

market price. 1. "The value of marketable goods which a trader holds in stock either for sale or consumption in his business": *B.S.C. Footwear* v *Ridgway* [1971] 2 All ER 534. 2. Price at which buyers and sellers are ready and willing to buy and sell in the ordinary course of trade.

market value. "The price of the commodity in the market as between the manufacturer and an ordinary purchaser": *Orchard* v *Simpson* (1857) 2 CBNS 299. See the Finance Act 1983, s. 21(11).

marriage. The act or rite based on a consensual union creating the legal and social status of husband and wife. "The voluntary union for life of one man and one woman to the exclusion of all others": Mat.C.A. 1857. Minimum age of parties is 16: Marriage Act 1949, s. 2. (For parental consent, see Sch 2.) Marriages in England must be registered. See the Marriage Acts 1949–1983; the Marriage (Enabling) Act 1960; and the Marriage (Registrar General's Licence) Act 1970.

marriage articles. Contract setting out terms upon which a marriage settlement (qv) is to be executed.

marriage, breakdown of. See BREAKDOWN OF MARRIAGE.

marriage brokage contract. Contract (qv) whereby a person undertakes, for a reward, to promote a marriage. No rights can arise under it: *Hermann v Charlesworth* [1905] 2 KB 123.

marriage, Church of England. Under the Marriage Act 1949, s. 5, a Church of England marriage is solemnised only after publication of banns or by authority of a common or special licence or superintendent registrar's certificate.

marriage, common-law. See COMMON-LAW MARRIAGE.

marriage, common licence for. Licence, which lasts for three months, issued under the authority of the bishop of a diocese enabling the parties to marry in the Church of England without waiting for the publication of banns (qv). See the Marriage Act 1949.

marriage consideration. Marriage is "the most valuable consideration imaginable": *A.-G.* v *Jacobs-Smith* [1895] 2 QB 341. Persons within the consideration are husband, wife, issue of the marriage and grandchildren. See *De Mestre* v *West* [1891] AC 264; *Re Plumptre's Settlement* [1910] 1 Ch 609; *Re Cook's Settlement Trusts* [1965] Ch 902. See CONSIDERATION.

marriage, consummation of. See CONSUMMATION OF A MARRIAGE.

marriage, mistake in. See MISTAKE AND MARRIAGE.

marriage, nullity of. See NULLITY OF MARRIAGE.

marriage, presumption of. See PRESUMPTION OF MARRIAGE VALIDITY.

marriage, proof of. Procedure where-

by a valid marriage is proved by the production of the marriage certificate and proof of identity; by declaration of a deceased person against interest or in the course of duty; by records (see the Civil Evidence Act 1968); by evidence of the ceremony given by one who was present; by presumption from cohabitation (see *Re Taylor* [1961] 1 WLR 9).

marriage, Registrar General's licence relating to. Under the Marriage (Registrar General's Licence) Act 1970, the Registrar General is empowered to licence a marriage to be solemnised elsewhere than in a registered building or register office. Used where the Registrar General is satisfied that one of the persons to be married is not expected to recover from an illness and cannot be moved to a place where a normal marriage would be solemnised.

marriage, registration of. Procedure whereby the following particulars of a marriage are officially recorded: date; surname, residence of parties; surname and profession of male parents; church where marriage takes place (in the case of a Church of England marriage).

marriage settlement. Deed executed in the consideration of a marriage which is to take place, relating to the settlement of property between the intended husband and wife. It can be varied under, eg, the Mat.C.A. 1973, s. 24 or the Inheritance (Provision for Family and Dependants) Act 1975, s. 2(1).

marriage, sham. See SHAM MARRIAGE.

marriage, special licence for. Special dispensation granted by the discretion of the Archbishop of Canterbury, enabling a marriage to be solemnised under Church of England rites at any convenient place and time. See the Marriage Act 1949, s. 79(9).

marriage, Superintendent-Registrar's certificate relating to. Certificate issued by the Superintendent-Registrar of the district in which the parties have lived for the preceding seven days. Notice is issued in a document open to public inspection and displayed on a notice-board for

21 days. If no caveat is entered, the certificate is issued for production to the person before whom the marriage is solemnised. See the Marriage Act 1949.

marriage, void and voidable. *See* NULLITY OF MARRIAGE.

marriage, will in contemplation of. In general, a will is revoked by a testator's marriage, but where it appears from the will that at the time it was made the testator was expecting to be married to a particular person and that he intended that the will should not be revoked by his marriage, the will is not revoked by his marriage to that person: W.A. 1837, s. 18(1), (3) (as substituted by the A.J.A. 1982, s. 18(1)).

married couple. A man and woman who are married to each other and are members of the same household. (An "unmarried couple" means a man and a woman who are not married to each other but are living together as husband and wife.) See the Family Income Supplements Act 1970, s. 17(1) (as amended by the S.S.A. 1980, s. 7(6)).

marshalling. Equitable principle under which, where there are two creditors of one debtor, and one creditor is entitled to resort to one fund only for payment of the debt, while the other creditor is entitled to resort to two funds, the funds will be marshalled by the court so that both creditors may be satisfied, as far as possible. Example: X mortgages Blackacre and Whiteacre to Y. Later X mortgages Blackacre to Z. If Y takes out of Blackacre money owing to him which he could have taken out of Whiteacre, then, to that extent, equity will give Z a charge on Whiteacre. Doctrine applies only where the mortgagor of both properties is the same person. See *Trimmer v Bayne (No. 2)* (1803) 9 Ves 209.

martial law. Rule by military authorities during an emergency when the civil authority cannot function. Not recognised under our constitution, according to Dicey. See *Ex p Marais* [1902] AC 109.

master and servant. Relationship, known now as "employer and employee", subsisting between one person and another who controls his work. Distinguished from "independent contractor" (qv). "The ultimate question is . . . who is entitled to give the orders as to how the work shall be done": *Mersey Docks and Harbour Board v Coggins & Griffiths Ltd* [1947] 1 AC 1. Indicia of the relationship were held in *Short v Henderson Ltd* (1946) 62 TLR 427 to be: master's power of selection of his servant; payment of wages or other remuneration; master's right to control the method of doing the work; master's right of suspension or dismissal. In a relationship of this kind a master's implied duties are to retain the servant for an agreed period, to pay agreed remuneration and to take reasonable care for servant's safety. See *Mathew v Bobbins* (1980) 256 EG 603. *See* SERVANT.

Master in Lunacy. Title formerly given to the Master of the Court of Protection (qv).

Master of the Crown Office. Appointed under the S.C.A. 1981, s. 89(2). He has custody of records relating to divisional court proceedings of Queen's Bench Division and is also registrar of criminal appeals. See O. 57.

Master of the Rolls. Formerly a keeper of records and, later, a judge of the Court of Chancery. Now a member of the High Court (qv) and *ex-officio* member of the Court of Appeal (qv). Presides over the Civil Division of the Court of Appeal: see the S.C.A. 1981, s. 10.

master, practice. *See* PRACTICE MASTER.

Master of the Bench. Full title of Benchers (qv).

Masters of the Supreme Court. Masters in the Chancery Division, Masters of the QBD and Masters who carry out taxation of costs and cases in the Chancery and QBD. A master has the general jurisdiction of a judge in chambers. District registrars carry out similar functions in the provinces. See the S.C.A. 1981, s. 89.

masters, taxing. *See* TAXING MASTERS.

material fact. "Every fact is material

which would, if known, reasonably affect the minds of prudent, experienced insurers in deciding whether they will accept the risk'': *Stroshein v Wawanesa Mutual Insurance Co* [1943] 3 WWR 509. See O. 18, r. 7.

material facts in pleadings. *See* PLEADINGS, MATERIAL FACTS IN.

maternity benefit. Grant and allowance paid under the S.S.A. 1975, ss. 21–23, to a woman who satisfies conditions under Sch 3, Part I and Sch 4, Part I. See the S.S.A. 1980, s. 5. The allowance is payable for 18 weeks, beginning with the 11th week before the expected confinement.

maternity leave, right to return to work after. Right of an employee to return to work after maternity leave: E.P.(C.)A. 1978, s, 33 and Employment Act 1980, s. 11. She must inform the employer of the expected date of confinement; if so requested within 49 days of the confinement, she must give written notice to employer of her intention to return within 14 days; she must give notice 21 days in advance of the date on which she expects to return: Employment Act 1980, s. 11. Failure to permit return may be treated as dismissal, but not in the case of a firm employing no more than five workers, or where it is not reasonably practical for the employer to permit a return: E.P.(C.)A. 1978, s. 56 (as amended by the 1980 Act, s. 12). See also *Lavery v Plessey Telecommunications Ltd* [1983] IRLR 202.

maternity pay. Payment under the E.P.(C.)A. 1978, Part III, (as amended by the Employment Act 1980, ss. 11, 12), made to a woman with two years' continuous service, absent from work because of pregnancy or confinement, if she continues to be employed until 11 weeks before the expected confinement and informs her employer in writing three weeks before. Amount is nine-tenths of a normal week's pay, less the standard maternity allowance.

matrimonial causes. Proceedings for divorce, judicial separation. Assigned generally to the Family Division of the High Court. *See* DIVORCE.

matrimonial home. Place in which a husband and wife have resided together. Under the Matrimonial Homes Act 1967, as amended, a spouse has a right of occupation to a house which the other is entitled to occupy by virtue of any estate or interest or contract or by virtue of any enactment giving him or her the right to remain in occupation. The right is registrable as a Class F land charge in the register of land charges (qv). See the Matrimonial Proceedings and Property Act 1970, s. 38; the L.C.A. 1972, s. 2(7); the Domestic Violence and Matrimonial Act 1976; the Matrimonial Homes and Property Act 1981; the Matrimonial Homes Act 1983; *Barnett v Hassett* [1981] 1 WLR 1385; and *Richards v Richards* [1983] 3 WLR 173.

matrimonial home, improvements to. ''Where a husband or wife contributes in money or money's worth to the improvement of real or personal property in which or in the proceeds of sale of which either or both of them has or have a beneficial interest, the husband or wife so contributing shall if the contribution is of a substantial nature . . . be treated as having then acquired by virtue of his or her contribution a share or enlarged share, as the case may be, in that beneficial interest . . .'': Matrimonial Proceedings and Property Act 1970, s. 37.

matrimonial home, order restricting occupation of. Order available under the Domestic Violence and Matrimonial Proceedings Act 1976, s. 4, prohibiting, suspending or restricting the exercise by one spouse, or requiring one spouse to permit the exercise by the other, of the right, by virtue of a legal estate vested in them jointly, or by virtue of contract, to occupy a dwelling-house in which the spouses have had a matrimonial home.

matrimonial injunctions. *See* INJUNCTIONS, MATRIMONIAL.

matrimonial offences. Basis of the pre-1971 law of divorce under which, subject to certain defences, divorce could be obtained upon proof of an ''offence'' such as adultery, desertion, insanity, cruelty, etc. See now, generally, the Mat.C.A. 1973. *See* DIVORCE.

matrimonial order. Order for separation, obtainable from magistrates under the D.P.A. 1978.

maturity. Time at which a bill of exchange (qv) becomes due.

maxims of equity. *See* EQUITY, MAXIMS OF.

mayhem. The malicious and violent deprivation of a member of the body so that one's effective capacity for self-defence is impaired. *See* MAIM.

mayor. Chairman of a city council elected by councillors. See the L.G.A. 1972, ss. 3–5, 245.

Mayor's and City of London Court. Local court formally abolished under the Courts Act 1971. The Act provides, however, that the county court for the City of London county court district is to be known as the Mayor's and City of London Court: s. 42.

McKenzie man. One who, according to the precedent of *McKenzie* v *McKenzie* [1971] P 33, is allowed to assist or prompt a litigant in person. Known, also colloquially, as "McKenzie lawyer". *See* LITIGANT, ASSISTANCE BY FRIEND OF.

measure of damages by reason of death. "The actual pecuniary loss of each individual entitled to sue can only be ascertained by balancing, on the one hand, the loss to him of the future pecuniary benefit, and on the other, any pecuniary advantage which from whatever source comes to him by reason of the death": *Davies* v *Powell Duffryn Associated Collieries Ltd* [1942] AC 601. The action is brought in the name of the executor or administrator of the deceased. It lies for the benefit of the wife, husband, children, grandchildren, father, mother, step-parents, grandparents, etc. See *Taylor* v *O'Connor* [1971] AC 115. But see also the A.J.A. 1982, s. 1.

measures of damages in contract. The principle upon which assessment of actual monetary compensation is to be paid for damage. In general, in the case of contract, there must be *restitutio in integrum* (qv), ie, compensation in full must be paid for the proximate damage suffered by the plaintiff. See *Hadley* v *Baxendale* (1854) 9 Exch 341; *Chaplin* v *Hicks* [1911] 2 KB 786; *Victoria Laundry Ltd* v *Newman Industries Ltd* [1949] 2 KB 528; *The Heron II* [1969] 1 AC 350; and *Photoproduction* v *Securicor* [1980] AC 627. *See* DAMAGES.

mediation. The act of a third party relating to the settling of a dispute between two contending parties.

medical examination. Where a decree of nullity of marriage (qv) is sought, resting on the ground that the marriage has not been consummated because of impotence or disability, the petitioner must apply to the registrar to determine whether a medical examination of the parties is necessary, save, eg, in the case of an undefended cause where the husband is the petitioner, or the wife is the petitioner and it appears that she has borne a child. See the Matrimonial Causes Rules 1977, r. 30.

medical examination, remand for. Adjournment of a case for 3 or 4 weeks to enable a medical examination and report to be made concerning a person on trial by a magistrates' court for an offence punishable on summary conviction with imprisonment: M.C.A. 1980, s. 30.

medical reports, exchange of. Procedure, often used in actions for personal injuries, whereby medical evidence is called for only if the essence of that evidence has been disclosed in the form of a written report to the other party. See O. 38; *Lane* v *Willis* [1972] 1 WLR 326.

mediums, fraudulent. *See* WITCHCRAFT.

meetings, board. *See* BOARD MEETINGS.

meetings, company. Meetings of a company (qv) attended by shareholders. (1) Annual general meetings (see the Cos.A. 1948, s. 131, Table A, art. 47) held each calendar year, with not more than 15 months between meetings. (2) Extraordinary general meetings, held whenever the directors wish (see Table A, art. 49) or on requisition by members holding at least one-tenth of the paid-up capital carrying right to vote. (3) Class meetings, called for a particular class of shareholder to discuss, eg, variation of class rights. See *Cane* v *Jones* [1981] 1 All ER 533.

melior est conditio possidentis et rei quam actoris. The position of the possessor is the better, and that of the defendant is better than that of the plaintiff.

Member of Parliament. One elected by a constituency to sit in the House of Commons (qv). Persons disqualified from membership of the Commons include, eg, most peers, judges, mental patients, certain classes of prisoner. See the House of Commons Disqualification Act 1975; and the Representation of the People Act 1983. *See* PARLIAMENT.

Members' interests, register of. Register, open to public inspection, of interests of Members of Parliament, including, eg, remuneration from employment, directorships, financial sponsorships.

members of a company. Those who have subscribed to a company's memorandum of association (qv), or have agreed to become members by applying for an allotment of shares or by taking a transfer from an existing member. Persons cease to be members by, eg, forfeiture, surrender, transfer, death. See the Cos.A. 1948, ss. 26, 112; the Cos.A. 1980, s. 75; *Re Bayswater Trading Co Ltd* [1970] 1 WLR 343; *Re Jermyn St Turkish Baths Ltd* [1970] 1 WLR 1194. *See* COMPANY.

members, register of. *See* REGISTER OF MEMBERS.

memorandum. A note recording the particulars of an event, eg, a commercial transaction.

memorandum in writing, relating to land. "No action may be brought upon any contract for the sale or other disposition of land or any interest in land, unless the agreement upon which such action is brought, or some memorandum or note thereof, is in writing, and signed by the party to be charged or by some person thereunto by him lawfully authorised": L.P.A. 1925, s. 40(1). See, eg, *Timmins* v *Moreland St Property Co Ltd* [1958] Ch 110; *New Hart Builders Ltd* v *Brindley* [1975] Ch 342.

memorandum of association. *See* ASSOCIATION, MEMORANDUM OF.

menaces, demand with. For the *actus reus* (qv) of blackmail see the Th.A. 1968, s. 21. "If the circumstances of the case were such that an ordinary reasonable man would understand that a demand for money was being made upon him and that the demand was accompanied by menaces—not perhaps direct, but veiled menaces— so that his ordinary balance of mind was upset, then you would be justified in coming to the conclusion that a demand for menaces had been made": *R* v *Collister* (1955) 39 Cr App R 100. *See* BLACKMAIL.

men, indecent assault on. *See* INDECENT ASSAULT ON MEN.

mensa et thoro. *See* A MENSA ET THORO.

mens rea. Translated as "guilty mind" or "wicked mind". More accurately, "criminal intention, or an intention to do the act which is made penal by statute or by the common law": *Allard* v *Selfridge Ltd* [1925] 1 KB 129. May include also recklessness relating to the circumstances and consequences of an act which comprise the *actus reus* (qv). See *R* v *Tolson* (1889) 23 QBD 168; *Sweet* v *Parsley* [1970] AC 132; *Albert* v *Lavin* [1981] 3 WLR 955; Law Commission Report No. 89, 1978. *See* ACTUS NON FACIT REUM NISI MENS SIT REA.

mental disorder. "Mental illness, arrested or incomplete development of mind, psychopathic disorder, and any other disorder or disability of mind": M.H.A. 1983, s. 1(2). A person may not be classified as mentally disordered by reason only of "promiscuity or other immoral conduct, sexual deviancy or dependence on alcohol or drugs": M.H.A. 1983, s. 1(3). Categories include mental illness, severe mental impairment, mental impairment and psychopathic disorder (qv). "Severe mental impairment" is "a state of arrested or incomplete development of mind which includes severe impairment of intelligence and social functioning and is associated with abnormally aggressive or seriously irresponsible conduct": M.H.A. 1983, s. 1(2). ("Mental impairment" is defined similarly—see s. 1(2)—but includes "significant impairment of intelligence"). See M.H.A. 1983 Part I.

Mental Health Commission. Authority set up under the M.H.A. 1983, s. 121 with a general protective function over detained patients. May visit and interview patients and investigate complaints.

Mental Health Review Tribunals, Area. Bodies set up under the M.H.A. 1959, consisting of doctors, lawyers and others, to consider applications for the discharge of a mental patient (qv) made by the patient or, eg, his nearest relative. See M.H.A. 1983, Part V.

mental patient. One who is suffering, or appears to be suffering, from a mental disorder. See the M.H.A. 1983, s. 145(1). For compulsory detention see the 1959 Act, s. 136; the M.H.(Amendment)A. 1982, ss. 3(3)(*b*), 4(2); M.H.A. 1983, Part III.

mercenary. "Any person who serves voluntarily and for pay in some armed force other than of Her Majesty in the right of the UK": *Report, of Privy Counsellors, 1976* (Cmnd 6569, para 7). *See* FOREIGN ENLISTMENT.

merchandise marks. Phrase used in relation to the marking of goods for sale. The Merchandise Marks Acts 1887–1953 were repealed by the Trade Descriptions Act 1968.

merchantable quality of goods. "Goods of any kind are of merchantable quality within the meaning of [this Act] if they are as fit for the purpose or purposes for which goods of that kind are commonly bought as it is reasonable to expect, having regard to any description applied to them, the price (if relevant) and all the other relevant circumstances": S.G.A. 1979, s. 14(6).

mercy killing. Offence, suggested by Criminal Law Revision Committee Report (August 1976) which would apply to one who, from compassion, unlawfully kills another who is believed by him to be (for example) permanently helpless or subject to rapid, incurable degeneration. It was rejected in the Committee's final report, 1980 (Cmnd 7844).

mercy, prerogative of. Power of the Crown, exercised through the Home Secretary, to commute, remit or suspend a sentence. *See* PARDON.

merger. 1. Acquisition of one firm by another, so that only one unit remains. Certain proposed mergers must be referred to the Monopolies Commission. See the Fair Trading Act 1973, ss. 57–77; and S.I. 1980/373. 2. Vesting of two estates or interests in property in one person by virtue of the same right. There is no merger by operation of law only of any estate the beneficial interest in which would not be deemed to be merged or extinguished in equity: L.P.A. 1925, s. 185. 3. No doctrine of merger (ie, of attempt with the full offence) remains in criminal law since the C.L.A. 1967: *Webley* v *Buxton* (1977) 121 SJ 153.

mesne. Middle; intermediate. A mesne lord was one who held of a superior and of whom an inferior held.

mesne profits, action for. Type of action for trespass brought, against an occupier of premises who remains in possession after the termination of his interest in those premises, to recover damages suffered by the plaintiff as the result of his having been out of possession. Damages are generally assessed on the basis of a rent representing fair value of premises during the relevant period of occupation. See *Dunlop* v *Macedo* (1891) 8 TLR 43; *Hall & Co Ltd* v *Pearlberg* [1956] 1 WLR 244; *Moore* v *Assignment Courier* [1977] 1 WLR 638.

messuage. A dwelling-house together with adjacent buildings, gardens, orchards.

metes and bounds. The boundaries of land, related to natural or artificial features, eg, streams, fences.

metropolitan stipendiary magistrates. Full-time, professional magistrates who sit as sole justices in Metropolitan Stipendiary Courts, ie, petty sessional courts in London. See the Justices of the Peace Act 1979, Part III. *See* STIPENDIARY MAGISTRATES.

Michaelmas Day. A quarter-day (qv). 29th September.

middlemen. Business intermediaries, eg, factors, brokers, wholesalers.

Middlesex, Bill of. *See* BILL OF MIDDLESEX.

Middle Temple. One of the Inns of Court (qv). It was granted its premises in perpetuity by James I in 1609.

Midsummer Day. A quarter-day (qv). 24th June.

military courts. Term applied to the old Court of Chivalry (qv) or courts-martial (qv).

military tenures. Tenures by knight service (qv), grand serjeanty (qv). Known also as "tenures in chivalry". Abolished (save for some honorary services of grand serjeanty) under the Tenures Abolition Act 1660.

military testament. A privileged will (qv) made by a soldier on active service.

mine. "An excavation or system of excavations made for the purpose of, or in connection with, the getting, wholly or substantially by means involving the employment of persons below ground, of minerals . . . or products of minerals": Mines and Quarries Act 1954, s. 180(1).

minerals. *See* MINING LEASE.

minimum subscription. Minimum amount of capital, decided on by directors or promoters of a company (qv) which will allow them to provide for preliminary expenses, underwriting commissions, price of property to be paid from proceeds of issue, working capital. Must be stated in the prospectus (qv): Cos.A. 1948, s. 47.

minimum wages. *See* WAGES, MINIMUM.

mining lease. A tenant for life (qv) may lease the whole or part of the land for 100 years in the case of a mining lease: S.L.A. 1925, s. 41. If the tenant is impeachable for waste (qv) relating to minerals, three-quarters of the rent becomes capital. "Minerals" include "all substances in, on or under the land, obtainable by underground or surface working": S.L.A. 1925, s. 117(1)(xv). For a definition of "mining operation", see the T.C.P.(Minerals)A. 1981, s. 1. See *Lonsdale (Earl)* v *A.-G.* [1982] 1 WLR 887.

minister, departmental. One entrusted by the Prime Minister (qv) with the management of a division of the government's activities. He holds office at the pleasure of the Crown and is usually appointed at a meeting of the Privy Council (qv). Ministers retire collectively upon a change of government. See the Ministers of the Crown Act 1975.

ministerial responsibility. Doctrine that ministers of the government are responsible to Parliament (qv) for the exercise of the powers and duties of their departments, whether personally authorised by ministers or not.

minister, junior. One who assists a senior minister, eg, by answering Parliamentary questions and assisting in Parliamentary duties. Known also as Parliamentary Secretary or Parliamentary Under-Secretary of State.

minister, non-departmental. A government minister who holds a traditional office, eg, Paymaster-General, Lord Privy Seal (qv), or Minister without Portfolio (qv).

Minister of State. A minister appointed in a subordinate position to a government department.

Minister without Portfolio. *See* PORTFOLIO.

Ministry. 1. The government, headed by the Prime Minister (qv). 2. A department of government.

minor. *See* INFANT.

minor interests. "The interests not capable of being disposed of or created by registered dispositions and capable of being overridden (whether or not a purchaser has notice thereof) by the proprietors unless protected as provided by this Act, and all rights and interests which are not registered or protected on the register and are not overriding interests": L.R.A. 1925, s. 3(xv). They may be protected by a notice, inhibition (qv), restriction or caution (qv). See *Murray* v *Two Strokes* [1973] 1 WLR 823.

minority. 1. The smaller group in number of those present at an assembly or other meeting. 2. Below 18 years of age: F.L.R.A. 1969.

minority, fraud on. *See* FRAUD ON MINORITY.

minority shareholders, oppression of. Conduct of a company (qv) unfairly prejudicial to the interests of some of its shareholders. See, eg, *Foss v Harbottle* (1843) 2 Ha 461; *Re Westbourne Galleries Ltd* [1970] 3 All ER 374; and *Eastmanco v GLC* [1982] 1 WLR 2. See the Cos.A. 1948, s. 210, superseded by the Cos.A. 1980, s. 75. *See* SHAREHOLDERS, PROTECTION OF.

minutes. Notes providing a record of proceedings. A company must keep minutes of its meetings. See the Cos.A. 1948, s. 145. Minutes signed by a chairman are usually prima facie evidence of proceedings. A computer may be used to keep company minutes: Stock Exchange (Completion of Bargains) Act 1976.

misadventure. An accident resulting from some lawful venture.

misappropriation. Dishonest appropriation of another's property. See the Th.A. 1968, s. 1.

miscarriage. 1. Failure in the administration of justice. 2. Synonym for abortion (qv). 3. Term used in the Statute of Frauds 1677, s. 4, relating to "that species of wrongful act for the consequences of which the law would make the party civilly responsible": *Kirkham v Marter* (1819) 2 B & Ald 613.

mischief. The "mischief of a statute" is the wrong for which it is intended to provide a remedy.

mischief rule. Method of construing a statute which necessitates asking: what was common law before the statute; what was the mischief (qv) for which common law did not provide; what remedy has Parliament resolved so as to cure it; what is the true reason of that remedy? See *Heydon's Case* (1584) 3 Co Rep 7a. See *Magdalen College Case* (1616) 11 Co Rep 71b; *Kruhlak v Kruhlak* [1958] 2 QB 32; *Maunsell v Olins* [1975] AC 373. *See* CONSTRUCTION.

misconduct, professional. *See* PROFESSIONAL MISCONDUCT.

misconduct, wilful. *See* WILFUL MISCONDUCT.

misdemeanours. Offences not amounting to felonies (qv). Under the C.L.A. 1967, s. 1, all distinctions between felony and misdemeanour are abolished.

misdescription. Usually refers to a description of the subject-matter of a contract which is false or misleading in some substantial way. In such a case the contract may be voidable at the option of the party who is misled.

misdirection. Failure by the judge to direct the jury adequately as to the issues requiring a decision, or the law applicable, or the legal effect of evidence, or total failure to direct: *Hobbs v Tinling* [1929] 2 KB 1. A conviction may be quashed on this ground: see, eg, *R v Trigg* [1963] 1 WLR 305. See O. 59, r. 11.

misfeasance. Improper performance of some essentially lawful act. See the Highways Act 1980, s. 58; *Griffiths v Liverpool Corporation* [1967] 1 QB 374. *See* MALFEASANCE.

misfeasance summons. The court may examine the conduct of a director, promoter, liquidator or officer of a company (qqv) who has misapplied the company's property or money or has been guilty of misfeasance. The official receiver (qv) or any creditor can apply to the court for a misfeasance summons. See the Cos.A. 1948, s. 333.

misjoinder of parties. The wrongful joining of parties in an action. "No cause or matter shall be defeated by reason of the misjoinder or non-joinder of any party": O. 15, r. 6(1).

misnomer. The giving of a wrong name to a person in pleadings. See O. 20.

mispleading. The omission in pleadings (qv) of that which is essential to the action.

misprision. *Mesprendre* = to make a mistake. Misprision of a felony was failure to report a felony (qv): *Sykes v DPP* [1962] AC 528. See the C.L.A. 1967, s. 5(1) by which the offence no longer exists generally. Misprision of treason remains as a common-law offence committed when a person knows, or has reasonable cause to believe that another has committed treason and fails within a reasonable time to inform an appropriate authority. *See* TREASON.

misrepresentation. A false statement which misrepresents a material fact; which is made before the conclusion of a contract with a view to inducing another to enter that contract; which is made with the intention that the person to whom it is addressed shall act on it; which is acted on, having induced the contract. "In my opinion any behaviour, by words or conduct, is sufficient to be a misrepresentation if it is such as to mislead the other party. If it conveys a false impression, that is enough": *per* Denning LJ in *Curtis* v *Chemical Cleaning and Dyeing Co Ltd* [1951] 1 KB 805. See the Misrepresentation Act 1967; *Hedley Byrne & Co* v *Heller & Partners* [1964] AC 465; *Esso Petroleum Ltd* v *Mardon* [1975] 1 All ER 203.

misrepresentation, fraudulent. A false representation made knowingly or without belief in its truth or recklessly, careless whether it be true or false: *Derry* v *Peek* (1889) 14 App Cas 337. See Misrepresentation Act 1967; *Polhill* v *Walter* (1832) 3 B & Ald 114; *Akerhielm* v *De Mare* [1959] AC 789.

misrepresentation, negligent. 1. A false statement made honestly, whether negligently or not. See *Watts* v *Spence* [1976] Ch 165. Remedies include damages and rescission (qqv). 2. A false statement made by a person who has no reasonable grounds for believing that statement to be true.

mistake. *Common mistake*—both parties make the same error relating to a fundamental fact. *Mutual mistake*—both parties fail to understand each other. *Unilateral mistake*—only one party is mistaken. "If mistake operates at all, it operates so as to negative or in some cases to nullify consent": *Bell* v *Lever Bros Ltd* [1932] AC 161. See the Lim.A. 1980, s. 32; *Couturier* v *Hastie* (1856) 5 HL Cas 673; *Raffles* v *Wichelhaus* (1864) 2 H & C 906; *Foster* v *Mackinnon* (1869) LR 4 CP 704; *Lewis* v *Averay* [1972] 1 QB 198; and *Centrovincial Estates PLC* v *Merchant Investors Assurance Co Ltd* (*The Times*, 8.3.1983).

mistake and marriage. A mistake is operative if it relates to the nature of the ceremony or the identity of the other party. See *Valier* v *Valier* (1925) 133 LT 830.

mistake of law. Error as to the law and its effects. Never a defence, since every person is presumed to know the law. See IGNORANTIA JURIS NEMINEM EXCUSAT.

mistake, operative. A mistake which operates so as to avoid a contract, eg, mistake as to the identity or existence of the subject-matter, or as to the nature of the document signed. See CONTRACT.

mistake, rectification in magistrates' court of. Power under common law and statute enabling magistrates to vary or rescind a sentence or other order imposed by them: see the M.C.A. 1980, s. 142; *R* v *West* [1964] 1 QB 15.

mistress. A woman who, without marriage, lives as a wife. "'Mistress', having lost its respectable if not reverential significance, came to mean a woman installed, in a clandestine way, by someone of substance, normally married, for his intermittent sexual enjoyment": *per* Lord Kilbrandon in *Davis* v *Johnson* [1978] 1 All ER 1132. See *Spindlow* v *Spindlow* [1979] 1 All ER 169.

mistrial. A false trial. "To constitute a mistrial the proceedings must have been abortive from beginning to end": *R* v *Middlesex Judges, ex p DPP* [1952] 2 QB 758. See *R* v *Townsend* [1982] 1 All ER 509.

mitigation. 1. Diminution, eg, of some penalty. Plea in mitigation of sentence may be heard at the end of the trial. 2. Mitigation of damages: it is the duty of the plaintiff to take all reasonable steps to mitigate the loss caused by a breach of contract (qv). See *Strutt* v *Whitnell* [1975] 1 WLR 870; and *R* v *Jones* [1980] Crim LR 58 (counsel's duty to make plea in mitigation).

mittimus. We send. 1. Writ (qv) authorising removal of records etc. 2. Order for the receiving and safe keeping of an accused person.

mixed action. An action which in its nature relates to both real and personal actions (qv).

mixed fund. A fund comprising the proceeds of the sale of real and personal property.

mixed property. Property compounded of realty and personalty and having some of the legal attributes of both.

M'Naghten Rules. Answers of the House of Lords relating to questions arising from the verdict in *R v M'Naghten* (1843) 10 C & F 200, where the accused, acting under insane delusion, killed the secretary of Sir Robert Peel and was found not guilty on the ground of insanity. The Rules remain legal criteria when insanity is pleaded as a defence. They state: (1) A person is presumed sane until the contrary is proved. (2) To establish a defence on the ground of insanity, it must be clearly proved that at the time of committing the offence, the accused was labouring under such a defect of reason, from disease of mind, as not to know the nature and quality of his act, or, if he did know it, that he did not know what he was doing was wrong. If the accused was conscious that the act was one he ought not to do and if that act was at the time contrary to law of the land, he is punishable. (3) Where a person under an insane delusion as to existing facts commits an offence in consequence thereof, and making the assumption that he labours under such partial delusion only, and is not in other respects insane, he is considered in the same situation as to responsibility as if the facts with respect to which the delusion exists were real. See *R v Codère* (1916) 12 Cr App R 21; *R v Windle* [1952] 2 QB 826; *R v Sullivan* [1983] 3 WLR 123.

mobility allowance. Non-contributory benefit payable under the S.S.A. 1975 to a person suffering from a physical disablement such that he is either unable to walk or is virtually unable to do so. The allowance is exempt from income tax after April 1982. See also the S.S.(Misc. Provs.)A. 1977, s. 13; and the S.S.A. 1979, s. 3.

mock auction. Auction during which articles are given away or offered as gifts, or the right to bid is restricted to persons who have bought or agreed to buy an article, or any lot is sold to a bidder at a price lower than the amount of his highest bid for it, or part of the price is repaid or credited to him. An offence under the Mock Auction Act 1961. A "lot" consists of or includes plate, linen, china, glass, books, furniture, jewellery, etc. See *R v Ingram* (1976) 64 Cr App R 116; *Allen v Simmons* [1978] 1 WLR 79. *See* AUCTION.

modo et forma. In the manner and form. A pleading, abolished under the J.A. 1875, whereby the defendant denied having done the thing on which the action was founded in the manner and form alleged.

modus operandi. Way of performing a task.

moiety. *Medius* = middle. One of two equal parts. See *Re Angus' Will Trusts* [1960] 1 WLR 1296.

molest. "A wide plain word which . . . if I had to find one synonym for it, I should select 'pester'": *per* Stephenson LJ in *Vaughan v Vaughan* [1973] 3 All ER 449.

molestation. Acts, the tendency of which is, in general, to injure or annoy, which were intended to injure or annoy the complainant. See the Domestic Violence and Matrimonial Proceedings Act 1976, s. 1(1); and *Horner v Horner* [1982] Fam 90. Used also to describe the following of a person in a persistent and disorderly manner, or by hiding his property, so as to compel him to do or abstain from doing an act.

molestation, non-, clause. *See* INJUNCTIONS, MATRIMONIAL.

molliter manus imposuit. He laid hands on him gently. Plea by the defendant (qv) sued for assault and battery (qqv) that he used only necessary and justifiable force.

monarchy. The institution of the Crown (qv). Dates of the reigns of England's monarchs are as shown in the following table:

House	Name	Year of accession
Normandy	William I	1066
	William II	1087
	Henry I	1100
	Stephen	1135
Plantagenet	Henry II	1154
	Richard I	1189
	John	1199
	Henry III	1216
	Edward I	1272
	Edward II	1307
	Edward III	1327
	Richard II	1377

House	Name	Year of accession
Lancaster	Henry IV	1399
	Henry V	1413
	Henry VI	1422
York	Edward IV	1461
	Edward V	1483
	Richard III	1483
Tudor	Henry VII	1485
	Henry VIII	1509
	Edward VI	1547
	Jane	1553
	Mary	1553
	Elizabeth I	1558
Stuart	James I	1603
	Charles I	1625
	{ The Commonwealth	1649}
	{ The Protectorate	1653}
Stuart	Charles II	1660
	James II	1685
	{William & Mary	1689–94 }
	{William III	1694–1702}
	Anne	1702
Hanover	George I	1714
	George II	1727
	George III	1760
	George IV	1820
	William IV	1830
	Victoria	1837
Saxe-Coburg	Edward VII	1901
Windsor	George V	1910
	Edward VIII	1936
	George VI	1936
	Elizabeth II	1952

money. That which by common consent is used as a medium of exchange, measure and store of value and standard of deferred payment. ''The word 'money' at the present time has a diversity of meanings, and when it is found in a will there is no presumption that it has one meaning rather than another'': *Perrin* v *Morgan* [1943] AC 399.

money Bill. A Bill (qv) usually introduced in the Commons which, in the opinion of the Speaker of the Commons, deals only with the imposition, repeal or alteration of taxation, the imposition of charges on the Consolidated Fund (qv), etc. If sent to the Lords and not passed by them, it is presented to the Crown and becomes an Act on the Royal Assent (qv) being signified: Parliament Act 1911. *See* PARLIAMENT.

money had and received. Action, derived from a writ of account, by which the plaintiff claimed a sum of money as ''had and received by defendant to his use'', eg, as where the defendant had received money on a consideration which had failed entirely.

moneylender. A person whose business is that of moneylending, or who advertises or announces himself or holds himself out in any way as carrying on that business. See the Moneylenders Acts 1900 and 1927 (repealed by the C.C.A. 1974). He must be licensed by the Director General of Fair Trading (qv) in his name at a registered address. See O. 83, r. 2 (action brought by moneylender or assignee); *London and Harrogate Securities* v *Pitts* [1976] 1 WLR 264.

money-lending company. A company, the ordinary business of which includes the making of loans or quasi-loans (qv) or the giving of guarantees in connection with them: Cos.A. 1980, s. 65(1).

money lodged in court. Money paid to the Court Funds Office (formerly the Supreme Court Pay Office) for transmission to the Bank of England. See Direction on Payments into Court (Postal Facilities), Sept. 1978; S.I. 1981/1589.

Monopolies and Mergers Commission. Appointed by the Secretary of State to investigate and report on any question referred to it under the Fair Trading Act 1973 with respect to: existence or possible existence of a monopoly situation (ie, where at least one-quarter of the market is controlled by a single firm); the creation or possible creation of a merger situation (ie, where two or more enterprises combine and the value of assets taken over exceeds (currently) £15m). See also the Monopolies and Restrictive Practices (Inquiry and Control) Act 1948; and S.I. 1980/373.

monopoly. 1. Market structure with only a single seller of a commodity or service. 2. Royal privilege for the buying, selling or making of a commodity, to be enjoyed by the grantee only. 3. Under the Fair Trading Act 1973, ''control of one-quarter of the sales in a market''.

monstrans de droit. Plea of right, abolished under the Crown Proceedings Act 1947, used to obtain possession of property from the Crown.

month. There is a statutory presumption that in all deeds and other instruments coming into force on or after 1st January 1926, "month" means "calendar month" unless the context otherwise provides. See the L.P.A. 1925, s. 61; O. 3, r. 1; the I.A. 1978, Sch 1; and *Dodds* v *Walker* [1981] 2 All ER 609.

moot. An assembly of members of an Inn of Court (qv) at which points of law are argued.

moratorium. An authorised period of delay in the performing of an obligation, eg, settling a debt.

morganatic marriage. Marriage between a royal or noble person and one of inferior rank (which remains unchanged), the children of which do not inherit a royal rank.

mort d'ancestor. Death of an ancestor. An action, abolished in 1833, whereby, if X died seised as of an estate in fee, and his heir, Y, should have been seised of that estate, then if Z obtained seisin (qv) before Y, Z was to be turned out and seisin restored to Y. The action was available only in the case of the death of a father, mother, brother, sister, uncle or aunt.

mortgage. The transfer of an estate or interest in land or other property in order to secure the payment of a debt or the discharge of some other obligation. Example: A borrows money from B and later conveys property to B as security for repayment of the loan; A is the *mortgagor*, B is the *mortgagee*. A mortgage may be legal (qv) or equitable (qv). It may be discharged by foreclosure (qv), redemption (qv), exercise of mortgagee's power of sale, merger (qv) or under the L.P.A. 1925, s. 115. See also the Rent Act 1977, Part X.

mortgage actions. Applications by mortgagees for possession of property or payment of principal, arrears, interest, etc. See O. 88; and the Lim.A. 1980, s. 29.

mortgage and consumer credit. A mortgage comes within the C.C.A. 1974 if it is in effect a regulated agreement (qv), ie, a personal credit agreement under which the debtor is supplied by the creditor with a credit not above £5,000 (but loans made by a building society or local authority for house purchase are exempt). An improperly executed agreement can be enforced against a debtor by court order only. The court can open an agreement considered extortionate. The debtor may redeem prematurely at any time, on giving notice to the creditor: s. 94. A security cannot be enforced by reason of breach of the regulated agreement without notice served on the debtor: s. 87. See also ss. 113, 177(2).

mortgage, building society. See BUILDING SOCIETY MORTGAGE.

mortgage, contributory. See CONTRIBUTORY MORTGAGE.

mortgage, controlled. See CONTROLLED MORTGAGE.

mortgagee. See MORTGAGE.

mortgage, equitable. See EQUITABLE MORTGAGE.

mortgagee's rights. Generally: to take possession; to sell; to foreclose; to lease; to hold title deeds; to appoint a receiver; to sue the mortgagor personally on covenants in the mortgage deed. See, eg, *Twentieth Century Banking Corporation* v *Wilkinson* [1977] Ch 99; *Western Bank* v *Schindler* [1977] Ch 1.

mortgage, instalment. The repayment of a mortgage loan by equal monthly payments for an agreed number of years, at the end of which capital and interest have been repaid fully.

mortgage, legal. See LEGAL MORTGAGE.

mortgage of registered land, protection of. See REGISTERED LAND, PROTECTION OF MORTGAGE OF.

mortgage, regulated. See REGULATED MORTGAGE.

mortgages, consolidation of. See CONSOLIDATION OF MORTGAGES.

mortgage, second. Mortgage subject to prior claims of a first mortgage.

mortgage, standing. Procedure whereby the borrower pays interest regularly on loan and repays capital in a single lump sum.

mortgage, Welsh. See WELSH MORTGAGE.

mortgagor. See MORTGAGE.

mortgagor's rights. Generally he is entitled to possession of the property, to receive income and profits, to redeem. See EQUITY OF REDEMPTION.

mortis causa, donatio. *See* DONATIO MORTIS CAUSA.

mortmain. Dead hand. Phrase used to refer to land which was considered inalienable. Under statutes prohibiting alienation in mortmain, the devise of lands to a corporation was void, except for charitable uses. Law relating to mortmain was abolished under the Charities Act 1960, s. 3.

mortuum vadium. Dead pledge. Early type of mortgage in which mortgagee took rents and profits in discharge of interest only.

motion. 1. Formal proposal made at a meeting. 2. Oral application to a judge or court requesting an order directing performance of an action in the applicant's favour. See, eg, O. 29: O. 53.

motive. That which incites to action. Not to be confused with *mens rea* (qv). Thus, X, in stealing Y's gloves may have as motive his desire for greater comfort, but this is not the *mens rea* required for the offence of stealing. The motive may be relevant as evidence or in deciding the punishment following conviction.

motor car. Mechanically-propelled vehicle, not being a motor cycle or invalid carriage, constructed to carry a load or passengers (not more than seven) with an unladen weight not in excess of 3 tonnes: Road Traffic Act 1972, s. 190.

motor cycle. Mechanically-propelled vehicle, not being an invalid carriage, with less than four wheels and an unladen weight not in excess of 8 cwt: Road Traffic Act 1972, s. 190. For "learner motor cycle", see the 1972 Act s. 88(2A)(as substituted by the Transport Act 1981, s. 23(2)).

motor dealer. *See* DEALER, MOTOR.

Motor Insurers' Bureau. Group of motor vehicle insurers which, by agreement with the Department of the Environment, undertakes to satisfy or cause to be satisfied, a judgment obtained against a motorist for a liability required to be covered by an insurance policy and which is not satisfied within seven days. The Bureau also makes payments relating to death or personal injury caused by a vehicle whose owner or driver cannot be traced. See the Road Traffic Act 1974, s. 20.

motor vehicle. Mechanically propelled vehicle intended or adapted for use on the roads. See the Road Traffic Act 1972, s. 190(1).

motor vehicle, taking of. The unauthorised taking of a vehicle is an offence under the Th.A. 1968, s. 12. *See* CONVEYANCE.

movables. Term generally applied to personal, as opposed to real (or "immovable"), property. See *R v Hoyles* [1911] 1 Ch 179.

M.P. Member of Parliament (qv).

M.R. Master of the Rolls (qv).

mugging. Colloquialism referring to robbery (qv) of an isolated pedestrian. See *R v Williams* (1982) 4 Cr App R(S) 156.

multiple admissibility. Principle of evidence (qv) stating that if evidence is admissible for one purpose it may not be rejected solely because it is not admissible for some other purpose. See, eg, *Morton v Morton* [1937] P 151.

multiple damages. An amount of damages (qv) calculated by multiplying the sum which might be truly compensatory. Under the Protection of Trading Interests Act 1980, s. 6, there is a right of action for a UK citizen or a person carrying on business in the UK or a body corporate incorporated in the UK to recoup payment made on account of a foreign award of multiple damages. See also the C.J.J.A. 1982, s. 38.

multiplicity of issues. Phrase relating to the exclusion of evidence (qv) which "raises side issues upon which the court cannot decide without injustice to other parties": *A.-G. v Nottingham Corporation* [1904] 1 Ch 673.

municipal law. The law of a nation or state, as distinguished from the law of nations (ie, international law). May be divided into *public* and *private* law (qqv).

muniments. Title deeds and other evidence relating to title to land. *See* TITLE.

murder. Unlawful homicide with malice aforethought (qv). Described by Coke as ". . . when any man of sound memory, and of the age of discretion, unlawfully killeth within any county of the realm any reasonable creature *in rerum natura* under the King's peace, with malice aforethought, either expressed by the party or implied by law, so as the party wounded, or hurt, etc., die of the wound or hurt, etc., within a year and a day after the same''. See *DPP* v *Smith* [1961] AC 290; *Hyam* v *DPP* [1975] AC 55; and *R* v *Williamson* (1978) 67 Cr App R 63.

murder, threats to. A person who without lawful excuse makes to another a threat, intending that that other would fear it would be carried out, to kill that other or a third person is guilty of an offence: O.P.A. 1861, s. 16. See *R* v *Cousins* [1982] QB 526.

murdrum. *Morth* = a secret killing. A heavy fine imposed by the Normans on a hundred (qv) in which a Norman had been slain and the murderer remained at large. The term came to signify the actual killing. *See* PRESENTMENT OF ENGLISHRY.

mutatis mutandis. 1. With the necessary changes made. 2. With consideration of the respective differences.

mute. When asked to plead, an accused person may stand mute. If considered to be mute of malice (ie, deliberately silent) a plea of not guilty is entered for him and the trial proceeds. If considered mute "by visitation of God" (ie, deaf and dumb) an attempt is made to make him understand and answer the charge by some means and where this fails, a plea of not guilty is entered for him. Where there is doubt a jury will decide. See *R* v *Paling* (1978) 67 Cr App R 229. See C.L.A. 1967, s. 6(1)(*c*).

mutiny. A combination between two or more persons subject to service law, or between persons, two at least of whom are subject to service law, to overthrow, or resist lawful authority in the Forces or any forces co-operating therewith, to disobey such authority so as to make the disobedience subversive of discipline, or to impede the performance of any duty or service in the Forces or in any forces co-operating therewith. See, eg, the Army Act 1955, s. 31(3).

mutual accounts. Where each of two parties has received and paid money on account of the other.

mutual dealings. Where there have been mutual dealings between a debtor and one of his creditors, account must be taken of what is due from one to the other, and the balance of the account (but no more) shall be paid or claimed. See the B.A. 1914, s. 31; *Rolls Razor Ltd* v *Cox* [1967] 1 QB 552.

mutual desertion. Result of each spouse, independently and without just cause, leaving the other. See *Hosegood* v *Hosegood* [1950] WN 218; *Price* v *Price* [1968] 3 All ER 543.

mutual wills. Wills made by two or more persons, conferring reciprocal benefits, and based on an agreement to make such wills and not to revoke them without consent of the other. See *Stone* v *Hoskins* [1905] P 194; *Re Oldham* [1925] Ch 75; *Re Cleaver* [1981] 1 WLR 939; and Law Reform Commission Report 1980 (Cmnd 7902). *See* WILL.

N

naked contract. *See* NUDUM PACTUM.

naked trust. Bare trust (qv).

name and arms clause. Clause in settlement (qv) or will (qv) directing forfeiture of a beneficiary's interests unless he takes and uses a stated surname on all occasions. See *Re Bouverie* [1952] Ch 69; *Re Neeld* [1962] Ch 643.

name, change of. A surname may be changed by operation of law (as on marriage), by statutory declaration, by deed poll, by advertisement (in, eg, a local newspaper). See *Dancer* v *Dancer* [1949] P 147 (change of name by repute); *Re T. (an infant)* [1963] Ch 238; *D.* v *B.* [1977] 2 WLR 1011. For change of a Christian name (ie, that given at baptism) see *Re Parrott* [1946] Ch 183. *See* SURNAME.

name, family. *See* SURNAME.

naming a Member. Parliamentary procedure whereby the Speaker (qv) or chairman of a committee of the House declares that a member of Parliament is guilty of irregular conduct.

National Health Services. *See* HEALTH SERVICES, NATIONAL.

national insurance. *See* SOCIAL SECURITY.

National Insurance Tribunals. *See* SOCIAL SECURITY TRIBUNALS.

nationalisation. The bringing of the ownership and management of firms or industries under state control. See, eg, the Transport Act 1947.

nationality. The legal relationship attaching to membership of a nation resulting from, eg, birth, naturalisation (qv), marriage. Generally implies duties of allegiance and protection by state. " 'Nationality' in the sense of citizenship of a certain state must not be confused with nationality as meaning membership of a certain nation in the sense of race": *London Borough of Ealing* v *Race Relations Board* [1972] 1 All ER 104. "Dual nationality" refers to citizenship held simultaneously in two countries. See the B.N.A. 1981.

nations, law of. International law (qv).

natural allegiance. The allegiance (qv) owed to his country by a subject. See *Joyce* v *DPP* [1946] AC 347.

natural child. Term applied generally to an illegitimate child (qv).

natural gas, offshore. *See* OFFSHORE NATURAL GAS.

naturalisation. Process resulting in an alien's receiving the status pertaining to a native citizen. In the UK it follows the grant of a certificate and the taking of an oath of allegiance. The alien must show that he is of good character, has a sufficient knowledge of English, Welsh or Gaelic, that his principal home will be in the UK, that he was in the UK at the beginning of the period of five years ending with the date of his application and that he has not been absent in that period from the UK for more than 450 days and has not been in breach of immigration laws: B.N.A. 1981, s. 6(1), Sch 1.

natural justice. *See* JUSTICE, NATURAL.

natural law. *See* LAW, NATURAL.

natural necessity. Term formerly used (see, eg, *R* v *Strattan* (1799) 21 St Tr) for self-defence (qv).

natural person. A human being, as contrasted with an artificial person (qv), eg, a corporation (qv).

natural rights. 1. Rights conferred upon man by the natural law (qv). 2. Those basic rights found commonly in the laws of civilised nations, eg, freedom of speech. *See* RIGHT.

naval court. Summoned by the commander of one of HM ships on a foreign station to investigate a complaint, or loss of a ship in the area and consisting of naval officers. Appeal lies to the Divisional Court and Court of Appeal (qv).

navigation, right of. Right of public to use a river as a highway for, eg, shipping. It is not a right of property, merely a right of way.

necessaries. 1. Goods suitable to the condition in life of an infant (qv) or minor or other person and to his actual requirements at the time of the sale and delivery. "A minor may bind himself to pay for his necessary meat, drink, apparel, necessary physic, and such other necessaries, and likewise for his good teaching and instruction, whereby he may profit himself afterwards": Co Litt 172a. See the S.G.A. 1979, s. 3; *Ryder v Wombwell* (1868) LR 4 Ex 32; *Nash v Inman* [1908] 2 KB 1. 2. In the case of husband and wife, "things that are really necessary and suitable to the style in which the husband chooses to live, in so far as the articles fall fairly within the domestic department which is ordinarily confided to the management of the wife": *Phillipson v Hayter* (1870) LR 6 CP 38.

necessaries, contracts made by wife for. A man is not generally liable on contracts made by his wife for necessaries if: the trader has been expressly warned not to supply her with goods on credit; she has been forbidden to pledge her husband's credit; she was supplied with the means to purchase necessaries without pledging her husband's credit; the trader gave credit exclusively to her; the husband had a sufficient supply of the goods purchased. The common law rules about a wife's agency of necessity were abrogated by the Matrimonial Proceedings and Property Act 1970, s. 41.

necessity. Circumstances compelling a course of action. As a defence, rejected in *R v Dudley and Stephens* (1884) 14 QBD 273 (shipwrecked mariners killing and eating boy so as to survive); *London Borough of Southwark v Williams* [1971] 2 All ER 175 (squatting by homeless persons). In the case of tort (qv) the defence may succeed where the damage has been caused to prevent a greater evil and the act was reasonable: *Leigh v Gladstone* (1909) 26 TLR 139; *Cope v Sharpe* [1912] 1 KB 496; *Cresswell v Sirl* [1948] 1 KB 241.

necessity, agent by. *See* AGENT.

neck verse. *See* BENEFIT OF CLERGY.

nec vi, nec clam, nec precario. Not by violence, stealth or entreaty. Phrase used in relation to user as of right, eg,

Gardner v Hodgson's Kingston Brewery Co [1903] AC 229.

ne exeat regno. That he shall not leave the kingdom. Writ (qv) restraining a person's leaving the realm, used in the case of political offenders and, later, debtors where there was probable cause to believe that they were about to leave the country. See, for a review of the law, *Lewis v Lewis* (1893) 68 LT 198; *Felton v Callis* [1969] 1 QB 200.

negative clearance. Procedure whereby parties to an agreement may seek a declaration that it does not come within the scope of, and therefore does not infringe, the Treaty of Rome 1957, art. 85 (prohibiting agreements which prevent, restrict or distort competition). See EEC Council Regulation No 17/62, art. 2; Commission Decision No 72/403/EEC [1973] CMLR 77. *See* EEC.

negative pregnant. A literal answer to an allegation in pleadings (qv) which evades answering its substance. Example: it is alleged that X received £100 from Y; X merely denies the stated amount, whereas the essence of the allegation is X's receipt of money and not merely the amount. See O. 18, r. 13; *Tildesley v Harper* (1878) 17 Ch D 403.

neglect. Culpable omission to perform a duty. One who undertakes the care of another who, by reason of sickness or age, is incapable of providing necessaries for himself, is criminally responsible if his conscious neglect causes the death of that other. See *R v Marriot* (1838) 3 C & P 425; *R v Instan* [1893] 1 QB 450; *R v Stone and Dobinson* [1977] QB 354 (in which it was held that in a case of manslaughter (qv) it is not necessary to prove that the defendant was reckless as to whether the victim might suffer serious bodily harm or death); and *R v Sheppard* [1980] 3 All ER 899.

neglect, wilful. *See* WILFUL NEGLECT.

negligence. "In strict legal analysis, negligence means more than heedless or careless conduct, whether in omission or commission; it properly connotes the complex concept of duty, breach and damage thereby suffered by the person to whom the duty was owing": per Lord Wright in *Lochgelly*

Iron & Coal v *M'Mullan* [1934] AC 1. Used in the Unfair Contract Terms Act 1977, s. 1(1) to mean the breach of any obligation arising from the express or implied terms of a contract, to take reasonable care or exercise reasonable skill in the performance of a contract, or the breach of any common-law duty to take reasonable care or exercise reasonable skill (but not any stricter duty), or the breach of the common duty of care imposed by the Occupiers' Liability Act 1957. *See* DUTY OF CARE.

negligence, advertent. Situation in which a tortfeasor (qv) displays ''an attitude of mental indifference to obvious risks'': *per* Eve J in *Hudston* v *Viney* [1921] 1 Ch 98. In a case of *in-advertent negligence*, the tortfeasor has displayed mere carelessness.

negligence, contributory. *See* CONTRIBUTORY NEGLIGENCE.

negligence, gross. *See* GROSS NEGLIGENCE.

negligence liability, avoidance of. By the Unfair Contract Terms Act 1977, s. 2(1) a person cannot by reference to any contract term or notice given to persons exclude or restrict his liability for death or personal injury resulting from negligence and, in the case of other loss or damage, he cannot so exclude or restrict his liability for negligence except in so far as the term or notice satisfies the requirement of reasonableness (which will be considered by reference to, eg, strength of bargaining position of parties relative to each other, whether goods were manufactured to the customer's special order, whether the customer knew or ought reasonably to have known of existence and extent of the term: Sch 2).

negligence, tort of. The breach of a legal duty to take care, resulting in damage to the plaintiff which was not desired by the defendant. ''The omission to do something which a reasonable man, guided upon those considerations which ordinarily regulate the conduct of human affairs, would do, or doing something which a prudent and reasonable man would not do'': *Blyth* v *Birmingham Waterworks Co* (1856) 11 Ex 781. Bur-

den of proof is generally on the plaintiff. See *Donoghue* v *Stevenson* [1932] AC 562; *Deyong* v *Shenburn* [1946] KB 227; *Home Office* v *Dorset Yacht Co* [1970] AC 10; and *McLaughlin* v *O'Brian* [1982] 2 WLR 82. *See* DUTY OF CARE.

negligent misstatement. A statement carelessly made in circumstances where there is a duty to be honest and careful, resulting in loss to some person to whom that duty is owed and who has acted on the statement. Liability for such a statement may arise in tort (qv) and contract (qv). See *Hedley Byrne & Co Ltd* v *Heller and Partners* [1964] AC 793; *Esso Petroleum Co Ltd* v *Mardon* [1976] QB 801.

negotiable instrument. An instrument with the following characteristics: (1) title to it passes on delivery; (2) holder for the time being may sue in his own name; (3) notice of assignment need not be given to person liable thereon; (4) bona fide holder for value takes free from any defect in title of predecessors. Examples: bills of exchange; promissory notes and cheques; dividend warrants; debentures payable to bearer (see *Bechuanaland Exploration Co* v *London Trading Bank Ltd* [1898] 2 QB 658). See the B.Ex.A. 1882, ss. 31, 32.

negotiation of a bill. The transferring of a bill of exchange (qv) from one person to another so that the transferee becomes the holder of the bill: B.Ex.A. 1882, s. 31(1).

negotiorum gestio. The management of affairs. *Negotiorum gestior* is one who interferes in the affairs of another for that other's advantage, but without authority. See *Falcke* v *Scottish Insurance* (1887) 34 Ch D 249.

neighbour, concept in law of. *See* DUTY OF CARE.

nemine contradicente. Abbreviated to *nem con.* No one saying otherwise, ie, unanimous.

nemo dat quod non habet. No one can give that which he has not. See S.G.A. 1979, s. 21(1). Thus, a person cannot give better title than he has. In some cases, however, a buyer acquires a good title, notwithstanding a defect in the seller's title. Examples: sale in market overt (qv);

sale under an order of the court; transfer of a negotiable instrument (qv) to a holder in due course; under the doctrine of estoppel (qv). See *Hollins v Fowler* (1875) LR 7HL 757; *Greenwood v Bennett* [1973] QB 195.

nemo debet bis puniri pro uno delicto. No man ought to be punished twice for one offence. See *R v Statutory Ctee of Pharmaceutical Society of Great Britain* [1981] 1 WLR 886.

nemo debet bis vexari. No man ought to be twice vexed. No person should be again prosecuted upon the same facts if he has been tried by a competent court. *See* AUTREFOIS ACQUIT.

nemo debet esse judex in propria causa. No person should be a judge in his own cause. The maxim applies also to a cause in which a person has an interest. See, eg, *Dimes v Grand Junction Canal Co* (1852) 3 HL 759; *R v Barnsley Metropolitan BC ex p Hook* [1976] 3 All ER 452.

nemo est heres viventis. A living person has no heir (since not until that person's death can his heir be ascertained). *See* HEIR APPARENT.

nemo tenetur seipsum accusare. No person is bound to incriminate himself. See *R v Scott* (1856) Dears & B 47; *Commissioners of Customs and Excise v Ingram* [1948] 1 All ER 927. *See* INCRIMINATE.

nervous shock. Actual illness in the form of physical symptoms or psychiatric illness. Regarded as bodily hurt, constituting a tort (qv). "It is now well recognised that an action will lie for injury by shock sustained through the medium of the eye or ear without direct contact": *Bourhill v Young* [1943] AC 92. See *King v Phillips* [1953] 1 QB 429; *Chadwick v British Rwys Board* [1967] 1 WLR 912; *Hinz v Berry* [1970] 2 QB 40; *McLaughlin v O'Brian* [1982] 2 WLR 982.

net estate. In relation to a deceased person, it includes: property which he had power to dispose of by will, less funeral, testamentary and administration expenses; property in respect of which he held a general power of appointment (qv) not exercised; sums which he nominated another to receive; *donationes mortis causa* (qv): Inheritance (Provision for Family and Dependants) Act 1975.

new trial. *See* TRIAL, NEW.

next friend. An adult through whom an infant (qv) or patient (within the meaning of the M.H.A. 1983) sues, eg, the infant's father or person *in loco parentis*, patient's receiver, or Official Solicitor (qqv). His name must appear on the writ (qv) and he must undertake to be responsible for costs. In the High Court, the next friend may not appear in person; a solicitor must be retained. See O. 80, rr. 1–3.

next of kin. Generally, one's nearest blood relations. "Statutory next of kin" may be construed technically, to denote next of kin who, on a person's death intestate, would have taken his personalty under the Statute of Distributions. See *Re Bilcock* [1916] 2 Ch 495; *Re Sutcliffe* [1929] 1 Ch 123.

nexus. Bond; connection.

night restriction. Supervision order (qv) requiring a young offender to remain for specified periods between 6 pm–6 am at a place or one of several places specified in the order: C.&Y.P.A. 1969, s. 12 as substituted by the C.J.A. 1982, s. 20.

nightwalker. Synonym for prostitute. See, eg, the Metropolitan Police Act 1839; and the C.L.A. 1967, s. 13 (abolishing the offence).

nihil debet. He owes nothing. Plea in former action of debt.

nisi. Unless. Not final or absolute.

nisi per legale judicium parium suorum, vel per legem terrae. [No freeman is to be taken, imprisoned or exiled] unless by the lawful judgment of his peers or [and] by the law of the land. Provision of Magna Carta (qv).

nisi prius. Unless before. Trial at *nisi prius* followed after the sheriff (qv) was commanded to secure the attendance of a jury at Westminster "unless before" that day the county should be visited by a judge of assize (qv). The term was used in recent years to refer to commission to try causes conferred on judges of assize.

no case to answer. Submission by the defendant, at the close of the plaintiff's case, that a prima facie case has not been made out. If the submission succeeds, judgment is entered for the defendant. It may be based on a point of law or absence of evidence relating to essential facts. See *R v Barker* (1975) 65 Cr App R 287; and *R v Galbraith* [1981] 1 WLR 1039.

noise. "Sound which is undesired by the recipient": *Wilson Report*, 1963. An action may lie in some circumstances for nuisance resulting from noise: see, eg, *Ball v Ray* (1873) LR 8 Ch 467; *Hammersmith BC v Magnum Automated Forecourts* [1978] 1 All ER 886; *Lambert Flat Management Ltd v Lomas* [1981] 1 WLR 898. See also the Control of Pollution Act 1974, s. 58.

noise abatement zone. Zone so designated by order of a local authority, confirmed by the Secretary of State, in which noise levels exceeding those registered (in a noise level register) may be penalised under the Control of Pollution Act 1974, s. 65. See the Land Compensation Act 1973, s. 1 (for the right to compensation where value of an interest is depreciated by noise); the L.G.P.L.A. 1980, Sch 2; the Control of Noise (Measurement and Registers) Regulations 1976 (S.I. 1976/37); *R v Fenny Stratford Justices ex p Watney Mann* (*Midlands*) *Ltd* [1976] 2 All ER 888.

nolens volens. Unwilling or willing.

nolle prosequi. Unwilling to prosecute. An undertaking by the plaintiff to discontinue an action. In a criminal case the entry of a *nolle prosequi*, which stays a prosecution on indictment (qv), is made only by the Attorney-General (qv) before judgment. It is not an acquittal, so that fresh proceedings may be brought on the same charge at a later date.

nolo contendere. I do not wish to contend. Generally, an implied confession of guilt.

nominal capital. A company's authorised capital (qv).

nominal damages. *See* DAMAGES.

nominal partner. Known also as "ostensible partner". One who holds himself out as having an interest in a business.

nomination. 1. The appointment of "a worthy clerk or man to a parson-age or vicarage": *Termes de la Ley*. 2. Designation or proposal by name for a vacant office. 3. A direction to a person who holds funds on behalf of another to pay them to a nominated person on the event of death. Nomination may be made by an adult or infant (qv) who has reached the age of 16. It is revoked on marriage, but not by will. See the Savings Certificates Regulations 1981, S.I. 1981/686.

nonage. 1. Below 18 years of age (ie, lacking the requisite legal age). 2. The ninth part of a deceased's movables, paid to the clergy.

non assumpsit. He did not promise. Plea in action of *assumpsit* (qv), stating that the defendant made no promise.

non-cohabitation order. Order made by a magistrates' court based upon the D.P.A. 1978, releasing one spouse from the obligation to cohabit with the other.

non-commercial agreement. "A consumer credit agreement or a consumer hire agreement (qqv) not made by the creditor or owner in the course of a business carried on by him": C.C.A. 1974, s. 189(1). Example: agreement for a loan made between friends and not in the course of a business transaction.

non compos mentis. Not of sound mind.

non constat. It is not clear. It does not follow.

non-contentious business. Business not contained within the definition of contentious business (qv), eg, drafting of a will, conveyancing. Mode and amount of remuneration are governed by orders under the Solicitors Act 1974, s. 56. See the S.C.A. 1981, s. 128.

non-contributory benefits. Benefits under the S.S.A. 1975, as amended, including: attendance allowance; invalid care allowance, mobility allowance; age addition (increase of pension for those over 80); guardian's allowance (payable, eg, to a guardian where both parents of a child are dead). *See* CONTRIBUTORY BENEFITS.

non-direction. Failure of a trial judge

to direct the jury on a necessary point of law.

non-disclosure. *See* DISCLOSURE, NON-.

non-discrimination notice. 1. Notice under the Race Relations Act 1976, s. 58, after investigation by the Commission for Racial Equality (qv) whereby a person who is committing or has committed an unlawful discriminatory act or an act contravening ss. 28–31, is required not to commit such acts. Appeal against notice may be made to an industrial tribunal (qv) or county court (qv). A register of such notices is established under s. 61. 2. Notice issued under the Sex Discrimination Act 1975, s. 67, by the Equal Opportunities Commission (qv) requiring a person not to commit an unlawful discriminatory act. There is a right of appeal under s. 68. See *Commission for Racial Equality* v *Amari Plastics Ltd* [1982] QB 1194.

non est factum. It is not [his] deed. Plea which denies that a deed is that of the defendant, eg, where there has been a mistake as to the nature of the transaction. See *Howatson* v *Webb* [1908] 1 Ch 1; *Blay* v *Pollard and Morris* [1930] 1 KB 628; *Gallie* v *Lee* [1971] AC 1004; and *Mills* v *IRC* [1972] 3 All ER 977. "A person who signs a document, and parts with it so that it may come into other hands, has a responsibility . . . to take care what he signs, which, if neglected, prevents him from denying his liability under the document": *United Dominions Trust Ltd* v *Western and Another* [1976] QB 513.

non est inventus. He has not been found. A return made by a sheriff (qv) to a writ of *capias* (qv) when the defendant cannot be found.

nonfeasance. Failure to perform an act which one is bound by law to do. "The distinction between misfeasance and nonfeasance is valid only in the case of highways repairable by the public at large. It does not apply to any other branch of law": *Pride of Derby Ltd* v *British Celanese Ltd* [1953] Ch 149. See also the Highways Act 1980, s. 58. *See* MISFEASANCE.

non-joinder. A plea in abatement which alleged that the plaintiff had failed to join in the action all those who ought to have been parties. Under O. 15, r. 6, "no cause or matter shall be defeated by reason of misjoinder or nonjoinder of any party".

non-jury list. A list in the QBD of cases to be tried by a judge sitting alone, or with assessors (qv).

non liquet. It is not clear.

non-molestation clause. *See* INJUNCTIONS, MATRIMONIAL.

non obstante. Notwithstanding. Term used to describe a doctrine by which the Crown attempted to extend its prerogative.

non obstante veredicto. Notwithstanding the verdict.

non placet. It does not please; it is not approved. Formula used by an assembly to record a negative vote.

non prosequitur. He does not follow up. Title of judgment for the defendant where the plaintiff did not take the proper steps within the prescribed period of time. See O. 19, r. 1.

non-provable debts in bankruptcy. Debts in respect of an illegal consideration (qv); maintenance payments due to the debtor's wife; debts barred under the Lim.A. 1939–80; demands in the nature of unliquidated damages (qv) arising otherwise than out of a contract or breach of trust; debts arising after commission of an act of bankruptcy (qv) where creditors knew of the act. See the B.A. 1914, s. 30. *See* BANKRUPTCY.

non sequitur. It does not follow.

non-suit. Phrase referring to the renouncing by the plaintiff of a suit before the verdict, eg, on discovery of a defect. Refers also to the withdrawal by a judge of the case from the jury, and the direction of the verdict in the defendant's favour. Non-suit in the High Court (qv) has been replaced by discontinuance (qv). See *Fox* v *Star Newspaper Co Ltd* [1900] AC 19; *Clack* v *Arthurs Engineering Ltd* [1959] 2 QB 211; and the County Court Rules 1981, O. 21, r. 2.

non-user. End of the exercise of rights. Thus, non-user may be evidence of abandonment of a private right of easement (qv). See *Swan* v *Sinclair* [1925] AC 227.

no-par value share. A share (qv)

252

which has no nominal value. In effect, its value is that determined on the Stock Exchange. Shares of this type may not be issued by a limited company: Cos.A. 1948, s. 2(4). *See* COMPANY.

norm. An authoritative standard or rule of behaviour. *See* LAW, PURE THEORY OF.

Norwich Guildhall Court. Local court, abolished under the Courts Act 1971, s. 43.

noscitur a sociis. Known from associates. A rule of interpretation whereby the meaning of a word may be ascertained by reference to its context. "English words derive colour from those which surround them": *Bourne* v *Norwich Crematorium Ltd* [1967] 2 All ER 576. See *Hunter* v *Wright* (1830) 10 B & C 714; *Pengelly* v *Bell Punch Co Ltd* [1964] 2 All ER 945.

notarial will. "Will made under a system which allows the testator either to dictate his last testamentary wishes to a notary or to hand the notary an instrument which he declares contains them. The notary then sees to the attestation requirements and records the transaction": Law Reform Committee Report 1980. The Report did not favour the introduction of such a system in the UK.

notary. Known also as "notary public". Usually a solicitor who attests deeds, or one, who, in the case of a dishonoured bill, notes or protests it. A "duly certificated notary public" is a notary public who has in force a practising certificate as a solicitor, and is duly entered in the Court of Faculties of the Archbishop of Canterbury: Solicitors Act 1974, s. 87(1). See *Re Champion* [1906] P 86.

not guilty. 1. Plea to an indictment which is, in essence, a challenge to the prosecution to establish guilt. It may be changed once the trial has started. 2. Verdict following trial, which, in effect, is an acquittal. The accused may be found not guilty of offences specifically charged in the indictment, but guilty of another offence arising from allegations therein. Where the defendant pleads not

guilty and the prosecution does not offer evidence, the judge may order the recording of a verdict of not guilty: C.J.A. 1967, s. 17. *See* GUILTY; VERDICT.

not guilty by reason of insanity. A special verdict which is, in form, an acquittal. The defendant may, nevertheless, appeal against it. See the Criminal Appeal Act 1968, ss. 12, 15.

notice. Knowledge of some fact. May be: (1) *actual*, as where, eg, a purchaser is made aware during negotiations of the existence of a prior interest (see *Reeves* v *Pope* [1914] 2 KB 284); (2) *constructive* (qv); (3) *imputed*, as where, eg, a purchaser employs a solicitor or other agent who obtains actual or constructive notice (see *Le Neve* v *Le Neve* (1747) 3 Atk 648).

notice, minimum periods of. Periods which an employer is required to give an employee if he wishes to terminate his contract—one week for each year of service up to maximum of 12 weeks after 12 years' service. See the E.P.(C.)A. 1978, Part IV.

notice of abandonment. Written or oral notice indicating that the assured (under a policy of marine insurance) abandons the subject-matter insured unconditionally to the insured. If notice is not given, the loss is considered as partial. Notice must be given with reasonable diligence. *See* ABANDONMENT.

notice of dishonour. Notice that a bill of exchange (qv) is dishonoured must be given to the parties whom the holder is seeking to hold liable. See the B.Ex.A. 1882, s. 49. *See* DISHONOUR OF BILL.

notice of intended prosecution. Notice sent to a person, within 14 days of his alleged offence, under, eg, the Road Traffic Act 1972, s. 179(2).

notice of title. Knowledge (actual, imputed, constructive) acquired by an intending purchaser that title is encumbered by rights or interests. *See* NOTICE; TITLE.

notice to admit. Notice calling on the party served to admit all or some specified part of another party's case or to admit to the authenticity of documents listed, but not to their truth. Failure to admit may result in the payment of costs of the proof of the issue(s) in question or of documents by the party served. See O. 27.

notice to produce. Notice by one party in an action to another to produce at the trial documents in his possession. In default of production, secondary evidence (qv) of documents may be given. See O. 24.

notice to quit. Notice required to be given by a landlord to a tenant (qv) prior to the determination of tenancy. No notice to quit premises let as a dwelling is valid unless in writing and contains information prescribed by the Secretary of State by statutory instrument, and is given not less than four weeks before the date on which it is to take effect: Protection from Eviction Act 1977, s. 5. See also the Rent Act 1977, ss. 103–106.

noting a bill. Process of attaching a memorandum to a bill of exchange by a notary (qv), giving the reason for its having been dishonoured, as the first step to a protest (qv). See the B.Ex.A. 1882, s. 51. *See* BILL OF EXCHANGE.

not negotiable. Words marked on, eg, a cheque or postal order, as a safeguard, so that the holder has no better right than the previous holder. See the B.Ex.A. 1882, s. 81; and *Great Western Rlwy Co* v *London & County Banking Co* [1900] 2 QB 464. *See* NEGOTIABLE INSTRUMENT.

notorious facts. Matters of common knowledge of which, generally, judicial notice (qv) will be taken, eg, that human gestation cannot be completed within 14 days (see *R* v *Luffe* (1807) 8 East 193).

not proven. Verdict, in Scots law only, which involves an acquittal.

nova causa interveniens. New intervening cause. See, eg, *Cummings* v *Sir William Arrol & Co Ltd* [1962] 1 All ER 623.

novation. Contract whereby a creditor at the request of a debtor agrees to take another person as debtor in place of the original debtor. The original debtor is thereby released from his obligations which fall on the new debtor. See *Re European Assurance Society* (1876) 3 Ch D 391; *Scarfe* v

Jardine (1882) 7 App Cas 345.

novel disseisin. An assize (qv) based on the complaint by P that D had, without judgment, unjustly disseised P of his freehold tenement. P requested that the King's court should give judgment to put him back into seisin (qv). Abolished by the Real Property Limitation Act 1833, s. 36. *See* DISSEISIN.

novus actus interveniens. New act intervening. General defence in an action in tort (qv). When the act of a third person intervenes between the original act or omission and the damage, that act or omission is considered as the direct cause of the damage if the act of the third person could have been expected in the particular circumstances: *Scott* v *Shepherd* (1733) 2 Wm Bl 892. There is a general duty to guard against a *novus actus interveniens*: *Davies* v *Liverpool Corporation* [1949] 2 All ER 175. See also *Sayers* v *Harlow UDC* [1958] 2 All ER 342; *Chadwick* v *British Rwys Board* [1967] 1 WLR 912; and *Knightley* v *Johns* [1982] 1 All ER 951; *R* v *Pagett* [1983] Crim LR 393. *See* CAUSA REMOTA.

noxal. Referring to an offence in ancient civil law committed by a slave or animal.

noxious. That which is offensive, or which causes or tends to cause injury to health. See the O.P.A. 1861, ss. 23, 24; and *R* v *Marcus* [1981] 1 WLR 774 (concept of a "noxious thing" depends not only on quality and nature of substance, but also the quantity administered).

N.P. *Nisi prius* (qv).

nuclear installations, operation of. No person other than the UK Atomic Energy Authority may use any site for purposes of nuclear plant operation unless a licence has been granted by the minister. See the Nuclear Installations Acts 1965 and 1969.

nudum pactum. A "nude" contract, ie, "a bare promise of a thing without any consideration": Cowel. *See* CONSIDERATION; EX NUDO PACTO.

nuisance. In law of torts, an unlawful interference with another's use of enjoyment of, or right over or in relation to, land, or damage resulting from such interference: *Read* v *Lyons & Co Ltd* [1945] KB 216. Nuisance may be *public* (in which case it is also a crime), eg, obstruction of a highway, or *private*, eg, causing unreasonable personal discomfort to another. Remedies include: abatement, action for damages, injunction (qqv). Defences include trivial injury only, result of lawful use of land (see *Bradford Corporation* v *Pickles* [1895] AC 587), prescriptive right. See the Public Health Act 1936, s. 92; the Noise Abatement Act 1960; the Public Health (Recurring Nuisances) Act 1969; *NCB* v *Thorne* [1976] 1 WLR 543; and *Coventry CC* v *Doyle* [1981] 2 All ER 184. *See* TORT.

nuisance, unreasonableness causing. "It is impossible to give any precise or universal formula, but it may broadly be said that a useful test is perhaps what is reasonable according to the ordinary usages of mankind living in society": *Sedleigh-Denfield* v *O'Callaghan* [1940] AC 880. "Those acts necessary for the common and ordinary use and occupation of land and houses may be done, if conveniently done, without subjecting those who do them to an action": *Bamford* v *Turnley* (1862) 3 B & S 66. See *Cavey* v *Ledbitter* (1863) 13 CB NS 470; *Moy* v *Stoop* (1909) 25 TLR 262.

nulla bona. No goods. Statement by a sheriff (qv) in return to a writ of *fieri facias* (qv) when there are no goods to be seized.

null and void. Having no force; invalid.

nulla poena sine lege. No punishment without legal authority.

nulle terre sans seigneur. No land without a lord. Basis of the principle that all land in England was owned by the Crown, and that tenants held, ultimately, from the Crown.

nullity decree, recognition of foreign. The decree is recognised if: granted by a court in the parties' common domicile; although granted elsewhere, is recognised as effective by courts of common domicile; granted by a court of the parties' common residence or a court of the country in which a void marriage was cele-

brated; at the time of the decree either party had a substantial connection with the country granting the decree. See *Gray* v *Formosa* [1962] P 259; *Indyka* v *Indyka* [1969] 1 AC 33. (Divorce and legal separation cases are separately provided for by the Recognition of Divorces and Legal Separations Act 1971).

nullity of marriage. Marriages may be rendered *void* (because the parties are within prohibited degrees of relationship (qv), or either party is under 16, or either was lawfully married at the time of the ceremony) or *voidable* (because of, eg, wilful refusal to consummate (qv), incapacity, pregnancy at time of marriage by some person other than the petitioner, lack of valid consent to the marriage). "A void marriage is one that will be regarded by every court in any case in which the existence of the marriage is in issue as never having taken place, and can be so treated by both parties to it without the necessity of any decree annulling it; a voidable marriage is one that will be regarded by every court as a valid and subsisting marriage until a decree annulling it has been pronounced": *De Reneville* v *De Reneville* [1948] P 100. See the Mat.C.A. 1973, ss. 11, 12.

nulli vendemus, nulli negabimus, aut differemus, rectum aut justitiam. To none will we sell, to none will we deny, to none will we delay either right or justice. Provision of Magna Carta (qv).

nullum crimen sine lege. No crime except in accordance with the law—the so-called "principle of legality". "The great leading rule of criminal law is that nothing is a crime unless it is plainly forbidden by law. This rule is no doubt subject to exceptions but they are rare, narrow, and to be admitted with the greatest reluctance, and only upon the strongest reasons": *R* v *Price* (1884) 12 QBD 247.

nullum tempus occurrit regi. Time does not run against the Crown. See, however, the Lim.A. 1980, s. 37.

nullus liber homo capiatur vel imprisonetur. No freeman shall be arrested or detained in prison [without a trial]. Provision of Magna Carta (qv).

nul tiel. No such; as in *nul tiel record* (traverse (qv) that there was "no such record").

nunc pro tunc. Now for then. Phrase relating to a judgment entered so that it takes effect as if entered at an earlier date. See O. 42, r. 3.

nuncupative will. *Nuncupare* = to name, declare. A verbal testament. Abolished under the W.A. 1837, s. 9, except in the case of privileged wills (qv) made by those on active service. See Law Reform Committee Report 1980, Cmnd 7902.

nunquam indebitatus. Never indebted. Plea in an action on contract in which the defendant denied facts on which alleged liability is based.

O

oath. A solemn appeal (usually to God) to witness that some statement is true or that some promise is binding. In general all evidence (qv) must be on oath. A witness's oath is: "I swear by Almighty God that the evidence which I shall give shall be the truth, the whole truth and nothing but the truth". See the Oaths Act 1978; the C. & Y.P.A. 1963, s. 28; and *R* v *Chapman* [1980] Crim LR 42. See AFFIRM; PERJURY.

oath, judge's. *See* JUDGE'S OATH.

oath, juror's. *See* JUROR'S OATH.

oath of allegiance. Oath taken, eg, by officers of the Crown on appointment. "I do swear that I will be faithful and bear true allegiance to Her Majesty Queen Elizabeth II, her heirs and successors, according to law." See the Promissory Oaths Acts 1868 and 1971. A somewhat similar oath is taken by an alien on obtaining a certificate of naturalisation.

Oaths, Commissioners for. *See* COMMISSIONERS FOR OATHS.

oath, unlawful. It was an offence to administer or assist in the administration of an oath to engage in any mutinous or seditious purpose, to disturb the public peace, etc: Unlawful Oaths Acts 1797 and 1812 (both repealed by the Statutue Law (Repeals) Act 1981).

obedience to orders, defence of. In some circumstances obedience to a superior's orders may be relevant in negativing *mens rea* (qv). In the case of orders given by a military superior, a soldier acting under those orders "not being necessarily or manifestly illegal" would be justified by them: *Keighley* v *Bell* (1868) 4 F & F 773. See *R* v *James* (1837) 8 C & P 131.

obiter dictum. Saying by the way. Refers to: a statement of the law based on facts which were not present, or not material, in a case (see, eg, the judgment of Denning J in *Central London Property Trust Ltd* v *High Trees House Ltd* 1947] KB 30); a statement of law based on facts as found, but not forming the basis of the decision (eg, a statement upon which a dissenting judgment is based). It will be of persuasive authority only. "Mere passing remarks of the judge, whereas [*judicial dicta*] consist of considered enunciations of the judge's opinion of the law on some point which does not arise for decision on the facts of the case before him, and so not part of the *ratio decidendi*": *West & Partners Ltd* v *Dick* [1969] 1 All ER 289. *See* RATIO DECIDENDI.

objection to indictment. Procedure whereby the accused attempts to show that the indictment (qv) is apparently open to legal objection, eg, because the court lacks jurisdiction to try that offence.

objects clause. Clause in the memorandum of association (qv) setting out the objects which a company (qv) has been formed to pursue. See the Cos.A. 1980, Sch 1. Under the Cos.A. 1948, s. 5, it may be altered by special resolution, eg, to enable the company to carry on business more economically or to amalgamate with another company.

objects of a power. Where an appointor is authorised to appoint an interest to the members of a generally restricted class (eg, "amongst the children of X"), those whom he may select are known as the "objects of the power." *See* APPOINTMENT, POWER OF.

obligation. 1. A duty, usually legal or moral and of one's choosing, to undertake a course of action. 2. A bond (qv) with a condition annexed, usually involving a penalty for non-fulfilment.

obligee. *See* BOND.

obligor. *See* BOND.

obliteration. That which has been made impossible to decipher. In the case of a will (qv), no obliteration is valid except so far as the words of the will before the obliteration are not apparent, unless the obliteration has been properly signed and attested. A complete obliteration is usually valid, so that probate (qv) will be granted as though the will contained blanks. See *In b Ibbetson* (1839) 2 Curt 337; *In b Horsford* (1872) LR 3 P & D 211.

obscenity. "An article shall be deemed to be obscene if its effect or (where the article comprises two or more distinct items) the effect of any one of its items is, if taken as a whole, such as to tend to deprave (qv) and corrupt persons who are likely, having regard to all relevant circumstances, to read, see or hear the matter contained or embodied in it": Obscene Publications Act 1959, s. 1(1). Obscenity is not confined to books, etc, dealing with sex: *Calder Publications Ltd* v *Powell* [1965] 1 QB 509. It is an offence: to possess an obscene article for publication for gain (Obscene Publications Act 1964, s. 1(1)); to send by post a packet containing any indecent or obscene print or article (Post Office Act 1953, s. 11). For cinematograph exhibition (qv), see the C.L.A. 1977, s. 53. For obscene phone calls, substituting a public nuisance, see *R* v *Norbury* [1978] Crim LR 435; and the British Telecommunications Act 1981, s. 49(1). See Williams Committee Report 1979 (Cmnd 7772); and *A.-G.'s Ref. (No. 5 of 1980)* [1980] 3 All ER 816. *See* PUBLICATION.

obstruction of highway. *See* HIGHWAY, OBSTRUCTION OF.

obstruction of police. *See* POLICE, OBSTRUCTION OF.

obstruction of recovery of premises. *See* RECOVERY OF PREMISES, OBSTRUCTION OF.

obtaining credit, undischarged bankrupt. An offence if the bankrupt obtains credit to the extent of £50 or over without informing the intending creditor that he is an undischarged bankrupt, or without disclosing the name under which he was adjudged bankrupt: B.A. 1914 s. 155, as amended by the Insolvency Act 1976, s. 1. *See* BANKRUPTCY.

obtaining pecuniary advantage. *See* DECEPTION, OBTAINING PROPERTY BY.

occupancy. The taking possession of, and acquiring title to, that which has no owner.

occupant. One who takes by occupancy.

occupant, general and special. *See* GENERAL OCCUPANT.

occupation. 1. A person's trade, calling. 2. The taking and controlling of enemy territory by the armed forces of the Crown. 3. Control, actual physical possession of land, or its use. A person was held to be "in actual occupation" only if that occupation was recognisable as such and apparent to a purchaser": *Hodgson* v *Marks* [1970] 3 All ER 513. "Occupation is a matter of fact and only exists where there is sufficient measure of control to prevent strangers from interfering": *Newcastle CC* v *Royal Newcastle Hospital* [1959] 1 All ER 734.

occupational pensions scheme. Any scheme or arrangement comprised in one or more instruments or agreements, relating to categories of employment and the provision of benefits in the form of pensions or otherwise payable on termination of service, or on death or retirement, to or in respect of earners with qualifying service in an employment of those categories: Social Security Pensions Act 1975, s. 66(1). See also the Social Security Act 1980, s. 4; and the Finance Act 1981, s. 3.

occupation road. *See* ROAD, OCCUPATION.

occupier. One who has possession as owner or tenant (qv) of land or a house.

occupier, residential. *See* RESIDENTIAL OCCUPIER.

occupiers' liability, principle of. An occupier has a common duty of care to all persons on his premises by his invitation or permission, express or implicit. "Wherever a person has a sufficient degree of control over premises to realise that any failure on his part to use care may result in injury to a person coming lawfully there, then he is an 'occupier' ": *Wheat* v *Lacon & Co* [1966] AC 552. See the Occupiers' Liability Act 1957; the Defective Premises Act 1972; *Indermaur* v *Dames* (1866) LR 1

CP 274; *Holden* v *White* [1982] 2 All ER 328; and *Collier* v *Anglian Water Authority* (*The Times*, 26.3.1983).

occupiers' liability to children. Occupiers' duty may require "the provision of an obstacle to their approach to the danger sufficiently difficult to surmount as to make it clear to the youngest unaccompanied child likely to approach the danger, that beyond the obstacle is forbidden territory": *British Rwys Board* v *Herrington* [1972] 1 All ER 749. In the case of a child lawfully on the land, a common duty of care under the Occupiers' Liability Act 1957 is owed to him. See *Pannett* v *McGuinness & Co Ltd* [1972] 2 QB 599.

occupiers' liability to trespassers. Occupiers owe a trespasser a duty to take those steps as would be dictated by common sense or common humanity, to exclude or warn or otherwise reduce or avert a danger within practicable, reasonable limits. See *British Rwys Board* v *Herrington* [1972] 1 All ER 749; *Westwood* v *Post Office* [1974] AC1; *Harris* v *Birkenhead Corporation* [1975] 1 All ER 1001.

occupying tenant. In relation to a dwelling, this means the person who is not an owner-occupier but who occupies or is entitled to occupy the dwelling as a lessee, or is a statutory tenant of the dwelling within the meaning of the Rent Act 1977, or occupies the dwelling as a residence under a restricted contract (qv) within the meaning of s. 19 of the 1977 Act or occupies or resides in the dwelling as part of his employment in agriculture: H.A. 1974, s. 104(1), as amended by the Rent Act 1977, Sch 23, para 65.

offence. Generally, that which is equivalent to a crime, ie, an act or omission punishable under criminal law: *Derbyshire CC* v *Derby* [1896] 2 QB 57; *Horsfield* v *Brown* [1932] 1 KB 355.

offences against international law and order. That group of crimes including genocide, piracy, hijacking (qqv).

offences against property. That group of crimes including theft, robbery, criminal damage, forgery, (qqv).

offences against public order. That group of crimes including riot and affray, (qqv).

offences against the person. That group of crimes including assault, infanticide, manslaughter, murder, (qqv).

offences against the state. That group of crimes relating to the safety or structure of the state, eg, sedition, treason (qqv), offences relating to state secrets.

offences, duplicated. *See* DUPLICATED OFFENCES.

offences, general classification of. Division of offences for purposes of criminal procedure into: indictable offences; summary offences; offences triable either way (qqv): C.L.A. 1977, s. 14.

offences relating to road traffic. Group of crimes arising largely from the Road Traffic Acts 1972 and 1974 (as amended), eg, reckless driving, driving while unfit, driving without insurance (qqv).

offences, sexual. That group of crimes comprising, eg, unlawful sexual intercourse, indecent assault, incest, sodomy (qqv). See Working Party Report 1980.

offences, street. *See* STREET OFFENCES.

offences triable either way. Offences which, if committed by an adult, are triable either on indictment (qv) or summarily (qv): C.L.A. 1977, s. 64(1) (*c*). See the M.C.A. 1980, s. 17, Sch 1; and *R* v *Islington North Juvenile Court ex p Daley* [1982] 3 WLR 344. For initial procedure on an information for offences triable either way see the M.C.A. 1980, s. 18. Some offences triable either way may be tried summarily if the value involved is small: M.C.A. 1980, s. 22. See the I.A. 1979, Sch 1.

offence, weapon of. "An article made or adapted for use for causing injury to or incapacitating a person, or intended by the person having it with him for such use": Th.A. 1968, s. 10(1) (*a*); C.L.A. 1977, s. 8(2). *See* OFFENSIVE WEAPON.

offender, fugitive. *See* FUGITIVE OFFENDER.

offender, persistent. *See* PERSISTENT OFFENDER.

offensive trades. Trades so defined

under the Public Health Act 1936, s. 107 (eg, glue-making) which may not be established without the consent of the local authority. See *Epping Forest DC* v *Essex Rendering Ltd* [1983] 1 WLR 158.

offensive weapon. "Any article made or adapted for use for causing injury to the person, or intended by the person having it with him for such use by him": Prevention of Crime Act 1953, s. 1(4). It is an offence to have, without lawful authority, or reasonable excuse, such an article in any public place: s. 1(1). See *Pittard* v *Mahoney* [1977] Crim LR 169; *Bates* v *Bullman* (1978) 68 CR App R 21; *R* v *Rapier* (1979) 70 Cr App R 17; *R* v *McCogg* [1982] Crim LR 685; and *Hills* v *Ellis* [1983] 2 WLR 235.

offer. A proposal to give or do something. It may be *express* or *implied* from conduct. The person making the offer is the *offeror*; the person to whom it is made is the *offeree*. General rules are: (1) an offer may be made to a definite person, definite class of persons or the world at large; (2) an offer must be communicated to the offeree before acceptance; (3) it is only made when it reaches the offeree, not when it might have reached him in ordinary course of post. See, eg, *Adams* v *Lindsell* (1818) 1 B & Ald 681; *Carlill* v *Carbolic Smoke Ball Co* [1893] 1 QB 256. *See* CONTRACT.

offer, counter-. Response of an offeree which, in effect, suggests an agreement on terms which differ from those of the offer. Example: 'You can have my car for £3,000.' "I'll give you £2,800 for it." See *Hyde* v *Wrench* (1840) 3 Beav 334; and *Butler Machine Tool Co* v *Ex-Cell-O Corp* [1979] 1 WLR 401.

offer for sale. Document offering shares to the public, issued by an issuing house which has bought the shares outright from a public company. See the Cos.A. 1948, s. 45.

offers, cross. Offers which cross, eg, in the post. Example: A and B discuss the sale and purchase of A's motor car; A then writes to B offering to sell the car for £2,000, and, simultaneously, B writes to A offering to buy it for £2,000. See

Timm v *Hoffman* (1873) 29 LT 271.

office of profit. A paid office under the Crown. Except as provided by the House of Commons Disqualification Act 1975, a person shall not be disqualified from membership of the House by reason of his holding an office or place of profit under the Crown or any other office or place: 1975 Act, s. 1(4).

office premises. A building or part of a building, the sole or principal use of which is as an office or for office purposes: Offices, Shops and Railway Premises Act 1963, s. 1. See also the H.S.W.A. 1974.

Official Custodian for Charities. Created under the Charities Act 1960, s. 3. Charity property may be vested in him by a court order; he does not exercise powers of management, but has, in general, the same powers as a custodian trustee (qv). *See* CHARITY.

Official Journal. Title of the EEC official publication, containing, eg, Community instruments. Usually published daily. Divided into parts dealing with legislation and communications. *See* EEC.

Official Petitioner. Title given to the DDP (qv) in relation to his function in cases in which a criminal bankruptcy order (qv) is made: P.C.C.A. 1973, ss. 39–41, Sch 2, Parts I–III. He considers whether it is in the public interest that he should himself present a petition, and he presents it where considered appropriate.

official receiver. Appointed by the Department of Trade. In relation to bankruptcy (qv), he investigates the debtor's conduct, takes part in his public examination (qv), acts as interim receiver and presides at the first meeting of creditors. In the case of the winding-up (qv) of a company, he becomes provisional liquidator as soon as winding-up order is made: Cos.A. 1948, s. 239.

official referee. An officer of the court, appointed to consider, eg, an arbitration agreement, trials involving substantial technical detail or documents or matters relating to accounts. See also the Arbitration Act 1950, s. 11. The office was abolished under the Courts Act 1971, s. 25, and jurisdiction conferred upon circuit judges nominated by the Lord Chancellor to take "official referees' business". See the S.C.A. 1981, s. 68; and O. 36. *See* REFEREE.

official search. Search by the registrar, made on requisition (qv), so as to discover the existence of registrable incumbrances on land. The issue of an official certificate is conclusive in favour of a purchaser or intending purchaser, so that he is free from liability arising from rights which the official search failed to disclose.

official secrets. Matters concerning state security, covered under the Official Secrets Act 1911–1939. It is an offence for a person to approach or inspect a prohibited place for any purpose prejudicial to the safety or interests of the state, to use certain types of information for the benefit of a foreign power or in another manner prejudicial to state interests. See the European Communities Act 1972, s. 11; *R* v *Parrott* (1913) 8 Cr App R 186; *Chandler* v *DPP* [1962] 2 All ER 314; *R* v *Bingham* [1973] QB 870.

Official Solicitor. An official who acts for those involved in High Court (qv) proceedings who are under a disability. He will appear as "next friend" (qv) where there is no other person willing or competent to do so. He may also defend, eg, a minor (qv) or patient (qv) as guardian *ad litem* (qv). He can be appointed as judicial trustee (qv) in proceedings relating to disputed trusts. See the S.C.A. 1981, s. 90.

officina justitiae. See ORIGINAL WRIT.

off-market deals. Defined in the Cos.A. 1980, s. 70, as dealings otherwise than on a recognised stock exchange in a company's advertised securities through an off-market dealer (ie, one holding a licence under the Prevention of Fraud (Investments) Act 1958, s. 3, or who is a member of a recognised stock exchange, or recognised association of dealers in securities, or who is an exempted dealer). See the Cos.A. 1981, s. 47. *See* INSIDER DEALINGS.

offshore natural gas. Natural gas won under the authority of licences issued under the Petroleum (Production) Act 1934, as applied by s. 1(3) of the Continental Shelf Act 1964: Energy Act 1976, s. 11(1) (*a*). "Natural gas" means "any gas derived from natural strata": s. 21. See the Oil and Gas (Enterprise) Act 1982, s. 24.

Old Bailey. Central Criminal Court (qv).

Ombudsman. Parliamentary Commissioner for Administration (qv).

Ombudsman, Local Government. Commissioners appointed under the L.G.A. 1974, s. 23, with jurisdiction involving, eg, the investigation of complaints against local councils. See eg, *Re Complaint against Liverpool CC* [1977] 2 All ER 650.

omission. 1. Failure to take action where it is required. It may constitute *actus reus* (qv), as in *R* v *Pittwood* (1902) 19 TLR 37 (railway crossing keeper omitted to close gate, resulting in the death of a person struck by a train). 2. A blank in a document. The general presumption (qv), where blanks are found to have been filled in a will by the testator, is that they were filled before the execution of the will. See *Birch* v *Birch* (1848) Not Cas 581; *Re Shearn* (1880) 50 LJP 15.

omne quod solo inaedificatur solo cedit. All that which is built into the soil is merged therein.

omnia praesumuntur contra spoliatorem. All things are presumed against a wrongdoer. See, eg, *Harwood* v *Goodwright* (1744) 1 Cowp 87. In criminal proceedings it becomes, in effect, a rebuttable presumption of fact: C.J.A. 1967, s. 8.

omnia praesumuntur rite et solemniter esse acta. All things are presumed to be done correctly and solemnly (ie, until the contrary shall be proved). The so-called presumption of legality. See, eg, *Piers* v *Piers* (1849) 2 HL Cas 331; *Scott* v *Baker* [1969] 1 QB 659; *Eaglehill Ltd* v *J. Needham Ltd* [1973] AC 992; *Campbell* v *Wallsend Slipway Co* [1977] Crim LR 351.

onus probandi. Burden of proof (qv). *See* PROOF.

op. cit. *Opere citato.* In the work quoted.

open contract. A contract for sale of

property which does not contain all the terms. In the case of a contract for sale of land it refers to one which merely contains, eg, names of parties, price, description of property. Certain conditions are implied by law, eg, that the vendor shall show good title. See *Clifton* v *Palumbo* [1944] 2 All ER 497; and *Bigg* v *Boyd Gibbins Ltd* [1971] 1 WLR 913. *See* FORMAL CONTRACT.

open court. Court to which public has access. See *R* v *Denbigh Justices* [1974] QB 759. *See* IN CAMERA.

opening speech. Speech made by prosecuting counsel comprising allegations against the defendant (in outline) and the evidence it is proposed to call. Defending counsel may make an opening speech unless he is calling a witness to fact, other than the defendant.

open justice. "It is not merely of some importance but is of fundamental importance that justice should not only be done, but should manifestly and undoubtedly be seen to be done": *per* Lord Hewart CJ in *R* v *Sussex Justices ex p McCarthy* [1924] 1 KB 256. See *Re B* [1975] 2 All ER 449; and *R* v *Weston-super-Mare Justices ex p Taylor* [1981] Crim LR 179.

open verdict. Verdict of coroner's jury leaving open the question of how a person met his death.

operative part. That part of a deed (qv) in which the principal object is effected (eg, actual conveyance of property) as contrasted with recitals (qv).

operative words. Words which create or transfer an estate (qv). *See* LIMITATION, WORDS OF.

opinion. Term applied to a judgment delivered by the Law Lords in the House of Lords (qv).

opinion, expert. *See* EXPERT OPINION.

opinions, EEC. *See* COMMUNITY LEGISLATION, FORMS OF.

opinions in evidence. Opinions of ordinary (non-expert) persons are generally irrelevant and inadmissible as evidence. Exceptions include: matters of identity; age; speed of a car; handwriting (where the witness has seen the accused person writing);

proof that the witness understood a libel to refer to the plaintiff. Under the Civil Evidence Act 1972, s. 3, in civil proceedings a non-expert witness may give his opinions on an ultimate issue in the form of a statement made as a way of conveying relevant facts personally perceived by him. *See* EXPERT OPINION.

Opposition, Leader of HM. "That member of the House [of Commons] who is for the time being the Leader in that House of the party in opposition to HM Government having the greatest numerical strength in the House of Commons": Ministerial and other Salaries Act 1975, s. 2(1).

oppression. "A disregard of the essentials of justice and the infliction of a penalty which is not properly related to the crime of which the party stands convicted, but is either to be regarded as merely vindictive or having proceeded upon some improper or irregular consideration": *Stewart* v *Cormack* 1941 SC(J) 73.

oppression leading to confession. "This word . . . imports something which tends to sap and has sapped that free will which must exist before a confession is voluntary . . . [including] such things as the length of time intervening between periods of questioning, whether the accused person had been given proper refreshment or not . . .": *R* v *Priestley* (1965) 51 Cr App R 1; *R* v *Prager* [1972] 1 All ER 1114. See *Judges' Rules* 1964. *See* CONFESSION.

option. A right which may be acquired by contract to accept or reject a present offer within a given period of time. Under the S.L.A. 1925, s. 51, a tenant for life (qv) may grant an option to purchase or take a lease of the settled land within 10 years. Provision that a mortgagee shall have an option to purchase the property is generally inconsistent with a mortgage and, therefore, void, but this may not be so if the option is part of an independent transaction: *Reeve* v *Lisle* [1902] AC 461. "Under an option, only one step is normally needed to accept a contract, namely the exercise of the option. Under a right of pre-emption two steps will usually be necessary, the making of the offer in accordance with the right of pre-emption, and the acceptance of that offer": *Brown* v *Gould* [1972] CH 53. See *United Scientific Holdings* v *Burnley BC* [1977] 2 All ER 62; and *Sudbrook Trading Estates Ltd* v *Eggleton* [1982] 3 WLR 315. See PRE-EMPTION.

option, call. See CALL OPTION.

oral agreement, modification of contract by. Following a written contract, the parties are free, by a later oral agreement, to "either altogether waive, dissolve or annul the former agreement, or in any manner to add to, or subtract from, or vary or qualify the terms of it, and thus to make a new contract; which is to be proved, partly by the subsequent verbal terms engrafted upon what will be thus left of the written agreement": *Goss* v *Nugent* (1833) 5 B & Ald 58. See also *J. Evans & Son Ltd* v *Andrea Merzario Ltd* [1976] 2 All ER 930. See CONTRACT.

oral evidence. See EVIDENCE, ORAL.

orality, principle of. Principle of the oral examination of witnesses, which is a fundamental feature of trial under English law. See, however, evidence given on affidavit (qv).

oral will. See NUNCUPATIVE WILL.

ordeal, trial by. Ancient procedure whereby an appeal was made to God to make manifest guilt or innocence of the accused. It was considered as *judicium Dei* (qv). It could involve, eg, ordeal *by fire* (in which guilt was established if the wounds of the accused sustained during the carrying of a heated iron for nine steps were not healed after three days), or *by water*, (in which the accused was bound with a rope and let down into the water, innocence being established if he sank to a knot tied in the rope). Virtually abolished in 1215.

order, matrimonial. See MATRIMONIAL ORDER.

order of discharge. Court order releasing a bankrupt from all the debts provable in the bankruptcy (save, eg, debts due to the Crown, debts incurred by means of fraud) and from liabilities of an undischarged bankrupt. Discharge may be suspensive and conditional. See the

B.A. 1914, s. 26; and the Insolvency Act 1976, ss. 7, 8 (automatic discharge five years after adjudication). See BANKRUPTCY.

order paper. Paper relating to the business of the Commons, published daily under the Speaker's authority.

orders. 1. Directions of the court. 2. Constituents of the procedural code of the Supreme Court.

Orders in Council. Orders made by the Sovereign and Privy Council (qqv) or by the government (which are sanctioned by the Privy Council). They may be used, eg, to bring Acts into force. See DELEGATED LEGISLATION; STATUTORY INSTRUMENTS.

Orders of Council. Orders made by the Privy Council (qv), in the absence of the Sovereign.

ordinance. Decree promulgated by Parliament (qv) without the consent of a constituent element (eg, Lords), or a declaration by the Sovereign made without Parliament's consent.

ordinarily resident. See RESIDENT IN UK.

Ordinary. Bishop who exercises jurisdiction in ecclesiastical matters.

ordinary meetings. See MEETINGS, COMPANY.

ordinary resolution. A resolution (qv) passed by a simple majority of those present at the general meeting of a company (qv). See EXTRAORDINARY RESOLUTION.

ordinary shares. Those which carry the greatest risk and rank for repayment of capital and payment of dividends after debenture-holders and preference shareholders. Preferred ordinary shares are a type of participating preference shares (qv) without priority for repayment of capital. See SHARE.

original writ. Ancient method of commencing a common-law action, by issue out of so-called *officina justitiae* (workshop of justice) controlled by the King's chancellor.

originating summons. "Every summons other than a summons in a pending cause or matter": O. 1, r. 4. Used to commence an action in Queen's Bench Division, eg, to obtain a decision on a point of law. See also O. 7, r. 2.

origin, country of, marking. Under S.I. 1981/121, some consumer goods (eg, textiles, clothing, footwear, domestic electrical appliances) must carry information on their country of origin. The instruction does not apply to second-hand goods or promotional "free gifts".

orse. Otherwise.

ostensible authority. Apparent authority. See, eg, *Waugh* v *Clifford & Sons* [1982] 2 WLR 679.

ostensible partner. Nominal partner (qv).

oust. To eject, dispossess, exclude, bar.

ouster. An act which wrongfully deprives a person of his freehold (qv) or other inheritance.

ouster clause. A clause in a statute which excludes the jurisdiction of the courts (eg, "This shall not be questioned in any legal proceedings whatsoever"). See, eg, *Anisminic* v *Foreign Compensation Commission* [1969] 2 AC 147.

ouster le main. Out of the hand. 1. Judgment against the Crown on a *monstrans de droit* (qv). 2. Ancient procedure whereby heirs or heiresses reaching the age of majority, had to "sue out their livery" by paying the lord (who had been entitled to wardship) half a year's profits so as to obtain delivery of their land.

ouster of jurisdiction. Removal from the court of its power to hear and determine an action. There is a presumption against a statute's ousting the jurisdiction of the courts: *Pyx Granite Co Ltd* v *Minister of Housing* [1960] AC 260.

outer Bar. Known also as "utter Bar". Term used to refer to junior barristers who are said to plead "outside the bar" and are known as "utter barristers". *See* BARRISTER.

outlawry. Procedure whereby an offender was placed outside the protection of the law. His property was forfeited and he lost all civil rights, being stigmatised as "an animal to be hunted and struck down if encountered". Criminal outlawry was abolished in 1838; outlawry in civil proceedings, in 1879.

outstanding offences. Those offences which are outstanding may be taken into account when the court is considering sentence. They must not be dissimilar offences, or offences in respect of which the court has no jurisdiction. See *R* v *McLean* (1911) 75 JP 127; *R* v *Simons* (1953) 117 JP 422.

outstanding term. A term of years (qv) which has not ended although the purpose for which it came into existence has been fulfilled. *See* SATISFIED TERM.

overcrowding. A dwelling-house is deemed to be overcrowded at any time when the number of persons sleeping there is such that any two of these persons, being persons 10 years old or more of opposite sexes and not being persons living together as husband and wife must sleep in the same room: H.A. 1957, s. 77(1), Sch 6. See the Rent Act 1977, s. 101; and the H.A. 1980, s. 146. See *Simmons* v *Pizzey* [1977] 2 All ER 432; and *Hackney LBC* v *Ezedinma* [1981] 3 All ER 438.

overdraft. Bank loan allowing a customer's current account to go into debit. See the C.C.A. 1974, s. 74(3), (3A) (inserted by the Banking Act 1979, s. 38(1)); and *Re Hone* [1951] Ch 85.

overdue bill. A bill which remains in circulation after the due date. A bill payable on demand is deemed overdue, for purposes of negotiation, if it appears to have been in circulation for an unreasonable length of time. "Unreasonable" is a question of fact: B.Ex.A. 1882, s. 36(3). *See* BILL OF EXCHANGE.

overdue cheque. *See* CHEQUE, OVERDUE.

over-insurance. *See* INSURANCE, OVER-.

overreaching. Device whereby, eg, land held on trust is sold to a purchaser free from the trust, even though he has notice of it. An equitable interest overreached is transferred from the land to money in the trustees' hands. Example: *ad hoc* trust for sale (qv). See, eg, *Caunce* v *Caunce* [1969] 1 WLR 286; *Shiloh Spinners Ltd* v *Harding* [1973] AC 80; and the S.L.A. 1925, s. 72.

overriding interests. Those encumbrances, interests, rights and powers not entered on the register but subject to which registered dispositions take effect. Hence, a registered proprietor, or his alienee, is bound by such rights, irrespective of registration and notice. Examples: rights of way, public rights. An overridden interest cannot be enforced against anyone; an overreached interest is transferred from land to money. See *Williams & Glyn's Bank* v *Boland* [1981] AC 487. See the L.R.A. 1925, s. 70.

overrule. To set aside. Thus, a decision may be overruled by statute, or a higher court. Overruling by the latter operates retrospectively; by the former, from the date on which the statute comes into operation. See, eg, *Button* v *DPP* [1966] AC 591; *Miliangos* v *George Frank Ltd* [1975] 3 All ER 801 (in which the House of Lords overruled one of its own decisions).

oversea company. A company incorporated outside Britain which has established a place of business in Britain. See the Cos.A. 1948, s. 406; the Cos.A. 1976, s. 9; and the Cos.A. 1981, Sch 3. *See* COMPANY.

oversea company, name of. The Secretary of State may, if of the opinion that it is or would be undesirable for an oversea company to carry on the business in Great Britain under its corporate name, cause a notice to that effect to be served on the company by the registrar of companies: Cos.A. 1976, s. 31(1) (amended by the Cos.A. 1981, s. 27).

overt. Open, as in overt act, market overt (qv).

owner-occupier of a dwelling. "The person who, as owner or as lessee under a long tenancy, occupies or is entitled to occupy the dwelling": H.A. 1974, s. 104(1).

owner of a dwelling. "The person who, otherwise than as a mortgagee in possession, is for the time being

entitled to dispose of the fee simple in the dwelling": H.A. 1974 s. 104(1). *See* FEE SIMPLE ABSOLUTE IN POSSESSION; MORTGAGE.

ownership. Right to the exclusive enjoyment of some thing based on rightful title. It may be *absolute* or *restricted, corporeal* (relating to, eg, a book, a car) or *incorporeal* (relating to, eg, the right to recover a debt), *legal* (as where A has fee simple absolute in possession (qv)) or *equitable* (as where A has a life interest), *vested* or *contingent*. In essence, it is based on a relationship *de jure* (qv), so that possession of the thing is not necessary. *See* POSSESSION.

ownership, acquisition of. Ownership may be acquired *originally* (eg, by asserting ownership over something not previously owned by anyone), *derivatively* (eg, by purchase), or *by succession* (eg, by inheritance).

ownership, legal and equitable. Term used in land law to distinguish estates in land capable of being conveyed or created at law (fee simple absolute in possession (qv) in case of freeholds, and term of years absolute (qv) in case of leaseholds) and all other ownership interests. See the L.P.A. 1925, s. 1.

ownership, proof of. Establishment of ownership or property by, eg, production of authenticated documents of title; proof of possession; proof of ownership of connected property (in the case of land) showing the probability that its owner would also own property in dispute.

ownership, reputed. *See* REPUTED OWNERSHIP.

oyer and terminer. To hear and determine. Commission issued to assize judges conferring criminal jurisdiction and directing them to hear and determine offences for which accused persons had been presented by grand juries. Effectively abolished under the Courts Act 1971. *See* ASSIZE.

P

P. President of the Family Division (qv), as in, eg, Sir George Baker P. See the S.C.A. 1981, s. 10.

pace. By leave, or with consent, of.

pact. A contract, promise, covenant, treaty between states.

pacta sunt servanda. Contracts are to be kept.

pactum, nudum. See NUDUM PACTUM.

paid-up capital. That part of the called-up capital which has been paid up by, or credited as paid up by, a company's shareholders. See the Cos.A. 1948, s. 124(1); and the European Communities Act 1972, s. 9(7). *See* CAPITAL; COMPANY.

pais. Pays = country. *Trial per pais* is a trial "by the country", ie, trial by jury.

palatine courts. Courts belonging to the counties palatine (*palatinus* = belonging to the palace), whose owners had sovereign rights, including the right to appoint judges, eg, Durham, Lancaster, Chester. Abolished under the Law Terms Act 1830 and the Courts Act 1971.

pannage, common of. Right to feed swine on acorns, etc, in another's forest or wood.

paramount. Superior. *Title paramount* is superior title. "It signifies in our law the highest lord of the fee": *Termes de la Ley.* Example: where X held land in fee of Y, and Y held that land in fee of Z, so that Z was lord paramount. A *paramount clause* in a charterparty or bill of lading (qqv) is a clause incorporating all the Hague Rules: *Nea Agrex SA v Baltic Shipping Co Ltd* [1976] QB 933.

paraphernalia. A wife's apparel, ornaments, including gifts from her husband. See *Tasker v Tasker* [1895] P 1.

parcels. 1. Plots of land. 2. Term used in a conveyance (qv) to indicate the clause giving a physical description of property conveyed, eg, "all that dwelling-house known as . . ." See *Scarfe v Adams* [1981] 1 All ER 843.

parceners. *See* COPARCENARY.

pardon. The excusing of an offence or remission of a punishment by the Sovereign (on the advice of the Home Secretary) or by Act of Parliament (qv). Plea that the defendant has been pardoned in respect of the offence charged may be raised on a motion to quash an indictment (qv). Some offences cannot be pardoned, eg, committing a person to prison beyond the seas (see the Habeas Corpus Act 1679). "A free pardon does not quash a conviction in the same way that the Court of Appeal can quash a conviction . . . it is, however, generally accepted that [it] has the effect of wiping out the conviction and all its consequences": Secretary of State for the Home Department (*Hansard*, 13.1.1977).

parens patriae. Parent of his country. Term applied to, eg, the Sovereign as guardian of those in need or who are under a legal disability.

parent. Father or mother. Used, eg, in the Child Benefit Act 1975 as including references to the natural parent or step-parent. See *R v Immigration Appeals Adjudicator ex p Crew* (*The Times*, 26.11.1982).

parental rights and duties. "As respects a particular child (whether legitimate or not), all the rights and duties which by law the mother and father have in relation to a legitimate child and his property": Ch.A. 1975, s. 85(1). Such rights and duties cannot generally be transferred, save, eg, under statute. See the I.A. 1978, Sch. 1; and the Child Care Act 1980, s. 3.

parental rights and duties, acquisition of. Under the Ch.A. 1948, s. 2, as amended by the Ch.A. 1975, s. 57, if it appears to a local authority with a child in its care that, eg, its parents are dead and he has no guardian or custodian, or that a parent has abandoned him or failed to discharge the obligation of a parent, the local authority is enabled to acquire parental rights over the child.

parent company. A controlling company that owns or actively operates a subsidiary enterprise. *See* COMPANY.

parents' identity, child's right to know. Adopted persons over 18 have a right to have access to a copy of their original birth certificate which will enable them to trace their natural parents: Ch.A. 1975, s. 26.

parents' liability for children's torts. Parents are not generally liable for their child's torts, save, eg, where the child is employed by a parent and commits a tort in the course of his employment and where torts are due to a parent's negligence, or if a parent had authorised the commission of the tort. See *Moon* v *Towers* (1860) 8 CB 611; *Bebee* v *Sales* (1916) 32 TLR 413.

pari passu. At the same rate; equal in every respect. Used in the sale of shares to describe a new issue in relation to shares already issued.

parish. Originally an ecclesiastical area, later a local government unit. Parish councils in England are constituted in a way similar to district and county councils (qqv). The number of councillors is determined by the district council; there must be a minimum of five members. Functions include responsibility for, eg, recreational facilities, cemeteries and crematoria. In Wales, parishes are replaced by communities (qv). Parish meetings must be held every March. See the L.G.A. 1933; and the L.G.A. 1972, Sch 1.

parium judicium. Judgment of [one's] peers.

Parliament. The supreme legislature of the United Kingdom of Great Britain and Northern Ireland (see the Royal and Parliamentary Titles Act 1927), consisting of the Queen, House of Lords and House of Commons. Its life is fixed for five years, divided into sessions (one or more each year). It can legislate as it pleases, since it is sovereign, for the whole of the UK or any constituent part. Legislation usually necessitates the concurrence of the Sovereign, Lords and Commons.

Parliamentary Commissioner for Administration. The "Ombudsman". Office created by the Parliamentary Commissioner Act 1967. The Commissioner, who is appointed by the Crown, investigates complaints by members of the public who believe they have suffered injustice as the result of maladministration arising from the functioning of government departments and public authorities. A written complaint is forwarded to a M.P. who sends it to the Commissioner. He then exercises his discretion whether or not to investigate. See *Annual Report of the Parliamentary Commissioner*; *Re Fletcher's Application* [1970] 2 All ER 527.

parliamentary committees. Committees of the whole House (eg, Committee of Ways and Means (qv)), standing committees to consider bills, select committees, appointed to enquire into a report to the House on special matters.

parliamentary control. Control of government is based on power exercised by the House of Commons which is able to force its resignation or to reject votes of confidence. Other aspects of control include, eg, question time, motions for adjournment.

parliamentary counsel. Barristers (qv) who are civil servants engaged in drafting government Bills, amendments by the government to those Bills, etc. They may advise government departments on parliamentary procedure.

parliamentary Papers. 1. Command Papers (qv) published by the government for Parliament's consideration (in theory, presented by Her Majesty's Command). They may be: "*white papers*", ie, statements of government policy or principles of a bill to be introduced; "*blue books*", ie, reports of committees, commissions; "*green papers*", ie, government plans intended for discussion. 2. Bills (qv). 3. House of Commons or House of Lords papers, published by order of the House, as reports of the Houses' own committees.

parliamentary privilege. Rights and immunities enjoyed by each House of Parliament, designed to allow members to carry out their duties unhindered. They apply collectively and individually to every M.P. Privileges include: the freedom of speech in debate; the right to control proceedings; right to penalise those who commit breach of privilege; the right to expel members whom Parliament considers unfit to serve. The absence of precedent does not prevent an act being considered a breach of privilege.

Parliament, European. *See* EUROPEAN PARLIAMENT.

Parliament, intention of. *See* INTENTION OF PARLIAMENT.

Parliament, legislative supremacy of. Doctrine that Parliament alone can, by statute, make or unmake any law. "The very keystone of the constitution": Dicey. Parliament can pass Acts of indemnity (qv) and retrospective legislation. No other body in the state can declare any Act invalid: see, eg, *Pickin* v *British Rwys Board* [1974] AC 765. It cannot, however, bind its successors.

parol. Executed orally. Formerly applied to a contract not under seal: *Rann* v *Hughes* (1788) 7 TR 350.

parol contract. Simple contract (qv).

parole. Refers to the revocable and conditional release of a prisoner serving his sentence. Prisoners serving fixed sentences are eligible to be considered for release on parole after having served one-third of their sentences (subject to a minimum of one year). A local review committee reports on each case to the Home Secretary who grants or refuses parole or refers cases to the Parole Board. See the C.J.A. 1967, ss. 59–64, (as amended by the C.L.A. 1977, and extended by the C.J.A. 1982, s. 32), the C.J.A. 1972, s. 35; and *Practice Direction* [1976] 1 WLR 122. See also *Payne* v *Lord Harris of Greenwich* [1981] 1 WLR 754. *See* LIFE IMPRISONMENT.

parol evidence rule. Rule that where the record of a transaction is embodied in a document, extrinsic evidence (qv) is not generally admissible to vary or interpret the document or as a substitute for it. See *Bank of Australasia* v *Palmer* [1898] AC 540.

Abolition of the rule was recommended by *Law Commission Working Paper* 1976, No 70. *See* EVIDENCE, PAROL.

parol lease. Lease (qv) taking effect in possession for a term not exceeding three years at the best rent which can be reasonably obtained without taking a fine: L.P.A. 1925, s. 54(2).

partial loss. *See* LOSS, LIABILITY IN MARINE INSURANCE FOR.

partibility. State of being capable of partition (qv). Term applied to the divisibility of inheritance among children.

particeps criminis. One who shares in a criminal act, ie, an accomplice (qv).

participation agreement. *See* AGREEMENT, PARTICIPATION.

participator in company. *See* CLOSE COMPANY.

particular average. *See* AVERAGE.

particular estate. An estate less than a fee simple (qv), given for a particular period of time. Term used to refer to an estate granted out of a larger estate. *See* ESTATE.

particular lien. Right to retain goods until all charges incurred in respect of them have been paid. Example: lien in respect of goods carried by common carriers. See *Bowmaker* v *Wycombe Motors Ltd* [1946] KB 505. *See* LIEN.

particulars. Matters concerning pleadings in an action needed by the other party so that he shall understand the case to be made. They may be applied for by letter or by summons for an order for further and better particulars. See O. 18, r. 12. They will not be ordered in relation to a matter not pleaded specifically. "The object of particulars is to enable the party asking for them to know what case he has to meet at the trial and so to save unnecessary expense": *Spedding* v *Fitzpatrick* (1888) 38 Ch D 413. *See* PLEADINGS.

particular tenant. The owner of a particular estate (qv).

parties. 1. "They that make a deed and they to whom it is made are called parties to the deed": *Termes de la Ley*. 2. Those persons who sue or are sued. Their names must be set out at the head of a writ (qv) and they form the title of the action. No one can appear on the record as both plaintiff and defendant: *Re Phillips* (1931) 101 LJ Ch 338.

partition. 1. Distribution, division. 2. Division of a governmental unit into two or more areas, each under a separate administration. 3. Term used in land law to refer to the disuniting of joint possession (qv) so that former co-tenants become separate owners. Now voluntary only, since compulsory partition was abolished by the repeal of the Partition Acts in 1925. See L.P.A. 1925, s. 28(3).

partition of chattels. Where chattels belong to persons in undivided shares, the persons interested may apply to the court for an order for the division of all or any of them: L.P.A. 1925, s. 188.

partner, salaried. A partner ''who receives a salary as remuneration, rather than a share of the profits, although he may, in addition to his salary, receive some bonus or other sum of money dependent on the profits'': *per* Megarry J in *Stekel* v *Ellice* [1973] 1 All ER 463.

partnership. The relationship which subsists between persons carrying on a business in common with a view of profit: Partnership Act 1890, s. 1. See *Keith Spicer Ltd* v *Mansell* [1970] 1 All ER 462. It cannot consist, in general, of more than 20 persons. See the Cos.A. 1967, ss. 120, 121 (exempting from this limit partnerships of solicitors, accountants, stockbrokers). The liability of each partner in respect of the partnership's contracts is joint; in respect of the partnership's wrongs, the liability is joint and several. A partnership may be dissolved by order of court or by the parties themselves. See the Partnership Act 1890, s. 32; O. 81. *See* LIMITED PARTNERSHIP.

partnership at will. A partnership determinable at will of either of the parties. See the Partnership Act 1980, s. 26; *Moss* v *Elphick* [1910] 1 KB 846; *Abbott* v *Abbott* [1936] 3 All ER 823.

partnership books, inspection of. Right given by the Partnership Act 1980, s. 24(9), to a partner to inspect and copy the partnership books. It

can be exercised by an agent of the parties.

partnership by estoppel. Any person who by spoken or written words or conduct represents himself, or allows himself to be represented as a partner in a particular firm, is liable as a partner to anyone who has on the faith of any such representation given credit to that firm: Partnership Act 1890, s. 14(1). See *Tower Cabinet Co Ltd* v *Ingram* [1949] 2 KB 397.

partnership, limited. *See* LIMITED PARTNERSHIP.

part payment rule. Payment of a lesser sum on the due day cannot be satisfaction for the whole debt. See *Pinnel's Case* (1602) 5 Co Rep 117; *Foakes* v *Beer* (1884) 9 App Cas 605; *D & C Builders* v *Rees* [1966] 2 QB 617; and the Lim.A. 1980, s. 29.

part performance. Equitable doctrine, restricted to contracts related preeminently to land, whereby the defendant (qv) who has acquiesced in the plaintiff's performance of a contract (qv) is barred from pleading absence of writing. The act of part performance must be exclusively referable to the contract and must be an act of real performance (not merely an act in preparation for the performance). See *Maddison* v *Alderson* (1883) 8 App Cas 467; *Wakeham* v *Mackenzie* [1968] 1 WLR 1175; *New Hart Builders* v *Brindle* [1975] Ch 342. *See* CONTRACT.

party and party costs. The ordinary basis of taxation of costs (qv). ''All such costs as were necessary or proper for the attainment of justice or for enforcing or defending the rights of the party whose costs are being taxed'' are allowed: O. 62, r. 28(2). No costs which may be considered as luxuries are allowed: *Smith* v *Bullen* (1875) LR 19 Eq 470. See *Garthwaite* v *Sherwood* [1976] 1 WLR 705.

party-wall. Generally, a wall of which the two adjoining owners were tenants in common. Under the L.P.A. 1925, s. 38, a wall would be deemed to be severed vertically as between the respective owners, each of whom has a right to support and user.

Passage, Court of. *See* LIVERPOOL COURT OF PASSAGE.

passenger. One who is carried in a conveyance for compensation. See, eg, the Merchant Shipping Act 1894, s. 267.

passim. Here and there. Used in relation to a reference appearing throughout a book or statute.

passing off. A tort (qv) committed by one person who, in a manner calculated to deceive, passes off his goods or business as those of another, eg, by imitating their appearance or selling them under a similar name or trade mark. The plaintiff's remedies include action for damages, injunction (qqv), account. See *Bollinger* v *Costa Brava Wine Co* [1960] Ch 262; *Habib Bank Ltd* v *Habib Bank AG Zurich* [1981] 2 All ER 650. See also the Cos.A. 1981, ss. 22 *et seq.* for regulation of the names of companies.

passive trust. A bare trust (qv).

passport. Document issued by the Foreign Office to citizens of the UK and British protected persons which is intended to ensure their safe passage from one country to another. In *Joyce* v *DPP* [1946] AC 347, it was held that the holder of a British passport owes allegiance to the Crown and that it is immaterial that he has no intention of availing himself of the Crown's protection.

past consideration. *See* CONSIDERATION, PAST.

pasture, common of. The right of feeding one's cattle on another's land. See *Tyrringham's Case* (1584) 4 Co Rep 36b. *See* PUR CAUSE DE VICINAGE.

patent. An exclusive right conferred on one who invents or discovers some process, machine, etc, to make, use, sell or assign it for a certain period of time (usually 20 years) which may be extended. See the Patents Acts 1949, 1957 and 1977. On the attitude of the EEC to patents, see the Treaty of Rome 1957, art. 85(1) and *Burroughs AG and Gehon-Werke GmBh's Agreement* [1972] CMLR D 72.

patent agent. An individual registered as a patent agent in the register, a company lawfully practising as a patent agent in the UK or a person who satisfies the conditions in s. 84(1)

or s. 104(3): Patents Act 1977, s. 104(4). For restrictions on practice, see s. 114.

patent ambiguity. *See* AMBIGUITY.

patent defect. *See* DEFECT.

patentee. A person registered as grantee or proprietor of a patent (qv).

patent, grant of. A patent may be granted only for an invention in respect of which the following conditions are satisfied: it must be new; it must involve an inventive step; it must be capable of industrial application; it must not be an invention which will encourage offensive, immoral or anti-social action; it must not consist of a scientific theory, computer program, aesthetic creation, etc.: Patents Act 1977, s. 1(1) (2) (3). It may be granted to the inventor, joint inventors, persons who by virtue of any enactment or treaty or agreement with the inventor were entitled to the whole of the property in it (other than equitable interests (qv)) in the UK, or successors in title of those persons: s. 7(2). The term of a patent is 20 years beginning with the date of filing of the application: s. 25. The application must contain a request for grant, specification, description, drawings and abstract: s. 14(2).

patent, infringement of. A patent is infringed where a person does one of the following without the consent of the patent's proprietor: where the invention is a product and he makes, disposes of, offers to dispose of, uses or imports the product or keeps it for disposal or otherwise; where the invention is a process and he uses, or offers it for use in the UK when he knows this is an infringement; where the invention is a process and he disposes of, offers to dispose of, uses or imports any product obtained directly by means of the process or keeps it for disposal or otherwise: Patents Act 1977, s. 60(1).

patent, revocation of. The court may revoke a patent on any one of the following grounds: that it is not a patentable invention; that the patent was granted to a person who was not the only person entitled to the grant; that the specification does not disclose the invention clearly and competently enough for it to be performed by a person skilled in the art; that the matter disclosed in the specification extends beyond that disclosed in the application for the patent; that the protection conferred by the patent has been extended by an amendment which should not have been allowed: Patents Act 1977, s. 72(1).

patent right. The right to do, or authorise the doing of, anything which, but for that right would be an infringement of a patent.

Patents Court. Constituted as part of the Chancery Division of the High Court (qv) "to take such proceedings relating to patents and other matters as may be prescribed by rules of court". Judges are puisne judges (qv) of the High Court nominated by the Lord Chancellor. Scientific advisers may be appointed to assist the Court: Patents Act 1977 s. 96(4). See the S.C.A. 1981, ss. 6, 70.

paternity, declaration of. Declaration that a stated person is the father of a stated child. See *S* v *S* [1970] 3 All ER 107; and *Re JS* [1980] 1 All ER 1061 (where the Court of Appeal denied the existence of a jurisdiction in wardship proceedings to grant a bare declaration of paternity).

patient. Term generally applied to a mental patient (qv).

patrial. Term denoting a person who has the right of abode in the UK. Replaced by "British citizen": B.N.A. 1981, s. 39.

patron. *See* ADVOWSON.

pawn. 1. An article subject to a pledge (qv): C.C.A. 1974, s. 189. 2. The delivery of a chattel (qv) by the pawnor to the pawnee as security for a loan. The chattel remains the property of the pawnor who has the right to redeem. See the C.C.A. 1974, ss. 114–122. The pawnee may retain possession until the debt is paid and can sell the chattel if the debt is not paid on the date fixed: s. 121.

pawnbroker. One who is engaged in the business of taking goods and chattels in pawn. A licence is required from the Director General of Fair Trading (qv). See the C.C.A. 1974, ss. 114–122.

pawn-receipt. Receipt in prescribed form given by a person who takes any article in pawn under a regulated agreement (qv) to the person from whom he receives it: C.C.A. 1974, s. 114(1).

pax regis. Peace of the King (qv).

payable at sight. *See* SIGHT, PAYABLE AT.

pay as you earn. System (known generally as PAYE) introduced in 1943 whereby wage and salary earners pay their income tax. Tax is deducted from earnings at source and accounted for to the Inland Revenue by the employer. See the Income and Corporation Taxes Act 1970; and *Clark* v *Oceanic Contractors* [1983] 2 WLR 94.

payee. One to whom a bill of exchange (qv) is made payable.

payment. The passing of money from payer to payee in satisfaction of some debt or obligation. For "payment under reserve", see *Banque de L'Indochine* v *JH Rayner Ltd* [1983] 1 All ER 1137.

payment in due course. Discharge of a bill of exchange (qv) by payment made at or after the maturity of bill by the acceptor to the holder thereof in good faith and without notice that his title is defective (if that is so): B.Ex.A. 1882, s. 59(1).

payment into court. Deposit of payment (through the Court Funds Office or the district registry) by the defendant (qv) in an action for debt or damages after entering an appearance and in satisfaction of all or any of the plaintiff's claims. See O. 22; O. 59, r. 12A; O. 62, r. 5(6); the County Court Rules 1981, O. 11; and the A.J.A. 1982, s. 38. The plaintiff must acknowledge receipt of the notice of payment within three days. The plaintiff may make payment into court in respect of any counterclaim made against him. Payment into court may not be disclosed during trial, except in an action to which a defence of tender before action is pleaded. See *Gaskins* v *British Aluminium Co* [1976] 1 All ER 208; *Pearl Furniture Co* v *Adrian Share Interiors* [1977] 1 WLR 464.

payment of wages. It is generally an

offence under the Truck Acts 1831–1940 to pay workmen their wages other than in coin of the realm. Other methods must fall within the Payment of Wages Act 1960, necessitating, eg, the request by an employee in writing for his wages to be paid by cheque or directly into his bank account. See the M.C.A. 1980, s. 100 (which provides for the use of a statement of wages as evidence). See WAGES.

payments, appropriation of. Where a debtor owes several debts to one creditor and payment is made, the debtor can appropriate the payment to a debt, expressly or by implication, at the time of payment. In absence of such appropriation, the creditor may appropriate at any time. See *Clayton's Case* (1816) 1 Mer 572; *Seymour v Pickett* [1905] 1 KB 715; and *Siebe Gormand Co v Barclays Bank* [1979] 2 Lloyd's Rep 142. For appropriation of payments under a hire-purchase contract, see the C.C.A. 1974, s. 81.

pay statement, itemised. Under E.P.(C.)A. 1978, ss. 8–9, at or before the time when the payment of wages or salary takes place, every employee is entitled to receive from his employer a statement showing: gross amount of wages or salary; net amount of wages or salary; amounts of fixed and variable deductions and purposes for which made.

P.C. Privy Council (qv). Privy Councillor.

peace, breach of. See BREACH OF THE PEACE.

peace of the King. The security in his realm promised by the Sovereign to his subjects. Originally attached to the royal palace and ''3,000 paces beyond the great road'', so that breaches of the peace there were punished. On the occasion of a church festival it was extended throughout the realm.

peculiar. A parish (qv) exempt from the jurisdiction of the Ordinary (qv).

pecuniary advantages. The cases in which a pecuniary advantage within the meaning of the Th.A. 1968, s. 16 (obtaining pecuniary advantage by deception) arises are where: any debt or charge for which a person makes himself liable (including one not legally enforceable) is reduced or in whole or in part evaded or deferred; a person is allowed to borrow by way of overdraft or to take out any policy of insurance or annuity contract, or obtains an improvement of the terms on which he is allowed to do so; a person is given the opportunity to earn remuneration or greater remuneration in an office or employment, or to win money by betting. See DECEPTION, OBTAINING SERVICES BY.

pecuniary legacy. See LEGACY.

pedigree. A line of ancestors. Statements, oral or written, by deceased persons, related by marriage or blood made before litigation was in contemplation, are admissible to prove matters concerning pedigree. See *Berkeley Peerage Case* (1811) 4 Camp 401. See DECLARATION CONCERNING PEDIGREE.

peer. The holder of a dignity entitling him to membership of the House of Lords (qv). A *peeress* is a woman who has the dignity of peerage as a result of marriage or in her own right. Grades, in ascending order, are baron, viscount, earl, marquess and duke.

peers, temporal. See HOUSE OF LORDS.

peers, trial by. Under Magna Carta (qv) a man was entitled to the judgment of his peers (ie, those of the same rank). ''Peer'' was apparently misinterpreted as referring to the barons. A peer could be tried before the House of Lords (qv). Thus, Lord De Clifford was tried and acquitted of manslaughter in 1935. Trial by peers in cases of treason and felony was abolished under the C.J.A. 1948, s. 30.

peine forte et dure. Strong and hard pain. A torture, consisting of piling weights on the body, administered so as to force the accused to accept jury trial. It may have originated in a misconstruing of the Statute of Westminster 1275, which ordered that such a person was to be ''remanded to a hard and strong prison''. The last fatal torture of this nature took place at Horsham Gaol in 1735. Abolished by the Felony and Piracy Act 1772.

penal actions. *See* ACTIONS CIVIL AND PENAL.

penal servitude. Substitute for transportation (qv) introduced by the Penal Servitude Act 1853. It involved imprisonment with compulsory labour. Abolished by the C.J.A. 1948.

penal statutes. 1. Statutes creating offences. 2. Statutes providing for the recovery of penalties in civil proceedings. There is a presumption in favour of the strict construction of a penal statute. See, eg, *Tuck & Sons v Priester* (1887) 19 QBD 629; *Salesmatic Ltd v Hinchcliffe* [1959] 3 All ER 401.

penalty. 1. A punishment. "Unless penalties are imposed in clear terms they are not enforceable": *A.-G. v Till* [1910] AC 50. 2. A threat, held over a party to a contract *in terrorem* (qv). The plaintiff who brings an action to enforce a penalty can generally recover only the damage suffered. Whether a sum is or is not a penalty is to be decided "upon the terms and inherent circumstances of each particular contract, judged of as at the time of making the contract, not as at the time of the breach": *Dunlop Pneumatic Tyre Co Ltd v New Garage & Motor Co Ltd* [1915] AC 79. See also *Robophone Facilities Ltd v Blank* [1966] 1 WLR 1428; and *ECGD v Universal Oil Products Co* [1983] 1 WLR 399.

penalty, enhanced. Penalty in the case of a conviction where, eg, the person committed is liable to imprisonment for a longer term in the case of a second or subsequent conviction. Generally abolished under the C.J.A. 1982, s. 35.

pendens lis. A pending action. See the L.C.A. 1972, ss. 5, 8; *Wigram v Buckley* (1894) 3 Ch 483.

pendente lite. While an action is pending.

pendente lite, **administration.** The court has power to appoint an administrator (qv) where there is a dispute as to the validity of a will (qv) or the right of administration. See the S.C.A. 1981, s. 117. The appointment will be made only where it can be shown to be necessary. The administrator *pendente lite* is entitled to remuneration. *See* LIS PENDENS.

pending actions. Actions or proceedings pending in court relating to land or any interest in or charge on land, which must be registered on the register of pending actions: L.C.A. 1972, s. 17(1). Actions of this type do not bind a purchaser without express notice of them, unless registered: s. 5(7). See *Taylor v Taylor* [1968] 1 All ER 843; *Selim Ltd v Bickenhall Engineering Ltd* [1981] 1 WLR 1318; and *Sowerby v Sowerby* (1982) 44 P & CR 192.

pension. Payments made periodically to a person on retirement from service. Generally taxable as earned income. See the Social Security Pensions Act 1975; the S.S. (Misc. Provs.) A. 1977; and the S.S.A. 1980, ss. 2–4.

pensionable age. *See* AGE, PENSIONABLE.

pension appeal tribunals. Bodies set up to determine appeals from decisions by the Minister of Pensions relating to pension claims in respect of war and service injuries. Each tribunal consists of three persons appointed by the Lord Chancellor. See the S.S.A. 1980, s. 16.

pensions, Civil List. *See* CIVIL LIST PENSIONS.

peppercorn rent. A nominal, usually insignificant, rent paid to keep alive a title. See the L.P.A. 1925, s. 99; and the S.L.A. 1925, s. 44.

per annum. By the year; annually.

per autre vie. See AUTRE VIE; CESTUI QUE VIE.

per capita. By heads. Individually, as in distribution *per capita*, where property is divided among those entitled to it, each receiving a share.

per curiam. Abbreviated to *per cur.* By the court. Refers to a decision of the court.

per diem. By the day.

peremptory challenge. *See* CHALLENGE TO JURY.

peremptory pleas. Pleas in bar (qv).

per eundem. By the same.

perfect and imperfect rights. Classification in jurisprudence (qv) of rights. A *perfect* right is one recognised and enforced by a legal system; an *imperfect* right is one recognised, but not enforced directly, by the law. (Example: although a statute-barred debt cannot be recovered generally in a court, if the debtor pays, he cannot subsequently sue for recovery of the money as having been paid without consideration.) *See* RIGHT.

perfection of gift. *See* GIFT, IMPERFECT.

perfect trust. An executed trust (qv).

performance. 1. The completion of an act. 2. An act which, in strict accordance with the terms of a contract, discharges it, eg, by tender (qv), payment.

performance bond. *See* BOND, PERFORMANCE.

performance, tender of. *See* TENDER OF PERFORMANCE.

perils, excepted. *See* EXCEPTED PERILS.

perils of the sea. An accident on the seas beyond the normal action of winds and waves. It includes damage caused by violent winds or storms, or striking a submerged rock. It does not include direct damage done to cargo by rats or bad stowage.

per incuriam. Through want of care. A mistaken decision of a court. It was held in *Young* v *Bristol Aeroplane Co Ltd* [1946] 1 All ER 98 that the Court of Appeal (qv) was not bound to follow one of its earlier decisions if satisfied that it was reached *per incuriam*. Application of the doctrine should be made only in the case of "decisions given in ignorance or forgetfulness of some inconsistent statutory provision or of some authority binding on the court concerned": *Morelle* v *Wakeling* [1955] 2 QB 379.

per infortunium. By mischance.

periodical payments. *See* FINANCIAL PROVISION ORDER DURING MARRIAGE.

periodic tenancy. A tenancy (qv) which continues for an original period and then for subsequent similar periods until determined by notice given by either party, eg, a tenancy from year to year. It may be created expressly or by implication.

perished goods. In a contract for the sale of specific goods the contract is void if, unknown to the seller, the goods have perished at the time of the making of the contract: S.G.A. 1979, s. 6. See *Couturier* v *Hastie* (1856) 5 HL Cas 673.

perjury. Offence committed by a person lawfully sworn as a witness or in-

terpreter in a judicial proceeding who wilfully makes a statement, material in that proceeding, which he knows to be false or does not believe to be true. See the Perjury Act 1911; *Welham* v *DPP* [1961] AC 103; *R* v *Dodge and Harris* [1971] 2 All ER 1523; *R* v *Cromack* [1978] Crim LR 217; and *R* v *Hall* (1982) 4 Cr App R (S) 153.

perjury, subornation of. *See* SUBORNATION.

per mensem. By the month.

per minas. By menaces.

permissive waste. That which arises from an omission by a tenant to do that which should be done, eg, failing to repair a building. A tenant for life (qv) is not liable for permissive waste unless the agreement indicates otherwise: *Re Cartwright* (1889) 41 Ch D 532. See *Powys* v *Blagrave* (1854) 4 De GM & G 448. *See* WASTE.

permit. "If a man permits a thing to be done, it means that he gives permission for it to be done, and if a man gives permission for a thing to be done, he knows what is to be done or is being done": *Lomas* v *Peek* [1947] 2 All ER 574.

per my et per tout. By the half and by all. Applied to a joint tenancy (qv) under which each joint tenant is possessed of the property *per my et per tout.* See the L.P.A. 1925, s. 36.

per pais. *See* PAIS.

perpetual injunction. *See* INJUNCTION.

perpetually renewable lease. Lease (qv) the holder of which was entitled to enforce the perpetual renewal thereof. Abolished under the L.P.A. 1922, as from 1st January 1926. Those existing on that date were converted into leases for 2,000 years from the date of commencement of the existing term. See *Marjorie Burnett Ltd* v *Barclay* (1981) 125 SJ 199.

perpetual trusts, rule against. *See* INALIENABILITY, RULE AGAINST.

perpetuating testimony. Procedure whereby evidence (qv) can be recorded where there is a danger of its loss and where it may be required for some future action. See O. 39.

perpetuities, rule against. Where there is a possibility that a future interest (qv) in property might vest after expiration of the perpetuity period, such an interest is generally void. The common-law period is lives in being (qv) at the time the instrument creating the interest becomes effective, plus 21 years and any gestation period. Under the P. & A.A. 1964, s. 1, the perpetuity period may be a fixed period of years not exceeding 80. See *Re Villar* [1928] Ch 471; *Re Atkin's Will Trusts* [1974] 1 WLR 761. *See* WAIT AND SEE PRINCIPLE.

perpetuities rule, exceptions to. The rule does not apply to: interests following an entailed interest; a gift to charity followed by a gift over to another charity on a certain event; covenants for renewal contained in a lease; postponement of the mortgagor's right to redeem; the right of the lessor to enter on a breach of covenant.

per quod. By reason of which.

per quod consortium et servitium amisit. By reason of which he lost her society and services. Action for damages brought by the husband against the person who had deprived him of his wife's society or services by some tortious act. Abolished by the A.J.A. 1982, s. 2. *See* CONSORTIUM.

per se. By itself; taken on its own.

persistent offender. Where the court is convinced that an offender convicted on indictment of an offence punishable with imprisonment for two years or more is likely to commit further offences and that the public should be protected from him for a substantial time, an extended period of imprisonment may be imposed. See the P.C.C.A. 1973, s. 28. It is essential that the offender shall have been convicted on indictment at least three times since reaching the age of 21: P.C.C.A. 1973, s. 28(1)(3). See also *R v Gooden* (*The Times*, 5.12.1979).

person. A *natural person* is a human being, capable of rights and duties. An *artificial person* is, eg, a corporation to which the law attributes personality. See the I.A. 1978, Sch 1.

personal action. *See* ACTIONS REAL AND PERSONAL.

personal Bill. A private Bill concerning the property or status of an individual. *See* BILL.

personal chattel. *See* CHATTELS.

personal credit agreement. An agreement between a debtor and creditor by which the creditor provides the debtor with credit of any amount: C.C.A. 1974, s. 8(1).

personal injuries. *See* INJURIES, PERSONAL, ACTION FOR.

personal injuries, provisional damages for. Provisional damages may be awarded if there is proved or admitted to be a chance that at some definite or indefinite time in the future the injured person will, as a result of the act or omission which gave rise to the cause of action, develop some serious deterioration in his physical or mental condition: S.C.A. 1981, s. 32A (inserted by the A.J.A. 1982, s. 6(1)).

personality. *Legal personality* is the sum total of a person's legal rights and duties ("his advantages and disadvantages"). *Corporate personality* is the sum of rights and duties borne by a corporate body.

personal property. Property other than land, eg, goods and chattels. Leasehold interests are classed as personal property. Divided into *choses in possession* and *choses in action* (qv). *See* PROPERTY.

personal representative. "The executor, original or by representation, or administrator for the time being of a deceased person": A.E.A. 1925, s. 55(1). See the S.C.A. 1981, s. 114. *See* ADMINISTRATOR; EXECUTOR.

personalty. Personal property (qv).

persona non grata. An unacceptable person, eg, a diplomatic official not acceptable to the government of the country to which he is accredited.

personation. Pretending to be another person for some improper motive. It is an offence, eg, to personate a juryman (see *R v Clark* (1918) 82 JP 295), to personate a woman's husband so as to have sexual intercourse with her (S.O.A. 1956, s. 1), to vote as some other person in an election (Representation of the People Act 1983, s. 60).

person in authority. A confession must be made voluntarily, without any threat of punishment held out by a person in authority. "Persons in authority'' have been held to include: prosecutor; prosecutor's spouse; police officer; magistrate; magistrate's clerk; but not a police officer's wife or a fellow prisoner or a prison chaplain. See *R* v *Cleary* (1963) 48 Cr App R 116; *Deokinanan* v *R* [1969] 1 AC 20. See CONFESSION.

person of unsound mind. One suffering from a mental disorder (qv).

per stirpes. According to stock. Refers to the distribution of property of an intestate divided among those entitled according to the stocks of descent.

persuade to murder. It is an offence under the O.P.A. 1861, s. 4, to persuade any person to murder any other person. See *R* v *Krause* (1902) 66 JP 121.

persuasive authorities. Precedents (qv) which are not binding. They include *obiter dicta*, decisions of inferior courts, decisions of Irish, Scottish, Commonwealth and foreign courts.

per subsequens matrimonium. See LEGITIMATION.

per totam curiam. By the entire court.

perverse verdict. A verdict altogether against the evidence, or one given by a jury which refuses to follow a judge's direction relating to a matter of law. See VERDICT.

perverting the course of justice. Acting in a way which has a tendency and is intended to pervert the administration of public justice. See, eg, *R* v *Bailey* [1956] NI 15 (false confession); *R* v *Rowell* [1978] 1 WLR 132 (attempting to pervert the course of justice is an offence known to law); and *R* v *Murray* (fabricating evidence) [1982] 1 WLR 475.

petition. A written application praying for relief or remedy, as in a petition for divorce, petition of right (qv). Available only where statute or the Rules of the Supreme Court specifically prescribe it as a mode of procedure. See O. 9.

petitioner, official. See OFFICIAL PETITIONER.

petition for winding up. Statement asking that a company (qv) be wound up by the court, presented by the company itself, or creditor(s), or contributories, or the Department of Trade, following an inspection of the company's affairs. See the Cos.A. 1948, s. 224; *Re Chesterfield Catering Co* [1976] 3 All ER 294. See WINDING-UP.

petition of right. 1. Declaration of the liberties of the people, made in 1628. 2. Procedure of obtaining restitution from the Crown or compensation in damages. See the Crown Proceedings Act 1947; *Franklin* v *R* [1974] QB 202 (in which the form of the petition is set out).

petit treason. See HIGH TREASON.

petty jury. See JURY, PETTY.

petty larceny. See GRAND LARCENY.

petty serjeanty. See GRAND SERJEANTY.

petty sessions. Court of summary jurisdiction, based initially on a statute of 1946. Now known as ''magistrates' court'' (qv). See the M.C.A. 1980; and the Justices of the Peace Act 1979, s. 4.

philanthropic purposes. Gifts for ''philanthropic'' or similar purposes have been held to be wider than gifts for ''charitable purposes'', so that they do not necessarily constitute a charity. ''It seems to me that 'philanthropic' is wide enough to comprise purposes not technically charitable'': *per* Stirling J in *Re Macduff* [1896] 2 Ch 451. See CHARITABLE TRUST.

phone tapping. See ELECTRONIC SURVEILLANCE.

photographs, use of in identification. Photographs of suspects must not be shown to witnesses for the purpose of identification if circumstances allow of a personal identification. Photographs used must be available for production in court. See *R* v *Dwyer* [1925] 2 KB 799.

picketing, peaceful. It is lawful for a person, in contemplation or furtherance of a trade dispute, to attend at or near his own place of work, or, if he is a union official, at or near the place of work of a member of that union whom he is accompanying and whom he represents, for the purpose only of peacefully obtaining or communicating information, or peacefully persuading any person to work or abstain from working: T.U.L.R.A. 1974, s. 15 (as substituted by the Employment Act 1980, s. 16(1)). Those who picket another's place of work lose their immunity in tort: T.U.L.R.A. 1974, s. 13 (as amended by the 1980 Act, s. 16). See *Duport Steels* v *Sirs* [1980] 1 WLR 142. *See* SECONDARY ACTION; STRIKE.

pin money. A regular allowance made to a wife on marriage for dress, personal expenses, etc.

pipe rolls. Rolls, so-called possibly because of their appearance when rolled up, which were originally the parchment Great Rolls of the Exchequer. Commenced *c.*1100 and continued until 1832. Contained information relating to Kings' debtors, administration, etc.

piracy. 1. Piracy *jure gentium* (piracy at common law) involves an act of armed violence committed upon the high seas within the jurisdiction of the Admiralty, and not being an act of war. The Piracy Act 1837 made piracy accompanied by dangerous violence or attempted murder a capital offence. (Term may include mutiny of passengers: *Naylor* v *Palmer* (1854) 10 Exch 382.) Piracy may also be committed against an aircraft: see the Aviation Security Act 1982, s. 5. See *Athens Maritime Enterprises* v *Hellenic Mutual War Risks Assn.* [1982] Com LR 188. (*The Times*, 1.7.82). 2. Infringement of a copyright: Copyright Act 1967, s. 21.

piscary, common of. Right to catch fish in waters belonging to another. *See* FISHERY.

places open to public, removal of articles from. "Where the public have access to a building in order to view the building or part of it, or a collection or part of a collection housed in it, any person who without lawful authority removes from the building or its grounds the whole or any part of any article displayed or kept for display to the public in the building or that part of it or in its grounds shall be guilty of an offence": Th.A. 1968, s. 11(1). See *R* v *Durkin* [1973] 2 All ER 872.

placing of shares. *See* SHARES, PLACING OF.

plaint. 1. Cause on which a complaint is based. 2. Written statement of an action.

plaintiff. One who brings an action into the court.

planning control, breach of. Development of land (qv) without appropriate planning permission. It can lead to a local planning authority serving an enforcement notice or stop notice (qqv) prohibiting specified operations on the land. See the T.C.P.A. 1971, s. 87.

planning permission. Formal consent of a local planning authority which must be sought by one who wishes to develop land. Permission may be granted unconditionally or subject to such conditions as the authority thinks fit, or may be refused. See, eg, the T.C.P.A. 1971, s. 23(1); and the T.C.P.(Minerals)A. 1981, s. 7. Planning inquiries should be held in public, subject to certain exemptions: see the Planning Inquiries (Attendance of Public) Act 1982, s. 1. *See* DEVELOPMENT.

plant. "It includes whatever apparatus is used by a businessman for carrying on a business. Not his stock in trade which he buys or makes for sale, but all goods and chattels, fixed or moveable, which he keeps for permanent employment in his business": *Yarmouth* v *France* (1887) 18 QBD 647. See the Capital Allowances Act 1968; the Finance Act 1971, s. 4(1) (*a*); *Munby* v *Furlong* [1977] Ch 359; *Benson* v *Yard Arm Club* [1979] 1 WLR 347; *IRC* v *Scottish & Newcastle Breweries Ltd* [1982] 1 WLR 322; and *Cole Bros* v *Phillips* [1982] 2 All ER 247. *See* MACHINERY AND PLANT.

plc. Abbreviation for "public limited company" (qv). *See* COMPANY'S NAME.

plea. An answer to the plaintiff's declaration in a common-law action; a defence; a pleading.

plea, ambiguous. A plea which, in response to an indictment, is not clear. Example: "Guilty, but I wasn't sure that the goods did not belong to me." If a plea remains ambiguous, a plea of not guilty is entered on behalf of the accused: C.L.A. 1967, s. 6(1).

plea bargaining. Informal procedure whereby the defendant may agree to plead guilty as an exchange for the prosecution's dropping other charges or agreeing to a summary trial. In *R* v *Turner* [1970] 2 QB 321, Lord Parker suggested certain applicable principles: counsel must not persuade a client to plead guilty if he has not committed those acts constituting the crime with which he has been charged; the accused must be completely free to make a choice as to his plea; discussions between counsel for the defence and the judge should take place only in the presence of counsel for the prosecution; the judge should never indicate the sentence he has in mind to impose where there is any suggestion that it might be different if the accused pleads guilty or not guilty, as the case may be. See *R* v *Cain* [1976] QB 486; *Practice Direction of Court of Appeal* [1976] Crim LR 561; and *R* v *Wise* [1979] RTR 57.

plea, change of. Change of plea by the accused at any stage of the trial. It must come from the accused personally. See *R* v *Heyes* [1951] 1 KB 29; *R* v *McNally* [1954] 1 WLR 933; and *R* v *Dodd* (1982) 74 Cr App R 50.

plead. To put forward a plea (qv); to allege in defence; to address the court.

pleading guilty by post. *See* POST, PLEA OF GUILTY BY.

pleadings. Formal written statements in a civil action, usually drafted by counsel, served by a party on his opponents, stating allegations of fact upon which the party pleading is claiming relief, but not the evidence by which the facts are to be proved. Must contain particulars of any claim on which party pleading relies. Usually consist of statement of claim; defence; reply (qqv). See O. 18. Intended to eradicate irrelevant matters, to state precisely issues in dispute and to allow the other party time to prepare reply.

pleadings, amendment of. Pleadings may be amended once without leave prior to the close of pleadings: O. 20, r. 3. An amended pleading must be served on the other party. After the close of pleadings, amendments may be made only with leave. See *Cropper* v *Smith* (1884) 26 Ch D 700.

pleadings, close of. Pleadings are deemed to be closed at the end of a period of 14 days after the service of reply or defence to counterclaim (qqv), or at the end of 14 days after the service of defence if neither reply nor defence to counterclaim has been served. See O. 18, r. 20.

pleadings, exchange of. Process of exchange between the plaintiff (qv) and defendant (qv) of the plaintiff's statement of claim, the defendant's defence and the plaintiff's reply. Further pleadings require leave (see O. 18, r. 4), eg, the defendant's rejoinder, the plaintiff's surrejoinder, the defendant's rebutter, and the plaintiff's surrebutter (qqv).

pleadings, formal requirements. Requirements under O. 18, r. 6, whereby every pleading must bear on its face: letter, number of action and year of issue; title of action; Division of High Court (qv) to which the action is assigned and the name of judge(s) to whom assigned; description of pleading and the date on which served. Pleadings must be divided into consecutively numbered paragraphs. Dates and other numbers must be in figures.

pleadings, material facts in. Pleadings must contain only material facts. "The word 'material' means necessary for formulating a complete cause of action, and if any one 'material' fact is omitted, the statement of claim is bad": *Bruce* v *Odhams Press Ltd* [1936] 1 KB 712.

pleadings, striking out. Under O. 18, r. 19, the defendant can apply to have the plaintiff's statement of claim struck out because, eg, it discloses no reasonable cause of action, or is frivolous, or may prejudice or delay the fair trial of action. Examples: action to recover payment apparently made by the plaintiff in contravention of statute (*Shaw* v *Shaw* [1965] 1 WLR 539); action against an M.P. for not presenting a petition to Parliament (*Chaffers* v *Goldsmid* [1894] 1 QB 186).

pleadings, subsequent. Pleadings subsequent to a reply or defence to counterclaim, served with leave of the court; the defendant's rejoinder; the plaintiff's surrejoinder; the defendant's rebutter; the plaintiff's surrebutter (qqv). See O. 18, r. 4.

pleadings, trial without. Procedure in any action commenced by a writ other than one based on a claim relating to libel, slander, malicious prosecution, false imprisonment or fraud, where the defendant has acknowledged service of the writ, where there is no substantial dispute, where parties agree on a statement of issues in dispute and where the court is satisfied that issues can be defined without pleadings. See O. 18, r. 21.

pleas in bar. Plea by the defendant in a trial on indictment, eg, *autrefois acquit, autrefois convict* (qqv).

pleas of the Crown. Term formerly used to refer to criminal prosecutions, ie, offences said to have been committed *contra pacem domini regis* (qv). Formerly such pleas were triable in the King's Courts only.

pledge. 1. A surety. 2. Transfer of a chattel (qv) as security for the payment of a debt incurred by a transferor, or performance of some engagement. 3. Pawnee's rights over an article taken in pawn: C.C.A. 1974, s. 189(1).

plenary. Full; complete; conclusive.

plene administravit. He has fully administered. Defence by an executor (qv) or administrator (qv) who is sued upon the testator's debts, claiming that he has administered the estate fully and has nothing left with which to satisfy the plaintiff's demands. See *Midland Bank Trust Co v Green (No. 2)* [1979] 1 All ER 726.

plenipotentiary. One invested with full powers, eg, as the Sovereign's representative.

plough bote. Wood employed in the repair of instruments of husbandry.

plurality. The holding by one person of two or more benefices (qv). See the Pluralities Acts 1838 and 1930; and the Pastoral Measure 1968.

poaching. Illegal taking of game or fish, and trespassing for that purpose. See the Night Poaching Act 1828; the Game Laws (Amendment) Act 1960; the Th.A. 1968, Sch 1; the Wild Creatures and Forest Laws Act 1971; the C.L.A. 1977, s. 15(4). Sch 12; the Deer Act 1980, s. 1; *Jones v Evans*

[1978] Crim LR 230; and *R v Smith* (1982) 4 Cr App R (S) 219.

point of law, objection in. A party may by his pleadings (qv) raise any point of law: O. 18, r. 11. See *Independent Automatic Sales Ltd v Knowles & Foster* [1962] 1 WLR 971.

poison. That which when administered is injurious to health or life. It is an offence under the O.P.A. 1861, s. 23, unlawfully to administer to a person any poison so as to endanger life or inflict grievous bodily harm. See also the Poisons Act 1972, which regulates the sale of poisons.

police authorities. Police committees controlling regular police forces. In England and Wales committees consist of local councillors and magistrates (qv). The police authority for the Metropolitan Police Force is the Home Secretary; for the City of London (qv), the Court of Common Council. It is the duty of an authority to provide an adequate police force for its area. Income comes largely from central government and a local police rate.

police cadet. "Any person appointed to undergo training with a view to becoming a constable": Race Relations Act 1976, s. 16(5). See *Wilts Police Authority v Wynn* [1981] QB 85 (cadets are not "employees").

Police Complaints Board. Body set up under the Police Act 1976, to deal with complaints by the public against police. Members do not include any person who is or has been a constable in the UK. Complaints are investigated by the police, after which a report is sent to the Board (unless referred to the DPP (qv)). The Board may direct that disciplinary proceedings be taken. A Disciplinary Tribunal, which includes the relevant Chief Officer and two Board members, considers disciplinary proceedings. See *R v Police Complaints Board ex p Madden* [1983] 1 WLR 447.

police court. Magistrates' court (qv).

police forces. There are 51 regular police forces in England, Scotland and Wales. Most counties have their own forces. The Metropolitan Police Force is responsible for the area within a radius of 24 km from Charing Cross; the City of London has its own force. Eventual control is with the Home Secretary, who is advised by the HM Chief Inspector and five Inspectors of Constabulary.

Police Negotiating Board. Board which represents the interests of authorities who maintain police forces and members of those forces (and cadets); it is appointed to consider questions concerning leave, pay and allowances, pensions, hours of duty: Police Negotiating Board Act 1980, s. 1(1).

police, obstruction of. It is an offence under the Police Act 1964, s. 51, unlawfully to obstruct a constable in the execution of his duty, and this is not confined to physical obstruction but includes "anything making it more difficult for the police to carry out their duties": *Hinchcliffe* v *Sheldon* [1955] 1 WLR 1207. "What the prosecution have to prove is that there was an obstructing of a constable; that the constable was at the time acting in the execution of his duty and that the person obstructing did so wilfully": *Rice* v *Connolly* [1966] 2 QB 414. See *Willmot* v *Atack* [1976] 3 WLR 753; *Green* v *Moore* [1982] 1 All ER 428; and *Hills* v *Ellis* [1983] 2 WLR 235.

police officer. One who, belonging to a police force, exercises by virtue of his office, powers as a constable (qv). His responsibilities include: protection of people and property (see *R* v *Dytham* [1979] QB 722); investigation of offences; apprehension of offenders. He is neither a servant nor an agent of the Crown.

police, right to detain for questioning. *See* QUESTIONING, DETAINING BY POLICE FOR.

policy holder. One who is the legal holder of a policy for securing a contract with an insurance company: Insurance Companies Act 1982, s. 96(1).

Policyholders Protection Board. Body corporate set up under the Policyholders Protection Act 1975. Its functions become exercisable when a resolution is passed or an order made for winding up an insur-

ance company. The Board is to secure payment of the full amount a company in liquidation is liable to pay to a UK policyholder in respect of a liability, subject to compulsory insurance. See *Policyholders Protection Board* v *Official Receiver* [1976] 1 WLR 447. *See* INSURANCE.

policy, life. *See* LIFE POLICY.

policy of insurance. The instrument containing the contract made by the insurer with the insured. See the Insurance Companies Act 1974, s. 85(1). *See* INSURANCE.

political fund. That part of a union's total funds used exclusively in the furtherance of political objects. A union member may decline to contribute by "contracting out" (qv). See *Parkin* v *ASTMS* [1980] IRLR 188; and *Richards* v *NUM* [1981] IRLR 281. See also the Employment Act 1982, s. 17(3).

political offence. Term used in relation to extradition (qv), which will not normally take place on the basis of a political offence. "In my opinion the idea that lies behind the phrase is that the fugitive is at odds with the state that applies for his extradition on some issue connected with the political control or government of the country": *per* Viscount Radcliffe in *Schtraks* v *Government of Israel* [1964] AC 556. See also; *R* v *Governor of Brixton Prison, ex p Kolczynski* [1955] 1 QB 540.

political offence, exclusion of cases from. Under the Suppression of Terrorism Act 1978, certain offences are not to be regarded as of a political character. They include: murder, manslaughter or culpable homicide, rape, kidnapping, false imprisonment, assault occasioning actual bodily harm or causing injury and wilful fire-raising; offences under the O.P.A. 1861 ss. 18, 20–24, 28–30, 48, 55–56; offences under the Explosive Substances Act 1883, ss. 2, 3; offences under the Hijacking Act 1971 and the Protection of Aircraft Act 1973, Part I; attempts to commit any of these offences. See the 1978 Act, Sch 1.

political uniforms. It is an offence to wear in any public place or public meeting a uniform "signifying association with any political organisation or the promotion of any political purpose": Public Order Act 1936, s. 1(1). See *O'Moran* v *DPP* [1975] QB 864.

poll. Procedure involved in taking, registering, counting votes and declaring the result in an election.

poll, deed. *See* DEED.

poll tax. Tax per person or head.

pollution. Action of rendering unclean. See, eg, the Prevention of Oil Pollution Act 1971; the Control of Pollution Act 1974 (amended by the L.G.P.L.A. 1980, Sch 2); the Dumping at Sea Act 1974; the Merchant Shipping Act 1979, s. 20; *Alphacell Ltd* v *Woodward* [1972] AC 82; and *Ashcroft* v *Cambro Ltd* [1981] 1 WLR 1349.

polygamy. Practice under which a person has several spouses. See the Matrimonial Proceedings (Polygamous Marriages) Act 1972; Mat.C.A. 1973, ss. 11, 47; the Matrimonial Causes Rules 1977, r. 108; and the Matrimonial Homes and Property Act 1981, s. 3. Polygamous marriages may be recognised in English law "unless there is some strong reason to the contrary": *Mohamed* v *Knott* [1969] 1 QB 1; Law Commission Working Paper 1982, No. 83; *Hussain* v *Hussain* [1982] 3 WLR 679.

pone. A writ, now obsolete, by which a cause was removed to the Court of Common Pleas (qv) or King's Bench.

pornography. Obscene material (books, films, etc.). See the Williams Report on Obscenity and Film Censorship 1979 (Cmnd 7772). *See* OBSCENITY.

port. Includes harbours, rivers, estuaries, havens, docks, canals or other places where persons are empowered under statute to make charges in respect of ships entering and using the facilities: S.C.A. 1981, s. 22(2).

portfolio. 1. Office of a minister of state. A Minister without Portfolio is one who is not in charge of a department of state. 2. List of securities owned by a person or financial institution.

portion. Gift of money or other property made to a child by a father or one *in loco parentis* (qv) so as to establish that child in life or to make a permanent provision for him. A "portion-debt" arises from a covenant to give a portion.

positive law. *See* LAW, NATURAL.

positivism, legal. Doctrine in legal theory based on the examination of man-made law, which is set down (ie, posited) by man for man. It is concerned, essentially, with law as it is, rather than as it ought to be.

posse comitatus. Power of the county. Group of able-bodied men who could be called together by a sheriff (qv), eg, to assist in keeping the peace, to pursue felons.

possession. Concept based on a degree of physical control and involving: *corpus* (that which is possessed) and *animus possidendi* (qv). May be prima facie evidence of ownership. Defined variously as, eg, "physical detention coupled with intention to use the thing detained as one's own" (Maine); "continuing exercise of a claim to the exclusive use of some material object" (Salmond). "In truth, English law has never worked on a completely logical and exhaustive definition of possession": *USA* v *Dollfus Mieg et Cie SA* [1952] 1 All ER 58. See *Lockyer* v *Gibb* [1967] 2 QB 243 (possession without mental element in relation to crime); *Warner* v *Metropolitan Police Commissioner* [1969] AC 256; *R* v *Ashton-Rickardt* [1978] 1 All ER 173. See OWNERSHIP.

possession, interest in. *See* INTEREST IN POSSESSION.

possession, quiet. *See* QUIET POSSESSION.

possession, recent. *See* RECENT POSSESSION.

possession, unity of. *See* UNITY OF POSSESSION.

possession, unlawful, of drugs. It is an offence under the Misuse of Drugs Act 1971: to have a controlled drug in one's possession (s. 5(1)); to have a controlled drug in one's possession, whether lawfully or not, with the intention to supply it to another in contravention of s. 4. "Possession" involves more than mere control; the person in control should know that the thing is in his control. See *Warner v Metropolitan Police Commissioner* [1969] AC 256; and *R v Chatwood* [1980] 1 All ER 467. *See* DRUGS, CONTROLLED.

possession, writ of. Writ directing a sheriff (qv) to enter upon land so as to give vacant possession to the plaintiff. Used for direct enforcement of order or judgment for possession of land. See O. 45, r. 3.

possessory action. Action, abolished in 1833, for regaining possession of land.

possessory lien. *See* LIEN.

possessory title. Title based on the possession of land where the applicant is, for the time being, unable to establish title in the usual way, eg, by title deeds. First registration of such title has the effect of registering land with absolute title, but that title will not affect any rights or interests subsisting or capable of arising at the time of registration. See the L.R.A. 1925, ss. 4, 6, 11. Possessory title to leasehold land may be granted to an applicant in possession or in receipt of rents and profits. See *Jessamine Investment Co v Schwartz* [1976] 3 All ER 521; *Basildon DG v Manning* (1976) 237 EG 879. *See* TITLE.

possibility. Term used in land law (eg, as in double possibility (qv)) to describe an interest in land which will arise on some uncertain event. "Bare possibility" described the expectation of an eldest son to succeed to his father's lands; "possibility coupled with an interest" refers to, eg, a contingent remainder (qv).

possibility of a reverter. Right of a grantor to land on determination of a determinable fee (qv).

post. After; following.

post, contracts by. Contracts made, eg, by letter or telegram. In general, an offer by post must be accepted by post unless the offer has indicated anything to the contrary. Acceptance is complete as soon as the letter is properly addressed, prepaid and posted, whether it reaches the offeror or not. See *Adams v Lindsell* (1818) 1 B & Ald 681.

post-date. To inscribe a document, eg, a bill or cheque, with a date

subsequent to that of its execution.

post-dated cheque. *See* CHEQUE, POST-DATED.

post diem. After the day.

posthumous child. A child born after the death of the father.

post litem motam. After the beginning of litigation.

post-mortem. After death. Term used to refer to the examination of a body after death so as to determine, eg, the cause of death. Known also as an "autopsy". See the Coroners Act 1877, s. 21; the Coroners (Amendment) Act 1929, s. 21; the Coroners Act 1980, s. 1; and S.I. 1980/557.

post-nuptial settlement. A settlement made after marriage for the financial benefit of one or both of the spouses. It may be varied by an order granted on a decree of divorce (qv) for the benefit of the parties to the marriage and children of the family.

post-obit bond. Bond payable on or after the death of some person other than the maker. See *Earl of Chesterfield v Janssen* (1751) 2 Ves Sen 125.

post, payment by. Generally not good payment where the letter is lost in post, unless the creditor requested payment by post. Such a request does not absolve the debtor from paying in a reasonable manner and in accordance with the accepted business practice. See *Pennington v Crossley & Son* (1897) 77 LT 43.

post, plea of guilty by. Procedure under the M.C.A. 1980, s. 12, often used in motoring cases. The prosecutor serves the summons and statement of facts to be placed before the court. The defendant must then inform the clerk that he wishes to plead guilty without appearance. (He may change his mind and appear.) The statement of facts read out in court must be exactly the same as that served on the defendant. The hearing is adjourned if the possibility of imprisonment or disqualification (motoring cases) arises.

post, service by. Where statute authorises or requires a document to be served by post, that service is deemed to be effected by properly addressing, pre-paying and posting a letter containing the document: I.A. 1978, s. 7.

potior est conditio defendentis. The condition of a defendant is the better.

potior est conditio possidentis. The condition of a possessor is the better. See *E India Co v Tritton* (1824) 3 B & C 280.

pound. Enclosure for the confining of stray cattle, etc.

poundage. Subsidy per pound on imports and exports, formerly granted to the Sovereign.

pound breach. Common-law offence of taking chattels (qv) from a pound before the satisfaction of a distrainor's claim. *See* DISTRESS.

power. Authority vested in the donee (of the power) to modify a legal relationship, as where one disposes of property for his own or another's benefit. May be: simply collateral (qv) (where the donee has no interest in the property); in gross (qv); appendant or appurtenant (qqv). *See* APPOINTMENT, POWER OF.

power, capricious. A power which is void because "it negatives a sensible consideration by the trustees of the exercise of the power": *Re Manisty's Settlement* [1974] Ch 17.

power coupled with interest. Power to perform some act, together with an interest (united in the same person) in the subject-matter of that act.

power of appointment. *See* APPOINTMENT, POWER OF.

power of attorney. Instrument authorising one person to act for another during the absence of that other. Under the Tr.A. 1925, s. 25, as amended by the Powers of Attorney Act 1971, a trustee (qv) has the power to delegate the exercise of his powers and discretions to an attorney.

power of sale. 1. Power of a tenant for life (qv) to sell settled land (qv) or any part thereof, or any easement, right or privilege over the land: S.L.A. 1925, s. 38. Sale must be made for the best consideration in money that can be obtained. 2. Power of trustee (qv), under the Tr.A. 1925, to sell or concur with any other person in selling all or part of the trust property. 3. Power of a mortgagee (qv), under the L.P.A. 1925, s. 101(1), to sell when the legal date for redemption (qv) has passed.

power of search. *See* SEARCH, POWER OF.

p.p. Abbreviation of *per procurationem* (by means of procuration). Used where one signs a document, eg, a receipt, as another's agent. See *Charles v Blackwell* (1877) 2 CPD 151.

practice. Formal procedures relating to proceedings in a court. Governed generally (in the Supreme Court) by the Rules of the Supreme Court (qv).

Practice Directions. Directions and notes, generally published in the law reports, indicating the views of the judges of the Court of Appeal or the judges, masters, registrars of the High Court, relating to matters of practice and procedure of the courts. They do not have any statutory authority.

practice, general and approved. Practice taken into account in determining standard of care in actions for negligence. "A defendant . . . can clear [himself] if he shows that he acted in accordance with general and approved practice": *per* Lord Alness in *Vancouver General Hospital v McDaniel* (1935) 152 LT 56.

practice master. A master who controls the business of the Central Office (qv). See O. 63, r. 2.

practising certificate. Annual certificate issued to a solicitor (qv) by the Law Society, entitling him to practice. See the Solicitors Act 1974, ss. 9–18; *Hudgell Yeates & Co v Weston* [1978] 2 All ER 363.

praecipe. Command. 1. Writ (qv), now abolished, ordering a person to perform some action, or to show the reason for non-performance. 2. Form used to secure the issue of various orders enforcing decisions of the High Court. See O. 45; O. 56.

praecipe, **tenant to the.** Procedure, now obsolete, whereby a tenant for life (qv) who was concurring in the barring of an entail (qv) conveyed the life estate to another so that a *praecipe* (qv) in recovery could be issued against that other, who was known as the *tenant to the praecipe.*

praemunire. *Praemoneri* = to be forewarned. Originally referred to an offence, punishable with life imprisonment and forfeiture of property, of asserting the supremacy of Pope over the English Sovereign. It was later applied to offences relating to, eg, the unlawful sending of a prisoner outside the realm to avoid the protection of Habeas Corpus Act (qv). See *Statute of Praemunire* 1392.

praemunire facias. Beginning of the writ of praemunire ("that you cause to be forewarned . . .").

praepositus. 1. One placed in authority. 2. One from whom descent might be traced.

praesumitur pro negante. It is presumed for the negative.

preamble. Introduction to a statute or Bill, explaining the facts and assumptions behind it. Where an operative part of a statute is ambiguous, the preamble may be resorted to so as to show, eg, the intention of the Act. "It is only when it conveys a clear and definite meaning in comparison with relatively obscure or indefinite enacting words that a preamble may legitimately prevail": *A.-G.* v *Prince Ernest Augustus of Hanover* [1957] 1 All ER 49. See also *Brett* v *Brett* (1826) 3 Add 210; *R* v *Bates* [1952] 2 All ER 842.

precarious possession. Possession simply at will. "What is 'precarious'?"—that which depends not on right, but on the will of another person": *Burrows* v *Lang* [1901] 2 Ch 511.

precatory trust. Trust arising as a result of the use of precatory words (qv) and their construction. *See* TRUST.

precatory words. *Precari* = to entreat. Words of an entreaty, prayer, desire, etc, which, when they accompany a transfer or bequest of property, suggest that the transferor had in mind the creation of a trust (qv), eg, "I most heartily beseech . . ."; "I will and desire that . . ." The court is guided by the intention of the testator (qv) apparent in the will, and not by any particular words in which the wishes of the testator are expressed: *Re Williams* [1897] 2 Ch 12. See also *Re Adams and Kensington Vestry* (1884) 27 Ch D 394; *Re Diggles* (1888) 39 Ch D 253. *See* WILL.

precedent. 1. Judgment or decision cited so as to justify a decision in a later, apparently similar, case. An *authoritative precedent* is generally binding and must be followed. A *persuasive precedent* (based, eg, on *obiter dicta*) need not be followed. A *declaratory precedent* merely applies an existing rule of law. An *original precedent* creates and applies a new rule of law. 2. Precedent as applied to the hierarchy of courts is as follows: *House of Lords*—generally bound by previous decisions (see *London Street Tramways Co.* v *LCC* [1898] AC 375) but will depart from such decisions where it appears right to do so; *Court of Appeal (Civil Division)*—bound by previous decisions, except where given *per incuriam* (qv) or where inconsistent with a subsequent House of Lords decision; *Court of Appeal (Criminal Division)*—apparently bound by previous decisions; *High Court and Crown Court*—bound by decisions of superior courts; *county courts and magistrates' courts*—bound by decisions of superior courts. See *Young* v *Bristol Aeroplane Co Ltd* [1944] KB 718; *Davis* v *Johnson* [1978] 1 All ER 1132. *See* STARE DECISIS.

precedent, condition. *See* CONDITION.

precept. 1. Command. 2. Written order. 3. Order referring specifically to the payment of rates: L.G.A. 1972, s. 149. (For the limitation of precepting powers see the Local Government Finance Act 1982).

precept, supplementary. "A precept issued by a precepting authority in respect of (or of part of) a financial year in respect of which it has already issued a precept, and by way of addition to and not in substitution for that previous precept": Local Government Finance Act 1982, s. 7(1).

predecessor. One (eg, a settlor; testator (qqv)) from whom benefit is derived of succession to property. A "predecessor in title" is one through whom another is able to trace a title in property.

pre-emption. Right to purchase before others. See the L.P.A. 1925, s. 186; the L.C.A. 1972, s. 2(4) (whereby it is registrable as an estate contract (qv)); *First National Securities* v *Chiltern DC* [1975] 2 All ER 786;

Pritchard v *Briggs* [1980] 1 All ER 294. For the statutory right of pre-emption on a new issue of equity securities, see the Cos.A. 1980, s. 17. *See* OPTION.

preference, fraudulent. *See* FRAUDULENT PREFERENCE.

preference, right of. Right of a personal representative (qv) to pay one creditor in preference to another of the same class. Abolished in relation to deaths occurring after 1971: A.E.A. 1971, s. 10.

preference shares. Shares ranking for payment after debentures (qv) and before ordinary shares (qv). See the Finance Act 1981, s. 67(1). For "fixed-rate" preference shares, see the Finance Act 1982, s. 54(5). *See* SHARE.

preferential debts. After payment of the costs of bankruptcy (qv), certain types of liabilities must be paid in priority to others, so that assets are applied in accordance with the provisions of the B.A. 1914 (in the case of rates, taxes, wages, salaries, etc). After preferential debts, ordinary liabilities of the bankrupt rank for dividend *pari passu inter se* (qv). See also the E.P.(C.)A. 1978, Part VII.

preferment. 1. Advancement or promotion. 2. Bringing or laying of a charge or bill of indictment (qv).

pregnancy, dismissal on grounds of. Dismissal from employment solely because of, or for any reason connected with, pregnancy. Treated as unfair dismissal: E.P.(C.).A. 1978, s. 60.

pregnancy *per alium*. Pregnancy by some other [person]. A marriage is voidable on the grounds that at the time of the marriage the respondent was pregnant by some person other than the petitioner. See the Mat.C.A. 1973, s. 12. *See* NULLITY OF MARRIAGE.

pre-hearing assessment. Procedure concerning industrial tribunal (qv) whereby either party, or the tribunal, may ask for a pre-hearing. If it is then decided that the originating application is "unlikely to succeed or that the submission or arguments put by either party have no reasonable prospect of success" and the applica-

tion is not withdrawn, costs may be awarded. See S.I. 1980/884; and *Mulvaney* v *London Transport Executive* [1981] ICR 351.

pre-incorporation contract. A contract made between a person acting as agent (qv) or trustee (qv) for a company about to be formed and another party. Neither the company nor the other party is generally bound by such a contract. See *Re English and Colonial Produce Co Ltd* [1906] 2 Ch 435. *See* CONTRACT.

prejudice. Preconceived judgment. "Without prejudice" is a term used so as to attempt to protect the writer of a document against the construing of its contents as an admission of liability and means, in effect, "without prejudice to rights of writer of the statement". See *Tomlin* v *Standard Telephones Ltd* [1969] 3 All ER 201; Law Reform Committee *Privilege in Civil Proceedings*, 1967 (Cmnd 3472).

preliminary investigation. Known also as "preliminary enquiry". Investigation by magistrates of a case which may go for trial to a higher court. The object is to establish whether the prosecution can show a prima facie case against the accused; if it can, the accused is committed for trial; if not, the defendant is discharged. See, eg, the M.C.A. 1980, ss. 4–7.

preliminary point of law. Point of law, eg, whether or not certain facts constitute the offence charged, considered by the judge who hears the argument on it, following a plea of not guilty and before the jury (qv) is empanelled. See *R* v *Vickers* [1975] 2 All ER 945.

Premier. The Prime Minister (qv).

premises. 1. Those operative parts of a deed (qv) which precede the habendum (qv) and set out, eg, the names of parties, property to be transferred. 2. Property, eg, land, buildings. 3. Propositions in an argument from which a conclusion is drawn.

premises, disposal of. *See* DISPOSAL OF PREMISES.

premises, domestic. *See* DOMESTIC PREMISES.

premises, industrial. *See* INDUSTRIAL PREMISES.

premium. 1. Periodical payment made for keeping up an insurance (qv). See *Lewis* v *Norwich Union* [1916] AC 509. 2. Reward. 3. Sum paid over and above a fixed wage or price. 4. "Any fine or other like sum and any other pecuniary consideration in addition to rent and any sum paid by way of a deposit, other than one which does not exceed one-sixth of the annual rent and is reasonable in relation to the potential liability in respect of which it is paid": Rent Act 1977, s. 128, (as substituted by the H.A. 1980, s. 79). Premiums and loans (secured or unsecured) on a grant of protected tenancies (qv) are prohibited under the 1977 Act, s. 119.

premium, issue of shares at a. Issue of shares at a price above par or nominal value. Premium must be transferred to share premium account: Cos.A. 1948, s. 56(1). See *Shearer* v *Bercain* [1980] 3 All ER 295.

prerogative orders. Mandamus (qv); prohibition (qv); certiorari (qv).

prerogative, royal. "The residue of discretionary or arbitrary authority which at any given time is legally left in the hands of the Crown": Dicey. Examples: summoning and dissolving Parliament; appointing bishops and judges; exemption from most statutes. These are, today, nominal rather than substantial. See *A.-G.* v *De Keyser's Royal Hotel* [1920] AC 508; *Moore* v *A.-G. for Irish Free State* [1935] AC 484.

prerogative writs. Prerogative orders (qv).

prescribe. 1. To claim by prescription (qv). 2. To set out under a regulation.

prescribed diseases. *See* DISEASES, PRESCRIBED.

prescribed limits of alcohol in blood, etc. Proportions of alcohol in blood, etc, in relation to driving offences. They include: 35 microgrammes of alcohol in 100 millilitres of breath; 80 milligrammes in 100 millilitres of blood; 107 milligrammes in 100 millilitres of urine: Road Traffic Act 1972, ss. 6–12 (as substituted by the Transport Act 1981, Sch 8).

prescription. Generally, acquisition or extinction of rights by lapse of time. Claim must be based on the actual and continuous user; enjoyment must be of right; the user must generally be by tenant in fee simple (qv) against another tenant in fee simple who has acquiesced in that user. Prescription at common law required proof of: user since time immemorial (qv); user *nec vi, nec clam, nec precario* (qv); continuous user. Under the Prescription Act 1832, in the case of easements (qv) other than light, the uninterrupted user for 60 years makes a claim to a *profit à prendre* indefeasible. See *Allen* v *Greenwood* [1980] Ch 119. *See* LOST MODERN GRANT.

present. To offer or tender.

presentment. 1. Presenting a bill of exchange (qv) to an acceptor for payment or to a drawee for acceptance. 2. Presentation to a benefice (qv). See the Pastoral Measure 1968.

presentment of Englishry. In the immediate post-Norman Conquest era, fines were levied on a community in which a person who was apparently Norman had been slain, but not where it could be proved that the dead man was English. The presumption was that he was Norman unless presentment of Englishry, ie, proof that he was English, was given. Abolished in 1340. *See* MURDRUM.

presents. As in the phrase "these presents". The phrase refers to the deed itself in which the words are contained.

preservation order. Order issued under the T.C.P.A. 1971 in relation to work needed for the preservation of an unoccupied listed building (qv), or in relation to a non-listed building of special architectural or historic interest which is threatened with demolition or alteration.

presiding judges. High Court judges assigned to circuits in England and Wales who have a general responsibility for a High Court and Crown Court centre.

presumption. 1. Assumption which must be made until the contrary is proved. 2. Conclusion that facts exist which must, or may, be drawn if other facts are proved or admitted.

presumption against a wrongdoer.

See OMNIA PRAESUMUNTUR CONTRA SPOLIATOREM.

presumption concerning ouster of jurisdiction. *See* OUSTER OF JURISDICTION.

presumption concerning penal statutes. *See* PENAL STATUTES.

presumption concerning vested rights. *See* VESTED RIGHTS.

presumption of accuracy. Presumption that instruments (eg, speedometers, watches) were in order on the occasion of the incident being investigated. See *Nicholas* v *Penny* [1950] 2 All ER 89.

presumption of advancement. *See* ADVANCEMENT.

presumption of continuance. Presumption of fact suggesting that any proved state of affairs can be presumed to have continued for some time. Thus, from the fact that a person was alive at one date it may be inferred that he was alive at some subsequent date. See *Re Forster's Settlement* [1942] Ch. 199.

presumption of death. "If a person has not been heard of for seven years, there is a presumption of law that he is dead": *Lal Chand Marwari* v *Mahant Ramrup Gir* (1925) 42 TLR. See the O.P.A. 1861, s. 57; the L.P.A. 1925, s. 184; the Mat.C.A. 1973, s. 19; *Chard* v *Chard* [1956] P 259; *Thompson* v *Thompson* [1956] 1 All ER 603; and *Kamouh* v *BAC Ltd* (*The Times,* 17.7.1982). *See* DEATH, PROOF OF.

presumption of good faith and value. The holder of a bill is prima facie presumed to be a holder in due course (qv): B.Ex.A. 1882, s. 30(2).

presumption of innocence. An accused person is presumed innocent until the prosecution has proved the case against him beyond reasonable doubt. See *Woolmington* v *DPP* [1935] AC 462.

presumption of lawful origin. Persuasive presumption that he who possesses property is its owner.

presumption of legality. *See* OMNIA PRAESUMUNTUR RITE ET SOLEMNITER ESSE ACTA.

presumption of legitimacy. A child born during lawful wedlock is presumed to be legitimate: *Banbury Peerage Case* (1811) 1 Sim & St 153.

The presumption may be rebutted only by strong preponderance of evidence, but "even weak evidence against legitimacy must prevail if there is not other evidence to counterbalance it": *S.* v *McC.* [1972] AC 24. "Any presumption of law as to the legitimacy of any person may in civil proceedings be rebutted by evidence which shows that it is more probable than not that that person is illegitimate or legitimate, as the case may be, and it shall not be necessary to prove that fact beyond reasonable doubt in order to rebut the presumption": F.L.R.A. 1969, s. 26.

presumption of marriage validity. "Where there is evidence of a ceremony of marriage having been followed by cohabitation of the parties, the validity of the marriage will be presumed, in the absence of decisive evidence to the contrary": *Russell* v *A.-G.* [1949] P 391. There is a presumption also that the marriage is monogamous: *Cheni* v *Cheni* [1965] P 85. See *Re Taplin* [1937] 3 All ER 105; *Blyth* v *Blyth* [1966] AC 643.

presumption of negligence. *See* RES IPSA LOQUITUR.

presumption of sanity. A presumption that a person is sane until the contrary is proved. *See* M'NAGHTEN RULES.

presumption of survivorship. *See* COMMORIENTES.

presumptions, classifications of. 1. *Traditional classification:* (*a*) *Praesumptiones juris et de jure,* ie, drawn by law and in an obligatory manner; inference of fact which cannot be contradicted; (*b*) *Praesumptiones juris sed non jure*: inferences of fact which hold good only where there is no contradictory evidence; (*c*) *Praesumptiones facti,* ie, inferences of fact which the court may, but need not, draw from the facts before it. 2. *Lord Denning's suggested classification* (see 61 LQR 379): (*a*) *Provisional,* ie, presumptions of fact; (*b*) *Conclusive,* ie, irrebuttable presumptions of law; (*c*) *Compelling,* ie, conclusions which must be drawn when basic facts are proved "unless the other side proves the contrary or proves some other fact which the law recognises as sufficient to rebut the presumption'' eg, the presumption of legitimacy (qv).

presumptions, conflicting. Two presumptions having application to the same set of facts, thereby creating conflicting results. In such a case they are effectively cancelled out. See *R v Willshire* (1881) 6 QBD 366.

presumptions, irrebuttable. Known also as conclusive presumptions. In effect, rules of substantive law (qv). Evidence to contradict them cannot be called. Example: the presumption that a child of under 10 cannot have a guilty mind.

presumptions, rebuttable. 1. *Of law*, which *must* be observed in the absence of evidence to the contrary, so that the burden of rebuttal is on opposing party. Example: the L.P.A. 1925, s. 184, regarding commorientes (qv). 2. *Of fact*, which *may* be observed in the absence of evidence to the contrary. Example: *omnia praesumuntur rite esse acta* (qv).

presumptions relating to construction of statutes. Presumptions laid down by the courts to assist in construing Acts of Parliament. They include: legislature does not make mistakes (see *Fisher* v *Bell* [1961] 1 QB 394); legislature does not intend what is unreasonable (see *Re A.B. & Co* [1900] 1 QB 541); words are presumed to be used in their popular sense in statutes (see *Re Hall's Settlement* [1954] 1 WLR 1185); Crown is unaffected by a statute unless expressly named therein (see *Ministry of Agriculture* v *Jenkins* [1963] 2 QB 317). *See* INTERPRETATION OF STATUTES.

presumptive heir. *See* HEIR PRESUMPTIVE.

presumptive title. Title arising only from occupancy (qv).

pretence, false. *See* FALSE PRETENCE.

pre-trial review. Procedure whereby, eg, in civil actions, the registrar makes a preliminary consideration of an action to be heard in a county court. He gives all such directions as appear to him "necessary or desirable for securing the just, expeditious and economical disposal of the action" (see the County Court Rules 1981, O. 17, r. 1). Evidence may be given by affidavit (qv). Failure of the defendant to appear combined with failure to deliver an admission or defence may result in the registrar's entering a judgment for the plaintiff. Comparable arrangements exist in the Crown Court and in some magistrates' courts with a view to simplifying (and therefore shortening) trials.

preventive detention. Introduced by the Prevention of Crime Act 1908. It involved an added period of detention where the jury found that the person convicted was a habitual criminal (qv). Abolished by the C.J.A. 1967.

previous consistent statements in civil cases, proof of. May be proved with leave of the court under the Civil Evidence Act 1968, ss. 2, 3, 4, or without leave if the statement is part of the *res gestae* (qv).

previous consistent statements in criminal cases, proof of. Certain previous consistent statements in criminal cases may be proved, eg, where they form part of the *res gestae* (qv); are complaints in charges of sexual offences; are made by the accused on arrest; are made at a date which tends to disprove the allegation that the witnesses' testimony had been recently concocted; are part of the identification of the accused by the prosecution witness. See *R* v *Osborne* [1905] 1 KB 551; *R* v *Benjamin* (1913) 8 Cr App R 146; *R* v *Roberts* [1942] 1 All ER 187. *See* EVIDENCE.

previous convictions, evidence of. Generally excluded as irrelevant, save where they form an essential ingredient of the offence, or where relevant to prove the offence itself, or in the course of cross-examination (qv) of the opposing witness as to credit, etc. See *Maxwell* v *DPP* [1935] AC 309; *Jones* v *DPP* [1962] AC 635; *R* v *Britzmann* [1983] 1 WLR 350. In civil proceedings a person's previous conviction may be relevant to prove that he committed the offence for which he was convicted: Civil Evidence Act 1968, s. 11. See the Criminal Evidence Act 1898, s. 1(*f*); the Official Secrets Act 1911, s. 1(2); the Th.A. 1968, s. 27(3); and the Rehabilitation of Offenders Act 1974 (relating to spent convictions (qv)).

previous statements, inconsistent. "When a witness is shown to have made previous statements inconsistent with the evidence given by that witness at the trial the jury should not merely be directed that the evidence given at the trial should be regarded as unreliable; they should also be directed that the previous statements whether sworn or unsworn do not constitute evidence upon which they can act": *R v Golder, Jones and Porritt* [1960] 3 All ER 457. See also the Civil Evidence Act 1968, s. 3(1) (*a*).

price. *See* SALE.

price in contract of sale. May be fixed by the contract or left to be fixed in a manner therein agreed, or may be determined by a course of dealing between the parties: S.G.A. 1979, s. 8(1). Where the price is not determined in accordance with the foregoing provision, the buyer must pay a reasonable price: s. 8(2).

prima facie. Of first appearance; on the face of it. Based on a first impression. A prima facie case is one in which the evidence in favour of a party is sufficient to call for an answer from his opponent.

prima facie evidence. *See* EVIDENCE, PRIMA FACIE.

primary evidence. *See* EVIDENCE, PRIMARY.

primary facts. *See* FACTS, PRIMARY.

Prime Minister. Conventional title of the Head of Her Majesty's Government, appointed by the Crown. He is usually the leader of the party with a majority in the House of Commons (qv) and, by convention, always sits in the Commons. His duties include presiding over the Cabinet (qv), exercising general supervision over government departments and speaking for the government in the Commons.

primer seisin. Profits of lands which had to be paid to the King by the heir of a tenant who died, when the heir reached full age. *See* SEISIN.

primogeniture. System of inheritance whereby preference was given to the eldest son and his issue. Abolished under the A.E.A. 1925, Part IV.

princes, restraints of. *See* RESTRAINTS OF PRINCES.

principal. 1. Sum of money invested. 2. One on whose behalf an agent (qv) works. 3. A principal in the *first degree* is the actual perpetrator of an offence; a principal in the *second degree* is one who, by being present, aids and abets.

principal clerks (in Chancery chambers). Officials who assist masters (qv), eg, in the preparation of orders on an *ex parte* application relating to matters such as garnishee orders nisi. Without reference to a master they may sign certificates of attendance in chambers for the purpose of the taxation of costs (qv).

principal, undisclosed. Where an agent (qv) conceals the fact that he is merely a representative, and has authority at the time of the contract to act on behalf of another, either the agent or principal when discovered can be sued and can sue the other party to the contract. See *Keighley, Maxsted & Co v Durant* [1901] AC 240.

priorities, rule concerning. The equitable rule by the application of which the rank of competing interests, eg, successive mortgages (qv) of an equitable interest in property, will be determined. The fundamental rule is *qui prior est tempore potior est jure* (qv) ie, priority is determined by the order of the creation of interests. The rule is qualified by the doctrine of purchaser without notice; fraud; negligence; estoppel (qv); registration of rights overreaching of interests. See the L.P.A. 1925, s. 137; *Dearle v Hall* (1828) 3 Russ 1; *Re Samuel Allen Ltd* [1907] 1 Ch 575.

priority caution. Caution entered in index of minor interests. Order of entry governs priority. *See* CAUTION.

priority inhibition. Inhibition entered in index of minor interests. Order of entry governs priority. *See* INHIBITION.

priority notice. A person who is entitled to apply for registration as the first proprietor of land may reserve priority for that application by a priority notice. See the L.R.A. 1925, s. 144; and the L.C.A. 1972, s. 11.

priority of debts of insolvent estate.

Governed by the A.E.A. 1925, s. 34(1), in accordance with Sch 1, Part I. Funeral, testamentary and administration expenses have priority. Subject to this, the same rules apply as to the administration of assets of a bankrupt (qv), where the priority is, rates, taxes, wages and salaries owing, accrued holiday remuneration, etc.

prison. Place of detention for those committed to custody under the law. Prison policy is administered by the Prison Department of the Home Office through a prison service headed by a Director-General. Reports on administration are made by boards of visitors (including magistrates) appointed by the Home Secretary.

privacy. The term is not defined by statute, but would seem to refer to an individual's personal seclusion. (An American comment is of interest: "The right to privacy is the right of the individual to decide for himself how much he will share with others his thoughts, feelings and the facts of his personal life"—Report to the United States President's Office of Science and Technology 1967, cited in the *Report on Privacy and Human Rights,* pub. Council of Europe 1973.) An unqualified right of personal privacy seems unknown in English law. See *Williams* v *Settle* [1960] 1 WLR 1072. The European Convention on Human Rights, signed in 1950, states: "Everyone has the right to respect for his private and family life, his home and his correspondence" (Article 8). See Council of Europe Convention (September, 1980) for Protection of Individuals with Regard to Automatic Processing of Personal Data.

private Act of Parliament. An Act concerning private persons, or a local Act passed on behalf of a public company or municipal corporation. It must not impinge on an issue of public policy or be of general application.

private Bill. *See* BILL.

private company. A company which is not a public company (qv): see the Cos.A. 1980, s. 1(1). By s. 15, it may not offer its debentures or shares to the public. The statutory minimum number of directors is one (Cos.A. 1948, s. 176). It cannot convert from a limited to an unlimited company (Cos.A. 1967, s. 43; Cos.A. 1980, Sch 3, para 43). No minimum authorised capital is required on registration (Cos.A. 1980, s. 3).

private defence. Where a person commits a tort (qv) in defence of himself or his property, he is not necessarily liable if the act has been, in the circumstances, of a reasonable nature. See *Cockcroft* v *Smith* (1705) 2 Salk 642; *Barnard* v *Evans* [1925] 1 KB 794.

private international law. That part of English law which deals with cases involving a foreign element and seeks to determine, eg, whether English courts have jurisdiction over a case; if so, what system of law must be applied; circumstances in which English courts will recognise and enforce judgments of foreign courts. Known also as "conflict of laws".

private law. Those areas of the law concerned primarily with duties and rights of individuals with which the state is not immediately and directly concerned, eg, the law of contract. *See* PUBLIC LAW.

private members' Bills. Bills of a public nature introduced, not by the government, but by private members of either House of Parliament.

private nuisance. *See* NUISANCE.

private persons' powers of arrest. *See* ARREST, POWERS OF PRIVATE PERSONS TO.

privilege. A special right or immunity conferred on some person or body, eg, members of Parliament; or a rule of evidence justifying a witness's refusal to produce a document or to answer a question. Some matters are protected from disclosure on the ground of privilege, eg, affairs of state, professional confidences. *See* PARLIAMENTARY PRIVILEGE.

privilege, absolute. Protection attaching to certain statements, which would otherwise be defamatory, so that no action lies even though the statements might have been false and malicious. Example: statements made in the course of judicial proceedings or in Parliament. See, eg,

Royal Aquarium v *Parkinson* [1892] 1 QB 442.

privilege, claim of. Claim entitling a person to refuse, eg, the production of documents for inspection. See O. 24, r. 13(2). It may apply to communications between solicitors and clients; opinions of counsel; incriminating documents; state papers. *See* DISCOVERY AND INSPECTION OF DOCUMENTS.

privileged communication. A communication which, although containing defamatory material, is protected, or one which is generally protected from disclosure in evidence (qv). See, eg, *D.* v *NSPCC* [1978] AC 171.

privileged will. The right of a soldier being in actual military service (qv), or a mariner or seaman being at sea to make a valid will without any formal requirements. The intention to make a will must be shown. See the W.A. 1837, s. 11; the Wills (Soldiers and Sailors) Act, 1918, s. 3(1); the F.L.R.A. 1969, s. 3(1) (*b*); *Re Yates* [1919] P 93; *Re Wingham* [1949] P 187; *Re Jones* [1981] Fam. 7; and *Re Hamilton* [1982] 6 NIJB. See Law Reform Commission Report 1980 (Cmnd 7902). *See* WILL.

privilege, legal professional. Right whereby communications between the client and legal adviser may not generally be given in evidence without the client's consent if made in relation to contemplated or pending litigation, or made to enable the adviser to give, or the client to receive, legal advice. See *R* v *Barton* [1972] 1 All ER 1192; *Alfred Crompton Amusement Machines* v *Customs and Excise Commissioners* [1974] AC 405; *Buttes Gas Co* v *Hammer (No. 3)* [1981] QB 223; *R* v *King* [1983] 1 WLR 411; and *Waugh* v *BR Board* [1980] AC 521.

privilege of witness. 1. Rule that a witness is not bound to answer certain types of question in legal proceedings. Examples: incriminating questions; questions relating to matters, publication of which might injure the state; questions relating to communications between counsel, solicitor and client on professional matters. 2. A witness is privileged (so that no action can be brought for defamation) to the extent of what he says during examination. "What he says before he enters or after he has left the witness box is not privileged": *Seaman* v *Netherclift* (1876) 2 CPD 56.

privilege, parliamentary. *See* PARLIAMENTARY PRIVILEGE.

privilege, public. Phrase used in a statement of principle excluding relevant evidence where disclosure could prejudice the public interest. See *Conway* v *Rimmer* [1968] AC 910; *D* v *NSPCC* [1978] AC 171; and *Buttes Gas Co* v *Hammer (No 3)* [1981] QB 223.

privilege, qualified. Protection afforded to the maker of a statement which may be defamatory, if made honestly, ie, without malice. Includes: fair and accurate reports of parliamentary and judicial proceedings and reports of public meetings; statements made in pursuance of a legal, moral or social duty; statements made to procure redress of a public grievance. See the Defamation Act 1952.

Privileges, Committee of. Committee set up by the House of Lords or Commons to consider matters relating to privileges of members. It ascertains facts and reports whether they constitute a breach of privilege (qv) or contempt. *See* PARLIAMENTARY PRIVILEGE.

privileges, marital. Privileges created by the Evidence (Amendment) Act 1853, s. 3, and the Criminal Evidence Act 1898, s. 1(*d*) whereby, during the marriage, one spouse could not be compelled to disclose communications made to him or her by the other, and by the Mat.C.A. 1965, s. 43(1) and the Mat.C.A. 1973, ss. 48, 54, whereby a spouse is competent but not compellable, to give evidence relating to sexual intercourse. These privileges relate only to criminal proceedings. See the Civil Evidence Act 1968, s. 16; *Rumping* v *DPP* [1964] AC 814.

privity. Relationships arising from participation in or knowledge of some transaction or event. See *The*

Eurysthenes [1976] 3 All ER 243.

privity of contract. Relationship subsisting between parties to a contract. "In the law of England certain principles are fundamental. One is that only a person who is a party to a contract may sue on it": *Dunlop Pneumatic Tyre Co Ltd v Selfridge Co Ltd* [1915] AC 47. See the L.P.A. 1925, s. 56(1); *Re Schebsman* [1944] Ch 83; *Beswick v Beswick* [1968] AC 58; and *Woodar v Wimpey* [1980] 1 All ER 571. *See* CONTRACT.

privity of estate. Relationship existing between persons whose estates constitute one estate in law, eg, lessor and lessee, tenant for life and remainderman.

privity, vertical and horizontal. Phrase used in the Law Commission Working Paper, No. 64, *Liability for Defective Products:* "If the manufactured product is thought of as descending a chain of distribution from the producer to the middleman and on to the retailer who sells to the public, 'vertical privity' is the privity which each of these persons has with his predecessor and successor, and 'horizontal privity' is the ensuing privity of contract between the retailer and the first domestic consumer who buys from him, and then between that consumer and any subconsumer, if such there be."

privy. Relating to participation in some act, or being in privity (qv) with another.

Privy Council. Until the eighteenth century the chief source of executive power in the state. Now plays a much-diminished role, advising the Sovereign on Orders in Council (qv), issue of Royal proclamations, etc. Headed by the Lord President of the Council, it consists of Cabinet ministers, Archbishops, Lord Chief Justice, Master of the Rolls, Speaker of the Commons, etc. The whole Council is called together on the death of the Sovereign. The Judicial Committee of the Privy Council (qv) has appellate jurisdiction.

Privy Council, Judicial, Committee of the. *See* JUDICIAL COMMITTEE OF THE PRIVY COUNCIL.

Privy Seal. Seal formerly used, eg, for letters patent (qv) before they passed under the Great Seal. Following the Great Seal Act 1844, s. 3, no instrument need now be passed under the Privy Seal.

prize competition. *See* COMPETITION FOR PRIZES.

prize courts. Courts specially set up to decide matters relating to the capture of ships in time of war. Appeal is to the Judicial Committee of the Privy Council (qv). See the Naval Prize Acts 1864–1916; and the S.C.A. 1981, s. 16(2).

prize of war. Enemy ship or other enemy property captured at sea.

pro. For.

probate. Document issued under the seal of the court as official evidence of the authority of an executor (qv). If the validity of a will (qv) is contested, probate is granted only after the court has pronounced in favour (grant "in solemn form"). Probate "in common form" is granted where litigation is unnecessary. Documents required in order to obtain probate include: Inland Revenue account; executor's oath; any renunciations by executors; engrossments; affidavit of due execution. See S.I. 1983/1180.

probate action. "An action for the grant of probate of a will, or letters of administration of the estate, of a deceased person, or for the revocation of such a grant, or for a decree pronouncing for or against the validity of an alleged will, not being an action which is non-contentious or common form probate business": O. 76, r. 1(2).

probate, ancillary. Subsidiary grant of probate relating to a grant obtained outside the UK, giving powers of administration to a foreign executor over property in the UK.

Probate, Court of. *See* COURT OF PROBATE.

Probate, Divorce and Admiralty Division. Former division of the High Court (qv), renamed the Family Division by the A.J.A. 1970. Admiralty jurisdiction is assigned to the QBD, to be exercised by the Admiralty Court. Probate (other than non-contentious, common form probate business) is assigned to the Chancery

Division. See now the S.C.A. 1981, s. 5(c).

probate, resealed. Certificate of probate sealed for a second time, eg, in order to give an executor (qv) powers of administration outside the UK.

probate rules. Rules of court made by the President of Family Division, concerned with regulating and prescribing the practice and procedure of the High Court with respect to non-contentious or common form probate business: S.C.A. 1981, s. 127. The current provisions are the Non-Contentious Probate Rules 1954 (S.T. 1954/796).

probation. Process designed to assist in the rehabilitation of offenders aged 17 or over who are willing to be bound by a probation order requiring them to remain under the supervision of probation officers for 6 months–3 years and to be of good behaviour. A probation order may require attendance at a specified day training centre. Failure to comply with the order may result in a sentence for the original offence. See the P.C.C.A. 1973, ss. 2–6. For right of appeal from order see *R* v *Tucker* [1974] 1 WLR 615; *R* v *Marquis* [1974] 1 WLR 1087. See also the C.L.A. 1977, s. 57(1), Sch 9; and the C.J.A. 1982, s. 66.

probationer. A person under supervision by virtue of a probation order.

probation hostel. Premises for the accommodation of persons who may be required to reside there by a probation order. Known also as "probation home". See the P.C.C.A. 1973, s. 57(1).

probation officer. One appointed to supervise probationers and others placed under their supervision "and to advise, assist and befriend them": P.C.C.A. 1973, Sch 3, Part I.

probative facts. *See* FACTS, INVESTITIVE.

procedendo. Prerogative writ issued when the judge of an inferior court (qv) delayed by refusing to give judgment.

procedure. Formal manner of conducting judicial proceedings. *See* RULES AND ORDERS OF THE SUPREME COURT.

proceedings, interlocutory. *See* INTERLOCUTORY PROCEEDINGS.

proceedings, stay of. *See* STAY OF PROCEEDINGS.

process. 1. Summons and warrant compelling the appearance of the defendant (qv). Before the issue of process, a magistrate (qv) must be satisfied that he has appropriate jurisdiction and that there is sufficient evidence against the person named to justify the issue. See the M.C.A. 1980, s. 1; and the S.C.A. 1981, s. 80. For the mode of commencing civil proceedings in the High Court see O. 5. 2. Mode of operation. Signifies "a substantial uniformity or system of treatment": *Vibroplant* v *Holland* [1982] 1 All ER 792.

process, abuse of. *See* ABUSE OF PROCESS.

proclamation, royal. Formal public announcement by the Crown. No law can be made or unmade in this manner unless a proclamation is issued by the authority of an Act of Parliament (qv). See *Case of Proclamations* (1611) 12 Co Rep 74; *Re Grazebrook* (1865) 4 De G J & S 662.

procreation, words of. Words which limit persons mentioned in a grant to the issue of a particular person, eg, "To Z and the heirs of his body".

procurement. It is an offence for a person to procure a woman by threats, intimidation, false pretences or false representations to have unlawful sexual intercourse in any part of the world: S.O.A. 1956, s. 2. Procuring involves bringing about conduct which the woman would not have embarked on of her own volition or spontaneously: *R* v *Broadfoot* [1976] 3 All ER 753. See *A.-G.'s Reference (No. 1 of 1975)* [1975] QB 773.

procuring an offence. Bringing about, instigating, a crime. It involves producing an offence "by some endeavour": *A.-G.'s Ref (No. 1 of 1975)* [1975] QB 773. The common law offence of procuring materials for crime was abolished under the Criminal Attempts Act 1981, s. 6(1). *See* AID OR ABET.

procuring breach of contract. *See* INDUCEMENT.

production of documents. Procedure ordered by court (see O. 24) by which documents and books must be produced for inspection. *See* DISCOVERY AND INSPECTION OF DOCUMENTS.

products liability. Under the *European Convention on Products Liability in regard to Personal Injury and Death* (January 1977), a producer shall be liable to pay compensation for death or personal injuries caused by a defect in his product. (A product has a "defect" when it does not provide the safety which a person is entitled to expect, having regard to all the circumstances including the presentation of the product.) See also the Law Commission Report on *Defective Products* (Cmnd 6831). See *Lambert* v *Lewis* [1980] 1 All ER 978.

profession. "A 'profession' in the present use of language involves the idea of an occupation requiring purely intellectual skill, or if any manual skill, as in painting and sculpture, or surgery, skill controlled by the intellectual skill of the operator": *per* Scrutton LJ in *IRC* v *Maxse* [1919] 1 KB 647. See also *Asher* v *London Film Productions* [1944] KB 133.

professional misconduct. Behaviour considered by the governing body of a profession to be unworthy of a member of that profession. May lead to removal from a professional register. See, eg, the Medical Act 1983, Part V; the Dentists Act 1983, s. 15. *See* STRIKING OFF.

profit and loss account. Yearly account, which must be compiled up to a date not more than nine months before the date of a company's meeting, in accordance with the requirements of the Cos.A. 1948, Sch 8, Part I, as amended by the Cos.A. 1967, Sch I. *See* COMPANY.

profits à prendre. Rights to take something off another's land (eg, rights of common). May be created, eg, by Act of Parliament or grant, and extinguished by statute, unity of seisin, release or alteration of dominant tenement (qqv). Cannot be claimed by custom (qv). See *White* v *Taylor* [1969] 1 Ch 160; and *Lady Dunsany* v *Bedworth* (1979) 38 P & CR 546. *See* COMMON, RIGHT OF.

profits available for distribution. Under the Cos.A. 1980, a company may make a distribution only of profits available for that purpose, ie, from accumulated realised profits less accumulated realised losses: s. 39. A distribution must be justified by the accounts. A public company may make a distribution only if, at the time, its net assets are not less than the aggregate of called-up share capital plus non-distributable reserves, and if the distribution does not reduce those assets to less than that aggregate.

profits, company's. "Profit for the year is regarded as any gains arising during the year which may be distributed while maintaining the amount of the shareholders' interest in the company at the beginning of the year, which is regarded as the company's capital": Inflation Accounting 1975 (Cmnd 6225, para 105).

profits, with. *See* WITH PROFITS.

prohibited degrees of relationships. *See* RELATIONSHIPS, PROHIBITED DEGREES OF.

prohibition. An order of the High Court (qv) preventing or prohibiting a body from acting, which will lie against an inferior tribunal or body in relation to decisions affecting an individual's rights. Issued, eg, to prohibit an imposition of sentence on the accused if there has been no proper trial. See *R* v *Electricity Commissioners* [1924] 1 KB 171; *Re Godden* [1971] 2 QB 662. For applications for an order see O. 53. See also the S.C.A. 1981, s. 29.

prohibition notice. Notice served by an inspector under the H.S.W.A. 1974, s. 22, stating that the inspector is of the opinion that activities involve or will involve a risk of serious personal injury and directing that the activities shall cease unless the matters specified are remedied. *See* IMPROVEMENT NOTICE.

prohibitory injunction. *See* INJUNCTION.

prolixity. Term applied to pleadings (qv) which are superfluous or of unnecessary length. The offending party may be liable for the costs arising.

promise. An undertaking relating to some event. Of no legal effect generally unless in the form of a contract (qv) or covenant (qv). A promise is made by a *promisor* to a *promisee*.

promissory estoppel. *See* ESTOPPEL.

promissory note. "An unconditional promise in writing made by one person to another, signed by the maker, engaging to pay on demand or at a fixed or determinable future time, a sum certain in money to or to the order of a specified person, or to bearer": B.Ex.A. 1882, s. 83. The note is ineffective until delivered to the payee.

promoter. 1. One who begins the procedure for the passing of a local, personal, private Bill (qv). 2. "One who undertakes to form a company with reference to a given project, and to set it going, and who takes the necessary steps to accomplish that purpose": *Twycross* v *Grant* (1877) 36 LT 812. He is neither trustee (qv) nor agent (qv) for the company, but stands in a fiduciary relationship to it. Whether a person is or is not a promoter is a question of fact in every case: *Jubilee Cotton Mills* v *Lewis* [1924] AC 958. See the Cos.A. 1948, ss. 38, 43(5), 188; the Cos.A. 1980, s. 24; and the Cos.A. 1981, s. 93 (disqualification of promoters).

proof. Method by which the existence or non-existence of a fact is established to the satisfaction of the court. Means of proof include: evidence; presumptions; judicial notice (qqv). "Evidence becomes proof when the jury accept it as being sufficient for proof": Williams.

proof beyond reasonable doubt. "Proof beyond reasonable doubt does not mean proof beyond the shadow of a doubt . . . If the evidence is so strong against a man as to leave only a remote possibility in his favour, which can be dismissed with the sentence 'of course it is possible but not in the least probable' the case is proved beyond reasonable doubt, but nothing short of that will suffice": *Miller* v *Minister of Pensions* [1947] 2 All ER 372.

proof, burden of. *See* BURDEN OF PROOF.

proof, standards of. *See* STANDARDS OF PROOF.

proper law of a contract. Phrase used in private international law (qv) to denote the system of law which governs a contract. Defined by Dicey as "the law, or laws, by which the parties intended, or may be fairly presumed to have intended, the contract to be governed". "It is the law which the parties intended to apply. Their intention will be ascertained by the intention expressed in the contract, if any, which will be conclusive": *R* v *International Trustee* [1937] 2 All ER 164. See *Vita Food Products* v *Unus* [1939] 1 All ER 513; *Amin Rashid Shipping* v *Kuwait Insurance* [1983] 3 WLR 241. See CONTRACT.

property. 1. That which can be owned. 2. Right to goods and land, etc. 3. An aggregate of rights having money value. 4. "Includes money and all other property, real or personal, including things in action and other intangible property": Th.A. 1968, s. 4(1). Classified as *real property* (realty); *personal property* (personalty) (qqv).

property adjustment order. Order made under the Mat.C.A. 1973, s. 21, relating to the transfer or settlement, of property or variation of settlement, on or after the grant of a decree of divorce (qv), nullity or judicial separation (qv).

property in goods. May be: (1) *General*, ie, title or ownership. ("Property means the general property in goods, and not merely a special property": S.G.A. 1979, s. 62(1).); (2) *Special*, eg, that which arises under a bailment (qv).

property register. *See* REGISTER AT LAND REGISTRY.

proponent. 1. The party who must raise an issue in the first instance (eg, the prosecutor, the plaintiff). 2. The party who bears the evidential burden of proof (qv) and, usually also, the legal burden.

propositus. 1. The person immediately concerned. 2. The person from whom descent is traced. 3. A testator (qv).

proprietary estoppel. *See* ESTOPPEL.

proprietary rights. Relating to private rights of ownership.

proprietor. One who has title to property.

proprietorship register. *See* REGISTER AT LAND REGISTRY.

propter defectum sanguinis. *See* ESCHEAT.

propter delictum tenentis. *See* ESCHEAT.

pro rata. Proportionately.

pro rata freight. *See* FREIGHT.

prorogation. The ending of a session of Parliament (qv) by exercise of the royal prerogative.

proscribed organisation. An organisation, association or combination of persons condemned or forbidden because its activities are harmful. See, eg, the Prevention of Terrorism (Temporary Provisions) Act 1974, s. 1.

prosecution. The instituting of criminal proceedings in the courts.

prosecutor. One who institutes criminal proceedings, usually in the name of the Crown.

prosecutor, Crown. *See* CROWN PROSECUTOR.

prosecutor, non-appearance of. If the accused appears for the trial of an information (qv) and the prosecutor fails to appear, the court may dismiss the information or, if evidence has been received on a previous occasion, proceed in the absence of the prosecutor: M.C.A. 1980, s. 15. If both parties fail to appear, the court may dismiss the information or proceed in their absence: s. 16. *See* ACCUSED, NON-APPEARANCE OF.

prospectus. Notice, circular, advertisement or other invitation offering to the public for subscription or purchase any shares or debentures of a company: Cos.A. 1948, s. 455. It must state, eg, the names and addresses of directors, the time of opening of subscription lists, the amount payable on application and allotment of shares. A dated copy should be filed with the Registrar before issue. See the Cos.A. 1948, s. 37; and the Cos.A. 1980, ss. 15, 16. *See* COMPANY.

prostitution. "Prostitution is proved if it be shown that a woman offers her body for purposes amounting to common lewdness for payment in return": *R* v *Webb* [1964] 1 QB 357. It is not limited to cases involving sexual intercourse. It is not, in itself, an offence, but it is an offence to cause others to become prostitutes or

to live on the earnings of prostitution: S.O.A. 1956. See *R* v *Clarke* [1976] 2 All ER 696; *R* v *Bell* [1978] Crim LR 233; Criminal Law Revision Committee Working Paper on Offences Relating to Prostitution (1982).

pro tanto. For so much; to a certain extent.

protected child. "Where a person gives notice in pursuance of s. 22(1) [of the Adoption Act 1976] . . . to apply for an adoption order in respect of a child, the child is . . . a protected child while he has his home with that person": 1976 Act, s. 32(1). See also the Adoption Act 1958, s. 37. Such a child must be visited from time to time by the local authority: 1976 Act, s. 33.

protected coin. A coin customarily used as money in any country or specified in an order made by the Treasury under the Forgery and Counterfeiting Act 1981. See s. 27(1)(*b*). *See* COUNTERFEITING.

protected furnished tenancy. A protected tenancy (qv) under which the dwelling-house concerned is *bona fide* let at a rent which includes payments in respect of furniture, and in respect of which the amount of rent which is fairly attributable to the use of furniture, having regard to the value of that use to the tenant, forms a substantial part of the whole rent: Rent Act 1977, s. 152(1).

protected goods. Goods which, under the C.C.A. 1974, s. 90, are the subject of a regulated hire purchase or credit sale agreement (qqv) and in relation to which the debtor has not terminated the agreement and has paid one-third or more of the total price in the goods. They cannot be recovered except by court order, or voluntary surrender by the debtor.

protected occupier. Phrase used in the Rent (Agriculture) Act 1976 referring to one whose occupation of a dwelling is protected by statute. A "protected occupier by succession", as referred to in the 1976 Act, s. 3, is the widow or other family member of a deceased protected occupier.

protected person. Head of State, member of body performing functions of Head of State, Head of Government or Minister of Foreign Affairs who is outside the territory of the state in which he holds office; persons who represent a state or international organisation of an intergovernmental character; person who is a member of the family of those mentioned above: Internationally Protected Persons Act 1978, s. 1(5). For offences relating to attacks and threats of attacks on them, see s. 1(1)–(4).

protected person, British. *See* BRITISH PROTECTED PERSON.

protected shorthold tenancy. Protected tenancy (qv) granted after the coming into force of the H.A. 1980, s. 52, for a term certain of 1–5 years; and which cannot be terminated by the landlord before the expiry of the term (except in pursuance of provisions for re-entry, forfeiture for non-payment of rent, or breach of other obligation), where the landlord has given the tenant (before the grant) valid notice that the tenancy is a protected shorthold one, and the rent is registered at the time of the grant, or an application for registration has been made, or a certificate of fair rent has been issued. See S.I. 1981/1578. *See* PROTECTED TENANCY.

protected states. Member states of the Commonwealth (qv) over whose external affairs the UK exerts full control, but who have a considerable measure of control over internal affairs.

protected tenancy. A contractual tenancy protected by the Rent Act 1977. Defined under the H.A. 1980, Sch 5(2) as "a protected tenancy within the meaning of the Rent Act 1977, other than one under which the landlord might recover possession of the dwelling-house under one of the Cases in Part II of Schedule 15 to that Act (cases where the court would order possession)". See *R v Rent Officer for Camden ex p Ebiri* [1981] 1 All ER 950.

protection and indemnity association. An association which undertakes to meet the cost of liabilities incidental to ship owning and not usually covered by insurance, in-

curred by members who contribute to its funds.

Protection, Court of. *See* COURT OF PROTECTION.

protection of trustees. *See* TRUSTEES, PROTECTION OF.

protection order. 1. Court order, under the C.C.A. 1974, s. 131, made on the application of creditor or owner under a regulated agreement (qv) to protect property from damage or depreciation pending the determination of proceedings under the Act. 2. Orders made under the D.P.A. 1978, ss. 16–18, and injunctions under the Domestic Violence and Matrimonial Proceedings Act 1976, s. 1.

protective award. Award by an industrial tribunal (qv) for remuneration to a dismissed employee where an employer has failed to take appropriate steps relating to consultation with union representatives in the event of redundancy: see the E.P.A. 1975, ss. 99–103.

protective trust. A trust for life, or any lesser period, determinable on the occurrence of certain events, eg, the beneficiary's bankruptcy, upon which the trust income will be applied at the absolute discretion of trustees for the support of the beneficiary and his family. Example: "Life interest to X until he shall become bankrupt." Can be created expressly or by implication. See the Tr.A. 1925, s. 33; and the F.L.R.A. 1969, s. 15(3). *See* TRUST.

protectorates, British. *See* BRITISH PROTECTORATES.

Protectorate, the. Era during which Cromwell was Lord Protector of the Commonwealth of England, Scotland and Ireland (1653–58). *See* COMMONWEALTH.

protector of settlement. One who could prevent a tenant in tail (qv) entitled only in remainder from disentailing. Today a tenant in tail in remainder can bar the entail (qv) by executing disentailing assurance with the protector's consent. Disentailment without the protector's consent will create a base fee (qv). See *Re Darnley's Will Trust* [1970] 1 WLR 405. *See* SETTLEMENT.

protest. 1. Document under seal made by a notary (qv) attesting the dishonour of a bill of exchange (qv). Accepted as proof that bill has been dishonoured. 2. Payment under protest is made where the payer will not agree that money is due from him.

protest, right to. "Everyone has the right publicly to protest against anything which displeases him and publicly to proclaim his views, whatever they might be. It does not matter whether there is any reasonable basis for his protest or whether his views are sensible or silly": *per* Salmon LJ in *Morris* v *Crown Office* [1970] 1 All ER 1079.

protocol. 1. An original draft or preliminary memorandum. 2. Minutes of a meeting setting out matters of agreement. 3. Code of procedure.

provable debts in bankruptcy. In general, all debts and liabilities present and future to which the debtor was subject at the date of the receiving order (qv) or to which he might become subject before his discharge, save those which under the B.A. 1914 are non-provable (qv). *See* BANKRUPTCY.

provident benefits. Includes any payment, expressly authorised by union rules, and made to a member during sickness, incapacity from personal injury or while unemployed, or by way of superannuation: Employment Act 1982, s. 17(3).

Provincial Courts. Ecclesiastical courts of the Archbishops of Canterbury and York, eg, the Court of Arches.

proving a debt. Establishing a debt due from the estate of a bankrupt (qv).

proving a will. Obtaining probate (qv) of a will.

provisional bid. *See* BID.

provisional liquidator. *See* LIQUIDATOR.

provisional orders. Orders which normally do not take effect until confirmed by Parliament (qv), issued by government departments relating, eg, to schemes of local authorities.

provision, financial. *See* FINANCIAL PROVISION, REASONABLE.

proviso. 1. In a deed (qv), a condition upon which its general validity is based. May begin: ". . . provided always that . . .". 2. In a statute, a clause qualifying or exempting from the enactment something which, but for the proviso, would have been included. It is construed with the preceding part of the clause to which it is attached. It never enlarges an enactment unless that is unavoidable: *Ex p Partington* (1844) 6 QB 649. See *West Derby Union* v *Metropolitan Life Assurance Society* [1897] AC 647; *Thomas* v *Dibdin* [1912] AC 533.

proviso, applying the. Where the Court of Appeal or House of Lords is satisfied that the point raised in an appeal should be decided in favour of the appellant, they may, nevertheless, dismiss that appeal if they consider that no miscarriage of justice has actually occurred: Criminal Appeal Act 1968, proviso to s. 2(1). Exercise of this power is known as "applying the proviso". Example: *DPP* v *Morgan* [1975] 2 All ER 347.

provocation. May be pleaded only on a charge of murder so as to reduce the charge to manslaughter (qv). "Provocation is some act or series of acts done by the dead man to the accused, which would cause in any reasonable person and actually causes in the accused, a sudden and temporary loss of self-control, rendering accused so subject to passion as to make him for the moment not master of his mind": *R* v *Duffy* [1949] 1 All ER 932. "The question whether the provocation was enough to make a reasonable man do as [accused] did shall be left to be determined by the jury; and in determining that question the jury shall take into account everything both done and said according to the effect which, in their opinion, it would have on a reasonable man": Homicide Act 1957, s. 3. A jury should be told that a reasonable man must have the power of self-control to be expected of an ordinary person of the age and sex of the accused, but in other respects must share such of the characteristics of the accused as they think would affect the gravity of the provocation to him: *DPP* v *Camplin* [1978] AC 705. See *Mancini* v *DPP* [1942] AC 1; *Bedder* v *DPP* [1954] 2 All ER 801 (no longer good authority); *Edwards* v *R* [1973] AC 648; *R* v *Whitfield* (1976) 62 Cr App R 39; *R* v *Newell* (1980) 71 Cr App R 331; and *R* v *Ibrams* (1982) 74 Cr App R 151. *See* MURDER.

proximate cause. *See* CAUSA PROXIMA.

proxy. 1. One appointed with authority or power to act for another in, eg, attendance at meetings. See the Cos.A. 1948, s. 136(1). 2. Document containing such an appointment.

psychopathic disorder. "A persistent disorder or disability of mind (whether or not including significant impairment of intelligence) which results in abnormally aggressive or seriously irresponsible conduct on the part of the person concerned": M.H.A. 1983, s. 1(2), replacing M.H. (Amendment) A. 1982, s. 2(1).

Public Accounts Committee. Set up first in 1861 to examine "the accounts showing the appropriation of the sums granted by Parliament to meet public expenditure", and consisting of members of Parliament. The chairman is usually a member of the Opposition.

public Act of Parliament. An Act (qv) which affects the public at large. Every Act passed after 1850 is a public Act unless it is expressly provided therein to the contrary: I.A. 1978, s. 3.

publication. 1. Term applied in relation to defamation (qv) to refer to the communication of words complained of to at least one other person than the person defamed. See *Huth* v *Huth* [1915] 3 KB 32; *Bata* v *Bata* [1948] WN 366. 2. Term applied in relation to the Obscene Publications Act 1959, whereby a person "publishes" an article who distributes, circulates, sells, lets on hire, gives, or lends it, or who offers it for sale or for letting on hire, or in the case of an article containing or embodying matter to be looked at, or a record, shows, plays or projects it. See the 1959 Act, s. 1(3); *A.-G.'s Reference (No. 2 of 1975)* [1975] 2 All ER 753. 3. In relation to the Copyright Act 1956, means making public that which has not previously been made public: *Infabrics* v *Jaytex* [1982] AC 1.

public benefit. A valid charitable trust must promote some public benefit, ie, "the benefit of the community or of an appreciably important class of the community": *Verge* v *Somerville* [1924] AC 496. A trust for the relief of poverty may be charitable, although not for the benefit of the public or even a "section" of it: *Re Coulthurst* [1951] 1 All ER 774. See *IRC* v *Educational Grants Association Ltd* [1967] Ch 123; *Neville Estates Ltd* v *Madden* [1962] Ch 832. *See* TRUST.

public Bill. *See* BILL.

public body. "A body . . . which has public or statutory duties to perform and which performs those duties and carries out its transactions for the benefit of the public and not for private profit": Halsbury, adopted in *DPP* v *Manners* [1978] AC 43. See also the Public Bodies Corrupt Practices Act 1889, s. 7, as amended; and *R* v *Newbould* [1962] 2 QB 102.

public company. Company (qv) either limited by shares or by guarantee with a share capital, provided that its memorandum states that it is to be a public company and the statutory provisions concerning registration are complied with: Cos.A. 1980, s. 1(1). It should have at least two directors: Cos.A. 1948, s. 176. Its shares are, in general, freely transferable.

public company, old. A company limited by shares or guarantee and having share capital, which did not exist on the day on which the Cos.A. 1980 came into operation, was not on that day a private company (according to the Cos.A. 1948, s. 28) and has not been re-registered as a public company or become a private company: Cos.A. 1980, s. 8. *See* COMPANY, RE-REGISTRATION OF.

public corporation. A business organisation created by an Act, responsible for the day-to-day operation of public enterprises, eg, the National Coal Board. Members are appointed by the relevant minister. Annual accounts must be placed before Parliament. Known also as "statutory corporation".

public decency. "I think that [the authorities] establish that it is an indictable offence to say or do or exhibit anything in public which outrages public decency, whether or not it also tends to corrupt and deprave those who see or hear it": *per* Lord Reid in *Shaw* v *DPP* [1961] 2 All ER 446. See also *Knuller Ltd* v *DPP* [1972] 2 All ER 898.

public document. "A document that is made for the purposes of the public making use of it, and being able to refer to it": *Sturla* v *Freccia* (1880) 5 App Cas 623. It is generally authenticated by a public officer. Examples: court records; public registers. Statements in a public document made by an officer in pursuance of a public duty are admissible evidence of the facts stated therein: Civil Evidence Act 1968, s. 9; Civil Evidence Act 1972. Bankers' books (qv) are not within the definition.

public duties, time off for. An employer is under a duty, under the E.P.(C.)A. 1978, s. 29, to give time off to certain employees, eg, those who are magistrates, members of local authorities.

public examination. The examination on oath of a debtor, after a receiving order (qv) in bankruptcy has been made, regarding his conduct, dealings, property, etc. The debtor must attend and the official receiver (qv) must take part in the examination. See the B.A. 1914, s. 15. An order dispensing with public examination may be made under the Insolvency Act 1976, s. 6(1), after the court has taken into account the number and nature of debts, public importance of the bankruptcy, etc. See *Re A Debtor (No. 37 of 1976)* [1980] 1 All ER 129. *See* BANKRUPTCY.

public good, defence of. Defence under the Obscene Publications Act 1964, s. 4(1), whereby a person will not be convicted of an offence of possessing obscene articles for publication for gain if it is proved that publication was justified as being for the public good on the ground that it is in the interests of science, literature, art or learning, or of other objects of general concern. See *DPP* v *Jordan* [1976] 3 All ER 775. "Learning" means "a product of scholarship":

A.-G.'s Ref (No. 3 of 1977) [1978] 1 WLR 1123.

public house. Premises licensed for the sale of intoxicating liquor for consumption on those premises where the sale of such liquor is, or is apart from any other trade or business ancillary or incidental to it, the only trade or business carried on there: L.G.A. 1966, s. 17(2).

public index map. Index of separate parcels of registered land, kept at the Land Registry and open to inspection by any person: Land Registration Rules 1925, rr. 8, 12.

public law. Those areas of the law concerned primarily with the state itself, eg, constitutional law. *See* PRIVATE LAW.

public lending right. Right conferred on authors by the Public Lending Right Act 1979, s. 1(1), to receive out of a central fund payment in respect of books lent out to the public by libraries in the UK. See S.I. 1982/719.

public limited company. *See* PUBLIC COMPANY.

public meeting. Any meeting in a public place and any meeting which the public or any section thereof are permitted to attend, whether on payment or otherwise: Public Order Act 1936, s. 9, as amended by the C.J.A. 1972.

public mischief. Formerly an offence tending to the prejudice of the community: *R* v *Manley* [1933] 1 KB 529 (false statements causing the police to waste their time). In *DPP* v *Withers* [1974] 3 All ER 984, the House of Lords held that the law does not recognise a crime in an individual accused of conduct tending to cause a public mischief.

public morals, courts and. "In the sphere of criminal law I entertain no doubt that there remains in the courts of law a residual power to enforce the supreme and fundamental purpose of the law, to conserve not only the safety and order but also the moral welfare of the state . . .": *per* Lord Simonds in *Shaw* v *DPP* [1961] 2 All ER 446.

public nuisance. *See* NUISANCE.

public officer. "An officer who discharges any duty in the discharge of which the public are interested, more clearly so if he is paid out of a fund provided by the public'': *R* v *Whitaker* [1914] 2 KB 1283.

public or general rights, declaration concerning. *See* DECLARATION CONCERNING PUBLIC OR GENERAL RIGHTS.

public place. Includes any highway and any other premises or place to which at the material time the public have or are permitted to have access, whether on payment or otherwise: C.J.A. 1972, s. 33, amending the Public Order Act 1936, s. 9. See *Cawley* v *Frost* [1976] 1 WLR 1207: *R* v *Edwards* [1978] Crim LR 564; and *Lawrenson* v *Oxford* [1982] Crim LR 185.

public policy. ''That principle of law which holds that no subject can lawfully do that which has a tendency to be injurious to the public, or against the public good'': *Egerton* v *Brownlow* (1853) 4 HL Cas 1. ''A very unruly horse, and when once you get astride it, you never know where it will carry you'': *per* Burrough J in *Richardson* v *Mellish* (1824) 2 Bing 229.

public privilege. *See* PRIVILEGE, PUBLIC.

public prosecutor. Director of Public Prosecutions (qv).

public service, contracts tending to injure. Contracts, eg, for the sale of public offices, for procurement of a title of honour for reward. See *Parkinson* v *College of Ambulance Ltd* [1925] 2 KB 1 (which led to the passing of the Honours (Prevention of Abuses) Act 1925).

public trust. A trust which has as its object the promotion of the public welfare, as opposed to a private trust, which is for the benefit of an individual or class. *See* TRUST.

Public Trustee. Appointed under the Public Trustee Act 1906 on the application of a beneficiary or trustee (qqv). He may be appointed as an ordinary trustee, or custodian trustee (qv), or personal representative (qv). He may decline to accept a trust, but not on the sole ground of its being of small value. Powers, duties and liabilities are those of an ordinary trustee. See S.I. 1983/1050.

publish. *See* PUBLICATION.

puffs. Exaggerated or vague statements or advertisements relating to merchandise or services. See, generally, the Trade Descriptions Act 1968; *Dimmock* v *Hallett* (1866) LR 2 Ch App 21; *Hawkins* v *Smith* [1978] Crim LR 578.

puisne. Junior, inferior. 1. A *puisne mortgage* is a local mortgage (qv) not protected by the deposit of documents relating to the legal estate affected, and is a Class C charge under the L.C.A. 1972. See the L.P.A. 1969, s. 30(1). 2. High Court judges are styled *puisne judges* or ''Justices of the High Court'': S.C.A. 1981, s. 4(2).

punctuation. The division of words in a document by stops, commas, etc. ''It is from the words and from the context, not from the punctuation, that the sense must be collected'': *Sandford* v *Raikes* (1816) 1 Mer 646. See *Re Narajansingh* [1962] 1 QB 211; *DPP* v *Schildkamp* [1971] AC 1; *Newman* v *Bennett* [1980] 3 All ER 449.

punishment. Penalty inflicted by a court on a convicted offender. The primary sanction of the criminal law.

pur autre vie. *See* AUTRE VIE.

pur cause de vicinage. Because of vicinity. A right of pasturage arising where there is a custom allowing animals to stray and feed freely on the common of a neighbour.

purchaser. 1. One who acquires goods or land in exchange for money. 2. Under the L.P.A. 1925, s. 205(1), a purchaser in good faith for valuable consideration, including a lessee and mortgagee. 3. Under the L.C.A. 1972, s. 17(1) ''any person (including a mortgagee or lessee) who, for valuable consideration, takes any interest in land or in a charge on land''. 4. One to whom land is expressly transferred other than by descent, ie, by the act of the parties by conveyance on sale, will, gift, etc.

purchaser for value without notice. One who purchases property *bona fide* for valuable consideration without notice of any prior right or title. ''Valuable consideration'' means any consideration (qv) in money, money's worth or marriage. He is generally entitled to priority at law and in equity. See *Pilcher* v *Rawlins* (1872) 7 Ch App 259.

purchase, words of. Words pointing out, by name or description, the transferee, ie, the person, who is to acquire an interest in land, eg, "to X and his heirs". (X is the "purchaser".) In effect, they are the words identifying the transferee or grantee.

pure theory of law. *See* LAW, PURE THEORY OF.

purpose trust. *See* TRUST, PURPOSE.

pushing shares. High-pressure selling of shares by exaggerated or false representation.

putative father. The person alleged to be the father of an illegitimate child. See the Affiliation Proceedings Act 1957, s. 4; the D.P.A. 1978, s. 50; and the Child Care Act 1980, s. 2(6).

pyramid selling. Scheme whereby a distributor collects franchise payments from others who are subsequently introduced, qualifying for special benefits and terms according to the number of sub-agents introduced. Under the Fair Trading Act 1973, these schemes are controlled by, eg, a ban on payments for training, the right of participants to require the promoter to buy back goods, a cooling-off period for those who join schemes, and written contracts for participants.

Q

Q.B. Queen's Bench.

Q.B.D. Queen's Bench Division (qv).

Q.C. Queen's Counsel (qv).

qua. In the character of.

quaere. See SED QUAERE.

qualification shares. The number of shares or amount of stock which, under a company's articles (qv) must be held by a person acting as director.

qualified acceptance. Refers, eg, to the conditional or partial acceptance of a bill of exchange (qv). See the B.Ex.A. 1882, s. 19.

qualified privilege. See PRIVILEGE, QUALIFIED.

qualified property. Limited rights of property, eg, chattel in possession of bailee.

qualified title. Title with which the applicant is registered under the L.R.A. 1925, where the registrar is unable to grant absolute, good leasehold, or possessory title.

qualifying capital interest. See CAPITAL INTEREST, QUALIFYING.

quality. In relation to goods, includes their state or condition: S.G.A. 1979, s. 61(1).

quamdiu se bene gesserit. For as long as he shall behave himself. Phrase used to indicate that an office (eg, that of a judge) will be held during good behaviour and will not be lost, therefore, save for bad behaviour. See the S.C.A. 1981, s. 11(3).

quantum. How much. A quantity, amount.

quantum meruit. As much as he has earned. On breach of contract (qv) the party injured may be entitled to claim for work done and services performed. See *Planche* v *Colburn* (1831) 8 Bing 14; *Craven-Ellis* v *Canons Ltd* [1936] 2 KB 403.

quantum valebat. As much as it was worth. Phrase referring to an action for goods supplied, where no price had been agreed on.

quarantine. Period of time (originally 40 days) in which ships and persons coming from a country in which serious infectious disease has spread are isolated. Some animals imported from abroad may be kept in quarantine for nine months.

quare clausum fregit. See CLAUSUM FREGIT, QUARE.

quare ejecit infra terminum. Wherefore he ejected [him] within the term. Writ whereby a lessee (qv) could claim protection against the lessor (qv), his heirs and the assignees of the lessor in a case of ejectment (qv). Abolished under the Real Property Limitation Act 1833.

quare impedit. Wherefore he hinders. Writ, abolished in 1880, used by one whose right of advowson (qv) had been disputed.

quarrel. Used formerly to mean "action" (qv).

quarter-days. These are Lady Day (March 25th), Midsummer Day (June 24th), Michaelmas Day (September 29th) and Christmas Day (December 25th). Certain quarterly rents are due on these days.

quartering. Penalty for high treason, involving the severance of the head of a traitor after death by hanging, and the division of body into quarters. Abolished in 1870. See HANGING, DRAWING AND QUARTERING.

quarter sessions. County quarter sessions and borough quarter sessions, consisting of county JPs, presided over by a legally qualified chairman and, in case of borough quarter sessions, a recorder (qv) sitting alone. They had civil, criminal, original and appellate jurisdiction. Abolished under the Courts Act 1971, s. 3.

quash. To annul; to make void.

quasi. As if; apparent; having some resemblance to, but lacking some requisites.

quasi-arbitrator. "Where a matter is left by two parties to the judgment of a third who is to determine their rights, and the task is not merely one of arithmetic, but involving technical skill and knowledge, that person is in the position of a quasi-arbitrator": *Stevenson* v *Watson* (1879) 4 CPD 148.

See *Sutcliffe* v *Thackrah* [1974] 1 All ER 859; *Arenson* v *Casson, Beckman Rutley & Co* [1975] 3 All ER 901.

quasi-contracts. Cases in which the law imposes on a person an obligation to make repayment, eg, when he has been enriched at the expense of another. Examples: where X has paid money to the use of Y; where X has paid money under a mistake of fact. See *Holt* v *Markham* [1923] 1 KB 504; *Shamia* v *Joory* [1958] 1 QB 448. *See* UNJUST ENRICHMENT.

quasi-easements. Where one person owns two or more adjoining and separate properties, rights which he may have been exercising over one or other of them are known as quasi-easements, since an owner cannot have an easement over his own land. See *Bolton* v *Bolton* (1879) 11 Ch D 968; *Ward* v *Kirkland* [1967] Ch 194. *See* EASEMENT.

quasi-entail. An estate *pur autre vie* (qv), for the life of A granted "to B and the heirs of his body". See *Ex p Sterne* (1801) 6 Ves 156. *See* FEE TAIL.

quasi ex contractu. As if arising out of a contract.

quasi-judicial. Having a character which is partly-judicial, eg, proceedings conducted by an arbitrator (qv).

quasi-loan. The term used in the Cos.A. 1980 to describe a transaction under which one party (the "creditor") agrees to pay, or pays otherwise than in pursuance of an agreement, a sum for another (the "borrower"), or agrees to reimburse, or reimburse otherwise than in pursuance of an agreement, expenditure incurred by another party for another (the "borrower") on terms that the borrower (or a person on his behalf) will reimburse the creditor, or in circumstances giving rise to a liability on the borrower to reimburse the creditor: s. 65(2). In general, a non-private company may not make a quasi-loan to any of its directors: s. 49. (For exceptions, see s. 50.)

Queen's Bench, Court of. *See* COURT OF KING'S (QUEEN'S) BENCH.

Queen's Bench Division. Division of the High Court, possessing civil, criminal, original, appellate and supervisory jurisdiction. It is pre-sided over by the Lord Chief Justice (qv) with a staff of puisne judges (qv). See the S.C.A. 1981, s. 5, Sch 1. *See* DIVISIONAL COURTS.

Queen's Counsel (or King's). A senior barrister appointed on the recommendation of the Lord Chancellor. He wears a silk gown (hence the phrase "to take silk") and takes precedence over the other barristers in court. He may appear in any case for or against the Crown.

Queen's evidence. Evidence for the Crown given by one co-accused who "turns Queen's evidence", ie, confesses guilt and acts as a competent witness against his associates. "It is the duty of the judge to warn the jury that, although they may convict upon his evidence, it is dangerous to do so unless it is corroborated": *Davis* v *DPP* [1965] AC 378.

Queen's Proctor. The solicitor (usually the Treasury Solicitor (qv)) representing the Crown who may intervene in the case of a petition for divorce. The court may direct papers to be sent to the Proctor who may instruct counsel to argue any question in relation to that case. Any person may, before the decree nisi (qv) is made absolute, give information to the Proctor or any matter relevant to the case, and the Proctor may then take such steps as are considered necessary. See the Mat.C.A. 1973, s. 8(15); and the Matrimonial Causes Rules 1977, rr. 61–62. *See* DECREE ABSOLUTE.

Queen's Remembrancer. One who performed duties relating to debts due to the Crown. Now involved in, eg, the selection of sheriffs. The office is held by a senior master of the Supreme Court. See the Queen's Remembrancer Act 1859; and the S.C.A. 1981, s. 89(4).

Queen's Speech. Speech, read by the Queen, at the opening of Parliament (qv), prepared by her ministers, setting out their proposals for legislation to be introduced during the session.

Queen, The. "Elizabeth the Second, by the Grace of God of the United Kingdom of Great Britain and Northern Ireland and of Her other Realms and Territories Queen, Head of the Commonwealth, Defender of the Faith'': Royal Titles Act 1953. Nominally, the supreme executive power; supreme head of the church; head of defence forces. A *queen regent* or *regnant* holds the Crown in her own right; a *queen consort* is the king's wife; a *queen dowager* is the widow of a deceased king. *See* CROWN; MONARCHY; SOVEREIGN.

que estate, prescription in. Prescription (qv) in which the claimant pleaded user by himself and ''those whose estate he had''—*ceux que estate il ad*. In effect, a right claimed by a prescription annexed to particular lands. *See Chesterfield v Harris* [1908] 2 Ch 397.

questioning, detaining by police for. Under the *Judges' Rules* 1964 (qv) the police may question anyone ''whether or not he has been taken into custody so long as he has not been charged with the offence or informed that he may be prosecuted for it''. ''If a person is put under restraint arbitrarily or for some expedient motive, he is, of course imprisoned. In a wide and inexact sense he may be said to be under arrest if the restraint is exercised by a police officer; but it may be neither a purported nor an actual arrest and the officer concerned may have to answer for his conduct in a court of law'': *R v Brown* [1977] RTR 160. See also *R v Inwood* [1973] 2 All ER 645. *See* SUSPECTS, QUESTIONING OF.

questioning of suspects. *See* SUSPECTS, QUESTIONING OF.

Question Time. An hour of Parliamentary time (usually on Mondays–Thursdays) in which ministers answer questions relating to their responsibilities.

quia emptores. Whereas purchasers [of lands and tenements] . . . Title of statute enacted in 1290, taking its name from the beginning of the preamble. It allowed freemen to alienate land (except by will) and without consent of the lord. Alienees held not of the alienor, but of the lord from whom the alienor had held previously. In effect, it abolished subinfeudation (qv).

qui approbat non reprobat. He who accepts cannot reject. *See* ELECTION.

quia timet. Because he fears. Action for injunction relating to a virtually irreparable wrong merely feared or threatened, but not yet committed. The plaintiff must show a very strong probability of grave damage accruing to him. The cost to the defendant must also be considered. ''What is aimed at is justice between the parties, having regard to all the circumstances'': *Hooper v Rogers* [1975] Ch 43. See *A.-G. v Corporation of Manchester* [1893] 2 Ch 87; *Redland Bricks Ltd v Morris* [1970] AC 652. *See* INJUNCTION.

quicquid plantatur solo, solo credit. Whatever is affixed to the soil, belongs to the soil. See *Simmons v Midford* [1969] 2 Ch 415; and *Royco v Eatonwill Construction* [1979] Ch 276.

quid pro quo. Something for something. Applied, eg, to the concept of consideration (qv) in contract.

quiet enjoyment. Implied obligations of a lessor that a lessee's peaceful enjoyment of the premises shall not be interfered with by the lessor or by any person who claims under him. ''Quiet'' is not restricted to an absence of noise. See *Markham v Paget* [1908] 1 Ch 697; *Kenny v Preen* [1963] 1 QB 499; and *Sampson v Hodson-Pressinger* [1981] 3 All ER 710. *See* LEASE.

quiet possession. In a contract of sale there is an implied warranty (qv) that the buyer will enjoy quiet possession of the goods except so far as it may be disturbed by the owner or other person entitled to the benefit of any charge or encumbrance so disclosed or known: S.G.A. 1979, s. 12(2)(*b*). See *Mason v Burningham* [1949] 2 KB 545; *Microbeads AG v Vinhurst Road Markings Ltd* [1975] 1 WLR 218.

qui facit per alium facit per se. He who does a thing through another does it himself.

qui prior est tempore potior est jure. He who is first in time is better in law. See the L.P.A. 1925, s. 137; *Dearle v Hall* (1823) 3 Russ 1. *See* PRIORITIES, RULE CONCERNING.

qui sentit commodum sentire debet et onus; et e contra. He who enjoys the benefit should bear the burden; and vice versa.

quit, notice to. *See* NOTICE TO QUIT.

quit rent. Fixed rent paid by a copy-holder to his lord in discharge of his obligation to perform agricultural services. See the L.P.A. 1925, ss. 121, 191. *See* COPYHOLD.

quittance. 1. Act of discharge from obligation or debt. 2. Document showing discharge.

quod hoc. As to this.

quod permittat. Title of writs to abate the nuisance (qv) to a neighbour's land caused by those who had built, eg, walls, houses. Abolished by the Real Property Limitation Act 1833.

quo jure. By what right. Writ (qv) re-lating to the title of common pasture (qv).

quo minus. By which the less. Title of a writ (qv), abolished in 1832.

quorum. Of whom. Referred formerly to the commission issued to justices of the peace (qv). Now used to indicate the specified number of members of a body, in the absence of which it cannot formally meet or act legally. See, eg, the Cos.A. 1948, s. 134; *Sharp* v *Dawes* (1876) 2 QBD 26; and *East* v *Bennett Bros Ltd* [1911] 1 Ch 163.

quotation. Term used in the C.C.A. 1974, ss. 152, 189(1) to refer to a document by which a person who carries on a consumer credit or hire business or business of credit broker-age or debt-adjusting gives prospec-tive customers information about terms on which he is prepared to do business. See the Quotations Regula-tions 1980 (S.I. 1980/55).

quoted company. *See* COMPANY, QUOTED.

quousque. Until. Refers to the right of a lord to seize land and profits where the heir of a copyhold tenant failed to pay any appropriate fines.

quo warranto. By what authority. Pre-rogative writ formerly issued by the King's Bench to enquire into the authority by which a public office was held or a franchise claimed. Replaced by information in nature of writ of *quo warranto* which was abolished by the A.J. (Misc. Provs.) A. 1938, s. 9. See now the S.C.A. 1981, s. 30; and O. 53, r. 1(1)(*b*).

qv. *Quod vide.* Which see.

R

R. Abbreviation for Rex (King) or Regina (Queen), as in *R* v *Smith*.

racial discrimination. *See* DISCRIMINATION, RACIAL.

Racial Equality, Commission for. Body of 8–15 individuals, set up under the Race Relations Act 1976, s. 43(1). Appointed by the Secretary of State to work towards the elimination of discrimination; to promote equality of opportunity and good relations between racial groups; to review the working of the 1976 Act. It is empowered to issue non-discrimination notices (qv) and apply for injunctions (qv) to restrain persistent discrimination.

racial group. "A group of persons defined by reference to colour, race, nationality or ethnic or national origins, and references to a person's racial group refer to any racial group within which he falls": Race Relations Act 1976, s. 3(1). See *Mandla* v *Dowell Lee* [1982] 3 WLR 932.

racial hatred, incitement to. An offence under the Race Relations Act 1976, s. 70, amending the Public Order Act 1936, committed by a person who publishes or distributes to the public at large, or to any section of the public not consisting exclusively of members of an association of which he is a member, abusive or insulting written matter or who uses threatening, abusive or insulting words in a public place or at a meeting where, having regard to all the circumstances, hatred is likely to be stirred up against any racial group in Great Britain by such matter or words. See *R* v *Pearce* (1980) 72 Cr App R 295.

rack rent. 1. A rent (qv) which is not less than two-thirds of the rent at which the premises might reasonably be expected to be let from year to year, free from all usual tenant's rates and taxes and tithe rentcharge (if any) and deducting therefrom the probable average annual cost of repairs, insurance and other expenses necessary to maintain the premises in a state to command such rent: Highways Act 1980, s. 329(1). 2. A rent raised to the highest level obtainable.

rank, rule of. Rule for construction of statutes, formulated by Blackstone. "A statute which treats of things or persons of an inferior rank cannot by any general words be extended to those of a superior": *Commentaries*, I, 104. *See* CONSTRUCTION.

ransom. Price paid for release from captivity. In feudal times it was an incident of knight service (qv).

rape. An offence under the S.O.A. 1956, s. 1(1). Defined under common law as unlawful sexual intercourse with a woman without her consent, by force, fear, fraud. Defined by the S.O. (Amendment) A. 1976, s. 1(1) as unlawful sexual intercourse with a woman who at the time of the intercourse does not consent to it, where at that time [the accused] knows that she does not consent to the intercourse or he is reckless as to whether she consents to it. See *R* v *Williams* [1923] 1 KB 340; *R* v *Miller* [1954] 2 All ER 529; *DPP* v *Morgan* [1975] 2 All ER 347; *R* v *Larger* [1981] Crim LR 577 (rape of wife); *R* v *Pigg* [1982] 1 WLR 762 ("recklessness" in rape); *R* v *Bashir* [1982] Crim LR 687; Working Party Report on Sexual Offences 1980.

rape, consent and. "Consent" in rape covers states of mind ranging from actual desire to reluctant acquiescence; it is no longer necessary in proving rape to establish that intercourse took place as a result of fear, fraud or force, but merely that it occurred without the woman's consent: *R* v *Olugboja* [1982] QB 320. See *R* v *Viola* [1982] 1 WLR 1138.

rape offence. "Rape, attempted rape, aiding, abetting, counselling and procuring rape or attempted rape, and incitement to rape'': S.O. (Amendment) A. 1976, s. 7(2). The Act imposes reporting restrictions in such cases.

rape, principles in sentencing for. Rape is a serious crime which, except in wholly exceptional circumstances, calls for an immediate custodial sentence, its length depending on all the circumstances. Aggravating factors include: threats of a brutal kind, group rape, very young or elderly victim, physical or mental injury of a serious nature sustained by the victim. See *R* v *Roberts* [1982] 1 WLR 133.

rashness. The mental state of one who ''thinks of the probable mischief; but in consequence of a missupposition begotten by insufficient advertence, he assumes that a mischief will not ensue in the given instance'': Austin.

rate rebate scheme, local and statutory. ''A scheme for the grant by a rating authority to residential occupiers of rebates from rates calculated in accordance with the provisions of the scheme by reference to their needs and resources'': L.G.A. 1974 s. 12(1). A statutory scheme is one made, for a similar purpose, by the Secretary of State with the consent of the Treasury: s. 11(1). See also the L.G.P.L.A. 1980, s. 45.

rates. Local taxes paid by the occupiers of lands, houses, etc, so as to help to meet the cost of local services. Each payment is calculated annually by multiplying rateable value of property by rate poundage (fixed by the local authority as an amount per £ of rateable value). Disputes relating to assessments are heard by local valuation courts and, on appeal, by the Lands Tribunal. See the General Rate Act 1967; the L.G.A. 1972; the L.G.A. 1974; the Rent Act 1977, s. 25; the S.S. and Housing Benefits Act 1982, Part II; and the Local Government Finance Act 1982 (limitation of rating powers).

rate support grant. Grant payable by government to local authorities, comprising domestic rate relief grant and the block grant: L.G.P.L.A. 1980, ss. 53–56.

ratification. Confirmation; approval.

In the case of ratification of a contract made by an agent (qv), the contract must be made on behalf of the principal; the principal must be competent at the time of the contract; there should have been an act capable of ratification. See the European Communities Act 1972, s. 9(2). *See* CONTRACT.

ratio decidendi. The reason for a judicial decision. Usually a statement of law applied to the problems of a particular case. In essence, the principle upon which a case is decided. (Goodhart suggests that this principle is to be found by taking account of the facts treated by the judge as material, and his decision as based on them: (1930) 40 Yale LJ 161.)

***ratio decidendi,* descriptive and prescriptive.** Distinction drawn by J. Stone (see (1959) 22 MLR 597) between the process of reasoning by which a decision is reached (the ''*descriptive*'' *ratio decidendi*) and that which identifies and delimits the reasoning which a later court will be bound to follow (the ''*prescriptive*'' *ratio decidendi*).

ratio legis. Reason for, or principle behind, a law.

re. In the matter of.

readings. The stages through which a Bill (qv) must pass before it becomes law.

real. 1. Relating to things (*res*), as distinct from persons. 2. Relating to land, and, specifically, freehold interests, as in ''real action''.

real action. *See* ACTIONS REAL AND PERSONAL.

real estate. ''Chattels real, and land in possession, remainder, or reversion (qqv), and every interest in or over land to which a deceased person was entitled at the time of his death; and real estate held on trust (including settled land (qv)) or by way of mortgage or security, but not money to arise under a trust for sale of land, nor money secured or charged on land'': A.E.A. 1925, s. 3(1).

real evidence. *See* EVIDENCE, REAL.

realised development value. Phrase used in the Development Land Tax Act 1976, referring to amount by which net proceeds of disposal of an interest in land exceed the relevant base value of that interest: s. 4(1). "Relevant base value" is one of a group of aggregates which gives the highest figure, eg, the aggregate of the cost of acquisition of the interest and expenditure on improvements and the amount by which the current use value of the interest at the time of disposal exceeds the current use value at the time of acquisition: s. 5. See the Finance Act 1981, s. 129.

real property. Property which could be recovered in a real action, ie, interests in land, more specifically, freehold interests.

real representative. One who is the representative of a deceased person in relation to his real property.

real security. A security charged on land. See the Tr.A. 1925, s. 5. *See* TRUST.

realty. Generally, freehold interest in land.

reasonable contemplation test. Principle relating to damages awarded for breach of contract (qv). "The damages...should be such as may fairly and reasonably be considered either arising naturally, ie, according to the usual course of things, from such breach of contract itself, or such as may reasonably be supposed to have been in the contemplation of both parties at the time they made the contract as the probable result of the breach": *Hadley* v *Baxendale* (1854) 9 Exch 341. It is a test of remoteness, not of quantification: *Re National Coffee Palace Co* (1883) 24 Ch D 367.

reasonable doubt. "That degree of doubt which would prevent a reasonable and just man from coming to a conclusion": *Bater* v *Bater* [1951] P 35. "It is far better, instead of using the words 'reasonable doubt' and then trying to say what is a reasonable doubt, to say to a jury: 'You must not convict unless you are satisfied by the evidence given by the prosecution that the offence has been committed'": *R* v *Summers* [1952] 1 TLR 1164.

reasonable financial provision. *See* FINANCIAL PROVISION, REASONABLE.

reasonable force. The degree of force reasonably necessary, eg, to effect an arrest, in all the circumstances. "A person may use such force as is reasonable in the circumstances in the prevention of crime, or in effecting or assisting in the lawful arrest of offenders or suspected offenders or of persons unlawfully at large": C.L.A. 1967, s. 3. See *R* v *Barrett* (1981) 72 CrAppR 212 (belief in right to use force).

reasonable man. "The fair and reasonable man who represents after all no more than the anthropomorphic conception of justice...": *Davis Contractors Ltd* v *Fareham UDC* [1956] AC 696. "It is left...to the judge to decide what, in the circumstances of the particular case, the reasonable man would have in contemplation, and what, accordingly, the party sought to be made liable ought to have foreseen... The standard of foresight of the reasonable man... eliminates the personal equation and is independent of the idiosyncrasies of the particular person whose conduct is in question": *Glasgow Corporation* v *Muir* [1943] AC 448.

reasonable man test in provocation. *See* PROVOCATION.

reasonable time. In relation to the delivery of goods, is a question of fact: S.G.A. 1979, s. 29(5). Where a contract does not refer specifically to time, there is an implication that the promised act will be carried out within a reasonable time: *Ford* v *Cotesworth* (1868) LR 4 QB 132. *See* TIME AS ESSENCE OF CONTRACT.

rebate. Refund; credit; discount. See the C.C.A. 1974 s. 94 (for an example of "statutory rebate").

rebates, rent. *See* RENT REBATES.

rebus sic stantibus. In these circumstances. Doctrine of international law, which assumes as a condition of all treaties that they will cease to be obligatory if there is a substantial change of the facts on which they were founded.

rebut. To oppose; contradict; disprove.

rebutter. A term used in pleading to indicate the defendant's answer to the plaintiff's surrejoinder (qv). *See*

PLEADINGS.

recall of witness. *See* WITNESS, RECALL OF.

recaption. The lawful retaking of one's chattels from another who has wrongfully taken and detained them. See, eg, *Anthony* v *Haney* (1832) 8 Bing 186; *Blades* v *Higgs* (1861) 10 CB NS 713.

receipt. Written acknowledgment of goods or money received.

receiver. 1. One appointed to enable a judgment creditor to obtain payment of a debt. The appointment of a receiver is not a winding-up (qv): *Moss Ltd* v *Whinney* [1912] AC 254. May be known as "receiver by way of equitable execution". See the S.C.A. 1981, s. 37; the A.J.A. 1977, s. 7; O. 30; O. 51. 2. One appointed to preserve property which is endangered, for the benefit of those entitled to it. 3. One who received stolen property. See the Th.A. 1968, s. 22.

receiving. The former offence of receiving stolen goods knowing them to have been stolen: Larceny Act 1916, s. 33. Now part of the offence of "handling" (qv). See *R* v *Smythe* (1980) 72 CrAppR 8.

receiving order. An order made at the hearing of a bankruptcy petition for the protection of the estate. It deprives creditors whose debts are provable in bankruptcy of remedy or action without the court's leave. On its being made, the official receiver (qv) becomes receiver of debtor's property. See the B.A. 1914, ss. 3, 7, 37; and the L.C.A. 1972, ss. 6, 8. *See* BANKRUPTCY.

recent possession. "Convenient but grammatically incorrect expression to describe the possession by someone of things which had recently been stolen": *R* v *Hobbs and Geoffrey-Smith* (1982) 132 NLJ 435. It may raise a presumption of theft or handling (qv). See *R* v *Ball* [1983] 1 WLR 801.

reciprocity. Term used in international law to denote agreement of states bestowing privileges on each other's subjects.

recitals. Part of a deed of conveyance on sale indicating the effect and purpose of that deed and stating the history of the property to be conveyed. They are not essential to the deed's validity. Recitals of particular facts may operate as an estoppel (qv): *Bensley* v *Burdon* (1830) 8 LJ Ch 85. See the L.P.A. 1925, s. 45(6).

reckless cycling. A person who rides a cycle, not being a motor vehicle, on a road recklessly is guilty of an offence: Road Traffic Act 1972 s. 17, as substituted by the C.L.A. 1977, s. 50(2).

reckless driving. *See* DRIVING, RECKLESS.

recklessness. Generally, the intentional creation of unjustifiable risk. "Recklessness on the part of the doer of an act does presuppose that there is something in the circumstances that would have drawn the attention of an ordinary prudent individual to the possibility that his act was capable of causing the kind of serious harmful consequences that the section which creates the offence was designed to prevent, and that the risk of those harmful consequences occurring was not so slight that an ordinary prudent individual would feel justified in treating them as negligible": *per* Lord Diplock in *R* v *Lawrence* [1982] AC 510. See *R* v *Caldwell* [1982] AC 341.

recognisance. Obligation or bond binding an offender to answer judgment when required to do so, or to keep the peace and be of good behaviour. See, eg, the M.C.A. 1980, Part VI; and the Bail Act 1976, s. 8.

recognisee. Person in whose favour a recognisance (qv) is made.

recognisor. One bound by a recognisance (qv).

recommendations of EEC. *See* COMMUNITY LEGISLATION, FORMS OF.

reconciliation. The act of harmonising differences and settling disputes. Thus, under the Mat. C.A. 1973, s. 6, provision is made by rules of court to require a solicitor acting for a petitioner for divorce to certify whether he has discussed with the petitioner the possibility of a reconciliation. Proceedings may be adjourned to enable attempts at reconciliation. A period of six months, or periods of up to a total of six months during which spouses may resume cohabitation without loss of the chance of subsequent divorce, are known as "reconciliation periods". See also the D.P.A. 1978, s. 26. *See* DIVORCE.

reconstruction of company. The transference of a company's assets to a new company under an arrangement whereby the shareholders of the old company receive shares, or similar interests, in the new company. It can be effected by, eg, a scheme of arrangement under the Cos.A. 1948, ss. 206, 287, 306. *See* COMPANY.

reconversion. Notional process whereby property which has been subject to notional conversion (qv) is treated as having been restored to its original state. Example: A devises land to B and C on trust to sell and pay the proceeds to D. D is then entitled (because of the doctrine of conversion) to the property in its converted form (ie, as personalty (qv)) at A's death. If D elects to take it as land, reconversion has taken place. See *Re Douglas and Powell's Contract* [1902] 2 Ch 296; *Re Cook* [1948] Ch 212.

reconveyance. Procedure whereby, before 1st January 1926, the mortgagee had to revest the legal estate in the mortgagor on redemption. A receipt on the mortgage deed now suffices to extinguish the mortgage. See the L.P.A. 1925, s. 115. *See* MORTGAGE.

record. 1. To make a written account. 2. An authentic account of some event(s). 3. A memorial of an action heard in a court of record (qv). See the Criminal Evidence Act 1965, s. 1(1); *R* v *Jones* [1978] 1 WLR 195.

record, contract of. *See* CONTRACT OF RECORD.

record, court of. *See* COURT OF RECORD.

Recorders. Appointed by the Queen on the recommendation of the Lord Chancellor to try criminal cases in the Crown Court (qv). Recorders may also sit as county court judges. They must be barristers or solicitors (qqv) of at least 10 years' standing. Appointed on a temporary basis, they

may be removed for failing to comply with the terms of the appointment. See the Courts Act 1971, s. 21. See also the Courts Act 1971, s. 24 (as substituted by the S.C.A. 1981, s. 146) for the appointment of assistant recorders.

records admissible in civil cases. Records, ie, documents (qv) containing information, admissible in evidence in civil proceedings. Under the Civil Evidence Act 1968, ss 4, 5, provision is made for the admissibility in evidence of documentary hearsay statements under certain conditions and of computerised records. See *Taylor* v *Taylor* [1970] 2 All ER 609; *H.* v *Schering Chemicals* [1983] 1 WLR 143. *See* EVIDENCE.

records admissible in criminal cases. Records in criminal proceedings which are admissible in evidence, ie, where they relate to a trade or business and have been compiled from information supplied by persons who have personal knowledge of the matters dealt with, where the person who supplied the information is, eg, dead or beyond the seas. See the Criminal Evidence Act 1965; *R* v *Gwilliam* [1968] 3 All ER 821; *R* v *Tirado* (1974) 59 Cr App R 80; *See* EVIDENCE.

recovery. 1. An action for the recovery of land—"the modern equivalent of the old action of ejectment": *Bramwell* v *Bramwell* [1942] 1 KB 370. The action must be brought within 12 years of accrual of the cause of action: Lim. A. 1980, s. 15. See *Moore Properties* v *McKeon* [1976] 1 WLR 1278. 2. A collusive action, known as common recovery (qv).

recovery of costs. *See* COSTS, RECOVERY OF.

recovery of premises, obstruction of. Resistance to or intentional obstruction of court officers executing process for possession against unauthorised occupiers is an offence under the C.L.A. 1977, s. 10(1). For defences, see s. 10(3).

recreational charity. A trust for the public benefit which provides facilities for recreation or other leisure time occupation in the interests of social welfare. See the

Recreational Charities Act 1958. *See* CHARITY; TRUST.

rectification. Where a written document does not accurately express an agreement between parties, as the result of some common mistake, equity has the power to rectify that mistake: *Craddock Bros v Hunt* [1923] 2 Ch 136. Rectification is not of the agreement itself, merely of the instrument recording the agreement. See *Frederick E Rose (London) v Pym* [1953] 2 QB 450; *Re Reynette-James* [1976] 1 WLR 116 (rectification of will); and *Re Slocock's WT* [1979] 1 All ER 358.

rectification of mistake in magistrates' court. *See* MISTAKE, RECTIFICATION IN MAGISTRATES' COURT OF.

rectification of will. If the court is satisfied that a will is so expressed that it fails to carry out the testator's intentions, in consequence of a clerical error or of a failure to understand his instructions, it may order rectification so as to carry out those intentions: A.J.A. 1982, s. 20(1).

reddendum. That which is to be paid. Clause in lease (qv) stating the amount of rent and when it is payable. See *King v King* (1980) 255 EG 1205.

redeemable preference shares. Preference shares (qv), first introduced by the Cos.A. 1929, that can be redeemed out of profits or out of a fresh issue of shares. Shares cannot be redeemed in this manner unless fully paid: Cos.A. 1948, s. 58, as amended by the Cos.A. 1981, s. 45(3). The terms of redemption must provide for payment on redemption: s. 45(4). *See* SHARE.

redeem up, foreclose down. Rule relating to redemption of mortgage (qv). Example: M has mortgaged property to L1, L2, L3, L4, L5, in that order of priority. L4 wishes to redeem L2. L4 must redeem those mortgages between him and the prior mortgage he wishes to redeem and he must also foreclose any subsequent mortgagees and the mortgagor. L3, L5 and M must be made parties to the action. L3 must be redeemed. L5 and M must be foreclosed and allowed an opportunity to pay off the prior mortgage. *See* MORTGAGE.

redemption. The recovery of mortgaged property on payment of the debt. The rights to redeem are: *legal* (right at law to redeem on the exact day fixed by the mortgage); *equitable* (right to redeem after that date has passed). *See* EQUITY OF REDEMPTION; MORTGAGE.

redemption period for a pawn. The longest of the following periods: six months after the pawn was taken; any period fixed by the parties for duration of credit secured by the pledge (qv) or for duration of redemption period: C.C.A. 1974, s. 116. *See* PAWN.

redress. *See* RELIEF; REMEDY.

reduction into possession. Conversion of a chose in action (qv) into a chose in possession (qv). Example: a debt which is paid.

reduction of capital. A company limited by shares may, if its articles permit, reduce its capital by means of a special resolution (qv) to be confirmed by the court: Cos.A. 1948, s. 66(1). It may be effected for reasons such as: loss of capital by wastage of assets and the company wishes to write off the loss; share capital issued may not be fully paid and the company has the capital it needs. See the Capital Gains Tax 1979, s. 77; and the Cos.A. 1980, s. 12. *See* COMPANY.

redundancy. 1. Irrelevant matter in pleadings (qv). 2. Dismissal of an employee because his job has ceased to exist. See the Redundancy Payments Act 1965; the E.P. (C.) A. 1978, Part VI, as amended by the Employment Act 1980; *Williams v Compair Maxam* [1982] IRLR, s. 83; and *Cowen v Haden* [1983] ICR 1.

redundancy payments. Payments made to employees in the event of their dismissal by reason of redundancy, ie, dismissal because of the actual or intended cessation of the business in which they are employed or the cessation of or decline for work of a particular kind. See the Redundancy Payments Act 1965; the E.P. (C.) A. 1978, Part VI; the Redundancy Rebates Act 1977; and the Redundancy Fund Act 1981. "The purpose of redundancy pay is to compensate a worker for loss of job, irrespective of whether that loss leads to unemployment. It is to compensate him for loss of security, possible loss of earnings and fringe benefits, and the uncertainty and anxiety of change of job": *Wynes* v *Southrepps Broiler Farm Ltd* [1968] ITR 407.

re-engagement order. Order under the E.P. (C.) A. 1978, s. 69, whereby a former employee has to be re-engaged by the employer in employment comparable to that from which he was dismissed or other suitable employment.

re-entry. Right of entry (qv).

re-examination. Examination of a witness (qv) by counsel or solicitor relating to matters arising out of his cross-examination (qv). In general, leading questions may not be asked and questions on new matter may not be asked save by leave of the judge. See the Civil Evidence Act 1968, s. 2; *Price* v *Samo* (1838) 7 LJ QB 123.

referee. 1. One to whom a dispute is referred for an opinion. In the case of statements by a referee: "If a man refers another upon any particular business to a third person, he is bound by what this third person says or does concerning it, as much as if that had been done or said by him": *Williams* v *Innes* (1804) 1 Camp 364. 2. One who provides a character reference for another.

referee, official. *See* OFFICIAL REFEREE.

reference. 1. Referring of a matter to an arbitrator (qv) for his decision. 2. Decision by an arbitrator or referee (qv).

reference, incorporation by. *See* INCORPORATION BY REFERENCE.

references, compulsory. *See* COMPULSORY REFERENCES.

referendum. The submission to popular vote of a question or a proposed legislative measure. See the Referendum Act 1975 (relating to the UK's membership of the EEC (qv)).

referential settlements. *See* SETTLEMENTS, REFERENTIAL.

refreshing memory. Permission granted to a witness under examina-

tion to refer to a document so as to recall some matter. The document must generally have been made by the witness, or under his supervision, or checked by him, substantially at the time of occurrence of the event in question and must be handed to the opposite party for inspection, on request. See *Jones* v *Stroud* (1825) 2 C & P 196; *R* v *Bass* [1953] 1 All ER 1064. A witness may refresh his memory from a note written by some other person as long as he adopts it as his own, particularly if he does so by signing it: *Groves* v *Redbart* [1975] RTR 268. See also the Civil Evidence Act 1968, s. 3(2); *R* v *Westwell* [1976] 2 All ER 812; *R* v *Cheng* (1976) 63 Cr App E 20; and *A.-G.'s Ref (No. 3 of 1979)* (1979) 69 Cr App R 411.

refusal, wilful. *See* WILFUL REFUSAL.

refuse disposal. Under the Refuse Disposal (Amenity) Act 1978, s. 1, a local authority has a duty to provide a place where refuse may be deposited free of charge by any person at all reasonable times.

regent. One appointed by Act of Parliament to fulfil royal functions if the Sovereign is under 18 on accession, or incapacitated. See the Regency Acts 1937 and 1953.

regional development aid. Assistance, generally incompatible with EEC objectives, save where intended to promote economic development where there is serious regional unemployment: Treaty of Rome 1957, art. 92. See Industrial Development Act 1982, Part II. *See* EEC.

register. Formal written records.

register at Land Registry. The register of title kept by the Land Registry, subdivided into *Property Register* (describing property and estate (qv) for which it is held); *Proprietorship Register* (stating class of title, eg, absolute, qualified); *Charges Register* (containing notices of charges or incumbrances). See the Land Registration Rules 1925, rr. 2–7. *See* LAND REGISTRATION.

register, dominion. *See* DOMINION REGISTER.

registered designs. *See* DESIGNS, REGISTERED.

registered land. Land, title to which is registered under the L.R.A. 1925–71. *See* LAND REGISTRATION.

registered land, protection of mortgage of. "Unless and until the mortgage becomes a registered charge it shall take effect only in equity and it shall be capable of being overridden as a minor interest unless protected by a notice under s. 49 or a caution under s. 54": L.R.A. 1925, s. 106 (as substituted by the A.J.A. 1977, s. 26). *See* CAUTION; MINOR INTERESTS; MORTGAGE.

registered office. A company's official address. It must be sent to the Registrar of Companies at the time the memorandum (qv) is submitted for registration: Cos.A. 1976, s. 23(1). The Registrar must be notified of any change within 14 days: s. 23(2). The address of a company's registered office, place and number of registration, must be mentioned "in legible characters in all business letters and order forms of the company": European Communities Act 1972, s. 9(7).

register of interests. Register, kept under the Cos.A. 1967, s. 34(1)(3), in which specified persons (see the Cos.A. 1967, s. 33(1) (as amended by the Cos.A. 1976, s. 26)) notify the company of interests in voting share capital.

register of members. A register, required under the Cos.A. 1948, s. 110, which must contain, eg, names and addresses of members and shares held by them, together with the amount paid up on shares. This must be kept at the company's registered office and may be inspected by any member during business hours.

registrar. An official responsible for compiling and keeping a register. In some cases he may be empowered to hear parties and make decisions.

registrar, county court. Appointed by the Lord Chancellor from solicitors of at least 7 years' standing. His functions are administrative (eg, keeping of court records and arranging for the issue of summonses) and judicial (eg, interlocutory matters and the taxation of costs (qv)). In modern provisions, however, except in relation to judicial acts, the term "registrar" has been replaced by "proper officer" (usually referring to the chief clerk): S.I. 1981/1687; as a result the county court registrar's functions are predominantly judicial.

registrars, district. *See* DISTRICT REGISTRARS.

registration of birth. *See* BIRTH, REGISTRATION OF.

registration of company. *See* COMPANY, REGISTRATION OF.

registration of death. *See* DEATH, REGISTRATION OF.

registration of marriage. *See* MARRIAGE, REGISTRATION OF.

registration of title. *See* LAND REGISTRATION.

registration, UK citizenship resulting from. *See* CITIZENSHIP, BRITISH, ACQUISITION BY REGISTRATION.

regularity, presumption of. *See* OMNIA PRAESUMUNTUR RITE ET SOLEMNITER ESSE ACTA.

regulated agreements. Agreements to which provisions of the C.C.A. 1974 relate, ie, consumer credit agreements; consumer hire agreements; credit token agreements (qqv). Regulations relating to form and content of such agreements may be made: s. 60. The agreements must be in writing, must contain all express terms in legible form, must comply with appropriate regulations and be signed by the debtor personally and by the other parties. Failure to comply renders agreements "improperly executed". See the Consumer Credit (Exempt Agreements) Order 1980 (S.I. 1980/52).

regulated mortgage. A mortgage which falls within the Rent Act 1977, s. 129(1) (a), is a regulated mortgage if it is a legal mortgage of land consisting of or including a dwelling-house which is let on or subject to a regulated tenancy (qv) and the regulated tenancy is binding on the mortgagee: Rent Act 1977, s. 131, amended by the H.A. 1980, Sch 26. For the court's powers to mitigate hardship to mortgagors under regulated mortgages, see the 1977 Act, s. 132. *See* MORTGAGE.

regulated tenancy. A protected or statutory tenancy (qqv): Rent Act

1977, s. 18(1) amended by the H.A. 1980, Sch 26.

regulated tenancy, registration of rents under. Scheme whereby the application for registration of rent is made to the rent officer by the landlord or tenant, or jointly by the landlord or tenant under a regulated tenancy. The register contains the rent payable, particulars relating to the tenancy and the specification of the dwelling-house. See the Rent Act 1977, ss. 62, 66, 67.

regulated tenancy, rent limit. Where a dwelling-house is registered under the Rent Act 1977, Part IV, the rent recoverable for any contractual period of a regulated tenancy is limited to the rent so registered: Rent Act 1977, s. 44(1).

regulations of EEC. *See* COMMUNITY LEGISLATION, FORMS OF.

rehabilitation order. Order made by a local authority, under the H.A. 1974, s. 114, and submitted to the Secretary of State, providing for the improvement up to full standard of amenities of a building included in a clearance area (qv). See the 1974 Act, Sch 10; and the H.A. 1980, Sch 25, para 26.

rehabilitation period. Periods of, eg, 5–10 years, depending on the sentence, running from conviction, during which a person may be "rehabilitated" and his convictions considered as "spent" under the Rehabilitation of Offenders Act 1974. There is no rehabilitation under the Act where the sentence was, eg, life imprisonment, or over 30 months' imprisonment or corrective training. *See* SPENT CONVICTIONS.

re-hearing. A second, or new, hearing of a case already adjudicated upon. Example: appeal to the Crown Court (qv) from conviction by a magistrates' court (qv), where there is a complete re-hearing and where fresh evidence may be introduced by either side without leave. See O. 59, r. 3 for the civil procedure in the Court of Appeal.

reinstatement. 1. Restoring of an employee to the position he occupied prior to dismissal. An order for reinstatement, stating that an employer shall treat the former employee in all respects as if he had not been dismissed may be made after hearing a complaint against unfair dismissal (qv) under the E.P. (C.) A. 1978, s. 69. 2. Replacement or repair of damaged property under insurance policy. See, eg, the Fires Prevention (Metropolis) Act 1774, s. 83; the L.P.A. 1925, ss. 47, 108(2); the Tr.A. 1925, s. 20(4); and *Pleasurama Ltd v Sun Alliance* [1979] 1 Lloyd's Rep 389.

reinsurance. Agreement between the reinsured (known as the "direct" or "primary" insurer) and the reinsurer whereby the reinsured undertakes to cede, and the reinsurer undertakes to accept, a fixed share of a risk. It takes the form of "facultative reinsurance", ie, reinsurance against liability on a stated policy, or "treaty reinsurance", ie, reinsurance against liabilities on policies in general.

rejection of offer. An offer (qv) is rejected: if the offeree communicates his rejection to the offeror; if the offeree accepts subject to conditions; if the offeree makes a counter-offer. See, eg, *Jordan v Newton* (1838) 4 M & W 155.

rejoinder. The defendant's answer to a reply by the plaintiff (qqv). It cannot be served without leave of court. See O. 18.

related company. *See* COMPANY, RELATED.

relation back. Principle whereby an act is referred to a prior date, from which time it is construed as being effective. Example: the rule that probate when granted relates back to the time of the testator's death: *Whitehead v Taylor* (1839) 10 A & E 210. See also the B.A. 1914, ss. 107(4), 130(8).

relations. Generally, the next of kin (qv). Those who would take under the intestacy laws: *Re Bridgen* [1938] Ch 205.

relationships, prohibited degrees of. Relationships within which a marriage celebrated after July 1971 is void: Mat.C.A. 1973, s. 11(a) (i). They are: *for a man*—mother, daughter, grandmother, granddaughter, sister, aunt, niece, father's or son's or grandfather's or grandson's wife, wife's mother or daughter or grandmother or granddaughter; *for a woman*—father, son, grandfather, grandson, brother, uncle, nephew, mother's or daughter's or grandmother's or granddaughter's husband, husband's father or son or grandfather or grandson. See the Marriage Act 1949 Sch 1, as amended by the Marriage (Enabling) Act 1960 and the Ch.A. 1975, Sch 3.

relatives. Relations (qv). The term usually includes persons who are relatives by marriage or adoption and persons who would be relatives if some persons born illegitimate had been born legitimate: S.S.A. 1975, Sch 20. See also the Adoption Act 1976, s. 72(1); and the Child Care Act 1980, s. 87(1).

relator. A private person at whose suggestion an action is commenced by the Attorney-General (qv) (as in the case of a matter of public interest, such as a public nuisance). See *LCC v A.-G.* [1902] AC 165; *Gouriet v UPW* [1978] AC 435. For relator actions, see O. 15, r. 11. *See* ATTORNEY-GENERAL AND RELATOR ACTIONS.

release. 1. "The giving or discharge of the right or action which any hath or claimeth against another, or his land": *Termes de la Ley*. As a defence in an action, it must be specifically pleaded. See O. 18, r. 8(1). 2. A document which acts as discharge of a claim. 3. Discharge from custody.

release of prisoners, early. The Secretary of State may order that persons of any class specified in the order shall be released from prison at such earlier time (but not more than six months earlier) than they would otherwise be released": C.J.A. 1982, s. 32(1). No order may be made in the case of those serving a life sentence, or those sentenced for an excluded offence (as specified in Sch 1, Part 1): s. 32(1).

release on licence. Release of a prisoner on the advice of the Parole Board. See the C.J.A. 1967, s. 60; and the C.J.A. 1982, s. 33. *See* PAROLE.

relevance. Known also as "relevancy", "logical relevancy". Term used in the law of evidence to refer to a connection or relationship between facts and events which ordinarily tends to render one probable from the very existence of the other. The general rule of relevance in evidence is that all facts which, though not in issue, may be given as evidence so that the court is enabled to reach a conclusion on facts in issue, are relevant. When one fact logically tends to prove a fact in issue it will be generally admissible unless excluded by some rule (exceptions include: hearsay (qv); opinion; reputation of the accused; conduct of the accused on other occasions). (Relevance must be distinguished from "admissibility".) *See* ADMISSIBILITY OF EVIDENCE; EVIDENCE.

relevant evidence. Evidence relating to facts in issue. "Any two facts to which [the term 'relevant'] is applied are so related to each other that according to the common course of events one either taken by itself or in connection with other facts proves or renders probable the past, present, or future existence or non-existence of the other": Stephen. "Evidence is relevant if it is logically probative or disprobative of some matter which requires proof": *per* Lord Simon in *DPP v Kilbourne* [1973] AC 729. Relevant evidence may be excluded on the grounds of estoppel (qv), public policy (eg, Crown privilege). *See* EVIDENCE.

relevant facts. *See* FACTS, RELEVANT.

relief. 1. Payment by a feudal tenant who succeeded to land on the death of a former tenant. 2. Remedial action of a court. 3. Tax allowance. See, eg, the Income and Corporation Taxes Act 1970. *See* REMEDY.

relief, financial. *See* FINANCIAL RELIEF.

relief, interim. *See* INTERIM RELIEF.

religion. "The Court of Chancery makes no distinction between one religion and another, unless the tenets of a particular sect inculcate doctrines adverse to the very foundations of all religions": *Thornton v Howe* (1862) 31 LJ Ch 767. "As between different religions the law stands neutral, but it seems that any religion is at least likely to be better than none": *Neville Estates Ltd* v *Madden* [1962] Ch 832. See *Re South Place Ethical Society* [1980] 1 WLR 1565.

religion, advancement of. "To advance religion means to promote it, to spread its message ever wider among mankind; to take some positive steps to sustain and increase religious belief; and these things are done in a variety of ways which may be comprehensively described as pastoral and missionary": *United Grand Lodge* v *Holborn BC* [1957] 1 WLR 1080.

remainder. "A residue of an estate in land depending upon a particular estate and created together with the same at one time": Coke. Example: "to X for life, then to Y in fee simple"—X is entitled to actual possession (his estate is the *particular estate*), Y's estate is a *remainder,* and Y is the *remainderman.* A *vested remainder* is one ready to come into possession immediately the particular estate is determined, as contrasted with a *contingent remainder* (qv).

remainder, common law rules. A remainder was void: if limited after a fee simple (qv); if not preceded by a particular freehold estate created under the same instrument; if limited so that it took effect by defeating the particular estate; if limited so that there was abeyance of seisin (qv).

remainderman. *See* REMAINDER.

remand. To dispose of the person of an individual charged with a crime, eg, on the adjournment of a hearing. Thus, magistrates may remand a defendant on bail (qv) or in custody when proceedings are adjourned. See, eg, the M.C.A. 1980, ss. 128–131; and the Bail Act 1976. The period of remand may not generally exceed eight days without the release of the accused on bail: M.C.A. 1980, s. 128(6). In general a person may not be remanded in custody without being brought before the court: see, however, the C.J.A. 1982, s. 59, Sch 9.

remand centres. Places for the detention of persons of 14–20 who are remanded or committed in custody

for trial or sentence: Prison Act 1952, s. 43(1) (*a*) (as substituted by the C.J.A. 1982, s. 11).

remand for medical examination. *See* MEDICAL EXAMINATION, REMAND FOR.

remedial rights. *See* ANTECEDENT RIGHTS.

remedial statute. A statute intended to remedy an existing defect in the law.

remedy. 1. The means provided by the law to recover rights or to obtain redress or compensation for a wrong, eg, action for damages. 2. The relief or redress given by a court.

remise. To release a claim; to surrender (by deed (qv)).

remission. 1. Pardoning of an offence. 2. Cancelling of the whole or part of some obligation. Remission of a prisoner's sentence, for good behaviour in prison, of up to one-third, is possible, save in the case of a life sentence, under the Prison Rules.

remoteness of damage. 1. In contract (qv), the general rule is that damages for breach will be too remote to be recovered unless such that the defendant, as a reasonable man, would have foreseen as likely to result: *Hadley* v *Baxendale* (1854) 9 Exch 341; *Parsons Ltd* v *Uttley Ingham & Co* [1978] 1 All ER 525. 2. In tort (qv), the general rule is that, once negligence (qv) is established, the defendant is liable for all the direct consequences, even though not foreseeable by an ordinary, reasonable man in similar circumstances: *Overseas Tankship (UK) Ltd* v *Morts Dock & Engineering Co Ltd* [1961] AC 388. See also *Re Polemis* [1921] 3 KB 560; *Lamb* v *Camden BC* [1981] QB 625; and *McLoughlin* v *O'Brian* [1982] 2 All ER 298.

remoteness, rules against. General rules affecting the period of time for which control over property may be exercised by a person. They include rules against perpetuities, inalienability, accumulations.

removal of action. Transfer of proceedings, eg, to the county court from the High Court (qqv) and vice versa.

remuneration. Consideration for services rendered, generally in the form of wages, salaries. Includes "any benefit, facility or advantage, whether in money or otherwise, provided by the employer": Remuneration, Charges and Grants Act 1975, s. 7. See *Perrott* v *Supplementary Benefits Commission* [1980] 3 All ER 110 (remuneration considered as arising from "work which is paid for, and not merely work resulting in a profit").

remuneration of directors. This must be stated in a company's balance sheet and prospectus: see the Cos.A. 1948, s. 196. Directors are not entitled to remuneration except by express agreement. Where the articles (qv) provide for remuneration there can be no change without a special resolution. *See* COMPANY.

remuneration of trustees. Not usually permitted except where authorised under the trust instrument, or by order of the court, or under statute: see the Tr.A. 1925, s. 42, and the Judicial T.A. 1896, s. 1(5). See *Re Sandys' WT* [1947] 2 All ER 302; *Dale* v *IRC* [1954] AC 11; *Boardman* v *Phipps* [1966] 2 AC 46; *Re Duke of Norfolk's Settlement* [1982] Ch 61; and *Re Keeler's ST* [1981] Ch 156.

renewal of lease. *See* LEASE, RENEWAL OF.

renewal of writ. A writ (qv) is valid for 12 months from the date of issue. On application (eg, where the defendant (qv) is untraceable) it may be renewed for a period of up to 12 months. See O. 6, r. 8; O. 46, r. 8.

renouncing probate. Refusal of executor (qv) to accept office. See the A.E.A. 1925, s. 5; *Re Russell* (1869) LR 1 P & D 634; *Re Biggs* [1966] P 118. *See* PROBATE.

rent. A periodic payment made by the tenant (qv) or other occupier of land to the owner for its possession and use.

rental period. "A period in respect of which a payment of rent falls to be made": H.A. 1980, s. 50(1).

rental purchase agreement. Agreement for the purchase of a dwelling-house under which the whole or part of purchase price is to be paid in three or more instalments and completion of the purchase is deferred until the

whole or a specified part of the purchase price has been paid: H.A. 1980, s. 88(4).

rent assessment committees. Committees, appointed by the Secretary of State, under the Rent Act 1977, s. 65 and Sch 10. See the H.A. 1980, s. 142.

rent book. Document usually recording the terms of tenancy and rent payments.

rentcharge. "Any annual or other periodic sum charged on or issuing out of land except rent reserved by a lease or tenancy or any sum payable by way of interest": Rentcharges Act 1977, s. 1. The creation of rentcharges is now prohibited, under s. 2(1), save in the case of, eg, the rentcharge having the effect of making land on which rent is charged settled land (qv) by virtue of the S.L.A. 1925, s. 1(1) (v), or an estate rentcharge for the purpose of making covenants to be performed by the owner of land affected by the rentcharge enforceable by the rent owner against the owner for the time being of the land. See s. 1(4). Rentcharges are extinguished at the expiry of 60 years beginning with the passing of the 1977 Act or the date on which the rentcharge first became payable, whichever is the later. For apportionment, see s. 4.

rent, chief. *See* CHIEF RENT.

rent, fair. *See* FAIR RENT.

rent, interim. *See* INTERIM RENT.

rent officers. Officers appointed under the Rent Act 1977, s. 63, with powers to keep registers of rents, consider applications relating to fair rents (qv), etc. See the H.A. 1980, s. 9.

rent rebates. Rebates from rent granted to persons who occupy as their homes dwellings let to them by a local authority (within its Housing Revenue Account), calculated in accordance with the provisions of the rent rebate scheme by reference to their needs and resources: Housing Finance Act 1972, s. 18(1). See the S.S. and Housing Benefits Act 1982, Part II.

rent restrictions. Statutory limitations on the amount of rent payable by a tenant (qv). See, eg, the Rent Acts 1974 and 1977. Under the Housing Rents and Subsidies Act 1975, s. 11(1): "An order may provide for restricting or preventing increases of rent for dwellings which would otherwise take place, or for restricting the amount of rent which would otherwise be payable on new lettings of dwellings." See the H.A. 1980, s. 60.

rent seck. Dry rent (qv).

rent service. Periodic payment made by a tenant (qv) to his landlord, deriving from tenure, unlike a rentcharge (qv) which is not attributable to tenure.

rents, registration of. The keeping of details of rents determined by rent tribunals (qv). See the Rent Act 1977, Sch 11; and the H.A. 1980, Sch 6.

rent tribunals. Appointed by the Secretary of State for the Environment under the Rent Acts 1974–1977 each consisting of a chairman and two other members, to consider references arising from rents under restricted contracts (qv). The procedure is generally informal.

renunciation. A statement of, or action amounting to, disclaimer (qv).

renvoi. Renvoyer = to send back. Doctrine in private international law (qv) involving the reference back of a question to English law. The concept of *partial renvoi* (where the court might make a reference to the whole of the foreign law and treat a remission to English law as a reference to English internal law) appears not to form a part of English law (but see *Re Johnson* [1903] 1 Ch 821). Where the court takes a reference to foreign law as meaning the law which the foreign court would, in fact, apply to the question, this is known as *"total"* or *"double" renvoi*. See *Re Annesley* [1926] Ch 692.

repair, covenant to. Where, in a lease (qv), there is an express covenant to repair, the covenantor must maintain the premises in a condition in which they would be maintained by a reasonably minded owner, taking into account their age and locality: *Proudfoot* v *Hart* (1890) 25

ABD 42. An order for specific performance (qv) may be made in the case of a plain breach of a landlord's covenant to repair: *Jeune* v *Queen's Cross Properties* [1974] Ch 97. See the L.P.A. 1925, s. 147(1); the H.A. 1974, ss. 125, 129; *Torrens* v *Walker* [1906] 2 Ch 166; *Campden Hill Towers Ltd* v *Gardner* [1977] QB 823; and *Smedley* v *Chumley and Hawkes* (1982) 44 P & CR 50.

repairs. Work of maintenance, decoration or restoration. " 'Repair' always involves renewal; renewal of a part, of a subordinate part": *Lurcott* v *Wakely* [1911] 1 KB 905.

reparations. Compensation, in money, materials and goods, paid by a defeated nation for damage sustained by the victor and others in a war between states.

repatriation. 1. The resumption of one's former nationality by leaving one country and settling in another. 2. Sending back a person to his own country.

repeal. To rescind or revoke. Refers, eg, to the express or implied abrogation of one statute by a later Act. "The test of whether there has been a repeal by implication by subsequent legislation is this: are the provisions of a later Act so inconsistent with, or repugnant to, the provisions of an earlier Act that the two cannot stand together": *West Ham Church Wardens* v *Fourth City Montreal Building Society* [1892] 1 QB 654. See the Statute Law (Repeals) Act 1978. Result of repealing a statute is that it is treated as though it had never been enacted, save for actions concluded prior to repeal: *Kay* v *Goodwin* (1836) 6 Bing 576. Where a person is charged under a repealed Act and convicted, the conviction will be quashed: *Stowers* v *Darnell* [1973] RTR 459. See also the I.A. 1978, ss. 15, 16.

replevin. *Replevire* = to give security. Formerly a remedy of re-delivery for one whose chattels had been wrongfully seized by way of distress (qv); later used in cases involving wrongful detention of chattels. Governed today by the County C.A. 1959 (see ss. 104–106) (as amended by the S.C.A. 1981, Sch 7) and may be sought, eg, where the plaintiff has been deprived of possession of chattels by act of trespass. See the Torts (Interference with Goods) Act 1977. See *Swaffer v Mulcahy* [1934] 1 KB 608.

replication. Reply (qv).

reply. 1. Plaintiff's statement in pleadings (qv), replying to a defence or counterclaim (qqv). It must be served within 14 days after the defence has been served. See O. 18. 2. Counsel's speech for the plaintiff (qv) or for the prosecution answering the defendant's points.

reporting of committal proceedings. *See* COMMITTAL PROCEEDINGS, REPORTING OF.

Reports, Law. *See* LAW REPORTS.

representation. 1. Taking the place of another, eg, as in the relationship of principal and agent (qqv). 2. Being represented in a legislative body (eg, the House of Commons (qv)). 3. A statement made by one party to another, relating to some past event or existing fact (but not as to law), which induces a course of action, eg, signing of a contract. It may be inferred from conduct. Includes, under the C.C.A. 1974, s. 189(1), any condition or warranty and any other statement or undertaking, whether oral or in writing. For representation in intestate succession, see the A.E.A. 1925, Part IV.

representation, chain of. *See* CHAIN OF REPRESENTATION.

representative. One who stands in the place of another, eg, a personal representative (qv). See O. 6, r. 3.

representative action. Action brought by one or more of a number of persons having the same interest in proceedings. Judgment is binding on all those represented if (as plaintiffs) they have a common grievance and are able to benefit from the relief claimed. See O. 15, r. 12; *John v Rees* [1970] Ch 345. (For a so-called "class action" for damages (not in use in the UK) see *City of Philadelphia v American Oil Co* 53 FRD 45 (1971).)

reprieve. Formal suspension of execution of a sentence.

republication of will. Where a testator (qv) desires that his unrevoked will should take effect as if written on a subsequent date, he may republish it with the formalities needed in the case of a will, by re-execution or by making a subsequent codicil (qv) showing the intention to republish. *See* WILL.

repudiation. Refusal to be bound by, eg, a contract. It generally amounts to a breach of contract (qv), as where a party states that he will not carry out a promise (see *Heyman v Darwins Ltd* [1952] 1 All ER 337) or does some act which disables him from performing his promise (an implied repudiation). See *Tai Hing Cotton Mill Ltd v Kamsing Knitting Factory* [1979] AC 91—date for assessing damages for repudiation; *Photo Production Ltd v Securicor* [1980] AC 827.

repugnancy. Inconsistency of two or more provisions in a deed (qv) or other document. The inconsistent provisions may be struck out by the court when no other method is possible to make effective the principal intention of the parties to the document (the so-called "main purpose" rule). If the court cannot say which of two provisions ought to be rejected, then the general rule is that, in the case of a will (qv), the later one remains, but in the case of a deed (qv), the earlier remains: *Gwynn v Neath Canal Co* (1865) LR 3 Ex 209. See *Glynn v Margetson & Co* [1893] AC 351; *Suisse Atlantique v NV Rotterdamsche KC* [1967] 1 AC 361; and *Evans & Son v Andrea Merzario* [1976] 1 WLR 1078.

reputation. The estimation in which a person is generally held. Disparagement of reputation may constitute defamation (qv). For the admissibility of evidence of reputation in civil proceedings, see, eg, the Civil Evidence Act 1968, s. 9(3), (4). *See* CHARACTER, EVIDENCE AS TO.

reputed ownership. Doctrine whereby a bankrupt trader is deemed to be the reputed owner of goods which at the commencement of the bankruptcy were in his possession. See the B.A. 1914, ss. 37(c), 38, 38A (added by the C.C.A. 1974, s. 192, Sch 4, para 6); *Ex p Hattersley* (1878) 8 Ch D 601; *Crawcrow v Salter* (1881) 18 Ch D

30. *See* BANKRUPTCY.

requesting court. Court or tribunal making application to a UK court for assistance in obtaining evidence for civil proceedings in that court: Evidence (Proceedings in Other Jurisdictions) Act 1975, s. 1.

request, letter of. *See* LETTER OF REQUEST.

Requests, Court of. *See* COURT OF REQUESTS.

requisition. 1. Demand by a purchaser for the official search relating to title (qv). See the L.P.A. 1925, s. 45(1) (*b*); and *Ogilvy* v *Hope-Davis* [1976] 1 All ER 683. 2. Request for supplies. 3. Compulsory taking of property, eg, for military purposes.

res. A thing.

resale price maintenance. The imposition of conditions for the maintenance of minimum prices at which goods are to be resold. An agreement of this nature is generally void unless it can be shown, eg, that the prices are such that, without them, the quality or variety of goods would be substantially reduced to the detriment of the public or that goods would be sold under conditions likely to cause danger to health. See the Resale Prices Acts 1964 and 1976; *Re Chocolate and Sugar Confectionery Reference* [1967] 3 All ER 261.

resale price maintenance, collective, prohibition of. Collective agreements by suppliers (carrying on the business of selling goods by wholesale or retail) based on the withholding of, or refusal to supply goods, save, eg, on terms and conditions less favourable than those applicable in the case of others, which are unlawful under the Resale Prices Act 1976, Part I. Goods may be exempted by the Restrictive Practices Court (qv) under s. 14.

resale price maintenance, exempted goods relating to. Goods exempted from the provisions of the Resale Prices Act 1976, following a successful application under the 1976 Act, s. 14 to the Restrictive Practices Court (qv). Grounds for exemption are, eg, that the detriment to consumers would outweigh the detriment to them resulting from the maintenance of minimum resale prices, eg, where the number of establishments in which the goods are sold by retail would be substantially reduced: s. 14.

resale price maintenance, individual, prohibition of. Terms or conditions of a contract for the sale of goods by the supplier to the dealer or agreements between them relating to such a sale which are void if they provide for the charging of minimum prices on the resale of goods in the UK: Resale Prices Act 1976, s. 9.

resale, right of. Right of the seller, under the S.G.A. 1979, s. 48, to resell even though ownership has passed to the original buyer, if the goods are perishable or if he has given notice to the original buyer of his intention to resell and the original buyer does not make payment.

rescission. Remedy for inducing a contract by innocent or fraudulent misrepresentation (qv), whereby the contract is abrogated. A party intending to rescind must notify the other party. Right of rescission is lost: if *restitutio in integrum* (qv) is impossible; if the injured party takes a benefit under the contract with the knowledge of the misrepresentation; if a third party has acquired for value rights under the contract. See the Misrepresentation Act 1967; *Lagunas Nitrate Co* v *Lagunas Syndicate* [1899] 2 Ch 392; *Car and Universal Finance Co* v *Caldwell* [1965] 1 QB 525; and *Hyundai Industries* v *Papadopoulos* [1980] 1 WLR 1129. *See* CONTRACT.

rescous. The rescue of distrained goods before they have reached the pound (qv).

rescue cases. Cases in which the plaintiff is injured while intervening in a situation so as to save the life or property endangered by the defendant's negligence. Generally, if the plaintiff's intervention is reasonable in the circumstances, it does not constitute an assumption of risk, but if unreasonable, *volenti non fit injuria* (qv) applies. See *Cutler* v *United Dairies Ltd* [1933] 2 KB 297; *Baker* v *Hopkins Ltd* [1959] 1 WLR 966; *Videan* v *BTC* [1963] 2 QB 650; and *The Ogopago* [1971] 2 Lloyd's Rep 410.

resealed probate. *See* PROBATE, RESEALED.

reservation. 1. Generally, a limiting condition. 2. Action by a vendor of land, selling part of it and wishing to reserve easements (qv) and profits. See the L.P.A. 1925, s. 65.

reserve capital. Uncalled capital which cannot be called in except on a winding-up (qv). It cannot be turned into ordinary capital without the leave of the court. See the Cos.A. 1948, ss. 60, 64; and the Cos.A. 1967, s. 44. *See* COMPANY.

reserve forces. They comprise: the Army Reserve; the Territorial Army; the Air Force Reserve; the Royal Auxiliary Air Force; the Royal Naval Reserve: see the Reserve Forces Act 1980, s. 10(4). They may be called out if national danger is imminent or a great emergency has arisen: s. 10(1). See also the Reserve Forces Act 1982.

reserves, undistributable. Included are a company's share premium account, capital redemption reserve fund, accumulated unrealised profits less accumulated realised losses, other reserves which a company may not distribute: see the Cos.A. 1980, s. 40.

reserve, without. *See* WITHOUT RESERVE.

res extincta. Phrase referring to the subject matter of an agreement which is, in fact, non-existent. In such a case no contract ensues. See, eg, *Couturier* v *Hastie* (1856) 5 HL Cas 673; *McRae* v *Commonwealth Disposals Commission* (1951) 84 CLR 377.

res gestae. Things done; the events which happened. All the facts constituting, accompanying or explaining a fact in issue (the "transaction"). See *R* v *Christie* [1914] AC 545; *Teper* v *R* [1952] 2 All ER 447. "As regards statements made after the event, it must be for the judge, by a preliminary ruling, to satisfy himself that the statement was so clearly made in circumstances of spontaneity or involvement in the event that the possibility of concoction can be disregarded... And the same must in principle be true of statements made before the event... The expression *res*

gestae may conveniently sum up these criteria, but the reality of them must always be kept in mind": *Ratten* v *R* [1972] AC 378.

residence. Place where a person abides, ie, where he has his home. A "residence" in the sense of a "dwelling-house" can comprise several dwellings not physically joined: *Batey* v *Wakefield* [1982] 1 All ER 61. See also *Tandon* v *Trustees of Spurgeons Homes* [1982] 2 WLR 735. In the case of a corporation, the place where its management is carried on. See the Income and Corporation Taxes Act 1970, ss. 49–51; *Frost* v *Feltham* [1981] 1 WLR 452; and *Gubay* v *Kingston* [1983] 1 WLR 709. *See* ABODE; DOMICILE.

residence, habitual. *See* HABITUAL RESIDENCE.

residential homes. Term referring to houses for disabled, old persons and mentally disordered persons (not including hospitals, nursing or mental nursing homes). They must be registered. See the Residential Homes Act 1980.

residential occupier. A person occupying premises as a residence whether under a contract or by virtue of any enactment or rule of law giving him the right to remain in occupation or restricting the right of any other person to recover possession of the premises: Protection from Eviction Act 1977, s. 1(1).

residential premises, adverse occupation of. *See* ADVERSE OCCUPATION OF RESIDENTIAL PREMISES.

resident in UK. "Ordinarily resident" refers to a man's abode in a particular place which he has adopted voluntarily and for settled purposes as part of the regular order of his life for the time being, whether of short or long duration: *per* Lord Scarman in *Akbarali* v *Brent London BC* (*The Times,* 17.12.1982). "Residence" implies lawful presence: see *R* v *Secretary of State ex p Marguerite* [1982] 3 WLR 954. A person who is resident in the UK for a period or periods totalling 183 days in any year is regarded as a resident in the UK for that year for tax purposes: Income and Corporation Taxes Act 1970, s.

51. See *Levene* v *IRC* [1982] AC 217.

residuary devise. *See* DEVISE.

residuary devisee. The devisee who takes the real property which remains after specific gifts of real property under a will (qv) have been satisfied. *See* DEVISE.

residuary estate. Testator's property not specifically bequeathed or devised. See the A.E.A. 1925, s. 33.

residuary legacy. *See* LEGACY.

residue. That which remains of an estate after payment of debts, funeral expenses, testamentary expenses, legacies, annuities, costs of administration, etc.

resile. To withdraw from (eg, an agreement).

res integra. A whole, "unopened", thing. A question on which there is no rule and no decision has been taken in a court of law and which must be resolved upon principle.

res inter alios acta alteri nocere non debet. A transaction between strangers should not prejudice another party. A special rule of evidence. Example: an admission generally binds only the person making it. See *Halcombe* v *Hewson* (1810) 2 Camp 391; *Beswick* v *Beswick* [1968] AC 58.

res ipsa loquitur. The thing speaks for itself. A rule of evidence in actions for injury where the mere fact of an accident occurring raises the inference of the defendant's negligence, so that a prima facie case exists. "You may presume negligence from the mere fact that it happens": *Ballard* v *N British Rwy* (1923) SC 43. See *Byrne* v *Boadle* (1863) 2 H & C 722 (barrel falling from an upper floor); *Mahon* v *Osborne* [1933] 2 KB 14 (swab left in a patient's body); *Henderson* v *Henry Jenkins & Sons* [1970] AC 282 (corrosion in a brake pipe); *Lloyde* v *W Midlands Gas Board* [1971] 1 WLR 749 (disintegration of a household gas system); *Ward* v *Tesco Ltd* [1976] 1 WLR 810 (slipping on a supermarket floor).

résistance abusive. Term in French law referring to a head of damages which can be awarded in France where a defendant has unreasonably refused to pay a claim. Held to be registrable

under Part I of the Foreign Judgments (Reciprocal Enforcement) Act 1933: *SA Consortium General Textiles* v *Sun & Sand Agencies Ltd* [1978] 2 WLR 1.

resisting arrest. *See* ARREST, RESISTING.

res judicata. A final judicial decision pronounced by a competent judicial tribunal. "It is a very substantial doctrine, and it is one of the most fundamental doctrines of all courts that there must be an end to all litigation, and that the parties have no right of their own accord, having tried a question between them, and obtained a decision of a court, to start that litigation over again on precisely the same question": *per* Brett MR in *Re May* (1885) 28 Ch D 516.

res nova. That which is not yet decided.

res nullius. A thing belonging to no one.

resolution. A formal expression of opinion by an organised body, eg, as in a meeting or assembly. In the case of companies, resolutions may be ordinary; extraordinary; special (qqv). See the Cos.A. 1948, s. 141. *See* VOTING AT MEETINGS.

res perit domino. The loss falls on the owner. See the S.G.A. 1979, ss. 7, 20, 32; and *Krell* v *Henry* [1903] 2 KB 740.

respondeat superior. Let the principal answer. In general, a master is responsible for the acts of his servant committed in the course of employment. *See* MASTER AND SERVANT.

respondent. One against whom a petition is presented or an appeal is brought.

responsibility. 1. Care and consideration for the outcome of one's actions. 2. Legal liability, ie, accountability for some state of affairs to which one's conduct has contributed, together with an obligation to repair any injury caused.

responsibility, collective. *See* COLLECTIVE RESPONSIBILITY.

responsibility, ministerial. *See* MINISTERIAL RESPONSIBILITY.

res sua. One's own goods. Phrase used, eg, where a person makes a contract (qv) to purchase that which, in fact, belongs to him. The contract is void. See *Bingham* v *Bingham* (1748) 1 Ves Sen 126; *Bligh* v *Martin* [1968] 1 WLR 804.

restitutio in integrum. Restoration to the original position. Right to rescind a contract for misrepresentation is lost if *restitutio in integrum* is not possible. Rescission must put parties *in statu quo ante* and restore things "as between them to the position in which they stood before the contract was entered into": *Abram Steamship Co* v *Westville Shipping Co* [1923] AC 773. See *Doyle* v *Olby Ironmongers Ltd* [1969] 2 QB 158.

restitution. 1. Restoration to rightful owner. Under the Th.A. 1968, s. 28, the court may order anyone in possession or control of stolen goods to restore them to any person entitled to recover them from him. See also the C.J.A. 1972, s. 6. 2. The equitable doctrine of restitution refers to the case, eg, of an infant who, having fraudulently obtained goods, is ordered to restore his ill-gotten gains. See *Nelson* v *Stocker* (1859) 4 De G & J 458; *Avon CC* v *Howlett* [1981] IRLR 447. 3. Writ (qv) restoring to a defendant (qv), who has appealed successfully against a judgment, that which he had lost following the execution of that judgment.

restitution of conjugal rights. *See* CONJUGAL RIGHTS, RESTITUTION OF.

restoration condition. Phrase used in relation to planning permission, referring to restoration of a site after working of minerals, by the use of subsoil, topsoil and soil-making material: see the T.C.P. (Minerals) A. 1981, s. 5. *See* AFTER CARE CONDITION.

restraint of marriage. An attempt to prevent a person marrying, by a condition in a contract, is void as contrary to public policy if in general restraint, but not necessarily so if in partial restraint. A condition in restraint of a second marriage may be valid: *Allen* v *Jackson* (1875) 1 Ch 399.

restraint of trade. "Any contract which interferes with the free exercise of [a person's] trade or business, by restricting him in the work he may do for others, or the arrangements which he may make with others, is a con-

tract in restraint of trade. It is invalid unless it is reasonable as between the parties and not injurious to the public interest": *Petrofina* v *Martin* [1966] Ch 146. Question of reasonableness is for the court, not for the jury: *Dowden* v *Pook* [1904] 1 KB 48. See *Morris Ltd* v *Saxelby* [1916] 1 AC 588; *Luck* v *Davenport-Smith* (1977) 242 EG 455; *Greig and Others* v *Insole and Others* [1978] 1 WLR 302.

restraint on alienation. *See* ALIENATION, RESTRAINT ON.

restraint on anticipation. *See* ANTICIPATION. RESTRAINT ON.

restraints of princes. Phrase used in some insurance policies to indicate interference with or frustration of some commercial endeavour (in connection with, eg, transport of goods by sea) as the result of activities of rulers of a country. See, eg, *British & Foreign Marine Insurance Co* v *Sanday* [1916] AC 650; *Rickards* v *Forestal Land Co* [1942] AC 50.

restricted contract. Contract (qv) whereby one person grants to another in consideration of a rent which includes payment for the use of furniture or for services (qv), the right to occupy a dwelling as a residence: Rent Act 1977, s. 19(2). Registers of rents under restricted contracts are kept by local authorities under the 1977 Act, s. 79(1). See the H.A. 1980, s. 69.

restricted-use credit agreement. A regulated consumer credit agreement (qv) to finance a transaction between a debtor and creditor, whether forming part of that agreement or not, or to finance a transaction between the debtor and a person other than the creditor, or to refinance any existing indebtedness of the debtor's whether to the creditor or another person: C.C.A. 1974, s. 11(1).

restriction order. An order based on a hospital order (qv) subjecting the offender to special restrictions for a specified or unlimited time. See *R* v *Toland* (1974) 58 Cr App R 453; M.H.A. 1983, s. 41.

restrictive covenant. 1. A covenant by which use of the covenantor's land is restricted for the benefit of the covenantee's adjoining land. The burden of such a covenant may bind an assignee of the covenantor's tenement, ie, it may be considered as a covenant running with the land (qv). 2. Covenant restraining an employee from exercising his skills on the termination of his employment. See, eg, *Littlewoods* v *Harris* [1978] 1 All ER 1026. *See* COVENANT.

restrictive covenants, discharge and modification of. Powers for discharge and modification of restrictive covenants concerning land are contained in the L.P.A. 1925, s. 84 (as amended by the L.P.A. 1969, s. 28). Application is made to the Lands Tribunal (qv). "For an application to succeed on the ground of public interest is so important and immediate as to justify the serious interference with private rights and the sanctity of contract": *Re Collins' Applications* (1975) 30 P & CR 527. See also *Texaco Antilles Ltd* v *Kernochan* [1973] AC 609.

restrictive indorsement. *See* ENDORSEMENT.

Restrictive Practices Court. A superior court of record (qv) created by the Restrictive Trade Practices Act 1956, presided over by a High Court judge and consisting of judges of the High Court, Court of Session, Supreme Court of N Ireland and lay members. Cases are referred to it by the Director General of Fair Trading (qv) or parties to a restrictive agreement who have been ordered to give particulars to the court. Its task is to declare whether a restriction is contrary to public interest and, if so, to declare it void. A restriction is deemed contrary to public interest unless shown to be, eg, reasonably necessary to protect the public against injury or to counteract measures taken by some person not a party to the restrictive agreement, etc. See the Restrictive Trade Practices Acts 1956, 1968, 1976 and 1977; the European Communities Act 1972, s. 10; the Fair Trading Act 1973; Restrictive Practices Court Act 1976; the Resale Prices Act 1976; the Competition Act 1980, ss. 25–29; *Re Galvanised Tank Manufacturer's Association Agreement* [1965] 1 WLR 1074; *Re Net Book Agreement* [1972] 3 All ER 751.

restrictive trade practices. Practices which must be registered with the Director General of Fair Trading (qv), under the Restrictive Trade Practices Acts 1956, 1968, 1976 and 1977, based on certain agreements relating to goods (eg, prices to be recommended, terms of supply, process of manufacture) or services. Agreements important to the national economy may be excepted: 1976 Act, s. 29. See SI 1976/98; the Participation Agreements Act 1978; and *RICS* v *DG of Fair Trading* [1981] Com LR 112.

resulting trust. A trust (qv) which arises in circumstances where the beneficial interest comes back ("results") to the person or his representatives who transferred the property to the trustee (qv) or who provided the means of obtaining property. Example: X transfers funds to trustees to be held on the trusts of a marriage settlement; the marriage is later declared void *ab initio* (qv), so that the fund is held on a resulting trust for X. See the L.P.A. 1925, s. 60; *Re Ames' Settlement* [1946] Ch 217; *Savage* v *Dunningham* [1974] Ch 181; and *Universe Tankships, etc.* v *ITWF* [1982] 2 WLR 803.

resulting use. An equitable interest arising where feoffment (qv) was made without declaring a use in favour of the feoffee (qv). See the L.P.A. 1925, s. 60(3). *See* USE.

retainer, right of. Rights of a personal representative (qv) to retain debts due to him in preference to paying other creditors of the same degree. Abolished by the A.E.A. 1971, s. 10.

retirement of jury. Period, following the summing-up (qv), in which the jury considers its verdict. No further evidence can be called once the jury has retired. "A jury shall deliberate in complete freedom, uninfluenced by any promise, unintimidated by any threat": *R* v *McKenna and Busby* (1960) 44 Cr App R 63.

retirement of trustees. A trustee (qv) can retire only under express power or statutory power conferred by the Tr.A. 1925, s. 39, or by the consent of all the beneficiaries, or by order of the court. *See* TRUSTEESHIP, TERMINATION OF.

retiring age, normal. The earliest age at which an employee could be required to retire; it is a matter of evidence, not depending exclusively on a contract of employment, although that provides the best evidence as to the normal retiring age: *Post Office* v *Wallser* [1981] 1 All ER 668; *Waite* v *Govt. Communications HQ* (*The Times*, 23.7.1983).

retour sans protêt. Return without protest. Request by the drawer of a bill that if it is dishonoured it can be returned without protest (qv). *See* BILL OF EXCHANGE.

retrial. *See* TRIAL, NEW.

retributive justice. *See* JUSTICE, RETRIBUTIVE.

retrospective legislation. Known also as "retroactive legislation". Laws which, expressly or by implication, operate so as to affect acts done prior to their having been passed. See, eg, *Blyth* v *Blyth* [1966] AC 643; *Commissioners of Customs and Excise* v *Thorn Electrical Industries Ltd* [1975] 3 All ER 881; and *Zainal bin Hashim* v *Govt of Malaysia* [1980] AC 734. There is a presumption (qv) against the retrospective operation of a statute relating to substantive law (qv): *Re Athlumney* [1898] 2 QB 547.

return. 1. Formal statement or report, eg, annual return (qv) required under the Cos.A. 1948. 2. Election of a member to serve in Parliament (qv).

return day. *See* INTERLOCUTORY RELIEF, APPLICATION FOR.

returning officer. A person (eg, sheriff, mayor (qqv)) who is responsible for the conduct of a parliamentary election. See the L.G.A. 1972, s. 40; *Greenway-Stanley* v *Paterson* [1977] 2 All ER 663.

return order. Court order for the return of goods to a creditor, under the C.C.A. 1974, s. 133(1) (*b*) (i). It may be made, eg, in an action brought by a creditor under a hire-purchase agreement to recover possession of the goods to which the agreement relates.

revenue. Income; yield of taxes; return on investment.

revenue statutes. Statutes concerned with, eg, taxation. The general rule is that "the subject is not to be taxed except by plain words". Where clearly worded they must be applied no matter what their effect on persons, but "if [a provision] is capable of two alternative meanings, courts will prefer that meaning more favourable to the subject": *IRC* v *Ross and Coulter* [1948] 1 All ER 616.

reversal of judgment. The altering of a judgment on appeal. See O. 59.

reversion. Known also as "reverter". Where X, owner of fee simple in Blackacre, grants Blackacre to Y for life, X retains reversion, ie, an interest which remains in him, since Blackacre will revert to him on Y's death. X is known as the "reversioner". A "reversionary interest" is defined under the Finance Act 1975, s. 51(1), as "a future interest under a settlement, whether it is vested or contingent."

reversionary lease. A lease (qv) which is to become effective at some future time. Grant of such a lease is now void unless it takes effect within 21 years from the date of the instrument creating it: L.P.A. 1925, s. 149(3).

reverter, possibility of. Possibility of a grantor's having an estate at some future time. It was destroyed if the determining event could not occur. Example: land is given "to X and his heirs until Y marries", and Y dies unmarried. See Cmnd 8410 (1981).

revival of will. Where a testator (qv) has revoked his will and wishes later to restore it to effect, he may revive it by re-execution with appropriate formalities or by a subsequent codicil (qv) showing the intention to revive. The revived will takes effect as though written at the date of revival. See the W.A. 1837, ss. 22, 34. *See* WILL.

revocation. An act by which one annuls something he has done.

revocation of offer. An offer may be revoked at any time before acceptance; after acceptance it is irrevocable. Revocation does not take effect until actually communicated to the offeree. See *Dickinson* v *Dodds* (1876) 2

Ch D 463; *Byrne* v *Van Tienhoven* (1880) 5 CPD 349. See OFFER.

revocation of probate. Revocation of a grant by the court when, eg, one of the executors has become incapable of acting, or probate has been obtained by fraud, or the testator is found to be alive. See the S.C.A. 1981, s. 121. See *Re Shaw* [1905] P 92. *See* PROBATE.

revocation of will. A will can always be revoked by the testator before his death. Revocation may be effected by the destruction of the will, or by the execution of another will or codicil (qv), or as a result of marriage. See the W.A. 1837, ss. 18–20, (as amended by the A.J.A. 1982, s. 18). (For revival of revoked will, see the W.A. 1837, s. 22). *Animus revocandi* (qv) at the time of the destruction of the will is essential. See *Cheese* v *Lovejoy* (1887) 37 LT 295; *Gill* v *Gill* [1909] P 157. *See* WILL; MARRIAGE, WILL IN CONTEMPLATION OF.

rewards for return of goods. Where a public advertisement of a reward for the return of lost or stolen goods uses words to the effect that no questions will be asked or that the person producing the goods will be safe from apprehension, an offence is committed under the Th.A. 1968, s. 23.

rex non potest peccare. The King can do no wrong. See, however, the Crown Proceedings Act 1947.

rex nunquam moritur. The King never dies. (In effect, there can be no interregnum.)

Richard Roe. *See* ROE, RICHARD.

rider. 1. Clause added to a Bill, or agenda. 2. Statement, eg, a recommendation, appended to a jury's verdict.

right. 1. That to which a person has a just or lawful claim. 2. An interest which will be recognised and protected by a rule of law, respect for which is a legal duty, violation of which is a legal wrong: Salmond.

right *ex lege*. Right created directly by law without the consent of those bound consequently, eg, right stemming from the law of torts.

right of action. 1. The right to bring an action. 2. Chose in action (qv).

right of entry. Right of resuming possession of land by entering. Proviso for re-entry in a lease indicates that a lessor (qv) may re-enter on a breach of covenant by the lessor. Under the L.P.A. 1925, s. 146, right of re-entry is not enforceable unless and until notice is served on the lessee and reasonable time is afforded to him to remedy the breach. See the Landlord and Tenant Act 1927, s. 18(2); *Hemmings* v *Stoke Poges Golf Club* [1920] 1 KB 720. It is unlawful to enforce a right of re-entry except through court proceedings while the occupier is lawfully residing in the premises: Protection from Eviction Act 1977, s. 2.

right of resale. *See* RESALE, RIGHT OF.

right of retainer. *See* RETAINER, RIGHT OF.

right of support. The natural right to have one's soil supported by the soil of one's neighbour's land. The right to the support of buildings by adjoining buildings or land may be acquired as an easement (qv). See *Dalton* v *Angus & Co* (1881) 6 App Cas 740.

right of way. The right to pass over another's land. A public right of way can be created by statute or by dedication and acceptance. For "prescriptive right of way", see *Ironside and Crabb* v *Cooke and Barefoot* [1981] 41 P & CR 326. See the Wildlife and Countryside Act 1981, Part III; and *Holden* v *White* [1982] 2 WLR 1030. *See* DEDICATION OF WAY.

right, petition of. *See* PETITION OF RIGHT.

rights, antecedent. *See* ANTECEDENT RIGHTS.

rights issue. Issue of shares whereby existing shareholders are given a prior right to take some part of the new issue at a price below the market value of the shares. *See* SHARE.

rights, natural. *See* NATURAL RIGHTS.

rights offer. An offer of shares in a company made by "letter of rights" sent by the company to existing members in proportion to their existing holdings, eg, two for one.

rights, perfect and imperfect. *See* PERFECT AND IMPERFECT RIGHTS.

rights, vested. *See* VESTED RIGHTS.

right to begin. Generally belongs to

the party on whom the burden of proof (qv) rests. In criminal cases the prosecution begins. In civil cases the plaintiff (qv) begins where the onus of proving an issue is on him, and where he claims substantial and un-liquidated damages. Where the onus of proving all issues is on a defendant (qv) he may generally begin. See O. 35, r. 7; *Mercer* v *Whall* (1845) 5 QBD 447.

right, writ of. Formerly used to claim right to lands in fee simple held unjustly by one other than the true owner. Abolished in 1833.

riot. An offence involving the follow-ing elements: three or more persons; a common purpose and execution or inception of that purpose; an intent by the participants to help one another by force if necessary against any person who may oppose them in the execution of the common pur-pose; force or violence displayed in such a manner as to alarm at least one person of reasonable firmness and courage. See *Field* v *Metropolitan Police District Receiver* [1907] 2 KB 853; *R* v *Sharp and Johnson* [1957] 1 QB 552.

riotous assembly. Under the Riot Act 1714, repealed by the Statute Law Repeals Act 1973, Part V, if an un-lawful assembly of 12 or more per-sons refused to disperse within one hour after a justice of the peace (qv) had read a proclamation set out in the Act calling on them to disperse, they became guilty of a felony (qv) punishable with imprisonment for life. Force could be used to suppress such an assembly.

riparian. Relating to the bank of a river or stream. A riparian owner may, under common law, take and use water for ordinary purposes relat-ing to tenement if the water is restored unaltered in character and substantially undiminished in value. *See* WATER, ABSTRACTION OF.

risk, transfer of. Principle whereby, in performance of a contract for the sale of goods, risk generally passes with the property, unless the parties agree otherwise. See the S.G.A. 1979, ss. 20, 33; *Pignataro* v *Gilroy* [1919] 1 KB 459; *Demby Hamilton* v

Barden [1949] 1 All ER 435.

road. "Any highway or any other road to which the public has access, and includes bridges over which a road passes": Road Traffic Act 1972, s. 196(1).

road, Crown. *See* CROWN ROAD.

road, occupation. A road, the right to use which is confined to occupiers of land and premises which it serves. See the Highways Act 1980, s. 31(3) (*b*); and *Fitch* v *Rawling* (1795) 2 Hy Bl 393.

robbery. Offence committed by one who steals and immediately before or at the time of doing so, and in order to do so, uses force on any person or puts or seeks to put any person in fear of being then and there subjected to force: Th.A. 1968, s. 8(1). See *R* v *Dawson* (1978) Cr App R 170.

Roe, Richard. Name of a fictitious defendant (qv) used in an action of ejectment (qv).

rogatory letter. *See* LETTER OF REQUEST.

rogues and vagabonds. Persons who, under the Vagrancy Act 1824 as sub-sequently amended, are found in a building or an enclosed yard for any unlawful purpose, or telling fortunes by palmistry to deceive, etc. See now the Criminal Attempts Act 1981, s. 8.

rolled-up plea. Plea used in the def-ence of fair comment (qv) in an action for libel, which states that in so far as the words complained of consist of statements of fact, they are true in substance and in fact; in so far as they consist of expressions of opinion they are fair comment made in good faith and without malice relating to facts which are a matter of public interest. See *Lord* v *Sunday Telegraph* [1971] 1 QB 235. See now O. 82, r. 3(2).

Romalpa clause. Stipulation in a contract of sale that the property in goods shall not leave the seller until he has received full payment. See *Aluminium Industrie Vaassen BV* v *Romalpa Ltd* [1976] 2 All ER 552 (remedy of tracing (qv) allowed); *Borden Ltd* v *Scottish Timber Products Ltd* [1979] 3 All ER 961; and *Re Bond Worth* [1980] Ch 228.

root of title. Document which des-cribes land to be sold so that it can be identified, which relates to the whole legal and equitable interest and which contains nothing to cast doubt on the title. See *Re Duce* [1937] Ch 642; and *Wimpey Ltd* v *Sohn* [1967] Ch 487. *See* TITLE.

rout. Offence committed when an unlawful assembly (qv) makes some move towards execution of its common purpose, eg, begins to march towards premises it intends to attack.

Royal Assent. This transforms a Bill into an Act of Parliament (qv) and takes the following forms: for ordinary bills, *la reyne (le roi) le veult* (the Queen (King) desires this...); for private bills, *soit fait comme il est désiré* (let it be done as it is wished...); for money bills, *la reyne remercie ses bons sujets, accepte leur benevolence, et ainsi le veult* (the Queen thanks her subjects, accepts their kindness and agrees that it be done...). Refusal of the Assent (last exercised by Queen Anne in 1707) takes the form: *la reine s'avisera* (the Queen will advise...).

Royal prerogative. *See* PREROGATIVE, ROYAL.

royalties. Share of a product or profit paid to the owner of property from which it arises. Refers, in particular, to payments to an author by a publisher, usually based on a (fixed) percentage of the selling-price.

Royal title. *See* QUEEN, THE.

Royal warrant. Authority issued to one who acts as a supplier of goods or services to a member of the Royal Family. See Trade Descriptions Act 1968, s. 2, which makes false representations as to Royal approval an offence.

R.S.C. Rules of the Supreme Court (qv).

rule. A regulation, principle, direction.

rule, main purpose. *See* REPUGNANCY.

rule of law. *See* LAW, RULE OF.

rules of court. Rules made by the authority having for the time being power to make rules or orders regulating the practice and procedure of a court: I.A. 1978, Sch 1.

Rules of the Supreme Court. Rules relating to practice and procedure in the Supreme Court made under the S.C.A. 1981, s. 84, by a Rule Committee, consisting of the Lord Chancellor, Lord Chief Justice, Master of the Rolls, President of the Family Division, Vice-Chancellor, judges, barristers and solicitors (qqv). The rules are set out in the White Book. Usually cited by Order and Rule, eg, ''O. 43, r. 1.'' See R.S.C. 1965.

run away. It is an offence knowingly to assist, induce or persistently attempt to induce a child in care to run away: Child Care Act 1980, s. 13.

running account credit. *See* CREDIT.

running days. Phrase referring to a charterparty (qv) in which days run consecutively, as contrasted with ''working days'' (which exclude Sundays and public holidays).

running with the land. *See* COVENANT RUNNING WITH THE LAND.

S

s. Abbreviation for a "section" (qv) of an Act, as in, eg, the Law of Property Act 1925, s. 1.

sabotage. Malicious destruction of or damage to property, so as to injure, eg, a business or the military potential of the state. "The saboteur just as much as the spy in the ordinary sense is contemplated as an offender under the Official Secrets Act": *Chandler* v *DPP* [1964] AC 763.

sacrilege. An offence consisting of breaking and entering and committing a felony in, or entering, committing a felony in and then breaking out of, any place of divine worship: Larceny Act 1916, s. 24 (repealed by the Th.A. 1968). See now the Th.A. 1968, s. 9.

safety at work. Under the H.S.W.A. 1974, a general duty is placed on an employer to ensure the health and safety and welfare at work of his employees: s. 2.

safety committee. Every employer must, if requested by safety representatives (qv), establish a safety committee in the place of work: H.S.W.A. 1974.

safety of goods. Under the Consumer Safety Act 1978, regulations may be issued concerning the composition, packing, marking of goods, designed to reduce the risk of death or personal injury. Items covered by such regulations include oil heaters, nightdresses, fireguards and electric blankets.

safety representatives. Appointed under the H.S.W.A. 1974 in factories, etc, to promote co-operation in achieving and maintaining safe working conditions.

salary. A fixed remuneration paid regularly for services performed.

sale. 1. The act of selling. 2. A contract for the sale of goods whereby the seller transfers or agrees to transfer the property in goods to the buyer for a money consideration called the price: S.G.A. 1979, s. 1(1). It includes "bargain and sale" as well as "sale and delivery": s. 6(1).

sale, bill of. *See* BILL OF SALE.

sale by the court. Sale of property following an order of the court, as in an action to enforce a mortgage.

sale of goods. *See* SALE.

sale or return. *See* APPROVAL, SALE ON.

sale, power of. *See* POWER OF SALE.

sale under voidable title. *See* VOIDABLE TITLE, SALE UNDER.

salus populi est suprema lex. The welfare of the people is the paramount law.

salvage. A reward to persons who save, or assist in saving, a ship, cargo or freight from shipwreck or similar jeopardy: *Wells* v *Owners of Whitton* [1897] AC 344. The amount payable is usually assessed by the court and is apportioned between owners, crew, officers and master of the salving vessel. It must be shown that any services rendered were voluntary, skilled and beneficial.

salvage of trust property. In a case of absolute necessity the court is able to sanction the mortgage or sale of part of an infant's beneficial interest for the benefit of property retained: *Re Jackson* (1882) 21 Ch D 786. *See* TRUST.

salvor. One who saves goods from a vessel in distress. *See* SALVAGE.

sample. Specimen presented for examination as evidence of the composition or quality of the whole. "The office of a sample is to present to the eye the real meaning and intention of the parties . . . The sample speaks for itself": *per* Lord Macnaghten in *Drummond* v *Van Ingen* (1887) 12 App Cas 297.

sample, sale by. Under the S.G.A. 1979, s. 15(2), it is implied in a contract of sale (qv) that the bulk shall correspond with the sample, that the buyer shall have a reasonable opportunity of comparing bulk and sample and that goods shall be free from any defect rendering them unmerchantable which would not be apparent on reasonable examination of sample.

See also the C.C.A. 1974, Sch 4. See, eg, *Ruben Ltd* v *Faire Bros & Co Ltd* [1949] 1 KB 254.

sanction. 1. A solemn agreement. 2. That which authorises or confirms. 3. Measure used to punish some action. 4. Measure adopted by nations to coerce into an acceptable course of action a state offending against international law.

sanctuary, right of. Right, formerly available to an accused person, to seek refuge in a consecrated place. Largely abolished in 1623, and finally in 1723.

sanity, presumption of. *See* PRESUMPTION OF SANITY.

sans frais. Without the incurring of expense.

sans nombre. Without number, as in, eg, common of pasture (qv) involving an unlimited number of cattle.

sans recours. Without recourse [to me]. Phrase used on a bill of exchange so that the endorser (eg, the agent endorsing for the principal) is not personally liable. See the B.Ex.A. 1882, s. 16. *See* BILL OF EXCHANGE.

satisfaction. 1. Extinguishing of a claim, eg, by performance. 2. Equitable doctrine, ie, "the donation of a thing with the intention that it is to be taken either wholly or in part in extinguishment of some prior claim of the donee": *Lord Chichester* v *Coventry* (1867) 36 LJ Ch 673. The general rule regarding satisfaction of debts by legacies (qv) is "if one, being indebted to another in a sum of money, does by his will give him a sum of money as great as, or greater than, the debt, without taking any notice at all of the debt, this shall, nevertheless, be in satisfaction of the debt, so that he shall not have both the debt and the legacy": *Talbot* v *Duke of Shrewsbury* (1714) Prec Ch 394.

satisfied term. A term of years (qv) created for a purpose which is now fulfilled. See the L.P.A. 1925, s. 5.

savings bank. A society formed in the UK for the purpose of accepting deposits of money, accumulating the produce of the deposits at compound interest and returning the deposits and produce to the depositors after deducting necessary expenses of

management but without deriving any benefit from the deposits or produce: Trustee Savings Bank Act 1981, s. 1(3).

scandalous statement. Matter of an abusive or irrelevant nature introduced in pleadings (qv) and affidavits (qv) which can be struck out. See O. 18, r. 19(1) (*b*); O. 41, r. 6.

scandalum magnatum. Slander of magnates. Offence, abolished under the Statute Law Revision Act 1888, committed by a person who published scandalous statements resulting in discord between the King and his subjects.

schedule. 1. A formal list. 2. An appendix to a Bill or Act. In the case of a contradiction between a schedule and a clause, the earlier enacted of the two prevails: *A.-G.* v *Lamplough* (1873) 3 Ex D 214. See *Buchanan & Co.* v *Babco Ltd* [1978] AC 141.

scheme. 1. A scheme of arrangement is an agreement between a debtor and creditors allowing the debts to be paid under that agreement, rather than his being adjudged bankrupt. 2. An arrangement for the administration of a charitable trust (qv), eg, so that it may be applied *cy-près* (qv). Whether it is ordered is in the discretion of the court: *Re Hanbey's Will Trusts* [1954] Ch 264.

scienter **rule.** *Sciens* = knowing. Common law ruling that an animal must be kept securely by its owner from causing damage where he knows or is presumed to know of its mischievous disposition. See the Animals Act 1971, s. 2(2); *May* v *Burdett* (1846) 9 QB 101; *Nichols* v *Marsland* (1875) LR 10 Ex 255; *Baker* v *Snell* [1908] 2 KB 825.

scilicet. Abbreviated to scil., or sc. That is to say.

scintilla juris. A spark, or trace, of a right.

scire facias. That you cause him to know. Title or writ (qv), abolished in 1947, requiring a person to show a cause why someone should not have "advantage of the record".

scire feci. I have caused to be warned. Return by a sheriff (qv) to a writ of *scire facias* (qv).

scrip. A certificate or memorandum of

shares held in a company. Generally a negotiable instrument (qv).

scrip issue. Bonus shares (qv) issue.

scrutiny. An enquiry into the votes (eg, number, validity) cast in an election.

scutage. *Scutagium* = shield money. A money payment, introduced *c.* 1166, levied, in commutation of providing the King's army with soldiers, on all tenants-in-chief, who collected it, in turn, from sub-tenants. Obsolete by the fourteenth century.

scuttling. 1. The cutting of holes through a ship so as to salvage cargo. 2. The sinking of a ship, eg, for the purpose of recovering insurance money. See *Probatina Shipping Co* v *Sun Insurance Office* [1974] QB 635.

seal. Wax impressed and attached to a document so as to authenticate it. See, eg, the Cos.A. 1948, s. 35(1).

seal, company's. *See* COMPANY'S COMMON SEAL.

seal, contract under. *See* CONTRACT UNDER SEAL.

sealing. Process essential to a deed (qv) based on signifying assent. "To constitute a sealing neither wax nor wafer nor a piece of paper, not even an impression is necessary": *Re Sandilands* (1871) LR 6 CP 411. The seal may be in the form of the word "seal" printed in a circle on the document. See *Re Balkis Consolidated Ltd* (1888) 36 WR 392; *First National Securities Ltd* v *Jones* [1978] Ch 109. See LOCUS SIGILLI.

search and seizure cases. Cases in which police entering premises under a search warrant may seize goods which afford some evidence of a criminal offence even though those goods are not of the description specified in that warrant. See *Chic Fashions* v *Jones* [1968] 1 All ER 229; *Ghani* v *Jones* [1970] 1 QB 698.

search before Crown Court. Where the Crown Court (qv) imposes a fine on a person or forfeits his recognisance (qv) or makes an order under the A.J.A. 1970, Sch 9, paras 3, 4 or 9 (as amended), the Crown Court may order him to be searched and money found on him may be applied towards payment of the fine or other sum payable by him, and any bal-

ance shall be returned to him: P.C.C.A. 1973, s. 34A(1) (2), inserted under the C.L.A. 1977, s. 49.

searches. Investigations made, eg, at the Land Charges Registry to check the existence of registrable encumbrances (qv).

search, power of. Power to seek out, procure and preserve real evidence for the prosecution. There is no statutory power given to private individuals to search persons or property. Statutory power is given to, eg, police officers, Department of Trade officials, customs officers. See, eg, the Customs and Excise Management Act 1979, ss.163, 164; the S.O.A. 1956, s. 42; the Firearms Act 1968, s. 47; the Th.A. 1968, s. 26; and the Criminal Damage Act 1971, s. 6. The police may search private premises without a warrant when, eg, they are given permission by the occupiers to do so, or in order to make an arrest or if in possession of a search authority issued by a senior police officer who believes that, eg, an offence under the Official Secrets Act 1911 is about to be or has been committed, or who wishes to look for evidence relating to terrorism where, under the Prevention of Terrorism Act 1976, immediate action is necessary in the state's interest. *See* ARREST, SEARCH UPON.

search upon arrest. *See* ARREST, SEARCH UPON.

search warrant. Warrant (qv) issued by magistrates, eg, for the search of premises for stolen goods, or drugs or firearms. See, eg, the Th.A. 1968, s. 26; and the Misuse of Drugs Act 1971, s. 23. There is no power vested in the police to search any person who is not under arrest, with the exception of search for firearms, drugs, stolen property, etc. See *Frank Truman Export* v *Metropolitan Police Commissioner* [1977] QB 952; *R* v *Adams* [1980] QB 575; and *McLorie* v *Oxford* [1982] 3 WLR 423.

seas, beyond the. *See* BEYOND THE SEAS.

sea, the. "Includes any area submerged at mean high water springs, and also includes, so far as the tide flows at mean high water springs, an estuary or an arm of the sea and the waters of any channel, creek, bay or river": Offshore Petroleum Development (Scotland) Act 1975, s. 20(2).

seaworthy. In the context of the Hague Rules (qv), means that the ship, with her master and crew, is fit to encounter the perils of the voyage and fit to carry her cargo safely on that voyage: *Actis Co* v *Stanko Steamship Co* [1982] 1 WLR 119.

seck rent. Dry rent (qv).

secondary action. Phrase used in the Employment Act 1980, s. 17, to refer to action in relation to a trade dispute (qv) involving the inducing of a breach of contract of employment with an employer who is not a party to the dispute. Tort immunities under the T.U.L.R.A. 1974, s. 13, do not apply where a commercial contract is interfered with by remote secondary action: 1980 Act, s. 17(1). See *Hadmor Productions* v *Hamilton* [1981] 2 All ER 724; and *Marina Shipping* v *Laughton* [1982] QB 1127. *See* PICKETING, PEACEFUL.

secondary party. One, other than the principal offender, who participates in the commission of a crime. *See* AID OR ABET.

secondary use. Shifting use (qv).

second marriage. Refers in the O.P.A. 1861, s. 57, to the second marriage charged in the indictment: *R* v *Taylor* [1950] 2 KB 368. *See* BIGAMY.

second mortgage. *See* MORTGAGE, SECOND.

Secretary of State. Member of the government in charge of a department. Appointed by the Crown and usually assisted by Parliamentary Under-Secretaries of State. See the I.A. 1978, Sch 1.

secret profits. Profits made by an agent acting in that capacity and not accounted for to his principal. See *Hippisley* v *Knee Bros* [1905] 1 KB 1; *Boardman* v *Phipps* [1967] 2 AC 46. *See* AGENT.

secret reserves. Reserves not disclosed in the balance sheet or accounts. See the Cos.A. 1948, Sch 8.

secret session. A sitting of the House of Lords or Commons, usually in time of war, from which all non-members are excluded.

secret trust. A trust which exists where

a will (qv) or other instrument discloses neither the existence of the trust nor its terms. Example: X bequeaths a legacy to Y and, during his (X's) lifetime Y promises that he will hold the subject-matter of the legacy on trust for Z. See *Moss* v *Cooper* (1861) 4 LT 790; *Re Stead* [1900] 1 Ch 237; *Blackwell* v *Blackwell* [1929] AC 318; *Re Snowden* [1979] Ch 528. *See* TRUST.

sections of an Act. Distinct, numbered sub-divisions of an Act of Parliament. "Every section of an Act takes effect as a substantive enactment without introductory words": I.A. 1978, s. 1 (applying to Acts passed after the commencement of the 1978 Act and to existing Acts passed after 1850).

secundum legem. According to law.

secured creditor. *See* CREDITOR.

secure tenant. *See* TENANT, SECURE.

securities. 1. Things deposited or pledged to ensure the fulfilling of an obligation. 2. Written evidence of ownership, eg, certificates. 3. Under the C.C.A. 1974, s. 189(1), in relation to an actual or prospective consumer credit or hire agreement, a security is a mortgage, charge, pledge, bond, debenture, indemnity, guarantee, bill, note or other right provided by the debtor or hirer to secure the carrying out of obligations under the agreement. Under the Aircraft and Shipbuilding Industries Act 1977, s. 56(1), for example, it means, in relation to a company, "any shares, debentures, debenture stock, loan stock, income notes, income stock, funding certificates and securities of a like nature".

securities, authorised. *See* AUTHORISED SECURITIES.

securities, listed. *See* LISTED SECURITIES.

security of tenure. *See* TENURE, SECURITY OF.

secus. Otherwise.

se defendendo. In self-defence (qv).

sedition. The publication, orally or in writing, of words intended "to bring into hatred or contempt, or to excite disaffection against the person of Her Majesty, her heirs, or successors, or the government and constitution of the UK . . . or either House of Parliament . . . or to raise discontent or disaffection amongst Her Majesty's subjects, or to promote feelings of ill-will and hostility between different classes of such subjects": *R* v *Burns* (1886) 16 Cox CC 335. See Law Commission Working Paper No 72, 1977.

seditious libel. Sedition (qv) in the form of printed words.

sed quaere. But question; enquire further.

seduction. Persuasion to disobedience, desertion or other disloyalty. The common-law action for the seduction of a wife was abolished in 1857. The right of action by a parent for the seduction of a child on the grounds of deprivation of services was abolished by the Law Reform (Misc. Provs.) Act 1970, s. 5. It is an offence under the Incitement to Disaffection Act 1934 to endeavour to seduce a member of the Forces from his duty and allegiance to the Crown. *See* PER QUOD CONSORTIUM ET SERVITIUM AMISIT.

seignory. Powers, rights, authority of a feudal lord.

seised. Feudal term referring to one possessed of a freehold (qv). *See* SEISIN.

seisin. *Saisir* = to seize. Feudal concept based on the physical occupation of land, so that an estate in freehold involved a right to seisin. Proof of seisin was required in actions for recovery of land. Abeyance of seisin was forbidden. *Seisin in law*: seisin possessed by an heir whose ancestor had died seised of the land. *Seisin in deed*: actual possession of the freehold.

seisin, abeyance of. Interruption of the tenancy of a freehold. Forbidden under early law, so that every transfer of land had to be open and necessitated public delivery of seisin.

seisina facit stipitem. Seisin makes the stock of descent. Prior to the Inheritance Act 1833, title by descent was to be traced, under this doctrine, from the person who had died last seised. *See* SEISIN.

seisin, livery of. *See* LIVERY OF SEISIN.

seisin, unity of. Situation whereby a person seised of land subject to an easement (qv) becomes seised of the land to which the easement is attached.

select committee. *See* COMMITTEE, SELECT.

self-build society. "A housing association whose object is to provide, for sale to, or occupation by, its members, dwellings built or improved principally with the use of its members' own labour": H.A. 1974, s. 12. *See* HOUSING ASSOCIATION.

self-defence. Acting so as to defend oneself, one's property or, possibly, some other person such as a parent, child, spouse, against violence or a reasonable apprehension of it. It may be an answer to a charge of, eg, homicide (qv) where no more force is used than is necessary and there is an honest belief based on reasonable grounds that force is necessary. It is not the law that the accused should have retreated as far as possible before the attack: *R* v *McInnes* [1971] 3 All ER 295. See the C.L.A. 1967, s. 3; the Animals Act 1971, s. (3); *Kenlin* v *Gardiner* [1967] 2 QB 510; *R* v *Duffy* [1967] 1 QB 63; and *R* v *Shannon* (1980) 71 Cr App R 192.

self-employed. An individual who works for gain or reward, otherwise than under a contract of employment, whether or not he himself employs others: H.S.W.A. 1974, s. 53(1). "A person who is gainfully employed in Great Britain otherwise than in employed earner's employment": S.S.A. 1975, s. 2(1) (*b*). See *Young & Woods Ltd* v *West* [1980] IRLR 201; and *Warner Holidays Ltd* v *Secretary of State for Social Services* [1983] ICR 440.

self-executing treaty. *See* TREATY, SELF-EXECUTING.

self-help. An extra-judicial remedy whereby, eg, in the case of trespass to land the person in possession may eject the trespasser using such force as is reasonable in the circumstances. See *Perry* v *Fitzhowe* (1846) 8 QB 757; *Hemmings* v *Stoke Poges Golf Club* [1920] 1 KB 720.

self-incrimination. The giving by a person of evidence or replies to questions, the result of which might lead that person to be prosecuted. "When giving evidence, an accused person shall not be asked, and if asked shall not be required to answer, any question tending to show that he has committed or been convicted of or been charged with any offence other than that wherewith he is then charged, or is of bad character'', unless, eg, he has given evidence against some other person charged with the same offence: Criminal Evidence Act 1898, s. 1(f) (as amended by the Criminal Evidence Act 1979). See, eg, *Khan* v *Khan* [1982] 1 WLR 513.

seller. Under the S.G.A. 1979, s. 61(1), one who sells or agrees to sell goods. It may include a person who is in the position of a seller, eg, as agent (qv).

seller, unpaid. *See* UNPAID SELLER.

semble. It seems. Word used to suggest that a particular point may be doubtful.

Senate of the Inns of Court and the Bar. Body formed in July 1974 to act as the governing body of the Bar (qv), consisting of 90 members (including the Attorney-General, Solicitor-General, Chairman of the Council of Legal Education, 24 Bench representatives, 12 Hall representatives, 39 Bar representatives and 12 additional persons). It regulates the admission of students and of the call to the Bar. It controls the policy of the Council of Legal Education.

sender. ''In relation to a letter or other communication, means the person whose communication it is'': British Telecommunications Act 1981, s. 66(5).

sentence. Punishment or penalty imposed on a person found guilty by the court. (It does not include committal in default of payment: M.C.A. 1980, s. 150(1).) Generally, save in case of murder or other offences for which penalty is fixed by law, the court has the discretion to select a sentence which it considers suitable in all the circumstances, eg, the nature and gravity of offence, background and needs of the offender. Principles applied in sentencing were said, in *R* v *Sergeant* (1974) SJ 753, to be retribution, deterrence, prevention and rehabilitation. See the comments of Hilbery J on sentencing, in *R* v *Blake* (1961) 45 Cr App R 292.

sentence, deferring of. *See* DEFERMENT OF SENTENCE.

sentence, procedure on. The accused is asked if he has anything to say before sentence and pleas in mitigation are heard. Antecedents of the accused (character, etc) are given. The accused may be remanded for a medical or social enquiry report before sentence. He may ask for other offences to be taken into consideration. Sentence is then given orally by the trial judge.

separate estate. Property given to a married woman for her personal and separate use, which she could charge or dispose of without her husband's consent. The doctrine was abolished under the Law Reform (Married Women and Tortfeasors) Act 1935, s. 2.

separate trials. *See* JOINDER OF OFFENDERS.

separation as ground for divorce. There is evidence that a marriage has broken down irretrievably if: the parties to the marriage have lived apart for a continuous period of at least two years immediately preceding the presentation of the petition and the respondent consents to the granting of a decree; the parties have lived apart for a continuous period of at least five years immediately preceding the presentation of the petition. See the Mat.C.A. 1973, s. 1. *See* BREAKDOWN OF MARRIAGE; DIVORCE.

separation, consensual. Consent to separation (qv). May be express (eg, separation agreement) or implied (eg, judicial separation). See *Joseph* v *Joseph* [1953] 1 WLR 1182.

separation, judicial. *See* JUDICIAL SEPARATION.

separation of powers. The division of functions of government—legislative, executive, judicial—between independent, separate institutions (see Montesquieu's *L'Esprit des Lois* (1748)). ''It cannot be too strongly emphasised that the British Constitution, though largely unwritten, is firmly based on the separation of powers'': *per* Lord Diplock in *Dupont Steels* v *Sirs* [1980] 1 All ER 529. See *Hinds* v *R* [1977] AC 195.

sequestration. Writ issued, eg, where a person fails to perform an act or disobeys an injunction (qv), commanding persons ("sequestrators") to enter upon and take possession of his estate and keep it under sequestration (ie, separated from the owner) until the judgment is complied with. See O. 45, r. 5.

serf. An unfree person whose service was attached to the soil and who could be sold with it.

seriatim. In order; serially.

serjeants-at-law. Formerly senior advocates, who had a monopoly of audience at the Court of Common Pleas (qv) and from whom judges were chosen. The Order of the Coif (to which they belonged) died out after the abolition of the monopoly by the J.A. 1873, s. 8.

serjeanty. *See* GRAND SERJEANTY.

servant. One whose work is under the control of another. "Any person employed by another to do work for him on the terms that he, the servant, is to be subject to the control and direction of his employer in respect of the manner in which his work is to be done" (Salmond, approved in *Hewitt* v *Bonvin* [1940] 1 KB 188). Implied duties are: to attend the place of work; to obey lawful orders; to conduct oneself properly; to exercise due care and skill; to observe good faith. See *Mersey Docks & Harbour Board* v *Coggins and Griffiths* (*Liverpool*) *Ltd* [1947] AC 1; *Ready Mixed Concrete Ltd* v *Ministry of Pensions* [1968] 2 QB 497. *See* INDEPENDENT CONTRACTOR.

servant, Crown. *See* CROWN SERVANT.

servant's duty of care. *See* CARE, SERVANT'S CONTRACTUAL DUTY OF.

service. 1. Duty owed by a tenant to his lord, or servant to his master. 2. Delivery of a writ or summons by personal service or service on the defendant's solicitor. Service more than 12 months from date of issue is irregular: O. 6, r. 8(1). See O. 10; O. 11; O. 65. *See* SUBSTITUTED SERVICE.

service, acknowledgment of. Procedure, replacing the entry of an appearance, introduced in 1979 (see S.I. 1979/1716). The defendant must acknowledge service of writ within 14 days of service and must indicate whether he intends to contest proceedings, giving "notice of intention

to defend": O. 12, r. 3. If he fails to return the acknowledgment within the prescribed time, or returns it without giving notice of intention to defend, the plaintiff can enter judgment immediately: O. 13.

service by post. *See* POST, SERVICE BY.

service charge. *See* LANDLORD, PROVISION OF SERVICES BY.

service, contract of. *See* CONTRACT OF SERVICE.

service, endorsement of. *See* ENDORSEMENT OF SERVICE.

service out of the jurisdiction. *See* JURISDICTION, SERVICE OUT OF THE.

services, loss of. *See* PER QUOD CONSORTIUM.

services provided by landlord. *See* LANDLORD, PROVISION OF SERVICES BY.

service, supply of a, contract for. "A contract under which a person agrees to carry out a service": Supply of Goods and Services Act 1982, s. 12(1). A contract of apprenticeship is excluded: s. 12(2). For implied terms concerning care and skill, see ss. 13–16.

servient tenement. Land over which a right *in alieno solo* is exercisable. *See* DOMINANT TENEMENT; EASEMENT.

servitudes. Rights over another's property, ie, easements (qv) and *profits à prendre* (qv).

sessions. Sittings of Parliament or the courts, eg, petty sessions (known also as "sessions of the peace").

set of bills. *See* BILLS IN A SET.

set-off. Pleading by way of defence to the whole or part of the plaintiff's claim. The defendant (qv) acknowledges the plaintiff's demand but sets up one which counterbalances it. Amount to be set off must have been due at the time of the issue of the writ: *Richards* v *James* (1848) 2 Exch 471. Nothing which is not a money claim may be set off. See O. 18, r. 17; *British Anzani Ltd* v *International Marine Management Ltd* [1980] QB 137.

setting aside. Cancelling; making void. Motion to the Court of Appeal (qv) to set aside a High Court judgment may be made by a party who alleges, eg, that the judgment is wrong. See also O. 13, r. 9, by which a judgment in default of acknowledgment may be set aside on such terms as the court thinks just.

setting down of action. Delivery to "the proper officer" (eg, head clerk at the Crown Office or District Registrar) of a request that an action be set down for trial in that place stated in order for trial. An action in the QBD (qv) is set down in the jury list, non-jury list, short-cause list, revenue list or commercial list. See O. 34.

settled. 1. With reference to an account, this means adjusted or paid. 2. With reference to a dispute, it means adjusted or ended.

settled account. *See* ACCOUNT, SETTLED.

settled land. Land which is the subject of a settlement (qv): S.L.A. 1925, s. 2.

Settled Land Act trustees. Those persons competent under the S.L.A. 1925, s. 30, to act as trustees of the settlement, ie, persons who under the settlement are trustees with the power of sale of the settled land; persons declared by settlement to be trustees; persons who under the settlement are trustees with the power of sale of any other land comprised in the settlement subject to the same limitations as the land being dealt with; persons who under the settlement are trustees with a future power of sale; persons appointed by deed by beneficiaries (who must be of full age and entitled to dispose of the entire settled estate).

settlement. 1. Limitation of property for persons usually by way of succession, eg, "to X for life, remainder to Y in fee simple". For the purposes of the S.L.A. 1925, a settlement is created when land stands: limited in trust for any persons by way of succession; limited in trust for any person in possession (eg, for a base or determinable fee (qv)); limited in trust for any person for an estate in fee simple for a term of years absolute (qv) contingently on the happening of an event; charged for the benefit of persons. 2. The documents used to create a settlement.

settlement, accumulation and maintenance. *See* ACCUMULATION AND MAINTENANCE SETTLEMENT.

settlement, compound. *See* COMPOUND SETTLEMENT.

settlement of action. Process whereby

parties to an action come to terms voluntarily. Settlement may be made without the court's consent by notice of withdrawal before trial. Settlement of an action on behalf of a patient (qv) or infant (qv) requires the court's approval: O. 80, r. 11. See *Green* v *Rozen* [1955] 1 WLR 741.

settlements, *ad hoc*. Under the S.L.A. 1925, s. 21, the owner of land can execute a vesting deed (qv) stating that the legal estate is vested in him on trust to give effect to those equitable interests affecting the estate. The deed must be executed by two or more trustees appointed by the court, or by a trust corporation (qv).

settlements, referential. Settlements (qv) which incorporate earlier settlements by reference: S.L.A. 1925, s. 32.

settlor. One who makes a settlement of his property.

several. Separate (in contrast to "joint").

several fishery. *See* FISHERY.

several tenancy. The separate holding of lands by a tenant (as contrasted with, eg, joint tenancy (qv)).

severalty. Separate and exclusive possession. Property is said to belong to X, Y and Z in severalty when the share of each is sole and exclusive (as contrasted with concurrent or joint ownership (qv)).

severance. 1. The conversion of a joint tenancy (qv) into a tenancy in common, eg, by alienation, contract to sever, acquisition of another interest in the land. See the L.P.A. 1925, s. 36(2). 2. Retention of the good points of a contract and rejection of the bad (eg, as in a partly-illegal contract). The promises must be separate and independent. See *Goldsoll* v *Goldman* [1915] 1 Ch 292; *Attwood* v *Lamont* [1920] 3 KB 571; *Bull* v *Pitney-Bowes Ltd* [1967] 1 WLR 273; and *Trigg* v *Staines UDC* [1969] 1 Ch 10. *See* BLUE PENCIL TEST.

severance pay. Payment to an employee whose contract of employment is terminated or whose contract of service has been cut short.

severance, words of. Words in a grant (qv) which served to show that tenants were to take a distinct share in the property, eg, "in equal shares", or "to be divided between", or "equally", or "respectively".

sex, change of. ". . . The biological sexual constitution of an individual is fixed at birth (at the latest) and cannot be changed, either by medical or surgical means . . . The only cases where the term 'change of sex' is appropriate are those in which a mistake as to sex is made at birth and subsequently revealed by further medical examination": *Corbett* v *Corbett* (*orse Ashley*) [1970] 2 All ER 33. See *White* v *British Sugar Corporation* [1977] IRLR 121; the Mat.C.A. 1973, s. 11(*c*); and *R* v *Tan* [1983] 2 All ER 12.

sex discrimination. *See* DISCRIMINATION, SEX.

sex establishments. Sex cinemas (ie, premises used to a significant degree for the exhibition of moving pictures concerned principally with the portrayal of, or intended to stimulate, sexual activity) and sex shops (ie, premises used to a significant degree for the selling or hiring of sex articles): see the Local Government (Misc. Provs.) Act 1982, Sch 3, paras 3, 4. For the licensing requirements, see para 6.

sexual immorality, contract for. An agreement to bring about, eg, illicit intercourse: *Benyon* v *Nettlefield* (1850) 3 Mac & G 94. Generally it will be void, even if under seal. See *Nye* v *Moseley* (1826) 6 B & C 133; *Ayerst* v *Jenkins* (1873) LR 16 Eq 275.

sexual intercourse, proof of. "Intercourse shall be deemed complete upon proof of penetration only": S.O.A. 1956, s. 44. Proof of rupture of the hymen is not necessary. See *R* v *Russen* (1777) 1 East PC 438; *R* v *Lines* (1844) 1 C & K 393.

sexual intercourse, unlawful. Illicit intercourse. As used in the S.O.A. 1956 it may mean extra-marital intercourse: *R* v *Chapman* [1958] 3 All ER 143. Unlawful intercourse within marriage may be such as creates grounds for separation or divorce (qv): *R* v *Clarence* (1888) 22 QBD 23. For the principles of sentencing in cases of unlawful sexual intercourse with under-age girls, see *R* v *Taylor and*

Others [1977] 1 WLR 612.

sexual offences. *See* OFFENCES, SEXUAL.

sham marriage. Known also as "marriage of convenience". Ceremony of marriage intended primarily to achieve some motive such as avoidance of a country's immigration regulations. See, eg, *Silver* v *Silver* [1955] 2 All ER 614; *R* v *Immigration Appeal Tribunal ex p Ullah* (*The Times*, 14.1.1983)—such marriages were held to be "not conducive to the public good".

sham plea. *See* FALSE PLEA.

share. "The interest of a shareholder in the company measured by a sum of money for the purpose of liability in the first place and of dividend in the second, but also consisting of a series of mutual covenants entered into by all the shareholders *inter se* in accordance with [the Companies Act]. The contract contained in the Articles of Association is one of the original incidents of the share": *Borland's Trustee* v *Steel Bros & Co Ltd* [1901] 1 Ch 279. A portion of the capital of a company giving shareholders the right to receive, in general, a proportion of the company's profits. Shares are classed as personal estate: Cos.A. 1948, s. 73. *See* COMPANY; SHARE, TYPES OF.

share capital. The total amount which a company's shareholders have contributed or are liable to contribute as payment for their shares. References on a company's stationery to its "share capital" must be to its paid-up share capital: European Communities Act 1972, s. 9(7).

share capital, equity. The issued share capital of a company, excluding any part which, neither as respects dividend nor as respects capital, carries any right to participate beyond a specified amount in a distribution: Cos.A. 1948, s. 154(5).

share certificate. *See* CERTIFICATE OF SHARES.

share certificate, exemption from obligation to prepare. Under the Stock Exchange (Completion of Bargains) Act 1976, s. 1, a company of which shares or debentures are allotted or debenture stock is allotted to a stock exchange nominee need not complete a certificate in pursuance of the Cos.A. 1948, s. 80(1).

share hawking. Also "share pushing". The personal offering of shares from house to house. Prohibited under the Prevention of Fraud (Investments) Act 1958.

shareholder. One who owns shares as a member of a company (qv).

shareholders, protection of. The Cos.A. 1980, s. 75 (superseding the Cos.A. 1948, s. 210) allows a member of a company to petition the court for an order on the ground of the company's affairs being, or having been, conducted in a way unfairly prejudicial to the interests of some part of the membership, including himself, or that an actual or proposed act of the company is or would be unfairly prejudicial.

share premium account. An account to which is transferred sums received from the issue of shares at a premium. The amount of the account appears in the balance sheet as part of the paid-up capital. See the Cos.A. 1948, s. 56.

shares, acquisition by a company of its own. A company may, subject to the Cos.A. 1981, ss. 46–52, purchase its own shares, but not if, as a result of that purchase, there would no longer be any member of the company holding shares other than redeemable shares.

shares at a discount. See DISCOUNT, SHARES AT A.

shares at a premium. See PREMIUM, SHARES AT A.

shares, bearer. See BEARER SHARES.

shares, forfeiture of. See FORFEITURE OF SHARES.

shares, lien on. A lien or other charge of a public company (qv) on its own shares (whether taken expressly or otherwise) is generally void: Cos.A. 1980, s. 38(1). For the permitted charges, see s. 38(2).

shares, payment for. Shares allotted by a company may be paid for in money or money's worth (eg, knowhow, goodwill (qqv)): Cos.A. 1980, s. 20(1). For the limitations applicable to a public company (qv), see the Cos.A. 1948, s. 47(2); and the Cos.A. 1980, ss. 20(2), 29.

shares, placing of. 1. Allocation of shares by a company to an issuing house which agrees to purchase and place them with clients. 2. "Stock Exchange placing" is the lodging of shares with jobbers so that they may be made available to brokers.

shares, surrender of. See SURRENDER OF SHARES.

shares, transfer of. See TRANSFER OF SHARES.

shares, transmission of. See TRANSMISSION OF SHARES.

share transfer. Document which must be prepared and furnished to a company when its shares are transferred, eg, a stock transfer form, a brokers' transfer form. See, eg, the Stock Transfer Act 1963. See TRANSFER OF SHARES.

share, types of. Generally: ordinary (qv); preference (qv); deferred (qv).

share warrant. See WARRANT, SHARE.

sheriff. Originally the "shire-reeve". He exercised civil and criminal jurisdiction as a judge of the sheriff's county court and sheriff's tourn. Today, he is the Crown's appointee and chief officer in the county. He is in charge of, eg, parliamentary elections, levying of forfeiture recognisances, and the execution of process issuing from criminal courts and the High Court (qv). See the L.G.A. 1972, s. 219.

sheriff's interpleader. See INTERPLEADER SUMMONS.

shifting use. A use which cut short a preceding interest. Example: "To X and his heirs to the use of Y and his heirs, but to the use of Z and his heirs as soon as Z shall become a doctor of medicine." See the L.P.A. 1925, ss. 1, 39; and the S.L.A. 1925, s. 1 (ii). See USE.

ship. Any type of vessel used in navigation, propelled otherwise than by oars: Merchant Shipping Act 1894, s. 742. Any vessel used for the carriage of goods by sea: Carriage of Goods by Sea Act 1924. For "British ship", see the Customs and Excise Management Act 1979, s. 1(1).

shipwreck. See WRECK.

shock, nervous. See NERVOUS SHOCK.

shop. Premises of which the sole and principal use is the carrying on there of retail trade or business; a building occupied by a wholesaler where goods are kept for sale, or part of a building so occupied; a building to which members of the public are invited to resort to deliver goods for repair or other treatment, or part of a building so used: Offices, Shops and Railway Premises Act 1963, s. 1(3) (*a*). See also the Shops Act 1950, s. 4 (as amended); *Thanet DC* v *Ninedrive* [1978] 1 All ER 703.

shop-lifting. Stealing goods from a shop. See the Th.A. 1968, ss. 1, 7. For circumstances under which custodial sentences are appropriate, see *R* v *Anderson* [1972] Crim LR 792. See *R* v *Leadley* (1976) 64 Cr App R 118; and *Davies* v *Leighton* (1978) 68 Cr App R 4. *See* THEFT.

shop steward. Elected, or appointed, union officer who represents members at a place of work. See the T.U.L.R.A. 1974, s. 30(1).

shore. That ground between the ordinary high-water and low-water mark: Hale.

short cause list. List in the QBD of cases to be tried without jury and which are unlikely to last more than four hours because the defence is relatively simple and short. See O. 14, r. 6; and *Practice Direction* [1981] 1 WLR 1296, para 5.

short committal. *See* COMMITTAL FOR TRIAL.

shorthold tenancy. *See* PROTECTED SHORTHOLD TENANCY.

short title. *See* TITLE, SHORT.

S.I. Statutory instrument (qv).

sic. So; thus. Used so as to indicate that a word or statement is intended as written, in spite of an obvious error or absurdity.

sick pay, statutory. Scheme instituted by the S.S. and Housing Benefits Act 1982 under which an employer becomes liable to pay to employees sick pay in a stipulated amount for the first eight weeks of a period of interruption of employment by reason of incapacity.

sic utere tuo ut alienum non laedas. So use your own property as not to interfere with that of your neighbour. But, "a balance has to be maintained between the right of the occupier to do

what he likes with his own, and the right of his neighbour not to be interferred with": *Sedleigh-Denfield* v *O'Callaghan* [1940] AC 880.

side by side rule. Rule, stated in *Sheers* v *Thimbleby & Sons* (1897) 76 LT 709, allowing documents signed by a defendant to be "read together" when placed side by side. See *Burgess* v *Cox* [1951] Ch 383, but note *Timmins* v *Moreland Street Property Co* [1958] Ch 110. *See* JOINDER OF DOCUMENTS.

side notes. Marginal notes (qv).

sight, payable at. In effect, a bill payable on demand. See the B.Ex.A. 1882, s. 10. *See* BILL OF EXCHANGE.

signature. 1. A person's name written in his own hand. 2. Sign or other mark impressed on a document.

signature of will. Under the W.A. 1837, s. 9 (as substituted by the A.J.A. 1982, s. 17), a will must be signed by the testator (or some person in his presence and at his direction) so that it appears that the testator intended by that signature to give effect to the will. The signature need not be written, so that a seal with the testator's initials affixed to the will has been held to suffice: *In b Emerson* (1882) 9 LR IR 443. See also *In b Finn* (1936) 105 LJP 36; *In b Chalcraft* [1948] P 222; *Re Harris* [1952] P 319; *Re Beadle* [1974] 1 All ER 493; *Law Reform Committee Report* 1980 (Cmnd 7902); and the A.J.A. 1982, ss. 17 *et seq.* (making new provisions for wills generally).

signing judgment. *See* JUDGMENT, ENTERING.

sign manual. The Sovereign's signature affixed to a document.

silence in relation to contract. Silence is not generally deemed consent: *Felthouse* v *Bindley* (1862) 11 CB NS 869. Mere silence is not generally misrepresentation, save in cases where it distorts a representation, or there is a fiduciary relationship between parties, or where contracts are *uberrimae fidei* (qv). See *Lindenau* v *Desborough* (1828) 8 B & C 586; *Dimmock* v *Hallett* (1866) 2 Ch App 21. *See* CONTRACT.

silence, right of accused to. "Undoubtedly when persons are speaking on even terms, and a charge is made, and the person charged says nothing, and expresses no indignation, and does nothing to repel the charge, that is some evidence to show that he admits the charge to be true": *R v Mitchell* (1892) 17 Cox CC 503. Generally, a person commits no offence by refusing to answer questions put by one attempting to discover by whom an offence has been committed (but see, for exceptions, the Official Secrets Act 1972, s. 162). Under the Criminal Evidence Act 1898, s. 1(*b*) the prosecution must not comment on an accused person's failure to testify. See *Hall* v *The Queen* [1971] 1 WLR 298; *Parkes* v *The Queen* [1976] 3 All ER 380. *See* INCRIMINATE.

silk, to take. *See* QUEEN'S COUNSEL.

similar facts evidence. *See* EVIDENCE, SIMILAR FACTS.

similiter. In like manner.

simony. See *Acts* viii:18. Purchase or sale of a church office. See the Simony Act 1913, repealed under the Statute Law (Repeals) Act 1971, Part II.

simple contract. Referred to also as "parol contract". Contract not under seal, and which requires consideration (qv) for its enforcement. May be oral or written. *See* CONTRACT.

simple trust. Bare trust (qv).

simplex commendatio non obligat. A mere recommendation [of goods by a seller] does not impose a liability upon him. See, eg, *Scott* v *Hanson* (1829) 1 Russ & M 128.

simpliciter. Absolutely; without qualification; simply.

sine die. Without day, ie, indefinitely.

sine qua non. Without which not. An indispensable condition.

single woman. Generally, an unmarried woman. See, however, the extended meaning given in the Affiliation Proceedings Act 1957, s. 1 (see also *Whitton* v *Garner* [1965] 1 All ER 70, in which the Divisional Court upheld the finding that the complainant was a single woman, within the 1959 Act, although married and living in the same household as her husband). "It seems to me that a woman whose husband has deserted her or cast her off can say to him, with as much force as she can say it to anyone else, that he has reduced her

to living as a single woman": *per* Devlin J in *Kruhlak* v *Kruhlak* [1958] 2 QB 32.

sit-in. Occupation of premises as an act of protest. Normally trespassory. See *Warwick University* v *De Graaf* [1975] 1 WLR 1126. See also the C.L.A. 1977, s. 9.

sittings. Periods during which the Supreme Court sits: Hilary; Easter; Trinity; Michaelmas. See O. 64, r. 1. *See* VACATIONS.

sittings of magistrates' courts. *See* MAGISTRATES' COURTS, SITTINGS OF.

slander. Words (or gestures) which amount to the tort of defamation (qv). Words are defined by the Defamation Act 1952 to include pictures, visual images, broadcasting. It may be actionable *per se*, ie, without proof of damage, in the case of, eg, imputation of a crime, unfitness, incompetence. See *Hellwig* v *Mitchell* [1910] 1 KB 609; *Jones* v *Jones* [1916] 2 AC 481.

slander of goods. Tort (qv) resulting from false and malicious comment on merchandise sold. See the Defamation Act 1952, s. 3(1); *White* v *Mellin* [1895] AC 154.

slander of title. Tort (qv) resulting from attacking a person's title to property. See the Defamation Act 1952, s. 3; *Riding* v *Smith* (1876) 1 Ex D 91.

slavery. Condition of unfree persons who have no rights and who are in the ownership of their masters. See *Sommersett's Case* (1772) 20 St Tr 1. "No one shall be held in slavery or servitude; slavery and the slave trade shall be prohibited in all their forms": Universal Declaration of Human Rights 1948, art. 4.

sleeping partner. *See* DORMANT PARTNER.

slip rule. Rule whereby a clerical error in an order or judgment, or an error based on an omission or accidental slip, may be corrected by the court on application by a motion or summons without appeal. See the L.R.R. 1925, r. 249; O. 20, r. 11; *Ainsworth* v *Wilding* [1896] 1 Ch 673. The rule has no application to a mistake of the court "of its own in law or otherwise". See O. 20.

small agreements. Term used under

the C.C.A. 1974, s. 17(1) to refer to agreements where the credit limit or payments under the agreement do not exceed (currently) £30 and are not regulated by the Act and do not constitute a hire purchase or conditional sale agreement (qv).

small claims. Claims usually involving consumers and based on £500 or less (or some other statutorily-fixed amount), heard by county courts under a simple and informal arbitration procedure. See the County Court Rules 1981, O. 19, rr. 1–6.

smuggling. Illegal export or import of merchandise, eg, without payment of duties. See the Customs and Excise Management Act 1979, s. 50.

socage tenure. *Soc* = ploughshare. A residual tenure, ie, one which was neither military, spiritual nor servile. The name was derived from socmen, who sought the protection of a lord in return for fealty. The Tenures Abolition Act 1660 transformed almost all tenures into free and common socage.

social inquiry report. Report based on the procedure under the P.C.C.A. 1973, s. 45, whereby the court takes into account any information relevant to a person's character, physical and mental condition, before sentencing him (if he has not previously served a prison sentence). See also the C.J.A. 1982, ss. 2, 62.

social policy rule. Interpretation of an Act (qv) by considering the social policy which gave rise to it. The courts do not generally favour the rule and it has been described as "a naked usurpation of the legislative function under the guise of interpretation": *Magor and St Mellors RDC v Newport Corporation* [1952] AC 189.

social security. Scheme, originally provided for under the National Insurance Acts, operating under the S.S.A. 1975. See also the S.S.A. 1979, 1980, 1981 and the S.S. and Housing Benefits Act 1982.

social security, categories of contributors. Classes of insured persons required to make contributions are: Class 1—earnings related contributions paid by employed earners, employers and others; Class 2—flat rate contributions payable weekly by self-employed earners; Class 3—contributions paid voluntarily by non-earners and some non-employed; Class 4—contributions payable in respect of profits, gains of a trade, profession or vocation, or in respect of equivalent earnings. See the Social Security (Contributions) Regulations 1979; the S.S.A. 1975; the S.S. (Contributions) A. 1982; and the S.S. and Housing Benefits Act 1982.

Social Security Tribunals. Originally called National Insurance Tribunals, they are the bodies which function under the S.S.A. 1975–1981. Local tribunals, each comprising a chairman and two panel members, hear appeals relating to, eg, disablement benefit claims. Appeal lies to the Social Security Commissioner (from whom appeal lies to the Court of Appeal). See the S.S.A. 1980, s. 14; and O. 59, r. 21.

societas leonina. Leonine partnership. One in which a partner is liable for losses, but has no right to share in profits. Agreements to this end are usually void.

society, friendly. *See* FRIENDLY SOCIETY.

sodomy. Buggery (qv). See *Genesis* xiii:13.

soit baillé aux seigneurs. Let it be handed to the Lords. Message used when a Bill (qv) is sent to the Lords from the Commons. When sent from the Lords to the Commons, it reads: *"Soit baillé aux communs".*

soit fait comme il est désiré. Let it be as it is desired. Form of Royal Assent (qv).

solatium. An additional allowance awarded for, eg, injured feelings.

soldier's will. *See* PRIVILEGED WILL.

sole. Unmarried; single; separate.

sole, corporation. *See* CORPORATION.

solemn form. *See* PROBATE.

solicit. To importune (qv).

solicitor. A solicitor of the Supreme Court. One who may conduct legal proceedings or give advice on legal problems, having passed the examinations of the Law Society and possessing a certificate, which is in force, authorising him to practise. He may be liable for any loss resulting from his breach of duty or negligence: *Marsh v Joseph* [1897] 1 Ch 213. He has a duty of care to his client and an obligation to preserve confidence relating to communications with clients: *Minter* v *Priest* [1930] AC 558. See the Solicitors Act 1974; *Ross* v *Caunters* [1980] Ch 297.

solicitor, access in police station to. Right of person under interrogation in a police station, apparently given by the *Judges' Rules* (qv). "... Every person at any stage of an investigation should be able to communicate and consult privately with a solicitor. This is so even if he is in custody, provided that in such a case no unreasonable delay or hindrance is caused to the process of investigation or the administration of justice by his doing so": *Preamble, Principle (c)*. "A person in custody should be allowed to speak on the telephone to his solicitor or to his friends": Administrative Directions, 7(a). See *R* v *Allen* [1977] Crim LR 163; *R* v *Lemsatef* [1977] 2 All ER 835; *R* v *King* [1980] Crim LR 40.

solicitor and own client basis of costs. Basis of taxation of costs (qv) applicable between a party to an action and his solicitor. All costs incurred with the express or implied approval of the client are presumed to have been reasonably incurred. See O. 62, r. 29.

Solicitor-General. a law officer of the Crown, subordinate to the Attorney-General. He is usually a member of the House of Commons (qv) and holds office at the pleasure of the Crown.

Solicitors Disciplinary Tribunal. Formerly the Solicitors Disciplinary Committee. Composed of practising solicitors of not less than 10 years' standing and lay members appointed by the Master of the Rolls (qv) to hear and determine complaints. The Tribunal may strike the name of a solicitor off the roll and restore to the roll the name of one formerly struck off. Appeal lies to the Master of the Rolls or High Court. See the Solicitors Act 1974, ss. 46–54.

solicitors, duty. *See* DUTY SOLICITORS.

solicitor's lien. Method by which a solicitor may protect his right to recover his costs from a client by: passive or retaining lien (ie, holding papers, deeds and other personal chattels); common law lien on personal property of the client preserved or recovered by his efforts in litigation; statutory lien enforceable by charging order under the Solicitors Act 1974, s. 73. *See* LIEN.

solicitor, sole. A solicitor who is the sole principal of a practice: Solicitors Act 1974, s. 87(1).

Solicitors Practice Rules. Rules made by the Council of the Law Society under the Solicitors Act 1974. The Council has power to waive in writing any of the provisions of the Rules.

solitary confinement. Imprisonment during which a prisoner is not allowed to communicate with any other prisoner. See the Prison Act 1952, s. 14; the Prison Rules 1964, r. 43; and *Williams* v *Home Office (No. 2)* [1981] 1 All ER 1211.

solus agreement. *Solus* = alone. Agreement whereby a retailer binds himself to buy a product from one source only. Example: garage proprietor agreeing to buy all his petrol from one oil company. See *Petrofina* v *Martin* [1966] Ch 146; *Esso Petroleum Co Ltd* v *Harper's Garage Ltd* [1968] AC 269; *Lobb Garages* v *Total Oil* [1983] 1 All ER 944. For the effect of the Treaty of Rome 1957, art. 85 on this type of agreement see *Brasserie* v *de Haecht SA (No. 1)* v *Wilkin* [1968] CMLR 26. *See* RESTRAINT OF TRADE.

solvent. Able to pay all debts or claims.

solvitur ambulando. It is proved as one goes along. The problem may be resolved by action.

somnambulism. A state in which actions are performed by a person who is, in fact, asleep. "Can anyone doubt that a man, who, though he might be perfectly sane, committed what would otherwise be a crime in a state of somnambulism, would be entitled to be acquitted? And why is this? Simply because he would not know what he was doing": *R* v *Tolson* (1889) 23 QBD 187.

Sovereign. The supreme ruler of the state, eg, King, Queen. "If a determinate human superior, not in a habit of obedience to a like superior, receive habitual obedience from the bulk of a given society, that determinate superior is sovereign in that society, and the society (including the superior) is a society political and independent'': Austin. See the I.A. 1978, s. 10. *See* MONARCHY.

sovereign authority. ''The person (or body) to whose directions the law attributes legal force, the person in whom resides as of right the ultimate power either of laying down general rules or of issuing isolated rules or commands whose authority is that of the law itself'': Bryce.

sovereignty. 1. Political and legal concept relating to ultimate authority in a state. 2. Freedom of a state from external control.

sovereignty of Parliament. Doctrine stating that Parliament is the supreme power in the state and possessed, therefore, of unlimited legal power. *See* PARLIAMENT.

space law. Binding rules accepted by some nations, relating to activities in outer space. See, eg, the Outer Space Treaty 1966.

Speaker of the House of Commons. Presiding officer of the Commons, elected by members of the House. He neither speaks nor votes save in an official capacity and is the channel through which the House communicates with the Crown. *See* PARLIAMENT.

Speaker of the House of Lords. The Lord Chancellor. *See* CHANCELLOR.

special acceptance. Acceptance of a bill of exchange (qv) as payable at a special place.

special administration. Limited administration (qv).

special agent. *See* AGENT, SPECIAL.

special business. Business of a company ''that is transacted at an extraordinary general meeting, with the exception of declaring a dividend, the consideration of accounts, and the reports of the directors and auditors, the election of the directors in the place of those retiring and the appointment of, and the fixing of the remuneration of, the auditors'': Cos.A. 1948, Table A, art. 52. *See* COMPANY.

special case. Procedure whereby parties to an action, after the issue of a summons, agree on a statement of facts for submission to the court for an opinion on the law relating to those facts. See O. 33, r. 3; the M.C.A. 1980, s. 111 (relating to the ''case stated'' procedure); *Duncan v Lambeth BC* [1968] 1 QB 747; and *Tilling v Whiteman* [1980] AC 1.

special damages. *See* GENERAL AND SPECIAL DAMAGES.

special defence. A defence which was peculiar to one type of action and which had to be specifically pleaded. Example: defences of fair comment, justification, in an action for defamation (qv).

special hospital. Institution which receives dangerous, violent or criminal persons requiring special security, eg, Broadmoor (qv), Rampton. See *R v Macfarlane* (1975) 60 Cr App R 320.

specialia generalibus derogant. Special words derogate from general words.

special jurisdiction, courts of. *See* COURTS OF SPECIAL JURISDICTION.

special jury. *See* JURY, SPECIAL.

special occupant. *See* GENERAL OCCUPANT.

special plea. Plea in bar, eg, plea of former acquittal. *See* AUTREFOIS ACQUIT.

special procedure orders. Orders usually relating to public authorities' operations, eg, acquisition of land, based on publication and parliamentary scrutiny and examination by the Select Committee on Statutory Instruments. See the Statutory Orders (Special Procedures) Act 1945, amended in 1965.

special resolution. One passed by a majority of not less than three-quarters of those members who are entitled to, and do, vote in person, or where proxies are allowed, by proxy, at a general meeting of which at least 21 days' notice has been given: Cos.A. 1948, s. 141(2). Necessary, eg, for altering the name, objects or articles of a company. See the Cos.A. 1980, ss. 5, 7, 10, 18. *See* COMPANY.

specialty. A contract under seal (''specialty contract'').

special verdict. 1. A verdict in which it is accepted that certain facts have been proved, but which leaves the court to apply the law to those facts. Such verdicts ought to be found only in very exceptional circumstances. See *R* v *Dudley and Stephens* (1884) 14 QBD 273; *R* v *Bourne* (1952) 36 Cr App R 125. 2. Verdict of "not guilty by reason of insanity" (qv) under the Criminal Procedure (Insanity) Act 1964—in fact, a form of acquittal. See *R* v *Sullivan* [1983] 2 WLR 392.

species, endangered. *See* ENDANGERED SPECIES.

specificatio. The making of a new article from the chattel of one person by the work of another.

specification. Form of information (relating to details of construction, operation, etc) required in the application for a patent (qv). See the Patents Act 1977.

specific delivery, writ of. *See* DELIVERY, WRIT OF.

specific devise. *See* DEVISE.

specific goods. *See* GOODS.

specific legacy. *See* LEGACY.

specific performance. Equitable, discretionary remedy *in personam* whereby a party to an agreement is ordered by the court to perform his obligations according to the terms of that agreement. Granted only where the appropriate remedy at law is inadequate, and will not be granted if the court has no jurisdiction to grant it: *Rushton* v *Smith* [1975] 2 All ER 905. Does not apply to contracts made for no consideration, or involving continuous supervision, or for personal services, etc. See the S.G.A. 1979, s. 52; the S.C.A. 1981, ss. 49, 50; O. 86; *Flint* v *Brandon* (1803) 8 Ves 159; *Lumley* v *Wagner* (1852) 1 De G M & G 604; *Marks* v *Lilley* [1959] 2 All ER 647; *Biggin* v *Minton* [1977] 2 All ER 647.

spent convictions. Convictions which, under the Rehabilitation of Offenders Act 1974, need not be disclosed, after a rehabilitation period (qv), and which are not proper grounds for dismissal from office, profession, occupation or employment: s. 4. No one should refer in open court to a spent conviction without the judge's authority, which authority should not be given unless the interests of justice so require: *Practice Direction* [1975] 1 WLR 1065; Rehabilitation of Offenders Act 1974 (Exceptions) Order 1975 (S.I. 1975/1023); Banking Act 1979, s. 53. See *Reynolds* v *Phoenix Assurance Co* [1978] 1 Lloyd's Rep 633; *R* v *Smallman* [1982] Crim LR 175; and *Property Guards* v *Taylor and Kershaw* [1982] IRLR 175.

spes successionis. Hope or expectation of succeeding to property, ie, as next of kin. It is not a title to property. See *Re Simpson* [1904] 1 Ch 1.

split orders for custody. *See* CUSTODY, SPLIT ORDERS FOR.

spouse. Husband or wife.

spouses, communications between. In a criminal case neither husband nor wife is generally compellable to disclose communications made between them during the marriage. See the Criminal Evidence Act 1898, s. 1(*d*); *Shenton* v *Tyler* [1939] Ch 620; *Rumping* v *DPP* [1964] AC 814. For the abolition of certain privileges in civil cases see the Civil Evidence Act 1968, s. 16.

spouses, questions relating to intercourse between. *See* INTERCOURSE, QUESTIONS TO SPOUSES RELATING TO.

springing use. A use intended to come into existence *in futuro*. Example: "to X and his heirs to the use of Y when he shall marry". *See* USE.

spying. Secretly obtaining information for purposes hostile to the security of the state. See the Official Secrets Act 1911, s. 1(1).

squatter. One who is wrongfully in occupation of land and claiming the right or title to it. See O. 113; *McPhail* v *Persons, Names Unknown* [1973] 3 All ER 393; *R* v *Wandsworth County Court* [1975] 3 All ER 390; *Swordheath Properties Ltd* v *Floydd* [1978] 1 All ER 721. *See* ADVERSE OCCUPATION OF RESIDENTIAL PREMISES.

squatter's title. Title acquired by one who has wrongfully occupied land without payment of rent. See *Scott* v *Scott* (1854) 4 HLC 1065; *Nisbet and Potts' Contract* [1906] 1 Ch 386.

S.R. & O. Statutory rules and orders. *See* STATUTORY INSTRUMENTS.

stag. Speculator who subscribes to an issue of shares with no intention of keeping those allotted to him, but in the hope that he can sell out at a profit. See *R* v *Greenstein* [1975] 1 WLR 1353 (process of "stagging").

stake. Sum of money risked for gain or loss on the outcome of some event attended by uncertainty.

stakeholder. One with whom a sum is deposited pending deciding of a wager.

stakeholder's interpleader. *See* INTER-PLEADER SUMMONS.

stale. Ineffective, usually because of lapse of time. *See* LACHES.

stale cheque. *See* CHEQUE, STALE.

stamp duties. Taxes on certain types of instruments (rather than on the transactions represented), eg, conveyances, first imposed by the Stamp Act 1765 (now repealed). The stamps may be *ad valorem*, ie, proportionate to the value of the property on which the instrument is based, or fixed in amount. See the Finance Act 1981, Part VI.

standard form contracts. Contracts (1) which set out terms on which mercantile transactions of common occurrence are to be carried out, eg, charterparties; (2) which are exemplified by the "ticket cases" of the nineteenth century (see, eg, *Parker* v *SE Rail Co* (1877) 2 CPD 416), the terms of which were not the subject of negotiations between the parties to them: *Schroeder Music Publishing Co* v *Macaulay* [1974] 1 WLR 1308.

standards of proof. In *civil cases*, generally proof on a preponderance of probabilities. See, eg, *Hornal* v *Neuberger Products Ltd* [1957] 1 QB 247. In *criminal cases*, where the burden of proof rests on the prosecution, proof beyond reasonable doubt (qv), but where the burden of proof is on the defence (see, eg, *R* v *Podala* [1960] 1 QB 325) it is proof on a preponderance of probabilities. In *matrimonial cases*, it is, apparently, proof on a preponderance of probabilities (see *Blyth* v *Blyth* [1966] 1 All ER 524). *See* PROOF; BALANCE OF PROBABILITIES.

standing by. Reference to the principle that where a person who knows what is happening is content to "stand by and see others fighting his battle", he ought to be bound by the result and should not be allowed to reopen the case. See *Wytcherley* v *Andrews* (1871) 2 P & D 327; *Nana Ofori Atta II* v *Nana Abu Bonsra II* [1958] AC 95.

standing civilian courts. Courts established under the Armed Forces Act 1976, s. 6, for the trial outside the UK of civilians to whom Part II of the Army Act 1955 or Part II of the Air Force Act 1955 is applied by s. 209 of either Act. Trial is before a magistrate, appointed from assistants to the Judge Advocate-General, and assessors selected from a panel: s. 6(4)–(15). See the 1976 Act, Sch 3; and the C.J.A. 1982, Sch 8.

standing committees. Committees appointed at the beginning of each parliamentary session by the Committee of Selection of the House of Commons (qv) to deal with public Bills at committee stage, or in the second reading and report stages. Each consists of at least 20 members.

standing mute. *See* MUTE.

standing orders. Orders formulated by a body, eg, the House of Commons (qv), for the conduct in formal manner of its proceedings.

stannaries. Districts in Cornwall and Devon in which tin was mined. Tinminers were exempted from any jurisdiction other than that of stannary courts, except in cases affecting "life, limb or land". The Stannaries Courts Abolition Act 1896 transferred the jurisdiction to the county courts (qv) of Cornwall. See *R* v *East Powder Justices ex p Lampshire* [1979] 2 WLR 479.

staple. Town appointed by Edward I and II to be an exclusive market for certain staple products, eg, wool and lead. Courts of the Staple were created in 1353 to settle disputes among merchants relating to debts, etc. See the A.J.A. 1977, s. 23, Sch 4 for restrictions on the business of such courts.

Star Chamber, Court of. Judicial body of the Tudor period. The name may be connected with *camera stellata* (room decorated with stars) in which it sat. It exercised criminal jurisdiction of the King in Council. Its procedure was inquisitorial and torture may have been used during some trials. Abolished in 1641.

stare decisis. To stand by decided matters. (*Stare decisis et non quieta movere* = to stand by precedent and not to disturb settled points.) Doctrine according to which previous judicial decisions must be followed. See, eg, *Williams* v *Home Office* (*No 2*) [1982] 2 All ER 564. *See* PRECEDENT.

state. 1. A politically organised community under a sovereign government. 2. Social position. 3. Estate (qv).

state immunity. *See* IMMUNITY FROM JURISDICTION, STATE.

stateless person. One who has no nationality. For provisions for reducing statelessness under the B.N.A. 1981, see s. 36, Sch 2.

statement. Includes any representation of fact, whether made in words or otherwise: Civil Evidence Act 1968, s. 10(1).

statement of affairs. Statement to be submitted by a debtor to the official receiver (qv) within three days of the receiving order (if presented by the debtor) or seven days (if presented by the creditor). It must include details of the debtor's assets, liabilities, names and addresses of creditors, etc. See the B.A. 1914, s. 14. *See* BANK-RUPTCY.

statement of claim. Statement by the plaintiff (qv) of the material facts upon which he relies and the relief he seeks. Costs need not be claimed specifically: O. 18, r. 15(1). It must be signed by counsel, if settled by him and, if not, by the party's solicitor, or by the party if he sues or defends in person: O. 18, r. 6(5). The statement of claim can be indorsed on a writ: see O. 18, r. 1 and O. 62, r. 7. *See* PLEADINGS.

statement of defence. In civil procedure the defendant must usually serve a statement of defence on the plaintiff within 14 days of receiving the statement of claim, or of the expiration of the time limited for acknowledging service of the writ. Each allegation in the plaintiff's statement must be dealt with by, eg, admission, traverse (qv), confession and avoidance (qv), objection in point of law.

statements, liability for careless. Liability resulting from the failure to observe a duty to avoid making careless statements resulting in harm to some person. See *Sharp* v *Avery and Kerwood* [1938] 4 All ER 85; *Hedley Byrne & Co Ltd* v *Heller & Partners Ltd* [1964] AC 465; *W. B. Anderson & Sons Ltd* v *Rhodes Ltd* [1967] 2 All ER 850.

statements, liability for false. *See* DECEIT.

state of emergency. *See* EMERGENCY POWERS.

status. 1. Legal personality and capacity, ie, a person's conditions and rights under the law. 2. Membership of a particular group or class. See *Re Luck's Settlement Trusts* [1940] Ch 864.

status quo ante. The same state as before.

statute. An Act of Parliament (qv).

statute-barred debt. Debts in respect of which a creditor may not bring proceedings because the periods of time stated in the Limitation Acts have passed. In the winding-up of a company (qv), the liquidator (qv) must not pay statute-barred debts if shareholders object: *Re Fleetwood Syndicate* [1915] 1 Ch 486.

statute book. Collective title of those Acts of Parliament which are in force.

statute, citation of. In early days statutes were cited by reference to the name of the place at which Parliament met, eg, the Provisions of Oxford 1258. Later they were cited by reference to the regnal year and chapter; thus the Perjury Act 1911 was cited as 1 & 2 Geo. V, c. 6 (ie, the sixth of the statutes passed in the parliamentary session of the first and second years of the reign of George V). Hence, the complete citation of a pre-1963 Act is, eg, Homicide Act 1957 (5 & 6 Eliz. II, c. 11), Following the Acts of Parliament Numbering and Citation Act 1962, an Act passed after 1st January 1963 is cited by reference to the calendar year in which it was passed, eg, the Criminal Damage Act 1971 (c. 48). See also the I.A. 1978, s. 19.

statute law. The body of law enacted by Parliament.

statutes, construction of. *See* INTERPRETATION OF STATUTES.

statutes, penal. *See* PENAL STATUTES.

statutes, presumptions relating to construction of. *See* PRESUMPTIONS RELATING TO CONSTRUCTION OF STATUTES.

statutes, revenue. *See* REVENUE STATUTES.

statutorily protected tenancy. A protected tenancy (qv) within the meaning of the Rent Act 1977 or a tenancy to which the Landlord and Tenant Act 1954, Part I applies; a protected occupancy or statutory tenancy as defined in the Rent (Agriculture) Act 1976; a tenancy to which the Landlord and Tenant Act 1954, Part II applies; a tenancy of an agricultural holding within the Agricultural Holdings Act 1948: Protection from Eviction Act 1977, s. 8(1). See also the H.A. 1980, Part II.

statutory authority, defence of. Defence in tort (qv), as where a statute authorises an action which interferes with some person's rights: see *A.-G. v Nottingham Corporation* [1904] 1 Ch 673; and *Allen v Gulf Oil Refining Ltd* [1981] AC 1001.

statutory books. Registers and other documents which a company must keep, ie: registers of members, directors and secretaries, directors' interests in debentures and shares, charges, interests in voting capital; minute books; directors' service contracts; records of receipts and expenditure; assets and liabilities, stock, sales and purchases. See the Cos.A. 1948, ss. 104, 110, 200; the Cos.A. 1967, ss. 26, 29; and the Cos.A. 1976, s. 12.

statutory company. A company whose objects and powers are defined under a special private Act. See the Companies Clauses Consolidation Act 1845. *See* COMPANY.

statutory corporation. Public corporation (qv).

statutory declaration. *See* DECLARATION.

statutory duty, breach of. Tort (qv) committed by one who injures another as the result of some breach of statute. The statutory duty must be owed to the plaintiff; the injury suffered must be of the nature which the statute was intended to prevent; the defendant must be guilty of a breach of his statutory obligation; the breach must have caused the damage. See *Denyer v Charles Skipper and East Ltd* [1970] 1 WLR 1087; *Linekar v Raleigh Industries* [1980] ICR 83; and *Lonrho Ltd v Shell Ltd* [1982] AC 173.

statutory instruments. Documents by which power to make subordinate legislation has been exercised by the Queen in Council or a minister. Known formerly as statutory rules and orders and are usually cited by calendar year, number and occasionally the title, eg, the Paraffin (Maximum Retail Prices) Order 1976, S.I. 1976/1204. (A "regulation" is a statutory instrument only where the parent Act declares the power to issue regulations is to be made by statutory instrument.) See the Statutory Orders (Special Procedure) Acts 1945 and 1965. *See* DELEGATED LEGISLATION.

statutory interpretation. *See* INTERPRETATION OF STATUTES.

statutory language, interpretation of. "Statutory language must always be given presumptively the most natural and ordinary meaning which is appropriate in the circumstances": *per* Lord Simon (dissenting judgment) in *Maunsell v Olins* [1975] AC 373.

statutory lives in being. Lives enumerated under the P. & A.A 1964, s. 3(5), for purposes of the perpetuities rule (qv) as: (1) the person who made the disposition; (2) the person to whom, or in whose favour, the disposition was made; (3) parents and grandparents of the beneficiaries, in certain cases; (4) any person on the failure or determination of whose prior interest the disposition is limited to take effect. See *Re Thomas Meadows & Co Ltd* [1971] Ch 278.

statutory owner. Term used in relation to a settlement to indicate those in whom, during a minority or where there is no tenant for life (qv), the legal estate is vested, ie: persons of full age upon whom powers are conferred by the settlement and, in any other case, the trustees of the settlement: S.L.A. 1925, ss. 23, 117. They have the powers of a tenant for life.

See SETTLEMENT.

statutory rules and orders. *See* STATUTORY INSTRUMENTS.

statutory tenancy. After the termination of a protected tenancy (qv) of a dwelling-house, the person who, immediately before that termination, was the protected tenant, shall, if and so long as he occupies the dwelling-house as his residence, be the statutory tenant of it and, when there is a statutory tenant of a dwelling-house that house is referred to as subject to a statutory tenancy: Rent Act 1977, s. 2(1) (*a*), (2).

statutory tenancy, terms and conditions of. So long as a statutory tenant retains possession he shall observe and be entitled to the benefit of all the terms and conditions of the original contract of tenancy, so far as they are consistent with the provisions of the 1977 Act: Rent Act 1977, s. 3(1).

statutory tenant. One who holds under a statutory tenancy (qv). *See* TENANT BY SUCCESSION, STATUTORY.

statutory trusts. 1. Trusts created or implied by statute, eg, under the L.P.A. 1925, s. 19, or the A.E.A. 1925, s. 33. 2. Under the A.E.A. 1925, s. 49 ("statutory trusts in favour of issue and other classes of relatives of an intestate"), part of the property is held by a personal representative (qv) to be divided equally among children who are alive at the death of the intestate as soon as they attain 18, or marry. *See* TRUST.

statutory undertakers. Persons authorised by any enactment to carry on transport, gas, electricity and other public undertakings. See, eg, the New Towns Act 1981, s. 79(1).

stay of execution. The suspending of operation of a judgment or order of the court. See O. 47; O. 59, r. 13. *See* JUDGMENTS, ENFORCEMENT OF.

stay of proceedings. The suspending of proceedings by the court, eg, where proceedings are obviously frivolous. See O. 18, r. 19; *Edmeades* v *Thames Board Mills* [1969] 2 All ER 127 (in which it was held that the court had jurisdiction to stay an action while the plaintiff unreasonably refused to submit to a medical examination requested by the defendant); *Lane* v *Willis* [1972] 1 WLR 326.

stealing. Theft (qv).

stealing, going equipped for. *See* GOING EQUIPPED FOR STEALING.

sterilisation. Surgical removal of, or obstruction of the functions of, the reproductive organs so as to prevent reproduction. Sterility is not in itself a ground for annulling a marriage. See *Bravery* v *Bravery* [1954] 1 WLR 1169 (petition for divorce on the grounds of cruelty alleging the husband had been sterilised without consultation with his wife); *R* v *Cowburn* [1959] 5 CL 353 (operation on a convicted sexual psychopath); *In Re D.* (*a minor*) [1976] 1 All ER 326 (proposed operation on an 11-year-old girl suffering from Sotos Syndrome).

stet. Let it stand.

stipendiary magistrates. Full-time, salaried magistrates who usually sit alone, who are appointed from barristers or solicitors of at least seven years' standing, by the recommendation of the Lord Chancellor, in Inner London and in some very large provincial centres (eg, Leeds, Liverpool, Birmingham). A stipendiary magistrate generally has all the powers of two lay magistrates: see the Justices of the Peace Act 1979, ss. 13–16.

stipulation. Agreement; bond; undertaking.

stirpes, per. See PER STIRPES.

stock. 1. Capital lent to the government or a local authority on which a fixed rate of interest is paid. 2. Fully-paid shares which have been converted and combined into one unit, so that a company's capital, consisting formerly of, eg, 100,000 separate shares of £1 each become stock worth £100,000. See the Cos.A. 1948, s. 455. 3. Goods available for sale. 4. A family, or line of descent.

stock exchange. Recognised company of stockbrokers and jobbers who engage in the purchase and sale of stocks, shares and securities. See the Stock Exchange (Completion of Bargains) Act 1976.

stock, inscribed. *See* INSCRIBED STOCK.

stop and search powers. Powers of the police to search persons so as to obtain evidence. See, eg, the Metropolitan

Police Act 1839, s. 66; and the Misuse of Drugs Act 1971.

stop list relating to planning control. Notice served by a local planning authority after the serving of an enforcement notice (qv) requiring a breach of the planning order to be remedied, where the authority considers it expedient to prevent some activity alleged by the notice to constitute a breach. It is an offence for a person to contravene the stop notice after it has been displayed as a site notice for more than 2 days after the stop notice has been served on him. See the T.C.P. (Amendment) A. 1977, s. 1.

stop list, trade. A list, usually drawn up by a trade association, of persons with whom members of the association are forbidden to deal. See *Ware & De Freville* v *Motor Trade Association* [1921] 3 KB 40; *Hardie and Lane Ltd* v *Chilton* [1928] 2 KB 306.

stop notice. A notice which can be served on, eg, a company ordering it not to register a transfer of shares without serving notice on the judgment creditors (qv). Issued so as to prevent a disposition of securities by a judgment debtor. See O. 50, relating to stop notices and orders prohibiting improper dealings with funds in the court, etc. See the Charging Orders Act 1979, s. 5; and the T.C.P.A. 1971, s. 90 (amended by the T.C.P. (Amendment) A. 1977) (stop notice for breach of planning order). See *R* v *Jenner* [1983] 2 All Er 46.

stoppage *in transitu. See* IN TRANSITU.

storm. "Some sort of violent wind usually accompanied by rain or hail or snow. Storm does not mean persistent bad weather nor does it mean heavy rain or persistent rain by itself": *per* Veale J in *Oddy* v *Phoenix Assurance Co Ltd* [1966] 1 Lloyd's Rep 134. See *S & M Hotels Ltd* v *Legal & General Assurance Ltd* [1972] 1 Lloyd's Rep 157.

stranger. One who is "not privy or party to an act": Cowel.

strangers in blood. Persons who have no degree of relationship to one another.

straw, man of. *See* MAN OF STRAW.

straying livestock. Where livestock belonging to any person strays on to land in the ownership or occupation of another and damages land or property thereon, or expenses are reasonably incurred by that other person in keeping the livestock (if, eg, it cannot be restored at once to the owner), the person to whom the livestock belongs is liable for damage or expenses: Animals Act 1971, s. 11. See also the Highways Act 1980, s. 155.

street. Public or private roadway running in front of houses or other buildings in a continuous line. It includes any highway, road, lane, footpath, square, court, alley or passage, whether a thoroughfare or not: Highways Act 1980, s. 329(1).

street offences. 1. Offences related to the obstruction of highways, disregard of police regulations. See, eg, the Metropolitan Police Act 1839, s. 54. 2. Importuning and loitering. *See* IMPORTUNE; LOITER.

streets, prohibited, licence, consent. Terms used in relation to street trading (qv) where such trading is totally prohibited, or prohibited without a licence granted by the district council, or prohibited without the consent of the district council: Local Government (Misc. Provs.) Act 1982, Sch 4.

street trading. The selling or exposing or offering for sale of any article (including a living thing) in a street: Local Government (Misc. Provs.) Act 1982, Sch 4, para 1.

stricti juris. According to strict right or law.

strict liability in criminal law. Term now preferred, rather than "absolute liability". "If a matter is made a criminal offence, it is essential that there should be something in the nature of *mens rea* . . . But there are exceptions to this rule . . . and the reason for this is, that the legislature has thought it so important to prevent the particular act from being committed that it absolutely forbids it to be done; and if it is done the offender is liable to a penalty whether he has any *mens rea* or not, and whether or not he intended to commit a breach of the law": *Pearks, Gunston & Tee Ltd* v *Ward* [1902] 2 KB 1. See *Meah* v

Roberts [1977] 1 WLR 1187. Where a statute is silent as to *mens rea*, the presumption that it is required may be rebutted, and in some cases (eg, the Trade Descriptions Act 1968, s. 24(1)) a statute imposing strict liability may also provide a defence.

strict liability in tort. *See* DANGEROUS THINGS, LIABILITY RELATING TO.

strict settlement. A settlement which was usually made on marriage whereby the husband received a life interest, the children of the marriage received entailed interests and the wife received pin money (qv) during her husband's life and an annual sum during widowhood. *See* SETTLEMENT.

strike. The cessation of work by a body of persons employed acting in combination, or a concerted refusal, or a refusal under a common undertaking, of any number of persons employed to continue to work for an employer in consequence of a dispute, done as a means of compelling their employer or any person or body of persons employed, to accept terms or conditions of or affecting employment. See the E.P.(C.) A. 1978, Sch 13; *Coates* v *Modern Methods Ltd* [1982] 3 WLR 764.

strike, official. A strike (qv) which is supported formally and financially by a recognised trade union (qv).

striking off. Removal from a register, eg, for misconduct in one's professional capacity. Under the Medical Act 1983, Part V, the Professional Conduct Committee of the General Medical Council may erase from the register a person convicted in the UK of a criminal offence, or who has been judged by the Committee to have been guilty of serious professional misconduct (qv).

student lettings. A tenancy of a dwelling-house is not a secure tenancy if granted for the purpose of enabling the tenant to attend a designated course at a university or establishment for further education and, if, before grant of the tenancy, the landlord notified him in writing of circumstances in which this exception applies, and that the proposed tenancy would probably fall within this exception: H.A. 1980, Sch 3, para

11. *See* TENANT, SECURE.

subinfeudation. A feudal tenure. King granted land to X, tenant in chief (qv) who created a sub-tenancy by transferring part of his holding to Y. Y created a further tenancy by transferring part of his holding to Z. In each case the transferee was a tenant of the transferor. *See* FEUDAL SYSTEM.

subject. Owing obedience to another (usually the Crown).

subject to contract. Generally, the use of this phrase prevents the document in which it is contained from being evidence of a concluded bargain. There may be a binding contract, however, if the court can conclude that all the terms of a bargain have been agreed and set down in writing and signed. See *Tiverton Estates Ltd* v *Wearwell Ltd* [1975] Ch 146; *Munton* v *GLC* [1976] 1 WLR 649; *Daulia* v *Four Millbank Nominees Ltd* [1978] Ch 231; *Cohen* v *Nessdale Ltd* [1982] 2 All ER 97; and *Lyus* v *Prowsa Development* [1982] 1 WLR 1044.

subject to survey. Use of the phrase in contract for the sale of property does not, apparently, prevent a binding contract from coming into existence. There is a duty on the purchaser, in such a case, to have a survey made. See *Ee* v *Kakar* (1980) 40 P & CR 223.

sub judice. Under judicial consideration; not yet decided.

sub judice **rule.** 1. Rule relating to contempt of court (qv) whereby the courts will act to prevent or punish the publishing of articles in the press which prejudice the fair trial of an action. See the Contempt of Court Act 1981, s. 1. 2. Principle of parliamentary procedure whereby a matter awaiting judicial decision is not generally referred to in debate nor as the subject of a question to a minister.

sub-lease. A lease emerging from, and shorter than, another leasehold interest. Known also as a "sub-tenancy" or "under-lease".

sub-letting. Leasing to a tenant (qv) of premises leased to him. An agreement not to sub-let is not broken by sub-leasing part of the premises: *Cook* v *Shoesmith* [1951] 1 KB 752. See also the H.A. 1980, ss. 35, 36; and *Scala House & District Property Co Ltd* v *Forbes* [1974] QB 575.

sub-modo. Under some restriction, modification or qualification.

sub-mortgage. The mortgage of a mortgage, eg, as where a mortgagee borrows money on the security of the mortgage. Under the L.P.A. 1925, s. 86, where the mortgage has been created by a grant of a term of years a legal sub-mortgage can be made only by a grant of a sub-term or a legal charge. *See* MORTGAGE.

sub nom. *Sub nomine.* Under the name.

subordinate legislation. Delegated legislation (qv).

subornation. The procuring of a person to commit a criminal act. Thus, subornation of perjury is the offence of procuring another to commit perjury: Perjury Act 1911, s. 7(1). See *R* v *Ellahi* (1979) 1 Cr App R (S) 164.

subpoena. *Sub poena* = under a penalty. A writ (qv) which may take the form of *subpoena duces tecum*, or *subpoena ad testificandum*, directing a person to give evidence and bring relevant documents (see O. 38, r. 14). See the S.C.A. 1981, ss. 36, 123.

subrogation. Substitution. Refers to, eg, an insurer's right to enforce a remedy which the assured could have enforced against a third party. See *Phoenix Assurance Co* v *Spooner* [1905] 2 KB 753; *Orakpo* v *Manson Investments* [1978] AC 95.

sub rosa. Under the rose (a symbol that those present at a meeting are sworn to secrecy). Confidentially.

subscribing witness. One who signs a document as an attesting witness. *See* ATTESTATION.

subscription, minimum. *See* MINIMUM SUBSCRIPTION.

subsequent condition. *See* CONDITION.

subsequent pleadings. *See* PLEADINGS, SUBSEQUENT.

subsidiary company. A company which is controlled by another, eg, where that other company is a member of it and controls the composition of its board of directors or holds more than one-half of its equity share capital. See the Cos.A. 1948, s. 154. *See* COMPANY.

subsidy. 1. Money formerly granted by Parliament to the Sovereign for extraordinary occasions. 2. Payment by the state to producers or distributors, intended to reduce prices paid by consumers.

sub silentio. Under silence; without notice having been given to some matter. For the use of the phrase, see *R* v *Gloucestershire CC* [1980] 2 All ER 746, referring to *Re DJMS* [1978] QB 120.

substantial damages. *See* DAMAGES.

substantive law. That part of the law concerned with the determination of rights, liabilities and duties, etc, as contrasted with adjective law (qv).

substantive offence. A definite, complete offence.

substituted service. Where the plaintiff (qv) cannot serve a writ on the defendant (qv) or his solicitor he may apply *ex parte* on affidavit to a master for an order for substituted service which, if made, states the form the service must take, eg, by press advertisement. See O. 65, r. 4. *See* SERVICE.

substitutional legacy. *See* LEGACY, SUBSTITUTIONAL.

substitutionary gift. Gift, eg, to children in equal shares which provides that the children of a deceased child will take the share of that child. (In such a case, those who are substituted take, in general, as joint tenants.) See *Re Bourke's WT* [1980] 1 All ER 219.

substitution, doctrine of. Principle that where there is limitation of property to persons in succession, ownership absolute and entire passes from beneficiary to beneficiary upon the prescribed event's occurrence.

sub-tenancy. Sub-lease (qv). See the Rent Act 1977, ss. 137–139.

sub-tenant. An under-lessee from the original tenant.

sub-tenant, unlawful. Person occupying under a lease or tenancy granted by the head tenant, in breach of some covenant or agreement against subletting, assigning or parting with possession. Recovery of possession may be sought under O. 113. See *Moore Properties (Ilford)* v *McKeon* [1976] 1 WLR 1278; *Leith Properties* v *Byrne* [1983] 2 WLR 67.

sub tit. *Sub titulo* = under the title of.

sub-trust. Known also as "derivate trust". Example: as where trustees A and B hold a fund in trust for C and D in equal shares, and C and D declare themselves trustees of their shares for their children. *See* TRUST.

sub voce. Under the title or heading.

succession. 1. The order in which persons succeed to property, or some title. 2. Term applied to the estate of a deceased person. 3. Process of becoming entitled to property of a deceased by operation of law or will. See the A.E.A. 1925.

sue. 1. To seek justice by the process of law. 2. To bring an action against some person(s).

sufferance, tenancy at. Tenancy created where a tenant is in occupation "by lawful demise and after his estate endeth continueth in possession and wrongfully holdeth over": Coke. In effect, mere possession, created only by construction of law, arising where a valid tenancy terminates but the tenant is holding over (qv) without the landlord's permission. See *Doe d Bennett* v *Turner* (1840) 7 M & W 226.

suffrage. Right or privilege to vote in an election.

suggestio falsi. Suggestion of falsehood.

suicide. The taking of one's own life intentionally and voluntarily. A crime until the Suicide Act 1961. It is a crime, however, for a person to aid, abet, counsel or procure the suicide of another: s. 2(1). See *R* v *McShane* (1977) 66 Cr App R 97. Suicide must be strictly proved at a coroner's inquest; it is not a verdict which ought to be reached as being the most likely cause of death: *R* v *City of London Coroner* [1975] 1 WLR 1310; *R* v *Reed* [1982] Crim LR 819.

suicide pact. An agreement between two or more persons having for its object the death of all of them, whether or not each is to take his own life: Homicide Act 1957, s. 4(3). See also the Suicide Act 1961, ss. 2, 3.

sui generis. Of its own right. Constituting a class of its own.

sui juris. Of one's own right. Having full legal capacity to act on one's own. *See* ALIENI JURIS.

suit. *Suite* = act of following. 1. Appeal to a superior (eg, the King) for justice. 2. Action in court in pursuance of a right or claim. 3. Litigation in general.

suit of court. Feudal obligation on a tenant to attend his lord's court and assist in its deliberations.

suitor. One who is a party to a suit.

summary conviction. Conviction before magistrates.

summary dismissal. Dismissal of an employer without giving the notice to which the employee is entitled by virtue of the contract of employment. It is justified if the employee's conduct is such that it prevents "further satisfactory continuance of the relationship": *Sinclair* v *Neighbour* [1967] 2 QB 279. See the E.P. (C.) A. 1978, s. 55(5).

summary judgment under Order 14. Procedure in an action begun by writ, except where it includes an allegation of fraud, libel, slander, malicious prosecution or false imprisonment. The plaintiff issues the summons having sworn to the belief that there is no defence to his claim. If the defendant contests the summons he must show that he has a triable defence. The master, at the hearing of the summons, may give judgment for the plaintiff unless the defendant shows that there is "an issue or question in dispute which ought to be tried or that there ought for some other reason to be a trial". He may give the defendant leave or unconditional leave to defend. See O. 14; O. 86 (relating to an analogous procedure for action for specific performance (qv) in the Chancery Division); see *European Asian Bank AG* v *Punjab Sind Bank* (*The Times*, 10.3.1983).

summary jurisdiction. Power of magistrates to try summary offences (qv). In general, the magistrates' court cannot try any information which was not laid within six months from the time of commission of the offence: M.C.A. 1980, s. 127.

summary jurisdiction, court of. *See* COURT OF SUMMARY JURISDICTION.

summary offence. An offence which, if committed by an adult, is triable only summarily: C.L.A. 1977, s.

64(1) (*b*). See the C.L.A. 1977, s. 15, Sch 6; and the M.C.A. 1980, ss. 9–15. For the procedure where summary trial appears more suitable, see the M.C.A. 1980, s. 21. See also the I.A. 1978, Sch 1.

summary trial. The trial of petty offences and other offences triable summarily by magistrates. See the M.C.A. 1980, ss. 9–15.

summing-up. The judge's summary of a case made following the closing speeches. It usually includes a direction on points of law, a review of the evidence (including, eg, onus of proof, effect of presumptions of law (qv), etc).

summons. 1. "A citation proceeding upon an information . . . laid before the magistrate who issues the summons, and conveying to the person cited the fact that the magistrate is satisfied that there is a prima facie case against him": *Dixon* v *Wells* (1890) 25 QBD 249. It must state the general matter of the information and the place and time the defendant is to appear and must be signed by the magistrate: *R* v *Brentford Justices, ex p Catlin* [1975] QB 455. See the C.L.A. 1977, s. 39; and the M.C.A. 1980, s. 1. 2. Application to a judge or master in chambers for a decision on the points of procedure before an action in court.

summons for directions. *See* DIRECTIONS, SUMMONS FOR.

summons, originating. *See* ORIGINATING SUMMONS.

summons, serving of. Procedure involving the delivery of a summons to the defendant or by leaving it with someone at his usual or last known place of abode, or by sending it by post to his usual or last known place of abode.

summons, writ of. The commencing stage of an action whereby the defendant is called on to acknowledge the claim being made by the plaintiff and to give notice of his intention to defend (if that be the case): see O. 12. It (rather than an originating summons (qv)) must be used in the case of a claim relating to tort (other than trespass to land) or to an allegation of fraud or to damages in respect of death or personal injury. See O. 5; O. 6. It must be endorsed with a statement of claim (special endorsement) or a statement of the nature of the claim or relief or remedy required (general endorsement). See R.S.C. (Writ and Appearance) S.I. 1979/1716.

summum jus, summa injuria. Extreme law is the greatest injury.

super altum mare. Upon the high sea.

superannuation scheme. Rules providing for payment of annuities or lump sums to persons on their retirement at a certain age, or earlier incapacitation, or to their personal representatives, widows, relatives or dependants: Wages Councils Act 1979, s. 28.

superficies solo cedit. That which is attached to the land forms a part of it. *See* FIXTURES.

superior courts. Courts with a jurisdiction not limited, eg, geographically or by value of the subject-matter of an action. They include, eg, the House of Lords, the Court of Appeal, the JCPC, the High Court, the Crown Court, the Restrictive Practices Court. *See* INFERIOR COURTS.

superior orders, obedience to. *See* OBEDIENCE TO ORDERS, DEFENCE OF.

supersedeas. You shall desist. Writ (qv) staying or ending the exercise of jurisdiction.

superstitious uses. A trust (qv) for celebrating or teaching doctrines and practices of a religion not generally tolerated by law, and, therefore, generally void. See, eg, *West* v *Shuttleworth* (1835) 2 Myl & K 684; *Bourne* v *Keane* [1919] AC 815; *Gilmour* v *Coats* [1949] AC 427.

supervening cause. *See* CAUSA REMOTA.

supervening event. That which takes place as something extraneous or additional.

supervision order. Order to a supervised person to comply with instructions given by a supervisor, eg, to live at a specified place for a specified period: C. & Y.P.A. 1969, s. 12(2) (3) (as substituted by the C.J.A. 1982, s. 20). See also the P.C.C.A. 1973, s. 26 (for suspended sentence supervision orders). *See* NIGHT RESTRICTION.

supplementary benefits. Supplementary allowances paid to persons over 16 in Great Britain, whose resources are insufficient to meet their requirements. See the Supplementary Benefits Acts 1966–75; the S.S.A. 1980, s. 6, Sch 2; and the S.S. and Housing Benefits Act 1982. Sch 4.

supplementary benefits and employment. Save in prescribed cases, the right of a person to a supplementary allowance is subject to his being registered and available for employment. No person engaged in remunerative full-time work is entitled to supplementary benefits: S.S.A. 1980, Sch 2.

supplier. "A person carrying on a business of selling goods other than a business in which goods are sold only by retail": Resale Prices Act 1976, s. 24(1).

Supply, Committee of. See COMMITTEE OF SUPPLY.

support, right of. See RIGHT OF SUPPORT.

suppression of documents, dishonest. Offence committed by a person who "dishonestly with a view to gain for himself or another or with intent to cause loss to another, destroys, defaces or conceals any valuable security, any will or other testamentary document or any original document of or belonging to, or filed or deposited in, any court of justice or any government department . . .": Th.A. 1968, s. 20(1).

suppressio veri, suggestio falsi. The suppression of truth is the suggestion of falsehood.

supra. Above; higher than; prior to.

supra protest. See ACCEPTANCE OF A BILL.

Supreme Court. This consists of the Court of Appeal, the High Court of Justice, and the Crown Court; the Lord Chancellor is President: S.C.A. 1981, s. 1.

Supreme Court, Masters of the. See MASTERS OF THE SUPREME COURT.

Supreme Court Procedure Committee. Set up by the Lord Chief Justice (in 1982) to consider and recommend reforms in practice and procedure which appear to be desirable for saving time and costs. Attached to it are subcommittees representing the Chancery, Queen's Bench and Family Divisions of the High Court (qqv).

Supreme Court Rule Committee. See RULES OF THE SUPREME COURT.

surcharge. The disallowing, following audits, of unauthorised expenditure.

surcharge and falsify. Term referring to an account in which there is an omission of a sum which ought to have been credited and of which proof of a wrongly-inserted item can be given. See O. 43; *Williamson v Barbour* (1877) 9 Ch D 529.

surety. A person who gives security for another. The procedure whereby magistrates bind over (qv) a person may involve his being ordered to find sureties for his keeping the peace. See the M.C.A. 1980, s. 115; and the Bail Act 1976.

surname. Family, as distinct from Christian, name. A child's surname is that of his father, and a wife is incompetent to change her child's surname by deed poll or registration of birth without the husband's consent or a court order: *D. v B.* [1977] Fam 145. See the Enrolment of Deeds (Change of Name) Amendment Regulations 1974. The name of a woman conferred by marriage is not lost upon her divorce: *Fendall v Goldsmid* (1877) 2 PD 263. See NAME, CHANGE OF.

surplusage. Unnecessary, irrelevant, excessive material in formal pleadings (qv).

surprise. Term applied, eg, to an event which may be grounds for a new trial. Examples: where an action comes on unexpectedly while the applicant's witnesses are not available, or where the plaintiff introduces allegations which had not been pleaded: *Lloyde v W Midlands Gas Board* [1971] 1 WLR 749. See O. 59, r. 11.

surrebutter. Term used in pleadings (qv) to indicate the plaintiff's answer to a rebutter (qv).

surrejoinder. Answer by the plaintiff to a rejoinder by the defendant. See REJOINDER.

surrender and admittance. Formerly a mode of conveyance of copyhold (qv). The copyhold was "surrendered" but, until admittance, legal estate remained in transferor. Prior to 1926 a legal mortgage (qv) of copyhold could be made in this way, involving the mortgagor's covenanting to surrender the property to the mortgagee's use on the condition that surrender was void if money and interest were not paid on a fixed date; this covenant was followed by formal surrender and admittance.

surrender of shares. The yielding up, and acceptance by the directors of a company, of shares, for the purpose of being cancelled, etc. If it involves a reduction of capital it is unlawful, except when sanctioned by the court. See the Cos.A. 1980, s. 37.

surrender of tenancy. A mode of determination of a tenancy (qv) whereby a tenant yields up his estate to the lessor. *Express surrender*, in the case of a lease exceeding 3 years, requires a deed: L.P.A. 1925, s. 52. *Implied surrender* occurs, eg, if the tenant delivers possession to the lessor who accepts it. See *Dodd* v *Acklom* (1843) 6 M & G 672; *Wallis* v *Heads* [1893] 2 Ch 75.

surrender value. The amount an insurance company will repay to a policy holder who wishes to discontinue prior to the date of maturity.

surrogate. One appointed to act in place of another.

survival of causes of action on death. *See* DEATH, SURVIVAL OF CAUSES OF ACTION ON.

survivors. "A word which has caused perhaps more difficulty in the interpretation of wills than any other in the language": *Re Pickworth* [1899] 1 Ch 642. When property is bequeathed to "the survivors" of individuals or members of a class, it is construed as meaning those who are living at the period of distribution: *Cripps* v *Wolcott* (1819) 4 Madd 11. See *Powell* v *Hellicar* [1919] 1 Ch 138; *Gilmour* v *MacPhillamy* [1930] 1 Ch 138.

survivorship, right of. The right of a survivor (eg, of joint tenants (qv)) to the whole property. *See* JUS ACCRESCENDI.

suspects, questioning of. The cross-examination of suspects by the police, usually when they are in custody. The *Judges' Rules* (qv) permit the questioning of a person, whether a suspect or not, in custody, provided that he has not been charged with or informed that he might be prosecuted for some offence to which the questions are related. *See* QUESTIONING, DETAINING BY POLICE FOR.

suspend. 1. To debar temporarily from the exercise of an office or occupation. 2. To revoke a law temporarily. See the Bill of Rights 1688, which condemned the use of the power to suspend laws: "The pretended power of dispensing with laws, or the execution of laws by regal authority . . . is illegal."

suspended sentence. Sentence ordered not to take effect immediately: P.C.C.A. 1973, s. 22. The sentence must be for a term of not more than two years and suspension can be for a period of not less than one year or more than two years from the date of the order. See *R* v *Goodlad* [1973] 2 All ER 1200. For partly-served and partly-suspended prison sentence, see the C.J.A. 1982, s. 30. For suspended sentence supervision orders see the P.C.C.A. 1973, s. 26.

suspended sentence, partly-. Where a court passes on an adult a sentence of imprisonment for a term of three months–two years, it may order that after he has served part of the sentence in prison, the remainder of it shall be held in suspense: C.L.A. 1977, s. 47(1) (as amended by the C.J.A. 1982, s. 30). The part held in suspense must be at least one-quarter of the whole term, the time to be served must be at least 28 days. For the principles governing the imposition of such sentences, see *R* v *Clarke* [1982] 1 WLR 1090.

sweepstake. A wager based on the outcome of some event, eg, result of a race. Held, in *Ellesmere* v *Wallace* [1929] 2 Ch 1, to be illegal as a lottery "if the winner is determined by chance, but not if the winner is determined by skill". See the Lotteries and Amusements Act 1976, s. 1; and *Imperial Tobacco* v *A.-G.* [1981] AC 718.

symbolic delivery. *See* DELIVERY.

synallagmatic contract. *Synallagmatikos* = of a contract. A reciprocal contract, ie, one characterised by mutual duties and rights. "Every synallagmatic contract contains in it the seeds of the problem: in what event will a party be relieved of his undertaking to do that which he has agreed to do but has not yet done?": *per* Diplock LJ in *Hong Kong Fir Shipping* v *Kawasaki* [1962] 2 QB 26. See *United Dominions Trust* v *Eagle Services Ltd* [1968] 1 All ER 104.

system, evidence of. Evidence given to show a propensity to commit a given crime by use of a certain technique. See, eg, *R* v *Rhodes* [1899] 1 QB 77; *R* v *Bond* [1906] 2 KB 389; *Thompson* v *R* [1918] AC 221; *R* v *Straffen* [1952] 2 QB 911.

T

Table A. Specimen set of articles (qv) for a company limited by shares, contained in the Cos.A. 1948, Sch 1. In so far as its contents are not excluded expressly, they are incorporated in the company's articles. (Part II of Table A was repealed by the Cos.A. 1980.)

Table B. Form of memorandum of association (qv) for a company limited by shares, set out in the Cos.A. 1948, Sch 1. In the case of a public company (qv), Table B is superseded by the Cos.A. 1980, Sch 1, Part I: 1980 Act, s. 2(4).

Table C. Form of memorandum and articles of association (qqv) for a company limited by guarantee, and not having a share capital, set out in the Cos.A. 1948, Sch 1.

Table D. Form of memorandum and articles of association (qqv) for a company limited by guarantee, and having a share capital, set out in the Cos.A. 1948, Sch 1. In the case of a public company (qv), Table D is superseded by the Cos.A. 1980, Sch 1 Part II: 1980 Act, s. 2(4).

Table E. Form of memorandum and articles of association (qqv) for an unlimited company having a share capital, set out in the Cos.A. 1948, Sch 1.

tabula in naufragio. Plank in a shipwreck. Doctrine, abolished by the L.P.A. 1925, s. 94, whereby if a legal mortgage to X was followed by an equitable mortgage to Y and then by an equitable mortgage to Z, then Z might obtain priority over Y by paying off X and acquiring legal estate from him. The legal estate was considered as a "plank in the shipwreck" by the use of which one mortgagee saved himself "while the other was drowned". (This applied only where Z did not know of an earlier mortgage to Y when he made the loan.) See MORTGAGE.

tacit. 1. Silent, implied. 2. Resulting without express agreement. 3. Arising by operation of law.

tacking. Prior to the L.P.A. 1925, a legal mortgagee who had made a further loan to the mortgagor could tack together both loans and recover them prior to the intervening mortgagee, if he had received no notice of the intervener. Under the 1925 Act s. 94, legal or equitable mortgagees may tack where intervening mortgagees concur, where further advance was made with no notice at the time of the intervening mortgage and where the mortgage involved an obligation to make a further advance. See _Burnes_ v _Trade Credits Ltd_ [1981] 1 WLR 805. _See_ MORTGAGE.

tail. _See_ FEE TAIL.

tail general. Widest form of entailed interest. Example: land limited "to X and the heirs of his body".

tail male general. Entailed interest which arises where land is limited "to X and the heirs male of his body begotten". Unlike the tail general (qv), only the _male heirs_ of X may succeed. In case of _tail female general,_ only _female heirs_ take.

tail male special. Entailed interest arising by grant "to X and Y and the heirs male of their two bodies begotten". In case of _tail female special,_ only _female heirs_ take.

take-over offer. Offer to all holders (other than the offeror and his nominees) of shares in a company to acquire those shares or a specified proportion of them, or to all the holders (other than the offeror and his nominees) of a particular class of shares to acquire them or a specified proportion of them: Cos.A. 1980, s. 73(5).

talaq. Repudiation, in Islamic law, of a wife by her husband by means of a formal, triple declaration. See _Quazi_ v _Quazi_ [1980] AC 744 (talaq recognized in England); and _Zaal_ v _Zaal_ (1983) 4 Fam Law 284.

tales. From the phrase _tales de circumstantibus_ = such (persons) of bystanders. Refers to the practice of making up the deficiency in the available number of jurors by commanding the sheriff (qv) to call others who can be found (known as *talesmen*). See now the Juries Act 1976, ss. 6, 11.

tam quam. Title of action also known as *qui tam* (qv).

tangible property. Corporeal property, eg, goods, as compared with intangible property, eg, choses in action (qv).

tape recorders in court. It is a contempt of court to use tape recorders in court, except by leave, or to publish a recording of legal proceedings made by means of such an instrument: Contempt of Court Act 1981, s. 9. See *Practice Direction* [1981] 1 WLR 1526.

tape-recording. Record of sound imprinted on magnetic tape. Notes of a tape-recording were given in evidence in, eg, *R* v *Mills* [1962] 3 All ER 298. Tape-recordings are treated as documents for the purposes of discovery and inspection of documents (qv): O. 24, r. 1; *Barker* v *Wilson* [1980] 1 WLR 884.

tautology. Unnecessary repetition of an idea or phrase. In a complicated matter, the presumption against tautology in statutory provisions is not strong: *Philipson-Stow* v *IRC* [1960] 3 All ER 814.

tax. A compulsory contribution by individuals and companies to the State, levied on goods, services, income and wealth. Local taxation imposed by local authorities is known as "rates" (qv).

taxation of costs. Procedure of examining, and altering where necessary, amounts payable by a party in an action. Usual bases are: (1) party and party (qv); (2) common fund (qv); (3) solicitor and own client (qv); (4) trustees' costs (qv). Where a party is dissatisfied with the taxation, an application may be made for a review of the decision. See O. 62; *Property and Reversionary Investment Corporation Ltd* v *Secretary of State for the Environment* [1975] 2 All ER 436; and *Treasury Solicitor* v *Regester* [1978] 1 WLR 446.

tax avoidance and evasion. Tax "avoidance" relates to the arrangement of one's affairs so that liability to tax is reduced or disappears. Tax "evasion" is the non-payment of taxes which one is under duty to pay, and is generally illegal. "The avoidance of tax may be lawful, but it is not yet a virtue": *Re Weston's Settlements* [1969] 1 Ch 223. See *W T Ramsay Ltd* v *IRC* [1982] AC 300; the Finance Act 1981, ss. 45, 46, 88; and *Cairns* v *MacDiarmid* [1983] STC 178.

tax haven. Nation or locality levying relatively low taxes, or none at all, on foreigners. Examples (at one time or another): Channel Islands, Lichtenstein, Panama. See the Income and Corporation Taxes Act 1970, s. 478; and *W T Ramsay Ltd* v *IRC* [1982] AC 300.

taximeter. "Any device for calculating the fare to be charged in respect of any journey in a hackney carriage or private hire vehicle by reference to the distance travelled or time elapsed since the start of the journey, or a combination of both": L.G. (Misc. Provs.) A. 1976, s. 80(1).

taxing masters. Salaried officials of the Supreme Court Taxing Office who consider taxation of costs (qv). See *R* v *Wilkinson* [1980] 1 All ER 597. They are usually appointed by the Lord Chancellor, with the agreement of the Treasury.

taxing statutes. Acts imposing taxation. They are construed as other statutes, but the tax must be imposed by plain words before persons will be held liable. "The Crown does not tax by analogy but by statute": *Ormond Investment Co* v *Betts* [1928] AC 143. A construction which helps evasion will be avoided. See *Simmons* v *Registrar of Probates* [1900] AC 323; *IRC* v *Wolfson* [1949] 1 All ER 865.

tax week. One of the successive periods in a tax year beginning with first day of that year and every seventh day thereafter; the last day of a tax year (or, in the case of a tax year ending in a leap year, the last two days) to be treated accordingly as a separate tax week: S.S.A. 1975, Sch 20.

tax year. The 12 months beginning

with 6th April in any year: S.S.A. 1975, Sch 20.

telephone, exchange of contracts by. Exchange can be effected in any manner recognised by the law as amounting to an exchange, and this includes telephone conversations: *Domb* v *Isoz* [1980] 1 All ER 942. See The Law Society's General Conditions of Sale (1980).

telephone tapping. Form of electronic surveillance (qv) carried out by security services after authorisation by the Home Secretary. See *Malone* v *Commissioner for Metropolis* [1979] 2 All ER 620; and Report on Interception of Communications 1980 (Cmnd 7873).

telex. Method of transmitting printed messages instantaneously by means of automatic teleprinters. Instantaneous telex communication should follow the general rule that a contract is made when and where acceptance is received: *Brinkibon Ltd* v *Stahag Stahl* [1982] 2 WLR 264.

tenancy. The relationship of a tenant (qv) to that land which he holds from another.

tenancy, assured. *See* ASSURED TENANCY.

tenancy at sufferance. *See* SUFFERANCE, TENANCY AT.

tenancy at will. *See* TENANT AT WILL.

tenancy by entireties. Where land was granted to a husband and wife so that, had they not been married, they would have taken as joint tenants, they were tenants by entireties; each was tenant of the whole land; when one died the land passed absolutely to the survivor. Abolished as a doctrine under the L.P.A. 1925, s. 37. Tenancies by entireties existing at that date were converted into joint tenancies (qv).

tenancy by estoppel. Where, eg, a mortgagor in possession grants a lease (qv) which does not satisfy the statutory provisions or the terms of the mortgage deed, the lease may bind the tenant and mortgagor (so that, eg, he may sue for rent) under the doctrine of estoppel (qv). See *Trent* v *Hunt* (1853) 9 Exch 14. *See* MORTGAGE.

tenancy, controlled. Tenancy under the Rent Act 1977, which becomes a regulated tenancy (qv) on commencement of the H.A. 1980, s. 64, save for one which qualifies for protection under the Landlord and Tenant Act 1954, Part II.

tenancy, enfranchisement of. *See* ENFRANCHISEMENT OF TENANCY.

tenancy, furnished, protected. *See* PROTECTED FURNISHED TENANCY.

tenancy, housing association. *See* HOUSING ASSOCIATION TENANCY.

tenancy, housing association, conversion into regular tenancy of. *See* HOUSING ASSOCIATION TENANCY, CONVERSION INTO REGULAR TENANCY OF.

tenancy, implied. Tenancy presumed from the payment and acceptance of a sum in the nature of rent. See *Longrigg Burrough* v *Smith* (1979) 251 EG 847.

tenancy in common. *See* COMMON, TENANCY IN.

tenancy, long. *See* LONG TENANCY.

tenancy, opposition to grant of new. Grounds upon which a landlord (qv) may oppose a grant under the Landlord and Tenant Act 1954, s. 26(2) include, eg, persistent delay in paying rent and other misbehaviour, such as failure to repair; availability of alternative accommodation; landlord's intention to reconstruct or demolish the premises.

tenancy, periodic. *See* PERIODIC TENANCY.

tenancy, protected. *See* PROTECTED TENANCY.

tenancy, protected shorthold. *See* PROTECTED SHORTHOLD TENANCY.

tenancy, regulated. *See* REGULATED TENANCY.

tenancy, regulated, registration of rents under. *See* REGULATED TENANCY, REGISTRATION OF RENTS UNDER.

tenancy, regulated, rent limit. *See* REGULATED TENANCY, RENT LIMIT.

tenancy, statutorily protected. *See* STATUTORILY PROTECTED TENANCY.

tenancy, statutory. *See* STATUTORY TENANCY.

tenancy, statutory, terms and conditions of. *See* STATUTORY TENANCY, TERMS AND CONDITIONS OF.

tenancy, surrender of. *See* SURRENDER OF TENANCY.

tenancy, weekly. *See* WEEKLY TENANCY.

tenant. One who holds land of another. A lessee (qv). Includes, under the Rent Act 1977, s. 152(1), "statutory tenant and also includes a subtenant and any person deriving title under the original tenant or subtenant". See the H.A. 1980, Sch 19, para 19.

tenantable repair. The quality of repair in a house rendering it fit for occupation by tenants. See the H.A. 1980, ss. 80, 81. *See* REPAIR, COVENANT TO.

tenant at sufferance. *See* SUFFERANCE, TENANCY AT.

tenant at will. One holding under a tenancy at will, which exists where the tenant (T) occupies L's land, with L's consent, on terms under which L or T may determine the tenancy at any time. "In this case the lessee is called tenant at will because he hath no certain or sure estate, for the lessor may put him out at what time it pleaseth him": Littleton. It may be created by express agreement or implication and may be ended by L or T if, eg, either should assign land, or die. See *James* v *Dean* (1805) 11 Ves 383; *Hagee Ltd* v *Erikson and Lawson* [1975] 3 All ER 234.

tenant by succession, statutory. After the termination of a protected tenancy (qv) of a dwelling-house, the person who, immediately before the termination, was the protected tenant of the dwelling-house is, so long as he occupied the house as his residence, the *statutory tenant* of it. One who, after the death of the statutory tenant, becomes the next statutory tenant is known as the "statutory tenant by succession". See the Rent Act 1977, s. 2, Sch 1.

tenant by the curtesy. *See* CURTESY.

tenant by the verge. Tenant who held copyhold (qv) after a symbolic surrender and delivery of a small rod (verge).

tenant for life. "The person of full age who is for the time being beneficially entitled under a settlement to possession of settled land for his life is for the purposes of this Act the tenant for life of that land and the tenant for life under that settlement": S.L.A. 1925, s. 19(1). Two or more persons of full age so entitled as joint tenants

together constitute the tenant for life for purposes of the Act: s. 19(2). *See* SETTLEMENT.

tenant for life, powers of. These are conferred by the S.L.A. 1925 and include power of sale and exchange, power to grant and accept leases, to borrow money and to apply capital money, to sell heirlooms and to compromise claims concerning settled land.

tenant for years. One who holds land for a term of years (qv).

tenant from year to year. One who holds a yearly tenancy, which may be created expressly ("to T from year to year") or by implication. It continues until ended by proper notice. See *Tickner* v *Buzzacott* [1965] Ch 426.

tenant, harassment of. *See* HARASSMENT OF OCCUPIER.

tenant-in-chief. *See* IN CAPITE.

tenant in tail. One who holds an estate in fee tail (qv).

tenant in tail after possibility. If a gift of land is made "to X and his heirs begotten by him on Y" and Y (X's wife) dies without leaving children, there exists no possibility of descendants of X and Y who could succeed. X (tenant in tail) is known as "tenant in tail after possibility of issue extinct" (or "tenant in tail after possibility"). X may not bar the entail in such a case, but he is given the statutory powers of a tenant for life (qv). See the S.L.A. 1925, s. 20(1) (*i*). *See* FEE TAIL.

tenant, occupying. *See* OCCUPYING TENANT.

tenant *pur autre vie.* *See* AUTRE VIE.

tenant, secure. Tenant of a local authority, a new town development corporation, the Development Board for Rural Wales and some housing associations, who, under the H.A. 1980, Part I, has the right to acquire the freehold or a long lease and the right to a mortgage. The person exercising the right to buy is entitled to a discount: s. 7. Security of tenure depends on fulfilment of "landlord and tenant conditions": s. 28. For exceptions to the right to buy, see Sch 1. A tenancy is not secure if it is a long tenancy, or one to which the Landlord and Tenant Act 1954, Part

II, applies: Sch 3. See *Harrison* v *Hammersmith and Fulham BC* [1981] 1 WLR 650.

tenant's fixtures. In general, a landlord is entitled to fixtures which have been attached by his tenant. There may be exceptions in the case of ornamental, domestic, agricultural and trade fixtures. See, eg, the Agricultural Holdings Act 1948; *Leach* v *Thomas* (1835) 7 C & P 327. It is an offence under the Th.A. 1968, s. 4(2) for a person who, being in possession of land under a tenancy, appropriates the whole or part of any fixture let to be used with the land. *See* FIXTURES.

tenant, statutory. *See* TENANT BY SUCCESSION, STATUTORY.

tenant, sub-. *See* SUB-TENANT.

tenant to the *praecipe*. *See* PRAECIPE, TENANT TO THE.

tender. 1. To offer for sale. 2. To offer money, etc, in payment or satisfaction of a debt or other obligation. "Payment extinguishes the debt; tender does not." There must be actual production of the exact sum of money, or a dispensation of such production. See O. 22, r. 8. 3. An offer relating to the supply of goods. Thus, X requires 1,000 ingots and invites tenders. If he accepts Y's tender, there is a contract for the sale of 1,000 ingots by Y to X. See *Percival Ltd* v *LCC* (1918) 87 LJKB 672. 4. Legal tender (qv).

tender before action, defence of. Plea by the defendant that he had offered to satisfy the plaintiff's claim before the issue of a writ, supported by payment into court of the amount alleged to have been tendered. See O. 18, r. 16.

tender of performance. Expressed readiness to perform an act in accordance with an obligation. See *Farquharson* v *Pear Insurance Co Ltd* [1937] 3 All ER 124.

tenement. 1. Property held by tenure. 2. House in use as dwelling.

tenendum. To be held. Clause in a conveyance (qv) formerly used to indicate the mode of tenure.

tenor. 1. The substance of some matter. 2. An exact copy of writing.

tenor, executor according to. *See* EXECUTOR.

tenure. A relationship of lord and tenant which determined the terms upon which land was held. The old tenures (free, lay, spiritual, unfree) were generally abolished by the land legislation of the 1920s, so that today there is one principal tenure only, ie, freehold, which is the name now used for free and common socage (qv). See the Tenures Abolition Act 1660; and the L.P.A. 1922, and 1925.

tenure, free. Spiritual (frankalmoign) and lay tenure (ie, by knight service, socage, sergeanty).

tenure, security of. Statutory protection, eg, under the Rent Act 1977, or the Protection from Eviction Act 1977, afforded to tenants, concerning rents and the landlord's right to recover possession. Under the Rent Act 1977, s. 98(1) a court will not make an order for possession of a dwelling-house let on a protected tenancy (qv) or subject to a statutory tenancy (qv) unless the court considers it reasonable to make the order and suitable alternative accommodation is available for the tenant, or the circumstances are as specified in Part I of Sch 15 of the Act. For application to the tribunal for security of tenure where notice to quit (qv) is served, see s. 104.

tenure, unfree. Copyhold tenure (known also as *villanagium* (qv)).

term. *Terminus* = limit or boundary. 1. A part of the year in which business could be transacted in the courts. Terms were abolished under the J.A. 1875, so that the year now comprises sittings (qv) and vacations (qv). 2. To "keep term" is to dine in an Inn of Court (qv) on a specified number of formal occasions, as part of the qualification for the call to the Bar (qv). 3. A fixed period of time. 4. Period for which an estate is granted. 5. Condition, provision or limitation. 6. Substantive part of a contract, creating a contractual obligation for whose breach an action lies.

term, express. *See* EXPRESS TERM.

term, fixed. *See* FIXED TERM.

term for years. Term of years (qv).

term, implied. *See* IMPLIED TERM.

term of years. Known also as "term

for years". A lease. In essence, an estate or interest in land limited to a certain fixed period, eg, a lease for 21 years. It must be created with required formalities (eg, a lease for more than three years must be created by deed); it must be based on a definite period (see *Swift* v *Macbean* [1942] 1 KB 375); it must confer on the lessee a right to exclusive possession (see *Crane* v *Morris* [1965] 1 WLR 1104). *See* LEASE.

term of years absolute. A term that is to last for a certain fixed period, although it may be liable to end before the expiration of that period by notice, re-entry, operation of law, etc. Includes a term for less than a year, or for a year or years and a fraction of a year or from year to year: L.P.A. 1925, s. 205(1) (xxvii).

termor. One holding land for a term of years (qv).

terre tenant. One who has actual possession of land, or is in occupation.

territorial extent, rule relating to. "An Act of Parliament only applies to transactions within the UK and not to transactions outside": *C.E. Draper & Sons Ltd* v *Edward Turner & Sons Ltd* [1964] 3 All ER 148. See, however, *Pugh* v *Pugh* [1951] P 482.

territoriality, principle of. Concept in international law that a Sovereign ought not to engage in jurisdictional acts outside the limits of his territory. See *British Nylon Spinners* v *ICI Ltd* [1954] 3 All ER 88.

territorial waters. Sea area adjacent to a state's shores and subject to its exclusive jurisdiction. See the Territorial Waters Jurisdiction Act 1878; the Sea Fisheries Act 1968, s. 6; *Post Office* v *Estuary Radio* [1968] 2 QB 740. Known also as "inland waters": see the S.C.A. 1981, s. 22.

terrorism. "The use of violence for political ends [including] any use of violence for the purpose of putting the public or any section of the public in fear": Prevention of Terrorism (Temporary Provisions) Act 1976, s. 14(1). See the Suppression of Terrorism Act 1978; European Convention on Suppression of Terrorism 1980 (Cmnd 7823); *R* v *Al-Mograbi* (1979)

70 Cr App R 24. See also Jellicoe Report (1983) (Cmnd 8803). *See* EXCLUSION ORDER.

testable. 1. Legally capable of making a will (qv) or bearing witness. 2. Disposable under a will.

testament. A will. "The true declaration of our last will, of that we would be done after our death": *Termes de la Ley*. A distinction is sometimes drawn between a will (a disposition of *real property*) and a testament (relating to *personal property*). *See* WILL.

testamentary capacity. The ability in law to make a valid will, based on, eg, the maker's being over 18, *animus testandi* (qv), and the ability to make a disposition of property "with understanding and reason". See *Re Simpson* (1977) 121 SJ 224.

testamentary expenses. Those incurred in the proper performance of an executor's duties. See *Re Treasure* [1900] 2 Ch 648; *Re Matthew's Will Trusts* [1961] 1 WLR 1415.

testamentary freedom. The right of a person to dispose of his property by will according to his wishes. Limited in practice by, eg, the Inheritance (Provision for Family and Dependants) Act 1975.

testamentary guardian. Guardian of an infant (qv) appointed by will. See the Guardianship of Minors Act 1971.

testamentary intention. Known also as *animus testandi* (qv). Essential for the validity of a will. Thus, a will executed in jest, or brought about by force, fear, fraud or undue influence will be set aside. See *Nichols* v *Nichols* (1814) 2 Phil 180; *Boyce* v *Rossborough* (1856) 6 HL Cas 2; *Parfitt* v *Lawless* (1872) LR 2 P & D 462.

testamentary trust. An express trust intended to operate after death. It must be contained in an attested or duly executed will or codicil. *See* TRUST.

testate. Having made and left one's will. *See* WILL.

testator. Fem: *testatrix*. One who makes a will. *See* WILL.

testator, presence of. Witnesses must attest and subscribe a will in the testator's presence: W.A. 1837, s. 9

(as substituted by the A.J.A. 1982, s. 17). "Presence" means that testator must be able to see witnesses subscribe and know what they are doing. See *Wyatt* v *Berry* [1893] P 5; *Re Colling* [1972] 3 All ER 729. *See* WILL; ATTESTATION.

testatum. The beginning of the operative part of a deed (qv): "Now this deed witnesseth that . . ."

test case. An action determining the legal position of many persons who are not parties to the action, as contrasted with, eg, a representative action (qv).

teste. *Teste meipso* = witness myself. The witnessing or concluding part of a writ (qv). See now O. 6, r. 1; S.I. 1979/1716.

testimonial evidence. *See* EVIDENCE, TESTIMONIAL.

testimonium. That final part of a deed stating that the parties have signed the deed "in witness" of what it contains.

testimony. Statement of a witness in court, generally sworn, and offered as evidence of the truth of that which he asserts. The essence of judicial evidence (qv).

testimony, perpetuating. *See* PERPETUATING TESTIMONY.

textbooks, authority of. General rule is that books may be cited in court, if at all, by way of evidence as to the correct interpretation of the law, but not as independent sources from which the law can be derived. Exceptions are "books of authority", eg, Coke, Blackstone. Some very few living writers are occasionally cited, but rarely referred to directly as authorities. Example of modern reliance on Coke: *Reid* v *Police Commissioner of the Metropolis* [1973] QB 551; example of adoption of contemporary writer's definition: *Re Ellenborough Park* [1956] Ch 131 ("easements", from Cheshire's *Modern Law of Real Property*). See also *Cordell* v *Second Clanfield Properties Ltd* [1968] 2 Ch 9.

theatre, obscenity in. It is an offence, under the Theatres Act 1968, to present or direct an obscene performance unless the performance can be justified as being for the public good on grounds of literary or other artistic merit.

theft. A person is guilty of theft "if he dishonestly appropriates property belonging to another with the intention of permanently depriving the other of it; and 'thief' and 'steal' shall be construed accordingly": Th.A. 1968, s. 1(1). *See* DISHONEST.

thing in action. Chose in action (qv).

third party. A person other than the principals in any proceedings. For "third party damages", see *Woodar Investment Ltd* v *Wimpey Ltd* [1980] 1 All ER 51.

third-party directions. Where a third party enters an appearance, the defendant who has issued a third-party notice must, by summons, apply to the court for directions: O. 16, r. 4(1).

third party, orders against. Orders issued under the A.J.A. 1970, s. 32 (County Court) or the S.C.A. 1981, ss. 33–35 (High Court), for the inspection, custody, etc, of property which is not the property of or in the possession of parties to the proceedings. Application for an order is by summons supported by affidavit (qv).

third-party proceedings. Proceedings brought by separate action for a remedy against a third party. Example: the plaintiff is the lessor and the defendant is being sued for breach of covenant; the defendant could claim relief from a third party, such as a sub-lessee. The third party, can counterclaim against the defendant, not against the plaintiff. See the County Court Rules 1981, O. 12; O. 16; *Barclays Bank* v *Tom* [1923] 1 KB 221.

third-party rights in land. Rights over another's land are binding on its successive owners, eg, easements, restrictive covenants (qqv).

third-party risks, insurance against. It is an offence to use, to cause or permit any other person to use, a motor vehicle on a road unless there is in force in relation to the use of the vehicle by that person a policy of insurance or some security in respect of third-party risks (ie, risks to persons not parties to the policy). See the Road Traffic Act 1972, s. 143(1) (as amended by the Road Traffic Act

1974, Schs 6 and 7).

threat. The expression of an intention to inflict unlawful injury or damage of some kind "so as to intimidate or overcome the will of the person to whom it is addressed".

three-tier system of Crown Court. Locations for sittings of the Crown Court (qv). The major centres (first-tier) have criminal and civil jurisdiction and are served by High Court judges, circuit judges and recorders. Second-tier centres have criminal jurisdiction only and are served as are first-tier centres. Third-tier centres have only criminal jurisdiction and are served by circuit judges and recorders.

ticket of leave. Permit formerly relating to the conditional release of a prisoner before the expiration of his sentence. See now the C.J.A. 1967, s. 61.

tidal waters. Those parts of the sea within territorial waters (qv) in which there is a real and perceptible ebb and flow of the tide. See the Salmon and Fisheries Act 1975, s. 6: *Ingram* v *Percival* [1969] 1 QB 548.

tied cottage. Dwelling belonging to and maintained by an employer for occupancy by his employee. Common at one time among workers on the land. A measure of security of tenure for agricultural workers housed by their employers and their successors is now afforded under the Rent (Agriculture) Act 1976 as amended by the Rent Act 1977. *See* PROTECTED OCCUPIER.

tied house. A public house, the lessee of which has covenanted with the lessor to buy all his supplies of beer, etc, only from that lessor.

timber. "Oak, ash and elm are timber, provided they are of the age of 20 years and upwards, provided also they are not so old as not to have a reasonable quantity of useable wood in them, sufficient to make a good post. Timber, that is, the kind of tree which may be called timber, may be varied by local custom": *Honywood* v *Honywood* (1874) LR 18 Eq 306. See also *Dashwood* v *Magniac* [1891] 3 Ch 306.

time as essence of a contract. Phrase referring to the common law principle that in absence of contrary intention, time is an essential condition in the performance of a contract: *Parkin* v *Thorold* (1852) 16 Beav 59. Equitable doctrine was that time was not of the essence unless made so expressly or impliedly. Under the L.P.A. 1925, s. 41: "Stipulations in a contract, as to time or otherwise, which according to rules of equity are not deemed to be or have become of the essence of the contract, are also construed and have effect at law in accordance with the same rules". See the S.G.A; 1979, ss. 10, 59, relating to stipulations as to time of payment (which are not generally of the essence of the contract in absence of contrary intention); *United Scientific Holdings* v *Burnley BC* [1978] AC 904.

time charter. A charterparty (qv) for a specified period (compared with one for a particular voyage).

time for performance of service contract. Where, under a contract for the supply of a service (qv) by a supplier acting in the course of a business, the time for the service to be carried out is not fixed by the contract, left to be fixed in a manner agreed by the contract or determined by the course of dealing between the parties, there is an implied term that the supplier will carry out the service within a reasonable time: Supply of Goods and Services Act 1982, s. 14(1). What is a "reasonable time" is a question of fact: s. 14(2).

time immemorial. Beyond legal memory, ie, "time whereof the memory of man runneth not to the contrary." Fixed by the Statute of Westminster 1275, as the first year of the reign of Richard I (1189).

time order. Order made by court under the C.C.A. 1974, s. 129, if it appears just to do so, allowing an extension of time on, eg, an application for an enforcement order or an application made by a debtor or hirer after service on him of a default notice.

time out of mind. Time immemorial (qv).

time policy. Policy of marine insurance where the contract is to insure for a fixed period of time. See the Finance Act 1959, repealing the Marine Insurance Act 1906, s. 25(2).

time, reasonable. *See* REASONABLE TIME.

tipstaff. Officer attached to the High Court, whose duties include arresting those responsible for contempt of court and enforcing orders in wardship proceedings.

tithes. "The tenth part of all fruits, praedial, personal, and mixt which are due to God, and consequently to his churches' ministers for their maintenance": Cowel. (*Praedial* = arising from the ground; *personal* = profits from labour; *mixt* = arising from things nourished from the ground, eg, eggs.) The Tithe Act 1936 replaced tithe rentcharges by redemption annuities. The Finance Act 1962 provided for compulsory redemption of such annuities on the sale of land. Their payment was ended under the Finance Act 1977, s. 56.

title. 1. Appellation of office or distinction. 2. Right to land or goods, or evidence of such right. 3. "Good title" indicates that the evidence of claim of title is conclusive. See *MEPC Ltd* v *Christian-Edwards* [1981] AC 205. 4. Title of an Act of Parliament (qv) is its heading. It is legitimate to use the title for the interpretation of the Act as a whole and to discover its scope: *Johnson* v *Upham* (1859) 2 E & E 263; *Vacher* v *London Society of Compositors* [1913] AC 107.

title, abstract of. *See* ABSTRACT AND EPITOME OF TITLE.

title, chain of. *See* CHAIN OF TITLE.

title deeds. Those documents constituting evidence of legal ownership of land. See, eg, the L.P.A. 1925, s. 45(9); *Clayton* v *Clayton* [1930] 2 Ch 12.

title, long. Formal title of an Act of Parliament (qv), eg, "An Act to consolidate the enactments relating to conveyancing and the law of property in England and Wales" (the long title of the Act, known generally by its short title of the Law of Property Act 1925).

title, paramount. *See* PARAMOUNT.

title, root of. *See* ROOT OF TITLE.

title, short. Title by which an Act is usually and conveniently cited. See the Short Titles Act 1896. Usually stated towards the end of the statute in a separate section, eg, the Th.A. 1968, s. 36(1). (1). It cannot be relied on for resolution of a doubt in construction. See *Re Boaler* [1915] 1 KB 21.

title to goods, transfer of. Where goods are sold by a person who is not their owner, and who does not sell them under the authority or with the consent of the owner, the buyer acquires no better title to the goods than the seller had, unless the owner of the goods is by his conduct precluded from denying the seller's authority to sell: S.G.A. 1979, s. 21(1).

title, voidable, sale under. *See* VOIDABLE TITLE, SALE UNDER.

toll. 1. Tax paid for some privilege. 2. Compensation for service provided.

Tolzey Court. *See* BRISTOL TOLZEY COURT.

Tomlin Order. Order (drafted by Tomlin J) in which the court records the voluntary settlement of an action and stays all further proceedings except for the purpose of carrying the agreed terms into effect. See *Practice Note* [1927] WN 276; *Dashwood* v *Dashwood* (1927) 64 LJNC 431; and *Re A Company (003324/1979)* [1981] 1 WLR 1059.

tonnage. 1. Tax formerly paid to the Crown on goods carried by ship. 2. A vessel's burden: Merchant Shipping Act 1965, s. 1.

tontine. An insurance scheme whereby contributors pay into a fund which is divided, at the end of a specified period, among the survivors by way of payment of capital or an annuity.

tools of trade. A bankrupt's tools of his trade are not generally available for creditors. See the B.A. 1914, s. 38(2). Under the Insolvency Act 1976, s. 1, Sch 1, a maximum value of £250 worth of a bankrupt's necessary goods is exempted from division amongst creditors.

tort. *Tortus* = twisted, distorted. A civil wrong independent of contract. Liability in tort arises from breach of a duty primarily fixed by law which is towards others generally, breach of which is redressible by an action for unliquidated damages (qv).

tortfeasor. One who commits a tort (qv).

tortious. Having the nature of a tort (qv).

tortious conveyance. Former device for destroying contingent remainders (qv), by which a tenant in tail or for life enlarged a fee simple (by fine and recovery of feoffment). Abolished by the Real Property Act 1845.

torts, classification of. 1. Wrongs to the person, eg, assault. 2. Wrongs to reputation, eg, defamation. 3. Wrongs to property, eg, trespass. 4. Wrongs to persons or property, eg, nuisance. 5. Wrongs of interference in contractual relations, eg, inducing breach of contract. 6. Abuse of legal procedure, eg, malicious prosecutions.

tort, waiver of. *See* WAIVER OF TORT.

total loss. *See* LOSS, LIABILITY IN MARINE INSURANCE FOR.

toties quoties. As many times as may happen. Repeatedly.

totting up. Procedure under the Transport Act 1981, s. 19; of adding together convictions involving the endorsement of licences under the Road Traffic Act 1972, and which may result in disqualification. See *Maynard* v *Andrews* [1973] RTR 398; *Dyson* v *Ellison* [1975] 1 All ER 278; and *Holland* v *Phipps* [1982] 1 WLR 1150.

touching and concerning land. *See* COVENANT RUNNING WITH THE LAND.

town. At one time a group of dwellings that "hath, or in time past hath had, a church and celebration of divine service, sacraments and burials": Coke. Now refers to a group of houses, etc, bigger than a village. A parish or community can resolve to adopt the status of a town: L.G.A. 1972, s. 245.

town planning. Principles related to the improvement of land in the general interests of the community. See the T.C.P.A. 1971, as amended; and the L.G.P.L.A. 1980, Part IX.

tracing trust property. Steps taken by beneficiaries to follow assets which have come into the hands of others. At common law the right to trace will be lost if the plaintiff's money has become mixed with another fund. In equity a charge can be imposed on the mixed fund to the full extent of the plaintiff's contribution. See *Re Hallett's Estate* (1879) 11 Ch D 772; *Re Diplock* [1948] Ch 495; and *Chase Manhattan Bank* v *Israel-British Bank* [1979] 3 All ER 1025. For the right to trace where there is no trust, but some other fiduciary element, see *Aluminium Industrie Vaassen BV* v *Romalpa Aluminium Ltd* [1976] 2 All ER 552.

trade. Business activity relating to the exchange of goods for money. For the purposes of the Finance Act 1980, the term does not include dealing in shares, securities, land, trades or commodity futures: Sch 18, Part VII, para 23(1). See *Blackmore* v *Bellamy* [1983] RTR 303.

trade association. Phrase used, eg, in the Resale Prices Act 1976, s. 24(1) to mean "a body of persons (whether incorporated or not) which is formed for the purpose of furthering the trade interests of its members or the persons represented by its members".

trade boards. Established by the Trade Boards Act 1909 and initially confined to a few "sweated industries". They were forerunners of the modern wages councils (qv) (and were so retitled in 1945).

trade description. Under the Trade Descriptions Act 1968, a description, direct or indirect, concerning goods, relating to: quantity, size, gauge; method of manufacture, production, etc; composition; fitness for purpose; other physical characteristics; testing and results; approval by any person: place or date of manufacture, production, etc; person by whom manufactured or produced, etc; other history. See *Stainthorpe* v *Bailey* [1980] RTR 7; S.I. 1981/121 (origin of goods marking); and *Westminster CC* v *Ray Alan Ltd* [1982] 1 WLR 383. *See* FALSE TRADE DESCRIPTION.

trade dispute. Under the T.U.L.R.A. 1974, s. 29(1) (as amended by the Employment Act 1982, s. 18(2)), a dispute between workers and their employers wholly or partly relating to: terms and conditions of employment, engagement or suspension of employment, allocation of work or other duties, discipline, union membership and non-membership, negotiating machinery and facilities for union officials.

trade dispute and tort. "An act done by a person in contemplation or furtherance of a trade dispute is not actionable in tort on the ground only that it is an interference with the trade, business or employment of another person, or with the right of another person to dispose of his capital or labour as he wills": T.U.L.R.A. 1974, s. 13(2). See the Employment Act 1980, s. 17; *Express Newspapers* v *McShane* [1980] ICR 42. See also the Employment Act 1982, s. 16 (limit on damages awarded against unions in actions in tort).

trade fixtures. A tenant may remove fixtures attached to the land for the purpose of conducting his trade. See *Poole's Case* (1703) 1 Salk 368; *Smith* v *City Petroleum Co* [1940] 1 All ER 260. *See* FIXTURES.

trade mark. "A mark used or proposed to be used in relation to goods for the purpose of indicating or so as to indicate a connection in the course of trade between the goods and some person having the right either as proprietor or registered user to use the mark, whether with or without any indication of the identity of that person": Trade Marks Act 1938, s. 68(1). "Mark" includes "a device, brand, heading, label, ticket, name, signature, word, letter, numeral, or any combination thereof". See, eg, *Baume & Co Ltd* v *Moore Ltd* [1958] RPC 226; *Re Waterford Trade Mark* [1972] RPC 149. For trade marks under EEC regulations, see, eg, *Van Zuylen Frères* v *Hag AG* [1974] 2 CMLR 127; *EMI Records Ltd* v *CBS UK Ltd* [1976] 1 CMLR 235.

trade mark at common law. A mark used so widely in connection with a group or class of goods that the public recognise goods carrying that mark as associated with the owner of the mark. A dispute relating to such a mark may result in a passing-off action (qv).

trade mark, registered. A trade mark

recorded on the Register. Part "A" registration relates to a mark containing or consisting of, eg, the name of a company represented in a special manner; the signature of the applicant for registration; an invented word. Part "B" relates to a mark which distinguishes the goods generally. Registration is for seven years and is renewable. See the Trade Marks Act 1938.

trade, restraint of. *See* RESTRAINT OF TRADE.

trade secret. Some manufacturing or productive process, knowledge of which is generally confined to a firm and utilisation of which provides an advantage over competitors. Disclosure of such information, as the result of a breach of confidence or where it has resulted from employment under contract, can be prevented by injunction. See *Cranleigh Precision Engineering* v *Bryant* [1964] 3 All ER 289; *Initial Service Ltd* v *Putterill* [1968] 1 QB 396. *See* CONFIDENCE, BREACH OF.

trade union. This means, under the T.U.L.R.A. 1974, s. 28(1), an organisation (whether permanent or temporary) which consists wholly or mainly of workers and is an organisation whose principal purposes include the regulation of relations between workers and employers or employers' associations, or consists wholly or mainly of constituent or affiliated organisations which fulfil the above conditions, or of representatives of such constituent or affiliated organisations. See, eg, *EETPU* v *The Times* [1980] 1 All ER 1097.

trade union ballots, funding of. Public funding of the secret ballots of independent unions in relation to matters such as amending union rules, ascertaining members' views on strikes, is provided for by the Employment Act 1980, s. 1. See S.I. 1982/953.

trade union duties and activities, time off for. The right under the E.P.(C.)A. 1978, ss. 27–28, allowing an official of an independent trade union to have paid time off for duties and an employee to have unpaid time off for trade union activities. See S.I.

1977/2076; *Beal* v *Beecham Ltd* [1982] 1 WLR 1005. *See* TRADE UNION OFFICIAL.

trade union, independent. This means, under the E.P. (C.) A. 1978, s. 153(1), a trade union which is not under the domination or control of an employer or group of employers or of one or more employers' associations, and is not liable to interference by an employer or any such group or association (arising out of the provision of financial or material support or by any other means whatsoever) tending towards such control. Genuine and effective independence of employers must be demonstrated: *Blue Circle Staff Association* v *Certification Officer* [1977] 1 WLR 239; *Association of HSD Employees* v *Certification Officer* [1978] ICR 21.

trade union membership, coercive recruitment of. Immunity in tort, granted to unions under the T.U.L.R.A. 1974, s. 13, is removed, under the Employment Act 1980, s. 18, where persons threaten to induce or induce workers to break contracts of employment with the objective of compelling others to join a particular union, and if those workers do not work for the same employer or at the same place of work as those who are being compelled to become members of the union.

trade union official. "Any person who is an officer of the union or of a branch or section of the union and who (not being such an officer) is a person elected or appointed in accordance with the rules of the union to be a representative of its members or of some of them including any person so elected or appointed who is an employee of the same employer as the members or one or more of the members, whom he is to represent": T.U.L.R.A. 1974, s. 30(1).

trade union, unreasonable exclusion or expulsion from. Every person who is, or is seeking to be, in employment with an employer whose practice it is to employ union members, has the right not to have an application for membership of a union unreasonably refused and not to be unreasonably expelled from a union: Employment Act 1980, s. 4(1), (2). A complaint may be pre-sented to an industrial tribunal (qv): s. 4(4). See *Cheall* v *APEX* [1983] 2 WLR 679.

trading certificate. Certificate to commence business issued by the registrar to a public company (qv) under the Cos.A. 1980, s. 4, following a statutory declaration by the company, stating: that the nominal value of its allotted share capital is not less than the authorised minimum; amount of company's preliminary expenses and who paid them; amount paid up on company's allotted share capital; any amount paid or benefit given to a promoter and his consideration for it. (A private company (qv) can commence business on incorporation.)

trading, fraudulent. *See* FRAUDULENT TRADING.

trading interests, protection of. Under the Protection of Trading Interests Act 1980, the Secretary of State may make orders prohibiting persons who carry on a business in the UK from complying with requirements or prohibitions which might damage the UK's trading interests, or infringe the UK's jurisdiction, or are otherwise prejudicial to the UK's sovereignty.

trading stamps. Stamps exchanged by a retailer's customer for free gifts from a stamp company. Under the Trading Stamps Act 1964, as amended, the stamp must be clearly marked with a monetary value and the name of the issuing organisation. Under the Supply of Goods (Implied Terms) Act 1973 there can be no exclusion, in the case of trading stamps, of an implied warranty (qv) on the part of the provider that he has a right to give the goods in exchange or that the goods are of merchantable quality (qv). See also the C.C.A. 1974, Sch 4, paras 24–26.

trading stock. Real or personal property, being either property such as is sold in the ordinary course of a trade, or would be sold if it were mature or if its manufacture, preparation or construction were complete, or materials such as are used in its manufacture, preparation or construction including work in progress (qv): Finance Act 1981, Sch 9, Part V, para 28(1).

traffic wardens. Persons appointed by police authorities to assist in control of road traffic. See the Road Traffic Act 1972, Sch 7; the Functions of Traffic Wardens Order 1970 (S.I. 1970/1958); and *R* v *Saunders* [1978] Crim LR 98.

transcript. A copy, usually in longhand, of notes taken, eg, in shorthand.

transfer. The conveyance of title or other interest in property from one person to another, eg, by sale or gift. See the S.G.A. 1979, Part III.

transferable. "The word 'transferable' is of the widest possible import, and includes every means by which property may be passed from one person to another": *Gathercole* v *Smith* (1875) 17 Ch D I.

transfer, blank. *See* BLANK TRANSFER.

transferee. "In relation to a contract for the transfer of goods means (depending on the context) a person to whom the property in the goods is transferred under the contract, or a person to whom the property is to be so transferred, or a person to whom the rights under the contract of either of those persons have passed": Supply of Goods and Services Act 1982, s. 18(1).

transfer of action. Removal of action (qv). See O. 16, r. 1.

transfer of shares. Shares are transferable subject to any restrictions in a company's articles (qv): Cos.A. 1948, s. 73. A transfer cannot be registered unless a proper instrument of transfer, correctly stamped, has been delivered to the company, executed by or on behalf of the transferor: s. 75. See the Stock Transfer Acts 1963 and 1982. *See* COMPANY; SHARE TRANSFER.

transferor. "In relation to a contract for the transfer of goods, means (depending on the context) a person who transfers the property in the goods under the contract, or a person who agrees to do so, or a person to whom the duties under the contract of either of those persons have passed": Supply of Goods and Services Act 1982, s. 18(1).

transfer order. Court order, under the C.C.A. 1974, s. 133(1) (*b*) (ii), for

the transfer to a debtor of a creditor's title to goods to which an agreement relates and the return to the creditor of the remainder of the goods.

transferred malice. *See* MALICE.

transformation, doctrine of. Doctrine that rules of international law are not to be considered a part of English law unless made a part of law by an Act of Parliament (qv), judges' decisions or long established customs, as contrasted with the doctrine of incorporation (qv). See *R* v *Keyn* (1876) 2 Ex D 63; *Chung Chi Cheung* v *The King* [1939] AC 160.

transit in rem judicatam. It passes into *res judicata* (qv). Refers to a clause of action disappearing as it is merged in a judgment.

transitu, stoppage in. See IN TRANSITU.

transmission of shares. The vesting of shares in another, not by virtue of transfer, but by the operation of law, eg, on the death or bankruptcy (qv) of a shareholder. See the Cos.A. 1948, ss. 75, 76, 82.

transportation. Penalty for serious crimes (eg, larceny) introduced in the reign of Elizabeth I whereby felons were transported overseas to a penal colony. Abolished and replaced by penal servitude under the Penal Servitude Act 1853, later by imprisonment.

transposing of words. Changing position of words in a sentence contained in a document. "The law... doth often transpose words contrary to their order to bring them to the intent of the parties": *Parkhurst* v *Smith* (1742) Willes 327. See *Re Bacharach* [1959] Ch 245.

travaux préparatoires. Phrase used in discussions of statutory interpretation to refer to the background of legislation, eg, reports of Royal Commissions, debates in Parliament. The judicial consideration of such matter has been generally forbidden in English law. See *Davis* v *Johnson* [1978] 1 All ER 1132. May now be used, apparently, in the interpretation of statutes: *Fothergill* v *Monarch Air Lines* [1981] AC 251.

traverse. An express and specific denial of an allegation of fact made in a statement of claim. Example:

"Plaintiff paid defendant £200"; traverse—"Plaintiff did not pay defendant £200 or any other sum". See O. 18, r. 13.

treachery. The offence under the Treachery Act 1940, which related to the Second World War, by those who did, conspired or attempted to do an act designed or likely to assist the military operations of the enemy or impede the operations of HM Forces.

treason. The capital offence under the Statute of Treasons 1351, which is, in essence, a breach of allegiance to the Crown. It comprises, eg, the levying of war against the King in his realm, being adherent to the King's enemies in his realm, giving them aid and comfort in the realm or elsewhere. See, eg, *R* v *Ahlers* [1915] 1 KB 616; *R* v *Casement* [1917] 1 KB 98; *Joyce* v *DPP* [1946] AC 347. A person charged with treason may not be granted bail except by order of a High Court judge or Secretary of State: M.C.A. 1980, s. 4.

treason felony. Offence under the Treason Felony Act 1848, committed by one within or without the realm, who compasses, imagines, devises or intends, to deprive or depose the Queen from the style or royal name of the imperial crown, to levy war against the Queen in the UK, to stir any foreigner to invade the UK.

treason, misprision of. *See* MISPRISION.

treasure trove. "When any money, gold, silver, plate or bullion is found in any place and no man knoweth to whom the property is, then the property thereof belongeth to the King": *Termes de la Ley*. It was a common-law offence to conceal treasure trove from the Crown. See now the Th.A. 1968, s. 32(1) (*a*). The coroner (qv) is empowered to hold an inquest relating to treasure trove: *A.-G.* v *Moore* [1893] 1 Ch 676. See *A.-G. of Duchy of Lancaster* v *Overton* [1982] 2 WLR 397 (only gold and silver are treasure trove).

Treasury. The government department, headed by the Chancellor of the Exchequer, concerned with the finances and economic and monetary policy of the nation. The Prime Minister (qv) is the First Lord of the Treasury. It includes divisions concerned with domestic economy, overseas finance and public services.

Treasury Counsel. Barristers (qv) nominated by the A.-G. who receive briefs from the DPP relating to prosecutions at the Central Criminal Court (qv).

Treasury, First Lord of the. A sinecure office, usually filled by convention by the Prime Minister (qv), who has no duties in connection with the department.

Treasury Solicitor. An official, who acts for the Treasury. See the Treasury Solicitors Act 1876. The office was separated from that of the DPP (qv) in 1908. He instructs parliamentary counsel (qv) on bills, advises on the interpretation of the law, may control the Statutory Publications Office and directs the work of the Queen's Proctor (qv).

treat, invitation to. *See* INVITATION TO TREAT.

treaty. Written agreement, governed by international law, concluded between two or more states, or other subjects of international law, possessed of treaty-making capacity. In English law a treaty can be made only through the Crown. "Treaties and declarations do not become part of our law until they are made law by Parliament": *per* Lord Denning in *R* v *Chief Immigration Officer ex p Bibi* [1976] 1 WLR 979.

treaty, self-executing. Treaty which does not require ancillary legislation to make it immediately effective.

trespass. An unjustifiable interference with possession. A tort involving "direct and forcible injury". "Every invasion of private property, be it ever so minute, is a trespass": *Entick* v *Carrington* (1765) 19 St Tr 1066. Known as "the fertile mother of actions", since from the writ of trespass (which appeared *c.* 1250) there developed a large number of personal actions.

trespass by relation. The fiction (qv) whereby a person being entitled to immediate possession, and entering upon the land, is deemed to have been in possession from the time that his right accrued. See *Dunlop v Macedo* (1891) 8 TLR 43.

trespasser *ab initio*. *See* AB INITIO.

trespasser, occupier's duty to. In general, a trespasser must take the land as he finds it. But the occupier owes the trespasser a duty to take such steps as common humanity or common sense would dictate, so as to exclude, warn, reduce or avert a danger: *British Rwys Board v Herrington* [1972] AC 877. See *Harris v Birkenhead Corporation and Another* [1975] 1 WLR 379. *See* OCCUPIERS' LIABILITY TO TRESPASSERS.

trespassing on premises of foreign missions. An offence under the C.L.A. 1977, s. 9.

trespassing with weapon of offence. "A person who is on any premises as a trespasser, after having entered as such, is guilty of an offence if, without lawful authority or reasonable excuse, he has with him on the premises any weapon of offence": C.L.A. 1977, s. 8. *See* OFFENCE, WEAPON OF.

trespass on the case. Formerly special writs of trespass based on indirect damage, eg, trover and *assumpsit* (qqv).

trespass to goods. A wrongful, direct (and not consequential) or negligent interference with possession of goods. Absence of intent is generally no excuse. See *Wilson v Lombank Ltd* [1963] 1 WLR 1294. See also the Torts (Interference with Goods) Act 1977.

trespass to land. Unjustifiable, direct and immediate interference with another's possession of land, eg by unauthorised walking on it, or improper use of a highway. See *Watson v Murray & Co* [1955] 2 QB 1; *Fowler v Lanning* [1959] 1 QB 426. For the purposes of the Th.A. 1968, s. 9(1)(*b*), a person is a trespasser if he enters the premises of another knowing that he is entering in excess of the permission given him or being reckless whether he is so doing: *R v Jones* [1976] 1 WLR 672.

trespass to the person. Some wrong suffered by a person, in the nature of assault, battery, false imprisonment, etc.

trial. The formal investigation and determination of matters in issue between parties before a court. See O. 33–35.

trial at bar. *See* BAR, TRIAL AT.

trial by battle. *See* BATTLE, TRIAL BY.

trial, new. 1. In the case of a civil appeal, under O. 59, r. 11, the Court of Appeal (qv) may order a new trial (on appeal from judge and jury, or judge alone) on grounds including: the improper admission or rejection of evidence; a perverse jury verdict; the discovery of fresh evidence (see *Skone v Skone* [1971] 2 All ER 582); some irregularity at trial (see *Brassington v Brassington* [1962] P 276). 2. Under the Criminal Appeal Act 1968, s. 7, a new trial may be ordered if the interests of justice so require. See the S.C.A. 1981, s. 17; *R v Flower* [1966] 1 QB 146; *R v Stafford* (1969) 53 Cr App R 1; *R v Rose* [1982] 3 WLR 192; and *Graham v Dodds* [1983] 1 WLR 808.

trial of action, modes of. Types of mode of trial of an action set out in O. 33, r. 2, include trial before judge alone, or judge with jury, or judge with the assistance of assessors, or official referee with or without the assistance of assessors, or master, or special referee.

trial of action, place of. Place in which civil proceedings will commence as determined by an order made on a summons for directions, ie, Royal Courts of Justice in London, or "one of the other places at which sittings of the High Court are authorised to be held for the trial of [those] proceedings or proceedings of the class to which they belong": O. 33, r. 1. For the place of trial on indictment, see the M.C.A. 1980, s. 7.

trial *per pais*. *See* IN PAIS.

trial, setting down for. *See* SETTING DOWN FOR ACTION.

trials, separate. *See* JOINDER OF OFFENDERS.

trials, separate, of separate issues. Procedure whereby the court may order separate trials of different questions or issues: O. 33, r. 4(2).

tribunals. Bodies outside the hierarchy of the courts with administrative or judicial functions, eg, industrial tribunals, rent tribunals (qqv). Their members include lawyers and laymen with specialised knowledge. In some cases chairmen are selected from a panel and appointed by the Lord Chancellor. Appeal may lie (where statute provides) to the High Court or, in some cases to the JCPC. See the Tribunals and Inquiries Act 1971.

tribunals, Council on. *See* COUNCIL ON TRIBUNALS.

tribunals of enquiry. *See* ENQUIRY, TRIBUNALS OF.

trigger clause. Term in an agreement which, when broken, activates some other term. See, eg, the CCA 1974, s. 88(3).

trinoda necessitas. Also *trimoda necessitas.* Necessity of three kinds. The threefold charge in Anglo-Saxon times on landholders, relating to repelling invasions, repairing highways and bridges and building castles.

trover. An action on the case (qv) brought "to recover the value of personal chattels wrongly converted to another by his use": *Cooper* v *Chitty* (1756) 1 Burr. The term is also applied to an action for conversion. See the Torts (Interference with Goods) Act 1977, s. 1. *See* CONVERSION, TORT OF.

truck system. Practice whereby wages were paid in goods or tokens, rather than money. Abolished by the Truck Acts 1831–1940. See the Payment of Wages Act 1960; *Kenyon* v *Darwen Cotton Manufacturing Co Ltd* [1936] 2 KB 193; *Williams* v *Butlers* [1975] 2 All ER 889 (agreed deduction of union contributions paid directly to union not illegal under the 1831 Act, s. 2).

trust. In essence, an equitable obligation which imposes on a person described as a trustee certain duties of dealing with property held and controlled by him for the benefit of the persons described as the beneficiaries, or, if there are not such persons, for some purpose recognised and enforceable at law. Example: A, the owner of Blackacre, conveys it to B in fee simple, directing B to hold it in trust for C; A is the *settlor,* B is the

trustee, C is the *beneficiary* (or *cestui que trust* (qv)), Blackacre is the *trust property.* For the domicile of a trust, see the C.J.J.A. 1982, s. 45.

trust, breach of. *See* BREACH OF TRUST.

trust, completely constitued. *See* COMPLETELY CONSTITUTED TRUST.

trust, controlled. *See* CONTROLLED TRUST.

trust corporation. A corporation entitled under the Public Trustee Rules 1926, including a corporation constituted under the law of the UK or any other member of state of the EEC (qv), and empowered under its constitution to undertake trust business in England and Wales. having one or more places of business in the UK, being a registered company with a capital of not less than (currently) £250,000 (or its equivalent in the currency of the state wherein it is registered) of which not less than (currently) £100,000, or the equivalent, is paid up in cash. The Treasury Solicitor, Official Solicitor and Public Trustee (qqv) are also included. See the Tr.A. 1925, s. 68; the S.L.A. 1925, s. 117(1); the L.P.(Amendment)A. 1926, s. 3; and the S.C.A. 1981, s. 115.

trust, derivative. *See* SUB-TRUST.

trustee. One who holds property on trust for another, known as *cestui que trust* (qv) or beneficiary. Capacity to be a trustee exists where there is capacity to take or hold property. Trustees may be appointed by the settlor, under express power conferred by a trust instrument, by court, under the Tr.A. 1925, s. 36. See Cmnd 8733 (1982). For "residence of trustees," see the Finance Act 1982, s. 94(1)(*c*).

trustee, acceptance of office by. Acceptance may be express or presumed. In general, in absence of evidence to the contrary, acceptance is presumed. Conduct may operate as acceptance. There can be no renunciation after acceptance. See *Conyngham* v *Conyngham* (1750) 1 Ves Sen 522; *Re Sharman's Will Trusts* [1942] Ch 311.

trustee de son tort. Where a person who is not a trustee and who has no authority from a trustee takes upon himself to intermeddle with trust matters or to carry out acts which are characteristic of the office of trustee, he makes himself a *trustee de son tort* ("of his own wrongdoing") and is held to be a constructive trustee. See *Re Barney* [1891] 2 Ch 265; *Barnes v Addy* (1874) LR 9 Ch 244; and *Re Bell's Indenture* [1980] 3 All ER 425.

trustee, duties of. Generally: to become acquainted with the terms of the trust; to ensure that the trust property is vested; to act gratuitously and not to profit from the trust; not to delegate; to act impartially in the interests of all beneficiaries.

trustee in bankruptcy. *See* BANKRUPTCY, TRUSTEE IN.

trustee investments. *See* INVESTMENT, TRUSTEES' POWERS OF.

Trustee, Public. *See* PUBLIC TRUSTEE.

trustees' costs basis. A basis for taxation of costs (qv) whereby a party may recover his costs out of the fund of which he is trustee. "No costs shall be disallowed except in so far as those costs or any part of their amount should not, in accordance with the duty of the trustee or personal representative as such, have been incurred or paid, or should for that or any other reason be borne by him personally": O. 62, r. 31(2).

trustees for sale, powers of. "Trustees for sale shall . . . have the powers of a tenant for life and the trustees of a settlement under the S.L.A. 1925, including in relation to the land the powers of management conferred by that Act during a minority": L.P.A. 1925, s. 28(1). See also the L.P.(Amendment)A. 1926, s. 7; *Re Wellsted's Will Trusts* [1949] Ch 296.

trusteeship. System of administration of certain non-self governing territories under the United Nations Charter, art. 75.

trusteeship, termination of. A trustee can retire under any express power, by statutory power conferred by the Tr.A. 1925, s. 39, by the consent of all beneficiaries, or by order of the court. He can be removed from office under any express power, under statutory power (see the Tr.A. 1925, ss. 36, 41), or by the court. Trusteeship terminates on death:

where there are two or more trustees and one dies, the rule of survivorship applies, so that the office devolves on the surviving trustees. On the death of the sole surviving trustee, the estate devolves on his personal representatives.

trustees of the settlement. *See* SETTLED LAND ACT TRUSTEES.

trustees, protection of. The court may relieve a trustee either wholly or partly from personal liability for breach of trust if he has acted honestly and reasonably and ought fairly to be excused. The burden of establishing this is on the trustee. See the Tr.A. 1925, s. 61; the Lim.A. 1980, s. 21; *Re Stuart* [1897] 2 Ch 583; *Marsden v Regan* [1954] 1 WLR 423.

trustees, remuneration of. *See* REMUNERATION OF TRUSTEES.

trustees, Settled Land Act. *See* SETTLED LAND ACT TRUSTEES.

trust, executed. *See* EXECUTED.

trust, executory. *See* EXECUTORY.

trust, express. *See* EXPRESS TRUST.

trust for sale. Means in relation to land "an immediate binding trust for sale, whether or not exercisable at the request or with the consent of any person, and with or without a power at discretion to postpone the sale; 'trustees for sale' means the persons (including a personal representative) holding land on trust for sale; and 'power to postpone a sale' means power to postpone in the exercise of a discretion": L.P.A. 1925, s. 205(1) (xxix). It may arise expressly or by operation of statute (eg, the A.E.A. 1925, s. 31(1), where a person dies intestate and the personal representative holds property "as to the real estate upon trust to sell the same; and as to the personal estate upon trust to call in, sell and convert into money such part thereof as may not consist of money").

trust, housing. *See* HOUSING TRUST.

trust instrument. The document used in the creation of a settlement (qv), which appoints trustees, contains the power to appoint new trustees and declares trusts affecting the settlement, etc. See the S.L.A. 1925, ss. 4, 9, 117(1).

trust, power in nature of. Known also as "trust-power". Created where the donor has demonstrated a clear intention that property is to pass to the objects in any event. Whether it has been created or not is a matter of "intention or presumed intention to be derived from the language of the instrument"; *Re Scarisbrick's Will Trusts* [1951] 1 All ER 822. See *Brown v Higgs* (1803) 8 Ves 561; *Re Brierley* (1894) 39 SJ 647. *See* POWER.

trust property. In general, all property, real or personal, legal or equitable, may be made the object of a trust. See *Lord Strathcona SS Co v Dominion SS Co* [1926] AC 108.

trust, public. *See* PUBLIC TRUST.

trust, purpose. Term applied to a trust not in favour of ascertainable individuals, eg, a charitable trust. See *Re Astor's Settlement Trusts* [1952] Ch 534; *Re Coxen* [1948] Ch 747; and *Re Grant's WT* [1979] 3 All ER 359.

trusts, classification of. 1. Imposed by statute. 2. Express. 3. Implied, or resulting and constructive. 4. Executed and executory. 5. Completely and incompletely constituted. 6. Private and public. 7. Simple and special. For an early classification by Lord Nottingham, see *Cook v Fountain* (1676) 3 Swan 585.

trust, sub-. *See* SUB-TRUST.

trusts, unenforceable. *See* UNENFORCE-ABLE TRUSTS.

trusts, unlawful. *See* UNLAWFUL TRUSTS.

trust, termination of by beneficiary. A beneficiary who is *sui juris* (qv) and absolutely entitled has the right to terminate a trust, irrespective of the wishes of the trustee or settlor. This applies also if there are several beneficiaries who are all *sui juris* and absolutely entitled: *Barton v Briscoe* (1822) Jac 603. Under these circumstances the trustees must convey the trust property, thus bringing the trust to an end. See *IRC v Executors of Hamilton-Russell* [1943] 1 All ER 474.

trust territory. Non-self governing territory, a former mandate under the League of Nations, administered under the Trusteeship Council of the United Nations. See the United Nations Charter, arts. 76, 87.

trust, variation of. *See* VARIATION OF TRUST.

trust, void. A trust which, because it is illegal or contrary to public policy, will not be enforced. Example: a trust which is to take effect on the future separation of a husband and wife (see *Westmeath v Westmeath* (1831) 1 Dow & Cl 519).

trust, voidable. A trust which, having been created as a result of, eg, fraud, mistake, duress, may be set aside or rectified in certain circumstances. Example: T, apparently about to die, executed a voluntary settlement which he did not understand, which was not read to him, and from which a power of revocation had been purposely omitted (see *Forshaw v Welsby* (1860) 30 Beav 243).

turbary, common of. Right to cut peat or turf on another's land, to be used as fuel.

turning Queen's evidence. *See* QUEEN'S EVIDENCE.

turpis causa. Base cause. Consideration that is base (eg, immoral) and that will not suffice to support a contractual obligation. *See* EX TURPI CAUSA.

two-counsel rule. Practice whereby the "freedom by a QC to supply his services without being accompanied by or assisted by a junior" is restricted: *Report of Monopolies and Mergers Commission on Barristers' Services* 1976. Abolished as from October 1977, following which a QC is entitled to accept instructions to appear alone in any particular case, but may refuse if by so doing he is unable to conduct the case in question, or in other cases, properly.

Tynwald, Court of. Governor, Legislative Council and Assembly (House of Keys) of the Isle of Man. See, for proof of Acts of Tynwald, Isle of Man Act 1979, s. 12. See the Isle of Man (Transfer of Functions) Order 1980 (S.I. 1980/399).

U

uberrimae fidei. Of the utmost good faith. Applies to a contract (eg, of insurance) in which the promisee must inform the promissor of all those facts and surrounding circumstances which could influence the promissor in deciding whether or not to enter the contract. See *Lindenau* v *Desborough* (1828) 2 Swann 400; and *Woolcott* v *Sun Alliance* [1978] 1 WLR 493. See also Cos.A. 1948, s. 38.

ubi jus ibi remedium. Where there is a right there is a remedy. See *Ashby* v *White* (1703) 2 Ld Raym 938.

ubi remedium ibi jus. Where there is a remedy there is a right.

ubi supra. At the place [mentioned] above.

UK. United Kingdom (qv).

ultimatum. A final demand or condition.

ultra. Beyond.

ultra vires. Beyond the powers. Term relating generally to the excess of legal powers or authority; specifically, the exercise by a corporation of powers beyond those conferred on it explicitly or implicitly. See *Ashbury Rail Carriage Co* v *Riche* (1875) LR 7 HL 653 (subject-matter not included in the memorandum (qv) and on which the contract was based was held to be *ultra vires*); *Baroness Wenlock* v *River Dee Co* (1885) 10 App Cas 354; *Bell Houses Ltd* v *City Wall Properties Ltd* [1966] 2 QB 656. Under the European Communities Act 1972, s. 9(1): "In favour of a person dealing with a company in good faith, any transaction decided on by the directors shall be deemed to be one which it is within the capacity of the company to enter into." See *International Sales* v *Marcus* [1982] 3 All ER 551.

umpire. *See* ARBITRATION.

UN. United Nations (qv).

unascertained goods. Goods defined by description only, eg, "1,000 tonnes of coal". Property in them does not pass until the goods are ascertained: S.G.A. 1979, s. 16. See

Pignatarou v *Gilroy* [1919] 1 KB 459.

unborn person, duty of care to. A doctor is under no legal obligation to a foetus to terminate its life; a child's claim for damages, having "suffered entry into a life in which her injuries are highly debilitating", was considered contrary to public policy as being a violation of the sanctity of human life: *McKay* v *Essex Area Health Authority* [1982] QB 1166.

unborn persons, killing of. It is an offence to kill any child capable of being born alive. See the O.P.A. 1861, s. 58; the Infant Life Preservation Act 1929, s. 1 (for the purposes of that Act evidence that a woman had been pregnant for 28 weeks is prima facie proof that she was pregnant of a child capable of being born alive); and the Abortion Act 1967. *See* ABORTION; CHILD DESTRUCTION.

uncalled capital. The amount remaining unpaid on the nominal value of a share.

uncertainty, void for. Term applied to a document (eg, a will) so ambiguous or obscure that it cannot be understood.

unchastity, imputation of. Actionable as slander (qv) without proof of special damage. See the Slander of Women Act 1891; *Kerr* v *Kennedy* [1942] 1 KB 409.

uncollected goods, disposal of. *See* DISPOSAL OF UNCOLLECTED GOODS.

unconscionable transaction. One "such as no man in his senses and not under delusion could make on the one hand, and no honest and fair man would accept on the other; which are unequitable and unconscientious bargains": *Earl of Chesterfield* v *Jannsen* (1750) 2 Ves Sen 125. See *Schroeder Music Publishing Co* v *Macaulay* [1974] 1 WLR 1308. "Was the bargain fair? . . . The test of fairness is, no doubt, whether the restrictions are both reasonably necessary for the protection of the legitimate interests of the promisee and commensurate with the benefits secured to the promisor under the contract. For the purposes of this test, all the provisions of the contract must be taken into consideration": *per* Lord Diplock. *See* CATCHING BARGAIN.

uncontrollable impulse. *See* IRRESISTIBLE IMPULSE, DEFENCE OF.

undefended cause. Cause in which the defendant fails to acknowledge service of the writ or other originating process or to give notice of his intention to defend the plaintiff's action, fails to put in statement of defence, or does not appear at the trial after having received notice. See O. 13, O. 19, O. 35.

undefended cause, in relation to matrimonial dispute. A case, under the Mat.C.A. 1973, s. 3, in which the respondent has not given notice of the intention to defend within the time limit, or, in any other case, a case in which no answer has been filed or any answer filed has been struck out or a case which is proceeding only on the respondent's answer and in which no reply or answer to the respondent's answer has been filed or any such reply or answer has been struck out: Matrimonial Causes Rules 1977, r. 2(2).

under-lease. A sub-lease (qv).

under protest. Acknowledgment of service of a writ while denying an obligation to participate in the case. Known also as "a conditional acknowledgment". See O. 12, rr. 7, 8.

undertakers, statutory. *See* STATUTORY UNDERTAKERS.

undertaking. 1. Promise, usually resulting in an obligation. 2. A business or project.

underwriter. One who subscribes his name to a policy of insurance against the sum for which he accepts liability. An underwriter of shares or debentures offers to take up shares and debentures not taken up by the public. A *sub-underwriting agreement* is a contract between an underwriter and another person which, in exchange for a commission, relieves the underwriter of liability. For the power of a company to pay underwriting commission, see the Cos.A. 1948, s. 53(1).

underwriting contract. "An agreement entered into before shares are brought before the public that in the event of the public not taking up the whole of them, or the number mentioned in the agreement, the underwriter will, for an agreed commission, take an allotment of such part of the shares as the public has not applied for": *Re Licensed Victuallers' Association* (1889) 42 Ch D 1.

undischarged bankrupt. *See* BANKRUPT, UNDISCHARGED.

undisclosed principal. *See* PRINCIPAL, UNDISCLOSED.

undivided share. Term relating to property held jointly or in common. Cannot now be created in land, except as settled land or behind trust for sale (qv): L.P.A. 1925, s. 34; S.L.A. 1925, s. 36. *See* JOINT TENANCY.

undue influence. Improper pressure on a person resulting in his not being an entirely free person in relation to some transaction. Such a transaction may be set aside by the court. "The law requires that influence, however natural and however right, shall not be unduly exercised—that is, shall be exercised only in due proportion to the surrounding circumstances and the strength of the person submitting to it. The more powerful influence or the weaker patient alike evokes a stronger application of the safeguard": *Allcard* v *Skinner* (1887) 36 Ch D 145. See also *Inche Noriah* v *Shaik Allie Bin Omar* [1929] AC 127; *Re Craig* [1971] Ch 95; *Lloyds Bank* v *Bundy* [1975] QB 326; *In re Sir Philip Lee Brocklehurst* [1978] Ch 14; *Roche* v *Sherrington* [1982] 2 All ER 426.

undue influence, presumption of. In the case of gifts *inter vivos* there is a presumption (qv) against the gift where there is a relationship resting on the inequality of bargaining power, eg, trustee and *cestui que trust* (qv), parent and child, doctor and patient, guardian and ward (but not husband and wife). See *Re Lloyds Bank* [1931] 1 Ch 289; *Lancashire Loans Ltd* v *Black* [1934] 1 KB 380; *Zamet* v *Hyman* [1961] 1 WLR 1442.

unemployment benefit. Benefit paid in respect of any day of unemployment which forms part of a period of interruption of employment: S.S.A.

1975, s. 14(1) (*a*). Generally payable after 3 days of interrupted employment; may cease to be payable after 312 days. see the S.S.(No.2) A. 1980, s. 5; *Crewe v SS Commissioner* [1982] 2 All ER 735.

unenforceable contract. A contract (qv) which although valid cannot be enforced by action because of some technical defect, eg, lapse of time.

unenforceable trusts. Trusts which cannot be enforced because, eg, there is no *cestui que trust* to enforce them and they are not charitable. See *Pettingall v Pettingall* (1842) 11 LJ Ch 178; *Re Astor's Settlement Trusts* [1952] Ch 534. *See* TRUST.

unfair consumer practices. "Contraventions of one or more enactments which impose duties, prohibitions or restrictions enforceable by criminal proceedings, whether any such duty, prohibition or restriction is imposed in relation to consumers as such or not and whether the person carrying on the business has or has not been convicted of any offence in respect of such contravention . . . or things done or omitted to be done in the course of that business in breach of contract or in breach of duty . . .": Fair Trading Act 1973, s. 34.

unfair contract terms. Contractual terms, eg, restricting or excluding liability for causing personal injury, or loss or damage resulting from negligence in manufacture of goods, and considered to be "unreasonable" in the circumstances which were or ought reasonably to have been known by, or in contemplation of, the parties when the contract was made. See the Unfair Contract Terms Act 1977.

unfair dismissal. *See* DISMISSAL.

unfavourable witness. One who, called by a party to prove a fact in issue (qv) or relevant to the issue, fails to prove that fact or proves an opposite fact. See *Ewer v Ambrose* (1825) 3 B & C 746. *See* WITNESS.

unfitness or incompetence, imputation of. Actionable as slander (qv) without proof of special damage. See the Defamation Act 1952, s. 2.

unfit to plead. Under the Criminal Procedure (Insanity) Act 1964, where the question arises of the accused being under a disability which could bar his being tried, consideration of the question can be postponed until any time up to the opening of the case for the defence. Generally, his fitness to plead is decided on arraignment by a jury other than that which tries him should the trial proceed. Where the Court of Appeal (qv) allows an appeal against unfitness to plead, the appellant can be tried for the offence with which he was originally charged: Criminal Appeal Act 1968, s. 16.

uniform, wearing of. It is generally an offence to wear in a public place or public meeting a uniform signifying one's association with a political organisation: Public Order Act 1936. See *O'Moran and Others v DPP* [1975] 1 All ER 473.

unilateral. One-sided.

unilateral contract. A contract (qv) arising where an offer is made in the form of a promise to pay in return for the performance of an act, so that the performance of the act is taken to imply assent. See, eg, *Carlill v Carbolic Smoke Ball Co* [1893] 1 QB 256; *United Dominions Trust v Eagle Aircraft* [1968] 1 WLR 74.

unilateral discharge. In a contract, the terms of which are carried out by X, but not by Y (the other party), the release of Y from his obligations by X.

unilateral mistake. *See* MISTAKE.

unincorporated bodies. *See* INCORPORATE.

unintentional defamation. Plea entered under the Defamation Act 1952, s. 4, whereby the defendant (qv) claims that he published the words innocently, that he did not intend to publish them and did not know of the circumstances by virtue of which the words might be understood to refer to the plaintiff (qv), or that the words were not defamatory on the face of them and that he did not know the circumstances by virtue of which they might be understood to be defamatory and that he exercised all reasonable care in relation to publication. He may then make an offer of amends. *See* DEFAMATION.

union, company. *See* COMPANY UNION.

union membership agreement. *See* CLOSED-SHOP AGREEMENT.

union, trade. See TRADE UNION.

United Kingdom. "The United Kingdom of Great Britain and Northern Ireland." It comprises England, Wales and Scotland (which make up Great Britain) plus Northern Ireland. See the I.A. 1978, Sch 1; and the B.N.A. 1981, s. 50(1).

United Nations. International organisation established on 24th October 1945, so as to maintain international peace and security, develop general welfare and relations among nations and encourage international co-operation in the solution of economic, social and humanitarian problems.

unities, four. See JOINT TENANCY.

unit trust. Commercial venture based on a trust deed between a management company (which manages the trust) and a trustee corporation, eg, bank, whereby subscriptions are invited from the public and used to buy a portfolio of investments held by trustees on behalf of the unit holders. See the Charging Orders Act 1979, s. 6(1).

unity of possession. Holding of one estate in undivided shares by two or more persons, or possession by one person of two or more rights based on separate titles.

unity of seisin. See SEISIN, UNITY OF.

universal agent. See AGENT, UNIVERSAL.

universal malice. See MALICE.

unjust enrichment. The unjust obtaining of money benefits at the expense of another. For the principles of restitution, see *Boissevain v Weil* [1950] AC 327. See QUASI-CONTRACTS.

unlawful assembly. Offence committed when there is an assembly of three or more persons gathered together with a common purpose, to commit a crime of violence or to achieve some other lawful or unlawful object in a manner which would cause reasonable persons to apprehend a breach of the peace. A misdemeanour at common law. See *R v Hunt* (1820) 1 St Tr NS 171; *R v Caird* (1970) 54 Cr App R 499; and *R v Chief Constable of Devon ex p Board* [1982] 3 WLR 967.

unlawful oath. See OATH, UNLAWFUL.

unlawful sexual intercourse. See SEXUAL INTERCOURSE, UNLAWFUL.

unlawful trusts. Trusts (qv) which are liable to be declared void, eg, as offending the rule against perpetuities (qv) or as preventing the carrying out of parental duties (see *Re Sandbrook* [1912] 2 Ch 471) or in restraint of marriage (see *Leong v Chye* [1955] AC 648).

unlawful wounding. It is an offence to unlawfully and maliciously wound a person with intent to do grievous bodily harm: O.P.A. 1861, s. 18. Provocation is no defence: *R v Cunningham* [1959] 1 QB 288. See WOUNDING; WOUNDING WITH INTENT.

unlimited company. Private company (qv) in which the liability of members is not limited. It need not have a share capital; it must have articles (qv). See the Cos.A. 1980, s. 1. See LIMITED COMPANY.

unliquidated damages. See DAMAGES.

unnatural offence. Synonym for buggery (qv).

uno flatu. With one breath (ie, on a single occasion, in a short space of time).

unopposed proceedings. Proceedings where a person who is entitled to oppose has been given the opportunity of doing so and has not done so.

unpaid seller. A seller in circumstances in which any portion of the price remains unpaid or where a negotiable instrument (qv) received as conditional payment has been dishonoured.

unpaid seller's rights. Even though the property in goods has passed to the buyer, the unpaid seller has a lien (qv) for the price, a right of stoppage *in transitu* (qv) if the buyer is insolvent and a right of resale (eg, where the goods are of a perishable nature: S.G.A. 1979, s. 39).

unread terms. In general, in the absence of fraud or misrepresentation (qv), a person who has not read the contents of a document or has chosen that they remain unread is bound by his signature to that document. See, eg, *L'Estrange v Graucob* [1934] 2 KB 394.

unreasonable. "No one can properly be labelled as unreasonable unless he is not only wrong but unreasonably wrong, so wrong that no reasonable person could sensibly take that view": *per* Lord Denning in *Secretary of State for Education and Science* v *Tameside Metropolitan BC* [1976] 3 All ER 665. "History is replete with genuine accusations of unreasonableness when all that is involved is disagreement": *per* Lord Russell.

unreasonable conduct. Under the Mat.C.A. 1973, s. 1(2) (*b*), conduct other than desertion or behaviour leading to desertion which will justify the conclusion that the marriage has broken down irretrievably: *Stringfellow* v *Stringfellow* [1976] 1 WLR 645. See *Katz* v *Katz* [1972] 3 All ER 210; *Livingstone-Stallard* v *Livingstone-Stallard* [1974] 2 All ER 766; *Bergin* v *Bergin* [1983] 1 WLR 279. *See* BREAK-DOWN OF MARRIAGE.

unregistered company. Any body corporate to which the provisions specified in the Cos.A. 1948, Sch 14, apply by virtue of s. 435 of that Act: Cos.A. 1980, s. 73(5).

unregistered land. Land, title to which has not been registered under the L.R.A. 1925–71 and Land Registration Rules 1925.

unreported cases. Transcripts of cases that do not appear in the published law reports. Such transcripts relating to the Court of Appeal (Civil Division) may not be cited on appeal to the House of Lords except with its leave: *Roberts Petroleum Ltd* v *Bernard Kenny Ltd* [1983] 2 WLR 305.

unrestricted-use credit. Any form of credit which is not restricted-use credit (qv): C.C.A. 1974, s. 11. Example: a bank overdraft.

unsecured creditor. *See* CREDITOR.

unsolicited goods. Goods sent to persons who had not asked for them. Under the Unsolicited Goods and Services Act 1971, if such goods are sent or delivered for sale or hire, they become the property of the recipient as though they were an unconditional gift if the sender does not take them back within six months of their receipt, or earlier if the recipient gives notice to the sender. It is an offence to demand payment for unsolicited goods where the person

making the demand has no cause to believe there is a right to payment. See also the Unsolicited Goods and Services (Amendment) Act 1975.

unsound mind, persons of. Referred to, since the M.H.A. 1959, as persons suffering from mental disorder (qv). "It is impossible to distinguish between unsoundness of mind and insanity": *per* Merriman P in *Smith* v *Smith* [1940] P 179.

unsworn evidence. *See* EVIDENCE, UNSWORN.

unsworn statement. Statement made by accused without being sworn. The right to make an unsworn statement was generally abolished (save for, eg, a statement by the accused by way of mitigation) by the C.J.A. 1982, s. 72.

unvalued policy. Policy of insurance (qv) where the value of the subject-matter is left to be ascertained later, subject to the limit of the amount insured.

Upper Bench. Title of the Court of King's Bench during the Protectorate (qv).

urban development areas. Land in a metropolitan district or an inner London borough or partly in an inner London borough and partly in an outer London borough which has a boundary in common with that inner London borough, designated by the Secretary of State, eg, for the purposes of regeneration. See the L.G.P.L.A. 1980, ss. 134–143.

urban servitudes. Servitudes of houses, ie, easements (qv) relating to the construction of houses, such as the right to light. *See* SERVITUDES.

urine test. A laboratory test carried out on the urine of a person arrested under the Road Traffic Act 1972, ss. 5, 8. See the Road Traffic Act 1972, ss. 6–12 (as substituted by the Transport Act 1981, Sch 8); *R* v *Taylor* [1974] RTR 554; *Ross* v *Hodges* [1975] RTR 55.

usage. A practice which has continued over a long period. " 'Usage' as a practice which the court will recognise is a mixed question of fact and law. For the practice to amount to such a recognised usage it must be certain, in the sense that the practice is clearly established; it must be notorious, in the sense that it is so well known in the market in which it is alleged to exist that those who conduct business in that market contract with usage as an implied term; and it must be reasonable. The burden lies on those alleging usage to establish it": *per* Ungoed-Thomas J in *Cunliffe-Owen* v *Teather* [1967] 3 All ER 561.

use. Term which may have originated in *opus (X tenet ad opus Y*—X holds for the benefit of Y). Example: Tenant, A, transferred land by common-law conveyance to the transferee, B, who undertook to hold it "to the use of" (ie, on behalf of) C. A was known as the *feoffor,* B was the *feoffee to uses* (ie, party to whom feoffment of land had been made), C was *cestui que use* (shortened version of *cestui à que use le feoffment fuit fait*—to whom feoffment had been made). Before the Statute of Uses 1535 (repealed by the L.P.A. 1925, Sch 7), B would have had the legal estate, C would have had the equitable estate. Following the Statute, C had the legal estate.

use and occupation. A claim which exists where one has used and occupied another's lands with his permission, but in the absence of a lease (qv) or agreement for a lease. See the Distress for Rent Act 1737, s. 14.

use classes. *See* DEVELOPMENT.

user. Use or enjoyment of property.

user as of right. *See* NEC VI, NEC CLAM, NEC PRECARIO.

user, evidence of. Evidence of the way in which parties to a document have acted before or after its execution. Will be received by the court: to show alterations by consent in a partnership deed; to remove uncertainty in a patent or latent ambiguity (qv); where there has been a change in the meaning of words used in an ancient document (see *NE Rwy* v *Lord Hastings* [1900] AC 260). *See* EVIDENCE.

use upon a use. Conveyance "to X and his heirs to the use of Y and his heirs to the use of Z and his heirs".

Void under *Tyrrel's Case* (1557) 2 Dy 115a, so that the entire legal and equitable interest was given to Y. Later, the second use was enforced in equity. See *Sambach* v *Dalston* (under *Morris* v *Darston* (1635) Nels 30). *See* USE.

usque ad medium filum aquae (viae). As far as the middle of the stream (or road). Refers to boundaries which are rivers or roads. In the absence of evidence to the contrary, each owner is presumed to own the river or road up to an imaginary line drawn through the centre of the river or road.

usual covenants. *See* COVENANTS, USUAL.

usucapion. Mode of acquiring title by uninterrupted possession. *See* PRESCRIPTION.

usufruct. Right of using and enjoying profits or fruits belonging to another.

usufructuary. One having a usufruct (qv) of property.

usurpation. Unauthorised or illegal assumption of rights, eg, by dispossession.

usury. An exorbitant or illegal amount or rate of interest. Statutes relating to usury were largely repealed in 1854. See now the C.C.A. 1974, ss. 137–140.

uterine. Relationship between persons born of the same mother, but having a different father.

ut infra. As [mentioned] below.

ut res magis valeat quam pereat. It is better for a thing to have effect than to be made void. See *Curtis* v *Stovin* (1889) 22 QBD 512.

ut supra. As [mentioned] above.

utter bar. Outer bar (qv).

u.x.b. "Unexpected balance of established development value." Term used after 1955 to represent the limit up to which the Secretary of State would pay compensation for depreciation resulting from restrictions on a new development. See the T.C.P.A. 1954 and 1974.

V

v. Versus (qv).

vacantia bona. See BONA VACANTIA.

vacant possession. Term applied to premises sold or offered for sale and not subject to a lease. The vendor must give vacant possession on completion, subject to an agreement to the contrary. Means more than "empty and unoccupied; property conveyed must be capable of occupation by a purchaser": *Topfell* v *Galley Properties* [1979] 1 WLR 446. See *Cook* v *Taylor* [1942] Ch 349.

vacations. Periods during which the Supreme Court (qv) does not sit for ordinary business, ie, Long Vacation and Whitsun Vacation. See O. 64.

vacation sittings. Senior judges of each division will direct judges to hear such business during vacations "as requires to be immediately or promptly heard". Judges may refuse to hear matters which they consider outside this description. See O. 64, r. 3; SI 1982/1111.

vadium, mortuum. *See* MORTUUM VADIUM.

vagabonds. *See* ROGUES AND VAGABONDS.

vagrant. One who, under the Vagrancy Act 1824, as amended, is found to be a rogue or vagabond, or an idle or disorderly person. See the C.J.A. 1982, s. 70.

valorem, ad. See AD VALOREM.

valuable consideration. *See* GOOD CONSIDERATION.

value. Generally, valuable consideration, as in "purchaser for value" (qv).

value-added tax. Tax introduced into the UK in 1973, under the Finance Act 1972. A broad, indirect tax falling on goods and services, with specified exemptions, levied at every stage of production and distribution on the value added at every point of sale. The rate is fixed in the annual Finance Acts. Local VAT tribunals hear disputes and appeal lies, on points of law only, to the High Court (qv). See Value Added Tax Act 1983.

value received. Phrase referring to the acceptance for value of a bill of exchange (qv).

vandalism. Malicious, ignorant injury to, or destruction of, property. See *Ferodo* v *Barnes* [1976] ICR 439 (employee dismissed on suspicion of vandalism).

variance. Disagreement or difference between a statement in the writ (qv) and pleadings (qv), or between a statement in pleadings and supporting evidence given at a later stage.

variation of trust. Under the Variation of Trusts Act 1958, the court may, if it thinks fit, approve any arrangement varying a trust, on behalf of persons unborn, persons having an interest in the trust but who are incapable of assenting, persons who may become entitled to an interest in the trust at some future date. "It is the agreement which has to be approved, not just the limited interest of the person on whose behalf the court's duty is to consider it": *Re Steed's Will Trusts* [1960] Ch 407. See the Tr.A. 1925, ss. 53, 57(1); the S.L.A. 1925, s. 64(1); the M.H.A. 1959, s. 103(1) (*d*); the Mat.C.A. 1973, s. 24(1); *Re Pettifor's Will Trusts* [1966] Ch 257; *Re Remnant's Settlement Trusts* [1970] Ch 560. *See* TRUST.

vassal. *Vassus* = servant. Person under the protection of a feudal lord, holding lands from him and bound to render appropriate services. *See* FEUDAL SYSTEM.

VAT. Value-added tax (qv).

V.-C. Vice-Chancellor (qv).

vehicle. That which can be, or is, used for the carriage of persons or things.

vehicle, immobilisation of illegally parked. A constable may fix an immobilisation device to an illegally parked vehicle and affix a notice specifying the steps to be taken to secure its release: Transport Act 1982, s. 53.

vehicle interference. Offence, under the Criminal Attempts Act 1981, s. 9, of interfering with a motor vehicle or trailer or with anything carried therein with the intention of theft of the vehicle or trailer or part of it, or its contents or taking and driving away without the consent of the owner. A constable may arrest without warrant anyone who is or whom he with reasonable cause suspects to be guilty of an offence under s. 9: s. 9(4). See *Reynolds and Warren* v *Metropolitan Police* [1982] Crim LR 831.

vehicle, motor. *See* MOTOR VEHICLE.

veil, lifting the. *See* LIFTING THE VEIL.

vendee. A buyer (of goods, or, more usually, land).

vendor. A seller (usually, of land).

vendor and purchaser summons. Procedure, introduced by the Vendor and Purchaser Act 1874, now governed by the L.P.A. 1925, s. 49(1), whereby parties to a contract for the sale of land who disagree on a matter which prevents completion of contract, eg, construction of terms, may apply to a judge in chambers for an order. The court may grant an order and any consequential reliefs, eg, the return of any deposit.

vendor's lien. *See* VENDOR'S RIGHTS.

vendor's rights. Pending the completion of the sale of land, the vendor possesses an equitable lien (qv) on the property for the full amount of the purchase money, and that lien arises at the date of the contract. He has a right to remain in possession until the purchase is paid, and to rents and profits until the time fixed for completion. See *Macreth* v *Symmons* (1808) 15 Ves 329; *Re Birmingham* [1959] Ch 523. See the S.G.A. 1979, ss. 38–43; and the L.C.A. 1972, s. 2(4) (iii).

venereal disease. Disease (eg, syphilis, gonorrhea) acquired as the result of sexual intercourse. It may be prima facie evidence of adultery (qv), the onus being on the respondent (qv) to rebut the presumption of its contraction as a result of intercourse with a person other than the petitioner: *Anthony* v *Anthony* (1919) 35 TLR 559. A marriage may be voidable on the ground that at the time of the marriage the respondent was suffering from a venereal disease in a communicable form: Mat.C.A. 1973,

s. 12(*e*). It may be a ground for a matrimonial order (qv) where the defendant, while knowingly suffering from a venereal disease, insisted on sexual intercourse between the complainant and defendant: *Rigby* v *Rigby* [1944] P 33.

venereal diseases, treatment of. Treatment of these diseases other than by a qualified medical practitioner is illegal: Venereal Disease Act 1917, s. 1.

venia aetatis. Privilege of age. Privilege allowed an infant (qv) whereby he may act as though of full age.

venire de novo. Writ directing a new trial. See *R* v *Neal* [1949] 2 KB 590; and *R* v *Rose* [1982] 3 WLR 192. *See* TRIAL, NEW.

venire facias. That you cause to come. Title of a writ or summons to appear and be arraigned.

venue. Place where a case is to be tried. Originally it signified "a place next to that where any thing that comes to be tried is supposed to be done": *Termes de la Ley.* See O. 33, r. 4.

verba chartarum fortius accipiuntur contra proferentem. The words of deeds should be interpreted most strongly against the person who uses them [provided that this works no wrong]. See *Stephens* v *Frost* (1837) 2 Y & C Ex 297; *Taylor* v *Corporation of St Helens* (1877) 6 Ch D 164; *Webster* v *Higgin* [1948] 2 All ER 127.

verba ita sunt intelligenda ut res magis valeat quam pereat. Words are to be understood so that the object may be carried out and not fail. See, eg, *Lloyd* v *Lloyd* (1837) 2 My & Cr 192.

verbals. Colloquialism for that which a suspect says to a police officer, or is heard to say to him. It may be admissible as evidence and can constitute an informal admission of guilt. *See* EVIDENCE.

verbatim. Word for word; exactly; precisely.

verdict. *Vere dictum* = truly said. Answer of a jury to a question committed to their examination and for their decision. Verdict is usually announced by the *foreman* (chosen by jury members to speak for them). The judge may not enquire into proceedings whereby the verdict was reached. Where the jury fails to agree they will be discharged and a new jury called to try the case. If there is yet another disagreement it is usual for the prosecution not to offer evidence in a third trial and the accused is then acquitted. See the C.J.A. 1967; the Juries Act 1974, s. 17; *A.-G. v New Statesman* [1981] QB 1; and *R v Reynolds* [1981] 3 All ER 849.

verdict, alternative. Verdict under the C.L.A. 1967, s. 6(3), whereby a jury is enabled to return a verdict of not guilty of the offence specifically charged in the indictment, but guilty of another offence, provided that the allegations in the indictment amount to or include (expressly or by implication) an allegation of another offence. Where the defendant (qv) is convicted of an offence and the jury, on that same indictment, could have found him guilty of another offence, the court may substitute a verdict of guilty of that other offence and pass sentence for it: Criminal Appeal Act 1968, s. 3(1).

verdict, finality of. A jury's verdict is considered complete as soon as it is announced. Evidence to show what has occurred in the jury room will not be considered by the Court of Appeal (qv): *R v Roads* [1967] 2 QB 108.

verdict, majority. Introduced under the C.J.A. 1967. The verdict need not be unanimous if, in a case where there are not less than 11 jurors, 10 of them agree on the verdict, or in a case where there are 10 jurors, 9 of them agree on the verdict. A majority verdict is not accepted unless it appears to the court that the jury have had not less than two hours for deliberation (or longer where considered appropriate) and unless the foreman states the numbers agreeing and disagreeing with the verdict: Juries Act 1974, s. 17. In civil cases majority verdicts were introduced by the Courts Act 1971, s. 39 (now repealed and replaced by the Juries Act 1974, s. 17). See also *R v Gilbert* [1978] Crim LR 216; *R v Mansfield* [1978] 1 All ER 134; *R v Pigg* [1983] 1 WLR 6; and *R v Modeste* (*The Times*, 25.7.1983).

verdict, open. *See* OPEN VERDICT.

verdict, perverse. *See* PERVERSE VERDICT.

verdict, special. *See* SPECIAL VERDICT.

verge, tenant by the. *See* TENANT BY THE VERGE.

versus. Against. Abbreviated to "v", as in *R v Jones*.

vest. 1. To put a person in possession of land. 2. To give legal rights to a person. See *Richardson v Robertson* (1826) 6 LT 75.

vested in interest. Term indicating a present right to future enjoyment, eg, "to X for life, remainder to Y for life, remainder to Z in fee simple should he survive Y". Y's interest is said to be "vested in interest". It is, in effect, a "vested remainder".

vested in possession. Term indicating an interest which gives a right of present enjoyment, eg, "to X for life, remainder to Y for life . . ." X's interest is vested in possession.

vested remainder. *See* VESTED IN INTEREST.

vested rights. Rights secured to their possessor. "The well-established presumption is that the legislature does not intend to limit vested rights further than clearly appears from the enactment": *Metropolitan Film Studios v Twickenham Film Studios* [1962] 3 All ER 508.

vesting assent. An assent in writing, but not under seal, whereby a personal representative (qv) vests settled land in the person entitled as tenant for life (qv) or statutory owner. See the S.L.A. 1925, ss. 8, 117(1) (xxx). *See* SETTLED LAND.

vesting, conditions of. A remainder (qv) is vested where the person entitled is ascertained and it is ready to take effect in possession at once. Where conditions are not satisfied the remainder is contingent only.

vesting declaration. Declaration under the Tr.A. 1925 during the appointment of new trustees (qv), that the property is to vest in the trustees. In the case of an appointment of new trustees by deed executed after 1925, such a declaration is implied in the absence of a statement to the contrary. Trust property (qv) cannot be transferred by vesting declaration where, eg, it consists of land held by trustees by way of a mortgage (qv) for securing trust property.

vesting deed. "Every settlement of a legal estate in land *inter vivos* shall, save as in this Act otherwise provided, be effected by two deeds, namely, a vesting deed and a trust instrument and if effected in any other way shall not operate to transfer or create a legal estate": S.L.A. 1925, s. 4(1). A vesting deed must contain, under s. 5(1): a description of settled land, the names of trustees of settlement, any additional powers conferred by the trust instrument, the name of any person entitled under trust instrument to appoint new trustees, and a statement that the settled land is vested in the person(s) to whom it is conveyed or in whom it is declared to be vested upon trusts from time to time affecting the settled land. It is known as the "principal vesting deed".

vesting deed, subsidiary. When other land is brought into a settlement (qv) which is in existence, a subsidiary vesting deed is needed, under the S.L.A. 1925, s. 10. It contains: particulars of principal vesting instrument, names of trustees of settlement and of those entitled to appoint new trustees, and a statement that the land conveyed is to be held subject to the same trusts as the land comprised in the principal vesting instrument.

vesting order. A court order having the effect of vesting, conveying or creating a legal estate (qv) as if the legal estate owner had executed a conveyance. See the L.P.A. 1925, s. 9; the Tr.A. 1925, s. 44; the S.L.A. 1925, ss. 12, 16; and the A.E.A. 1925, s. 38.

veto. 1. Power to prohibit or refuse. 2. Refusal to assent to a parliamentary Bill. 3. Power of any permanent members of the Security Council of the United Nations (qv) to refuse to agree to a proposed course of action.

vexata quaestio. A problem which has not been settled and which has been discussed repeatedly.

vexatious action. An action which is brought (by a "vexatious litigant") merely to annoy an opponent, or which is frivolous. The court is em-

powered to stay such an action. See the S.C.A. 1981, s. 42; *Re Wilson* [1973] 1 WLR 314; *Re Becker* [1975] 1 WLR 842.

vicarious. Performed by one person as a substitute for, or for the benefit of, another.

vicarious immunity. See IMMUNITY, VICARIOUS.

vicarious liability. See LIABILITY, VICARIOUS.

vicarious performance of contract. Performance of a contract (qv) based on the delegation of work to a third person. Vicarious performance does not release the contracting party; obligations "cannot be shifted off the shoulders of a contractor or on to those of another without the consent of the contractee": *Tolhurst v Associated Portland Cement Manufacturers* [1902] 2 KB 660. Vicarious performance of a personal contract is generally no performance if personal performance is of the essence of the contract: *Davies v Collins* [1945] 1 All ER 247.

vicarious responsibility. See LIABILITY, VICARIOUS.

Vice-Chancellor. One of those first appointed in 1813 to assist the Lord Chancellor in the Court of Chancery (qv). They were transferred to the High Court in 1873 as judges of the Chancery Division. A Vice-Chancellor is appointed, with responsibility to the Lord Chancellor, for the organisation and management of Chancery Division business. See the S.C.A. 1981, s. 10.

vice, inherent. See INHERENT VICE.

viceroy. One who stands in place of the Sovereign.

vicinage. An adjacent or neighbouring area.

vicious propensity. Tendency of animal to act so as to endanger persons or property. See the Animals Act 1971, s. 2(2); and *Wallace v Newton* [1982] 1 WLR 375.

videlicet. Namely; that is to say. Abbreviated to viz.

viduity. Widowhood.

vi et armis. With force and arms. Words used to describe trespass resulting from the use of actual violence.

view. An inspection by a judge of

some object or place outside the court where the characteristics of the object or place constitute facts from which facts in issue (qv) may be inferred. See O. 35. *See* INSPECTION BY JUDGE.

viewing the scene. *See* INSPECTION BY JUDGE.

vigilantibus non dormientibus jura subveniunt. The laws give help to those who are watchful, not to those who sleep. Principle of the doctrine of laches (qv).

village green. Land which has been allotted for the exercise or recreation of the inhabitants of any locality: Commons Registration Act 1965, s. 22(1). See *Re The Rye, High Wycombe* (1977) 242 EG 811.

villanagium. Non-free tenure, later known as copyhold (qv).

villeinage. Villein tenure (qv).

villein tenure. *Villa* = farm. An unfree tenure in early days. *Privileged villein tenure* involved duties usually of an agricultural or domestic character, servile in nature and fixed in character and time. *Pure villein tenure* involved services uncertain in character and time. A tenant in these conditions was known as a villein (or villain).

vinculo matrimonii. *See* A VINCULO MATRIMONII.

vindictive damages. *See* DAMAGES.

violence, criminal. *See* CRIMINAL VIOLENCE.

violence, domestic. *See* INJUNCTIONS, MATRIMONIAL.

violence for securing entry. *See* ENTRY, VIOLENCE FOR SECURING.

virement. A transfer of budgetary funds from one heading to another.

virtute officii. By virtue of office.

visa. Endorsement on a passport indicating that it has been examined and found correct. Usually made by a foreign authority for the purpose of allowing entry to a country.

vis et metus. Force and fear.

visitor. A person appointed to visit other persons and inspect institutions. See *Patel* v *Bradford University* [1978] 1 WLR 1488; and *Casson* v *Aston University* [1983] 1 All ER 88. See also the Child Care Act 1980, s. 11; the S.C.A. 1981, s. 44; and the M.H.A. 1983, s. 103.

vis major. Greater force; irresistible

force, eg, a storm which, because it cannot be prevented, may relieve parties to a contract from some obligations.

vivum vadium. Living pledge. The mortgagee could take possession of land, while rents and profits could be taken in discharge of principal and interest. *See* MORTGAGE.

viz. Abbreviation of *videlicet* (qv).

vocation. "The way in which a person passes his life": *per* Denman J in *Partridge* v *Mallandaine* (1886) 18 QBD 276. See also *Nagle* v *Fielden* [1966] 2 QB 633.

void. Empty; without force; of no legal effect. "A void contract is a paradox; in truth there is no contract at all": *Fawcett* v *Star Car Sales Ltd* [1960] NZLR 406.

voidable. Capable of being voided, ie, set aside. A voidable contract has legal effect until avoided.

voidable marriage. *See* NULLITY OF MARRIAGE.

voidable title, sale under. When the seller of goods has a voidable title to them, but his title has not been avoided at the time of the sale, the buyer acquires a good title to the goods, provided he buys them in good faith and without notice of the seller's defect of title: S.G.A. 1979, s. 23.

voidable trust. *See* TRUST, VOIDABLE.

void marriage. *See* NULLITY OF MARRIAGE.

void trust. *See* TRUST, VOID.

voir dire. Also *voire dire*. *Vrai dire* = to speak the truth. Preliminary examination of a witness by the judge, eg, to determine whether a confession was voluntary; ie, the trial of incidental issues ("trial within a trial"). See *R* v *Francis* (1959) 43 Cr App R 174; and *R* v *Brophy* [1982] AC 476.

voisinage. Rules and practices in international law governing the conduct of neighbouring states.

volenti non fit injuria. That to which a person consents cannot be considered an injury. Term referring to the harm suffered with the plaintiff's freely-given assent and, hence, a defence in tort. Knowledge is not assent, but merely evidence of assent: *Dann* v *Hamilton* [1939] 1 KB 509. A person does not necessarily assent to a situation because he has knowledge of its potential danger: *Baker* v *James* [1921] 2 KB 674. "Knowledge of the risk of injury is not enough. Nor is a willingness to take the risk of injury. Nothing will suffice short of an agreement to waive any claim for negligence": *Nettleship* v *Weston* [1971] 3 All ER 581. See *Hall* v *Brooklands Racing Club* [1933] 1 KB 205; *Murray* v *Harringay Arena Ltd* [1951] 2 KB 529.

voluntary. 1. Proceeding from some exercise of the will and involving an act of choice. 2. Without valuable consideration (qv).

voluntary bill procedure. See BILL PROCEDURE, VOLUNTARY.

voluntary conduct. Conduct resulting from the exercise of one's will. In general, a person will not be held liable for any harmful result produced by conduct which was not voluntary.

voluntary confession. See CONFESSION.

voluntary conveyance. See VOLUNTARY DISPOSITION.

voluntary disposition. A disposition of land not founded upon valuable consideration (qv). "Every voluntary disposition of land made with intent to defraud a subsequent purchaser is voidable at the instance of that purchaser": L.P.A. 1925, s. 173(1). See also the B.A. 1914, s. 42.

voluntary liquidation. See VOLUNTARY WINDING-UP.

voluntary settlement. A settlement (qv) made without valuable consideration.

voluntary waste. Waste (qv) arising from an injury to land actively caused by the tenant (qv), eg, cutting timber. See *Honywood* v *Honywood* (1874) LR 18 Eq 306. A tenant for years, yearly tenant, tenant at sufferance, will be liable for voluntary waste.

voluntary winding-up. The winding-up of a company (qv) so that company and creditors may settle their affairs before coming to court. It may be carried out when: the period fixed for the duration of the company has ended; the company has passed a special resolution to wind up voluntarily; the company has passed an extraordinary resolution that it is expedient that the company be wound up. Voluntary winding-up dates from the passing of a resolution authorising it. The resolution must be advertised in the *London Gazette* within 14 days. See the Cos.A. 1948, ss. 278–80.

volunteer. One who takes under a disposition for which neither he nor anyone on his behalf has given valuable consideration (qv). Equity will not aid a volunteer. See, eg, *Plumptre's Marriage Settlement* [1910] 1 Ch 609.

vote. 1. To express one's opinion, as at an election: see the Parliamentary and Municipal Elections Act 1872 and the Representation of the People Act 1983, Part I. 2. That which is voted, eg, a grant of money.

voting at meetings. Generally by show of hands. In the case of a registered company (see Table A, arts. 58, 62) a resolution (qv) is decided on by show of hands, unless a poll (qv) is demanded. See the Cos.A. 1948, s. 136.

voting shares, disclosure of interests in. Where a person, to his knowledge, acquires an interest in, or ceases to be interested in, a public company's relevant share capital, he must notify this to the company: Cos.A. 1981, s. 63(1). "Relevant share capital" means a five per cent interest in voting shares.

vouch. 1. To summon. 2. To bear witness. 3. To answer for.

vouchee. One who is summoned.

voucher. 1. Receipt. 2. Process of vouching to warranty (qv).

vouching to warranty. Calling to court a person who has warranted land to another. A process used in the old common recovery (qv).

voyage, change of. See CHANGE OF VOYAGE.

voyage charter. A charterparty (qv) under which a ship is hired for one or more voyages (as compared with a time charter (qv)).

voyage policy. Term in marine insurance indicating a policy in which the subject-matter is insured for a particular voyage only.

W

wage. 1. A pledge. 2. Money remuneration.

wager. A bet (qv).

wagering contract. "One by which two persons, professing to hold opposite views touching the issue of a future, uncertain event, mutually agree that, dependent upon the determination of that event, one shall win from the other, and the other shall pay or hand over to him, a sum of money or other stake; neither of the contracting parties having any other interest in that contract than the sum or stake he will so win or lose, there being no other real consideration for the making of such contract by either of the parties": *Carlill* v *Carbolic Smoke Ball Co* [1892] 2 QB 484. Null and void under, eg, the Gaming Act 1845, s. 18. See *Hill* v *William Hill Ltd* [1949] AC 530. *See* BET.

wagering policy. A policy of assurance in the subject-matter of which the assured person does not have an interest, or for purposes of gambling. Example: insuring of a stranger's life. See the Life Assurance Act 1774.

wager of battle. *See* BATTLE, TRIAL BY.

wager of law. Procedure of compurgation (qv).

wages. Monetary remuneration of an employee paid by his employer for labour or other services rendered. "Any money or other thing had or contracted to be paid, delivered or given as a recompense, reward or remuneration for any labour done or to be done, whether within a certain time or to a certain amount, or for a time or an amount uncertain, shall be deemed or taken to be the 'wages' of such labour": Truck Act 1831, s. 25.

wages councils. Bodies, comprising employers, employees and independent members, set up by the Secretary of State where no adequate machinery exists for the effective regulation of remuneration of workers. See the Wages Councils Act 1979. Under the 1979 Act, s. 10, they can be converted into statutory joint industrial councils.

wages, minimum. Minimum wage levels prescribed generally in industries which do not possess adequate bargaining machinery. See the Trade Board Acts 1909 and 1918; and the Wages Councils Act 1979, s. 14.

wages, payment of. *See* PAYMENT OF WAGES.

waif. 1. Property which has no apparent owner. 2. Right to property apparently without an owner. 3. "Waifs" were stolen property abandoned by a thief in flight, which could be claimed by the King or lord of the manor. They were recoverable by an owner who successfully prosecuted the thief.

wait and see principle. Rule relating to perpetuities. Under common law there was no "wait and see", so that a limitation was void if it could *possibly* fail to vest during the perpetuity period. Under the P. & A.A. 1964, s. 3, the principle applies to instruments which become effective after July 1964 in the following cases: an interest capable of vesting after the perpetuity period will not be treated as void under the perpetuity rule until it is established that it will vest, if at all, after the end of the perpetuity period; in the case of a general power of appointment (qv) which could possibly be exercised after the end of the perpetuity period, the power will be treated as valid until such time (if any) as it becomes established that the power will not be exercised in the perpetuity period; in the case of a disposition consisting of the conferring of power, option or other right which might be exercised after the end of the perpetuity period, such disposition will be void only if, and so far as, the right is not fully exercised within that period. *See* PERPETUITIES, RULE AGAINST.

waive. 1. To relinquish a right freely.

2. To forego the enforcing of a claim.

waiver. 1. Relinquishing of a claim. "The abandonment of a right in such a way that the other party is entitled to plead the abandonment by way of confession and avoidance if the right is thereafter asserted": *Banning* v *Wright* [1972] 2 All ER 987. "A waiver must be an intentional act with knowledge": *Darnley* v *London, Chatham and Dover Rwy* (1867) 16 LT 217. 2. The instrument which declares an act of waiving. 3. Surrender by operation of law. 4. Variation of a contract (see *Hickman* v *Haynes* (1875) LR 10 CP 598).

waiver clause. Clause in, eg, a company prospectus waiving shareholders' claims against directors for damages resulting from the issue of the prospectus. Void under the Cos.A. 1984, s. 38(2).

waiver of tort. The foregoing by a person of a remedy in tort in favour of some other remedy (eg, an action based on a quasi-contract). The waiver extinguishes the right of action in tort. See *Rice* v *Reed* [1900] 1 QB 54; *Re Simmons* [1934] 1 Ch 24. *See* TORT.

wall, party-. *See* PARTY-WALL.

war crimes. Offences against the law of nations relating to: crimes against peace (eg, waging of a war of aggression); conventional war crimes (eg, violation of customs of war, or the murder of prisoners of war); crimes against humanity (eg, enslavement). See the Nuremberg Trial Indictment 1945.

ward. One under the protection or care of another.

ward of court. Person under the care of a guardian appointed by the court, or an infant (qv) brought under the authority of the protection of the court. See O. 90; the Mat.C.A. 1973, s. 42(1); the S.C.A. 1981, s. 41; the A.J.A. 1982, s. 50; and *M.* v *Humberside CC* [1979] 2 All ER 744.

wardship. 1. The exercise of care and protection of a ward (qv). "The golden thread running through the courts' jurisdiction is the child's welfare, considered first, last and all the time": *Re D.* [1977] Fam 158; and *A.* v *Liverpool CC* [1982] AC 363.

2. Right, exercised in feudal times, of the custody of a ward and the ward's property.

warning of caveat. Notice to one who has entered a caveat (qv) to appear so as to declare his interest.

warrant. 1. Document authorising some action, eg, payment of money. 2. Document issued by a magistrate (qv) ordering that a person be arrested and brought before the court. The person must be mentioned by name, or described otherwise. It must contain a statement of the offence charged and it should be signed by the issuing magistrate. See the C.L.A. 1977, s. 38; and the M.C.A. 1980, s. 1.

warrant, arrest with and without. *See* ARREST AND WARRANT.

warrant backed for bail. *See* BACKED FOR BAIL.

warrant, entry without. Right, under common law or statute, of a constable to enter a dwelling-house or other premises without warrant. See *Thomas* v *Sawkins* [1935] 2 KB 249; *Davis* v *Lisle* [1936] 2 All ER 213; and *McLorie* v *Oxford* [1982] 3 WLR 423.

warrant, general. *See* GENERAL WARRANT.

warrantor. One who gives a warranty (qv).

warrant, Royal. *See* ROYAL WARRANT.

warrant, search. *See* SEARCH WARRANT.

warrant, share. Document under seal stating that the bearer is entitled to shares specified therein. A warrant is a negotiable instrument (qv). See the Cos.A. 1948, ss. 83, 112, 185; *Bechuanaland Expedition Co* v *London Trading Bank Ltd* [1898] 2 QB 658.

warranty. An agreement with reference to goods which are the subject of a contract of sale, but collateral to the main purpose of such contract, the breach of which gives rise to a claim for damages, but not to a right to reject the goods and treat the contract as repudiated: S.G.A. 1979, s. 61(1). It may be express or implied. See *Wallis* v *Pratt* [1910] 2 KB 1012; *Finnegan* v *Allen* [1943] KB 425; *Oscar Chess* v *Williams* [1957] 1 WLR 370; and *Wickman Machine Tools* v *L. Schuler AG* [1974] AC 235.

warranty defence. Defence (in matters related to consumer legislation) available where the person charged can show that he purchased the food, medicines, etc, from an immediate vendor with a written warranty. See *Hargreaves* v *Spackman* (1907) 87 LT 41; and *Rochdale MBC* v *FM (Meat) Ltd* [1980] 1 WLR 461.

warranty, vouching to. *See* VOUCHING TO WARRANTY.

waste. 1. Acts or omissions by a tenant which alter the nature of land or houses. They may be voluntary; permissive; ameliorating; equitable (qqv). 2. Includes any substance which constitutes a scrap material or an effluent or other unwanted surplus substance arising from the application of any process and any substance or article which requires to be disposed of as being broken, worn out, contaminated or otherwise spoiled: Control of Pollution Act 1974, s. 30(1).

waste land of a manor. "The open, uncultivated and unoccupied lands parcel of the manor, or open lands parcel of the manor other than the demesne lands of the manor": *A.-G.* v *Hammer* (1858) 27 LJ Ch 837, applied in *Re Britford Common* [1977] 1 WLR 39.

waste, unlicensed disposal of. Except in prescribed cases, a person must not deposit on any land controlled waste (ie, household, industrial and commercial waste): Control of Pollution Act 1974, ss. 3, 30.

wasting assets. Assets or securities which are subject to depletion, or which have a terminating nature, eg, leaseholds. See *Howe* v *Dartmouth* (1802) 7 Ves 137; and the Capital Gains Tax Act 1979, ss. 37, 127. *See* CONVERT, DUTY TO.

watch committee. Local authority committee set up to control a police force. See the Police Act 1964, s. 2; and the L.G.A. 1972, s. 196.

watching and besetting. An offence which was committed by watching or besetting a house or other place where another resides or works or carries on business or happens to be: Conspiracy and Protection of Property Act 1875, s. 7. See *Mersey Docks & Harbour Co* v *Verrinder* [1982]

IRLR 152. *See* PICKETING, PEACEFUL.

water, abstraction of. "No person shall abstract water from any source of supply in a water authority area, or cause or permit any other person so to abstract any water, except in pursuance of a licence . . . granted by the water authority and in accordance with the provisions of that lease": Water Resources Act 1963, s. 23(1), amended by the Water Act 1973, s. 9. Exceptions include the abstraction of a quantity not exceeding 1,000 gallons (1963 Act, s. 24(1)), water for domestic purposes of a household and agricultural purposes other than spray irrigation. See Water Act 1983.

water, classification of. At common law: tidal rivers and the sea; non-tidal (rivers, streams lakes, ponds, water in artificial channels, etc.). Under statute (Water Resources Act 1963): inland waters; waters in an underground stratum.

watercourse. "Includes all rivers and streams and all ditches, drains, cuts, culverts, dikes, sluices, sewers (other than public sewers within the meaning of the Public Health Act 1936) and passages, through which water flows": Land Drainage Act 1976, s. 116(1).

water ordeal. *See* ORDEAL, TRIAL BY.

waters, coastal. *See* COASTAL WATERS.

waters, inland. *See* TERRITORIAL WATERS.

waters, territorial. *See* TERRITORIAL WATERS.

waters, tidal. *See* TIDAL WATERS.

way, right of. *See* RIGHT OF WAY.

Ways and Means, Committee of. *See* COMMITTEE OF WAYS AND MEANS.

weapon, offensive. *See* OFFENSIVE WEAPON.

weapon of offence. *See* OFFENCE, WEAPON OF.

wear and tear. Deterioration or depreciation of a thing resulting from its ordinary reasonable use. *See* FAIR WEAR AND TEAR.

week. A period of seven days, beginning with midnight between Saturday and Sunday (except where otherwise defined): S.S.A. 1975, Sch 20.

weekly tenancy. A tenancy from week to week, which can be created similarly to a yearly tenancy, eg, by express agreement, or by inference. *See* TENANCY.

weights and measures. Units and standards of measurement referred to in the Weights and Measures Acts 1963–1979, under which, eg, customers must be properly informed as to the weight and quantity of goods on sale. See the L.G.P.L.A. 1980, Sch 4.

welfare law. The area of law concerned with social security legislation, factory safety and welfare of workers, public health, housing, consumer protection, security of employment, preservation of amenities, legal aid, etc.

Welsh language, use in court proceedings of. Under the Welsh Language Act 1967, s. 1, the Welsh language may be used in any legal proceedings in Wales or Monmouthshire by any party desiring to use it.

Welsh mortgage. A mortgage (qv) in which there was no covenant for repayment of the loan and the mortgagee could not compel redemption or foreclosure (qqv). See now the L.P.A. 1925, s. 85.

whip. 1. Government or Opposition official responsible for controlling the presence of MPs at debates and votes, arranging pairs, etc. 2. A command to an MP to attend a House of Commons (qv) vote. A "three-line whip" is an urgent command (underlined three times) to attend a vote. *See* PARLIAMENT.

White Book, The. *See* RULES OF THE SUPREME COURT.

white paper. *See* PARLIAMENTARY PAPERS.

white slave traffic. International traffic in prostitution.

Whitley Councils. Joint Industrial Councils set up following the *Report of the Committee on Relations between Employers and Employed* 1917, under the chairmanship of J. H. Whitley.

whole blood. *See* BLOOD RELATIONSHIP.

widow's benefit. Payable under the S.S.A. 1975, comprising: widow's allowance payable to a widow under 65 for a period of 26 weeks from her husband's death; widowed mother's allowance payable to a widow not entitled to the widow's allowance, with children under 19; widow's pension paid to a widow who was 40–65 at her husband's death, but not entitled to the widow's allowance or widowed mother's allowance.

wife, provision for. Under the Inheritance (Provision for Family and Dependants) Act 1975, the wife or former wife of the deceased may apply for financial provision from the deceased's estate if the disposition of that estate effected by his will or the law relating to intestacy (qv) is not such as to make reasonable financial provision for the applicant: ss. 1, 2.

wife's services, loss of. *See* PER QUOD CONSORTIUM.

wild creatures, theft of. A person cannot steal a wild creature not tamed nor ordinarily kept in captivity unless it has been reduced into possession by or on behalf of another person and possession has not since been lost or abandoned: Th.A. 1968, s. 4(4).

wilful. Term used to refer to the deliberate conduct of a person who is a free agent, knows what he is doing and intends to do what he is doing. "If a man permits a thing to be done, it means that he gives permission for it to be done, he knows what is to be done or is being done, and, if he knows that, it follows that it is wilful": *Lomas* v *Peck* [1947] 2 All ER 574. Used synonymously with "intentional" in *Wheeler* v *New Merton Mills* [1933] 2 KB 669. "Wilfully" means "that the act is done deliberately and intentionally, not by accident or inadvertence, but so that the mind of the person who does the act goes with it": *per* Lord Russell in *R* v *Senior* [1899] 1 QB 480. See *Dibble* v *Ingleton* [1972] 1 QB 480.

wilful default. "Either a conscious-ness of negligence or breach of duty, or a recklessness in the performance of a duty": *Re City Equitable Fire Insurance Co* [1925] Ch 407.

wilful misconduct. "To be guilty of wilful misconduct the person concerned must appreciate that he is acting wrongfully, or is wrongfully omitting to act, and yet persists in so acting or omitting to act regardless of the consequences, or acts or omits to act with reckless indifference as to what the results may be": *Horabin v BOAC* [1952] 2 All ER 1016.

wilful neglect. Intentional or purposeful omission to do a thing. Wilful neglect of a child (under the C. & Y.P.A. 1933, s. 1(1)) is not an absolute offence: *R v Sheppard* [1981] AC 349. See also *R v Gittins* [1982] RTR 363.

wilful refusal. A refusal without adequate cause. For the imposition of imprisonment upon wilful refusal to pay a fine see the M.C.A. 1980, ss. 76 *et seq.*

wilful refusal to consummate. "A wilful, determined and steadfast refusal to perform the obligations and to carry out the duties which the matrimonial contract involves": *Dickinson v Dickinson* [1913] P 198. See also *Horton v Horton* [1948] WN 3; *Jodla v Jodla* [1960] 1 All ER 625. *See* CONSUMMATION OF A MARRIAGE.

will. A revocable declaration, made in the prescribed form, of the intentions of the maker concerning the disposition and devolution of his property, and other matters, which he desires should become effective on and after the event of his death. "The word 'will' shall extend to a testament, and to a codicil (qv), and to an appointment by will or by writing in the nature of a will in exercise of a power . . . and to any other testamentary disposition": W.A. 1837, s. 1.

will, conditional. *See* CONDITIONAL WILL.

will, forfeiture of benefit under. *See* FORFEITURE OF BENEFIT UNDER WILL.

will in contemplation of marriage. *See* MARRIAGE, WILL IN CONTEMPLATION OF.

will, international. Will made in accordance with Annex to Convention on International Wills as set out in the A.J.A. 1982, Sch 2. It is valid as regards form, irrespective particularly of the place where it is made, of the location of the assets and of the testator's nationality, domicile or residence.

will, notarial. *See* NOTARIAL WILL.

will, nuncupative. *See* NUNCUPATIVE WILL.

will, partnership at. *See* PARTNERSHIP AT WILL.

will, privileged. *See* PRIVILEGED WILL.

will, rectification of. *See* RECTIFICATION OF WILL.

will, republication of. *See* REPUBLICATION OF WILL.

will, revival of. *See* REVIVAL OF WILL.

will, revocation of. *See* REVOCATION OF WILL.

wills, mutual. *See* MUTUAL WILLS.

will, tenant at. *See* TENANT AT WILL.

will, validity of. "No will shall be valid unless—(*a*) it is in writing, and signed by the testator, or by some other person in his presence and by his direction; and (*b*) it appears that the testator intended by his signature to give effect to the will; and (*c*) the signature is made or acknowledged by the testator in the presence of two or more witnesses present at the same time; and (*d*) each witness either (i) attests and signs the will; or (ii) acknowledges his signature, in the presence of the testator (but not necessarily in the presence of any other witness), but no form of attestation shall be necessary": W.A. 1837, s. 9 (as substituted by the A.J.A. 1982, s. 17).

windfalls. Trees and their fruit blown down by the wind. They belong, in general, to the owner of the inheritance; but dotards (qv) may be taken by the tenant (qv). See *Herlakenden's Case* (1589) 4 Co Rep 62; *Re Harrison's Trusts* (1885) 28 Ch D 220.

winding-up. Process whereby a company is brought to an end, eg, following insolvency. It may be: compulsory winding-up by the court (qv); winding-up under the court's supervision; voluntary winding-up (qv). Thus, a company may be wound up for any cause if a sufficient number of members pass a special resolution to that end. An alternative remedy to winding-up was provided by the Cos.A. 1948, s. 210. Its place has been taken by the Cos.A. 1980, s. 75. See also the Cos.A. 1948, s. 222 (as amended by the Cos.A. 1980, Sch 4).

winding-up, compulsory. *See* COMPULSORY WINDING-UP BY THE COURT.

winding-up, voluntary. *See* VOLUNTARY WINDING-UP.

witchcraft. Prior to the Witchcraft Act 1735, a capital offence. The Fraudulent Mediums Act 1961 repealed the 1735 Act and provided that it is an offence for a person with intent to deceive and for reward to purport to act as a medium and in so purporting to act, to use a fraudulent device. See *R* v *Duncan and Others* [1944] KB 713 (charge of conspiracy to pretend to exercise or use a kind of conjuration, contrary to the 1735 Act).

with costs. Term referring to a successful party's entitlement to recover costs from the othe party. *See* COSTS.

withdrawal of acknowledgment. withdrawal of an acknowledgment, with leave of the court, by a party who has acknowledged service of a writ in an action. See O. 21, r. 1; *Somportex* v *Philadelphia Chewing Gum Corporation* [1968] 3 All ER 26; and *Castanho* v *Brown and Root* [1981] 1 All ER 143.

withdrawal of defence. Procedure whereby the defendant serves notice on the plaintiff that he is not proceeding with his entire claim, or with some part of it. See O. 21, r. 2(*a*). *See* DISCONTINUANCE, NOTICE OF.

withdrawal of issue from jury. Procedure whereby a judge, who is not satisfied that there is sufficient evidence in support of a proponent's contention, discharges the jury and enters judgment for the opponent, or directs the jury to return a verdict in the opponent's favour. See *Ryder* v *Wombwell* (1868) LSR 4 Ex 32; *R* v *Abbott* [1955] 2 QB 497.

without day. *See* SINE DIE.

without prejudice. *See* PREJUDICE.

without recourse to me. *See* SANS RECOURS.

without reserve. Phrase used in a sale by auction (qv), showing that no price has been reserved.

with profits. Title of the insurance policy under which bonuses from profits of the insurance company are used to increase the value of the policy.

witness. 1. To give evidence or proof. 2. To attest by signature. 3. One who gives formal or sworn evidence at a hearing.

witnesses, adverse. *See* ADVERSE WITNESSES.

witnesses, compellable. Those who are obliged to give evidence. For the case of a wife whose husband has been charged with violence on her, see *Hoskyn* v *Metropolitan Police Commissioner* [1979] AC 474. A witness is not generally compellable to answer a question which might expose him to a criminal charge: *R* v *Boyes* (1861). 30 LJQB 301. See also *R* v *Bathurst* [1968] 1 All ER 1175; *R* v *Wickham* (1971) 55 Cr App R 199; *R* v *Sparrow* [1973] 2 All ER 129.

witnesses, competence of. In general, all persons are competent to give evidence. Exceptions include, the Sovereign in his own cause, the mentally ill (unless the judge is sure that they understand the duty of telling the truth on oath), judges or jurors in a case they are hearing and spouses (in the case of the prosecution, except in a trial relating to national insurance, some offences against children, etc.). An accused is not generally a competent witness for the prosecution.

witnesses, order of calling. Generally an advocate is entitled to call witnesses in order of his choice. ". . . [This is] solely a matter for counsel. It is a grave responsibility and it rests on him and him alone": *Briscoe* v *Briscoe* [1966] 1 All ER 465. See also *Barnes* v *BPC Ltd* [1975] 1 WLR 1565.

witnesses, securing attendance of. *See* WITNESS ORDER.

witness, eye. *See* EYE WITNESS.

witness, hostile. *See* HOSTILE WITNESS.

witness, interfering with. *See* INTERFERING WITH WITNESSES.

witness, intimidation of. *See* INTIMIDATION.

witness order. Procedure for the compelling of attendance by witnesses in criminal trials at the court, failure to comply with which is a contempt of court (qv): Criminal Procedure (Attendance of Witnesses) Act 1965. A "conditional witness order" requires him to attend only if given notice.

witness, privilege of. *See* PRIVILEGE OF WITNESS.

witness, recall of. The judge has a discretionary power to allow the recall of a witness after the close of a party's case to allow evidence in rebuttal. See, eg, *R v Flynn* (1957) 42 Cr App R 15.

witness's oath. *See* OATH.

witness, unfavourable. *See* UNFAVOURABLE WITNESS.

witness warrant. A notice ordering a witness who is required to attend before the Crown Court (qv) to attend forthwith or at a time specified in the future. See the Criminal Procedure (Attendance of Witnesses) Act 1965; and the M.C.A. 1980, s. 97 (procuring attendance of witnesses at magistrates' courts).

witness, zealous. *See* ZEALOUS WITNESS.

woman. A female adult person. In the Sex Discrimination Act 1975, s. 81(1), it is used to include a female "of any age".

women, abduction of. *See* ABDUCTION.

women, indecent assault on. *See* INDECENT ASSAULT ON WOMEN.

women, procurement of. *See* PROCUREMENT.

woolsack. The seat of the Lord Chancellor in the House of Lords (qv). Technically, not within the House, so that when the Lord Chancellor wishes to address the House he must stand aside from it.

words of art. Words which have a particular, fixed legal meaning, not generally modified by their context. See, eg, *Barclays Bank v Cole* [1967] 2 QB 738 (meaning of "fraud").

words of limitation. *See* LIMITATION, WORDS OF.

words of procreation. *See* PROCREATION, WORDS OF.

words of purchase. *See* PURCHASE, WORDS OF.

words of severance. *See* SEVERANCE, WORDS OF.

words, operative. *See* OPERATIVE WORDS.

words, precatory. *See* PRECATORY WORDS.

words, primary and secondary meanings of. Phrase used in reference to the ordinary and extended meanings of words. "The first question to ask always is what is the ordinary meaning of [a] word or phrase in its context in the statute. It is only when that meaning leads to some result which cannot reasonably be sup-

posed to have been the intention of the legislature that it is proper to look for some other permissible meaning of the word or phrase": *Pinner v Everett* [1962] 3 All ER 257 ("There is no word the primary meaning of which may not be modified by the context": *per* Griffith CJ in *Nicol v Chant* (1909) 7 CLR 69.) See also *Barnard v Gorman* [1941] AC 378; *IRC v Hinchy* [1960] AC 748; *Wiltshire v Barrett* [1966] 1 QB 312.

work. "Either the labour which a man bestows upon a thing, or the thing upon which the labour is bestowed": *Atkinson v Lumb* [1903] 1 KB 861. "An employee is 'at work' throughout the time when he is in the course of his employment but not otherwise; and the self-employed person is at work throughout such time as he devotes to work as a self-employed person": H.S.W.A. 1974, s. 52. See *Clear v Smith* [1981] 1 WLR 399.

work done and materials supplied, contracts for. Contracts in which there is an implied condition that work is to be properly done in the manner contemplated and that materials supplied are to be reasonably fit for the purpose contemplated. Example: it was an implied condition that dentures would fit the person for whom they were made (*Samuels v Davis* [1943] 1 KB 526).

worker. One who works or normally works or seeks to work under a contract of employment or under any other contract (express or implied, oral or in writing) whereby he undertakes to do or perform personally any work or services for another party to the contract who is not a professional client of his: T.U.L.R.A. 1974, s. 30(1). See *Murphy & Sons v Southwark LBC* (1938) 127 SJ 119. See also the Employment Act 1982, s. 18(6).

workers, freedom of movement for. Under the Treaty of Rome 1957, art. 48, there is a right to work freely within the territory of member states and this involves "the abolition of any discrimination based on nationality between the workers of member states [of the EEC] as regards employment, remuneration and other conditions of work and employment". This does not apply to employment in the public service. See *R v Pieck* [1981] QB 571.

work-in. A type of industrial action, in which employees occupy their place of work and continue production. Normally trespassory. Injunctions (qv) to restrain this type of action can be given. See *Re Briant Colour Printing Ltd* [1977] 1 WLR 942—company owning factory occupied as a work-in not liable for rates.

working day. Any day other than: Saturday or Sunday; Good Friday or Easter Monday; last Monday in May and August; Christmas Day; 26th December (if it is not a Sunday); or 27th December in a year in which either 25th or 26th December is a Sunday. See the Banking and Financial Dealings Act 1971. *See* BANK HOLIDAYS.

working life. The period between (inclusive) the year in which a person attained the age of 16 and (exclusive) the year in which he attained pensionable age or died under that age: S.S.A. 1975, s. 27(2).

working to rule. *See* GO-SLOW.

work in progress. Any services performed in the ordinary course of a trade, the performance of which was partly completed at a material time and for which it would be reasonable to expect that a charge will subsequently be made, and any article produced, and any such material as is used, in the performance of any such services: Finance Act 1981, Sch 9, Part V.

work to rule. A type of industrial action in which employees work in literal compliance with the terms of their contracts, so that the pace of work is slowed down or brought to a halt. See *Henthorn v CEGB* [1980] IRLR 36.

World Court. International Court of Justice (qv).

worthier title, doctrine of. Principle, whereby if a person could take by purchase or descent, the law preferred title by descent. Abolished under the Inheritance Act 1833, s. 3. See the L.P.A. 1925, s. 132.

wounding. The infliction of an injury which breaks the continuity of the skin, internal or external. A scratch or burn is not a wound. See *R v Wood* (1830) 4 C & P 381; *JJC v Eisenhower* [1983] Crim LR 567.

wounding, malicious. *See* MALICIOUS WOUNDING.

wounding with intent. It is an offence under the O.P.A. 1861, s. 18, as amended by the C.L.A. 1967, Sch 3, Part III, unlawfully and maliciously by any means whatsoever to wound or cause any grievous bodily harm to any person or with intent to resist or prevent the lawful apprehension or detainer of any person. See *R v Belfon* [1976] 1 WLR 741.

wreck. 1. The damage of a ship so that she ceases to be of service. 2. Goods which, after shipwreck, are cast on land. See the Merchant Shipping Act 1894, s. 510; and the Protection of Wrecks Act 1973.

writ. 1. Instrument under seal issued in the name of the Sovereign, declaring some command. 2. Order in the name of the Sovereign or court, ordering some action or forbearance from some action. 3. A *judicial writ* is issued by a court to originate some actions. See O. 5, r. 2. Writs originated in the granting by the King to a suitor of a right to petition where justice had been denied in the local courts. A Register of Writs was created and writs enforceable in the King's courts were increased in number.

writ, amendment of. Under O. 20 the plaintiff may amend a writ once without leave prior to the close of pleadings (qv) and the amended version must be served on the defendant.

writ, concurrent. *See* CONCURRENT WRITS.

writ, endorsement of. *See* ENDORSEMENT OF WRIT, FORMAL.

writing. Term includes printing, lithography, photography and other modes of representation or reproduction of words in a variable form: I.A. 1978, Sch 1.

writ, issuing of. Procedure following the preparation and endorsement of a writ, so that it becomes an official document emanating from the court. The writ must be in the prescribed form: O. 6, r. 1. Leave to issue is necessary, eg, if the defendant is beyond the jurisdiction. The plaintiff sends two copies to the Central Office or a District Registry, where one copy is stamped and the other returned to him. See O. 6, r. 7.

writ of right. *See* RIGHT, WRIT OF.

writ of summons. *See* SUMMONS, WRIT OF.

writ of summons, leave to issue. Permission required, eg, if the defendant is outside the jurisdiction, or if the plaintiff is designated by the High Court as a vexatious litigant.

writ, service of. *See* SERVICE.

wrong. 1. An act contrary to the rules of legal justice. 2. A tort (qv) involving the infringement of a right. 3. In the M'Naghten Rules (qv) "wrong means contrary to law and not 'wrong' according to the opinion of one man or of a number of people on the question whether a particular act might or might not be justified": *R* v *Windle* [1952] 2 QB 826.

wrongful dismissal. Dismissal of an employee without justification which is, in effect, a repudiation of the contract. See *General Billposting Co* v *Atkinson* [1909] AC 118. *See* DISMISSAL.

wrongful interference with goods. *See* INTERFERENCE WITH GOODS, WRONGFUL.

X

xc. Stock Exchange abbreviation for *ex capitalisation* (qv).

xd. Stock Exchange abbreviation for *ex dividend. See* EX DIV.

xr. Stock Exchange abbreviation for *ex rights* (qv).

Y

year. A period of 12 calendar months calculated either from 1st January or some other stated day and consisting of 365 days (or 366 in a leap year). See *IRC* v *Hobhouse* [1956] 1 WLR 1393.

year and thereafter. The expression "to T for a year and thereafter from year to year" confers a minimum tenancy of two years upon T, ie, an express term of one year plus a yearly tenancy which may be terminated not earlier than the end of the second year. See *Re Searle* [1912] 1 Ch 610.

Year Books. A series of reports, authors unknown, running from 1282–1536, spanning the reigns of Edward I and Henry VIII. The title is derived from their being grouped under the regnal years of the Sovereigns in whose reigns the cases reported were decided.

year, day and waste. Term applied to a royal prerogative, now abolished, allowing the monarch to take the profits for one year and one day of persons convicted of felony or petty treason (qqv) and to commit waste (qv) on that person's lands.

year, executor's. *See* EXECUTOR'S YEAR.

year, financial. *See* FINANCIAL YEAR.

year, half a. Where a tenancy (qv) begins on a quarter-day (qv), the phrase means the interval between a quarter-day and the next quarter-day but one.

year, legal. *See* LEGAL YEAR.

yearly tenancy. *See* TENANT FROM YEAR TO YEAR.

years, estate for. An estate (qv) granted for a term of years (qv).

year to year. *See* TENANT FROM YEAR TO YEAR.

yield. The annual return on an investment expressed as a percentage of its market price or cost, known also as the "flat" or "gross running yield". The "net running yield" is the flat yield less income tax at the standard rate.

York–Antwerp rules. Shipping code, formulated in 1877, referring to rules of general average (qv) etc., which is usually incorporated in contracts of affreightment (qv). The current rules were issued in 1974.

young adult offenders. Offenders aged 17–20. There are special types of custodial treatment for this group, eg, attendance centres (qv). See also the A.J.A. 1982, Part I.

young offenders, fining of. Pecuniary penalties imposed on young offenders under, eg, the C.J.A. 1961, s. 8(3) the C. & Y.P.A. 1969, s. 6(3), as amended by the C.L.A. 1977, s. 58, and the M.C.A. 1980, s. 36. Where a magistrates' court would, but for restrictions on the imprisonment of young offenders, have power to imprison a person under 17 for default consisting of failure to pay, or want of sufficient distress (qv) to satisfy, a sum adjudged to be paid by a conviction, the court may make an order requiring the defaulter's parent or guardian to enter into a recognisance (qv) to ensure that the defaulter pays or directing the sum unpaid to be paid by the defaulter's parent or guardian: C.L.A. 1977, s. 36; see also the M.C.A. 1980, s. 81, and the A.J.A. 1982, ss. 26, 28.

young offenders, imprisonment of. *See* IMPRISONMENT OF YOUNG OFFENDERS.

young person. Generally one who has reached 14 and is under 17: C. & Y.P.A. 1933, s. 107(1). Under the Factories Act 1961, one over compulsory school age, but not yet 18.

youth custody centres. Places in which offenders aged 15–20 may be detained and given training, instruction and work and prepared for their release: Prison Act 1952, s. 43 (as substituted by the C.J.A. 1982, s. 11).

youth custody sentence. Sentence passed under the C.J.A. 1982, s. 6, on offenders of 15–20. The usual term exceeds 4 months: s. 7(5).

Where such an offender is convicted of murder or any other offence carrying life imprisonment, the court must sentence him to custody for life unless he is liable to be detained under the C. & Y.P.A. 1933, s. 53(1). For conversion of youth custody sentences to sentences of imprisonment, see the C.J.A. 1982, s. 13.

Z

zealous witness. A witness who attempts to give evidence in a manner which makes it as favourable as possible for a party to the proceedings. *See* WITNESS.

zebra crossing. A road crossing, the presence and limits of which are indicated in accordance with the provisions of S.I. 1971/1524, Sch 2. An "uncontrolled zebra crossing" is a zebra crossing at which traffic is not for the time being controlled by a police constable in uniform or by a traffic warden: S.I. 1971/1524, reg. 3(1). See *Connor* v *Paterson* [1977] 1 All ER 516.

zero rating. Term used in the administration of value-added tax (qv) to indicate that no tax is levied on certain goods sold to final customers and that any tax charged on an input used to produce those goods can be recovered. Principal zero-rated categories include exports, food, books and newspapers. See the Finance Act 1972; *British Rwys Board* v *Customs and Excise Commissioners* [1977] 1 WLR 588; *A.C.T. Construction Ltd* v *Commissioners* [1981] 1 WLR 1562; *Customs and Excise Commissioners* v *Sutton Housing Trust* [1983] STC 399; Value Added Tax Act 1983, s. 16.

APPENDIX

List of abbreviated titles of selected principal law reports.

Abbreviation	Reports	Date
Abr Ca Eq	Equity Cases Abridged	1667–1744
AC	Appeal Cases	1891 to present
Ad & E	Adolphus & Ellis	1834–40
A & E	Adolphus & Ellis	1834–40
ALJ	Australian Law Journal	1927 to present
All ER	All England Law Reports	1936 to present
App Cas	Appeal Cases	1875–90
Atk	Atkyns	1736–55
B	Beavan	1838–66
B & A	Barnewall & Alderson	1817–22
B & Ad.	Barnewall & Adolphus	1830–4
Barn	Barnardiston	1726–34
Barn & Adol.	Barnewall & Adolphus	1830–4
Barn & Ald	Barnewall & Alderson	1817–22
Barnard	Barnardiston	1726–34
Barn & Cress	Barnewall & Cresswell	1822–30
BC	British Columbia Law Reports	1867–1947
B & C	Barnewall & Cresswell	1822–30
BCC	Brown's Chancery Cases	1778–94
B & CR	Bankruptcy and Companies Cases	1918–41
Beav	Beavan	1838–66
Bell	Bell	1842–50
Benl	Benloe	1530–1627
Bing	Bingham	1822–34
Bing NC	Bingham, New Cases	1834–40
Blackst	Blackstone	1746–80
Bli	Bligh	1819–21
Bli NS	Bligh, New Series	1826–37
B NC	Bingham, New Cases	1834–40
BPC	Brown's Parliamentary Cases	1702–1801
Brac	Bracton's Note Book	1217–40
Brod & B	Broderip & Bingham	1819–22
B & S	Best & Smith	1861–70
BTR	British Tax Review	1956 to present
Bulstr	Bulstrode	1610–38
Burr	Burrow	1756–72
BWCC	Butterworth's Workmen's Compensation Cases	1908–50
Can LR	Canadian Law Review	1901–7
Car & P	Carrington & Payne	1823–41
Cas Eq Abr	Equity Cases Abridged	1667–1744
CB	Common Bench	1845–56
CB NS	Common Bench, New Series	1856–65
CCC	Cox's Criminal Cases	1844–1941
CC Chron	County Courts Chronicle	1848–59
CCC Sess Pap	Central Criminal Court Session Papers	1834–1913
CCR	Crown Cases Reserved	1865–75
C & F	Clark & Finnelly	1831–46
Ch	Chancery	1891 to present
Ch App	Chancery Appeal Cases	1865–75

Abbreviation	*Reports*	*Date*
Ch D	Chancery Division	1875–90
C & K	Carrington & Kirwan	1843–53
Cl & F	Clark & Finnelly	1831–46
CLJ	Cambridge Law Journal	1921 to present
CLR	Commonwealth Law Reports	1903 to present
CLYB	Current Law Year Book	1947 to present
C & M	Crompton & Meeson	1832–4
CMLR	Common Market Law Reports	1962 to present
Co	Coke	1572–1616
Com	Comyns	1695–1740
Com Cas	Commercial Cases	1895–1941
Com LR	Common Law Reports	1853–5
Conv NS	Conveyancer & Property Law, New Series	1936 to present
Co Rep	Coke	1572–1616
Cox CC	Cox's Criminal Cases	1843–1941
Cox Cty CC	Cox's County Court Cases	1860–1919
C & P	Carrington & Payne	1823–41
C & R	Clifford & Rickards	1873–84
Cr App R	Criminal Appeal Reports	1908 to present
Crim LR	Criminal Law Review	1954 to present
Cro Car	Croke	1625–41
Cro Eliz	Croke	1582–1603
Cro Jac	Croke	1603–25
Cromp & M	Crompton & Meeson	1832–4
Curt	Curteis	1834–44
D & B	Dearsly & Bell	1856–8
D & Ch	Deacon & Chitty	1832–5
D & E	Durnford & East's Reports	1785–1800
DLR	Dominion Law Reports	1912 to present
DM & J	De Gex, MacNaghten & Gordon	1851–7
Doug	Douglas	1778–85
Dunn	Dunning	1753–4
Durn & E	Durnford & East's Reports	1785–1800
E	East's Term Reports	1800–12
E & B	Ellis & Blackburn	1851–8
E & E	Ellis & Ellis	1858–61
EG	Estates Gazette	1858 to present
Eq	Equity Cases	1866–75
Eq Cas	Equity Modern Reports	1722–55
Esp	Espinasse	1793–1807
Ex	Exchequer Reports	1847–56
Ex	Exchequer Cases	1865–75
Exch Rep	Exchequer Reports	1847–56
Ex D	Exchequer Division	1875–80
Fam	Family Division	1972 to present
F & F	Foster & Finlayson	1856–67
For	Forrester's Chancery Reports	1735–8
Fost & Fin	Foster & Finlayson	1856–67
FSR	Fleet Street Patent Law Reports	1963 to present
Gal & Dav	Gale & Davison	1841–3
Giff	Gifford	1857–65
Gl & J	Glyn & Jameson	1819–28
Godb	Godbolt	1575–1638
H	Hare	1841–53
Hale Prec	Hale's Precedents	1475–1640

Abbreviation	*Reports*	*Date*
Hare	Hare	1841–53
H & C	Hurlstone & Coltman	1862–6
HL	House of Lords Appeals	1866–75
HL Cas	House of Lords Cases	1847–66
H & M	Hemming & Miller	1862–5
H & N	Hurlstone & Norman	1856–62
Hodg	Hodges	1835–7
Ho Lords C	House of Lords Cases	1847–66
Horn & H	Horn & Hurlstone	1838–9
Hurl and Nor	Hurlstone & Norman	1856–62
H & W	Harrison & Wollaston	1835–6
ICR	Industrial Cases Reports	1972 to present
IJ	Irish Jurist	1935 to present
ILJ	Industrial Law Journal	1972 to present
ILR	International Law Reports	1950 to present
IR	Irish Reports	1838 to present
IRLR	Industrial Relations Law Reports	1972 to date
Ir LT	Irish Law Times	1867 to date
ITR	Industrial Tribunal Reports	1966 to date
Jac & W	Jacob & Walker	1819–20
Jenk Cent	Jenkins' Reports	1220–1623
JP	Justice of the Peace & Local Government Review	1837 to present
JPL	Journal of Planning Law	1948 to present
Jur	Jurist Reports	1837–54
Jur NS	Jurist Reports, New Series	1855–66
K	Kenyon	1753–9
KB (or QB)	King's or Queen's Bench	1841 to present
Keb	Keble	1661–79
Keny	Kenyon	1753–9
K & J	Kay & Johnson	1854–8
Ld Ken	Kenyon	1753–9
Ld Ray	Raymond	1694–1732
Lew	Lewin	1822–38
LGR	Local Government Reports	1903 to present
LJ Adm	Law Journal Reports, Admiralty	1866–75
LJ Bk	Law Journal Reports, Bankruptcy	1832–80
LJ Ch	Law Journal Reports, Chancery	1822–1946
LJ CP	Law Journal Reports, Common Pleas	1822–80
LJ Ecc	Law Journal Reports, Ecclesiastical	1865–75
LJ KB(QB)	Law Journal Reports, King's (Queen's) Bench	1831–1946
LJ OS	Law Journal Reports, Old Series	1822–31
LJ PC	Law Journal Reports, Privy Council	1865–1946
LJ PD & A	Law Journal Reports, Probate, Divorce & Admiralty	1876–1946
LJ P&M	Law Journal Reports, Probate & Matrimonial	1858–75
Ll LR	Lloyd's List Law Reports	1919–50
Lloyd's Rep	Lloyd's List Law Reports	1951 to present
Lofft	Lofft's Reports	1772–4
LQR	Law Quarterly Review	1885 to present
LR	Law Reports	1865 to present
LR A & E	Law Reports, Admiralty & Ecclesiastical Cases	1865–75
LR CCR	Law Reports, Crown Cases Reserved	1865–75

Abbreviation	Reports	Date
LR Ch App	Law Reports, Chancery Appeal Cases	1865–75
LR CP	Law Reports, Common Pleas Cases	1865–75
LR Eq	Law Reports, Equity Cases	1865–75
LR Ex	Law Reports, Exchequer Cases	1865–75
LR HL	Law Reports, House of Lords	1865–75
LR PC	Law Reports, Privy Council Appeals	1865–75
LR P & D	Law Reports, Probate & Divorce Cases	1865–75
LR QB	Law Reports, Queen's Bench	1865–75
LR RP	Law Reports, Restrictive Practices Cases	1958 to present
LS Gaz	Law Society Gazette	1903 to present
LT	Law Times Reports	1859–1947
Lush	Lushington	1859–62
Madd	Maddock	1815–22
Mau & S	Maule & Selwyn	1813–17
M & C	Mylne & Craig	1835–41
M & G	Manning & Granger	1840–4
M & K	Mylne & Keen	1832–5
MLR	Modern Law Review	1937 to present
Mod Cas	Modern Cases	1702–45
Mod Rep	Modern Reports	1669–1755
Moo	Moody	1824–44
Moo	Moore	1817–27
Moo CC	Moody	1824–44
Moo & P	Moody & Payne	1827–31
Moo PC	Moore	1836–62
Morr	Morrell	1884–93
M & P	Moore & Payne	1827–31
M & S	Maule & Selwyn	1813–17
M & W	Meeson & Welsby	1836–47
Myl & Cr	Mylne & Craig	1835–41
Myl & K	Mylne & Keen	1832–5
Nev & M	Neville & Manning	1832–6
New Rep	New Reports	1862–5
NJL	New Law Journal	1965 to present
N & McN	Neville & MacNamara	1855–1928
Not Cas	Thornton's Notes of Cases	1841–50
NR	New Reports	1862–5
NSWLR	New South Wales Law Reports	1880–1900
NSWSR	New South Wales State Reports	1901 to present
NZLR	New Zealand Law Reports	1883 to present
P	Probate	1891–1971
P & CR	Planning & Compensation Reports	1949 to present
PD	Probate Division	1875–90
P D & A	Probate, Divorce & Admiralty	1875–90
Pea	Peake	1790–4
Per & D	Perry & Davison	1838–41
Phil Ecc R	Phillimore's Reports	1809–21
Pl	Plowden's Commentaries	1550–80
Pr	Price	1814–24
QB (or KB)	Queen's or King's Bench	1841 to present
QBD	Queen's Bench Division	1875–90
Qd R	Queensland Law Reports	1958 to present
Rep	Coke	1572–1616
RHC	Road Haulage Cases	1950 to present
R & IT	Rating & Income Tax Reports	1924–60

Abbreviation	*Reports*	*Date*
Rom	Romilly's Notes on Cases	1767–87
RPC	Reports of Patents Cases	1884 to present
RTR	Road Traffic Reports	1970 to present
Russ	Russell	1823–9
Russ & M	Russell & Mylne	1829–31
Russ & R	Russell & Ryan	1799–1824
R & VR	Rating & Valuation Reports	1960 to present
Ry & M	Ryan & Moody	1823–6
Salk	Salkeld	1689–1712
SALR	South African Law Reports	1948 to present
SC	Sessions Cases	1906 to present
Sc	Scott	1834–40
SCC	Select Cases in Chancery	1724–33
Scot Jur	Scottish Jurist	1829–73
SCT	Scots Law Times	1893 to present
Sim	Simons	1826–52
SJ	Solicitors' Journal	1857 to present
Sol	The Solicitor	1934 to present
Sol J	Solicitors' Journal	1857 to present
S & S	Simons & Stuart	1822–6
St Tr	State Trials	1163–1820
St Tr NS	State Trials, New Series	1820–58
Swan	Swanston	1818–19
Tal	Talbot's Cases in Equity	1733–8
Taun	Taunton	1807–19
TC	Tax Cases	1875 to present
TLR	Times Law Reports	1884–1952
Tot	Tothill	1559–1646
TR	Taxation Reports	1939 to present
TR	Term Reports	1785–1800
Tyr	Tyrwhitt	1830–5
VATTR	Value Added Tax Tribunal Reports	1973 to present
Ves & B	Vesey & Beames	1812–14
Ves Jr	Vesey Junior	1789–1817
Ves Sen	Vesey Senior	1747–56
VLR	Victoria Law Reports	1875 to present
W Bl	Blackstone	1746–80
Wilm	Wilmot's Case Notes	1757–70
WLR	Weekly Law Reports	1953 to present
Wm Bl	Blackstone	1746–80
WN	Weekly Notes	1866–1952
WR	Weekly Reporter	1853–1906
W & W	Wyatt & Webb	1861–3
Y & C	Younge & Collyer	1834–43